A Holocaust Reader

Responses to the Nazi Extermination

EDITED BY

Michael L. Morgan

Indiana University, Bloomington

New York   Oxford
OXFORD UNIVERSITY PRESS
2001

To Debbie and Sara

Oxford University Press

Oxford New York
Athens Auckland Bangkok Bogotá Buenos Aires Calcutta
Cape Town Chennai Dar es Salaam Delhi Florence Hong Kong Istanbul
Karachi Kuala Lumpur Madrid Melbourne Mexico City Mumbai
Nairobi Paris São Paulo Singapore Taipei Tokyo Toronto Warsaw

and associated companies in
Berlin Ibadan

Copyright © 2001 by Oxford University Press, Inc.

Published by Oxford University Press, Inc.,
198 Madison Avenue, New York, New York, 10016
http://www.oup-usa.org

Oxford is a registered trademark of Oxford University Press

Library of Congress Cataloging-in-Publication Data

A Holocaust reader : responses to the Nazi extermination / edited by Michael L. Morgan.
     p. cm.
   Includes bibliographical references and index.
   ISBN 978-0-19-505958-8

     1. Holocaust, Jewish (1939–1945) 2. Holocaust (Jewish theology) 3. Holocaust, Jewish
(1939–1945)—Influence. I. Morgan, Michael L., 1944–

D804.3.H6484 2000
940.53'18—dc21   99-086797

Printed in the United States of America
on acid-free paper

CONTENTS

3   DEVELOPMENTS: THE 1970s AND 1980s   159

4   THE HOLOCAUST AND WESTERN CULTURE: THE 1980s AND 1990s   271

PREFACE

For twenty years, I have been teaching a course that deals with philosophical and religious responses to the Holocaust. From the outset, I gathered materials from a variety of sources for my students to examine and discuss, and I yearned for an excellent anthology. As the years have passed, the need for a collection of intellectual responses has not waned, although it has changed. For during the past two decades, the Holocaust has cast its shadow farther and farther into our intellectual culture—invoking responses by literary critics, a wider range of philosophers, historians, psychologists, anthropologists, sociologists, students of material culture, and more. The present anthology is an attempt to meet that need today. If history is a good guide, then as time goes on the need will change and future editions of this anthology may change with it. For now, it is my hope that it will serve usefully students of the Holocaust and its impact on our thinking, in universities and elsewhere.

Thanks must go to my students over these two decades, who have helped me to understand what works are most exciting and challenging as one tries to grapple with the impact of the Holocaust on our understanding of ourselves and our world. Early on I discussed materials with Roy Eckardt, Irving Greenberg, David Tracy, Clark Williamson, and a host of others; friends have given me insight into how such a collection should be organized and what should be included—Dan Frank, Ken Seeskin, David Ellenson, Arnie Eisen, Mike Meyer, Rabbi Michael Stroh, and Rabbi Peter Knobel, among many others. As always, my deepest thanks must go to Emil Fackenheim, my teacher and my friend. In the venue of post-Holocaust reflection, Emil's corpus of work is monumental; it dwarfs everything else. I have been fortunate to know him well for more than thirty years and to have been close to his thinking and indeed to him.

I would like to thank Jeff Wolin for permission to use his striking photograph for the cover; the photo first appeared in Jeffrey A. Wolin, *Written in Memory: Portraits of the Holocaust* (San Francisco: Chronicle Books, 1997). Many years ago Cynthia Read at Oxford encouraged and supported this project; Robert Miller, Elissa Morris, and Christine D'Antonio have helped me to bring it to completion. They have been the best of editors and the best of support. Audrey, I am sure, never had their confidence, but she should take a good deal of credit for the finished product. Our cat Amanda did what she could to obstruct my quest for permissions, while Aud's love and support have made my own work possible, enjoyable, and ultimately worthwhile.

When I was young, growing up in upstate New York, I was from time to time brought to our synagogue to see films, taken by the liberating Allied forces, of people and places whose world I sarcely understood. I do not remember the purposes of those occasions, and there were many, nor do I recall exactly my feelings either before or after other than to say that I was horrified then and am horrified still, when those images flood into my memory. And I do remember the images: emaciated figures, hauntingly thin, with large, deep, dark hollows where eyes would normally be, staring, reaching out. And bulldozers, plowing through huge mounds of what looked like strange logs or lumber, until one looked again, when they appeared as what they were: corpses, barely recognizable human bodies.[1]

These images have stayed with me over the years, and when I read essays and chapters, like the ones included in this volume, my reading and thinking must always compete with the involuntary return of those faces, those huge mounds, and more. And, if my thinking about this dark event has taught me anything, it is that this is rightly so. Detached reflection should never, in this case, be too detached, and controlled thinking should never, in this case, be too controlled. The Holocaust, the *Shoah*, the *Endlösung*, call it what you will, is no abstraction to be comprehended, examined, analyzed, and understood, its particularity taken up in camouflaging adjectives, descriptions, categories, and models. It is neither disposable nor assimilable; rather it intrudes, and ought to. Thought, like a monarch, may expect subordination, but the Holocaust, unlike any slave or servant, gives none. Rather it makes demands, whether we like it or not, and is relentless.

In this volume I have collected writings of a variety of thinkers who have sensed that demand and responded to it. Some are theologians or religious thinkers; others are philosophers or political theorists or literary critics. Some lived during the event and were victims, onlookers, or possibly accomplices; others respond largely out of distance and memory. But all, to one degree or another, testify to the burden that history brings, that this particular event, with its myriad episodes of horror and heroism, of suffering and dignity, brings to them and, if they are right, to us all. Indeed, in their writing and in the writing of others—historians, victims, poets, novelists—we can not only recognize a sense of burden and obligation, but also see the creation of new images, new

emblems that join the images of the survivors and victims as obstacles to forgetfulness and to facile abstraction. In responding to the Holocaust, these writers
add not only to our understanding of its momentous impact on subsequent life
and thought; they also testify to its concrete horror and provide us with vehicles
for keeping that concreteness ever before us. Both tasks are vitally important.

The fall of Nazi Germany and the liberation of the death camps took place
over 50 years ago. In a sense, the Holocaust, the Nazi attempt to destroy the Jews
and ultimately to purify Germany, Europe, and the world of all those they considered undesirables, has found its place in our culture. Or to be more precise it
has found a variety of places. The terminology of Holocaust, death camps, and
genocide is an unremarkable part of our everyday culture and vocabulary. We
have television specials and movies about the death camps, about the Nazi
machinery of death, and myriad books, historical, fictional, and both. Everyone
"knows" all about the Holocaust; people are no longer surprised or shocked
when another Nazi perpetrator, now old and seemingly benign, is located,
exposed, brought to trial, and convicted. There is some sympathy for these
"old" criminals; they have, we hear it said, paid their debt; their past is past.
Indeed, their lives and the lives of the arch-criminals, from Hitler to Goebbels to
Heydrich to Himmler, are sensationalized, vulgarized, and popularized in magazines, pulp novels, and elsewhere. Like a speck of dirt that finds its way into a
clam, the Holocaust is being counteracted and coopted into something of value.[2]

Not all, however, think so or have thought so. From the period of the event
itself to this day, there are many who have deeply and seriously confronted the
Holocaust, honestly seeking to understand it, its implications for our understanding of human nature or the human condition, for our understanding of
God, religiosity, morality, destiny, hope, and more. For these thinkers, the Holocaust is complex and foreboding. It demands to be taken seriously and honestly;
it submits to some questions but not to others. It shapes our world, and hence to
ignore or falsify it is to foresake any understanding of our own situation, its possibilities, its character, and its future.

In this anthology I have tried to collect and organize writings from these
thinkers, from all of the central ones and from many others too. To my knowledge there is no other volume at this stage that tries to do just this, to draw on all
that has been written by philosophers, political and literary theorists, Christian
theologians, and Jewish thinkers during the event itself and the five decades
that have followed it in order to provide an opportunity to examine and study
the intellectual-existential phenomenon of post-Holocaust thought. This anthology wants to provide such an opportunity. Hence, in it I have selected articles,
chapters, and much else, in order to expose the reader to the most important
pieces and thinkers, to the central ideas and strategies, to the development of
thinking that confronted the Holocaust, and to the most advanced or sophisticated stages of our thinking. In making the selections, I have imagined that we
have arrived at a distinguishable stage of thinking and that the volume should
show how we got here, why, and with what outcome. This overall goal has
guided the selections and the order of the selections; of course much had to be

omitted, given restrictions of space and size. But I have tried to meet that goal nonetheless.

On the one hand, or from one point of view, intellectual responses to the Holocaust are part of a larger genus: intellectual responses to catastrophic, horrifying, transforming events. Some of the thinkers represented in this collection think that this is so. They, like many others, treat the Holocaust as a catastrophic event such as the destruction of the Second Temple, the crucifixion of Jesus, the Crusades, the Inquisition, the First World War, and so on. Gershom Scholem's work on the Lurianic Kabbalah and then the importance of the false messianism of Shabbetai Zevi provides a model for how such thinking works, and Jacob Neusner has written extensively about the variety of responses to the destruction of the Second Temple, including of course Rabbinic Judaism and Christianity. David Roskies and Alan Mintz have also discussed this phenomenon, with special consideration of literary responses.

Doubtless there are a variety of reasons for this posture, among them a conviction that the center of gravity of Jewish life has shifted away from Europe and should not be determined by a major event in the life of European Jewry. There are academic sorts of reasons too, guided by the social scientific attitude that what is most interesting and most valuable about events are the general truths we can identify and explore as a result of studying them, not the special concatenation that makes each event distinguishable and remarkable. In the end, however, most of the writers and thinkers whom I have selected begin with the utter particularity of Nazism, the assault on Judaism and Jewry, the death camps, and all that went to make up the Holocaust, and proceed to thinking that tries to cope with it by understanding man, God, and Western culture but without ever abandoning its starting point, the recognition of the event's particularity.

Hence, from a second point of view, the Holocaust is not a member of a larger genus but is rather sui generis. Or, to be more precise, it is a member of a host of genera, but what is important is not this fact but rather the distinguishable character of this particular collection of features, attitudes, methods, and so forth. To use a term that will appear and reappear, the Holocaust is unprecedented. Its proper context is history, and it occurs, like all historical events, in time. But its concatenation of features and characteristics never occurred before; indeed, it was not "authorized" by precedent. But part of its horror is that by having occurred, it authorizes. As Hans Jonas once said, at Auschwitz more was actual than was possible. Now we can say, after Auschwitz more is possible than was possible, and indeed more is necessary. At least part of its unprecedented or unique character lies in this, the fact that life after Auschwitz occurs in a new epoch, that the character and dimension and depth of the Holocaust has altered our world in fundamental and important ways, unavoidable ways, and that any thinking that does not acknowledge its epoch-making character is somehow deficient and inadequate and even inauthentic.

It is not, of course, the mere fact of change or alteration that signals the importance of the Holocaust as a watershed event. After all, other events have also changed things irrevocably and made the future *wholly different* from the past. From the invention of the automobile or the television to the American and Russian Revolutions and the discovery of nuclear power, events have been and will continue to be momentous, in this sense. What distinguishes the Holocaust, I think, is that its momentousness, if we call it that, touches fundamental conceptions of human living, including our understanding of what human nature or the human condition is and how, if at all, the divine is related to the human. It concerns too the relationship between history and thought, between experience and event, on the one hand, and principles and ideas and ideals, on the other. And, deeply, the Holocaust concerns evil—what we take it to be, its degrees, its content, and its role in our lives and in our destiny. In short, the Holocaust is not merely momentous; it is seriously or deeply momentous.

Arguably there have been other seriously or deeply momentous events in history; indeed, it would be foolish to deny that there have been. But, as the majority of thinkers in this collection seem to agree, the Holocaust is uniquely one of these. Its particular concatenation of features, occurring at its precise moment in history, involving its precise set of victims, perpetrators, and bystanders, and figuring as it does into modern life and modern history—all this constitutes, to use Arthur Cohen's term, a "caesura" or interruption. It is a *novum*, an event that distinguishes one epoch from another. Life and thought after Auschwitz are not and cannot be the same as life was before this event, in important and transforming ways. This is something that many of the thinkers represented here believe.

But they do not all believe it, nor do they all believe it in the same way or at the same time. It is one of the distinguishing features of post-Holocaust thought that the role and effectiveness of this idea of uniqueness differs from thinker to thinker. One way of assessing a response is in terms of what the thinker believes about the Holocaust's particularity or unprecedented character, what role that plays, and to what depth its influence carries.

If we stand back from this matter a bit, we can see that from a certain detached point of view the issue is one of parochialism and even relativism. From another point of view, it is one of abstractness and escapism. Indeed, the deep lines are drawn in such a way that the fears and passions of both sides tend to prohibit open conversation and good will. By and large, the thinkers represented in this volume oppose escapism and avoidance and would have little sympathy for any post-Holocaust posture that fails to appreciate the utter particularly of the hatred, the guilt, the responsibility, and the implications of the event. Not all may agree with this set of convictions, but if one thinks deeply enough about what is being said, one can at least understand and appreciate it.

When does an event end? In a sense, we set the limits for ourselves, by our definition of the notion of event and by our understanding of the event in question. Hence, for some the Holocaust still goes on. But for most of us it ended over five decades ago; all that follows is *thereafter*.

The major or central responses to the Holocaust were literary, scholarly, and theological, and they did not occur immediately after the event. The theological responses came years after the event, first in the late 1950s, then in the 1960s and early 1970s. Who of us really knows why this delay occurred? Surely it was partly a cultural, historical matter, that neither the survivors themselves nor world Jewry, especially in Israel and the United States, nor the churches nor the world at large, was ready to reflect on this dark moment in its recent past. There had been a victory of sorts, and no one wants or dares to mitigate a victory. And the memories were so awful, so horrifying, that there probably seemed to be no reason to dredge them up and no encouragement to do so. Moreover, there were individual, psychological reasons for suppressing the memories and avoiding intellectual response, aside from an unwillingness to admit that what had happened had happened, to face one's survival—undeserved and traumatic and guilt-ridden—in the face of the death of the victims. It seemed so inexplicable, so terrifyingly awesome, that one might have wondered whether the mind was capable of grasping and dealing with it at all, and if not, then one feared a sense of personal annihilation. Perhaps the torturers and murderers had not only destroyed human bodies; perhaps they had also destroyed human transcendence, the intellect, the mind, the soul. Perhaps, in the end, they and not we had been the real victors. One can imagine that such thoughts immobilized many intellectuals and forced a deferral.

Still, in the 1960s and early 1970s, the implications of the Holocaust for our conceptions of God, human nature and destiny, and religious and moral life came to be addressed. Elie Wiesel's *Night* was one of the first works to address these themes, and it did so in an especially powerful and indeed classic way, through autobiographical fiction. To this day, *Night* is probably the most recommended introductory text concerning the reality of the death camps and religious-intellectual reflections on the Holocaust experience. Then, there were others: Richard Rubenstein, Roy Eckardt, Emil Fackenheim, Eliezer Berkovits, Frank Littell, and Irving Greenberg.

The organization of this anthology stems from an appreciation of this fact, that there were indeed a set of important statements, some more developed, some less, that came to the fore during the late 1950s to early 1970s, and that these statements form the core of post-Holocaust thought. The earliest theological publications were articles of Richard Rubenstein from the early 1960s, the influence of which was only really felt after 1966, when his collection of essays, *After Auschwitz*, was published. By this time, Frank Littell and Roy Eckardt had already been writing on a new Christian attitude toward Judaism and the Jewish people, at least in part as a recognition of the role of the church in the Holocaust. Then, approximately at the time of the Six Day War, in 1967, we find a new surge of published thinking, including the articles and book by Emil Fackenheim, Eliezer Berkovits's book, and the thinking of Irving Greenberg. Although there is some looseness in looking at it this way, I take these major theological statements and reflections to form a core. What preceded them can be considered preparatory, in a sense, and what follows them can be understood as development, ramification, and critique.

I have called the preparation "early reflections." I have sought to collect here important early statements or understandings with which we ought to be familiar. They are by a variety of types of intellectuals, from philosophers in the technical sense to political theorists, historians, and literary or cultural critics. Frequently later developments build on these accounts. Often these responses introduce themes that later become important. At times, they give some indication of how more contemporary thinkers, from differing points of view, begin the process of coming to grips with the darkest side of Nazism. They raise a host of questions, only some of which are dealt with later, by theologians, philosophers, and others. My belief is that the core statements and the developments of the 1970s through the 1990s can best be understood against the background of these early reflections.

I shall say something about the specific readings in the introductions to each section.

Whatever the next stage of reflection on the Holocaust, I am convinced that it should be mediated by the existing thinking represented by the selections in this anthology. In a sense, one of the book's purposes is to articulate the tradition of interpretation that has developed as philosophers, theologians, literary and cultural critics, political thinkers, and historians have begun to confront the event and reflect on what man, God, society, and history can and must be like thereafter. Once that tradition is defined and presented, all of us who now attempt to understand these matters for our own day and the future can do so by returning to the past with our interpretive situation clearly in hand. In part, we shall want to try to confront the event itself, to the degree that such a confrontation is possible, through film, memoir, diary, and more. Then we shall want to understand our own world in terms of that event and the subsequent interpretations that it has stimulated. We shall try both to return to the event itself and to return via the interpretive reflections of those represented in this volume. Only once all of this is accomplished shall we venture beyond the abyss to the past that lies stretched out, to the sources of our thinking and our faith, from Western Europe to the Renaissance to the Middle Ages and back to antiquity. In short, we shall interpretively recover our past for the present only once we have encountered honestly and openly the events that have given shape and character to our own historical situation, and one of those is surely the Holocaust and the thinking which it has provoked.

Often anthologies such as this arise out of need, and this one is a case in point. I am a member of a department of philosophy and a Jewish studies program. All of my courses are offered within the philosophy department and are, for this reason, bound by the standards, expectations, and traditions of that department. For many years, while I taught courses in Jewish philosophy that were primarily historical and dealt with themes often discussed in courses in the philosophy of religion, I was reluctant to introduce a course on the impact of the Holocaust on recent Jewish thought. When I finally became bold enough to do so, I came to realize that the best such course would embrace a variety of types of intellectual reflection and would require reading far beyond any one set of traditional boundaries. Fortunately, these days such courses, often called "interdisciplinary," are common, and I felt no reluctance in introducing this one, which would read some theological, philosophical, and literary-critical material, as well as other types. Immediately I saw the need for a collection of readings that was unlike any existing anthology. With few exceptions, what ones there are focus on historical and literary materials and generally give only token attention to philosophical and theological reflection. One could hardly castigate the editors, for their intent in general was to provide sources for studying the Holocaust as a total phenomenon; it was not to focus exclusively on the impact of the Holocaust on our conceptions of human nature, society, ethics, religion, and God.

For nearly twenty years, then, I have worked to collect materials for this volume. Many people have been a great help to me in the project, some by sending reprints, others by making suggestions about their own work and that of others, others by sending me lists of pieces they found most useful and important. Based on their advice and my own experience, I made some hard decisions; the present volume is the result. In the end, it is meant to be useful to students and teachers, and I am hopeful that it will be and eager to alter future editions in order to better achieve that goal.

As I mentioned earlier, some may argue that the Holocaust, via its deep resonances in the soul of our society, may still not have come to an end. But most believe that 1945 marked its historical terminus. It is less easy to define the historical parameters of the intellectual event or episode that is the theme of this book: the encounter between that horror and the human mind. Surely, in a sense, that event has not come to an end and should not. But, perhaps, a stage of it has or something akin to a stage. If so, then there is good reason for us to summarize, to look carefully and thoughtfully at where we have been and where we have arrived. In part, this volume is an attempt to do that, and hence by looking backwards to help us to live into the future, an epoch unavoidably and relentlessly burdened by the reality of Auschwitz.

NOTES

1. See Alfred Kazin's recollection of the films of Bergen-Belsen, quoted in Richard H. Pells, *The Liberal Mind in a Conservative Age* (New York: Harper & Row, 1985), 471, from Alfred Kazin, *Starting Out in the Thirties* (Boston: Little, Brown and Company, 1965), 166. Also the reflections on the newsreels, the films of Bergen-Belsen, Dachau, Mauthausen, and Buchenwald, Jorge Semprun, *Literature of Life* (New York: Viking, 1997), 198–201.

2. See the exemplary books by Saul Friedlander, *Reflections of Nazism: An Essay on Kitsch and Death* (New York: Harper & Row, 1984), and Alvin Rosenfeld, *Imagining Hitler* (Bloomington: Indiana University Press, 1985), on the cultural appropriation of Hitler and Nazism. Also, see Ron Rosenbaum, *Explaining Hitler* (New York: Random House, 1998).

PART 1

◼ Early Reflections

Martin Heidegger, in his classic philosophical work *Being and Time*, characterizes human existence as being-toward-death and hence as marked by a consciousness of mortality and finitude. We all know that some day we shall die, and part of human living is to live with and despite a recognition of this fact, the undeniability of death. But death of course comes in different ways, suddenly for some, slowly and painfully for others. Heidegger himself died of natural causes at an old age, as did Martin Buber and Hannah Arendt. Not so Paul Celan, probably the darkest and most powerful poetic voice to come out of the Holocaust, or Jean Améry or Primo Levi. They all committed suicide.

I do not want to draw any precise lessons from this fact; indeed, I am not sure what such lessons might be. But it is a chilling and deeply moving fact nonetheless, that three powerful intellects, all of whom experienced the horrors of the death camps and survived, all of whom have left us incomparable memoirs, images, reflections, and testimony concerning the events of those dark times, chose to take their own lives. There was a time for each one when, for whatever reasons, continued existence and the responsibility to witness to the victims became too great a burden to bear, perhaps because no future was possible without the past and because it was in the end the memory of past that was too great a burden to bear. We do not know this of course, but it is possible and, given the deeply unsettling character of their works, perhaps more than possible.

Intellectual reflection, whether it is scholarly analysis or philosophical interpretation or theological construction, involves a certain kind of detachment. The thinker stands back from the event, examines it, views it from different points of view, asks questions of it, and seeks to place it within some pattern or other. In short, the thinker tries to understand by comprehending, by stepping away and circumscribing in thought. Individual, particular events or persons or acts or whatever can engage the thinker only as a disengaged spectator and examiner; the object of inquiry is to strip the particular of all that distinguishes it and thereby to swallow it up in the generality of theory, of thinking itself.

Many of the figures that are represented in this volume struggle with the tension that the very activity of thought introduces when we focus it on the Holocaust, the death camps, and the Nazi enterprise of extermination. By its nature, thinking wants to be detached from the experience of the event and ultimately wants to plunder the event of its special character; at the same time, the thinker's interest in the event depends upon its particularity, what makes it distinctive and different. Hence, the thinker is drawn to the event or it compels him only qua particular event, while his thinking about it moves him to treat it qua universal type.

This tension is no better represented than in the writings of Primo Levi and Jean Améry. Both experienced the Nazi assault through torture, deprivation, manipulation, and more. Both wrote with power and depth about what they experienced, describing episodes of horror with a wrenching clarity that fixes an image forever in one's memory. And both were well-educated intellectuals, who thought about what was happening to them and others while it was happening and after and who wrote about what they took the meaning of their experiences to be, for them and for our conceptions of human dignity, human worth, and more. Hence, in Levi and Améry, in remarkable ways, we have vivid and powerful examples of intellectual detachment coupled with relentless involvement. Indeed, in Améry we even have an example of someone who thinks about the special problems that the intellectual had to face in the camps precisely because of his intellect and his thinking. If Améry is right, then the camps exposed the anti-Aristotelian truth that rational thought can be the nemesis of human life.

Levi is a secular humanist, and what impresses him deeply is the assault on human dignity and the struggle to maintain it. Often, in *Survival in Auschwitz*, he recalls incidents that dramatize the Nazi effort to dehumanize their victims as part of their program to annihilate them. Levi exhibits a theme that Terrence Des Pres will brilliantly illuminate in *The Survivor*: that it was part of the Nazi plan to force their victims to live in filth and indeed their own exrement, so that they would come to abhor themselves as objects of disgust and loathing. But Levi's clear, evocative prose not only focuses on the dehumanizing program of the perpetrators; he also and prominently emphasizes the endeavor to oppose it. Some, he shows, understood the Nazi goal, to make them wretched and disgusting in their own eyes, and refused to succumb. Human dignity and a sense of their own worthiness as human beings became the prize in a constant battle, and Levi is at his best when he recalls and describes the contestants in that battle, both the victors and the victims. Later thinkers, in trying to understand the depth of the evil of the death camps, will focus on Levi's portrait of the ultimate victim, where the human condition is so transformed that even death is no longer a dignified possibility.

Jean Améry was a resistance fighter, a philosopher, and later a journalist. His essays are like no others in their depth and subtlety. Levi is a writer, and his prose, with its stark clarity and simplicity, moves and conveys by understatement; Améry is a thinker and philosopher, and his essays move by the power of the thought. Three themes are worth special mention. First, as I indicated, he explores in a subtle and revealing way the special debilities of the intellectual, how the intellectual thinks too much and places himself at risk by his thinking, his rational examination of alternatives, which will not let him hope or accept but leads him to resist and hence to suffer. It is a brilliant portrait of how human transcendence becomes the agent of its own ruin.

Secondly, Améry gives a horrifying, chilling account of torture and its effects on one's sense of social solidarity and isolation. Reading the passage in which he does this is sufficient to send chills up one's spine.

> In the bunker there hung from the vaulted ceiling a chain that above ran into a roll. At its bottom end it bore a heavy, broadly curved iron hook. I was led to the instrument. The hook gripped into the shackle that held my hands together behind my back. Then I was raised with the chain until I hung about a meter above the floor. In such a position, or rather, when hanging this way, with your hands behind your back, for a short time you can hold at a half-oblique through muscular force. During these few minutes, when you are already expending your utmost strength, when sweat has already appeared on your forehead and lips, and you are breathing in gasps, you will not answer any questions. Accomplices? Addresses? Meeting places? You hardly hear it. All your life is gathered in a single, limited area of the body, the shoulder joints, and it does not react; for it exhausts itself completely in the expenditure of energy. But this cannot last long, even with people who have a strong physical constitution. As for me, I had to give up rather quickly. And now there was a crackling and splintering in my shoulders that my body has not forgotten until this hour. The balls sprang from their sockets. My own body weight caused luxation; I fell into a void and now hung by my dislocated arms, which had been torn high from behind and were now twisted over my head. Torture, from Latin *torquere*, to twist.[1]

Améry says a great deal about torture, but nothing can compete with the juxtaposition of this description and its etymological coda. Torture is an old phenomenon, and there are doubtless many modes of it that are more awful and more unnerving than this example. But it is hard to leave this passage without an indelible association of Nazism with immeasurable suffering, the fracturing of human dignity, and the utter incommensurability of all of this with the human intellect.

Finally, in his brilliant essay "On the Necessity and Impossibility of Being a Jew," Améry provides an unforgettable portrait of a post-Holocaust secular Judaism. He has no Jewish memories, no Jewish past nor Jewish associations. But from Nuremberg on, Améry recognizes that for him being Jewish is both impossible, in one sense, and necessary, in another. Torture may have destroyed any sense of solidarity with humankind, but being the object of Nazi hatred and dehumanization, he must respond, and the only possible response is as a Jew and a victim, in opposition to the attack on human dignity. So, Améry must be a Jew, who expresses his solidarity with those who fight for human dignity in the only way he now can do so, as a Jew and as a Zionist. Later, when Fackenheim and Greenberg portray the subtle interrelation between religiosity and secularity in the Jewish secularist, one can hardly find a better example than Améry of what they have in mind.

Like these selections, the others in this first or preparatory stage raise important questions that will continue to be powerful motives for serious reflection. Adorno, for example, raises serious questions about the venue of Nazism, that this overwhelming form of degradation and assault, which sought to annihilate human dignity in an unencumbered act of domination, grew out of the richest soil of European civilization and culture. Like many others, Adorno finds this an astounding fact and asks how it was possible and what its implications are for our understanding of the capacities of culture to oppose evil—the depth of the humaneness of culture, as it were. Has this event paralyzed the metaphysical capacity, as Adorno suggests; is poetry after it possible? And is the assault on the Jew, who played such a central role in European culture, an act of self-destruction, an explosion of self-hatred? These and other questions mark a central crux: Can an historical event limit thought, culture, creativity? Are there places where the mind is simply not at home, an utter alien, forbidden? And if there are, then what are they like? Can we describe them, understand them, or is our only response a foreboding silence? Or must it be an inarticulate or prearticulate opposition?

The contributions of Hannah Arendt and Martin Buber to these early reflections are specially important. Both of course are controversial figures, Arendt especially, and there are those who have been so offended and enraged by her treatment of the Judenrate and the notion of complicity that they fail to appreciate properly her earlier work on the nature of Nazi criminality and the nature of the death camps. But there is no denying, I think, that Arendt's examination of the Nazi perpetrators and the functioning of the death camps is a tremendously important set of reflections. But let me begin with Buber.

During the First World War, in the course of efforts in behalf of peace and reconciliation, Buber had diagnosed the sickness of mankind as "massive decisionlessness," and he prescribed the cure, "direction" or "singleness of purpose"[2] that is discovered by openness to reality or the present situation.[3] He was also convinced of the loss of true community, the "voluntary coming together of men in direct relationship,"[4] and its replacement in people's lives by the models of Soviet Russia, Weimar Germany, and capitalist America—what he called "phantom[s] of community."[5] Already, during the First World War, Buber was wrestling with the human and theological problems of evil, of "how 'evil' belongs to the coming of the kingdom."[6]

> In an essay on the Hebrew theater, written in 1929, Buber describes Judaism this way: What saved Judaism is not . . . the fact that it failed to experience "the tragedy," the contradiction in the world's process, deeply enough; but rather that it experienced that "tragedy" in the dialogical situation. . . . This very world, this very contradiction, unabridged, unmitigated, unsmoothed, unsimplified, unreduced, this world shall be—not overcome—but consummated. . . . It is a redemption not from evil but of the evil.[7]

Perhaps it is not amazing to find Buber, in 1929, so optimistic about man's capacity to redeem evil itself. Perhaps, in these years before the victory of

Nazism, his conviction is reasonable, that evil is relative—to be transformed, not transcended or rejected. But, as the years pass, it is surprising that Buber's personal encounter with the reality of the evil of Nazism does not succeed in altering his view.

The surprise begins with Buber's understanding of Hitler. In 1942, in an essay called "People and Leader," Buber attacks Hitler as the leader who does not teach. "When one looks at Hitler, one is seized by dizziness," for when he speaks to the masses he is in the grip of a kind of hysteria. He castrates his followers, who become mute, dumb followers. "What distinguishes man as man, that he himself may judge concerning what he does and what he leaves undone, has been superseded in Nazism."[8] To Buber, Hitler is like Jacob Frank, a man with no beliefs, who demands only unconditional obedience—for his own sake.

For Buber, evil resides in lack of direction, of decision, and of purpose. The core of Buber's play *Elijah*, written in 1956 and published in 1963, is "the demand for decision," and it is this that lies at the heart of Buber's conception of good and evil.[9] In one of his responses in *Philosophical Interrogations*, Buber says "evil proper is the affirmation and strengthening of one's own decisionlessness against the God who demands decision. . . . One does not decide for Baal, one falls to him. . . . Adolf Hitler, the Baalish man, is precisely the exemplary living being with whom a dialogue is no longer possible."[10]

Against the background of this view of evil, it is no wonder that in 1965 Buber could say that while he held no one to be "absolutely" unredeemable by God, he felt radically separated from Hitler: "[S]peaking not 'of God, but solely of myself and this man [Hitler],' there was no possibility of dialogue. Hitler is not my antagonist in the sense of a partner 'whom I can confirm in opposing him' . . . , for he is incapable of really addressing one and incapable of really listening to one."[11] In short, Hitler, although as evil as one could be, is nonetheless not beyond redemption; while he is beyond man, he is not beyond God.

There is a haunting symmetry between Buber's understanding of Hitler and his understanding of his victims. In 1936, Buber published 23 psalms in Hebrew with his translation, "Out of the Depths I Call Unto Thee." There he could say that God seems to have forsaken the Jewish people, but they await his salvation nonetheless. Even in His absence, then, one could and indeed should wait for Him. Years later he was to restate this same sentiment. In the fall of 1951, during his first visit to America, Buber gave three new talks on Judaism, under the auspices of the Jewish Theological Seminary. At the end of the third, "The Dialogue between Heaven and Earth," which we include in this collection, he characterized the hour as one in which God hid His face, a time of eclipse, and yet, he ended with an affirmation of how life with God is possible in such an age. "We do not put up with earthly being: we struggle for its redemption, and struggling we appeal to the help of our Lord, who is again and still a hiding one"—'again,' as He was to the survivors of Auschwitz—to whom we dare to recommend, 'Give thanks unto the Lord, for He is good.'"[12]

For Buber, then, just as one dares to recommend to the victims of Nazism a receptivity to divine help, so one is forced to admit to the Nazi perpetrators the possibility of divine redemption. In the course of responses to critics in *Philosophical Interrogations*, Buber said, "I confess that I can hold no one to be 'absolutely' unredeemable." Evil may become radical, and we can help "deradicalize it" but not wholly succeed. Man can never redeem human existence fully and completely, but he can and must aim at fulfillment by making dialogue real in it.[13] But there are limits to our ability to succeed in so doing and even in our trying. In his speech "Genuine Dialogue and the Possibilities of Peace," accepting the Peace Prize of the German Book Trade (1953), Buber distinguished between those Germans who were weak, those who were ignorant, and those who killed millions of Jews. "I . . . have only in a formal sense a common humanity with those who took part in this action. . . . They have so radically removed themselves from the human sphere . . . , that not even hatred . . . was able to arise in me. And what am I that I could here presume to 'forgive'!"[14] God may forgive but not man, a sentiment Buber was to repeat about Hitler himself a dozen years later.

In the end, then, Buber finds himself unable to sever the relationship between God and evil. Ultimately, it may be that nothing is so evil that God cannot or will not redeem it. In 1956, Buber said: "The time of Hitler was the most terrible that I have lived through, but even in that time there was a holy meaning in history, there was God . . . only I cannot say how and where."[15]

Buber often returns to this same view of evil and the comprehensiveness of the divine. If *I and Thou* is Buber's great literary response to the First World War, his novel *For the Sake of Heaven* is his response to Nazism and the Second World War.[16] In retelling and weaving this cycle of messianic Hasidic tales, Buber portrays the tragic confrontation between two views of redemption, two men, and a view about redemption from evil. That view—still with Buber—is that "redemption must be of evil and not just from it,"[17] and it is wrought through the love and the conflict of dialogical encounter and the openness that waits for a path to appear where none is yet visible. For Buber, there simply is no such thing as being absolutely separated from God. In *Moses*, for example, Buber characterizes the religion of Moses as that of one "who learned to recognize the demonic as one of the forms by which the divine functions."[18] "Moses," Friedman comments, "is one who withstood evil not because he recognized it as Satan but precisely because he recognized it as God. . . . Even Hitler and the Nazis that Buber had to endure he did not attribute to a devil utterly sundered from God."[19]

The implications of Buber's view are powerful ones. First, it implies that certain acts, certain crimes, are beyond human solution. In 1961, in an interview regarding the Eichmann trial, Buber denied that the trial had revealed any new evil. Yet he did indicate that the crimes were so monstrous that there is no penalty, no punishment for them.[20] Secondly, they are beyond human understanding. In 1938, Buber responded to Gandhi, who had said that the Nazi persecutions were "an exact parallel" to those of the Indians in South Africa in 1905. After methodically distinguishing the Nazi assault and chastising Gandhi for the comparison and the suggestion that the Jews resist, Buber said, "A diabolic universal steam-roller cannot thus be understood."[21]

Finally, however, such crimes can be confronted; they can be the objects of response and responsibility. Friedman interprets *The Question to the Single One* (1936) as an act of "spiritual resistance to Nazism,"[22] a "radical criticism of collectivism." Each individual is potential existence (freedom) in a limited situation. Evil is the shirking of direction to one's freedom and potentialities. When the state exploits this shirking and capitalizes on the loss of authentic direction, then governments such as that formed by the Nazis arise. Only the responsible individual, the Single One, can "answer for the direction of the concrete situation." The state cannot supersede the individual's responsibility in this task.[23]

A glance at these comments indicates how anthropocentric and yet optimistic Buber's conception of evil always remained. The special reality of the Nazi death camps, so brilliantly examined by others, does not significantly alter that conception. Indeed, one wonders how much of that event remained hidden from him. This myopia becomes apparent when one recalls that in 1948, in a letter to Ernst Simon, Buber compared the Arab-Israeli tensions in Jerusalem to the Nazi era in this way: "Next to surrender of the soul to the irreconcilable contradiction, everything that I have experienced before, for example in Hitler Germany, was a gentle idyll."[24] According to Friedman, Buber's reason for this judgment had to do with their different character, for the former was organized terror while the latter was "simply anarchy."

Indeed, it is just at this point that Hannah Arendt's remarkable contribution has its effect. She tries to understand the unprecedented character of the death camps as residing precisely in their organization and the bureaucratic criminals who were their administrators. It is just these facts that are the core of the unique horror of Nazism, of a totalitarianism whose goal is unlimited domination and whose primary resources are normal, everyday workers, whose talents and commitment are employed to heinous purposes as long as their philistine desires and needs are satisfied. Indeed, the Nazi criminal, she argues, does not do evil for evil's sake; rather he does evil without intending it at all. What he intends is to make a decent living, to live a secure and relaxing life with his family, to pay his insurance premiums, and to enjoy his evenings and weekends with his wife and children. This is the real criminal, the new, great criminal of the twentieth century. His real intentions and goals are personal and self-interested. And he is capable of the most horrifying acts as long as his needs and desires are satisfied and he is assured that he is not responsible for what he does. He is a philistine and a bureaucrat, an automaton, the final corruption of the ideal of rational agency. And it is because of him, in part, that Buber's judgment must be wrong, that organized evil is worse than anarchy.

Arendt puts it this way in her 1945 article "Organized Guilt and Universal Responsibility":

> Heinrich Himmler is not one of those intellectuals stemming from the dim No-Man's Land between the Bohemian and the Pimp. . . . He is neither a Bohemian

like Goebbels, nor a sex criminal like Streicher, nor a perverted fanatic like Hitler, nor an adventurer like Goering. He is a "bourgeois" with all the outer aspect of respectability, all the habits of a good *paterfamilias* who does not betray his wife and anxiously seeks to secure a decent future for his children; and he has consciously built up his new terror organization, covering the whole country, on the assumption that most people are not Bohemians nor fanatics, nor adventurers, nor sex maniacs, nor sadists, but, first and foremost job-holders, and good family-men. . . . It became clear that for the sake of his pension, his life insurance, the security of his wife and children, such a man was ready to sacrifice his beliefs, his honor, and his human dignity. It needed only the satanic genius of Himmler to discover that after such degradation he was entirely prepared to do literally anything when the ante was raised and the bare existence of his family was threatened. The only condition he put was that he should be fully exempted from responsibility for his acts.[25]

To this powerful and disturbing account of Nazi criminality, with its critique of modern, post–seventeenth century society and the primacy of self-interest and acquisitiveness, an account that provides the real foundation for her controversial portrait of Eichmann and her description of his evil as "banal," Arendt appends an analysis of the death camps. Here, in *The Origins of Totalitarianism*, she explores the implications of the harrowing judgment, that "the concentration and extermination camps of totalitarian regimes serve as the laboratories in which the fundamental belief of totalitarianism that everything is possible is being verified."[26] But, as Arendt shows, this notion of unlimited possibility has a precise focus for totalitarianism: "not the transformation of the outside world or the revolutionizing transmutation of society, but the transformation of human nature itself. The concentration are the laboratories where changes in human nature are tested."[27] It is Arendt's special contribution in these pages that she examines how these experiments are conducted, by subjecting human capacity, experience, and even human death to manipulation and distortion, so that the end is to separate the criminals totally from the pale of human solidarity. And then, as she ends the work, Arendt gropes to say what this radical evil is. But, she is brought to admit, "we actually have nothing to fall back on in order to understand a phenomenon that nevertheless confronts us with its overpowering reality and breaks down all standards we know."[28]

Once more, then, with Arendt as with Celan, Levi, Améry, and others, we return to the theme of silence, of incomprehensibility, and of meaning. How indeed, once one has examined and explored and looked again and again, does one understand? What do we learn about radical evil by treating the camps as the central and essential institutions of totalitarianism and hence of Nazi domination? What do we learn by thinking to a limit and finding oneself unable to go further? Are there patterns of thinking, worldviews, philosophical systems or religious ones, that enable us to assimilate this event, to bring thinking to a point of rest, of satisfaction, of composure? Or not? Is there a deep, unresolvable incommensurability between the Holocaust and its conduct, on the one hand, and thinking, on the other? From the earliest reflections we collect here to those of the 1950s, questions like these impose themselves and resist facile disposal. The intellectual reflections of this period typically arise out of a theoretical posture that seeks to expose the horrors of totalitarianism or modernity or whatever and then to oppose these nemeses of genuine modern life. But, at a certain point, each such attempt breaks down. Or, more precisely, the event and its character breaks the bonds of the system of thought employed to encompass and comprehend it.

Here perhaps is the most important lesson of these early thoughts. Like a carpenter whose saw strains and finally shatters, its teeth crumbling, as he tries to cut through an unknown piece of wood that proves too hard, too impenetrable, too uncompromising, these thinkers take it for granted that their tools will work, that their systems, views, and theories will comprehend and illuminate this event as they would any other. But then something happens; either they or we can see the strain, the struggle, and finally the failure, the limit, where all that is revealed and clarified reaches an impasse, an *aporia,* and the question is raised, is the metaphysical capacity paralyzed? What can thought do with this event?

In a sense, the central theological responses, which we shall turn to in the second section, do not solve this question. It is the fundamental question for all post-Holocaust thinking and reflection, and it is not solved as much as confronted and negotiated, in a variety of ways. The theologians, as we shall see, confront it from a different direction, and then they go on, with all the uncertainty and the hope that going on requires. And in going on, they provide a set of alternatives and options that are then taken up, clarified, developed, and often rejected in the thinking that follows.

NOTES

1. Jean Améry, *At the Mind's Limits* (Bloomington: Indiana University Press, 1980), 32.

2. Maurice Friedman, *The Early Years, 1878–1923,* vol. 1 of *Martin Buber's Life and Work* (Detroit: Wayne State University Press, 1987), 180–181.

3. Friedman, *Early Years,* 167.

4. Friedman, *Early Years,* 238; cf. 234–235.

5. Friedman, *Early Years,* 240.

6. Maurice Friedman, *The Middle Years, 1923–1945,* vol. 2 of *Martin Buber's Life and Work* (Detroit: Wayne State University Press, 1987), 35.

7. Friedman, *Middle Years,* 87.

8. Friedman, *Middle Years,* 299.

9. Maurice Friedman, *The Later Years, 1945–1965,* vol. 3 of *Martin Buber's Life and Work* (Detroit: Wayne State University Press, 1987), 463.

10. Friedman, *Later Years,* 463.

11. Friedman, *Middle Years,* 176.

12. Friedman, *Later Years*, 146–147.

13. Friedman, *Later Years*, 278–279.

14. Friedman, *Later Years*, 119.

15. Friedman, *Middle Years*, 170.

16. Cf. Friedman, *Middle Years*, 309–325.

17. Friedman, *Middle Years*, 315.

18. Friedman, *Later Years*, 37.

19. Friedman, *Later Years*, 37.

20. Friedman, *Later Years*, 359.

21. Friedman, *Middle Years*, 173.

22. Friedman, *Middle Years*, 188.

23. Friedman, *Middle Years*, 192.

24. Friedman, *Later Years*, 25.

25. Hannah Arendt, "Organized Guilt and Universal Responsibility," in *The Jew as Pariah*, ed. Ron H. Feldman (New York: Grove, 1978), 231–232.

26. Hannah Arendt, *The Origins of Totalitarianism* (1951; reprint, New York: Harcourt Brace Jovanovich, 1973), 437.

27. Arendt, *Origins of Totalitarianism*, 458.

28. Arendt, *Origins of Totalitarianism*, 459.

▣ Survival in Auschwitz

ON THE BOTTOM

The journey did not last more than twenty minutes. Then the lorry stopped, and we saw a large door, and above it a sign, brightly illuminated (its memory still strikes me in my dreams): *Arbeit Macht Frei,* work gives freedom.

We climb down, they make us enter an enormous empty room that is poorly heated. We have a terrible thirst. The weak gurgle of the water in the radiators makes us ferocious; we have had nothing to drink for four days. But there is also a tap—and above it a card which says that it is forbidden to drink as the water is dirty. Nonsense. It seems obvious that the card is a joke, "they" know that we are dying of thirst and they put us in a room, and there is a tap, and *Wassertrinken Verboten.* I drink and I incite my companions to do likewise, but I have to spit it out, the water is tepid and sweetish, with the smell of a swamp.

This is hell. Today, in our times, hell must be like this. A huge, empty room: we are tired, standing on our feet, with a tap which drips while we cannot drink the water, and we wait for something which will certainly be terrible, and nothing happens and nothing continues to happen. What can one think about? One cannot think anymore, it is like being already dead. Someone sits down on the ground. The time passes drop by drop.

We are not dead. The door is opened and an SS man enters, smoking. He looks at us slowly and asks, *"Wer kann Deutsch?"* One of us whom I have never seen, named Flesch, moves forward; he will be our interpreter. The SS man makes a long calm speech; the interpreter translates. We have to form rows of five, with intervals of two yards between man and man; then we have to undress and make a bundle of the clothes in a special manner, the woollen garments on one side, all the rest on the other; we must take off our shoes but pay great attention that they are not stolen.

Stolen by whom? Why should our shoes be stolen? And what about our documents, the few things we have in our pockets, our watches? We all look at the interpreter, and the interpreter asks the German, and the German smokes and looks him through and through as if he were transparent, as if no one had spoken.

I had never seen old men naked. Mr. Bergmann wore a truss and asked the interpreter if he should take it off, and the interpreter hesitated. But the German understood and spoke seriously to the interpreter pointing to someone. We saw the interpreter swallow and then he said: "The officer says, take off the truss, and you will be given that of Mr. Coen." One could see the words coming bitterly out of Flesch's mouth; this was the German manner of laughing.

Now another German comes and tells us to put the shoes in a certain corner, and we put them there, because now it is all over and we feel outside this world and the only thing is to obey. Someone comes with a broom and sweeps away all the shoes, outside the door in a heap. He is crazy, he is mixing them all together, ninety-six pairs, they will be all mixed up. The outside door opens, a freezing wind enters and we are naked and cover ourselves up with our arms. The wind blows and slams the door; the German reopens it and stands watching with interest how we writhe to hide from the wind, one behind the other. Then he leaves and closes it.

Now the second act begins. Four men with razors, soap-brushes and clippers burst in; they have trousers and jackets with stripes, with a number sewn on the front; perhaps they are the same sort as those others of this evening (this evening or yesterday evening?); but these are robust and flourishing. We ask many questions but they catch hold of us and in a moment we find ourselves shaved and sheared. What comic faces we have without hair! The four speak a language which does not seem of this world. It is certainly not German, for I understand a little German.

Finally another door is opened: here we are, locked in, naked, sheared and standing, with our feet in water—it is a shower-room. We are alone. Slowly the astonishment dissolves, and we speak, and everyone asks questions and no one answers. If we are naked in a shower-room, it means that we will have a shower. If we have a shower it is because they are not going to kill us yet. But why then do they keep us standing, and give us nothing to drink, while nobody explains anything, and we have no shoes or clothes, but we are all naked with our feet in the water, and we have been travelling five days and cannot even sit down.

And our women?

Mr. Levi asks me if I think that our women are like us at this moment, and where they are, and if we will be able to see them again. I say yes, because he is married and has a daughter; certainly we will see them again. But by now my belief is that all this is a game to mock and sneer at us. Clearly they will kill us, whoever thinks he is going to live is mad, it means that he has swallowed the bait, but I have not; I have understood that it will soon all be over, perhaps in this same room, when they get bored of seeing us naked, dancing from foot to foot and trying every now and again to sit down on the floor. But there are two inches of cold water and we cannot sit down.

We walk up and down without sense, and we talk, everybody talks to everybody else, we make a great noise. The door opens, and a German enters; it is the officer of before. He speaks briefly, the interpreter translates. "The officer says you must be quiet, because this is not a rabbinical school." One sees the words which are not his, the bad words, twist his mouth as they come out, as if he was spitting out a foul taste. We beg him to ask what we are waiting for, how long we will stay here, about our women, everything; but he says no, that he does not want to ask. This Flesch, who is most unwilling to translate into Italian the hard cold German phrases and refuses to turn into German our questions because he knows that it is useless, is a German Jew of about fifty, who has a large scar on his face from a wound received fighting the Italians on the Piave. He is a closed, taciturn man, for whom I feel an instinctive respect as I feel that he has begun to suffer before us.

The German goes and we remain silent, although we are a little ashamed of our silence. It is still night and we wonder if the day will ever come. The door opens again, and someone else dressed in stripes comes in. He is different from the others, older, with glasses, a more civilized face, and much less robust. He speaks to us in Italian.

By now we are tired of being amazed. We seem to be watching some mad play, one of those plays in which the witches, the Holy Spirit and the devil appear. He speaks Italian badly, with a strong foreign accent. He makes a long speech, is very polite, and tries to reply to all our questions.

We are at Monowitz, near Auschwitz, in Upper Silesia, a region inhabited by both Poles and Germans. This camp is a work-camp, in German one says *Arbeitslager*; all the prisoners (there are about ten thousand) work in a factory which produces a type of rubber called Buna, so that the camp itself is called Buna.

We will be given shoes and clothes—no, not our own,—other shoes, other clothes, like his. We are naked now because we are waiting for the shower and the disinfection, which will take place immediately after the reveille, because one cannot enter the camp without being disinfected.

Certainly there will be work to do, everyone must work here. But there is work and work: he, for example, acts as doctor. He is a Hungarian doctor who studied in Italy and he is the dentist of the Lager. He has been in the Lager for four and a half years (not in this one: Buna has only been open for a year and a half), but we can see that he is still quite well, not very thin. Why is he in the Lager? Is he Jewish like us? "No," he says simply, "I am a criminal."

We ask him many questions. He laughs, replies to some and not to others, and it is clear that he avoids certain subjects. He does not speak of the women: he says they are well, that we will see them again soon, but he does not say how or where. Instead he tells us other things, strange and crazy things, perhaps he too is playing with us. Perhaps he is mad—one goes mad in the Lager. He says that every Sunday there are concerts and football matches. He says that whoever boxes well can become cook. He says that whoever works well receives prize-coupons with which to buy tobacco and soap. He says that the water is really not drinkable, and that instead a coffee substitute is distributed every day, but generally nobody drinks it as the soup itself is sufficiently watery to quench thirst. We beg him to find us something to drink, but he says that he cannot, that he has come to see us secretly, against SS orders, as we still have to be disinfected, and that he must leave at once; he has come because he has a liking for Italians, and because, he says, he "has a little heart." We ask him if there are other Italians in the camp and he says there are some, a few, he does not know how many; and he at once changes the subject. Meanwhile a bell rang and he immediately hurried off and left us stunned and disconcerted. Some feel refreshed but I do not. I still think that even this dentist, this incomprehensible person, wanted to amuse himself at our expense, and I do not want to believe a word of what he said.

At the sound of the bell, we can hear the still dark camp waking up. Unexpectedly the water gushes out boiling from the showers—five minutes of bliss; but immediately after, four men (perhaps they are the barbers) burst in yelling and shoving and drive us out, wet and steaming, into the adjoining room which is freezing; here other shouting people throw at us unrecognizable rags and thrust into our hands a pair of broken-down boots with wooden soles; we have no time to understand and we already find ourselves in the open, in the blue and icy snow of dawn, barefoot and naked, with all our clothing in our hands, with a hundred yards to run to the next hut. There we are finally allowed to get dressed.

When we finish, everyone remains in his own corner and we do not dare lift our eyes to look at one another. There is nowhere to look in a mirror, but our appearance stands in front of us, reflected in a hundred livid faces, in a hundred miserable and sordid puppets. We are transformed into the phantoms glimpsed yesterday evening.

Then for the first time we became aware that our language lacks words to express this offence, the demolition of a man. In a moment, with almost prophetic intuition, the reality was revealed to us: we had reached the bottom. It is not possible to sink lower than this; no human condition is more miserable than this, nor could it conceivably be so. Nothing belongs to us anymore; they have taken away our clothes, our shoes, even our hair; if we speak, they will not listen to us, and if they listen, they will not understand. They will even take away our name: and if we want to keep it, we will have to find in ourselves the strength to do so, to manage somehow so that behind the name something of us, of us as we were, still remains.

We know that we will have difficulty in being understood, and this is as it should be. But consider what value, what meaning is enclosed even in the smallest of our daily habits, in the hundred possessions which even the poorest beggar owns: a handkerchief, an old letter, the photo of a cherished person. These things are part of us, almost like limbs of our body; nor is it conceivable that we can be deprived of them in our world, for we immediately find others to substitute the old ones, other objects which are ours in their personification and evocation of our memories.

Imagine now a man who is deprived of everyone he loves, and at the same time of his house, his habits, his clothes, in short, of everything he possesses: he will be a hollow man, reduced to suffering and needs, forgetful of dignity and restraint, for he who loses all often easily loses himself. He will be a man whose life or death can be lightly decided with no sense of human affinity, in the most fortunate of cases, on the basis of a pure judgment of utility. It is in this way that one can understand the double sense of the term "extermination camp," and it is now clear what we seek to express with the phrase: "to lie on the bottom."

The washroom is far from attractive. It is badly lighted, full of draughts, with the brick floor covered by a layer of mud. The water is not drinkable; it has a revolting smell and often fails for many hours. The walls are covered by curious didactic frescoes: for example, there is the good Häftling,[1] portrayed stripped to the waist, about to diligently soap his sheared and rosy cranium, and the bad Häftling, with a strong Semitic nose and a greenish colour, bundled up in his ostentatiously stained clothes with a beret on his head, who cautiously dips a finger into the water of the washbasin. Under the first is written: *"So bist du rein"* (like this you are clean), and under the second: *"So gehst du ein"* (like this you come to a bad end); and lower down, in doubtful French but in Gothic script: *"La propreté, c'est la santé."*

On the opposite wall an enormous white, red and black louse encamps, with the writing: *"Eine Laus, dein Tod"* (a louse is your death), and the inspired distich:

Nach dem Abort, vor dem Essen
Hände waschen, nicht vergessen.

(After the latrine, before eating, wash your hands, do not forget.)

For many weeks I considered these warnings about hygiene as pure examples of the Teutonic sense of humour, in the style of the dialogue about the truss which we had heard on our entry into the Lager. But later I understood that their unknown authors, perhaps without realizing it, were not far from some very important truths. In this place it is practically pointless to wash every day in the turbid water of the filthy washbasins for purposes of cleanliness and health; but it is most important as a symptom of remaining vitality, and necessary as an instrument of moral survival.

I must confess it: after only one week of prison, the instinct for cleanliness disappeared in me. I wander aimlessly around the washroom when I suddenly see Steinlauf, my friend aged almost fifty, with nude torso, scrub his neck and shoulders with little success (he has no soap) but great energy. Steinlauf sees me and greets me, and without preamble asks me severely why I do not wash. Why should I wash? Would I be better off than I am? Would I please someone more? Would I live a day, an hour longer? I would probably live a shorter time, because to wash is an effort, a waste of energy and warmth. Does not Steinlauf know that after half an hour with the coal sacks every difference between him and me will have disappeared? The more I think about it, the more washing one's face in our condition seems a stupid feat, even frivolous: a mechanical habit, or worse, a dismal repetition of an extinct rite. We will all die, we are all about to die: if they give me ten minutes between the reveille and work, I want to dedicate them to something else, to draw into myself, to weigh up things, or merely to look at the sky and think that I am looking at it perhaps for the last time; or even to let myself live, to indulge myself in the luxury of an idle moment.

But Steinlauf interrupts me. He has finished washing and is now drying himself with his cloth jacket which he was holding before wrapped up between his knees and which he will soon put on. And without interrupting the operation he administers me a complete lesson.

It grieves me now that I have forgotten his plain, outspoken words, the words of ex-sergeant Steinlauf of the Austro-Hungarian army, Iron Cross of the '14–'18 war. It grieves me because it means that I have to translate his uncertain Italian and his quiet manner of speaking of a good soldier into my language of an incredulous man. But this was the sense, not forgotten either then or later: that precisely because the Lager was a great machine to reduce us to beasts, we must not become beasts; that even in this place one can survive, and therefore one must want to survive, to tell the story, to bear witness; and that to survive we must force ourselves to save at least the skeleton, the scaffolding, the form of civilization. We are slaves, deprived of every right, exposed to every insult, condemned to certain death, but we still possess one power, and we must defend it with all our strength for it is the last—the power to refuse our consent. So we must certainly wash our faces without soap in dirty water and dry ourselves on our jackets. We must polish our shoes, not because the regulation states it, but for dignity and propriety. We must walk erect, without dragging our feet, not in homage to Prussian discipline but to remain alive, not to begin to die.

These things Steinlauf, a man of good will, told me; strange things to my unaccustomed ear, understood and accepted only in part, and softened by an easier, more flexible and blander doctrine, which for centuries has found its dwelling place on the other side of the Alps; according to which, among other things, nothing is of greater vanity than to force oneself to swallow whole a moral system elaborated by others, under another sky. No, the wisdom and virtue of Steinlauf, certainly good for him, is not enough for me. In the face of this complicated world my ideas of damnation are confused; is it really necessary to elaborate a system and put it into practice? Or would it not be better to acknowledge one's lack of a system?

THE DROWNED AND THE SAVED

What we have so far said and will say concerns the ambiguous life of the Lager. In our days many men have lived in this cruel manner, crushed against the bottom, but each for a relatively short period; so that we can perhaps ask ourselves if it is necessary or good to retain any memory of this exceptional human state.

To this question we feel that we have to reply in the affirmative. We are in fact convinced that no human experience is without meaning or unworthy of analysis, and that fundamental values, even if they are not positive, can be deduced from this particular world which we are describing. We would also like to consider that the Lager was pre-eminently a gigantic biological and social experiment.

Thousands of individuals, differing in age, condition, origin, language, culture and customs are enclosed within barbed wire: there they live a regular, controlled life which is identical for all and inadequate to all needs, and which is much more rigorous than any experimenter could have set up to establish what is essential and what adventitious to the conduct of the human animal in the struggle for life.

We do not believe in the most obvious and facile deduction: that man is fundamentally brutal, egoistic and stupid in his conduct once every civilized institution is taken away, and that the Häftling is consequently nothing but a man without inhibitions. We believe, rather, that the only conclusion to be drawn is that in the face of driving necessity and physical disabilities many social habits and instincts are reduced to silence.

But another fact seems to us worthy of attention: there comes to light the existence of two particularly well differentiated categories among men—the saved and the drowned. Other pairs of opposites (the good and the bad, the wise and the foolish, the cowards and the courageous, the unlucky and the fortunate) are considerably less distinct, they seem less essential, and above all they allow for more numerous and complex intermediary gradations.

This division is much less evident in ordinary life; for there it rarely happens that a man loses himself. A man is normally not alone, and in his rise or fall is tied to the destinies of his neighbours; so that it is exceptional for anyone to acquire unlimited power, or to fall by a succession of defeats into utter ruin. Moreover, everyone is normally in possession of such spiritual, physical and even financial resources that the probabilities of a shipwreck, of total inadequacy in the face of life, are relatively small. And one must take into account a definite cushioning effect exercised both by the law, and by the moral sense which constitutes a self-imposed law; for a country is considered the more civilized the more the wisdom and efficiency of its laws hinder a weak man from becoming too weak or a powerful one too powerful.

But in the Lager things are different: here the struggle to survive is without respite, because everyone is desperately and ferociously alone. If some Null Achtzehn vacillates, he will find no one to extend a helping hand; on the contrary, someone will knock him aside, because it is in no one's interest that there be one more "mussulman"[2] dragging himself to work every day; and if someone, by a miracle of savage patience and cunning, finds a new method of avoiding the hardest work, a new art which yields him an ounce of bread, he will try to keep his method secret, and he will be esteemed and respected for this, and will derive from it an exclusive, personal benefit; he will become stronger and so will be feared, and who is feared is, ipso facto, a candidate for survival.

In history and in life one sometimes seems to glimpse a ferocious law which states: "To he that has, will be given; to he that has not, will be taken away." In the Lager, where man is alone and where the struggle for life is reduced to its primordial mechanism, this unjust law is openly in force, is recognized by all. With the adaptable, the strong and astute individuals, even the leaders willingly keep contact, sometimes even friendly contact, because they hope later to perhaps derive some benefit. But with the mussulmans, the men in decay, it is not even worth speaking, because one knows already that they will complain and will speak about what they used to eat at home. Even less worthwhile is it to make friends with them, because they have no distinguished acquaintances in camp, they do not gain any extra rations, they do not work in profitable Kommandos and they know no secret method of organizing. And in any case, one knows that they are only here on a visit, that in a few weeks nothing will remain of them but a handful of ashes in some near-by field and a crossed-out number on a register. Although engulfed and swept along without rest by the innumerable crowd of those similar to them, they suffer and drag themselves along in an opaque intimate solitude, and in solitude they die or disappear, without leaving a trace in anyone's memory.

The result of this pitiless process of natural selection could be read in the statistics of Lager population movements. At Auschwitz, in 1944, of the old Jewish prisoners (we will not speak of the others here, as their condition was different), "kleine Nummer," low numbers less than 150,000, only a few hundred had survived; not one was an ordinary Häftling, vegetating in the ordinary Kommandos, and subsisting on the normal ration. There remained only the doctors, tailors, shoemakers, musicians, cooks, young attractive homosexuals, friends or compatriots of some authority in the camp; or they were particularly pitiless, vigorous and inhuman individuals, installed (following an investiture by the SS command, which showed itself in such choices to possess satanic knowledge of human beings) in the posts of Kapos, Blockältester, etc.; or finally, those who, without fulfilling particular functions, had always succeeded through their astuteness and energy in successfully organizing, gaining in this way, besides material advantages and reputation, the indulgence and esteem of the powerful people in the camp. Whosoever does not know how to become an "Organisator," "Kombinator," "Prominent" (the savage eloquence of these words!) soon becomes a "mussulman." In life, a third way exists, and is in fact the rule; it does not exist in the concentration camp.

To sink is the easiest of matters; it is enough to carry out all the orders one receives, to eat only the ration, to observe the discipline of the work and the camp. Experience showed that only exceptionally could one survive more than three months in this way. All the mussulmans who finished in the gas chambers have the same story, or more exactly, have no story; they followed the slope down to the bottom, like streams that run down to the sea. On their entry into the camp, through basic incapacity, or by misfortune, or through some banal incident, they are overcome before they can adapt themselves; they are beaten by time, they do not begin to learn German, to disentangle the infernal knot of laws and prohibitions until their body is already in decay, and nothing can save them from selections or from death by exhaustion. Their life is short, but their number is endless; they, the *Muselmänner*, the drowned, form the backbone of the camp, an anonymous mass, continually renewed and always identical, of non-men who march and labour in silence, the divine spark dead within them, already too empty to really suffer. One hesitates to call them living: one hesitates to call their death death, in the face of which they have no fear, as they are too tired to understand.

They crowd my memory with their faceless presences, and if I could enclose all the evil of our time in our image, I would choose this image which is familiar to me: an emaciated man, with head dropped and shoulders curved, on whose face and in whose eyes not a trace of a thought is to be seen.

NOTES

1. A prisoner.
2. This word *"Muselmann,"* I do not know why, was used by the old ones of the camp to describe the weak, the inept, those doomed to selection.

JEAN AMÉRY

◲ On the Necessity and Impossibility of Being a Jew

Not seldom, when in conversation my partner draws me into a plural—that is, as soon as he includes my person in whatever connection and says to me: "We Jews . . ."—I feel a not exactly tormenting, but nonetheless deep-seated discomfort. I have long tried to get to the bottom of this disconcerting psychic state, and it has not been very easy for me. Can it be, is it thinkable that I, the former Auschwitz inmate, who truly has not lacked occasion to recognize what he is and what he must be, still did not want to be a Jew, as decades ago, when I wore white half socks and leather breeches and nervously eyed myself in the mirror,

---

From Jean Améry, *At the Mind's Limits* (Bloomington: Indiana University Press).

hoping it would show me an impressive German youth? Naturally not. The foolishness of my masquerading in Austrian dress—although it was, after all, part of my heritage—belongs to the distant past. It is all right with me that I was not a German youth and am not a German man. No matter how the disguise may have looked on me, it now lies in the attic. If today discomfort arises in me when a Jew takes it for granted, legitimately, that I am part of his community, then it is not because I don't want to be a Jew, but only because I cannot be one. And yet must be one. And I do not merely submit to this necessity, but expressly claim it as part of my person. The necessity and impossibility of being a Jew, that is what causes me indistinct pain. It is with this necessity, this impossibility, this oppression, this inability that I must deal here, and in doing so I can only hope, without certainty, that my individual story is exemplary enough also to reach those who neither are nor have to be Jews.

First of all, concerning the impossibility. If being a Jew means sharing a religious creed with other Jews, participating in Jewish cultural and family tradition, cultivating a Jewish national ideal, then I find myself in a hopeless situation. I don't believe in the God of Israel. I know very little about Jewish culture. I see myself as a boy at Christmas, plodding through a snow-covered village to midnight mass; I don't see myself in a synagogue. I hear my mother appealing to Jesus, Mary, and Joseph when a minor household misfortune occurred; I hear no adjuration of the Lord in Hebrew. The picture of my father—whom I hardly knew, since he remained where his Kaiser had sent him and his fatherland deemed him to be in the safest care—did not show me a bearded Jewish sage, but rather a Tyrolean Imperial Rifleman in the uniform of the First World War. I was nineteen years old when I heard of the existence of a Yiddish language, although on the other hand I knew full well that my religiously and ethnically very mixed family was regarded by the neighbors as Jewish, and that no one in my home thought of denying or hiding what was unconcealable anyhow. I was a Jew, just as one of my schoolmates was the son of a bankrupt innkeeper: when the boy was alone the financial ruin of his family may have meant next to nothing to him; when he joined us others he retreated, as we did, into resentful embarrassment.

If being a Jew implies having a cultural heritage or religious ties, then I was not one and can never become one. Certainly, it could be argued that a heritage can be acquired, ties established, and that therefore to be a Jew could be a matter of a voluntary decision. Who would possibly prevent me from learning the Hebrew language, from reading Jewish history and tales, and from participating—even without belief—in Jewish ritual, which is both religious and national? Well supplied with all the requisite knowledge of Jewish culture from the prophets to Martin Buber, I could emigrate to Israel and call myself Yochanan. I have the freedom to choose to be a Jew, and this freedom is my very personal and universally human privilege. That is what I am assured of.

But do I really have it? I don't believe so. Would Yochanan, the proud bearer of a new self-acquired identity, be made immune on the 24th of December by his supposedly thorough knowledge of chassidism against thoughts of a Christmas tree with gilded nuts? Would the up-right Israeli, conversing fluently in Hebrew, be able so completely to obliterate the white-stockinged youth who once took such pains to speak a local dialect? In modern literature the switch of identity is quite a stimulating game, but in my case it is a challenge that one meets with no certainty of success, in one's human totality, without the chance of an interim solution, and would—it seems to me—be wholly predestined to fail. One can reestablish the link with a tradition that one has lost, but one cannot freely invent it for oneself, that is the problem. Since I was not a Jew, I am not one; and since I am not one, I won't be able to become one. A Yochanan on Mt. Carmel, haunted and spirited home by memories of Alpine valleys and folk rituals, would be even more inauthentic than was once the youth with his knee socks. To be who one is by becoming the person one should be and wants to be: for me this dialectical process of self-realization is obstructed. Because being Something, not as metaphysical essence, but as the simple summation of early experience, absolutely has priority. Everyone must be who he was in the first years of his life, even if later these were buried under. No one can become what he cannot find in his memories.

Thus I am not permitted to be a Jew. But since all the same I must be one and since this compulsion excludes the possibilities that might allow me to be something other than a Jew, can I not find myself at all? Must I acquiesce, without a past, as a shadow of the universal-abstract (which does not exist) and take refuge in the empty phrase that I am simply a human being? But patience, we haven't reached that point yet. Since the necessity exists—and how compelling it is!—perhaps the impossibility can be resolved. After all, one wants to live without hiding, as I did when I was in the underground, and without dissolving into the abstract. A human being? Certainly, who would not want to be one. But you are a human being only if you are a German, a Frenchman, a Christian, a member of whatever identifiable social group. I must be a Jew and will be one, with or without religion, within or outside a tradition, whether as Jean, Hans, or Yochanan. Why I must be one is what will be told here.

It didn't begin when schoolmates said to the boy: You're Jews anyway. Nor with the fight on the ramp of the university, during which, long before Hitler's ascent to power, a Nazi fist knocked out one of my teeth. Yes, we are Jews, and what of it? I answered my schoolmate. Today my tooth, tomorrow yours, and the devil take you, I thought to myself after the beating, and bore the gap proudly like an interesting duelling scar.

It didn't begin until 1935, when I was sitting over a newspaper in a Vienna coffeehouse and was studying the Nuremberg Laws, which had just been enacted across the border in Germany. I needed only to skim them and already I could perceive that they applied to me. Society, concretized in the National Socialist German state, which the world recognized absolutely as the legitimate representative of the German people, had just made me formally and beyond any question a Jew, or rather it had given a new dimension to what I had already known earlier, but which at the time was of no great consequence to me, namely, that I was a Jew.

What sort of new dimension? Not one that was immediately fathomable. After I had read the Nuremberg Laws I was no more Jewish than a half hour before. My features had not become more Mediterranean-Semitic, my frame of reference had not suddenly been filled by magic power with Hebrew allusions, the Christmas tree had not wondrously transformed itself into the seven-armed candelabra. If the sentence that society had passed on me had a tangible meaning, it could only be that henceforth I was a quarry of Death. Well, sooner or later it claims all of us. But the Jew—and I now was one by decree of law and society—was more firmly promised to death, already in the midst of life. His days were a period of false grace that could be revoked at any second. I do not believe that I am inadmissibly projecting Auschwitz and the Final Solution back to 1935 when I advance these thoughts today. Rather, I am certain that in that year, at that moment when I read the Laws, I did indeed already hear the death threat— better, the death sentence—and certainly no special sensitivity toward history was required for that. Had I not already heard a hundred times the appeal to fate—coupled with the call for Germany's awakening—that the Jew should perish? "Juda verrecke!"—that was something completely different than the almost cheerful "L'aristocrat, à la laterne!" Even if one did not consider or did not know that historically it linked up with countless pogroms of the past, it was not a revolutionary clamor, but rather the carefully considered demand of a people, compressed into a slogan, a war cry! Also in those same days I had once seen in a German magazine the photo of a Winter Relief event in a Rhenish town, and in the foreground, in front of the tree gleaming with electric lights, there was proudly displayed a banner with the text: "No one shall go hungry, no one shall freeze, but the Jews shall die like dogs." And only three years later, on the day of Austria's incorporation into the *Grossdeutsches Reich*, I heard Joseph Goebbels screaming on the radio that one really ought not to make such a fuss about the fact that in Vienna a few Jews were now committing suicide.

To be a Jew, that meant for me, from this moment on, to be a dead man on leave, someone to be murdered, who only by chance was not yet where he properly belonged; and so it has remained, in many variations, in various degrees of intensity, until today. The death threat, which I felt for the first time with complete clarity while reading the Nuremberg Laws, included what is commonly referred to as the methodic "degradation" of the Jews by the Nazis. Formulated differently: the denial of human dignity sounded the death threat. Daily, for years on end, we could read and hear that we were lazy, evil, ugly, capable only of misdeed, clever only to the extent that we pulled one over on others. We were incapable of founding a state, but also by no means suited to assimilate with our host nations. By their very presence, our bodies—hairy, fat, and bowlegged— befouled public swimming pools, yes, even park benches. Our hideous faces, depraved and spoilt by protruding ears and hanging noses, were disgusting to our fellow men, fellow citizens of yesterday. We were not worthy of love and thus also not of life. Our sole right, our sole duty was to disappear from the face of the earth.

The degradation of the Jews was, I am convinced, identical with the death threat long before Auschwitz. In this regard Jean-Paul Sartre, already in 1946 in his book *Anti-Semite and Jew*, offered a few perceptions that are still valid today. There is no "Jewish Problem," he said, only a problem of antisemitism; the anti-semite forced the Jew into a situation in which he permitted his enemy to stamp him with a self-image. Both points appear to me to be unassailable. But in his short phenomenological sketch Sartre could not describe the total, crushing force of antisemitism, a force that had brought the Jew to that point, quite aside from the fact that the great author himself probably did not comprehend it in its entire overwhelming might. The Jew—and Sartre speaks here, without making a value judgment, of the "inauthentic" Jew, that is, the Jew who has fallen victim to the myth of the "universal man"—subjugates himself, in his flight from the Jewish fate, to the power of his oppressor. But one must say in his favor that in the years of the Third Reich the Jew stood with his back to the wall, and it too was hostile. There was no way out. Because it was not only radical Nazis, offi-cially certified by the party, who denied that we were worthy of being loved and thereby worthy of life. All of Germany—but what am I saying!—the whole world nodded its head in approval of the undertaking, even if here and there with a certain superficial regret.

One must remember: when after World War II streams of refugees poured out of the various communist-ruled lands into the West, the countries of the pro-claimed free world outdid one another in their willingness to grant asylum and aid, although among all the emigrants there was only a handful whose lives would have been directly threatened in their homeland. But even when it long since should have been clear to any discerning person what awaited us in the German Reich, no one wanted to have us. Thus, it necessarily had to reach the point where the Jews, whether authentic or not, whether secure in the illusion of a God and a national hope, or assimilated, found within themselves no powers of resistance when their enemy burned the image from Streicher's *Stürmer* into their skin. It should be noted that this weakness had only little to do with the classical Jewish self-hatred of those German Jews of the time before the outbreak of Nazism who were not only willing but craving to assimilate. The self-haters had believed that they were unable to be what they so much wanted to be: Ger-mans, and therefore they rejected themselves. They had not wanted to accept their existence as non-Germans, but no one had forced them to reject themselves as Jews. When, on the other hand, between 1933 and 1945 precisely the bright-est and most upright Jewish minds, authentic or inauthentic, capitulated to Streicher, that was a wholly different act of resignation, no longer moral, but rather social and philosophic in nature. This, so they must have told themselves, is how the world sees us, as lazy, ugly, useless, and evil; in view of such univer-sal agreement what sense does it still make to object and say that we *are* not that way! The surrender of the Jews to the *Stürmer* image of themselves was nothing other than the acknowledgment of a social reality. To oppose it with a self-evaluation based on other standards at times had to appear ridiculous or mad.

In order to discuss it, however, one must have experienced it. When I think about the social reality of the wall of rejection that arose before us everywhere,

my stay in Auschwitz-Monowitz comes to mind. In the camp itself, but also
among the so-called free workers at the worksite, there was a strict ethnic hierarchy, imposed by the Nazis on all of us. A German from the Reich was regarded
more highly than a German from an Eastern country. A Flemish Belgian was
worth more than a Walloon. A Ukrainian from occupied Poland ranked higher
than his Polish compatriot. A forced laborer from Eastern Europe was more
poorly regarded than an Italian. Far down on the bottom rungs of the ladder
were the concentration camp inmates, and among them, in turn, the Jews had
the lowest rank. There was not a single non-Jewish professional criminal, no
matter how degenerate he may have been, who did not stand high above us.
The Poles, whether they were genuine freedom fighters who had been thrown
into the camp after the ill-fated Warsaw insurrection, or merely small-time pick-
pockets, despised us unanimously. So did half-illiterate White Russian workers.
But also Frenchmen. I still hear a free French worker conversing with a Jewish-
French concentration camp inmate: "I'm French," the inmate said. "Français,
toi? Mais, tu es juif, mon ami," his countryman retorted objectively and without
hostility; for in a mixture of fear and indifference he had absorbed the teachings
of Europe's German masters. I repeat: the world approved of the place to which
the Germans had assigned us, the small world of the camp and the wide world
outside, which but rarely, in individual heroic instances, arose in protest when
we were taken at night from our homes in Vienna or Berlin, in Amsterdam,
Paris, or Brussels.

The degradation proceedings directed against us Jews, which began with
the proclamation of the Nuremberg Laws and as a direct result led all the way to
Treblinka, met on our, on my side with an equivalent proceedings aimed at the
reattainment of dignity. For me, until today, this case is not closed. Let my
endeavor to gain clarity concerning its stages and its preliminary result be
recorded here, and permit me to request of the reader that he accompany me
awhile along this path. It is short, but difficult to tread, and full of obstacles and
traps. For what, after all, actually is the nature of the dignity that was first
denied me in 1935, officially withheld from me until 1945, and that perhaps even
today one does not want to grant me, and that I must therefore attain through
my own effort? What is dignity, really?

One can try to answer by inverting the above-formulated identification of
degradation and death threat. If I was correct that the deprivation of dignity was
nothing other than the potential deprivation of life, then dignity would have to
be the right to live. If it was also correct when I said that the granting and
depriving of dignity are acts of social agreement, sentences against which there
is no appeal on the grounds of one's "self-understanding," so that it would be
senseless to argue against the social body that deprives us of our dignity with
the claim that we do indeed "feel" worthy—if all of this were valid, then every
effort to regain our dignity would have been of no value, and it would still be so
today. Degradation, that is, living under the threat of death, would be an
inescapable fate. But luckily, things are not entirely the way this logic claims. It

is certainly true that dignity can be bestowed only by society, whether it be the dignity of some office, a professional or, very generally speaking, civil dignity; and the merely individual, subjective claim ("I am a human being and as such I have my dignity, no matter what you may do or say!") is an empty academic game, or madness. Still, the degraded person, threatened with death, is able— and here we break through the logic of the final sentencing—to convince society of his dignity by taking his fate upon himself and at the same time rising in revolt against it.

The first step must be the unqualified recognition that the verdict of the social group is a given reality. When I read the Nuremberg Laws in 1935 and realized not only that they applied to me but also that they were the expression, concentrated in legal-textual form, of the verdict "Death to the Jews!" which already earlier had been pronounced by German society, I could have taken intellectual flight, turned on the defense mechanisms, and thereby have lost my case for rehabilitation. Then I would have told myself: well, well, so this is the will of the National Socialist state, of the German *pays légal;* but it has nothing to do with the real Germany, the *pays réel,* which has no thought whatever of ostra-cizing me. Or I could have argued that it was only Germany, a land unfortu-nately sinking into a bloody madness, that was so absurdly stamping me as sub-human (in the literal sense of the word), whereas to my good fortune the great wide world outside, in which there are Englishmen, Frenchmen, Americans, and Russians, is immune to the collective paranoia scourging Germany. Or finally, even if I had abandoned the illusion both of a German *pays réel* and of a world immune against the German mental disorder, I could have comforted myself with the thought: no matter what they say about me, it isn't true. I am true only as I see and understand myself deep within; I am what I am for myself and in myself, and nothing else.

I am not saying that now and then I did not succumb to such temptation. I can only testify that finally I learned to resist it and that already at that time, in 1935. I vaguely felt the necessity to convince the world of my dignity, the world that by no means indignantly and unanimously broke off all relations with the Third Reich. I understood, even if unclearly, that while I had to accept the ver-dict as such, I could force the world to revise it. I accepted the judgment of the world, with the decision to overcome it through revolt.

Revolt; well, of course, that is another one of those high-sounding words. It could lead the reader to believe that I was a hero or that I falsely want to present myself as one. I certainly was no hero. When the little grey Volkswagen with the POL license plate crossed my path, first in Vienna, then in Brussels, I was so afraid that I couldn't breathe. When the Kapo drew back his arm to strike me, I didn't stand firm like a cliff, but ducked. And still, I tried to initiate proceedings to regain my dignity, and beyond physical survival that provided me with just the slightest chance to survive the nightmare morally also. There is not much that I can present in my favor, but let it be noted anyhow. I took it upon myself to be a Jew, even though there would have been possibilities for a compromise settlement. I joined a resistance movement whose prospects for success were very dim. Also, I finally relearned what I and my kind often had forgotten and what was more crucial than the moral power to resist: to hit back.

Before me I see the prisoner foreman Juszek, a Polish professional criminal of horrifying vigor. In Auschwitz he once hit me in the face because of a trifle; that is how he was used to dealing with all the Jews under his command. At this moment—I felt it with piercing clarity—it was up to me to go a step further in my prolonged appeals case against society. In open revolt I struck Juszek in the face in turn. My human dignity lay in this punch to his jaw—and that it was in the end I, the physically much weaker man, who succumbed and was woefully thrashed, meant nothing to me. Painfully beaten, I was satisfied with myself. But not, as one might think, for reasons of courage and honor, but only because I had grasped well that there are situations in life in which our body is our entire self and our entire fate. I was my body and nothing else: in hunger, in the blow that I suffered, in the blow that I dealt. My body, debilitated and crusted with filth, was my calamity. My body, when it tensed to strike, was my physical and metaphysical dignity. In situations like mine, physical violence is the sole means for restoring a disjointed personality. In the punch, I was myself—for myself and for my opponent. What I later read in Frantz Fanon's *Les damnés de la terre*, in a theoretical analysis of the behavior of colonized peoples, I anticipated back then when I gave concrete social form to my dignity by punching a human face. To be a Jew meant the acceptance of the death sentence imposed by the world as a world verdict. To flee before it by withdrawing into one's self would have been nothing but a disgrace, whereas acceptance was simultaneously the physical revolt against it. I became a person not by subjectively appealing to my abstract humanity but by discovering myself within the given social reality as a rebelling Jew and by realizing myself as one.

The proceedings, I said, went on and still go on. At present, I have neither won nor lost the case. After the collapse of the National Socialist Reich there was a brief global hour in which I was able to believe that from the bottom up everything was transformed. For a short time in those days I was able to foster the illusion that my dignity was totally restored, through my own, no matter how modest, activity in the resistance movement, through the heroic uprising in the Warsaw Ghetto, but above all through the contempt that the world showed toward those who had stripped me of my dignity. I could believe that the deprivation of dignity that we had experienced had been a historical error, an aberration, a collective sickness of the world, from which the latter had recovered at the moment when in Reims German generals signed the declaration of surrender in the presence of Eisenhower. Soon I learned worse. In Poland and in the Ukraine, while they were still discovering Jewish mass graves, there were antisemitic disturbances. In France the ever sickly petty bourgeoisie had allowed itself to be infected by the occupiers. When survivors and refugees returned and demanded their old dwellings, it happened that simple housewives, in a peculiar mixture of satisfaction and chagrin, said: "Tiens, ils reviennent, on ne les a tout de même tué." Even in countries that previously had hardly known any antisemitism, as in Holland, there suddenly existed as a relict of the German propaganda a "Jewish Problem," though scarcely any more Jews. England barred its Mandate of Palestine to those Jews who had escaped from the camps and jails and who tried to immigrate. In a very short time I was forced to recognize that little had changed, that I was still the man condemned to be murdered in due time, even though the potential executioner now cautiously restrained himself or, at best, even loudly protested his disapproval of what had happened.

I understood reality. But should this perhaps have occasioned me to come to grips with the problem of antisemitism? Not at all. Antisemitism and the Jewish Question, as historical, socially determined conceptual phenomena, were not and are not any concern of mine. They are entirely a matter for the antisemites, their disgrace or their sickness. The antisemites have something to overcome, not I. I would play into their unclean hands if I began investigating what share religious, economic, or other factors have in the persecution of the Jews. If I were to engage in such investigations I would only be falling for the intellectual dupery of so-called historical objectivity, according to which the murdered are as guilty as the murderers, if not even more guilty. A wound was inflicted on me. I must disinfect and bind it, not contemplate why the ruffian raised his club, and, through the inferred "That's Why," in the end partly absolve him.

It was not the antisemites who concerned me, it was only with my own existence that I had to cope. That was hard enough. Certain possibilities, which had emerged for me in the war years, no longer existed. From 1945 to 1947 I could not very well sew on a yellow star without appearing foolish or eccentric to myself. There also was no longer any opportunity to punch the enemy in his face, for he was not so easy to recognize anymore. The reattainment of dignity, just as urgent as in the previous years of war and National Socialism, but now— in a climate of deceptive peace—infinitely more difficult, remained a compulsion and desire. Except that I had to recognize even more clearly than in the days when physical revolt was at least possible that I was confronted with necessity and impossibility.

At this point I must stop for a moment and separate myself from all those Jews who do not speak from the realm of my own experience. In his book *La condition réflexive de l'homme juif* the French philosopher Robert Misrahi said: "The Nazi Holocaust is henceforth the absolute and radical reference point for the existence of every Jew." That is not to be doubted, yet I am convinced that not every Jew is capable of thinking out this relationship. Only those who have lived through a fate like mine, and no one else, can refer their lives to the years 1933–45. By no means do I say this with pride. It would be ridiculous enough to boast of something that one did not do but only underwent. Rather it is with a certain shame that I assert my sad privilege and suggest that while the Holocaust is truly the existential reference point for all Jews, only we, the sacrificed, are able to spiritually relive the catastrophic event as it was or fully picture it as it could be again. Let others not be prevented from empathizing. Let them contemplate a fate that yesterday could have been and tomorrow can be theirs. Their intellectual efforts will meet with our respect, but it will be a sceptical one, and in conversation with them we will soon grow silent and say to ourselves: go ahead, good people, trouble your heads as much as you want; you still sound like a blind man talking about color.

The parentheses are now closed. I am once again alone with myself and a few good comrades. I find myself in the postwar years, which no longer permitted any of us to react with violence to something that refused to reveal itself clearly to us. Again I see myself confronted with necessity and impossibility.

That this impossibility does not apply to all is obvious. Among the Jews of this time, whether they be workers in Kiev, storekeepers in Brooklyn, or farmers in the Negev, there are enough men and women for whom being a Jew was and always remained a positive fact. They speak Yiddish or Hebrew. They celebrate the sabbath. They explicate the Talmud or stand at attention as young soldiers under the blue-and-white banner with the Star of David. Whether religiously or nationally or merely in personal reverence before the picture of their grandfather with his sidelocks, they are *Jews* as members of a community. One could briefly digress perhaps and, together with the sociologist Georges Friedmann, ask the secondary question of whether their progeny will still be Jews and whether the end of the Jewish people may not be imminent in that Mediterranean country where the Israeli is already displacing the Jew, as well as in the Diaspora, where perhaps the total assimilation of the Jews—not so much to their host peoples, who for their part are losing their national character, but to the larger unity of the technical-industrial world—could take place.

I'll not pursue this question further. The existence or the disappearance of the Jewish people as an ethnic-religious community does not excite me. In my deliberations I am unable to consider Jews who are Jews because they are sheltered by tradition. I can speak solely for myself—and, even if with caution, for contemporaries, probably numbering into the millions, whose being Jewish burst upon them with elemental force, and who must stand this test without God, without history, without messianic-national hope. For them, for me, being a Jew means feeling the tragedy of yesterday as an inner oppression. On my left forearm I bear the Auschwitz number; it reads more briefly than the Pentateuch or the Talmud and yet provides more thorough information. It is also more binding than basic formulas of Jewish existence. If to myself and the world, including the religious and nationally minded Jews, who do not regard me as one of their own, I say: I am a Jew, then I mean by that those realities and possibilities that are summed up in the Auschwitz number.

In the two decades that have passed since my liberation I have gradually come to realize that it does not matter whether an existence can be positively defined. Sartre had already said once that a Jew is a person who is regarded by others as a Jew, and later Max Frisch dramatically portrayed this in *Andorra*. This view does not need to be corrected, but perhaps one may amplify it. For even if the others do not decide that I am a Jew, as they did with the poor devil in *Andorra*, who would have liked to become a carpenter and whom they permitted only to be a merchant, I am still a Jew by the mere fact that the world around me does not expressly designate me as a non-Jew. To be something can mean that one is *not* something else. As a Non-non-Jew, I am a Jew; I must be one and must want to be one. I must accept this and affirm it in my daily existence, whether—showing my colors—I butt into a conversation when stupid things are said about Jews at the greengrocery, whether I address an unknown audience on the radio, or whether I write for a magazine.

But since being a Jew not only means that I bear within me a catastrophe that occurred yesterday and cannot be ruled out for tomorrow, it is—beyond being a duty—also *fear*. Every morning when I get up I can read the Auschwitz number on my forearm, something that touches the deepest and most closely intertwined roots of my existence; indeed I am not even sure if this is not my entire existence. Then I feel approximately as I did back then when I got a taste of the first blow from a policeman's fist. Every day anew I lose my trust in the world. The Jew without positive determinants, the Catastrophe Jew, as we will unhesitatingly call him, must get along without trust in the world. My neighbor greets me in a friendly fashion, *Bonjour, Monsieur*; I doff my hat, *Bonjour, Madame*. But Madame and Monsieur are separated by interstellar distances; for yesterday a Madame looked away when they led off a Monsieur, and through the barred windows of the departing car a Monsieur viewed a Madame as if she were a stone angel from a bright and stern heaven, which is forever closed for the Jew. I read an official announcement in which "la population" is called upon to do something or other, told that the trash cans are to be put out on time or that the flag is to be displayed on a national holiday. *La population*. Still another one of those unearthly realms that I can enter as little as I can Kafka's castle; for yesterday "la population" had great fear of hiding me, and whether tomorrow it would have more courage if I knocked at the door, unfortunately is not certain.

Twenty years have passed since the Holocaust. Glorious years for such as us. Nobel prize winners in abundance. There were French presidents named René Mayer and Pierre Mendès-France; an American UN delegate by the name of Goldberg practices a most dignified anticommunist American patriotism. I don't trust this peace. Declarations of human rights, democratic constitutions, the free world and the free press, nothing can again lull me into the slumber of security from which I awoke in 1935. As a Jew I go through life like a sick man with one of those ailments that cause no great hardships but are certain to end fatally. He didn't always suffer from that sickness. When he attempts, like Peer Gynt, to peel his self out of the onion, he doesn't discover the malady. His first walk to school, his first love, his first verses had nothing to do with it. But now he is a sick man, first and foremost and more deeply than he is a tailor, a book-keeper, or a poet. Thus, I too am precisely what I am not, because I did not exist until I became it, above all else: a Jew. Death, from which the sick man will be unable to escape, is what threatens me. *Bonjour, Madame, Bonjour, Monsieur*, they greet each other. But she cannot and will not relieve her sick neighbor of his mortal illness at the cost of suffering to death from it herself. And so they remain strangers to one another.

Without trust in the world I face my surroundings as a Jew who is alien and alone, and all that I can manage is to get along within my foreignness. I must accept being foreign as an essential element of my personality, insist upon it as if upon an inalienable possession. Still and each day anew I find myself alone. I was unable to force yesterday's murderers and tomorrow's potential aggressors to recognize the moral truth of their crimes, because the world, in its totality, did not help me to do it. Thus I am alone, as I was when they tortured me. Those around me do not appear to me as antihumans, as did my former torturers; they are my co-humans, not affected by me and the danger prowling at my side. I pass them with a greeting and without hostility. I cannot rely on them, only on a Jewish identity that is without positive determinants, my burden and my support.

Where there is a common bond between me and the world, whose still unrevoked death sentence I acknowledge as a social reality, it dissolves in polemics. You don't want to listen? Listen anyhow. You don't want to know to where your indifference can again lead you and me at any time? I'll tell you. What happened is no concern of yours because you didn't know, or were too young, or not even born yet? You should have seen, and your youth gives you no special privilege, and break with your father.

Once again I must ask myself the question that I already raised fleetingly in my essay "Resentments": am I perhaps mentally ill and am I not suffering from an incurable ailment, from hysteria? The question is merely rhetorical. I have long since provided myself with a fully conclusive answer. I know that what oppresses me is no neurosis, but rather precisely reflected reality. Those were no hysteric hallucinations when I heard the Germans call for the Jews to "die like a dog!" and, in passing, heard how people said that there really must be something suspicious about the Jews, because otherwise they would hardly be treated so severely. "They are being arrested, so they must have done something," said a proper social-democratic worker's wife in Vienna. "How horrible, what they are doing with the Jews, *mais enfin* . . . ," speculated a humane and patriotic-minded man in Brussels. I am thus forced to conclude that I am not deranged and was not deranged, but rather that the neurosis is on the part of the historical occurrence. The others are the madmen, and I am left standing around helplessly among them, a fully sane person who joined a tour through a psychiatric clinic and suddenly lost sight of the doctors and orderlies. But since the sentence passed on me by the madmen can, after all, be carried out at any moment, it is totally binding, and my own mental lucidity is entirely irrelevant.

These reflections are nearing their end. Now that I have explained how I manage in this world, it is time to testify how I relate to my kinsmen, the Jews. But are they really related to me after all? Whatever an ethnologist may determine—for example, that my external appearance presents one or another Jewish characteristic—may be relevant if I land in a screaming mob that is hounding Jews. It loses all significance when I am alone or among Jews. Do I have a Jewish nose? That could become a calamity if a pogrom breaks out again. But that does not align me with a single other Jewish nose anywhere. The Jewish appearance that I may or may not have—I don't know if I do—is a matter for the others and becomes my concern only in the objective relationship they establish toward me. If I were to look like I had stepped out of Johann von Leers's book

Juden sehen euch an[1] it would have no subjective reality for me; it would, to be sure, establish a community of fate, but no positive community between me and my fellow Jews. Thus there remains only the intellectual—more correctly, the consciously perceived—relationship of Jews, Judaism, and myself.

That it is a nonrelationship I have already stated at the outset. With Jews as Jews I share practically nothing: no language, no cultural tradition, no childhood memories. In the Austrian region of Vorarlberg there was an innkeeper and butcher of whom I was told that he spoke fluent Hebrew. He was my great-grandfather. I never saw him and it must be nearly a hundred years since he died. Before the Holocaust my interest in Jewish things and Jews was so slight that with the best of intentions I could not say today which of my acquaintances at that time was a Jew and which was not. However I might try to find in Jewish history my own past, in Jewish culture my own heritage, in Jewish folklore my personal recollections, the result would be nil. The environment in which I had lived in the years when one acquires one's self was not Jewish, and that cannot be reversed. But the fruitlessness of the search for my Jewish self by no means stands as a barrier between me and my solidarity with every threatened Jew in this world.

I read in the paper that in Moscow they discovered an illegally operating bakery for unleavened Jewish Passover bread and arrested the bakers. As a means of nourishment the ritual matzoth of the Jews interest me somewhat less than rye crisps. Nevertheless, the action of the Soviet authorities fills me with uneasiness, indeed with indignation. Some American country club, so I hear, does not accept Jews as members. Not for the world would I wish to belong to this obviously dismal middle-class association, but the cause of the Jews who demand permission to join becomes mine. That some Arab statesman calls for Israel to be wiped off the map cuts me to the quick, even though I have never visited the state of Israel and do not feel the slightest inclination to live there. My solidarity with every Jew whose freedom, equal rights, or perhaps even physical existence is threatened is *also*, but *not only*, a reaction to antisemitism, which, according to Sartre, is not an opinion but the predisposition and readiness to commit the crime of genocide. This solidarity is part of my person and a weapon in the battle to regain my dignity. Without being a Jew in the sense of a positive identification, it is not until I am a Jew in the recognition and acknowledgment of the world verdict on the Jews and not until I finally participate in the historical appeals process that I may speak of freedom.

Solidarity in the face of threat is all that links me with my Jewish contemporaries, the believers as well as the nonbelievers, the national-minded as well as those ready to assimilate. For them that is perhaps little or nothing at all. For me and my continued existence it means much, more probably than my appreciation of Proust's books or my affection for the stories of Schnitzler or my joy in seeing the Flemish landscape. Without Proust and Schnitzler and the wind-bent poplars at the North Sea I would be poorer than I am, but I would still be human. Without the feeling of belonging to the threatened I would be a self-surrendering fugitive from reality.

I say reality, with emphasis, because in the end that is what matters to me. Antisemitism, which made a Jew of me, may be a form of madness; that is not what is in question here. Whether it is a madness or not, it is in any event a historical and social fact. I was, after all, really in Auschwitz and not in Himmler's imagination. And antisemitism is still a reality; only someone with complete social and historical blindness could deny it. It is a reality in its core countries, Austria and Germany, where Nazi war criminals either are not convicted or receive ridiculously mild prison sentences, of which for the most part they serve hardly a third. It is a reality in England and the United States, where one tolerates the Jews, but would not be unhappy to be rid of them. It is a reality, and with what dire consequences, in the spiritual global domain of the Catholic Church. The complexity and confusion of the Vatican Council's consultations on the so-called Declaration on the Jews were, despite the honorable effort of so many a prelate, grievously shameful.

It may well be—but in view of the given circumstances one can by no means count on it—that in the Nazi death factories the final act was played in the vast historical drama of Jewish persecution. I believe that the dramaturgy of antisemitism continues to exist. A new mass extermination of Jews cannot be ruled out as a possibility. What would happen if in a war against the small land of Israel the Arab countries, today supported by arms shipments from East and West, were to gain a total victory? What would an America that had come under the sway of military fascism mean not only for the Negroes but also for the Jews? What would the fate of the Jews have been in France, the European country with their greatest number, if at the beginning of this decade not de Gaulle had triumphed, but the OAS?

With some reluctance I read in the study of a very young Dutch Jew the following definition of the Jew: "A Jew can be described as someone who has more fear, mistrust, and vexation than his fellow citizens who were never persecuted." The apparently correct definition is rendered false by the absence of an indispensable extension, which would have to read: ". . . for with good reason he awaits a new catastrophe at any moment." The awareness of the last cataclysm and the legitimate fear of a new one is what it all amounts to. I, who bear both within me—and the latter with double weight, since it was only by chance that I escaped the former—am not "traumatized," but rather my spiritual and psychic condition corresponds completely to reality. The consciousness of my being a Holocaust Jew is not an ideology. It may be compared to the class consciousness that Marx tried to reveal to the proletarians of the nineteenth century. I experienced in my existence and exemplify through it a historical reality of my epoch, and since I experienced it more deeply than most other Jews, I can also shed more light on it. That is not to my credit and not because I am so wise, but only because of the chance of fate.

Everything could be borne more easily if my bond with other Jews were not limited to the solidarity of revolt, if the necessity did not constantly run up against the impossibility. I know it only too well: I was sitting next to a Jewish friend at a performance of Arnold Schönberg's "A Survivor From Warsaw" when, accompanied by the sounds of trumpets, the chorus intoned the words "Sch'ma Israel"; my friend turned as white as chalk and beads of perspiration appeared on his brow. My heart did not beat faster, yet I felt myself to be more wanting than my comrade, whom the Jewish prayer, sung to the blasts of trumpets, had powerfully affected. To be a deeply stirred Jew, I thought to myself afterwards, is not possible for me, I can be a Jew only in fear and anger, when—in order to attain dignity—fear transforms itself into anger. "Hear, oh Israel" is not my concern. Only a "hear, oh world" wants angrily to break out from within me. The six-digit number on my forearm demands it. That is what the awareness of catastrophe, the dominant force of my existence, requires.

Often I have asked myself whether one can live humanly in the tension between fear and anger. Those who have followed these deliberations may well see their author as a monster, if not of vengeance, then at least of bitterness. There may be a trace of truth in such a judgment, but only a trace. Whoever attempts to be a Jew in my way and under the conditions imposed on me, whoever hopes, by clarifying his own Holocaust-determined existence, to draw together and shape within himself the reality of the so-called Jewish Question, is wholly void of naïveté. Honey-sweet humane pronouncements do not flow from his lips. He is not good at gestures of magnanimity. But this does not mean that fear and anger condemn him to be less righteous than his ethically inspired contemporaries are. He is able to have friends and he has them, even among members of just those nations who hung him forever on the torture hook between fear and anger. He can also read books and listen to music as do the uninjured, and with no less feeling than they. If moral questions are involved, he will probably prove to be more sensitive to injustice of every kind than his fellow man. He will certainly react more excitably to a photo of club-swinging South African policemen or American sheriffs who sick howling dogs on black civil rights protesters. Because it became hard for me to be a human being does not mean that I have become a monster.

In the end, nothing else differentiates me from the people among whom I pass my days than a vague, sometimes more, sometimes less perceptible restiveness. But it is a *social* unrest, not a metaphysical one. It is not Being that oppresses me, or Nothingness, or God, or the Absence of God, only society. For it and only it caused the disturbance in my existential balance, which I am trying to oppose with an upright gait. It and only it robbed me of my trust in the world. Metaphysical distress is a fashionable concern of the highest standing. Let it remain a matter for those who have always known who and what they are, why they are that way, and that they are permitted to remain so. I must leave it to them—and it is not for that reason that I feel needy in their presence.

In my incessant effort to explore the basic condition of being a victim, in conflict with the necessity to be a Jew and the impossibility of being one, I believe to have recognized that the most extreme expectations and demands directed at us are of a physical and social nature. That such knowledge has made me unfit for profound and lofty speculation, I know. It is my hope that it has better equipped me to recognize reality.

NOTE

1. The racist diatribe *Juden sehen dich an* ("Jews Are Watching You") by the Nazi propagandist Johann von Leers (1902–) first appeared in 1933. (In his text, Améry has slightly misquoted the title.) (trans. note.)

THEODOR W. ADORNO

▣ Meditations on Metaphysics

1. AFTER AUSCHWITZ

We cannot say any more that the immutable is truth, and that the mobile, transitory is appearance. The mutual indifference of temporality and eternal ideas is no longer tenable even with the bold Hegelian explanation that temporal existence, by virtue of the destruction inherent in its concept, serves the eternal represented by the eternity of destruction. One of the mystical impulses secularized in dialectics was the doctrine that the intramundane and historic is relevant to what traditional metaphysics distinguished as transcendence—or at least, less gnostically and radically put, that it is relevant to the position taken by human consciousness on the questions which the canon of philosophy assigned to metaphysics. After Auschwitz, our feelings resist any claim of the positivity of existence as sanctimonious, as wronging the victims; they balk at squeezing any kind of sense, however bleached, out of the victims' fate. And these feelings do have an objective side after events that make a mockery of the construction of immanence as endowed with a meaning radiated by an affirmatively posited transcendence.

Such a construction would affirm absolute negativity and would assist its ideological survival—as in reality that negativity survives anyway, in the principle of society as it exists until its self-destruction. The earthquake of Lisbon sufficed to cure Voltaire of the theodicy of Leibniz, and the visible disaster of the first nature was insignificant in comparison with the second, social one, which defies human imagination as it distills a real hell from human evil. Our meta-

---

From *Negative Dialectics* by Theodor W. Adorno. Reprinted by permission of the Continuum Publishing Company.

physical faculty is paralyzed because actual events have shattered the basis on which speculative metaphysical thought could be reconciled with experience. Once again, the dialectical motif of quantity recoiling into quality scores an unspeakable triumph. The administrative murder of millions made of death a thing one had never yet to fear in just this fashion. There is no chance any more for death to come into the individuals' empirical life as somehow conformable with the course of that life. The last, the poorest possession left to the individual is expropriated. That in the concentration camps it was no longer an individual who died, but a specimen—this is a fact bound to affect the dying of those who escaped the administrative measure.

Genocide is the absolute integration. It is on its way wherever men are leveled off—"polished off," as the German military called it—until one exterminates them literally, as deviations from the concept of their total nullity. Auschwitz confirmed the philosopheme of pure identity as death. The most far out dictum from Beckett's *End Game,* that there really is not so much to be feared any more, reacts to a practice whose first sample was given in the concentration camps, and in whose concept—venerable once upon a time—the destruction of nonidentity is ideologically lurking. Absolute negativity is in plain sight and has ceased to surprise anyone. Fear used to be tied to the *principium individuationis* of self-preservation, and that principle, by its own consistency, abolishes itself. What the sadists in the camps foretold their victims, "Tomorrow you'll be wiggling skyward as smoke from this chimney," bespeaks the indifference of each individual life that is the direction of history. Even in his formal freedom, the individual is as fungible and replaceable as he will be under the liquidators' boots.

But since, in a world whose law is universal individual profit, the individual has nothing but this self that has become indifferent, the performance of the old, familiar tendency is at the same time the most dreadful of things. There is no getting out of this, no more than out of the electrified barbed wire around the camps. Perennial suffering has as much right to expression as a tortured man has to scream; hence it may have been wrong to say that after Auschwitz you could no longer write poems. But it is not wrong to raise the less cultural question whether after Auschwitz you can go on living—especially whether one who escaped by accident, one who by rights should have been killed, may go on living. His mere survival calls for the coldness, the basic principle of bourgeois subjectivity, without which there could have been no Auschwitz; this is the drastic guilt of him who was spared. By way of atonement he will be plagued by dreams such as that he is no longer living at all, that he was sent to the ovens in 1944 and his whole existence since has been imaginary, an emanation of the insane wish of a man killed twenty years earlier.

Thinking men and artists have not infrequently described a sense of being not quite there, of not playing along, a feeling as if they were not themselves at all, but a kind of spectator. Others often find this repulsive; it was the basis of Kierkegaard's polemic against what he called the esthetic sphere. A critique of

philosophical personalism indicates, however, that this attitude toward immediacy, this disavowal of every existential posture, has a moment of objective
truth that goes beyond the appearance of the self-preserving motive. "What
does it really matter?" is a line we like to associate with bourgeois callousness,
but it is the line most likely to make the individual aware, without dread, of the
insignificance of his existence. The inhuman part of it, the ability to keep one's
distance as a spectator and to rise above things, is in the final analysis the human
part, the very part resisted by its ideologists.

It is not altogether implausible that the immortal part is the one that acts in
this fashion. The scene of Shaw on his way to the theater, showing a beggar his
identification with the hurried remark, "Press," hides a sense of that beneath the
cynicism. It would help to explain the fact that startled Schopenhauer: that
affections in the face of death, not only other people's but our own, are frequently so feeble. People, of course, are spellbound without exception, and none
of them are capable of love, which is why everyone feels loved too little. But the
spectator's posture simultaneously expresses doubt that this could be all—
when the individual, so relevant to himself in his delusion, still has nothing but
that poor and emotionally animal-like ephemerality.

Spellbound, the living have a choice between involuntary ataraxy—an
esthetic life due to weakness—and the bestiality of the involved. Both are wrong
ways of living. But some of both would be required for the right désinvolture and
sympathy. Once overcome, the culpable self-preservation urge has been confirmed, confirmed precisely, perhaps, by the threat that has come to be cease-
lessly present. The only trouble with self-preservation is that we cannot help
suspecting the life to which it attaches us of turning into something that makes
us shudder: into a specter, a piece of the world of ghosts, which our waking consciousness perceives to be nonexistent. The guilt of a life which purely as a fact
will strangle other life, according to statistics that eke out an overwhelming
number of killed with a minimal number of rescued, as if this were provided in
the theory of probabilities—this guilt is irreconcilable with living. And the guilt
does not cease to reproduce itself, because not for an instant can it be made fully,
presently conscious.

This, nothing else, is what compels us to philosophize. And in philosophy
we experience a shock: the deeper, the more vigorous its penetration, the greater
our suspicion that philosophy removes us from things as they are—that an
unveiling of the essence might enable the most superficial and trivial views to
prevail over the views that aim at the essence. This throws a glaring light on
truth itself. In speculation we feel a certain duty to grant the position of a corrective to common sense, the opponent of speculation. Life feeds the horror of a
premonition: what must come to be known may resemble the down-to-earth
more than it resembles the sublime; it might be that this premonition will be
confirmed even beyond the pedestrian realm, although the happiness of
thought, the promise of its truth, lies in sublimity alone.

If the pedestrian had the last word, if it were the truth, truth would be
degraded. The trivial consciousness, as it is theoretically expressed in positivism

and unreflected nominalism, may be closer than the sublime consciousness to an *adaequatio rei atque cogitationis*; its sneering mockery of truth may be truer than a superior consciousness, unless the formation of a truth concept other than that of *adaequatio* should succeed. The innervation that metaphysics might win only by discarding itself applies to such other truth, and it is not the last among the motivations for the passage to materialism. We can trace the leaning to it from the Hegelian Marx to Benjamin's rescue of induction; Kafka's work may be the apotheosis of the trend. If negative dialectics calls for the self-reflection of thinking, the tangible implication is that if thinking is to be true—if it is to be true today, in any case—it must also be a thinking against itself. If thought is not measured by the extremity that eludes the concept, it is from the outset in the nature of the musical accompaniment with which the SS liked to drown out the screams of its victims.

2. METAPHYSICS AND CULTURE

A new categorical imperative has been imposed by Hitler upon unfree mankind: to arrange their thoughts and actions so that Auschwitz will not repeat itself, so that nothing similar will happen. When we want to find reasons for it, this imperative is as refractory as the given one of Kant was once upon a time. Dealing discursively with it would be an outrage, for the new imperative gives us a bodily sensation of the moral addendum—bodily, because it is now the practical abhorrence of the unbearable physical agony to which individuals are exposed even with individuality about to vanish as a form of mental reflection. It is in the unvarnished materialistic motive only that morality survives.

The course of history forces materialism upon metaphysics, traditionally the direct antithesis of materialism. What the mind once boasted of defining or construing as its like moves in the direction of what is unlike the mind, in the direction of that which eludes the rule of the mind and yet manifests that rule as absolute evil. The somatic, unmeaningful stratum of life is the stage of suffering, of the suffering which in the camps, without any consolation, burned every soothing feature out of the mind, and out of culture, the mind's objectification. The point of no return has been reached in the process which irresistibly forced metaphysics to join what it was once conceived against. Not since the youthful Hegel has philosophy—unless selling out for authorized cerebration—been able to repress how very much it slipped into material questions of existence.

Children sense some of this in the fascination that issues from the flayer's zone, from carcasses, from the repulsively sweet odor of putrefaction, and from the opprobrious terms used for that zone. The unconscious power of that realm may be as great as that of infantile sexuality; the two intermingle in the anal fixation, but they are scarcely the same. An unconscious knowledge whispers to the child what is repressed by civilized education; this is what matters, says the whispering voice. And the wretched physical existence strikes a spark in the supreme interest that is scarcely less repressed; it kindles a "What is that?" and

"Where is it going?" The man who managed to recall what used to strike him in the words "dung hill" and "pig sty" might be closer to absolute knowledge than Hegel's chapter in which readers are promised such knowledge only to have it withheld with a superior mien. The integration of physical death into culture should be rescinded in theory—not, however, for the sake of an ontologically pure being named Death, but for the sake of that which the stench of cadavers expresses and we are fooled about by their transfiguration into "remains."

A child, fond of an innkeeper named Adam, watched him club the rats pouring out of holes in the courtyard; it was in his image that the child made its own image of the first man. That this has been forgotten, that we no longer know what we used to feel before the dogcatcher's van, is both the triumph of culture and its failure. Culture, which keeps emulating the old Adam, cannot bear to be reminded of that zone, and precisely this is not to be reconciled with the conception that culture has of itself. It abhors stench because it stinks—because, as Brecht put it in a magnificent line, its mansion is built of dogshit. Years after that line was written, Auschwitz demonstrated irrefutably that culture has failed.

That this could happen in the midst of the traditions of philosophy, of art, and of the enlightening sciences says more than that these traditions and their spirit lacked the power to take hold of men and work a change in them. There is untruth in those fields themselves, in the autarky that is emphatically claimed for them. All post-Auschwitz culture, including its urgent critique, is garbage. In restoring itself after the things that happened without resistance in its own countryside, culture has turned entirely into the ideology it had been potentially—had been ever since it presumed, in opposition to material existence, to inspire that existence with the light denied it by the separation of the mind from manual labor. Whoever pleads for the maintenance of this radically culpable and shabby culture becomes its accomplice, while the man who says no to culture is directly furthering the barbarism which our culture showed itself to be.

Not even silence gets us out of the circle. In silence we simply use the state of objective truth to rationalize our subjective incapacity, once more degrading truth into a lie. When countries of the East, for all their drivel to the contrary, abolished culture or transformed it into rubbish as a mere means of control, the culture that moans about it is getting what it deserves, and what on its part, in the name of people's democratic right to their own likeness, it is zealously heading for. The only difference is that when the apparatchiks over there acclaim their administrative barbarism as culture and guard its mischief as an inalienable heritage, they convict its reality, the infrastructure, of being as barbarian as the superstructure they are dismantling by taking it under their management. In the West, at least, one is allowed to say so.

The theology of the crisis registered the fact it was abstractly and therefore idly rebelling against: that metaphysics has merged with culture. The aureole of culture, the principle that the mind is absolute, was the same which tirelessly violated what it was pretending to express. After Auschwitz there is no word tinged from on high, not even a theological one, that has any right unless it underwent a transformation. The judgment passed on the ideas long before, by Nietzsche, was carried out on the victims, reiterating the challenge of the traditional words and the test whether God would permit this without intervening in his wrath.

A man whose admirable strength enabled him to survive Auschwitz and other camps said in an outburst against Beckett that if Beckett had been in Auschwitz he would be writing differently, more positively, with the front-line creed of the escapee. The escapee is right in a fashion other than he thinks. Beckett, and whoever else remained in control of himself, would have been broken in Auschwitz and probably forced to confess that frontline creed which the escapee clothed in the words "Trying to give men courage"—as if this were up to any structure of the mind; as if the intent to address men, to adjust to them, did not rob them of what is their due even if they believe the contrary. That is what we have come to in metaphysics.

HANNAH ARENDT

▣ The Concentration Camps

The SS has made the camp the most
totalitarian society in existence up to now.
DAVID ROUSSET.

I

There are three possible approaches to the reality of the concentration camp: the inmate's experience of immediate suffering, the recollection of the survivor, and the fearful anticipation of those who dread the concentration camp as a possibility for the future.

Immediate experience is expressed in the reports which "record but do not communicate" things that evade human understanding and human experience; things therefore that, when suffered by men, transform them into "uncomplaining animals" (*The Dark Side of the Moon*, New York, 1947). There are numerous such reports by survivors; only a few have been published, partly because, quite

---

Reprinted by permission of the Hannah Arendt Literary Trust.

understandably, the world wants to hear no more of these things, but also because they all leave the reader cold, that is, as apathetic and baffled as the writer himself, and fail to inspire those passions of outrage and sympathy through which men have always been mobilized for justice, for "Misery that goes too deep arouses not compassion but repugnance and hatred" (Rousset).

Der SS-Staat by Eugen Kogon and *Les Jours de notre mort* by David Rousset are products of assimilated recollection.* Both authors have consciously written for the world of the living, both wish to make themselves understood at any cost, and both have cast off the insane contempt for those "who never went through it," that in the direct reports so often substitutes for communication. This conscious good will is the only guaranty that those who return will not, after a brief period of sullen resentment against humanity in general, adapt themselves to the real world and become once more the exact same unsuspecting fools that they were when they entered the camps. Both books are indispensable for an understanding not only of the concentration camps, but of the totalitarian regime as a whole. They become useless and even dangerous as soon as they attempt a positive interpretation—Kogon because he cites apparent historical precedents and believes that the camps can be understood psychologically, Rousset because he seeks the consolation of an "extreme experience" in a kind of suffering which, strictly speaking, no longer permits of experience, and thus arrives at a meaningless affirmation of life that is extremely dangerous because it romanticizes and transfigures what must never under any circumstances be repeated on this earth.[1] What is really true, on the contrary, was recently remarked by Isaac Rosenfeld in *The New Leader* (February 14, 1948): "We still don't understand what happened to the Jews of Europe, and perhaps we never will. . . . By now we know all there is to know. But it hasn't helped . . . as there is no response great enough to equal the facts that provoked it. There is nothing but numbness, and in the respect of numbness we . . . are no different from the murderers who went ahead and did their business and paid no attention to the screams."

Fearful anticipation is the most widespread and perhaps the only fitting approach to the reality of the concentration camp. It certainly has a great deal to do with the attitudes of men under the totalitarian terror, although it always seems to go hand in hand with a remarkable and very characteristic uncertainty which impedes both rebellion and any clear, articulated understanding of the thing feared. Kogon reports: "Only a very, very few of those who entered a concentration camp for the first time had the slightest idea . . . of what awaited them. [Some] were prepared for the worst. But these ideas were always nebulous; the reality far exceeded them." The reason for the uncertainty was pre-

---

*Editor's Note: Eugen Kogon, *Der SS-Staat* (Stockholm: Bermann-Fischer Verlag, 1947); appeared in English as *The Theory and Practice of Hell* (New York: Farrar, Straus and Cudahy, Inc., 1950). David Rousset, *Les jours de notre mort* (Paris: Editions du Parios, 1947); appeared in English as *The Other Kingdom* (New York: Reynal & Hitchcock, 1947).

cisely that this reality was utterly incredible and inconceivable. In totalitarian regimes, uncertainty as well as fear is manufactured and fostered by the propagandistic treatment of the institution of terror. "There was hardly anything connected with the SS that was not kept secret. The biggest secret of all was the routine of the concentration camps . . . whose only purpose was to spread an anonymous terror of a general political character" (Kogon). Concentration camps and everything connected with them are systematically publicized and at the same time kept absolutely secret. They are used as a threat, but all actual reports about them are suppressed or denounced as fantastic.

It is not surprising that those who made terror the actual foundation of their power should know how to exploit it through publicity and propaganda. The surprising thing is that the psychological and political effects of this propaganda could survive the collapse of the Nazi regime and the opening up of the concentration camps. One would think that the eye-witness reports and, to an even greater degree, the works of ordered recollection which substantiate one another and speak directly to the reader, in Rousset's case most persuasively, should have punctured the propagandist claim that such things were absurd horror stories. This, as we all know, is not the case. Despite overwhelming proofs, anyone speaking or writing about concentration camps is still regarded as suspect; and if the speaker has resolutely returned to the world of the living, he himself is often assailed by doubts with regard to his own truthfulness, as though he had mistaken a nightmare for reality.

This doubt of people concerning themselves and the reality of their own experience only reveals what the Nazis have always known: that men determined to commit crimes will find it expedient to organize them on the vastest, most improbable scale. Not only because this renders all punishments provided by the legal system inadequate and absurd; but because the very immensity of the crimes guarantees that the murderers who proclaim their innocence with all manner of lies will be more readily believed than the victims who tell the truth. The Nazis did not even consider it necessary to keep this discovery to themselves. Hitler circulated millions of copies of his book in which he stated that to be successful, a lie must be enormous—which did not prevent people from believing him as, similarly, the Nazis' proclamations, repeated ad nauseam, that the Jews would be exterminated like bedbugs (i.e., with poison gas), prevented anybody from *not* believing them.

There is a great temptation to explain away the intrinsically incredible by means of liberal rationalizations. In each one of us, there lurks such a liberal, wheedling us with the voice of common sense. We attempt to understand elements in present or recollected experience that simply surpass our powers of understanding. We attempt to classify as criminal a thing which, as we all feel, no such category was ever intended to cover. What meaning has the concept of murder when we are confronted with the mass production of corpses? We attempt to understand the behavior of concentration camp inmates and SS men psychologically, when the very thing that must be realized is that the psyche (or character) *can* be destroyed even without the destruction of the physical man;

that, indeed, as Rousset convincingly shows, psyche, character, or individuality seem under certain circumstances to express themselves only through the rapidity or slowness with which they disintegrate. The end result in any case is inanimate men, i.e., men who can no longer be psychologically understood, whose return to the psychologically or otherwise intelligibly human world closely resembles the resurrection of Lazarus—as Rousset indicates in the title of his book. All statements of common sense, whether of a psychological or sociological nature, serve only to encourage those who think it "superficial" to "dwell on horrors" (Georges Bataille, in *Critique,* January 1948).

If it is true that the concentration camps are the most consequential institution of totalitarian rule, "dwelling on horrors" would seem to be indispensable for the understanding of totalitarianism. But recollection can no more do this than can the uncommunicative eyewitness report. In both these genres there is an inherent tendency to run away from the experience; instinctively or rationally, both types of writer are so much aware of the terrible abyss that separates the world of the living from that of the living dead, that they cannot supply anything more than a series of remembered occurrences that must seem just as incredible to those who relate them as to their audience. Only the fearful imagination of those who have been aroused by such reports but have not actually been smitten in their own flesh, of those who are consequently free from the bestial, desperate terror which, when confronted by real, present horror, inexorably paralyzes everything that is not mere reaction, can afford to keep thinking about horrors. Such thoughts are useful only for the perception of political contexts and the mobilization of political passions. A change of personality of any sort whatever can no more be induced by thinking about horrors than by the real experience of horror. The reduction of a man to a bundle of reactions separates him as radically as mental disease from everything within him that is personality or character. When, like Lazarus, he rises from the dead, he finds his personality or character unchanged, just as he had left it.

Nor can horror or thinking about horrors become a basis for a political community or a party in the narrower sense. Attempts have failed to create a European elite with a program of inter-European understanding on the basis of the common experience of the concentration camp, much in the same way that similar attempts after the First World War failed to draw political consequences from the experience of the front-line soldier. In both cases it developed that the experiences themselves could impart only nihilistic platitudes, such as: "Victim and executioner are alike ignoble; the lesson of the camps is the brotherhood of abjection; if you haven't acted with the same degree of ignominy, it's only because you didn't have time . . . but the underlying rot that rises, rises, rises, is absolutely, terrifyingly the same" (Rousset). Political consequences like postwar pacifism followed from the universal fear of war, not from experience of the war. An insight, led and mobilized by fear, into the structure of modern war would have led not to a pacifism without reality, but to the view that the only acceptable ground for modern war is to fight against conditions under which we no longer wish to live—and our knowledge of the camps and torture chambers of totalitarian regimes has convinced us only too well that such conditions are possible. An insight into the nature of totalitarian rule, directed by our fear of the concentration camp, might serve to devaluate all outmoded political shadings from right to left and, beside and above them, to introduce the most essential political criterion for judging the events of our time: Will it lead to totalitarian rule or will it not?

In any case fearful anticipation has the great advantage that it dispels the sophistical-dialectical interpretations of politics, which all rest on the superstition that some good can come out of evil. Such dialectical acrobatics retained at least an appearance of justification as long as the worst evil that man could inflict on man was murder. But murder, as we know today, is still a limited evil. The murderer who kills a man who must die in any event, moves within the familiar realm of life and death, between which there is a necessary relation that is the basis of dialectics, although dialecticians are not always aware of it. The murderer leaves a corpse and does not claim that his victim never existed; he may obscure the traces of his own identity, but he does not efface the memory and grief of those who loved his victim; he destroys a life, but he does not destroy the very fact of its ever having existed.

The horror of the concentration and extermination camps can never be fully embraced by the imagination for the very reason that it stands outside of life and death. The inmates are more effectively cut off from the world of the living than if they were dead, because terror compels oblivion among those who know them or love them. "What extraordinary women you are here," exclaimed the Soviet police when Polish women insisted on knowing the whereabouts of their husbands who had disappeared. "In our country, when the husband is arrested, the wife sues for divorce and looks for another man" (*The Dark Side of the Moon*). Murder in the camps is as impersonal as the squashing of a gnat, a mere technique of management, as when a camp is overcrowded and is liquidated—or an accidental by-product, as when a prisoner succumbs to torture. Systematic torture and systematic starvation create an atmosphere of permanent dying, in which death as well as life is effectively obstructed.

The fear of the absolute Evil which permits of no escape knows that this is the end of dialectical evolutions and developments. It knows that modern politics revolves around a question which, strictly speaking, should never enter into politics, the question of all or nothing: of all, that is, a human society rich with infinite possibilities; or exactly nothing, that is, the end of mankind.

II

There are no parallels to the life of the concentration camps. All seeming parallels create confusion and distract attention from what is essential. Forced labor in prisons and penal colonies, banishment, slavery, all seem for a moment to offer helpful comparisons, but on closer examination lead nowhere.

Forced labor as a punishment is limited as to time and intensity. The convict retains his rights over his body; he is not absolutely tortured and he is not absolutely dominated. Banishment banishes only from one part of the world to another part of the world, also inhabited by human beings; it does not exclude from the human world altogether. Throughout history slavery has been an institution within a social order; slaves were not, like concentration camp inmates, withdrawn from the sight and hence the protection of their fellow men; as instruments of labor they had a definite price and as property a definite value. The concentration camp inmate has no price, because he can always be replaced and he belongs to no one. From the point of view of normal society he is absolutely superfluous, although in times of acute labor shortage, as in Russia and in Germany during the war, he is used for work.

The concentration camp as an institution was not established for the sake of any possible labor yield; the only permanent economic function of the camps has been the financing of their own supervisory apparatus; thus from the economic point of view the concentration camps exist mostly for their own sake. Any work that has been performed could have been done much better and more cheaply under different conditions.[2] The example of Russia, whose concentration camps are usually referred to as forced labor camps, because the Soviet bureaucracy has given them this flattering title, shows most clearly that the main point is not forced labor; forced labor is the normal condition of the whole Russian proletariat which has been deprived of freedom of movement and can be mobilized anywhere at any time.

The incredibility of the horrors is closely bound up with their economic uselessness. The Nazis carried this uselessness to the point of open antiutility when in the midst of the war, despite the shortage of rolling stock, they transported millions of Jews to the east and set up enormous, costly extermination factories. In the midst of a strictly utilitarian world the obvious contradiction between these acts and military expediency gave the whole enterprise an air of mad unreality.

However, such unreality, created by an apparent lack of purpose, is the very basis of all forms of concentration camp. Seen from outside, they and the things that happen in them can be described only in images drawn from a life after death, that is, a life removed from earthly purposes. Concentration camps can very aptly be divided into three types corresponding to three basic Western conceptions of a life after death: Hades, purgatory, and hell. To Hades correspond those relatively mild forms, once popular even in nontotalitarian countries, for getting undesirable elements of all sorts—refugees, stateless persons, the asocial and the unemployed—out of the way; as DP camps, which are nothing other than camps for persons who have become superfluous and bothersome, they have survived the war. Purgatory is represented by the Soviet Union's labor camps, where neglect is combined with chaotic forced labor. Hell in the most literal sense was embodied by those types of camp perfected by the Nazis, in which the whole of life was thoroughly and systematically organized with a view to the greatest possible torment.

All three types have one thing in common: the human masses sealed off in them are treated as if they no longer existed, as if what happened to them were no longer of any interest to anybody, as if they were already dead and some evil spirit gone mad were amusing himself by stopping them for a while between life and death before admitting them to eternal peace.

It is not so much the barbed wire as the skillfully manufactured unreality of those whom it fences in that provokes such enormous cruelties and ultimately makes extermination look like a perfectly normal measure. Everything that was done in the camps is known to us from the world of perverse, malignant fantasies. The difficult thing to understand is that, like such fantasies, these gruesome crimes took place in a phantom world, in a world in which there were neither consequences nor responsibilities; and finally neither the tormentors nor the tormented, and least of all the outsider, could be aware that what was happening was anything more than a cruel game or an absurd dream.

The films which the Allies circulated in Germany and elsewhere after the war showed clearly that this atmosphere of insanity and unreality is not dispelled by pure reportage. To the unprejudiced observer they are just about as convincing as the pictures of mysterious substances taken at spiritualist séances. Common sense reacted to the horrors of Buchenwald and Auschwitz with the plausible argument: "What crime must these people have committed that such things were done to them!"; or, in Germany and Austria, in the midst of starvation, overpopulation, and general hatred: "Too bad that they've stopped gassing the Jews"; and everywhere with the skeptical shrug that greets ineffectual propaganda.

If the propaganda of truth fails to convince the average Philistine precisely because it is too monstrous, it is positively dangerous to those who know from their own imaginings that they themselves are capable of doing such things and are therefore perfectly willing to believe in the reality of what they have seen. Suddenly it becomes evident that things which for thousands of years the human imagination had banished to a realm beyond human competence, can be manufactured right here on earth. Hell and purgatory, and even a shadow of their perpetual duration, can be established by the most modern methods of destruction and therapy. When people of this sort, who are far more numerous in any large city than we like to think, see these films, or read reports of the same things, the thought that comes to their minds is that the power of man is far greater than they ever dared to think and that men can realize hellish fantasies without making the sky fall or the earth open.

The one thing that cannot be reproduced is what made the traditional conceptions of hell tolerable to man: the Last Judgment, the idea of an absolute standard of justice combined with the infinite possibility of grace. For in the human estimation there is no crime and no sin commensurable with the everlasting torments of hell. Hence the discomfiture of common sense, which asks: What crime must these people have committed in order to suffer so inhumanly? Hence also the absolute innocence of the victims: no man ever deserved this. Hence finally the grotesque haphazardness with which concentration camp victims were chosen in the perfected terror state: such "punishment" can, with equal justice and injustice, be inflicted on anyone.

III

In comparison with the insane end-result—concentration camp society—the process by which men are prepared for this end, and the methods by which individuals are adapted to these conditions, are transparent and logical. The insane mass manufacture of corpses is preceded by the historically and politically intelligible preparation of living corpses.

In another connection it might be possible, indeed it would be necessary, to describe this preparatory process as a consequence of the political upheavals of our century. The impetus and, what is more important, the silent consent to such unprecedented conditions in the heart of Europe are the products of those events which in a period of political disintegration suddenly and unexpectedly made hundreds of thousands of human beings homeless, stateless, outlawed and unwanted, while millions of human beings were made economically superfluous and socially burdensome by unemployment. This in turn could only happen because the rights of man, which had never been philosophically established but merely formulated, which had never been politically secured but merely proclaimed, have, in their traditional form, lost all validity.

Meanwhile, however, totalitarian regimes exploited these developments for their own purposes. In order to understand these purposes, we must examine the process of preparing living corpses in its entirety. After all, loss of passport, residence, and the right to work, was only a very provisional, summary preparation, which could hardly have produced adequate results.

The first essential step was to kill the juridical person in man; this was done by placing the concentration camp outside the normal penal system, and by selecting its inmates outside the normal judicial procedure in which a definite crime entails a predictable penalty. Thus criminals, who for other reasons are an essential element in concentration camp society, are ordinarily sent to a camp only on completion of their prison sentence. Deviations from this rule in Russia must be attributed to the catastrophic shortage of prisons and to a desire, so far unrealized, to transform the whole penal system into a system of concentration camps.

The inclusion of criminals is necessary in order to make plausible the propagandistic claim that the institution exists for asocial elements. It is equally essential, as long as there is a penal system in the country, that they should be sent to the camps only on completion of their sentence, that is, when they are actually entitled to their freedom. It is, paradoxically, harder to kill the juridical person in a man who is guilty of some crime than in a totally innocent man. The stateless persons who in all European countries have lost their civil rights along with their nationality, have learned this only too well; their legal position improved automatically as soon as they committed a theft: then they were no longer without rights but had the same rights as all other thieves. In order to kill the juridical person in man, the concentration camp must under no circumstance become a calculable punishment for definite offenses. Criminals do not properly belong in the concentration camps; if nevertheless they constitute the sole permanent category among the inmates, it is a concession of the totalitarian state to the prejudices of society which can in this way most readily be accustomed to the existence of the camps. The amalgamation of criminals with all other categories has moreover the advantage of making it shockingly evident to all other arrivals that they have landed in the lowest level of society. It soon turns out, to be sure, that they have every reason to envy the lowest thief and murderer; but meanwhile the lowest level is a good beginning. Moreover it is an effective means of camouflage: this happens only to criminals and nothing worse is happening than what deservedly happens to criminals.[3]

The criminals everywhere constitute the aristocracy of the camps. (In Germany, during the war, they were replaced in the leadership by the Communists, because not even a minimum of rational work could be performed under the chaotic conditions created by a criminal administration. This was merely a temporary transformation of concentration camps into forced labor camps, a thoroughly atypical phenomenon of limited duration. With his limited, wartime experience of Nazi concentration camps, Rousset overestimates the influence and power of the Communists.) What places the criminals in the leadership is not so much the affinity between supervisory personnel and criminal elements—in the Soviet Union apparently the supervisors are not, like the SS, a special elite of criminals—as the fact that only criminals have been sent to the camp in connection with some definite activity and that in them consequently the destruction of the juridical person cannot be fully successful, since they at least know why they are in a concentration camp. For the politicals this is only subjectively true; their actions, in so far as they were actions and not mere opinions or someone else's vague suspicions, or accidental membership in a politically disapproved group, are as a rule not covered by the normal legal system of the country and not juridically defined.

To the amalgam of politicals and criminals, with which concentration camps in Russia and Germany started out, was added at an early date a third element which was soon to constitute the majority of all concentration camp inmates. This largest group has consisted ever since of people who had done nothing whatsoever that, either in their own consciousness or the consciousness of their tormentors, had any rational connection with their arrest. In Germany, after 1938, this element was represented by masses of Jews, in Russia by any groups which, for any reason having nothing to do with their actions, had incurred the disfavor of the authorities. These groups, innocent in every sense, are the most suitable for thorough experimentation in disfranchisement and destruction of the juridical person, and therefore they are both qualitatively and quantitatively the most essential category of the camp population. This principle was most fully realized in the gas chambers which, if only because of their enormous capacity, could not be intended for individual cases but only for people in general. In this connection, the following dialogue sums up the situation of the individual: "For what purpose, may I ask, do the gas chambers exist?"—"For what purpose were you born?" (Rousset). It is this third group of the totally innocent who in every case fare the worst in the camps. Criminals and politicals are assimilated to this category; thus deprived of the protective distinction that comes of their having done something, they are utterly exposed to the arbitrary.

Contrasting with the complete haphazardness with which the inmates are selected are the categories, meaningless in themselves but useful from the standpoint of organization, into which they are usually divided on their arrival. In the German camps there were criminals, politicals, asocial elements, religious offenders, and Jews, all distinguished by insignia. When the French set up concentration camps after the Spanish civil war, they immediately introduced the typical totalitarian amalgam of politicals with criminals and the innocent (in this case the stateless), and despite their inexperience proved remarkably inventive in devising meaningless categories of inmates. Originally devised in order to prevent any growth of solidarity among the inmates, this technique proved particularly valuable because no one could know whether his own category was better or worse than someone else's. In Germany this eternally shifting though pedantically organized edifice was given an appearance of solidity by the fact that under any and all circumstances the Jews were the lowest category. The gruesome and grotesque part of it was that the inmates identified themselves with these categories, as though they represented a last authentic remnant of their juridical person. It is no wonder that a Communist of 1933 should have come out of the camps more Communistic than he went in, a Jew more Jewish.

While the classification of inmates by categories is only a tactical, organizational measure, the arbitrary selection of victims indicates the essential principle of the institution. If the concentration camps had been dependent on the existence of political adversaries, they would scarcely have survived the first years of the totalitarian regimes. "The camps would have died out if in making its arrests the Gestapo had considered only the principle of opposition" (Kogon). But the existence of a political opposition is for a concentration camp system only a pretext, and the purpose of the system is not achieved even when under the most monstrous terror, the population becomes more or less voluntarily coordinated, i.e., relinquishes its political rights. The aim of an arbitrary system is to destroy the civil rights of the whole population, who ultimately become just as outlawed in their own country as the stateless and homeless. The destruction of a man's rights, the killing of the juridical person in him, is a prerequisite for dominating him entirely. For even free consent is an obstacle; and this applies not only to special categories such as criminals, political opponents, Jews, but to every inhabitant of a totalitarian state.

Any, even the most tyrannical, restriction of this arbitrary persecution to certain opinions of a religious or political nature, to certain modes of intellectual or erotic social behavior, to certain freshly invented "crimes," would render the camps superfluous, because in the long run no attitude and no opinion can withstand the threat of so much horror; and above all it would make for a new system of justice, which, given any stability at all, could not fail to produce a new juridical person in man, that would elude the totalitarian domination. The so-called "Volksnutzen" of the Nazis, constantly fluctuating (because what is useful today can be injurious tomorrow) and the eternally shifting party line of

the Soviet Union which, being retroactive, almost daily makes new groups of
people available for the concentration camps, are the only guaranty for the continued existence of the concentration camps and hence for the continued total
disfranchisement of man.

IV

The next decisive step in the preparation of living corpses is the murder of the
moral person in man. This is done in the main by making martyrdom, for the
first time in history, impossible. Rousset writes:

> How many people here still believe that a protest has even historic importance?
> This skepticism is the real masterpiece of the SS. Their great accomplishment.
> They have corrupted all human solidarity. Here the night has fallen on the
> future. When no witnesses are left, there can be no testimony. To demonstrate
> when death can no longer be postponed is an attempt to give death a meaning,
> to act beyond one's own death. In order to be successful, a gesture must have
> social meaning. There are hundreds of thousands of us here, all living in
> absolute solitude. That is why we are subdued no matter what happens.

The camps and the murder of political adversaries are only part of organized oblivion that not only embraces carriers of public opinion such as the spoken and the written word, but extends even to the families and friends of the
victim. Grief and remembrance are forbidden. In the Soviet Union a woman will
sue for divorce immediately after her husband's arrest in order to save the lives
of her children; if her husband chances to come back, she will indignantly turn
him out of the house. The Western world has hitherto, even in its darkest periods, granted the slain enemy the right to be remembered as a self-evident
acknowledgment of the fact that we are all men (and *only* men). It is only because even Achilles set out for Hector's funeral, only because the most despotic
governments honored the slain enemy, only because the Romans allowed the
Christians to write their martyrologies, only because the Church kept its
heretics alive in the memory of men, that all was not lost and never could be lost.
The concentration camps, by making death itself anonymous—in the Soviet
Union it is almost impossible even to find out whether a prisoner is dead or
alive—robbed death of the meaning which it had always been possible for it to
have. In a sense they took away the individual's own death, proving that henceforth nothing belonged to him and he belonged to no one. His death merely set
a seal on the fact that he had never really existed.
    This attack on the moral person might still have been opposed by man's
conscience which tells him that it is better to die a victim than to live as a
bureaucrat of murder. The totalitarian governments have cut the moral person
off from this individualist escape by making the decisions of conscience
absolutely questionable and equivocal.

When a man is faced with the alternative of betraying and thus murdering his friends or of sending his wife and children, for whom he is in every sense responsible, to their death; when even suicide would mean the immediate murder of his own family—how is he to decide? The alternative is no longer between good and evil, but between murder and murder. In perhaps the only article which really gets to the core of this matter, Camus (in *Twice a Year*, 1947) tells of a woman in Greece, who was allowed by the Nazis to choose which among her three children should be killed.

Through the creation of conditions under which conscience ceases to be adequate and to do good becomes utterly impossible, the consciously organized complicity of all men in the crimes of totalitarian regimes is extended to the victims and thus made really total. The SS implicated concentration camp inmates—criminals, politicals, Jews—in their crimes by making them responsible for a large part of the administration, thus confronting them with the hopeless dilemma whether to send their friends to their death, or to help murder other men who happened to be strangers.

Once the moral person has been killed, the one thing that still prevents men from being made into living corpses is the differentiation of the individual, his unique identity. In a sterile form such individuality can be preserved through a persistent stoicism, and it is certain that many men under totalitarian rule have taken and are each day still taking refuge in this absolute isolation of a personality without rights or conscience. There is no doubt that this part of the human person, precisely because it depends so essentially on nature and on forces that cannot be controlled by the will, is the hardest to destroy (and when destroyed is most easily repaired).

The methods of dealing with this uniqueness of the human person are numerous and we shall not attempt to list them all. They begin with the monstrous conditions in the transports to the camps, when hundreds of human beings are packed into a cattle car stark naked, glued to each other, and shunted back and forth over the countryside for days on end; they continue upon arrival at the camp, the well-organized shock of the first hours, the shaving of the head, the grotesque camp clothing; and they end in the utterly unimaginable tortures so gauged as not to kill the body, at any event not quickly. The aim of all these methods, in any case, is to manipulate the human body—with its infinite possibilities of suffering—in such a way as to make it destroy the human person as inexorably as certain mental diseases of organic origin.

It is here that the utter lunacy of the entire process becomes most apparent. Torture, to be sure, is an essential feature of the whole totalitarian police and judiciary apparatus; it is used every day to make people talk. This type of torture, since it pursues a definite, rational aim, has certain limitations: either the prisoner talks within a certain time, or he is killed. But to this rationally conducted torture another, irrational, sadistic type was added in the first Nazi concentration camps and in the cellars of the Gestapo. Carried on for the most part by the SA, it pursued no aims and was not systematic, but depended on the initiative of largely abnormal elements. The mortality was so high that only a few concentration camp inmates of 1933 survived these first years. This type of torture seemed to be not so much a calculated political institution as a concession of the regime to its criminal and abnormal elements, who were thus rewarded for services rendered. Behind the blind bestiality of the SA, there often lay a deep hatred and resentment against all those who were socially, intellectually, or physically better off than themselves and who now, as if in fulfillment of their wildest dreams, were in their power. This resentment, which never died out entirely in the camps, strikes us as a last remnant of humanly understandable feeling.

The real horror began, however, when the SS took over the administration of the camps. The old spontaneous bestiality gave way to an absolutely cold and systematic destruction of human bodies calculated to destroy human dignity; death was avoided or postponed indefinitely. The camps were no longer amusement parks for beasts in human form, that is, for men who really belonged in mental institutions and prisons; the reverse became true: they were turned into "drill grounds" (Kogon), on which perfectly normal men were trained to be full-fledged members of the SS.

The killing of man's individuality, of the uniqueness shaped in equal parts by nature, will, and destiny, which has become so self-evident a premise for all human relations that even identical twins inspire a certain uneasiness, creates a horror that vastly overshadows the outrage of the juridical-political person and the despair of the moral person. It is this horror that gives rise to the nihilistic generalizations which maintain plausibly enough that essentially all men alike are beasts. Actually the experience of the concentration camps does show that human beings can be transformed into specimens of the human beast, and that man's "nature" is only "human" in so far as it opens up to man the possibility of becoming something highly unnatural, that is, a man.

After murder of the moral person and annihilation of the juridical person, the destruction of the individuality is almost always successful. Conceivably some laws of mass psychology may be found to explain why millions of human beings allowed themselves to be marched unresistingly into the gas chambers, although these laws would explain nothing else but the destruction of individuality. It is more significant that those individually condemned to death very seldom attempted to take one of their executioners with them, that there were scarcely any serious revolts, and that even in the moment of liberation there were very few spontaneous massacres of the SS men. For to destroy individuality is to destroy spontaneity, man's power to begin something new out of his own resources, something new that cannot be explained on the basis of reactions to environment and events. Nothing then remains but ghastly marionettes with human faces, which all behave like the dog in Pavlov's experiments, which all react with perfect reliability even when going to their own death, and which do nothing but react. This is the real triumph of the system—:

The triumph of the SS demands that the tortured victim allow himself to be led to the noose without protesting, that he renounce and abandon himself to the point of ceasing to affirm his identity. And it is not for nothing. It is not gratu- itously, out of sheer sadism, that the SS men desire this defeat. They know that the system which succeeds in destroying its victim before he mounts the scaf- fold . . . is incomparably the best for keeping a whole people in slavery. In sub- mission. Nothing is more terrible than these processions of human beings going like dummies to their death. The man who sees this says to himself: "For them to be thus reduced, what power must be concealed in the hands of the masters," and he turns away, full of bitterness but defeated. (Rousset).

V

It is characteristic of totalitarian terror that it increases as the regime becomes more secured, and accordingly concentration camps are expanded as political opposition decreases.[4] Totalitarian demands do not seem to be satisfied by polit- ical success in establishing a one-party state, and it seems as though political opposition were by no means the cause of terror but rather a barrier to its full development. This seems absurd only if we apply to modern totalitarian move- ments those standards of utility which they themselves expressly reject as obso- lete, sentimental, and bourgeois.

If on the contrary we take totalitarian aspirations seriously and refuse to be misled by the common-sense assertion that they are utopian and unrealizable, it develops that the society of the dying established in the camps is the only form of society in which it is possible to dominate man entirely. Those who aspire to total domination must liquidate all spontaneity, such as the mere existence of individuality will always engender, and track it down in its most private forms, regardless of how unpolitical and harmless these may seem. Pavlov's dog, the human specimen reduced to the most elementary reactions, the bundle of reac- tions that can always be liquidated and replaced by other bundles of reactions that behave in exactly the same way, is the model "citizen" of a totalitarian state and such a citizen can be produced only imperfectly outside of the camps.

The uselessness of the camps, their cynically admitted antiutility, is only apparent. In reality they are more essential to the preservation of the regime's power than any of its other institutions. Without concentration camps, without the undefined fear they inspire and the very well-defined training they offer in totalitarian domination, which has nowhere else been fully tested with all of its most radical possibilities, a totalitarian state can neither inspire its nuclear troops with fanaticism nor maintain a whole people in complete apathy. The dominat- ing and the dominated would only too quickly sink back into the "old bourgeois routine"; after early "excesses," they would succumb to everyday life with its human laws; in short, they would develop in the direction which all observers counseled by common sense were so prone to predict. The tragic fallacy of all these prophecies originating in a world that was still safe, was to suppose that there was such a thing as one human nature established for all time to identify this human nature with history and thus declare that the idea of total domination was not only inhuman but also unrealistic. Meanwhile we have learned that the power of man is so great that he really can be what he wishes to be.

It is in the very nature of totalitarian regimes to demand unlimited power. Such power can only be secured if literally all men, without a single exception, are reliably dominated in every aspect of their life. In the realm of foreign affairs new neutral territories must constantly be subjugated, while at home ever-new human groups must be mastered in expanding concentration camps, or, when circumstances require, liquidated to make room for others. Here the question of opposition is unimportant both in foreign and domestic affairs. Any neutrality, indeed any spontaneously given friendship is from the standpoint of totalitarian domination just as dangerous as open hostility, precisely because spontaneity as such, with its incalculability, is the greatest of all obstacles to total domination over man. The Communists of non-Communist countries, who fled or were called to Moscow, learned by bitter experience that they constituted a menace to the Soviet Union. Convinced Communists are in this sense, which alone has any reality today, just as ridiculous and just as menacing to the regime in Russia as for example the convinced Nazis of the Roehm faction were to the Nazis.

What makes conviction and opinion of any sort so ridiculous and dangerous under totalitarian conditions is that totalitarian regimes take the greatest pride in having no need of them, or of any human help of any kind. Men insofar as they are more than animal reaction and fulfillment of functions are entirely superfluous to totalitarian regimes. Totalitarianism strives not toward despotic rule over men, but toward a system in which men are superfluous. Total power can be achieved and safeguarded only in a world of conditioned reflexes, of marionettes without the slightest trace of spontaneity. Precisely because man's resources are so great, he can be fully dominated only when he becomes a specimen of the animal-species man.

Therefore character is a threat and even the most unjust legal rules are an obstacle; but individuality, anything indeed that distinguishes one man from another, is intolerable. As long as all men have not been made equally superfluous—and this has been accomplished only in concentration camps—the ideal of totalitarian domination has not been achieved. Totalitarian states strive constantly, though never with complete success, to establish the superfluity of man—by the arbitrary selection of various groups for concentration camps, by constant purges of the ruling apparatus, by mass liquidations. Common sense protests desperately that the masses are submissive and that all this gigantic apparatus of terror is therefore superfluous; if they were capable of telling the truth, the totalitarian rulers would reply: The apparatus seems superfluous to you only because it serves to make men superfluous.

They will not speak so frankly. But the concentration camps, and even more so the corpse factories invented by the Nazis speak only too clearly. Today, with population almost everywhere on the increase, masses of people are continuously being rendered superfluous by political, social, and economic events. At such a time the instruments devised for making human beings superfluous are

bound to offer a great temptation: why not use these same instruments to liquidate human beings who have already become superfluous?

This side of the matter is only too well understood by the common sense of
the mob which in most countries is too desperate to retain much fear of death.
The Nazis, who were well aware that their defeat would not solve the problems
of Europe, knew exactly what they were doing when, toward the end of the
war—which by then they knew they had lost—they set up those factories of
annihilation which demonstrated the swiftest possible solution to the problem
of superfluous human masses. There is no doubt that this solution will from
now on occur to millions of people whenever it seems impossible to alleviate
political, or social, or economic misery in a manner worthy of man.

NOTES

1. That Rousset's purely literary vitalism could survive the years in Buchenwald would
seem to be striking proof of Kogon's thesis that "most of the prisoners [left] the concentration camps with exactly the same convictions that they had before; if anything,
these convictions became more accentuated" (p. 302). David Rousset concludes 702
pages of horror, which prove many times over that it is possible to kill man's humanity without killing his body, with a short paragraph of "triumph," that sounds as if it
had been written by a literary hack who had never set foot outside of Paris. "We never
blasphemed against life. Our systems of the world were not alike, but more profoundly, more remotely, our affirmation of the power and creative grandeur of life, our
absolute faith in its triumph remained intact. We never believed in the final disaster of
humanity. For collectively it is the highest, strongest expression of the vital gesture in
the history of the universe." It is not surprising that this "vital gesture" should have
appealed to Georges Bataille with his theory of "extreme experience"—yet it is somehow surprising that the proponents of extremity and meaninglessness should not
have changed their mind in the face of a reality that surpassed all their dreams. Bataille
(Critique, October 1947) writes: "One of Rousset's most unexpected reactions is his
exultation, almost to the point of euphoria, before the idea of participating in an experience that made no sense. Nothing could be more virile, more healthy." The translation
is quoted from Instead (No. 1, 1948); it would seem to be no accident that this pseudo-
profound reflection was the first break in the silence that the intellectuals have maintained on this whole matter.

2. Kogon has the following to say of working conditions in the Nazi camps, which presumably were better organized from this point of view than those of the Soviet Union:
"A large part of the work exacted in the concentration camps was useless; either it was
superfluous or it was so miserably planned that it had to be done over two or three
times. Buildings often had to be begun several times because the foundations kept cav-
ing in" (p. 58). As for Russian conditions, even Dallin (Forced Labor in Soviet Russia, p.
105) who has built his whole book on the thesis that the purpose of the Russian camps
was to provide cheap labor, is forced to admit: "Actually, the efficiency of forced labor,
despite incentives and compulsion, was and is on an extremely low level. The average
efficiency of a slave laborer has certainly been below 50 per cent of that of a free Russian worker, whose productivity in turn has never been high."

3. "Gestapo and SS have always attached great importance to mixing the categories of

inmates in the camps. In no camp have the inmates belonged exclusively to one category" (Kogon, p. 19). In Russia it has also been customary from the first to mix political prisoners and criminals. During the first ten years of Soviet power, the leftist political groups enjoyed certain privileges as compared with counter-revolutionaries and criminals. But "after the end of the twenties, the politicals were even officially treated as inferior to the common criminals" (Dallin, 177 ff).

4. This is evident in Russia as well as in Germany. In Russia, the concentration camps, which were originally intended for enemies of the regime, began to swell enormously after 1930, i.e., at a time when not only all armed resistance had been quelled, but when all opposition to Stalin within the Party had been liquidated. In the first years there were in Germany at most ten camps with a total of no more than ten thousand inmates. All effective resistance against the Nazis ceased by the end of 1936. But at the outbreak of the war there were more than a hundred concentration camps, which after 1940 seem to have maintained an average population of one million.

MARTIN BUBER

◼ The Dialogue between
Heaven and Earth

I

The most important of all that the biblical view of existence has opened up for all times is clearly recognized by a comparison of Israel's Holy Writ with those holy books of the nations that originated independently of it. None of those books is, like it, full of a dialogue between heaven and earth. It tells us how again and again God addresses man and is addressed by him. God announces to man what plan He has for the world; as the earliest of the "literary" prophets puts it (Amos 4:13), God lets him know "his soliloquy." He discloses to him His will and calls upon him to take part in its realization. But man is no blind tool; he was created as a free being—free also vis-à-vis God, free to surrender to Him or to refuse himself to Him. To God's sovereign address, man gives his autonomous answer; if he remains silent, his silence, too, is an answer. Very

---

often we hear God's voice alone, as in much of the books of the prophets, where only in isolated cases—in certain accounts of visions, or in the diary-like records of Jeremiah—does the prophet's reply become articulate, and sometimes these records actually assume a dialogic form. But even in all those passages where God alone speaks, we are made to feel that the person addressed by Him answers with his wordless soul, that is to say, that he stands in the dialogic situation. And again, very often we hear the voice of man alone, as generally in the Psalms, where only in isolated cases the worshipper indicates the divine reply; but here, too, the dialogic situation is apparent: it is apparent to us that man, lamenting, suppliant, thanks-giving, praise-singing man, experiences himself as heard and understood, accepted and confirmed, by Him to whom he addresses himself. The basic teaching that fills the Hebrew Bible is that our life is a dialogue between the above and the below.

But does this still apply to our present-day life? Believers and unbelievers deny it. A view common among believers is that though everything contained in Scripture is literally true, though God did certainly speak to the men chosen by Him, yet, since then, the holy spirit has been taken from us; heaven is silent to us, and only through the books of the written and oral tradition is God's will made known to us as to what we shall do or not do. Certainly, even today, the worshipper stands immediately before his Creator, but how could he dare, like the Psalmist, to report to the world words of personal reply, of personal granting, as spoken immediately to him? And as for the unbelievers, it goes without saying that the atheists need not be mentioned at all, but only the adherents of a more or less philosophic God-concept, with which they cannot reconcile the idea of God's addressing and being addressed by man; to them, the entire dialogics of Scripture is nothing but a mythical figment, instructive from the point of view of the history of the human mind, but inapplicable to our life.

As against either opinion, a faithful and unbiased reader of Scripture must endorse the view he has learned from it: what happened once happens now and always, and the fact of its happening to us is a guarantee of its having happened. The Bible has, in the form of a glorified remembrance, given vivid, decisive expression to an ever recurrent happening. In the infinite language of events and situations, eternally changing, but plain to the truly attentive, transcendence speaks to our hearts at the essential moments of personal life. And there is a language in which we can answer it; it is the language of our actions and attitudes, our reactions and our abstentions. The totality of these responses is what we may call our responsibility in the proper sense of the word. This fundamental interpretation of our existence we owe to the Hebrew Bible; and whenever we truly read it, our self-understanding is renewed and deepened. . . .

IV

But there is, in the biblical view [another] sphere of divine utterance. God speaks not only to the individual and to the community, within the limits and under the conditions of a particular biographical or historical situation. Everything, being and becoming, nature and history, is essentially a divine pronouncement (*Aussprache*), an infinite context of signs meant to be perceived and understood by perceiving and understanding creatures.

But here a fundamental difference exists between nature and human history. Nature, as a whole and in all its elements, enunciates something that may be regarded as a self-communication of God to all those ready to receive it. This is what the psalm means that has heaven and earth "declare," wordlessly, the glory of God.[1] Not so human history—not only because mankind, being placed in freedom, cooperates incessantly in shaping its course, but quite especially because, in nature, it is God the Creator who speaks, and His creative act is never interrupted; in history, on the other hand, it is the revealing God who speaks, and revelation is essentially not a continuous process, but breaks in again and again upon the course of events and irradiates it. Nature is full of God's utterance, if one but hears it, but what is said here is always that one, though all-inclusive, something, that which the psalm calls the glory of God; in history, however, times of great utterance, when the mark of divine direction is recognizable in the conjunction of events, alternate with, as it were, mute times, when everything that occurs in the human world and pretends to historical significance appears to us as empty of God, with nowhere a beckoning of His finger, nowhere a sign that He is present and acts upon this our historical hour. In such times it is difficult for the individual, and more so for the people, to understand oneself to be addressed by God; the experience of concrete responsibility recedes more and more, because, in the seemingly God-forsaken space of history, man unlearns taking the relationship between God and himself seriously in the dialogic sense.

In an hour when the exiles in Babylon perceived God's passage through world history, in the hour when Cyrus was about to release them and send them home, the anonymous Prophet of the Exile, who like none before him felt called upon to interpret the history of peoples, in one of his pamphlets made God say to Israel: "From the beginning I have not spoken in secret" (Isaiah 48:16). God's utterance in history is unconcealed, for it is intended to be heard by the peoples. But Isaiah, to whose book the pronouncements of the anonymous prophet have been attached, not only speaks of a time when God "hideth His face from the house of Jacob" (8:17), but he also knows (28:21) that there are times when we are unable to recognize and acknowledge God's own deeds in history as His deeds, so uncanny and "barbarous" do they seem to us. And the same chapter of the Prophet of the Exile, in which God says, "Ask Me of the things to come" (45:11), states that in the hour of the liberation of peoples the masses whom Egypt put to forced labor and Ethiopia sold as slaves will immediately, with the chains of serfdom still on their bodies, as it were, turn to God, throw themselves down, and pray: "Verily Thou art a God that hideth Himself, O God of Israel, Savior!" (45:15). During the long periods of enslavement it seemed to them as though there were nothing divine any more and the world were irretrievably abandoned to the forces of tyranny; only now do they recognize that there is a

Savior, and that He is one—the Lord of History. And now they know and profess: He is a God that hides himself, or more exactly, the God that hides Himself
and reveals Himself.

The Bible knows of God's hiding His face, of times when the contact
between heaven and earth seems to be interrupted. God seems to withdraw
Himself utterly from the earth and no longer to participate in its existence. The
space of history is then full of noise, but empty of the divine breath. For one who
believes in the living God, who knows about Him, and is fated to spend his life
in a time of His hiddenness, it is very difficult to live.

There is a psalm, the 82nd, in which life in a time of God's hiddenness is
described in a picture of startling cruelty. It is assumed that God has entrusted
the government of mankind to a host of angels and commanded them to realize
justice on earth and to protect the weak, the poor, and the helpless from the
encroachments of the wrongdoers. But they "judge unjustly" and "respect the
persons of the wicked." Now the Psalmist envisions how God draws the unfaithful angels before His seat, judges them, and passes sentence upon them: they
are to become mortal. But the Psalmist awakes from his vision and looks about
him: iniquity still reigns on earth with unlimited power. And he cries to God:
"Arise, O God, judge the earth!"

This cry is to be understood as a late, but even more powerful, echo of that
bold speech of the patriarch arguing with God: "The judge of all the earth, will
He not do justice?!"[2] It reinforces and augments that speech; its implication is:
Will He allow injustice to reign further? And so the cry transmitted to us by
Scripture becomes our own cry, which bursts from our hearts and rises to our
lips in a time of God's hiddenness. For this is what the biblical word does to us:
it confronts us with the human address as one that in spite of everything is
heard and in spite of everything may expect an answer.

In this our own time, one asks again and again: How is a Jewish life still possible after Auschwitz? I would like to frame this question more correctly: how is
a life with God still possible in a time in which there is an Auschwitz? The
estrangement has become too cruel, the hiddenness too deep. One can still
"believe" in the God who allowed those things to happen, but can one still speak
to Him? Can one still hear His word? Can one still, as an individual and as a people, enter at all into a dialogic relationship with Him? Can one still call to Him?
Dare we recommend to the survivors of Auschwitz, the Job of the gas chambers:
"Give thanks unto the Lord, for He is good; for His mercy endureth forever"?[3]

But how about Job himself? He not only laments, but he charges that the
"cruel" God (30:21) has "removed his right" from him (27:2) and thus that the
judge of all the earth acts against justice. And he receives an answer from God.
But what God says to him does not answer the charge; it does not even touch
upon it. The true answer that Job receives is God's appearance only, only this
that distance turns into nearness, that "his eye sees Him" (42:5), that he knows
Him again. Nothing is explained, nothing adjusted; wrong has not become
right, nor cruelty kindness. Nothing has happened but that man again hears
God's address.

The mystery has remained unsolved, but it has become his, it has become man's.

And we?

We—by that is meant all those who have not got over what happened and will not get over it. How is it with us? Do we stand overcome before the hidden face of God like the tragic hero of the Greeks before faceless fate? No, rather even now we contend, we too, with God, even with Him, the Lord of Being, whom we once, we here, chose for our Lord. We do not put up with earthly being; we struggle for its redemption, and struggling we appeal to the help of our Lord, who is again and still a hiding one. In such a state we await His voice, whether it comes out of the storm or out of a stillness that follows it. Though His coming appearance resemble no earlier one, we shall recognize again our cruel and merciful Lord.

NOTES

1. Psalm 19:2.
2. Genesis 18:25.
3. Psalm 106:1.

ELIE WIESEL

▣ A Plea for the Dead

In recent times, many people are beginning to raise questions about the problem of the incomprehensible if not enigmatic behavior of Jews in what was concentration-camp Europe. Why did they march into the night the way cattle go to the slaughterhouse? Important, if not essential, for it touches on timeless truth; this question torments men of good conscience who feel the need to be quickly reassured, to have the guilty parties named and their crimes defined, to have unraveled for them the meaning of a history which they had not experienced except through intermediaries. And so those millions of Jews, whom so-called civilized society had abandoned to despair and to agonize in silence and

Reprinted by permission of Georges Borchardt, Inc., Literary Agency.

then in oblivion, suddenly are all brought back up to the surface to be drowned in a flood of words. And since we live at a time when small talk is king, the dead offer no resistance. The role of ghost is imposed upon them and they are bombarded with questions: "Well, now, what was it really like? How did you feel in Minsk and in Kiev and in Kolomea, when the earth, opening up before your eyes, swallowed up your sons and your prayers? What did you think when you saw blood—your own blood—gushing from the bowels of the earth, rising up to the sun? Tell us, speak up, we want to know, to suffer with you, we have a few tears in reserve, they pain us, we want to get rid of them."

One is sometimes reduced to regretting the good old days when this subject, still in the domain of sacred memory, was considered taboo, reserved for the initiates, who spoke of it only with hesitation and fear, always lowering their eyes, and always trembling with humility, knowing themselves unworthy and recognizing the limits of their language, spoken and unspoken.

Now in the name of objectivity, not to mention historical research, everyone takes up the subject without the slightest embarrassment. Accessible to every mind, to every intellect in search of stimulation, this has become the topic of fashionable conversation. Why not? It replaces Brecht, Kafka, and communism, which are now overdone, overworked. In intellectual, or pseudo-intellectual circles, in New York and elsewhere too, no cocktail party can really be called a success unless Auschwitz, sooner or later, figures in the discussion. Excellent remedy for boredom; a good way to ignite passions. Drop the names of a few recent works on this subject, and watch minds come alive, one more brilliant, more arrogant then the next. Psychiatrists, comedians, and novelists, all have their own ideas about the subject, all are clear, each is ready to provide all the answers, to explain all the mysteries: the cold cruelty of the executioner and the cry which strangled the victim, and even the fate that united them to play on the same stage, in the same cemetery. It is as simple as saying hello. As hunger, thirst, and hate. One need only understand history, sociology, politics, psychology, economics; one need know only how to add. And to accept the axiom that everywhere $A + B = C$. If the dead are dead, if so many dead are dead, that is because they desired their own death, they were lured, driven by their own instincts. Beyond the diversity of all the theories, the self-assurance of which cannot but arouse anger, all unanimously conclude that the victims, by participating in the executioner's game, in varying degrees shared responsibility.

The novelty of this view cannot fail to be striking. Until recently, Jews have been held responsible for everything under the sun, the death of Jesus, civil wars, famines, unemployment, and revolutions: they were thought to embody evil; now, they are held responsible for their own death: they embody that death. Thus, we see that the Jewish problem continues to be a kind of no-man's land of the mind where anyone can say anything in any way at all—a game in which everyone wins. Only the dead are the losers.

And in this game—it is really nothing else—it is quite easy to blame the dead, to accuse them of cowardice or complicity (in either the concrete or metaphysical sense of that term). Now, this game has a humiliating aspect. To insist on speaking in the name of the dead—and to say: these are their motivations, these the considerations that weakened their wills, to speak in their name—this is precisely to humiliate them. The dead have earned something other than this posthumous humiliation. I never before wholly understood why, in the Jewish faith, anything that touches corpses is impure. Now I begin to understand.

Let us leave them alone. We will not dig up those corpses without coffins. Leave them there where they must forever be and such as they must be: wounds, immeasurable pain at the very depth of our being. Be content they do not wake up, that they do not come back to the earth to judge the living. The day that they would begin to tell what they have seen and heard, and what they have taken most to heart, we will not know where to run, we will stop up our ears, so great will be our fear, so sharp our shame.

I could understand the desire to dissect history, the strong urge to close in on the past and the forces shaping it; nothing is more natural. No question is more important for our generation which is the generation of Auschwitz, or of Hiroshima, tomorrow's Hiroshima. The future frightens us, the past fills us with shame: and these two feelings, like those two events, are closely linked, like cause to effect. It is Auschwitz that will produce Hiroshima, and if the human race should perish by the nuclear bomb, this will be the punishment for Auschwitz, where, in the ashes, the hope of man was extinguished.

And Lot's apprehensive wife, she was right to want to look back and not be afraid to carry the burning of doomed hope. "Know where you come from," the sages of Israel said. But everything depends on the inner attitude of whoever looks back to the beginning: if he does so purely out of intellectual curiosity, his vision will make of him a statue in some salon. Unfortunately, we do not lack statues these days; and what is worse, they speak, as if from the top of the mountain.

And so I read and I listen to these eminent scholars and professors who, having read all the books and confronted all the theories, proclaim their erudition and their power to figure everything out, to explain everything, simply by performing an exercise in classification.

At times, especially at dawn, when I am awakened by the first cry I heard the first night behind barbed wire, a desire comes over me to say to all these illustrious writers who claim to go to the bottom of it all: "I admire you, for I myself stumble when I walk this road; you claim to know everything, there again I admire you: as for me, I know nothing. What is to be done, I know I am still incapable of deciphering—for to do so would be to blaspheme—the frightened smile of that child torn away from his mother and transformed into a flaming torch; nor have I been able, nor will I ever be able, to grasp the shadow which, at that moment, invaded the mother's eyes. You can, undoubtedly. You are fortunate, I ought to envy you, but I do not. I prefer to stand on the side of the child and of the mother who died before they understood the formulas and phraseology which are the basis of your science."

Also, I prefer to take my place on the side of Job, who chose questions and not answers, silence and not speeches. Job never understood his own tragedy which, after all, was only that of an individual betrayed by God; to be betrayed by one's fellow men is much more serious. Yet, the silence of this man, alone and defeated, lasted for seven days and seven nights; only afterward, when he identified himself with his pain, did he feel he had earned the right to question God. Confronted with Job, our silence should extend beyond the centuries to come. And we dare speak on behalf of our knowledge? We dare say: "*I know*"? This is how and why victims were victims and executioners executioners? We dare interpret the agony and anguish, the self-sacrifice before the faith and the faith itself of six million human beings, all named Job? Who are we to judge them?

One of my friends, in the prime of life, spent a night studying accounts of the holocaust, especially the Warsaw Ghetto. In the morning he looked at himself in the mirror and saw a stranger: his hair had turned white. Another lost not his youth but his reason. He plunged back into the past and remains there still. From time to time I visit him in his hospital room; we look at one another and we are silent. One day, he shook himself and said to me: "Perhaps one should learn to cry."

I should envy those scholars and thinkers who pride themselves on understanding this tragedy in terms of an entire people; I myself have not yet succeeded in explaining the tragedy of a single one of its sons, no matter which.

I have nothing against questions: they are useful. What is more, they alone are. To turn away from them would be to fail in our duty, to lose our only chance to be able one day to lead an authentic life. It is against the answers that I protest, regardless of their basis. Answers: I say there are none. Each of these theories contains perhaps a fraction of truth, but their sum still remains beneath and outside what, in that night, was truth. The events obeyed no law and no law can be derived from them. The subject matter to be studied is made up of death and mystery, it slips away between our fingers, it runs faster than our perception: it is everywhere and nowhere. Answers only intensify the question: ideas and words must finally come up against a wall higher than the sky, a wall of human bodies extending to infinity.

For more than twenty years, I have been struggling with these questions. To find one answer or another, nothing is easier: language can mend anything. What the answers have in common is that they bear no relation to the questions. I cannot believe that an entire generation of fathers and sons could vanish into the abyss without creating, by their very disappearance, a mystery which exceeds and overwhelms us. I still do not understand what happened, or how, or why. All the words in all the mouths of the philosophers and psychologists are not worth the silent tears of that child and his mother, who live their own death twice. What can be done? In my calculations, all the figures always add up to the same number: six million.

Some time ago, in Jerusalem, I met by chance one of the three judges in the Eichmann trial. This wise and lucid man, of uncompromising character, is, to use an expression dear to Camus, at once a person and a personage. He is, in addition, a conscience.

He refused to discuss the technical or legal aspects of the trial. Having told him that side was of no interest to me, I asked him the following question:

"Given your role in this trial, you ought to know more about the scope of the holocaust than any living person, more even than those who lived through it in the flesh and in their memory. You have studied all the documents, read all the secret reports, interrogated all the witnesses. Now tell me: do you *understand* this fragment of the past, those few pages of history?"

He shuddered imperceptibly, then, in a soft voice, infinitely humble, he confessed:

"No, not at all. I know the facts and the events that served as their framework; I know how the tragedy unfolded minute by minute, but this knowledge, as if coming from outside, has nothing to do with understanding. There is in all this a portion which will always remain a mystery; a kind of forbidden zone, inaccessible to reason. Fortunately, as it happens. Without that . . ."

He broke off suddenly. Then, with a smile a bit timid, a bit sad, he added:

"Who knows, perhaps that's the gift which God, in a moment of grace, gave to man: it prevents him from understanding everything, thus saving him from madness, or from suicide."

In truth, Auschwitz signifies not only the failure of two thousand years of Christian civilization, but also the defeat of the intellect that wants to find a Meaning—with a capital M—in history. What Auschwitz embodied has none. The executioner killed for nothing, the victim died for nothing. No God ordered the one to prepare the stake, nor the other to mount it. During the Middle Ages, the Jews, when they chose death, were convinced that by their sacrifice they were glorifying and sanctifying God's name. At Auschwitz the sacrifices were without point, without faith, without divine inspiration. If the suffering of one human being has any meaning, that of six million has none. Numbers have their own importance; they prove, according to Piotr Rawicz, that God has gone mad.

I attended the Eichmann trial, I heard the prosecutor try to get the witnesses to talk by forcing them to expose themselves and to probe the innermost recesses of their being: Why didn't you resist? Why didn't you attack your assassins when you still outnumbered them?

Pale, embarrassed, ill at ease, the survivors all responded in the same way: "You cannot understand. Anyone who was not there cannot imagine it."

Well, I was there. And I still do not understand. I do not understand that child in the Warsaw Ghetto who wrote in his diary: "I'm hungry, I'm cold; when I grow up I want to be a German, and then I won't be hungry anymore, and I won't be cold anymore."

I still do not understand why I did not throw myself on the Kapo who was beating my father before my very eyes. In Galicia, Jews dug their own graves and lined up, without any trace of panic, at the edge of the trench to await the machine-gun barrage. I do not understand their calm. And that woman, that mother, in the bunker somewhere in Poland, I do not understand her either; her companions smothered her child for fear its cries might betray their presence; that woman, that mother, having lived this scene of biblical intensity, did not go mad. I do not understand her: why, and by what right, and in the name of what, did she not go mad?

I do not know why, but I forbid us to ask her the question. The world kept silent while the Jews were being massacred, while they were being reduced to the state of objects good for the fire; let the world at least have the decency to keep silent now as well. Its questions come a bit late; they should have been addressed to the executioner. Do they trouble us? Do they keep us from sleeping in peace? So much the better. We want to know, to understand, so we can turn the page: is that not true? So we can say to ourselves: the matter is closed and everything is back in order. Do not wait for the dead to come to our rescue. Their silence will survive them.

We have questions? Very good. We do not want to put them to the executioner—who lives in happiness if not in glory at home in Germany—well then, pass them on to those who claim they never participated in the game, to those who became accomplices through their passivity. Their "ignorance" of the facts hardly excuses them, it was willful.

In London and in Washington, in Basel and in Stockholm, high officials had up-to-date information about every transport carrying its human cargo to the realm of ashes, to the kingdom of mist. In 1942–1943, they already possessed photographs documenting the reports; all were declared "confidential" and their publication prohibited.

Not many voices were raised to warn the executioner that the day of punishment is at hand; not many voices were raised to effectively console the victims: that there will be punishment and that the reign of night is only temporary. . . .

If I dwell so long on the culpability of the world, it is not to lessen that of the Germans, nor to "explain" the behavior of their victims. We tend to forget.

The fact, for example, that in the spring of 1944 we, in Transylvania, knew nothing about what was happening in Germany is proof of the world's guilt. We listened to the short-wave radio, from London and Moscow: not a single broadcast warned us not to leave with the transports, not one disclosed the existence, not even the name of Auschwitz. In 1943, when she read three lines in a Hungarian newspaper concerning the Warsaw Ghetto uprising, my mother remarked: "But why did they do it? Why didn't they wait *peacefully* for the end of hostilities?" Had we known what was happening there, we might have been able to flee, to hide: the Russian front was only thirty kilometers away. But we were kept in the dark.

At the risk of offending, it must be emphasized that the victims suffered more, and more profoundly, from the indifference of the onlookers than from the brutality of the executioner. The cruelty of the enemy would have been incapable of breaking the prisoner; it was the silence of those he believed to be his friends—cruelty more cowardly, more subtle—which broke his heart.

There was no longer anyone on whom to count: even in the camps this became evident. *"From now on we shall live in the wilderness, in the void: blotted out of history."* It was this conviction which poisoned the desire to live. If this is the world we were born into, why cling to it? If this is the human society we come from—and are now abandoned by—why seek to return?

At Auschwitz, not only man died, but also the idea of man. To live in a world where there is nothing anymore, where the executioner acts as god, as judge—many wanted no part of it. It was its own heart the world incinerated at Auschwitz.

Let no one misinterpret. I speak without hatred, without bitterness. If at times I do not succeed in containing my anger, it is because I find it shocking if not indecent that one must plead to protect the dead. For this is the issue: they are being dug up in order to be pilloried. The questions asked of them are only reproaches. They are being blamed, these corpses, for having acted as they did: they should have played their roles differently, if only to reassure the living who might thus go on believing in the nobility of man. We do not like those men and women for whom the sky became a common grave. We speak of them without pity, without compassion, without love. We juggle their thousand ways of dying as if performing intellectual acrobatics: our heart is not in it. More than that: we despise them. For the sake of convenience, and also to satisfy our mania to classify and define everything, we make some distinctions: between the Germans and the *Judenrat*, between the Kapos and the ghetto police, between the nameless victim and the victim who obtained a reprieve for a week, for a month. We judge them and we hand out certificates for good or bad conduct. We detest some more than others: we are on the other side of the wall, and we know exactly the degree of guilt of each of them. On the whole, they inspire our disgust rather than our anger.

That is what I reproach us for: our boundless arrogance in thinking we know everything. And that we have the right to pass judgment on an event which should, on the contrary, serve as proof that we are poor, and that our dreams are barren—when they are not bloody.

I plead for the dead and I do not say they are innocent; that is neither my intention nor aim. I say simply we have no right to judge them; to confer innocence upon them is already to judge them. I saw them die and if I feel the need to speak of guilt, it is always of my own that I speak. I saw them go away and I remained behind. Often I do not forgive myself for that.

Of course, in the camps I saw men conquered, weak, cruel. I do not hesitate to admit I hated them, they frightened me; for me, they represented a danger greater than the Germans. Yes, I have known sadistic Kapos; yes, I have seen Jews, a savage gleam burning in their eyes, whipping their own brothers. But, though they played the executioner's game, they died as victims. When I think about it, I am still astonished that so few souls were lost, so few hearts poisoned, in that kingdom of the night, where one breathed only hate, contempt, and self-disgust. What would have become of me had I stayed in the camps longer, five years, or seven, or twelve? I have been trying to answer that question for more than twenty years and at times, after a sleepless night, I am afraid of the answer. But many people are not afraid. These questions, which are discussed as one might discuss a theorem or a scientific problem, do not frighten us. For that, too, I reproach us.

Since the end of the nightmare I search the past, whose prisoner I shall no doubt forever remain. I am afraid, but I still pursue my quest. The further I go, the less I understand. Perhaps there is nothing to understand.

On the other hand, the further I go, the more I learn of the scope of the betrayal by the world of the living against the world of the dead. I take my head in my hands and I think: it is insanity, that is the explanation, the only conceivable one. When so great a number of men carry their indifference to such an extreme, it becomes sickness, it resembles madness.

Otherwise how to explain the Roosevelts, the Churchills, the Eisenhowers, who never expressed their indignation? How to explain the silence of the Pope? How to explain the failure of certain attempts in London, in Washington, to obtain from the Allies an aerial bombardment of the death factories, or at least of the railway lines leading to them?

One of the saddest episodes of that war, not lacking in sad episodes, had as hero a Polish Jewish leader exiled in London: to protest the inaction of the Allies, and also to alert public opinion, Arthur Ziegelbaum, member of the "National Committee to Free Poland," put a bullet through his head in broad daylight in front of the entrance to the House of Commons. In his will he expressed his hope that his protest would be heard.

He was quickly forgotten, his death proved useless. Had he believed his refusal to live among men voluntarily blind would move them, he had been wrong. Ziegelbaum dead or Ziegelbaum living: to those hearts of stone it was all the same. For them he was only a Polish Jew talking about Jews and living their agony; for them he might just as well have perished over there, with the others. Arthur Ziegelbaum died for nothing. Life went on, so did the war: against the Axis powers, which continued their own war against the Jews. And the world stopped up its ears and lowered its eyes. Sometimes the newspapers printed a small item: the Ghetto of Lodz had been liquidated, the number of European Jews massacred already exceeded two or three million. This news was published as if these were normal events, almost without comment, without anguish. It seemed normal that Jews should be killed by the Nazis. Never had the Jewish people been so alone.

The more I search, the more reasons I find for losing hope. I am often afraid to reopen this Pandora's box, there are always the newly guilty to emerge from it. Is there no bottom to this evil box? No.

I repeat: hatred is no solution. There would be too many targets. The Hungarians put more passion than did the Germans into the persecution of Jews; the Rumanians displayed more savagery than the Germans; the Slovaks, the Poles, the Ukrainians: they hunted down Jews cunningly, as if with love. Perhaps I should hate them, it would cure me. But I am incapable. Were hatred a solution, the survivors, when they came out of the camps, would have had to burn down the whole world.

Now almost everywhere I am told: you mustn't bear a grudge against us, we didn't know, we didn't believe it, we were powerless to do anything. If these justifications suffice to assuage people's consciences, too bad for them. I could answer that they did not want to know, that they refused to believe, that they could have forced their governments to break the conspiracy of silence. But that would open the door to discussion. It is too late, in any case: the time for discussion is past.

Now, I shall simply ask: is it any surprise that the Jews did not choose resistance? And die fighting like soldiers for the victory of their cause? But what victory and what cause?

Let me reveal a secret, one among a thousand, about why Jews did not resist: to punish us, to prepare a vengeance for us for later. We were not worth their sacrifice. If, in every town and every village, in the Ukraine and in Galicia, in Hungary and in Czechoslovakia, Jews formed endless nightly processions and marched on to eternity as if carrying within themselves a pure joy, one which heralds the approach of ecstasy, it is precisely to reveal to us the ultimate truth about those who are sacrificed on the margins of history. In staying alive, at that price, we deserve neither salvation nor atonement. Nor do we even deserve that lesson of solemn dignity and lofty courage which, in spite of everything, in their own way, they gave us by making their way toward death, staring it full in the face, point blank, their heads high in the joy of bearing this strength, this pride within themselves.

Let us, therefore, not make an effort to understand, but rather to lower our eyes and not understand. Every rational explanation would be more esoteric than if it were mystical. Not to understand the dead is a way of paying them an ancient debt; it is the only way to ask their pardon.

I have before me a photograph, taken by a German officer fond of souvenirs, of a father who, an instant before the burst of rifle fire, was still speaking calmly to his son, while pointing to the sky. Sometimes I think I hear his dreamy voice: "You see, my son, we are going to die and the sky is beautiful. Do not forget there is a connection between these two facts." Or perhaps: "We are going to die, my son, yet the sky, so serene, is not collapsing in an end-of-the-world crash. Do you hear its silence? Listen to it, you must not forget it." It occurs to me that were I to ask him a question, any question, that same father would answer me. But I bury my eyes in what remains of him and I am silent.

Just as I am silent every time the image comes to my mind of the Rebbe in Warsaw who stood erect, unyielding, unconquerable, before a group of SS; they were amusing themselves by making him suffer, by humiliating him; he suffered, but did not let himself be humiliated. One of them, laughing, cut off his beard, but the Rebbe stared right into his eyes without flinching; there was pain in this expression, but also defiance, the expression of a man stronger than evil, even when evil is triumphant, stronger than death, even when death assumes

the face of a comedian playing a farce—the expression of a man who owes nothing to anyone, not even to God.

I have long since carried that expression buried within me. I have not been
able to part with it, I no longer want to part with it, as though wanting always to
remember there are still, there will always be, somewhere in the world, expressions I will never understand. And when such an expression lights upon me, at
the dinner table, at a concert, or beside a happy woman, I give myself up to it in
silence.

For the older I grow, the more I know that we can do little for the dead; the
least we can do is to leave them alone, not project our own guilt onto them. We
like to think the dead have found eternal rest: let them be. It is dangerous to
wake them. They, too, have questions, questions equal to our own.

My plea is coming to an end, but it would be incomplete if I said nothing
about the armed assaults which, in spite of what the prosecution may think,
Jews did carry out against the Germans. If I have difficulty understanding how
multitudes went to their death without defending themselves, that difficulty
becomes insurmountable when it comes to understanding those of their companions who chose to fight.

How, in the ghettos and camps, they were able to find the means to fight
when the whole world was against them—that will always remain a mystery.

For those who claim that all the Jews submitted to their murderers, to
fate, in common cowardice or common resignation, those people do not know
what they are saying or—what is worse—knowingly falsify the facts only
to illustrate a sociological theory, or to justify a morbid hatred which is always
self-hatred.

In truth, there was among the victims an active elite of fighters composed of
men and women and children who, with pitiful means, stood up against the
Germans. They were a minority, granted. But is there any society where the
active elite is not a minority? Such groups existed in Warsaw, in Bialystock, in
Grodno, and—God alone knows how—even in Treblinka, in Sobivor, and in
Auschwitz. Authenticated documents and eye-witness accounts do exist, relat-
ing the acts of war of those poor desperadoes; reading them, one does not know
whether to rejoice with admiration or to weep with rage. One wonders: but how
did they do it, those starving youngsters, those hunted men, those battered
women, how were they able to confront, with weapons in hand, the Nazi army,
which at that time seemed invincible, marching from victory to victory? Where
did they take their sheer physical endurance, their moral strength? What was
their secret and what is its name?

We say: weapons in hand. But what weapons? They had hardly any. They
had to pay in pure gold for a single revolver. In Bialystok, the legendary Mordecai Tenenbaum-Tamaroff, leader of the ghetto resistance, describes in his journal—miraculously rediscovered—the moment he obtained the first rifle, the
first ammunition: twenty-five bullets. "Tears came to my eyes. I felt my heart
burst with joy." It was thus with one rifle and twenty-five bullets that he and his
companions were going to contain the vast onslaught of the German army. It is

easy to imagine what might have happened had every warrior in every ghetto obtained one rifle.

All the underground networks in the occupied countries received arms, money, and radio equipment from London, and secret agents came regularly to teach them the art of sabotage: they felt themselves organically linked to the outside world. In France or Norway a member of the resistance who was caught could comfort himself with the thought that somewhere in that town as well as on the other shore, there were people who feared for his life, who lived in anxiety because of him, who would move heaven and earth to save him: his acts registered somewhere, left traces, marks of sorrow, produced results. But the Jews were alone: only they were alone.

They alone did not receive help or encouragement; neither arms nor messages were sent them; they were not spoken to, no one was concerned with them; they did not exist. They cried for help, but the appeals they issued by radio or by mail fell on deaf ears. Cut off from the world, from the war itself, the Jewish fighters participated, fully aware they were not wanted, they had already been written off; they threw themselves into battle knowing they could count on no one, help would never arrive, they would receive no support, there would be no place to retreat. And yet, with their backs to the burning wall, they defied the Germans. Some battles are won even when they are lost.

Yes, competent elite existed even at Sobivor, where they organized an escape; at Treblinka, where they revolted; and at Auschwitz, where they blew up the crematoria. The Auschwitz insurgents attempted an escape, but in the struggle with the SS, who obviously had an advantage of superiority in weapons and men, all were killed. Later the Germans arrested the four young Jewish girls from Warsaw who had obtained the explosives for the insurgents. They were tortured, condemned to death, and hanged at a public ceremony. They died without fear. The oldest was sixteen, the youngest twelve.

We can only lower our heads and be silent. And end this sickening posthumous trial which intellectual acrobats everywhere are carrying on against those whose death numbs the mind. Do we want to understand? There is no longer anything to understand. Do we want to know? There is nothing to know anymore. It is not by playing with words and the dead that we will understand and know. Quite the contrary. As the ancients said: "Those who know do not speak; those who speak do not know."

But we prefer to speak and to judge. We wish to be strong and invulnerable. The lesson of the holocaust—if there is any—is that our strength is only illusory, and that in each of us is a victim who is afraid, who is cold, who is hungry. Who is also ashamed.

The Talmud teaches man never to judge his friend until he has been in his place. But, for the world, the Jews are not friends. They have never been. Because they had no friends they are dead.

So, learn to be silent.

PART 2

▣ Central Theological Responses

In the late 1950s through the early 1970s, a number of Jewish and Christian theologians began to confront the Holocaust and to reflect on its implications for religious belief and conduct. As we indicated in the general introduction, there are many reasons why this response was delayed and really reached a peak only after the Six Day War in 1967. Many of these reasons are psychological and historical, but some were surely intellectual and theoretical, so to speak, reasons having to do with what could be said and what ought to be said and how and with what implications.

It is not surprising that this serious and open response was made in large part by Jewish thinkers, for after all the Holocaust as an expression of hatred and an intention of unconditional destruction was aimed at the Jewish people and the historical results—social, political, and psychological—were felt most deeply by Jews. Nor is it totally surprising that the earliest responses, literary and theological, were negative. That is, that they raised the obvious and yet probing question of God's role vis à vis Auschwitz, the suffering, the dehumanization, and the technology of death. The problem of evil as a cognitive problem of holding together beliefs about God and about atrocity and suffering is not only an old problem; it is perennial in part because it is deep and serious and because rational consistency is a very deep-seated desire for most of us. Hence, in both the early writings of Elie Wiesel and in the essays collected in Rubenstein's *After Auschwitz*, the framework of confrontation was at least in part the traditional problem of evil and its implication, that the Jewish commitment to a covenantal God, a divine partner with historical responsibilities to protect and save his people, was destroyed at Auschwitz. In a memorable scene depicted in *Night*, Wiesel has created a classic image of this response, of God hanging on the gallows as the body of a small boy twitches and jerks before the eyes of the passing inmates. To be sure, Wiesel's views about God after the Holocaust do change, but here, in this early work, his belief in and trust in God is destroyed. This, or something like it, is Rubenstein's position, that the God of history and the religion of history are dead, and that a new type of Judaism, perhaps even with a new notion of God, must take its place.

No strictly historical or chronological display of these central theological options seemed possible, and so I have chosen a quasi-historical alternative. That is, I have selected several thinkers whose work first took shape in this period, and offer major options. Among Jewish thinkers, this group includes Rubenstein, Fackenheim, Berkovits, and Greenberg. Among Christian theologians, it includes Roy Eckardt and Franklin Littell. Even though some of these thinkers have continued to think about these issues and developed their thinking in the later 1970s and 1980s, I generally selected from all of their writings one or more pieces that indicate the overall character of their views. In general, I was unable to indicate important shifts and changes. To see this, one should check the bibliography and look at articles and books from different periods. In some cases—for example, Fackenheim and Eckardt—the development is extensive and important, and one should note the dates of publication of the selections. I shall say a word about them and their development shortly. But generally I set these thinkers out as major, developed post-Holocaust theological options that began to take shape at a fairly early stage in the 1960s.

This strategy of presentation should not lead the reader to think that no other developed, important positions are available. Later in the 1970s and 1980s, other thinkers did make important, innovative contributions to reflection on the religious implications of Auschwitz, and I have tried to include many of the important ones in the third section. But they are latecomers, in a sense, and their thinking arises after this first important wave and partially in response to it as well as to the event. To put it differently, the thinkers in this second section constitute a vocabulary for discussing the Holocaust and its religious and moral implications; they fix the terms and strategies and alternatives, as it were. Those who follow either reject or revise or embrace the terms and concepts and strategies of these earlier thinkers, to one degree or another.

I have said that these religious thinkers provide us with major options for confronting and coping with the Holocaust. While I think that this is true, it is not simple to understand why and how this is so, for it is not easy to grasp what each thinker is doing and precisely what type of option he is setting out. This much is true: Although each one had been involved in theological reflection prior to exposing his thought to Auschwitz, each takes the event with utter seriousness. The event is not simply swept up into a system of thought or a theory. Indeed, part of what makes these figures so important is that the event threatens to shatter their thought and that they struggle with this possibility but do not avoid or coopt it. Some intellectuals, that is, treat the Holocaust as a case or instance of something, ultimately wanting to make a point by using it as a particularly powerful example. But these thinkers are not of this sort. To them, the event imposes itself and refuses to be "softened" or coopted. They come to it with a view of Judaism or Christianity or modernity or whatever, and they realize that some or all of that view may have to be abandoned or revised once the encounter is conducted, for the event is a watershed; that is just undeniable.

But they do provide a spectrum of response, at least insofar as they differ on how much the Holocaust demands that they abandon or revise or on how much *can* be abandoned or revised, without losing everything. In the end, they may differ basically and fundamentally in the degree of optimism or pessimism they accept concerning the very relationship between thought and history itself.

What I mean is this. When Rubenstein confronts the Holocaust, he has already come to an understanding of Judaism and religion that is shaped by existential philosophy, Freud, modern literary imagination, and reconstructionism, that movement of Jewish naturalism developed by Mordecai Kaplan in the thirties. In a sense, then, Rubenstein already was seeking a naturalistic understanding of Jewish practise and belief, and he had found it, to a degree, by conceiving of Judaism as a variegated response to the problematic of the human condition, as that is clarified by thinkers such as Sartre, Freud, Camus, Dostoyevsky, Tillich, and Eliade. Rubenstein at times seems to present his abandonment of a covenantal theology, the God of history, and a Judaism of providence and historical development as the direct result of his confrontation with the Holocaust and hence as the outcome of the problem of evil. But, at other times, the Holocaust seems to be a confirmation of a set of views about Judaism, religion, man's existential condition, and so forth that he had already developed. On this view, the Holocaust is the epitome of the modern human predicament; it underlines and dramatizes the needs that religion is created to solve and endorses the rejection of a transcendent hope in favor of human institutions, both ritual and political. Hence, while Rubenstein looks like someone who believes that thought is completely refutable by history—for even the belief in a transcendent God can be destroyed by historical suffering and atrocity—he really may be saying that the Holocaust tends to confirm an already accepted naturalism. The real question, then, remains open.

Part of the greatness of the thinking of Roy Eckardt and Emil Fackenheim comes from the fact that both recognize precisely what this question means and what role it plays. That is, both have thought about the exposure of thought to history and hence about the "necessity" of historicity. Fackenheim often has stated that the most important shift in his thinking came when he recognized and admitted that all Jewish thought and possibly philosophy too must be open to historical refutation. Eckardt has both said and shown by argument that no Christian doctrine or belief is immune to the transforming impact of the Shoah. Both realize that Judaism and Christianity must now hold firm to something but that in principle everything is negotiable. We might call this an "unconditioned historicism" or an "absolutist relativism," just to underscore the struggle that deeply invades the thoughts of both men and renders their writings powerful, serious, and always challenging.

Eckardt comes to the Holocaust with a strong commitment to liberal Christian theology and with an uncompromising desire to understand Christianity in terms of its relationship to Judaism. But the Judaism he has in mind is not simply ancient, nor are the Jews he seeks to understand long dead and buried. Rather, Eckardt seeks a living relationship between contemporary Jews and the Church, and hence he takes seriously the Christian role in historical antisemitism, in modern Jewish history, and ultimately in the Holocaust and with regard to the reestablishment of the Jewish state. In the end, for Eckardt, no Christian doctrine is immune to the vicissitudes of the historical interaction between Christianity and the Jewish people, so that at an extreme moment he can say that the only remaining authentic Christian theology is Jewish theology. Everything, from the notion of Christian love to the doctrine of the resurrection and of Christology, can be and perhaps should be abandoned, in order for an honest, authentic post-Holocaust Christian theology to maintain its integrity.

Rubenstein, at one time, seems to have conceived of his disposal of a transcendent God and naturalistic affirmation of Jewish ritual and statehood as a Jewish version of death-of-God theology, a short-lived movement of the sixties. Certainly, Eckardt never conceived of his own thought that way. Yet, Eckardt is far more radical, I think, as he slowly gropes from a passionate resolve for a Christian openness to the Jewish people and to responsibility for the Shoah to a grudging willingness to give up everything, if honesty demands it. Perhaps another way to describe their relationship is this way: both thinkers expose their thinking to modernity and the scientific world-view that includes psychological, social, and scientific critique of religion and revelation and also to the Holocaust, but while Rubenstein's Judaism is decisively altered by the former, Eckardt's is decisively altered by the latter.

Fackenheim's Judaism is decisively altered by both, but one is a transformation sponsored by external criticism and attack, while the other is a transformation sponsored by an internal event in which everything, from covenant and providence to human purpose and nature, is called into question. Fackenheim's Jewish thought exhibits a depth and profundity and richness matchless among those who have thought about the Holocaust and its implications for us all, Jews, Germans, Americans, scholars, laypeople, survivors, and bystanders. He has written six books and dozens of articles on the subject; my selections only scratch the surface of his complex and subtle thinking.

In the late sixties, when Fackenheim first publicly began to articulate a Jewish response to the Holocaust, he had already established himself as a formidable student of German idealism and especially of Hegel, and as a serious Jewish theologian.[1] Probably the two issues that had commanded most of his attention were the articulation and development of an acceptable concept of revelation for contemporary Jewish experience and the philosophical confrontation with historicism and the possibility of philosophical transcendence. Both of these issues play a major role in his subsequent thinking, but while he continues to accept an account of revelation as an unmediated divine-human encounter, the role of that notion and of revelation changes as the role of history and historicity become more central.

As I indicated earlier, Fackenheim often remembers that the crucial change in his thinking came when he acknowledged that all Jewish belief, including the belief in God, covenant, and all that these entail, is immersed in history and hence subject to historical refutation. In short, what this means is that he had come to realize that nothing is a priori and immune to history. He does not clarify whether this change is the outcome of an open and serious exposure to Auschwitz or a theoretical shift regarding the lack of a compelling argument against historicism. But the result is transforming.

In a series of writings of the late 1960s, Fackenheim develops a line of thinking that he has continued to develop, enrich, and ramify to this day. Perhaps the clearest formulation of it can be found in an article we have reprinted below, "Jewish Faith and the Holocaust: A Fragment." Fackenheim's basic strategy is this: Suppose the theologian or the thinker confronts Auschwitz and tries to grasp its meaning. This means trying to incorporate the Holocaust—described precisely in terms of its crimes, the criminals, the victims, and all others implicated as accomplices or bystanders—into some theoretical perspective, religious, historical, psychological, philosophical, or otherwise. What is the outcome of this confrontation between thought and the Shoah? Impasse. That is, the event turns out to be unprecedented in a sufficient number of ways to "paralyze" thought and prohibit any satisfying placement in a system of thought; it is, in short, meaningless; it cannot be understood. What does thought do then? Fackenheim, drawing on Schelling and Buber, notes that this kind of meaning, call it incorporative or systematic meaning, is not the exclusive kind of meaning. There is another, what an event means to those who respond to it. In other words, thought, immobilized by the event, must turn elsewhere or come to an end. But, wanting to respond, thought needs direction and content; where does it find these? At this early stage in his thinking, Fackenheim found the direction and content of responding thought in the lives of Jews whose conduct, no matter how minimal, can be interpreted by the theologian as responsive to the Nazi assault. Fackenheim's thinking, then, moves this way: from (1) later conduct to (2) the interpretation of that conduct as responsive to the Holocaust to (3) the interpretation of its motive as an imposed imperative to (4) the interpretation of that imperative's source as a divine voice and finally to (5) the manifold interpretation of the content of the imperative as four-fold, in behalf of Judaism, the Jewish people, the victims, and ultimately human dignity. I realize that this is condensed, but a careful reading of the article will show that this is the way Fackenheim proceeds. And it is a line of thinking that he develops further in chapter three of *God's Presence in History*, reiterates and reformulates in numerous articles in the 1970s, and finally revises and deepens importantly in *To Mend the World*.[2]

It is tempting to separate Fackenheim's results from this line of thinking that grounds those results, as some commentators have done. Hence, some call Fackenheim a traditional theist, as if his belief in God and divine providence is traditional and is never threatened. Some call Fackenheim ethnocentric, treating a parochial event as having some kind of universal significance. Others find him conservative and even reactionary or too secular. Typically, these judgments may conceal a kernel of truth, usually invisible to the critic just because the route of the justification, the ground that supports the results that are being criticized, is not appreciated. To put the issue differently, Fackenheim spends little time on interpretive theory or hermeneutics and a great deal of subtle energy on the interpretive encounter between thought and the event and how that encounter gives rise to a certain understanding of what subsequent Jewish life and thought—and indeed much else including Christianity, historiography, German life, and philosophy—ought to be like. Like all interpretations, these encounters carry no guarantees; they persuade or fail to persuade on the basis of analysis, demonstration, and so forth. But in order to grasp the role of these inquiries, one needs to know how they fit in and where. For this an appreciation of the line of thinking I traced above is essential.

In his important article, reprinted below, Irving Greenberg at one point distinguishes Fackenheim, Rubenstein, and Berkovits this way: Rubenstein is an atheist, while Fackenheim and Berkovits are both traditional theists. At best, this assessment gets only Berkovits right. Rubenstein is no atheist; at least, not in any classic sense. And Fackenheim is surely no traditional theist; indeed, after the all-too-facile introduction of God into the scheme in his early papers, Fackenheim speaks only rarely about God. Recently it has become clear that the role of God in Jewish life and thought today is far more complex and uncertain than he had earlier appreciated.

Both Berkovits and Greenberg are orthodox Jewish thinkers, one a philosopher and the other a historian. It is tempting to take that distinction to be the root of what distinguishes their thought, and to a certain degree it is. For Berkovits, for all his quaintness and rhetorical chauvinism, is certainly more precise and disciplined a thinker, while Greenberg, for all his lack of precision and organization and clarity, is more moving and concretely imaginative. But these are superficial differences, in the end. The real distinction between them lies elsewhere, in their respective attitudes, not really critically exposed, concerning the relationship between thought and history.

Berkovits is an excellent example of a theologian of traditional Jewish commitments who nonetheless struggles to take the Holocaust seriously. At the same time that he must say that the Holocaust poses no greater problem for the Jewish doctrine of divine providence and the Jewish conception of history than the death of one innocent child, Berkovits feels deeply the torment and agony of the victims and understands the tremendous need to acknowledge the special power of the extermination camps. The grandeur in his thinking comes with his solution to this tension, and it is a grandeur worthy of respect. In the end, Berkovits is bound to the transcendent, absolute character of Jewish faith and yet also to its historical role. Hence, he can admit that the Holocaust has no effect on that faith but only on its effectiveness. In short, for Berkovits the Holocaust plays a psychological but not a theological role in Jewish experience.

What exactly does this mean? According to Berkovits, the Holocaust poses no unique threat to traditional Jewish thought. The Jewish conception of history is moral in character. God has charged the Jewish people with the task of bringing moral probity to the arena of history, where power and self-interest have been and are dominant. The Jewish responsibility is to take up the prophetic task of chiding the administrators and advocates of policies, practises, and conduct that are oriented by principles of acquisitiveness and self-interest, the descendants of the Hobbesian universe, and encouraging the priority of principles of justice, equality, and peace. In effect, this is the Jewish contribution to the project of perfecting creation, a project that assumes human freedom and a moral direction. Hence, evil—that is, moral evil—is as possible as good, but if free choice entails the possibility of moral evil as it does of moral good, then so be it. That is a consequence of God's choice to leave the perfection of creation only partial and to mandate human solidarity with His purposes. Berkovits solicits the help of the Biblical notion of *hester panim*, God's hiding of His face, to show that the traditional Jewish notion of providence involves God's paradoxical presence, an absence in presence, where Divine creativity is followed by human freedom and hence a Divine absence.

The Holocaust, according to Berkovits, occurs as the epitome of power history, of those trends in human history that are oriented by self-interest and acquisitiveness and power. Whether explicit or not, one can see the influence of Arendt here and all those social and political thinkers who see modern technological society and especially twentieth century totalitarian regimes as the outcome of a modern conception of man and society that goes back to Macchiavelli and Hobbes and is rooted in modern economic and political developments. Hence, the Holocaust is at once the highest expression of the forces that oppose Divine creation and its perfection and a psychological trauma for the Jewish people, whose task it is to assist the Divine plan. The impact of the Holocaust is not theological; no traditional Jewish theory is altered by it. But it does have a major psychological influence, for it demoralizes the Jews and all but destroys their motivation to continue their religious task. What was needed, after Auschwitz, was a Divine event that would serve to rejuvenate Jewish motivation and sense of purpose, that would show that all moral effort was not in vain. This, according to Berkovits, was the role of the reestablishment of the state of Israel, a virtual miracle of psychological renewal.

Berkovits, then, provides an excellent example of a traditional Jewish thinker who refuses to allow the Holocaust to modify his beliefs but at the same time takes it seriously in a deep and significant way. His writing, to be sure, is archaic at times and uses outmoded distinctions without sufficient awareness and self-criticism; he is also chauvanistic in an uncomfortable way. Nonetheless, Berkovits is clear and systematic, and his thinking stakes out an important option.

Somewhere between Fackenheim and Berkovits, between a total openness to historical exposure and a closed theological system, we find the thought of Irving Greenberg. The former pair are both trained philosophers, and while they are capable of distinctly different types of rhetoric, their thinking is generally systematic and disciplined. Greenberg is not a philosopher but an historian and theologian, and his work gives the appearance of system without being systematic. Often, reading Greenberg, one is impressed by a formulation or an illustration or image, only to find on examination that issues are blurred or unclear or ambiguous. Still, the outcome is both interesting and provocative and marks off new territory for post-Holocaust thought.

At the same time that Greenberg is steeped in Jewish traditional thought, he is totally exposed to Auschwitz and its transforming importance for contemporary religious thought and indeed for modernity as a whole. In the article we have selected, probably his most important and cited statement, Greenberg claims that both Judaism and Christianity must be open to historical refutation, for both are religions of history. Moreover, once the Holocaust has occurred, there is no ignoring it, for to ignore is already to respond. He establishes two principles for authentic post-Holocaust theological thought. One is put metaphorically this way: Given the account of the children burned alive at Auschwitz, ostensively to save money, we should accept only those theological statements that could be uttered in the presence of the burning children. The second is substantive, that only dialectical statements of faith are acceptable after Auschwitz. Greenberg neither clarifies these statements very well nor argues for them or their interconnection. His point, however, might be paraphrased this way: All theological statements—e.g., about God, the covenant, salvation, and hope—must be understood in terms of the Holocaust and whatever we take it to imply about God, man, and the Jewish people. Moreover, when this mandate is heeded, the result will be dialectical statements. It is not easy to determine what Greenberg means by "dialectical," but two interpretations seem possible. The first is that any statement of faith be at one time confident, then dubious and uncertain, and so forth. The second is that any statement of faith be simultaneously positive and negative, certain and uncertain. This latter seems to be the point of his reflections on Wiesel's character Sarah, who is at the same time both a whore and a saint. Hence, a genuine post-Holocaust faith must be both confident and riddled with uncertainty and doubt. The outcome of this, Greenberg suggests, is an attempt to recover by revision traditional models of response and a new understanding of the dialectical compresence of secularity and religiosity in the post-Holocaust commitment to human dignity and worth.

Greenberg, then, seems to believe that Auschwitz has changed everything or could, in principle, but at the same time he retains a great deal, but in revised form. Whatever faith is, it must now be dialectically complex; whatever the covenant now is, it must be dialectically complex, mixing secularity with religiosity. But the commitment to the divine image and to human dignity persists. When one asks for justification for all of this, however, one rarely gets it, and in the end Greenberg appears as a passionate spokesperson for sensitivity and fidelity, where novel formulations and images replace justification and ground.

As one reads these central figures, whose primary concern is to open religious thought to the Holocaust and raise the question of epoch-making transformation and revision, one might come to think of these responses as parochial and narrow. But certainly these thinkers have not viewed their work this way. All, to one degree or another, take the Holocaust to be a "world-historical" event with profound implications for all who live thereafter. While they tend to begin with the impact of the Holocaust for Jewish and Christian self-understanding, they all believe that it has important implications for others—for historians, political theorists, psychologists, philosophers, moral thinkers, for Germans, Americans, and so forth. In short, they imply that religious response is somehow central and reflects the categories or principles which will have implications for others as well. In *To Mend the World,* Fackenheim is very clear about this; there and elsewhere he sketches out the way in which authentic responses to the Holocaust will be conducted.[3]

Something should be said about how these thinkers have developed their thought in the nearly three decades that have passed. Rubenstein has written extensively but in ways that extend beyond the boundaries of Jewish thought and that move far from being responses to the Holocaust. In *Morality and Eros,* for example, he engages in a psychological analysis and moral critique of contemporary society and culture, and in *The Age of Triage* he continues this line of moral and cultural criticism, a line of thinking that extends back to his appropriation of Freud, Sartre, Camus, and others in order to advance the contemporary assessment of the human condition. Perhaps the most interesting of Rubenstein's subsequent work, for our purposes, is *The Cunning of History: The Holocaust and the American Future.* Here he treats the Holocaust as part of a history of slavery and domination, indeed as a stage in the process of cultural decay. This tendency to place the Holocaust within a social-scientific critique of modernity is not surprising and fits well Rubenstein's deep commitment to naturalistic analysis. In Arendt's *The Origins of Totalitarianism,* she says the following:

> There are no parallels to the life in the concentration camps. Its horror can never be fully embraced by the imagination for the very reason that it stands outside of life and death. . . . It is as though he had a story to tell of another planet. . . . Therefore all parallels create confusion and distract attention from what is essential. *Forced labor in prisons and penal colonies, banishment, slavery, all seem for a moment to offer helpful comparisons, but on closer examination lead nowhere.*[4]

Rubenstein's book can be interpreted as a response to this claim and the argument that follows, an effort to show that in fact the camps fit into the history of these very institutions of domination and disposal. If there is a lack of parallel, there is no lack of fit, and Rubenstein wants to show how this is so.

Rubenstein's thinking, then, has moved away from the narrowly religious into larger domains of cultural and historical criticism. Greenberg's various essays, often in semi-popular journals or magazines, has continued to be theological and historical, in the very special way that he combines the two. Berkovits's subsequent book *With Faith in Hell* attempts to document cases of Jewish faithfulness in the death camps, ghettoes, and concentration camps during the Holocaust, as evidence, as it were, of the strength of Jewish faith even during great adversity and trauma.

We find the richest elaboration, revision, and enrichment in the many books and articles of Fackenheim and Eckardt. Viewed broadly, Fackenheim has subjected the line of thinking that I outlined above to deep and serious critique and revision. The most important stage in that process occurs in *To Mend the World,* on which Fackenheim worked from the mid-1970s until its publication in 1982. There he reencounters his major predecessors, from Spinoza and Rosenzweig to Hegel, Heidegger, Buber, and others, in order to assess without restriction the capacity of thought to comprehend the Holocaust. He then thinks through the event, especially by tracing the actions and thought of victims and survivors, so that thought in the end can encompass the whole of horror to the degree that is possible, to recoil, to respond in opposition, and ultimately to become transformed into an imperative of resistance and a life of resistance. The role of God and a recovered faith is here displaced to a later stage of thinking and living, when it arises only with the proper uncertainty and when it plays a different role in the process of recovery.

At the same time that Fackenheim was rethinking the foundations of his response, he was exploring its diversity, the way in which his thinking could apply to the richness of Jewish life and the various constituents of it, from traditional texts to moral questions to the State of Israel and beyond. In two books, *The Jewish Return into History* and *What Is Judaism?*, he shows how rich are the applications, as it were, of his post-Holocaust thinking to the complexities and diversity of Jewish life.[5] And in a further book, *Jewish and Christian Reading of the Bible after Auschwitz*, he turns to the recovery of texts, in particular the biblical text itself.

Eckardt's work has, in a sense, followed a similar path. He has deepened and extended his reevaluation of Christianity in the light of the Shoah in a variety of articles and books, especially in *Long Day's Journey into Night*, coauthored with Alice Eckardt. At the same time, he has extended the scope of his thinking to cover liberation theology and woman's rights. As always, Eckardt's dominant tendency is toward moral issues and ethical reflection, all of which has come to a culmination in *For Righteousness' Sake*, a major effort to articulate Christian morality in a post-Holocaust age.

I remember Roy Eckardt once remarking that he had become a philosopher and no longer was a theologian. Reading his works, one might find that self-assessment remarkable and baffling. For in his writings, Eckardt draws on religious texts and ideas and seems to move primarily within the orbit of theological thought. But there is sense in what he said. If a philosopher is one who relentlessly follows the movement of rational thought and does not balk, no matter how difficult, when thought leads to critique or demands rejection and refutation, then Eckardt does appear often to be philosophical. When he takes the implications of the Holocaust to the core of Christian affirmation and takes honesty and intellectual probity to demand the rejection of even central Christian beliefs, then perhaps Eckardt is a philosopher and no longer a theologian.

Surely, Fackenheim is both, and the drama of how he integrates and struggles with the philosophical and Jewish dimensions of his thinking is one of the impressive facets of his thinking. Indeed, one is probably too glib and too facile in trying to categorize these thinkers as theologians. To be sure, their thinking does arise out of a felt need to expose their deep sense of religiosity and their understanding of Judaism or Christianity to the stark horror of Auschwitz, but the special features of their thinking arise only when one realizes that each thinker brings to the task a unique set of understandings and postures and orientations and methods of inquiry. In the end, this central set of statements is not narrowly theological in any traditional sense. In part, no doubt, this accounts for their importance.

NOTES

1. See Michael L. Morgan, *The Jewish Thought of Emil Fackenheim* (Detroit: Wayne State University Press, 1987); also Emil L. Fackenheim, *Quest for Past and Future* (Bloomington: Indiana University Press, 1968), and *The Religious Dimension of Hegel's Thought* (Bloomington: Indiana University Press, 1967).

2. See Morgan, *Jewish Thought of Emil Fackenheim*, pt. 3, with my introduction.

3. See Emil L. Fackenheim, *To Mend the World*, 3rd ed. (Bloomington: Indiana University Press, 1994), 262–313, and "Concerning Authentic and Inauthentic Responses to the Holocaust," *Holocaust and Genocide Studies* 1 (1):101–120 (1986).

4. Hannah Arendt, *The Origins of Totalitarianism* (1951; reprint, New York: Harcourt Brace Jovanovich, 1973), 444.

5. See also Morgan, *Jewish Thought of Emil Fackenheim*, pt. 4, where I try to display this diversity of application.

RICHARD RUBENSTEIN

◼ The Making of a Rabbi

. . . I can remember distinctly the objective issues which brought about my disenchantment with classical Reform and my eventual turning to a more traditional Judaism. By the fall of 1944, the facts about the Nazi death camps had become generally known. Reports of the capture of the camp at Madjdanek, Poland, with its huge piles of ownerless shoes, left an indelible impression upon me. I read about Madjdanek at about the same time I was preparing to serve as a student rabbi for the High Holy days in Tupelo, Mississippi.

The revelation of the death camps caused me to reject the whole optimistic theology of liberal religion. People weren't getting any better, nor did I believe they ever would. The evil rooted in human nature would never entirely disappear. Like the plague in Albert Camus's novel, radical evil might lie dormant for long periods but it remained forever capable of disrupting the pathetically weak fragments of reason and decency with which men have constructed their fragile civilization. My generation might add to the treasury of knowledge, but it was incapable of adding significantly to humanity's store of goodness. Each generation had to confront the choice between good and evil unaided by those who went before.

The death camps spelled the end of my optimism concerning the human condition. Though twenty years have passed, I see little reason to alter my pessimism. I regarded the camps and Nazism as far more than a sport of history. They revealed the full potentiality of the demonic as a permanent aspect of human nature. I was all the more shaken because I began to recognize that the difference between the Germans and other men was not very great. Given similar conditions of political and social stress, most of us could commit very terrible crimes. Moral nihilism had, in any event, been one of the deepest strains in my nature. I had struggled to overcome it from childhood, but the anarchic creature of infantile desire within me had never been put to death. During my years at the Hebrew Union College, it had been suppressed by the regnant liberal optimism. The discovery of the Nazi camps again demonstrated its potency to me. The polite, optimistic religion of a prosperous middle class hardly offered much hope against the deep strains of disorder I saw in the world and in myself.

The shock of the extermination camps was paralleled by the shock of realization of the degree to which both the occupied peoples and even the Allies had, to a degree, cooperated in or assented to the Nazi holocaust. I began to understand the relationship between the Christian theology of history and the deep and abiding hatred of the Jew in the Occident. When the death camps were followed by Britain's refusal to permit the entry of the survivors into Palestine, I came to understand the inadequacy of any definition of Jewish life which rested on religious confession alone. Perhaps the healthiest aspect of my understanding of the ethnic aspect of Jewish life was that I could now see myself and the Jews of eastern Europe as united by ties of common fate and psychology. I had become and remain unimpressed with American Jewish life as a special case. . . .

Only death perfects life and ends its problems. God can redeem only by slaying. We have nothing to hope for beyond what we are capable of creating in the time we have allotted to us. Of course, this leaves room for much doing and much creating. Nevertheless, in the final analysis all things crumble away into the nothingness which is at the beginning and end of creation.

If existence is ultimately devoid of hope and God offers us absolutely nothing, why bother with religion at all? I must confess that at a significant level I have much sympathy with the contemporary "death of God" Protestant theologians, though many of their concerns are specifically rooted in the ethos of Christianity, which has had to grapple with the meaning of the death of God involved in the crucifixion of Jesus. The question, "Why religion?" probably is meaningless. There are men and women devoid of all illusion who nevertheless regard withdrawal from the religious community as unthinkable. I am one of them. The decision to partake of the life of a community rests upon forces within the psyche which have little to do with rational argument. There is absolutely no reason for those who can do without religion to bother. At a certain tribal level, religion is inescapable in the United States. Our identities are shaped by the religious groups into which we are born. Our religions are less what we profess than what we inherit. There are Protestant, Catholic, and Jewish atheists. Jewish "death of God" theology is very different from its Christian counterpart. At the level of religious philosophy, Jewish and Christian radical theologians make similar denials. Their life styles inevitably reflect the communities they come from. Was it not Santayana who declared that there is no God but Mary is his mother? Nowhere in America can one find abstract men who are Americans without any other qualification.

Inheritance may influence personal identity. It does not necessarily compel religious commitment or affiliation. Undoubtedly the need for a community of manageable proportions to which one can belong and in which one is welcome has had a lot to do with the proliferation of churches and synagogues in middle-class America. For me, another need determined my affiliation. Like the Polish Jew in the East European *Shtedtl*, the tribesman in an African tribe untouched by "civilization," and the Spanish peasant, I cannot dispense with the institution through which I can dramatize, make meaningful, and share the decisive moments of my life. For me that institution is the synagogue; for all men it is the religious community they have inherited. Of course there is something absurd and irrational about this. I did not choose to be Jewish. It has been one of the givens of my nature, but no religious institution other than the synagogue is psychologically and culturally appropriate for my need to celebrate and share the decisive moments of existence. These moments include birth, puberty, marriage, temporary or permanent infirmity, the marking of time irretrievably past, the rearing of children, the need to express and find catharsis for feelings of guilt, the need for personal renewal, and the feeling of awe and wonder which overcomes me when I think about God's nothingness as the ultimate source and the final end.

This may be a highly subjective rationale for synagogue participation, but such subjectivity need not be solipsistic. I suspect other people find the life and liturgy of the synagogue meaningful for similar reasons. Each of the crises I have enumerated tends to be emotionally overdetermined and requires a significant context in which our emotions concerning it can be expressed, objectified, and clarified. Over the years I have come to question the adequacy of nontraditional liturgy for this purpose. The very fact that so much of liberal Jewish liturgy is in the vernacular suggests that it is in the language appropriate to the conscious level of response. There are other levels of response which require drama, grandeur, and mystery. I have found increasingly that the traditional Jewish liturgy, with the fewest possible rationalistic alterations, is the most appropriate vehicle for the expression of both my conscious and my unconscious feelings toward the crises I have enumerated. Myth and ritual are the domains in which we express and project our unconscious feelings concerning the dilemmas of existence. They are indispensable vehicles of expression in an institution in which the decisive moments of existence are to be shared and celebrated at both the conscious and unconscious levels.

I have not said much about the details of my spiritual development after the revelation of the death camps at Madjdanek. Much has happened of religious importance since then. I left Reform and completed my rabbinical studies at the Jewish Theological Seminary, ultimately finding academic and intellectual work more suitable to my capacities than the congregational rabbinate. Nevertheless, I prefer to conclude the recital of personal details, insofar as they are relevant to my religious development, with Madjdanek. That is as it should be. I am convinced that the problem of God and the death camps is the central problem for Jewish theology in the twentieth century. The one pre-eminent measure of the adequacy of all contemporary Jewish theologies is the seriousness with which they deal with this supreme problem of Jewish history. The fact of the death camps cannot be dismissed or swept under an intellectual rug. It will not be forgotten. On the contrary, we have yet to experience the full religious impact of the terrible happenings of World War II. The catastrophe of 1939–45 represents a psychological and religious time bomb which has yet to explode fully in the midst of Jewish religious life.

Already there are clear and unmistakable symptoms of Jewish reaction to what took place. The birth of Israel is the most obvious. Another has been the massive defection of young Jews from Jewish life in both Europe and the United States. Young Jews tend to be highly intelligent and well educated. They have learned all the lessons of contemporary skepticism. They know how terrible the price of being a Jew can be in an age of murderous technology. Many of them have said to themselves, especially in western Europe, "If being Jewish involves the threat of a future death camp for my children, I will use the respite between the explosions of anti-Semitism to marry outside the Jewish community and give my children a decent chance to escape this fate." Judaism is simply no longer worth the price of martyrdom for far more young Jews than most of us can possibly imagine. One of the results of the age of "broken symbols," as Paul Tillich has called it, is that martyrdom has gone out of fashion among Jews and has been replaced by the possibility of massive defection.

I suspect that many of us remain Jewish because we have concluded that self-contempt and self-falsification are too great a price to pay for safety. I must affirm my identity as a Jew. I have no choice. That is the kind of man I am. Nevertheless, I see no special virtue in my decision. It is simply my pathway to authenticity as a human being. There have been rewards. Self-acceptance as a Jew has made it possible for me to accept myself as a man and to learn how to live, given a decent respect for the necessities of society, in terms of my own needs and my own perspectives. Had I rejected myself as a Jew, I would have had to enthrone the opinions of others as ultimately decisive for my inner life. I could not grant the world that tyranny over me. I am prepared to do many things that society requires of me, granted their consistency with the canons of human decency, but I am not prepared to bestow upon others the right to determine how I shall think of myself or my community. By accepting myself as a Jew, I have liberated myself from the most futile and degrading of servilities, that of forever attempting to appease the irrational mythology that the Christian world has constructed of the Jew. As long as the Christian world regards a Palestinian Jew as God incarnate, it will find it excessively difficult to see Jews in terms devoid of mythic distortion. The only way I can live free of such distortion is through self-acceptance as a Jew.

I believe I have, against surprising odds, found myself insofar as this is possible. The death camps helped me to understand the religious meaning of our era. Ours is the time of the death of God. That time which Nietzsche's madman had said was too far off has come upon us. I understood the meaning of the death of God when I understood the meaning of Auschwitz and Madjdanek. The terrible fact is that the Germans set out to annihilate European Jewry and they succeeded quite well. Most of the participants in the most monstrous crime in history sleep undisturbed in comfortable and even luxurious beds in their newly prosperous fatherland. There has been no real retribution nor will there be. I doubt that there are even real pangs of conscience. On the contrary, when the *Alte Kameraden* gather together to discuss the good old days in the SS, they undoubtedly recall their murders in the same good spirit as hunters regaling each other with tales of the hunt. God really died at Auschwitz. This does not mean that God is not the beginning and will not be the end. It does mean that nothing in human choice, decision, value, or meaning can any longer have vertical reference to transcendent standards. We are alone in a silent, unfeeling cosmos. Our actions are human actions. Their entailments are human entailments. Morality and religion can no longer rest upon the conviction that divinely validated norms offer a measure against which what we do can be judged. As Jean Paul Sartre has shown in *The Flies*, if we are prepared to accept the consequences of our actions, nothing prevents us from carrying out any crime, even matricide. Though most of us will refrain from antisocial behavior, we do so because of the fear of ourselves and others rather than fear of God.

What then of Judaism? It is the way we Jews share our lives in an unfeeling and silent cosmos. It is the flickering candle we have lighted in the dark to enlighten and to warm us. Somehow it will continue for a very long time because there will always be some men who will accept and affirm what they were born to be. Ultimately, as with all things, it will pass away, for omnipotent Nothingness is Lord of All Creation.

RICHARD RUBENSTEIN

◙ Symposium on Jewish Belief

. . . I believe the greatest single challenge to modern Judaism arises out of the question of God and the death camps. I am amazed at the silence of contemporary Jewish theologians on this most crucial and agonizing of all Jewish issues. How can Jews believe in an omnipotent, beneficent God after Auschwitz? Traditional Jewish theology maintains that God is the ultimate, omnipotent actor in the historical drama. It has interpreted every major catastrophe in Jewish history as God's punishment of a sinful Israel. I fail to see how this position can be

---

After Auschwitz: Radical Theology and Contemporary Judaism by Richard Rubenstein, ©
1966. Reprinted by permission of Prentice-Hall, Inc., Upper Saddle River, N.J.

maintained without regarding Hitler and the SS as instruments of God's will. The agony of European Jewry cannot be likened to the testing of Job. To see any purpose in the death camps, the traditional believer is forced to regard the most demonic, antihuman explosion in all history as a meaningful expression of God's purposes. The idea is simply too obscene for me to accept. I do not think that the full impact of Auschwitz has yet been felt in Jewish theology or Jewish life. Great religious revolutions have their own period of gestation. No man knows the hour when the full impact of Auschwitz will be felt, but no religious community can endure so hideous a wounding without undergoing vast inner disorders.

Though I believe that a void stands where once we experienced God's presence, I do not think Judaism has lost its meaning or its power. I do not believe that a theistic God is necessary for Jewish religious life. Dietrich Bonhoeffer has written that our problem is how to speak of God in an age of no religion. I believe that our problem is how to speak of religion in an age of no God. I have suggested that Judaism is the way in which we share the decisive times and crises of life through the traditions of our inherited community. The need for that sharing is not diminished in the time of the death of God. We no longer believe in the God who has the power to annul the tragic necessities of existence; the need religiously to share that existence remains.

Finally, the time of the death of God does not mean the end of all gods. It means the demise of the God who was the ultimate actor in history. I believe in God, the Holy Nothingness known to mystics of all ages, out of which we have come and to which we shall ultimately return. I concur with atheistic existentialists such as Sartre and Camus in much of their analysis of the broken condition of human finitude. We must endure that condition without illusion or hope. I do not part company with them on their analysis of the human predicament. I part company on the issue of the necessity of religion as the way in which we share that predicament. Their analysis of human hopelessness leads me to look to the religious community as the institution in which that condition can be shared in depth. The limitations of finitude can be overcome only when we return to the Nothingness out of which we have been thrust. In the final analysis, omnipotent Nothingness is Lord of all creation.

ELIEZER BERKOVITS

▣ Faith after the Holocaust

APPROACHING THE HOLOCAUST

There are two principle approaches to the holocaust of European Jewry: the attitude of pious submission to it as a manifestation of the divine will, and the more frequently met attitude of questioning and doubt, a position that may ultimately lead to outright rebellion against the very idea of a beneficent providence. The rebellion may reach quite deep, in which case it may appear as the Jewish version of contemporary radical theology. Its final emphasis may lie in the phrases that God is dead, and life, absurd. In truth, however, the decisive question is rather: Who is the one who truly relates to this awesome issue? is it not the person who actually experienced it himself, in his own body and soul? who actually entered the hell of the ghettos, the concentration camps, and the crematoria, with his wife and children, his family and friends, with innumerable fellow Jews from all over Europe, who lived, suffered, and endured, or who perished there? Or is it someone who read about it, heard about it, may have, perhaps, even experienced it in his identifying imagination? The response of these two cannot—dare not—be the same. Those who were there responded on the basis of their own experience, which was unique, incomparable, that stands in all human history in a class by itself. However much, and however deeply, those who were not there may identify with the sufferings of the victims, their experience remains forever, merely a vicarious shadow of the actual event, as removed from the reality of the holocaust as is the rather comfortable scholarship of the radical theologians of our day from the universe of the concentration camps and the crematoria. Their response, based on their vicarious experience, will be as shadowy and unreal as the experience itself. Needless to say, what applies to the rebellion of the radical theologian applies with equal validity to the pious submission and the acceptance of the holocaust as an act of faith, by those who were not there either. Their response is no less unrelated to the actual event than is the response of the rebels and disbelievers. Neither of them succeeds in establishing genuine contact with the world of the *Shoa*.

From Berkovits, *Faith after the Holocaust* (1973). Reprinted by permission of KATV Publishing House, Inc.

Those of us who were not there must, before anything else, heed the response of those who were, for theirs alone are the authentic ones. Many who were there lost their faith. I can understand them. A Hell fiercer than Dante's was their lot. I believe that God himself understands and does not hold their loss of faith against them. Such is my faith in God. Can I, therefore, adopt their attitude for myself and rebel and reject? I was not there myself. I am not Job. I am only his brother. I cannot reject because there were others, too, in the thousands, in the tens of thousands, who were there and did not lose their faith; who accepted what happened to them in awesome submission to the will of God. I, who was not there, cannot reject, because to reject would be a desecration of the sacrifice of the myriads who accepted their lot in faith. How dare I reject, if they accepted! Neither can I accept. I who was not there, because I was not there, dare not accept, dare not submit, because my brothers in their tens of thousands, who did go through that hell, did rebel and did reject. How dare I, who was not there, accept their superhuman suffering and submit to it in faith!

I stand in awe before the memory of the k'doshim who walked into the gas chambers with the Ani Ma'amin—I believe!—on their lips. How dare I question, if they did not question! I believe, because they believed. And I stand in awe before the k'doshim, before the memory of the untold suffering of innocent human beings who walked to the gas chambers without faith, because what was imposed upon them was more than man can endure. They could not believe any longer; and now I do not know how to believe, so well do I understand their disbelief. In fact, I find it easier to understand the loss of faith in the "Kz" than the faith preserved and affirmed. The faith affirmed was superhuman; the loss of faith—in the circumstances—human. Since I am only human, what is human is nearer to me than the superhuman. The faith is holy; but so, also, is the disbelief and the religious rebellion of the concentration camps holy. The disbelief was not intellectual but faith crushed, shattered, pulverized; and faith murdered a millionfold is holy disbelief. Those who were not there and, yet, readily accept the holocaust as the will of God that must not be questioned, desecrate the holy disbelief of those whose faith was murdered. And those who were not there, and yet join with self-assurance the rank of the disbelievers, desecrate the holy faith of the believers.

One may, perhaps, go even further and say: The pious believer who was not there but meekly submits, not to his own destruction, but to that of six million of his brethren, insults with his faith the faith of the concentration camps. The k'doshim, who affirmed their faith in the God of Israel in the light of the doom that surrounded them may well say to such an eager believer: "What do you know about believing, about having faith? How dare you submit into suffering that is not yours. Calm yourselves and be silent." But they, too, who were not there and yet declare from the housetops their disbelief in the God of Israel, insult the holy disbelief of the concentration camps. They who lost their faith there may well turn to our radical theologians, saying: "How dare you speak about loss of faith, what do you know about losing faith, you who have never known what we have known, who never experienced what we have experienced?" In the presence of the holy faith of the crematoria, the ready faith of those who were not there, is vulgarity. But the disbelief of the sophisticated intellectual in the midst of an affluent society—in the light of the holy disbelief of the crematoria—is obscenity.

We are not Job and we dare not speak and respond as if we were. We are only Job's brother. We must believe, because our brother Job believed; and we must question, because our brother Job so often could not believe any longer. This is not a comfortable situation; but it is our condition in this era after the holocaust. In it alone do we stand at the threshold to an adequate response to the *Shoa*—if there be one. It is from this threshold alone that the break in and the breakthrough must come. It must come without the desecration of the holy faith or of the holy loss of faith of the Jewish people in the European hell. And if there be no breakthrough, the honest thing is to remain at the threshold. If there is no answer, it is better to live without it than to find peace either in the sham of an insensitive faith or in the humbug of a disbelief entertained by people who have eaten their fill at the tables of a satiated society. . . .

The question after the holocaust ought not to be, how could God tolerate so much evil? The proper question is whether, after Auschwitz, the Jewish people may still be witnesses to God's elusive presence in history as we understand the concept. What of the nemesis of history and what of Jewish survival?

The Nazi crime of the German people attempted to eradicate the last vestiges of a possible innate sense of humanity, it sought the conscious extirpation from human nature of the last reminder of the fear of God in any form. It was the ultimate rebellion of nihilism against all moral emotion and all ethical values. However, this up to now mightiest and most morbid manifestation of human hubris too was overtaken by its complete and inescapable nemesis. In every field the very opposite of its goals has been accomplished. "Das Tausendjährige Reich," the empire for a millenium, was in ashes after twelve terrible years. Instead of the much heralded "Gross Deutschland" there is a divided Germany with greatly reduced frontiers. The nemesis is not limited to Nazi Germany alone, it has overtaken Western civilization itself. The holocaust is not exclusively the guilt of Germany; the entire West has a goodly share in it. One of the most tragic aspects of the world catastrophe of nazism is to be seen in the fact that it was able to assume its vast dimensions of calamity mainly because of the tolerance and "understanding" that it enjoyed in the world community of nations for many years. During the period of favorable international climate nazified Germany was able to create one of the most powerful war machines in all history, to poison the minds of vast sections of the world's population, and to corrupt governments and public officials in many lands. This was possible partly because, with the help of the antisemitic heritage of the West, Nazi Germany was able to bring about the moral disintegration of many peoples with diabolical efficiency and speed and partly—and not altogether independently of it—because of the cynical calculations of worldwide power politics. Germany was meant to become the bulwark of the West against the threat of Russian communism. To this end many were willing to ignore the German-Nazi challenge to elementary justice and humanity. After all, its worst venom was directed against the Jews only. Even after the Second World War had already pursued its horrifying course in Europe for several years, there were still influential forces in the high seats of power, and even on the throne of so-called "spiritual grandeur," that hoped for a rapprochement between Nazi Germany and the Western powers. They thought it politically wise to go slow on Nazi-German criminality, piously hoping to bring off the brotherly alliance that would enable them to launch the greatest of all crusades, that against Soviet communism. Thus they became accomplices in the criminality of Auschwitz and the gas chambers. Nothing of what they had hoped for has been achieved. Instead of a curbing of communism, for which Germany and her sympathizers hoped, communism has reached its widest penetration the world over. This is not stated with any partiality for communism, but solely from the point of view of an observer who tries to detect the functioning of nemesis in history. Nazi Germany could have been stopped early in its track had there been less indifference toward the plight of the Jews and a better understanding of the demoralizing power of antisemitism. But antisemitism had long been a respectable trait in Western civilization. Thus, the Second World War became inevitable, as a result of which all the formerly great powers of Europe had been reduced to second and third rank. And even Russia and the United States who came out of the war as superpowers dwarfing all others, what have they gained if, as a result of their overwhelming might, they render each other's future, as well as that of all mankind, rather questionable? It is no mere coincidence that having countenanced the Final Solution to the Jewish problem, partly with glee and partly with equanimity, the world is now confronted with the serious possibility of a Final Solution to the entire problematic existence of a man on this planet. Every one of the ambitions that the forces of power history have been pursuing have been weighed and found wanting. Had the nations and their churches not been silent and indifferent to what was recognizably afoot in the early days of nazism, world history would have taken an entirely different course and mankind would not now be balancing on the very edge of the thermonuclear abyss. This post-holocaust era is charged with the nemesis of history. This is the ignoble twilight hour of a disintegrating civilization.

It is true the Jewish people had to pay a terrible price for the crimes of mankind and to-day, too, as part of mankind, they are themselves deeply involved in the crisis of the human race, yet the Final Solution intended for it is far from being final. Though truncated, Israel survived this vilest of all degradations of the human race. Not only has it survived, but rising from one of its most calamitous defeats, it has emerged to new dignity and historic vindication in the state of Israel.

The most significant aspect of the establishment of the state of Israel is the fact that Jews through the ages knew that it was to come. They were waiting for it during their wanderings for long and dark centuries. There was little rational basis for their faith in the eventual return to the land of their fathers. Yet they knew that one day the faith would be translated into historical reality. They lived with that faith in the sure knowledge of divine concern. For the Jew, for whom Jewish history neither begins with Auschwitz nor ends with it, Jewish survival through the ages and the ingathering of the exiles into the land of their fathers after the holocaust proclaim God's holy presence at the very heart of his inscrutable hiddenness. We recognized in it the hand of divine providence because it was exactly what, after the holocaust, the Jewish people needed in order to survive. Broken and shattered in spirit even more than in body, we could not have been able to continue on our Jewish way through history without some vindication of our faith that the "Guardian of Israel neither slumbers nor sleeps." The state of Israel came at a moment in history when nothing else could have saved Israel from extinction through hopelessness. It is our lifeline to the future.

Confronting the Holocaust, the relevant consideration is the full realization that it does not preempt the entire course of Jewish history. One dare not struggle with the problem of faith as if the holocaust were all we knew about the Jew and his relation to God. There is a pre-holocaust past, a post-holocaust present, and there is also a future, which is, to a large extent, Israel's own responsibility. Auschwitz does not contain the entire history of Israel; it is not the all-comprehensive Jewish experience. As to the past, we should also bear in mind that the Jew, who has known so much of the "Hiding of the Face," has also seen the divine countenance revealed to him. Notwithstanding Auschwitz, the life of the patriarchs is still with him; the Exodus did not turn into a mirage; Sinai has not come tumbling down; the prophets have not become charlatans; the return from Babylon has not proved to be a fairy tale. It is, of course, possible for people to secularize the history of Israel and deny the manifestation of a divine presence in it. However, such secularization is independent of the holocaust. It is not very meaningful to interpret the entire course of Jewish history exclusively on the basis of the death-camp experience of European Jewry. If the believer's faith in Israel's "encounters" with God in history is false, it must be so not on account of Auschwitz, but because the "encounters" just did not happen. On the other hand, if these manifestations of the divine presence did occur, then they are true events and will not become lies because of the holocaust.

For the person who does not recognize the presence of God in the Exodus, at Sinai, in the words of the prophets, in innumerable events of Jewish history, Auschwitz presents no problem of faith. For him God is forever absent. Only the Jew who has known of the presence of God is baffled and confounded by Auschwitz. What conclusions is he to draw from this terrifying absence of divine concern? Is God indifferent to human destiny? But the Jew knows otherwise. He knows of the most intimate divine concern. Has God, perhaps, died? Is it possible that once upon a time there was a God who was not indifferent toward Israel, but that now something has happened to him, he has gone away, he is no longer? This is plain silly. It is possible for a human being to lose faith in God. But it is not possible for God to die. He either is and therefore, will ever be;

or he is not and, therefore never was. But if God who was, is, and will ever be, is it possible that at Auschwitz he rejected Israel, he turned away from Israel as a punishment for its sins? To believe this would be a desecration of the Divine Name. No matter what the sins of European Jewry might have been, they were human failings. If the holocaust was a punishment, it was a thousandfold inhuman. The only crime of man for which such punishment might be conceivable would be the Nazi crime of Germany, and even there, one would hesitate to impose it.

The Jew of faith is thus left with the perplexing duality of his knowledge of God. He knows of the numerous revelations of the divine presence as he knows of the overlong phases of God's absence. Auschwitz does not stand by itself. Notwithstanding its unique position as perhaps the most horrifying manifestation of divine silence, it has its place in Jewish history beside the other silences of God together with the utterances of his concern. The Jew was called into being by the revelation of the divine in history. It is because God allowed his countenance to shine upon man that he is what he is. Only because of that does he know of the absence of God. But thanks to that, he also knows that God's absence, even at Auschwitz, is not absolute. Because of that it was possible for many to know God even along the path to the gas chambers. There were many who found him even in his hiding. Because of the knowledge of God's presence, the Jew can find God even in his absence.

No, the holocaust is not all of Jewish history, nor is it its final chapter. That it did not become the Final Solution as was planned by the powers of darkness enables the Jew who has known of the divine presence to discern intimations of familiar divine concern in the very midst of his abandonment. This, too, is essentially an old Jewish insight.

Yet all this does not exonerate God for all the suffering of the innocent in history. God is responsible for having created a world in which man is free to make history. There must be a dimension beyond history in which all suffering finds its redemption through God. This is essential to the faith of a Jew. The Jew does not doubt God's presence, though he is unable to set limits to the duration and intensity of his absence. This is no justification for the ways of providence, but its acceptance. It is not a willingness to forgive the unheard cries of millions, but a trust that in God the tragedy of man may find its transformation. Within time and history that cry is unforgivable. One of the teachers of the Talmud notes that when God asks Abraham to offer him his son Isaac as a sacrifice, the exact rendering of the biblical words reads: "Take, I pray thee, thy son."[1] In the view of this teacher the "binding of Isaac" was not a command of God, but a request that Abraham take upon himself this most exacting of all God's impositions. In a sense, we see in this a recognition that the sacrificial way of the innocent through history is not to be vindicated or justified! It remains unforgivable. God himself has to ask an Abraham to favor him by accepting the imposition of such a sacrifice. The divine request accompanies all those through history who suffer for the only reason that God created man, whom God himself has to endure. Within time and history God remains indebted to his people; he may be long-suffering only at their expense. It was hardly ever as true as in our own days, after the holocaust. Is it perhaps what God desires—a people, to whom he owes so much, who yet acknowledge him? children, who have every reason to condemn his creation, yet accept the creator in the faith that in the fullness of time the divine indebtedness will be redeemed and the divine adventure with man will be approved even by its martyred victims?

NOTE

1. *Talmud Babli, Sanhedrin* 89b.

IRVING GREENBERG

▣ Cloud of Smoke, Pillar of Fire

Judaism, Christianity, and Modernity after the Holocaust

JUDAISM AND CHRISTIANITY: RELIGIONS OF REDEMPTION AND THE CHALLENGE OF HISTORY

Both Judaism and Christianity are religions of redemption. Both religions come to this affirmation about human fate out of central events in history. For Jews, the basic orientating experience has been the Exodus. Out of the overwhelming experience of God's deliverance of His people came the judgment that the ultimate truth is not the fact that most humans live nameless and burdened lives and die in poverty and oppression. Rather, the decisive truth is that man is of infinite value and will be redeemed. Every act of life is to be lived by that realization.

For Christians, the great paradigm of this meaning is the life, death, and resurrection of Jesus Christ. By its implications, all of life is lived.

From Fleischner (ed.), *Auschwitz: Beginning of a New Era*. Reprinted by permission of KTAV Publishing House, Inc.

The central events of both religions occur and affect humans in history. The shocking contrast of the event of salvation come and the cruel realities of actual historical existence have tempted Christians to cut loose from earthly time. Yet both religions ultimately have stood by the claim that redemption will be realized in actual human history. This view has had enormous impact on the general Western and modern view that human liberation can and will be realized in the here and now.

Implicit in both religions is the realization that events happen in history which change our perception of human fate, events from which we draw the fundamental norms by which we act and interpret what happens to us. One such event is the Holocaust—the destruction of European Jewry from 1933 to 1945.

The Challenge of the Holocaust

Both religions have always sought to isolate their central events—Exodus and Easter—from further revelations or from the challenge of the demonic counter-experience of evil in history. By and large, both religions have continued since 1945 as if nothing had happened to change their central understanding. It is increasingly obvious that this is impossible, that the Holocaust cannot be ignored.

By its very nature, the Holocaust is obviously central for Jews. The destruction cut so deeply that it is a question whether the community can recover from it. When Adolf Eichmann went into hiding in 1945, he told his accomplice, Dieter Wisliceny, that if caught, he would leap into his grave laughing. He believed that although he had not completed the total destruction of Jewry, he had accomplished his basic goal—because the Jews could never recover from this devastation of their life center. Indeed, Eichmann had destroyed 90 percent of East European Jewry, the spiritual and biological vital center of prewar world Jewry. Six million Jews were killed—some 30 percent of the Jewish people in 1939; but among the dead were over 80 percent of the Jewish scholars, rabbis, full-time students and teachers of Torah alive in 1939.[1] Since there can be no covenant without the covenant people, the fundamental existence of Jews and Judaism is thrown into question by this genocide. For this reason alone, the trauma of the Holocaust cannot be overcome without some basic reorientation in light of it by the surviving Jewish community. Recent studies by Prof. Simon Herman, an Israeli social psychologist, have indicated that the perception of this event and its implications for the Jews' own fate has become a most widespread and powerful factor in individual Jewish consciousness and identity.[2]

The Holocaust as Radical Counter-Testimony to Judaism and Christianity

For Christians, it is easier to continue living as if the event did not make any difference, as if the crime belongs to the history of another people and faith. But such a conclusion would be and is sheer self-deception. The magnitude of suffering and the manifest worthlessness of human life radically contradict the fundamental statements of human value and divine concern in both religions. Failure to confront and account for this evil, then, would turn both religions into empty, Pollyanna assertions, credible only because believers ignore the realities of human history. It would be comparable to preaching that this is the best of all possible worlds to a well-fed, smug congregation, while next door little children starve slowly to death.

Judaism and Christianity do not merely tell of God's love for man, but stand or fall on their fundamental claim that the human being is, therefore, of ultimate and absolute value. ("He who saves one life it is as if he saved an entire world"—B.T. Sanhedrin 37a; "God so loved the world that He gave His only begotten son"—John 3:16.) It is the contradiction of this intrinsic value and the reality of human suffering that validates the absolute centrality and necessity of redemption, of the Messianic hope. But speak of the value of human life and hear the testimony of S. Szmaglewska, a Polish guard at Auschwitz, about the summer of 1944. The passage (from the Nuremburg trial record) deserves commentary:

WITNESS: . . . women carrying children were [always] sent with them to the crematorium. [Children were of no labor value so they were killed. The mothers were sent along, too, because separation might lead to panic, hysteria—which might slow up the destruction process, and this could not be afforded. It was simpler to condemn the mothers too and keep things quiet and smooth.] The children were then torn from their parents outside the crematorium and sent to the gas chambers separately. [At that point, crowding more people into the gas chambers became the most urgent consideration. Separating meant that more children could be packed in separately, or they could be thrown in over the heads of adults once the chamber was packed.] When the extermination of the Jews in the gas chambers was at its height, orders were issued that children were to be thrown straight into the crematorium furnaces, or into a pit near the crematorium, without being gassed first.

SMIRNOV: (Russian prosecutor): How am I to understand this? Did they throw them into the fire alive, or did they kill them first?

WITNESS: They threw them in alive. Their screams could be heard at the camp. It is difficult to say how many children were destroyed in this way.

SMIRNOV: Why did they do this?

WITNESS: It's very difficult to say. We don't know whether they wanted to economize on gas, or if it was because there was not enough room in the gas chambers.[3]

A word must be said on the decision to economize on gas. By the summer of 1944, the collapse of the Eastern front meant that the destruction of European Jewry might not be completed before the advancing Allied armies arrived. So Hungarian Jewry was killed at maximum speed—at the rate of up to ten thousand people a day. Priority was given to transports of death over trains with reinforcements and munitions needed for the Wehrmacht. There was no time for selections of the healthy, of young Jews for labor, or even for registering the number of victims. Entire trainloads were marched straight to the gas chambers.

The gas used—Zyklon B—causes death by internal asphyxiation, with damage to the centers of respiration, accompanied by feelings of fear, dizziness, and vomiting. In the chamber, when released, "the gas climbs gradually to the ceiling, forcing the victims to claw and trample upon one another in their struggle to reach upward. Those on the top are the last to succumb. . . . The corpses are piled one on top of another in an enormous heap . . . at the bottom of the pile are babies and children, women and old people. . . ."[4]

The sheer volume of gas used in the summer of 1944 depleted the gas supply. In addition, the Nazis deemed the costs excessive. Therefore, in that summer, the dosage of gas was halved from twelve boxes to six per gassing. When the concentration of the gas is quite high, death occurs quickly. The decision to cut the dosage in half was to more than double the agony.

How much did it cost to kill a person? The Nazi killing machine was orderly and kept records. The gas was produced by the Deutsche Gesellschaft fur Schadlingsbekampfung m.b.H. (German Vermin-Combating Corporation, called DEGESCH for short). It was a highly profitable business, which paid dividends of 100 percent to 200 percent per year (100 percent in 1940 and 1941; 200 percent in 1942, 1943) to I. G. Farben, one of the three corporations which owned it.[5] The bills for Zyklon B came to 195 kilograms for 975 marks = 5 marks per kilogram. Approximately 5.5 kilograms were used on every chamber-load, about fifteen hundred people. This means 27.5 marks per fifteen hundred people. With the mark equal to 25 cents, this yields $6.75 per fifteen hundred people, or forty-five hundreths of a cent per person. In the summer of 1944, a Jewish child's life was not worth the two-fifths of a cent it would have cost to put it to death rather than burn it alive. There, in its starkest form, is the ultimate denial.

In short, the Holocaust poses the most radical counter-testimony to both Judaism and Christianity. Elie Wiesel has stated it most profoundly:

> Never shall I forget the little faces of the children, whose bodies I saw turned into wreaths of smoke beneath a silent blue sky.
> Never shall I forget those flames which consumed my faith forever.
> Never shall I forget that nocturnal silence which deprived me, for all eternity, of the desire to live.
> Never shall I forget those moments which murdered my God and my soul and turned my dreams to dust.
> Never shall I forget these things, even if I am condemned to live as long as God Himself. Never.[6]

The cruelty and the killing raise the question whether even those who believe after such an event dare talk about God who loves and cares without making a mockery of those who suffered. . . .

THE HOLOCAUST AS ORIENTING EVENT AND REVELATION

Not to Confront Is to Repeat

For both Judaism and Christianity (and other religions of salvation—both secular and sacred) there is no choice but to confront the Holocaust, because it happened, and because the first Holocaust is the hardest. The fact of the Holocaust makes a repetition more likely—a limit was broken, a control or awe is gone—and the murder procedure is now better laid out and understood. Failure to confront it makes repetition all the more likely. So evil is the Holocaust, and so powerful a challenge to all other norms, that it forces a response, willy-nilly; not to respond is to collaborate in its repetition. This irony of human history which is already at work, is intensified by the radical power of the Holocaust. Because the world has not made the Holocaust a central point of departure for moral and political policy, the survivors of the Holocaust and their people have lived continually under the direct threat of another Holocaust throughout the past thirty years. Muslims who feel that the event is a Western problem and that Christian guilt has been imposed on them have been tempted to try to stage a repeat performance. They lack the guilt and concern, and that in itself leads to guilt.

The nemesis of denial is culpability. Pope John XXIII, who tried strongly to save Jews in the Holocaust (he made representations and protests, issued false baptismal papers, helped Jews escape), felt guilty and deeply regretted the Catholic Church's past treatment of Jews. This pope did more than any other pope had ever done to remove the possibility of another destruction (through the Vatican II Declaration, revising Catholic instruction and liturgy with reference to the Jews, dialogue, etc.).[7] Pope Paul VI, who denied the complicity or guilt of Pius XII in the Holocaust, was tempted thereby into a set of policies (he watered down the Declaration, referred to Jews in the old Passion story terms, refused to recognize Israel's de jure political existence, maintained silence in the face of the threat of genocide), which brings the dreadful guilt of collaboration in genocide so much closer.

This principle applies to secular religions of salvation as well. Thus, the German Democratic Republic (East Germany) has denied any responsibility for the Holocaust, on the grounds that it was carried out by fascist and right-wing circles, whereas East Germany is socialist. As a result, it has allowed Nazis back into government with even more impunity than West Germany. Whereas West Germany has given back billions of dollars of Jewish money in the form of reparations (it is estimated that many more billions were directly stolen and spoiled), the GDR, having no guilty conscience, has yielded up none of the ill-gotten gains of mass murder. In fact, East Germany and its "socialist" allies have pursued policies which have kept the genocide of the Jewish people in Israel a live option to this day. Thus, failure to respond to the Holocaust turns a hallowed ideology of liberation into a cover for not returning robbed goods and for keeping alive the dream of another mass murder.

This is not to say that all-out support for Israel is the only way to avoid complicity in attempted genocide. The Communist world could have pursued a pro-

Arab policy on its merits. Had they felt as guilty as they should have—as they actually were—they would have made a sine qua non the giving up of all genocidal hopes and talk by the Arabs. In actual fact, the opposite occurred. Several times, when such extreme possibilities were about to be dropped by the Arab world, Russian intervention, with no such policy conditions attached (or with tacit encouragement of destructive goals), restored this abominable option.

The Holocaust cannot be used for triumphalism. Its moral challenge must also be applied to Jews. Those Jews who feel no guilt for the Holocaust are also tempted to moral apathy. Religious Jews who use the Holocaust to morally impugn every other religious group but their own are the ones who are tempted thereby into indifference at the Holocaust of others (cf. the general policy of the American Orthodox rabbinate on United States Vietnam policy). Those Israelis who place as much distance as possible between the weak, passive Diaspora victims and the "mighty Sabras" are tempted to use Israeli strength indiscriminately (i.e., beyond what is absolutely inescapable for self-defense and survival), which is to risk turning other people into victims of the Jews. Neither faith nor morality can function without serious twisting of perspective, even to the point of becoming demonic, unless they are illuminated by the fires of Auschwitz and Treblinka.

The Dialectical Revelation of the Holocaust

The Holocaust challenges the claims of all the standards that compete for modern man's loyalties. Nor does it give simple, clear answers or definitive solutions. To claim that it does is not to take burning children seriously. This surd will—and should—undercut the ultimate adequacy of any category, unless there were one (religious, political, intellectual) that consistently produced the proper response of resistance and horror at the Holocaust. No such category exists, to my knowledge. To use the catastrophe to uphold the univocal validity of any category is to turn it into grist for propaganda mills. The Nazis turned their Jewish victims into soap and fertilizer after they were dead. The same moral gorge rises at turning them into propaganda. The Holocaust offers us only dialectical moves and understandings—often moves that stretch our capacity to the limit and torment us with their irresolvable tensions. In a way, it is the only morally tenable way for survivors and those guilty of bystanding to live. Woe to those so at ease that they feel no guilt or tension. Often this is the sign of the death of the soul. I have met many Germans motivated by guilt who came to Israel on pilgrimages of repentance. I have been struck that frequently these were young people, too young to have participated in the genocide; or, more often, persons or the children of persons who had been anti-Nazi or even imprisoned for resistance. I have yet to meet such a penitent who was himself an SS man or even a train official who transported Jews. Living in the dialectic becomes one of the verification principles for alternative theories after the Holocaust.

Let us offer, then, as working principle the following: No statement, theological or otherwise, should be made that would not be credible in the presence of the burning children. In his novel *The Accident*, Elie Wiesel has written of the encounter of a survivor with Sarah, a prostitute who is also a survivor. She began her career at twelve, when she was separated from her parents and sent to a special barracks for the camp officers' pleasure. Her life was spared because there were German officers who liked to make love to little girls her age. Every night she reenacts the first drunken officer's use of a twelve-year-old girl. Yet she lives on, with both life feeling and self-loathing. And she retains enough feeling to offer herself to a shy survivor boy, without money. "You are a saint," he says. "You are mad," she shrieks. He concludes, "Whoever listens to Sarah and doesn't change, whoever enters Sarah's world and doesn't invent new gods and new religions, deserves death and destruction. Sarah alone has the right to decide what is good and what is evil, the right to differentiate between what is true and what usurps the appearance of truth."[8]

In this story Wiesel has given us an extraordinary phenomenology of the dialectic in which we live after the Holocaust. Sarah's life of prostitution, religiously and morally negative in classic terms, undergoes a moral reversal of category. It is suffering sainthood in the context of her life and her ongoing response to the Holocaust experience. Yet this scene grants us no easy Sabbatianism, in which every act that can wrap itself in the garment of the Holocaust is justified and the old categories are no longer valid. The ultimate tension of the dialectic is maintained, and the moral disgust which Sarah's life inspires in her (and Wiesel? and us?) is not omitted either. The more we analyze the passage the more it throws us from pole to pole in ceaseless tension. The very disgust may, in fact, be the outcome of Sarah's mistaken judgment; she continues to judge herself by the categories in which she was raised before the event. This is suggested in the narrator's compassion and love for her. Yet he himself is overcome by moral nausea—or is it pity?—or protest?—until it is too late and Sarah is lost. There is no peace or surcease and no lightly grasped guide to action in this world. To enter into Sarah's world in fear and trembling, and to remain there before and in acting and speech, is the essence of religious response today, as much as when normative Judaism bids us enter into the Exodus, and Christianity asks we enter into Easter and remain there before and in acting or speaking. The classic normative experiences themselves are not dismissed by Wiesel. They are tested and reformulated—dialectically attacked and affirmed—as they pass through the fires of the new revelatory event.[9] . . .

JEWISH THEOLOGICAL RESPONSES TO THE HOLOCAUST

A Critique

There have been some notable Jewish theological responses that have correctly grasped the centrality of the Holocaust to Jewish thought and faith. The two primary positions are polar. One witness upholds the God of History. Emil Fackenheim has described the Commanding Voice of Auschwitz, which bids us not to hand Hitler any posthumous victories, such as repudiating the covenant and retrospectively declaring Judaism to have been an illusion. Eliezer Berkovits has stressed that Jewish survival testifies to the Lord of History. The other witness affirms the death of God and the loss of all hope. Richard Rubenstein has written: "We learned in the crisis that we were totally and nakedly alone, that we could expect neither support nor succor from God nor from our fellow creatures. Therefore, the world will forever remain a place of pain, suffering, alienation and ultimate defeat."[10] These are genuine important responses to the Holocaust, but they fall afoul of the dialectical principle. Both positions give a definitive interpretation of the Holocaust which subsumes it under known classical categories. Neither classical theism nor atheism is adequate to incorporate the incommensurability of the Holocaust; neither produced a consistently proper response; neither is credible alone—in the presence of the burning children.

Rubenstein's definitiveness is part of this writer's disagreement with him. Rubenstein concluded that "Jewish history has written the *final chapter* in the terrible story of the God of History"; that "the world will *forever* remain a place of pain . . . and *ultimate defeat*," and that the "pathetic hope (of coming to grips with Auschwitz through the framework of traditional Judaism) *will never be realized*" (italics supplied).[11] After the Holocaust, there should be no final solutions, not even theological ones. I could not be more sympathetic to Rubenstein's positions, or more unsympathetic to his conclusions. That Auschwitz and the rebirth of Israel are normative; that there are traditional positions which Auschwitz moves us to repudiate (such as "We were punished for our sins") is a profoundly, authentically Jewish response. To declare that the destruction closes out hope forever is to claim divine omniscience and to use the Holocaust for theological grist. Contra Rubenstein, I would argue that it is not so much that any affirmations (or denials) cannot be made, but that they can be made authentically only if they are made after working through the Holocaust experience. In the same sense, however, the relationship to the God of the convenant cannot be unaffected.

Dialectical Faith, or "Moment Faiths"

Faith is living life in the presence of the Redeemer, even when the world is unredeemed. After Auschwitz, faith means there are times when faith is overcome. Buber has spoken of "moment gods": God is known only at the moment when Presence and awareness are fused in vital life. This knowledge is interspersed with moments when only natural, self-contained, routine existence is present. We now have to speak of "moment faiths," moments when Redeemer and vision of redemption are present, interspersed with times when the flames and smoke of the burning children blot out faith—though it flickers again. Such a moment is described in an extraordinary passage of *Night*, as the young boy sentenced to death but too light to hang struggles slowly on the rope. Eliezer finally responds to the man asking, "Where is God now?" by saying, "Here He is—He is hanging here on this gallows . . ."[12]

This ends the easy dichotomy of atheist/theist, the confusion of faith with doctrine or demonstration. It makes clear that faith is a life response of the whole person to the Presence in life and history. Like life, this response ebbs and flows. The difference between the skeptic and the believer is frequency of faith, and not certitude of position. The rejection of the unbeliever by the believer is literally the denial or attempted suppression of what is within oneself. The ability to live with moment faith is the ability to live with pluralism and without the self-flattering, ethnocentric solutions which warp religion, or make it a source of hatred for the other. . . .

THE CENTRAL RELIGIOUS TESTIMONY AFTER THE HOLOCAUST

Recreating Human Life

In the silence of God and of theology, there is one fundamental testimony that can still be given—the testimony of human life itself. This was always the basic evidence, but after Auschwitz its import is incredibly heightened. In fact, it is the only testimony that can still be heard.

The vast number of dead and morally destroyed is the phenomenology of absurdity and radical evil, the continuing statement of human worthlessness and meaninglessness that shouts down all talk of God and human worth. The Holocaust is even model and pedagogy for future generations that genocide can be carried out with impunity—one need fear neither God nor man. There is one response to such overwhelming tragedy: the reaffirmation of meaningfulness, worth, and life—through acts of love and life-giving. The act of creating a life or enhancing its dignity is the counter-testimony to Auschwitz. To talk of love and of a God who cares in the presence of the burning children is obscene and incredible; to leap in and pull a child out of a pit, to clean its face and heal its body, is to make the most powerful statement—the only statement that counts.

In the first moment after the Flood, with its testimony of absurd and mass human death, Noah is given two instructions—the only two that can testify after such an event. "Be fruitful and multiply and replenish the earth" (Gen. 9:1–7), and "but your life blood I will hold you responsible for"—"who sheds man's blood, shall his blood be shed; for in the image of God made He man" (Gen. 9:5–6). Each act of creating a life, each act of enhancing or holding people responsible for human life, becomes multiplied in its resonance because it contradicts the mass graves of biblical Shinar—or Treblinka.

Recreating the Image of God

This becomes the critical religious act. Only a million or billion such acts can begin to right the balance of testimony so drastically shifted by the mass weight of six million dead. In an age when one is ashamed or embarrassed to talk about God in the presence of the burning children, the image of God, which points beyond itself to transcendence, is the only statement about God that one can make. And it is human life itself that makes the statement—words will not help.

Put it another way: the overwhelming testimony of the six million is so strong that it all but irretrievably closes out religious language. Therefore the religious enterprise after this event must see itself as a desperate attempt to create, save, and heal the image of God wherever it still exists—lest further evidence of meaninglessness finally tilt the scale irreversibly. Before this calling, all other "religious" activity is dwarfed.

But where does one find the strength to have a child after Auschwitz? Why bring a child into a world where Auschwitz is possible? Why expose it to such a risk again? The perspective of Auschwitz sheds new light on the nature of childrearing and faith. It takes enormous faith in ultimate redemption and meaningfulness to choose to create or even enhance life again. In fact, faith is revealed by this not to be a belief or even an emotion, but an ontological life-force that reaffirms creation and life in the teeth of overwhelming death. One must silently assume redemption in order to have the child—and having the child makes the statement of redemption.

There is a Jewish tradition that unashamedly traces the lineage of the Messiah to Lot's two daughters (Gen. 19:30 ff.), the survivors of the brimstone-and-fire catastrophe of Sodom. Lot and the two daughters believed that they were the only survivors of another world catastrophe (ibid., v. 31). What is the point, then, of still conceiving? What possible meaning or value can there be to life? The answer to absurd death is unreasoning life; it is *chesed*—lovingkindness that seeks to create an object of its love, that sees that life and love can overcome the present reality, which points to and proves a new creation and final redemption. So the daughters stopped at nothing—getting their own father drunk, seducing him, committing drunken incest—yet conceiving the Messiah. (Jewish tradition traces the Messiah from Moab to Ruth, to David, to the final Redeemer.)[13] It is quite a contrast to the Immaculate Conception, but it is truer to human reality and redemption out of the human condition. In the welter of grubby human reality, with evil and death rampant, with mixed human motives and lusts, the Redeemer comes out of the ground of new creation and hope. "On the day the Temple was destroyed, the Messiah was born."[14] After the war, one of the highest birth-rates in the world prevailed in the displaced-persons camps, where survivors lived in their erstwhile concentration camps.

The reborn State of Israel is this fundamental act of life and meaning of the Jewish people after Auschwitz. To fail to grasp that inextricable connection and response is to utterly fail to comprehend the theological significance of Israel. The most bitterly secular atheist involved in Israel's upbuilding is the front line of the Messianic life-force struggling to give renewed testimony to the Exodus as ultimate reality. Israel was built by rehabilitating a half-million survivors of the Holocaust. Each one of those lives had to be rebuilt, given opportunity for trust restored. I have been told of an Israeli Youth Aliyah village settled by orphan children from the European camps, which suffered from an infestation of mice for a long time. There were children in this village who had lived through the shattering effect of the total uprooting and destruction of their reality, of the overnight transition from affluence to permanent hunger. Ten years after the Holocaust, some of these children would still sneak bread out of the dining room and hide it in their quarters. They could not believe that this fragile world of love would not again be shattered at any time. They were determined not to be caught without a supply of bread. And neither reassurances nor constant searches could uncover the bread; it was hidden in evermore clever caches—only to bring the mice. Yet these half a million—and the eight hundred thousand Jewish refugees from Arab countries—were absorbed and given new opportunity and dignity. (They found enough strength to live under the shadow of another genocide aimed at themselves for more than twenty-five years.)

The Context of an Image of God

In a world of overpopulation and mass starvation and of zero population growth, something further must be said. I, for one, believe that in the light of the crematoria, the Jewish people are called to re-create life. Nor is such testimony easily given. One knows the risk to the children.

But it is not only the act of creating life that speaks. To bring a child into a world in which it will be hungry and diseased and neglected, is to torment and debase the image of God. We also face the challenge to create the conditions under which human beings will grow as an image of God; to build a world in which wealth and resources are created and distributed to provide the matrix for existence as an image of God.

We also face the urgent call to eliminate every stereotype discrimination that reduces—and denies—this image in the other. It was the ability to distinguish some people as human and others as not that enabled the Nazis to segregate and then destroy the "subhumans" (Jews, Gypsies, Slavs). The ability to differentiate the foreign Jews from French-born Jews paved the way for the deportation first of foreign-born, then of native, French Jews. This differentiation stilled conscience, stilled the church, stilled even some French Jews. The indivisibility of human dignity and equality becomes an essential bulwark against the repetition of another Holocaust. It is the command rising out of Auschwitz.

This means a vigorous self-criticism, and review of every cultural or religious framework that may sustain some devaluation or denial of the absolute and equal dignity of the other. This is the overriding command and the essential criterion for religious existence, to whoever walks by the light of the flames. Without this testimony and the creation of facts that give it persuasiveness, the act of the religious enterprise simply lacks credibility. To the extent that religion may extend or justify the evils of dignity denied, it becomes the devil's testimony. Whoever joins in the work of creation and rehabilitation of the image of God is, therefore, participating in "restoring to God his scepter and crown." Whoever does not support—or opposes—this process is seeking to complete the attack on God's presence in the world. These must be seen as the central religious acts. They shed a pitiless light on popes who deny birth control to starving millions because of a need to uphold the religious authority of the magisterium; or on rabbis who deny women's dignity out of loyalty to divinely given traditions. . . .

LIVING WITH THE DIALECTIC

The dialectic I have outlined is incredibly difficult to live by. How can we reconcile such extraordinary human and moral tensions? The classical traditions of Judaism and Christianity suggest: by reenacting constantly the event which is normative and revelatory. Only those who experience the normative event in their bones—through the community of the faith—will live by it.[15] I would suggest, then, that in the decades and centuries to come, Jews and others who seek to orient themselves by the Holocaust will unfold another sacral round. Men and women will gather to eat the putrid bread of Auschwitz, the potato-peelings of Bergen-Belsen. They will tell of the children who went, the starvation and hunger of the ghettoes, the darkening of the light in the Mussulmen's eyes. To enable people to reenact and relive Auschwitz there are records, pictures, even films—some taken by the murderers, some by the victims. That this pain will be incorporated in the round of life we regret; yet we may hope that it will not destroy hope but rather strengthen responsibility, will, and faith.

After Auschwitz, one must beware of easy hope. Israel is a perfect symbol for this. On the one hand, it validates the right to hope and speak of life renewed after destruction. On the other hand, it has been threatened with genocide all along. At the moment it is at a low point—yet prospects for a peace also suddenly emerge. Any hope must be sober, and built on the sands of despair, free from illusions. Yet Jewish history affirms hope.

I dare to use another biblical image. The cloud of smoke of the bodies by day and the pillar of fire of the crematoria by night may yet guide humanity to a goal and a day when human beings are attached to each other; and have so much shared each other's pain, and have so purified and criticized themselves, that *never again will a Holocaust be possible.* Perhaps we can pray that out of the welter of blood and pain will come a chastened mankind and faith that may take some tentative and mutual steps toward redemption. Then truly will the Messiah be here among us. Perhaps then the silence will be broken. At the prospect of such hope, however, certainly in our time, it is more appropiate to fall silent.

NOTES

1. Dieter Wisliceny, affidavit dated November 29, 1945, printed in *Nazi Conspiracy and Aggression* (Washington: Government Printing Office, 1946), 8:610; he quotes Eichmann as follows: "I laugh when I jump into the grave because of the feeling I have killed 5,000,000 Jews. That gives me great satisfaction and gratification." Rudolf Hoess, the head of Auschwitz, reports Eichmann's joy grew out of his conviction that

he had landed a fatal blow by devastating Jewry's life center. In Hoess's responses to Dr. Jan Sehn, the examining judge, printed as appendix 3 in Hoess's autobiography, *Commandant of Auschwitz* (London: Weidenfeld & Nicolson, 1959), p. 215. The estimate of Jewish scholars, rabbis, and full-time students killed is by Rabbi M. J. Itamar (Wohlgelernter), formerly secretary-general of the Chief Rabbinate of Israel. Heydrich, the original head of the Final Solution project and its driving force until his death by assassination, instructed the Einsatzgruppen that in killing the Jews of Eastern Europe, they would be killing the "intellectual reservoir of the Jews."

2. Simon Herman, *Israelis and Jews: A Study in the Continuity of an Identity* (New York: Random House, 1970), pp. 78–80, 175, 186, 191, 203–4, 211–13; idem, lecture given at the annual meeting of the Memorial Foundation for Jewish Culture in Geneva, July 9, 1974, published in 1975 *Proceedings of the Memorial Foundation for Jewish Culture;* idem, "Ethnic Identity and Historical Time Perspective: An Illustrated Case Study; the Impact of the Holocaust (Destruction of European Jewry) on Jewish Identity," mimeographed (Jerusalem, 1972); idem, research in progress.

3. S. Szmaglewska, in *Trial of the Major War Criminals before the International Military Tribunal* (Nuremberg, 1947–49), 8:319–20, quoted in Erich Kulka and Uta Kraus, *The Death Factory* (Oxford: Pergamon, 1966), p. 114. (In the IMT record she is listed as Shmaglevskaya); cf. also Hoess, *Commandant of Auschwitz*, pp. 149–51.

4. S. Szmaglewska, ibid.

5. Raul Hilberg, *The Destruction of the European Jews* (Chicago: Quadrangle, 1966); Hilberg, ibid., p. 569, fn. 65, cites 5.28 RM per kg. for TESTA's price from DEGESCH before resale to Gerstein, the chief disinfection officer in the office of the hygienic chief of the Waffen-SS, for use in Auschwitz. However, a photograph of an invoice from DEGESCH to Kurt Gerstein dated March 13, 1944, published in *La Deportation* (n.d., n.p., published by Fédération Nationale des Déportés et Internis Resistants et Patriots), p. 138, clearly shows a price of 5 RM per kg. (210 kg. for 1,050 RM).

6. Elie Wiesel, *Night* (New York: Hill & Wang, 1960), pp. 43–44.

7. Writing under a pseudonym, a priest who had served as ghost writer for Pope John published a report on Vatican II which stated that John had composed a prayer about the Jews. The text, to be read in all Catholic churches, said: "We are conscious today that many centuries of blindness have cloaked our eyes so that we can no longer see the beauty of Thy chosen people. . . . We realize that the mark of Cain stands on our foreheads. Across the centuries our Brother Abel has lain in blood which we drew, or shed tears we caused, forgetting Thy love. Forgive us for crucifying Thee a second time in their flesh. For we knew not what we did . . ." (F. E. Cartus [pseudo], "Vatican II and the Jews," *Commentary*, January 1965, p. 21.) While the prayer is apocryphal (no trace of it has been found in John's papers), widespread acceptance of its attribution reflects John's known regret and concern.

8. Elie Wiesel, *The Accident* (New York: Hill & Wang, 1962), p. 91.

9. Elie Wiesel, "The Death of My Father," in *Legends of our Time* (New York: Holt, Rinehart & Winston, 1968), pp. 2, 4, 5, 6, 7; idem, *The Gates of the Forest* (New York: Holt, Rinehart & Winston, 1966), pp. 194, 196, 197, 198, 224, 225–26.

10. Eliezer Berkovits, *Faith After the Holocaust* (New York: KTAV, 1973); Emil Fackenheim, *God's Presence in History* (New York: New York University Press, 1970); Richard Rubenstein, *After Auschwitz* (Indianapolis: Bobbs-Merrill, 1968), especially pp. 128–29.

11. Richard Rubenstein, "Homeland and Holocaust," in *The Religious Situation 1968* (Boston: Beacon Press, 1969), pp. 39–111.

12. Wiesel, *Night*, p. 71.

13. Cf. *Bereshith Raba, Seder VaYera*, parsha 50, par. 16; also ibid., parsha 51, par. 10; B. T. Yevamot 77a; see Z. Y. Lipovitz, *Commentary on the Book of Ruth* (Tel Aviv, 1959).

14. Talmud Yerushalmi, *Berakhot* 15b (chap. 2, halakhah 4); *Aychah Rabba*, parsha 1, sec. 51.

15. Haggadah of Pesach; Exod. 12:13, 20:1–14, 22:21; Lev. 11, esp. v. 45, 19:33–36, 23:42–43, 25:34–55; Deut. 4:30–45, 5:6–18, 15:12–18, 16:1–12, 26:1–11; Josh. 24; Judg. 2:1–5, 11–12; Jer. 2:1–9, 7:22–27, 11:1–8, 16:14–15, 22:7–8, 31:3–33, 32:16–22, 34:8–22; Ezek. 20; Neh. 9.

EMIL L. FACKENHEIM

◩ Jewish Faith and the Holocaust

A Fragment

I

Within the past two centuries, three events have shaken and are still shaking Jewish religious existence—the Emancipation and its aftereffects, the Nazi Holocaust, and the rise of the first Jewish state in two thousand years—and of these, two have occurred in our own generation. From the point of view of Jewish religious existence, as from so many other points of view, the Holocaust is the most shattering. Doubtless the Emancipation and all its works have posed and continue to pose powerful challenges, with which Jewish thought has been wrestling all along—scientific agnosticism, secularism, assimilation, and the like. The Emancipation presents, however, a challenge *ab extra*, from without, and for all its well-demonstrated power to weaken and undermine Jewish religious existence, I have long been convinced that the challenge can be met, religiously and intellectually. The state of Israel, by contrast, is a challenge *ab intra*, from within—at least to much that Jewish existence has been throughout two

Reprinted by permission of Georges Borchardt, Inc., Literary Agency.

millennia. But this challenge is positive—the fact that in one sense (if not in many others) a long exile has ended. That it represents a positive challenge was revealed during and immediately after the Six Day War, when biblical (i.e., pre-exilic) language suddenly came to life.

The Holocaust, too, challenges Jewish faith from within, but the negativity of its challenge is total, without light or relief. After the events associated with the name of Auschwitz, everything is shaken, nothing is safe.

To avoid Auschwitz, or to act as though it had never occurred, would be blasphemous. Yet how face it and be faithful to its victims? No precedent exists either within Jewish history or outside it. Even when a Jewish religious thinker barely begins to face Auschwitz, he perceives the possibility of a desperate choice between the faith of a millenial Jewish past, which has so far persisted through every trial, and faithfulness to the victims of the present. But at the edge of this abyss there must be a great pause, a lengthy silence, and an endurance.

II

Men shun the scandal of the particularity of Auschwitz. Germans link it with Dresden; American liberals, with Hiroshima. Christians deplore antisemitism-in-general, while Communists erect monuments to victims-of-Fascism-in-general, depriving the dead of Auschwitz of their Jewish identity even in death. Rather than face Auschwitz, men everywhere seek refuge in generalities, comfortable precisely because they are generalities. And such is the extent to which reality is shunned that no cries of protest are heard even when in the world community's own forum obscene comparisons are made between Israeli soldiers and Nazi murderers.

The Gentile world shuns Auschwitz because of the terror of Auschwitz—and because of real or imagined implication in the guilt for Auschwitz. But Jews shun Auschwitz as well. Only after many years did significant Jewish responses begin to appear. Little of real significance is being or can be said even now. Perhaps there should still be silence. It is certain, however, that the voices, now beginning to be heard, will grow ever louder and more numerous. For Jews now know that they must ever after remember Auschwitz, and be its witnesses to the world. Not to be a witness would be a betrayal. In the murder camps the victims often rebelled with no other hope than that one of them might escape to tell the tale. For Jews now to refrain from telling the tale would be unthinkable. Jewish faith still recalls the Exodus, Sinai, the two destructions of the Temple. A Judaism that survived at the price of ignoring Auschwitz would not deserve to survive.

It is because the world shrinks so fully from the truth that once a Jew begins to speak at all he must say the most obvious. Must he say that the death of a Jewish child at Auschwitz is no more lamentable than the death of a German child at Dresden? He must say it. And in saying it, he must also refuse to dissolve Auschwitz into suffering-in-general, even though he is almost sure to be considered a Jewish particularist who cares about Jews but not about mankind. Must he distinguish between the mass-killing at Hiroshima and that at Auschwitz? At the risk of being thought a sacrilegious quibbler, he must, with endless patience, forever repeat that Eichmann was moved by no such "rational" objective as victory when he diverted trains needed for military purposes in order to dispatch Jews to their death. He must add that there was no "irrational" objective either. Torquemada burned bodies in order to save souls. Eichmann sought to destroy both bodies and souls. Where else and at what other time have executioners ever separated those to be murdered now from those to be murdered later to the strain of Viennese waltzes? Where else has human skin ever been made into lampshades, and human body-fat into soap—not by isolated perverts but under the direction of ordinary bureaucrats? Auschwitz is a unique descent into hell. It is an unprecedented celebration of evil. It is evil for evil's sake.

A Jew must bear witness to this truth. Nor may he conceal the fact that Jews in their particularity were the singled-out victims. Of course, they were by no means the sole victims. And a Jew would infinitely prefer to think that to the Nazis, Jews were merely a species of the genus "inferior race." This indeed was the theme of Allied wartime propaganda, and it is still perpetuated by liberals, Communists, and guilt-ridden Christian theologians. Indeed, "liberal"-minded Jews themselves perpetuate it. The superficial reason is that this view of Auschwitz unites victims of all races and creeds: it is "brotherly" propaganda. Under the surface, however, there broods at least in Jewish if not in some Gentile minds an idea horrible beyond all description. Would even Nazis have singled out Jews for such a terrible fate unless Jews had done *something* to bring it upon themselves? Most of the blame attaches to the murderers: must not at least some measure of blame attach to the victims as well? Such are the wounds that Nazism has inflicted on some Jewish minds. And such is the extent to which Nazism has defiled the world that, while it should have destroyed every vestige of antisemitism in every Gentile mind on earth, Auschwitz has, in some Gentile minds, actually increased it.[1]

These wounds and this defilement can be confronted only with the truth. And the ineluctable truth is that Jews at Auschwitz were not a species of the genus "inferior race," but rather the prototype by which "inferior race" was defined. Not until the Nazi revolution had become an anti-Jewish revolution did it begin to succeed as a movement; and when all its other works came crashing down only one of its goals remained: the murder of Jews.[2] This is the scandal that requires, of Germans, a ruthless examination of their whole history; of Christians, a pitiless reckoning with the history of Christian antisemitism; of the whole world, an inquiry into the grounds of its indifference for twelve long years. Resort to theories of suffering-in-general or persecution-in-general permits such investigations to be evaded.

Yet even where the quest for explanations is genuine there is not, and never will be, an adequate explanation. Auschwitz is the scandal of evil for evil's sake, an eruption of demonism without analogy; and the singling-out of Jews, ultimately, is an unparalleled expression of what the rabbis call groundless hate. This is the rock on which throughout eternity all rational explanations will crash and break apart.

How can a Jew respond to thus having been singled out, and to being singled out even now whenever he tries to bear witness? Resisting rational explanations, Auschwitz will forever resist religious explanations as well. Attempts to find rational causes succeed, at least up to a point, and the search for the religious, ideological, social, and economic factors leading to Auschwitz must be relentlessly pressed. In contrast, the search for a purpose in Auschwitz is foredoomed to total failure. Not that good men in their despair have not made the attempt. Good Orthodox Jews have resorted to the ancient "for our sins we are punished," but this recourse, unacceptable already to Job, is in this case all the more impossible. A good Christian theologian sees the purpose of Auschwitz as a divine reminder of the sufferings of Christ, but this testifies to a moving sense of desperation—and to an incredible lapse of theological judgment. A good Jewish secularist will connect the Holocaust with the rise of the state of Israel, but while to see a causal connection here is possible and necessary, to see a purpose is intolerable. A total and uncompromising sweep must be made of these and other explanations, all designed to give purpose to Auschwitz. No purpose, religious or non-religious, will ever be found in Auschwitz. The very attempt to find one is blasphemous.

Yet it is of the utmost importance to recognize that seeking a purpose is one thing, but seeking a response quite another. The first is wholly out of the question. The second is inescapable. Even after two decades any sort of adequate response may as yet transcend the power of any Jew. But his faith, his destiny, his very survival will depend on whether, in the end, he will be able to respond.

How can a Jew begin to seek a response? Looking for precedents, he finds none either in Jewish or in non-Jewish history. Jewish (like Christian) martyrs have died for their faith, certain that God needs martyrs. Job suffered despite his faith, able to protest within the sphere of faith. Black Christians have died for their race, unshaken in a faith which was not at issue. The one million Jewish children murdered in the Nazi Holocaust died neither because of their faith, nor in spite of their faith, nor for reasons unrelated to faith. They were murdered because of the faith of their great-grandparents. Had these great-grandparents abandoned their Jewish faith, and failed to bring up Jewish children, then their fourth-generation descendants might have been among the Nazi executioners, but not among their Jewish victims. Like Abraham of old, European Jews some time in the mid–nineteenth century offered a human sacrifice, by the mere minimal commitment to the Jewish faith of bringing up Jewish children. But unlike Abraham they did not know what they were doing, and there was no reprieve. This is the brute fact which makes all comparisons odious or irrelevant. This is what makes Jewish religious existence today unique, without support from analogies anywhere in the past. This is the scandal of the particularity of Auschwitz which, once confronted by Jewish faith, threatens total despair.

I confess that it took me twenty years until I was able to look at this scandal, but when at length I did, I made what to me was, and still is, a momentous discovery: that while religious thinkers were vainly struggling for a response to Auschwitz, Jews throughout the world—rich and poor, learned and ignorant, religious and nonreligious—had to some degree been responding all along. For twelve long years Jews had been exposed to a murderous hate which was as groundless as it was implacable. For twelve long years the world had been luke-warm or indifferent, unconcerned over the prospect of a world without Jews. For twelve long years the whole world had conspired to make Jews wish to cease to be Jews wherever, whenever, and in whatever way they could. Yet to this unprecedented invitation to group suicide, Jews responded with an unexpected will to live—with, under the circumstances, an incredible commitment to Jewish group survival.

In ordinary times, a commitment of this kind may be a mere mixture of nostalgia and vague loyalties not far removed from tribalism; and, unable to face Auschwitz, I had myself long viewed it as such, placing little value on a Jewish survival which was, or seemed to be, only survival for survival's sake. I was wrong, and even the shallowest Jewish survivalist philosophy of the postwar period was right by comparison. For in the age of Auschwitz a Jewish commitment to Jewish survival is in itself a monumental act of faithfulness, as well as a monumental, albeit as yet fragmentary, act of faith. Even to do no more than remain a Jew after Auschwitz is to confront the demons of Auschwitz in all their guises, and to bear witness against them. It is to believe that these demons cannot, will not, and must not prevail, and to stake on that belief one's own life and the lives of one's children, and of one's children's children. To be a Jew after Auschwitz is to have wrested hope—for the Jew and for the world—from the abyss of total despair. In the words of a speaker at a recent gathering of Bergen-Belsen survivors, the Jew after Auschwitz has a second *Shema Yisrael*: no second Auschwitz, no second Bergen-Belsen, no second Buchenwald—anywhere in the world, for anyone in the world!

What accounts for this commitment to Jewish existence when there might have been, and by every rule of human logic should have been, a terrified and demoralized flight from Jewish existence? Why, since Auschwitz, have all previous distinctions among Jews—between religious and secularist, Orthodox and liberal—diminished in importance, to be replaced by a new major distinction between Jews committed to Jewish survival, willing to be singled out and counted, and Jews in flight, who rationalize this flight as a rise to humanity-in-general? In my view, nothing less will do than to say that a commanding Voice speaks from Auschwitz, and that there are Jews who hear it and Jews who stop their ears.

The ultimate question is: where was God at Auschwitz? For years I sought refuge in Buber's image of an eclipse of God. This image, still meaningful in other respects, no longer seems to me applicable to Auschwitz. Most assuredly no *redeeming* Voice is heard from Auschwitz, or ever will be heard. However, a *commanding* Voice is being heard, and has, however faintly, been heard from the start. Religious Jews hear it, and they identify its source. Secularist Jews also hear it, even though perforce they leave it unidentified. At Auschwitz, Jews came face to face with absolute evil. They were and still are singled out by it, but in the midst of it they hear an absolute commandment: *Jews are forbidden to grant posthumous victories to Hitler.* They are commanded to survive as Jews, lest the Jewish people perish. They are commanded to remember the victims of Auschwitz, lest their memory perish. They are forbidden to despair of man and his world, and to escape into either cynicism or otherworldliness, less they cooperate in delivering the world over to the forces of Auschwitz. Finally, they are forbidden to despair of the God of Israel, lest Judaism perish. A secularist Jew cannot make himself believe by a mere act of will, nor can he be commanded to do so; yet he can perform the commandment of Auschwitz. And a religious Jew who has stayed with his God may be forced into new, possibly revolutionary, relationships with him. One possibility, however, is wholly unthinkable. A Jew may not respond to Hitler's attempt to destroy Judaism by himself cooperating in its destruction. In ancient times, the unthinkable Jewish sin was idolatry. Today, it is to respond to Hitler by doing his work.

In the Midrash, God is, even in time of unrelieved tragedy, only "seemingly" powerless, for the Messiah is still expected. In Elie Wiesel's *Night*, God hangs on the gallows, and for the hero of Wiesel's *The Gates of the Forest*, a Messiah who is able to come, and yet at Auschwitz failed to come, is not to be conceived. Yet this same hero asserts that precisely because it is too late we are commanded to hope. He also says the Kaddish, "that solemn affirmation, filled with grandeur and serenity, by which man returns to God His crown and His scepter." But how a Jew after Auschwitz can return these to God is not yet known. Nor is it yet known how God can receive them. . . .

On another public occasion, in March 1967, I asked the following question: Would we [like Job] be able to say that the question of Auschwitz will be answered in any sense whatever in case the eclipse of God were ended and He appeared to us? An impossible and intolerable question.[3] Less than three months later this purely hypothetical question had become actual, when at Jerusalem the threat of total annihilation gave way to sudden salvation, atheists spoke of miracles, and hardboiled Western reporters resorted to biblical images.

The question *is* impossible and intolerable. Even Job's question is not answered by God's presence, and to him children are restored. The children of Auschwitz will not be restored, and the question of Auschwitz will not be answered by a saving divine presence.

And yet, is a Jew after Auschwitz permitted to despair of salvation because of Auschwitz? Is it permitted him to cast out all hope and all joy? But on the other side, can there be any hope and any joy, purchased at the price of forgetting? Any one of these responses would be further victories handed to Hitler, and are thus impossible.

It was into precisely this impossible and intolerable contradiction that believing Jews were placed by the events at Jerusalem in May and June 1967. Those events cast into clear relief the whole as yet unassimilated fact of an embattled, endangered, but nevertheless free Jewish state, emerging from ashes and catastrophe. Solely because of the connection of the events of May and June with Auschwitz did a military victory (rarely applauded in Judaism, and never for its own sake) acquire an inescapable religious dimension.

In this context, let me quote from a letter I recently received from Professor Harold Fisch of Bar-Ilan University in Israel:

> May I report to you a conversation I had last summer with a colleague, a psychologist, who had served during the war as an artillery officer in Sinai. I asked him how he accounted for the remarkable heroism of the quite ordinary soldier of the line, for, as you may know, exemplary heroism was the normal thing at that time; mere carrying out of duty was the exception. Where, I asked him, was the psychological spring? To my surprise, he answered that what deeply motivated each and every soldier was the memory of the Holocaust, and the feeling that *above all this must never happen again.* There had been an ominous similarity between the statements of Arab leaders, their radio, and newspapers, and the remembered threats of the Nazis: we had entered into a *Shoah* (holocaust) psychosis, all around us enemies threatening us with extermination and having both the means and the will to carry out their threat. As the ring closed in and help seemed far, one noticed one's neighbors who had been in Auschwitz and Bergen-Belsen going about whitefaced. It was all too obvious what was the source of their dread. The years in between had momentarily fallen away, and they were back in that veritable nightmare world. The dark night of the soul was upon us. *And it was the commandment which the Lord of history had, so to speak, pronounced at Auschwitz which saved us.* [Italics added.] I told my friend that I could not entirely accept his explanation because I knew that a majority of the soldiers had no personal or family recollections of the European Holocaust: they had come from North Africa or Yemen, or even the neighboring Arab countries where at that time such horrors were unknown. How could they feel the force of the analogy as could the survivors of Buchenwald? He told me that the intervening twenty years had brought it about that the Holocaust had become a collective experience pressing consciously and unconsciously on the minds of all, even the young, for whom Jewish history in the Diaspora had come to an end with the beginnings of Israeli independence.

It is solely because of this connection of the events of May and June with Auschwitz that a Jew must both tremble and rejoice. He must tremble lest he permit any light after Auschwitz to relieve the darkness of Auschwitz. He must rejoice, lest he add to the darkness of Auschwitz. Rejoicing after Auschwitz and because of Auschwitz, the Jew must be a Jew, *Am Yisrael Chai* ("the people Israel, alive"), a witness to the world, preparing a way for God.

NOTES

1. Witness the recent Polish propaganda campaign—tantamount to a rewriting of Holocaust history—in which it was suggested that the Jews had cooperated with the Nazis in their own destruction. Since I wrote these words, the idea of a Nazi-Zionist axis has become standard Soviet propaganda.
2. See, e.g., George L. Mosse, *The Crisis of German Ideology* (New York: Universal Library, 1964), especially chap. 17.
3. See *Judaism*, vol. 16, no. 3, Summer Issue 1967, p. 296.

EMIL L. FACKENHEIM

◨ Holocaust

Holocaust is the term currently most widely employed for the persecution of the Jewish people by Nazi Germany from 1933 to 1945, first in Germany itself and subsequently in Nazi-occupied Europe, culminating in "extermination" camps and resulting in the murder of nearly six million Jews. However, the Hebrew term *Shoah* (total destruction) would be more fitting, since *Holocaust* also connotes "burnt sacrifice." It is true that, like ancient Moloch worshipers, German Nazis and their non-German henchmen at Auschwitz threw children into the flames alive. These were not, however, their own children, thrown in acts of sacrifice, but those of Jews, thrown in acts of murder.

Is the Holocaust unique? The concept *unprecedented* is preferable, as it refers to the same facts but avoids not only well-known difficulties about the concept of *uniqueness* but also the temptation of taking the event out of history and thus mystifying it.[1] To be sure, Auschwitz was "like another planet," in the words of "Katzetnik 135683," the pen name of the novelist Yechiel Dinur, that is, a world of its own, with laws, modes of behavior, and even a language of its own. Even so, as *unprecedented*, rather than *unique*, it is placed firmly into history. Historians are obliged, so far as possible, to search for precedents; and thoughtful people, by no means historians only, are obliged to ask if the Holocaust itself may become a precedent for future processes, whether as yet only possible or already

---

actual. Manés Sperber, for example, has written: "Encouraged by the way Hitler had practiced genocide without encountering resistance, the Arabs [in 1948] surged in upon the nascent Israeli nation to exterminate it and make themselves its immediate heirs."[2]

The most obvious recent precedent of the Holocaust is the Turkish genocide of the Armenians in World War I. Like the Nazi genocide of the Jews in World War II, this was an attempt to destroy a whole people, carried out under the cover of a war with maximum secrecy, and with the victims being deported to isolated places prior to their murder, all of which provoked few countermeasures or even verbal protests on the part of the civilized world. Doubtless the Nazis both learned from, and were encouraged by, the Armenian precedent.

But unlike the Armenian genocide, the Holocaust was intended, planned, and executed as the "final solution" of a "problem." Thus, whereas, for example, the roundup of Armenians in Istanbul, the very heart of the Turkish empire, was discontinued after a while, Nazi Germany, had it won the war or even managed to prolong it, would have succeeded in murdering every Jew. North American Indians have survived in reservations; Jewish reservations in a victorious Nazi empire are inconceivable. Thus the Holocaust may be said to belong, with other catastrophes, to the species *genocide*. Within the species, defined as intended, planned, and largely executed extermination, it is without precedent and, thus far at least, without sequel. It is—here the term really must be employed— unique.

Equally unique are the means without which this project could not have been planned or carried out. These include: a scholastically precise definition of the victims; juridical procedures, enlisting the finest minds of the legal profession, aimed at the total elimination of the victims' rights; a technical apparatus, including murder trains and gas chambers, and, most importantly, a veritable army not only of actual murderers but also of witting and unwitting accomplices—clerks, lawyers, journalists, bank managers, army officers, railway conductors, entrepreneurs, and an endless list of others.

All these means and accomplices were required for the *how* of the "Final Solution." Its *why* required an army of historians, philosophers, and theologians. The historians rewrote history. The philosophers refuted the idea that mankind is human before it is Aryan or non-Aryan. And the theologians were divided into Christians who made Jesus into an Aryan and neopagans who rejected Christianity itself as non-Aryan. (Their differences were slight compared to their shared commitments.) Such were the shock troops of this army. Equally necessary, however, were its remaining troops: historians, philosophers, and theologians who knew differently but betrayed their calling by holding their peace.

What was the *why* of the Holocaust? Even the shock troops never quite faced it, although they had no reason or excuse for not doing so. As early as 1936 Julius Streicher was on record to the effect that "who fights the Jew fights the devil" and "who masters the devil conquers heaven."[3] Streicher was only expressing more succinctly Hitler's assertion in *Mein Kampf* that "if the Jew will be victorious" in his cosmic struggle with mankind, his "crown" will be the "funeral wreath of humanity, and this planet will, as it did millions of years ago, move through the ether devoid of human beings."[4]

Planet Auschwitz was as good as Streicher's word. When the Third Reich was at the height of its power, the conquest of heaven seemed to lie in the apotheosis of the master race; even then, however, the mastery of the Jewish devil was a necessary condition of the conquest. When the Third Reich collapsed and the apocalypse was at hand, Planet Auschwitz continued to operate until the end, and Hitler's last will and testament made the fight against the Jewish people mandatory for future generations. The mastery of the Jewish devil, it seems, had become the sufficient condition for the "conquest of heaven," if indeed not identical with it.

To be sure, this advent of salvation in the Auschwitz gas chambers was but for relatively few eyes to see. What could be heard by all, however, was the promise of it years earlier, when the streets of Germany resounded to the storm troopers' hymn: "When Jewish blood spurts from our knives, our well-being will redouble."

Never before in history had a state attempted to make a whole country— indeed, as in this case, a whole continent—*rein* (free) of every member of a whole people, man, woman, and child. Never have attempts resembling the Holocaust been pursued with methods so thorough and with such unswerving goal-directedness. It is difficult to imagine and impossible to believe that, this having happened, world history can ever be the same. The Holocaust is not only an unprecedented event. It is also of an unfathomable magnitude. It is world historical.

As a world-historical event, the Holocaust poses new problems for philosophical thought. To begin with reflections on historiography, if, by near-common philosophical consent, to explain an event historically is to show how it was possible, then, to the philosopher, the Holocaust historian emerges sooner or later as asserting the possibility of the Holocaust solely because it was actual. He thus exposes the historian's explanation as being, in fact, circular. This impasse, to be sure, is often evaded, most obviously when, as in many histories of World War II, the Holocaust is relegated to a few footnotes. An impasse is even explicitly denied when, as in Marxist ideological history, Nazism-equals-fascism-equals-the-last-stage-of-capitalism, or when, as in liberalistic ideological history, the Holocaust is flattened out into man's-inhumanity-to-man-especially-in-wartime. (Arnold Toynbee, for example, considered that "what the Nazis did was nothing peculiar.")[5] The philosopher, however, must penetrate beyond these evasions and ideological distortions. And when such a philosopher finds a solid historian who states, correctly enough, that "the extermination grew out of the biologistic insanity of Nazi ideology, and for that reason is completely unlike the terrors of revolutions and wars of the past,"[6] he must ponder whether "biologistic insanity" has explanatory force or is rather a metaphor whose chief significance is that explanation has come to an end. As he ponders this, he may well be led to wonder "whether even in a thousand years people will understand Hitler, Auschwitz, Maidanek, and Treblinka better than we do now. . . . Posterity may understand it even less than we do."[7]

Such questions turn philosophical thought from methodological to substantive issues, and above all to the subject of man. Premodern philosophy was prepared to posit a permanent human nature that was unaffected by historical change. More deeply immersed in the varieties and vicissitudes of history, modern philosophy generally has perceived, in abstraction from historical change, only a human condition, which was considered permanent only insofar as beyond it was the humanly impossible. At Auschwitz, however, "more was real than is possible,"[8] and the impossible was done by some and suffered by others. Thus, prior to the Holocaust, the human condition, while including the necessity of dying, was seen as also including at least one inalienable freedom—that of each individual's dying his own death.[9] "With the administrative murder of millions" in the death camps, however, "death has become something that was never to be feared in this way before. . . . The individual is robbed of the last and poorest that until then still remained his own. In the camps it was no longer the individual that died; he was made into a specimen."[10]

As well as a new way of dying, the Auschwitz administrators also manufactured a new way of living. Prior to the Holocaust no aspect of the human condition could make so strong a claim to permanency as the distinction between life and death, between still-being-here and being-no-more. The Holocaust, however, produced the *Muselmann* (Muslim; pl., *Muselmänner*)—camp slang for a prisoner near death, the skin-and-bone walking corpse, or living dead, the vast "anonymous mass, continuously renewed and always identical, of non-men who march and labor in silence, the divine spark dead within them, already too empty really to suffer. One hesitates to call them living. One hesitates to call their death death."[11] The *Muselmann* may be called the most truly original contribution of the Third Reich to civilization.

From these new ways of being human—those of the victims—philosophical thought is turned to another new way of being human, that of the victimizers. Philosophy has all along been acquainted with the quasi-evil of sadism (a mere sickness), the semievil of moral weakness, the superficial evil of ignorance, and even—hardest to understand and, therefore often ignored or denied—the radical or demonic evil that is done and celebrated for its own sake. Prior to the Holocaust, however, it was unacquainted with the "banality of evil"[12] practiced by numberless individuals who, having been ordinary or even respected citizens, committed at Auschwitz crimes on a scale previously unimaginable, only to become, in the Holocaust's aftermath, ordinary and respectable once more—without showing signs of any moral anguish.

The evil is banal by dint not of the nature of the crimes but of the people who committed them: these, it is said, were made to do what they did by the system. This, however, is only half a philosophical thought, for who made the system—conceived, planned, created, perpetuated, and escalated it—if not such as Himmler and Eichmann, Stangl and Hoess, to say nothing of the unknown-soldier-become-S.S.-murderer? Already having difficulty with radical or demonic evil, philosophical thought is driven by the "banal" evil of the Holocaust from the operators to the system, and from the system back to the operators. In this circular movement, to be sure, banal evil, except for ceasing to be banal, does not become intelligible. Yet the effort to understand is not without result, for from it the Holocaust emerges as a world or, rather, as the anti-world par excellence. The human condition does not dwell in a vacuum. It "always-already-is" within a world, that is, within a structured whole that exists at all because it is geared to life and that is structured because it is governed by laws of life. Innocent so long as they obey the law, the inhabitants of a world have a right to life, and forfeit it, if at all, only by an act of will—the breach of the law. The Holocaust antiworld, while structured, is governed by a law of death. For some—Jews—existence itself was a capital crime (a hitherto unheard-of proposition) and the sole raison d'être of the others was to mete out their punishment. In this world, the degradation, torture, and eventual murder of some human beings at the hands of others was not a by-product of, or means to, some higher, more ultimate purpose. They were its whole essence.

Modern philosophers, we have said previously, were able to conceive of a human condition because not all things were considered humanly possible. Even so, some of their number, possibly with modern history in mind, have not hesitated to ascribe to man a "perfectibility" that is infinite. Auschwitz exacts a new concession from future philosophy: whether or not man is infinitely perfectible, he is in any case infinitely depravable. The Holocaust is not only a world-historical event. It is also a "watershed,"[13] or "caesura,"[14] or "rupture"[15] in man's history on earth.

Is the Holocaust a rupture in the sight of theology? This question requires a separate inquiry. Theology, to be sure, at least if it is Jewish or Christian, is bound up with history. But it can be, and has been, argued that this is a *Heilgeschichte* immune to all merely secular historical events. Thus, for Franz Rosenzweig nothing crucial could happen for Jews between Sinai and the Messianic days. And for Karl Barth it was "always Good Friday *after* Easter," the implication being that the crucial saving event of Christianity has already occurred and is unassailable ever after.

Is the Holocaust a rupture for Christianity? German Christians, and possibly Christians as a whole, "can no longer speak evangelically to Jews."[16] They cannot "get behind" Auschwitz; they can get "beyond it" if at all only "in company with the victims," and this latter only if they identify with the state of Israel as being a Jewish "house against death" and the "last Jewish refuge."[17] Christians must relate "positively" to Jews, not "despite" Jewish nonacceptance of the Christ but "because" of it.[18] Even to go only this far and no further with their theologians (it seems fitting here to cite only German theologians) is for Christians to recognize a post-Holocaust rupture in their faith, for the step demanded—renunciation of Christian missions to the Jews, as such and in principle—is, within Christian history, unprecedented. (Of the Christian theologians who find it necessary to go much further, A. Roy Eckardt is, perhaps, the most theologically oriented.) To refuse even this one step, that is, for Christians to stay with the idea of mission to the Jews in principle, even if suspending it altogether in practice, is either to ignore the Holocaust, or else sooner or later to reach some such view as that mission to the Jews "is the sole possibility of a genuine and meaningful restitution (*Wiedergutmachung*) on the part of German Christendom."[19] Can Christians view such a stance as other than a theological obscenity? The Jewish stance toward Christian missionizing attempts directed at them, in any case, cannot be what it once was. Prior to the Holocaust, Jews could respect such attempts, although of course considering them misguided. After the Holocaust, they can only view them as trying in one way what Hitler undertook in another.

It would seem, then, that for Christians Good Friday can no longer be always *after* Easter. As for Jews, was the Holocaust a crucial event, occurring though it did between Sinai and the Messianic days? Franz Rosenzweig's Jewish truth, it emerges in our time, was a truth not of Judaism but of *Galut* (exile) Judaism only, albeit its most profound modern statement. *Galut* Judaism, however, has ceased to be tenable.

Galut Judaism may be characterized as follows:

1. A Jew can appease or bribe, hide or flee from an enemy and, having succeeded, can thank God for having been saved.

2. When in *extremis* such salvation is impossible, when death can be averted only through apostasy, he can still choose death, thus becoming a martyr; and then he is secure in the knowledge that, while no Jew should seek death, *kiddush ha-Shem* (sanctifying God's name by dying for it) is the highest stage of which he can be worthy.[20]

3. Exile, though painful, is bearable, for it is meaningful, whether its meaning consists in punishment for Jewish sins, vicarious suffering for the sins of others, or whether it is simply inscrutable, a meaning known only to God.

4. *Galut* will not last forever. If not he himself or even his children's children, at any rate some Jews' distant offspring will live to see the Messianic end.

These are the chief conditions and commitments of *Galut* Judaism. Existing in the conditions and armed by the commitments, a Jew in past centuries was able to survive the poverty of the eastern European ghetto; the slander, ideologically embellished and embroidered, of anti-Semitism in modern Germany and France; the medieval expulsions; the Roman Emperor Hadrian's attempt once and for all to extirpate the Jewish faith; and, of course, the fateful destruction of the Jerusalem Temple in 70 C.E., to which *Galut* Judaism was the normative and epoch-making response. All these *Galut* Judaism was able to survive. The Holocaust, however, already shown by us to be unprecedented simply as an historical event, is unprecedented also as a threat to the Jewish faith, and *Galut* Judaism is unable to meet it.

1. The Holocaust was not a gigantic pogrom from which one could hide until the visitation of the drunken Cossacks had passed. This enemy was coldly sober, systematic rather than haphazard; except for the lucky few, there was no hiding.

2. The Holocaust was not a vast expulsion, causing to arise the necessity, but also the possibility, of once again resorting to wandering, with the Torah as "portable fatherland."[21] Even when the Third Reich was still satisfied with expelling Jews there was, except for the fortunate or prescient, no place to go; and when the Reich became dissatisfied with mere expulsions, a place of refuge, had such been available, would have been beyond reach.

3. The Holocaust was not an assault calling for bribing or appeasing the enemy. This enemy was an "idealist" who could not be bribed, and he remained unappeasable until the last Jew's death.

4. The Holocaust was not a challenge to Jewish martyrdom but, on the contrary, an attempt to destroy martyrdom forever. Hadrian had decreed death for the crime of practicing Judaism and thereby inspired the martyrdom of such as Rabbi Akiva, which in turn inspired countless Jewish generations. Hitler, like Hadrian, sought to destroy Jews but, unlike Hadrian, was too cunning to repeat the ancient emperor's folly. He decreed death for Jews, not for doing or even believing, but rather for being—for the crime of possessing Jewish ancestors. Thus, Jewish martyrdom was made irrelevant. Moreover, no effort was spared to make martyrdom impossible as well, and the supreme effort in this direction was the manufacture of *Muselmänner*. A martyr chooses to die; as regards the *Muselmänner*, "one hesitates to call them living; one hesitates to call their death death."

It cannot be stressed enough that, despite these unprecedented, superhuman efforts to murder Jewish martyrdom, countless nameless Akivas managed to sanctify God's name by choosing how to die, even though robbed of the choice of whether to die; their memory must have a special sacredness to God and man. Such memory is abused, however, if it is used to blot out, minimize, or even divert attention from the death of the children as yet unable to choose and the death of the *Muselmänner* who could choose no more.

That these four *nova* have made *Galut* Judaism untenable has found admirable expression in an ancient midrash that was originally intended to expound the then-new form of Judaism. In this midrash God, at the beginning of the great exile initiated by the destruction of the Temple in 70 C.E., exacts three oaths, one from the gentiles and two from the Jews. The gentiles are made to swear not to persecute the Jews, now stateless and helpless, excessively. The Jews are made to swear not to resist their persecutors, and not to "climb the wall," that is, prematurely to return to Jerusalem.

But what, one must ask, if not Auschwitz, is "excessive persecution"? In response, some have said that the Jews broke their oath by climbing the wall, that is, by committing the sin of Zionism, and that in consequence God at

Auschwitz released the gentiles from obligation. Any such attempt to save *Galut* Judaism, however, reflects mere desperation, for it lapses into two blasphemies: toward the innocent children and the guiltless *Muselmänner*, and toward a God who is pictured as deliberately, callously, consigning them to their fate. There remains, therefore, only a bold and forthright taking leave from *Galut* Judaism. It was the gentiles at Auschwitz who broke their oath, and the Jews in consequence are now released from theirs.

A "post-*Galut* Judaism" Judaism is, unmistakably, in the making in our time. Its most obvious aspects are that "resisting" the persecutors and "climbing the wall" have become not only rights but also ineluctable duties. After the Holocaust, Jews owe anti-Semites, as well as, of course, their own children, the duty of not encouraging murderous instincts by their own powerlessness. And after the absolute homelessness of the twelve Nazi years that were equal to a thousand, they owe the whole world, as well as, of course, their own children, the duty to say no to Jewish wandering, to return home, to rebuild a Jewish state.

These aspects of the Judaism in the making are moral and political. Their inner source is spiritual and religious. In the Warsaw Ghetto Rabbi Isaac Nissenbaum, a famous and respected orthodox rabbi, made the statement—much quoted by Jews of all persuasions in their desperate efforts to defend, preserve, and hallow Jewish life against an enemy sworn to destroy it all—that this was a time not for *kiddush ha-Shem* (martyrdom) but rather for *kiddush ha-hayyim* (the sanctification of life). It is a time for *kiddush ha-hayyim* still. The Jewish people have passed through the Nazi antiworld of death; thereafter, by any standard, religious or secular, Jewish life ranks higher than Jewish death, even if it is for the sake of the divine name. The Jewish people have experienced exile in a form more horrendous than ever dreamt of by the apocalyptic imagination; thereafter, to have ended exile bespeaks a fidelity and a will to live that, taken together, give a new dimension to piety. The product of this fidelity—the Jewish state—is fragile still, and embattled wherever the world is hostile or does not understand. Yet Jews both religious and secular know in their hearts that Israel—the renewed people, the reborn language, the replanted land, the rebuilt city, the state itself—is a new and unique celebration of life. There are many reasons why Israel has become the center of the Jewish people in our time; not least is that it is indispensable to a future Judaism. If a Jewish state had not arisen in the wake of the Holocaust, it would be a religious necessity—although, one fears, a political near-impossibility—to create it now.

NOTES

1. See the warnings voiced by Yehuda Bauer.
2. Manés Sperber, . . . *Than a Tear in the Sea* (1967), xiii.
3. Quoted in *The Yellow Spot: The Extermination of the Jews in Germany* (1936), 47.
4. Hitler, *Mein Kampf*, trans. R. Mannheim (1943), 60.

5. In a debate with Yaacov Herzog. See Yaacov Herzog, *A People That Dwells Alone* (1975), 31.

6. K. D. Bracher, *The German Dictatorship* (1971), 430.

7. Isaac Deutscher, *The Non-Jewish Jew* (1968), 163 ff.

8. A statement by Hans Jonas, made to Ernst Simon as reported in the latter's "Revisionist History of the Jewish Catastrophe," *Judaism*, 12, no. 4 (Summer 1963), 395.

9. See esp. Martin Heidegger's *Sein und Zeit* (1935), sec. II, chap. 1.

10. Theodor Adorno, *Negative Dialektik* (1966), 354 ff.

11. Primo Levi, *Survival in Auschwitz*, trans. Stuart Woolf (1959), 82.

12. See, e.g., Hannah Arendt, *Eichmann in Jerusalem: A Report on the Banality of Evil* (1977).

13. Franklin Littell, *The Crucifixion of the Jews* (1975).

14. Arthur A. Cohen, *The Tremendum* (1981).

15. Emil L. Fackenheim, *To Mend the World: Foundations of Future Jewish Thought* (1982).

16. Dietrich Bonhoeffer as quoted in *The German Church Struggle and the Holocaust*, ed. Franklin H. Littell and Hubert G. Locke (1974), 288.

17. Johann Baptist Metz in *Gott Nach Auschwitz* (1979), 124 ff., 139 ff.

18. H. H. Henrix, F. M. Marquardt, M. Stoehr, all in personal conversation with this writer. The formulation is Henrix's.

19. The German Lutheran theologian Martin Wittenberg, as quoted in *Auschwitz als Herausforderung für Juden und Christen*, ed. G. B. Ginzel (1980), 566.

20. See Maimonides in his *Responsum on Martyrdom*.

21. A celebrated and much-quoted dictum by the German Jewish poet Heinrich Heine.

EMIL L. FACKENHEIM

◼ The Holocaust and the State of Israel

Their Relation

I. HOPE

> Our Father in Heaven, the Rock of Israel and her Redeemer, bless Thou the state
> of Israel, the beginning of the dawn of our redemption. . . .

This prayer by the Israeli Chief Rabbinate does not hesitate to describe the
state of Israel as "the beginning of the dawn of the redemption" of the Jewish
people. That the official rabbinate of Israel should formulate such a prayer
is in itself surprising: what is positively astonishing, however, is its wide acceptance by Jews everywhere. Religious Jews inside and outside Israel recite it
in the synagogue, and secularist Israelis, who neither frequent synagogues nor
recite prayers, recite *this* prayer, as it were, not with their lips but with their
lives. . . .

The modern Zionist movement originally appears on the scene as another
normalization effort, and, indeed, at one extreme one so radical as total assimilation is at the other. No Jewish self-classification as "religious denomination"
or "ethnic subculture" can ever be quite successful, not the one because one is
born a Jew, not the other because one is somehow obliged to remain one, and
various identity-crises reflect these difficulties. In contrast, Zionism characteris-
tically seems to come on the scene with the aim of making Jews "a nation like
any other nation," just as, at the opposite extreme, assimilationism aims at dissolving Jews *into* other nations. Thus Jewish "normalization" seems complete
only at the extremes.

However, as Zionism unfolds in thought and action, it gradually emerges
that the messianic future, ignored or even repudiated, lives on within it, changed
or unchanged, as the hidden inspiration without which the movement cannot
survive. To be sure, Herzl's "If you will it, it is no dream" is a strikingly secularist appeal, exalting as it does the will above all else: it may even be understood
as an anti-religious protest. Yet the goal aimed at by this will is so radically at

---

Reprinted by permission of Georges Borchardt, Inc., Literary Agency.

odds with all the "natural" trends of modern history as to require a mainspring far deeper and more original than the imitation of the varieties of nineteenth-century European nationalism, and one more positive and radical than escape into "normalcy" from what was then known as antisemitism. To this day this deeper inspiration has found little articulation in Zionist *thought*. Yet had it not existed throughout Zionist *life*—from the days of the early settlers through the Yom Kippur War—Herzl's dream would either not have become real at all or else not have stayed real for long. No other twentieth-century "liberation movement" has had to contend with all (or any) of these problems: the reuniting of a people rent apart by vast culture gaps of centuries; the reviving of an ancient language; the recreation, virtually overnight, of self-government and self-defense in a people robbed of these arts for two millennia; to say nothing of defending a young state for a whole generation against overwhelming odds, and on a territory virtually indefensible. Only a will in touch with an absolute dimension could have come anywhere near solving these problems; and even those acting on this will may well be astonished by its accomplishments. Hence it has come to pass that the categories "religious" and "secularist" (whatever their undiminished validity in other contexts) have been radically shaken by the Zionist reality, a fact that has produced strange bedfellows. On one side, ultra-religious Jews waiting for God's Messiah and secularist Jews wanting neither God nor Messiah are united in hostility to the will that animates the Zionist reality, obtuse to its meaning. On the other side, religious Zionists do not count on miracles, while secularist Zionists have been known to be astonished. These two are united as well, if not when things appear normal, at any rate in those extreme moments when all appearances fall away and only truth remains.

IIA. CATASTROPHE

The Holocaust is unique in history, and therefore in Jewish history. Previously, genocide has been a means to such human (if evil) ends as power, greed, an extreme of nationalist or imperialist self-assertion, and at times this means may even have become, demonically, an end *beside* these others. In the Holocaust Kingdom genocide showed itself gradually to be *the sole ultimate end* to which all else—power, greed, and even "Aryan" self-assertion—were sacrificed, for "Aryan" had no other clear meaning than "not-non-Aryan." And since the Nazis were not antisemites because they were "racists" but rather racists because they were antisemites, the "non-Aryan" was, paradigmatically, the Jew. Thus the event belongs to Jewish and world history alike.

   Nor is "genocide" adequate to describe the Holocaust Kingdom. Torquemada burned Jewish bodies to save Jewish souls. Eichmann created a system which, by torturing with terror and hope, by assailing all human dignity and self-respect, was designed to destroy the souls of all available Jewish men, women, and children before consigning their bodies to the gas chambers. The Holocaust Kingdom was a celebration of degradation as much as of death, and of death as much as of degradation. The celebrants willingly or even enthusiastically descended into hell themselves, even as they created hell for their victims. As for the world—it tolerated the criminals and abandoned the innocents. Thus the Holocaust is not only a unique event: it is epoch-making. The world, just as the Jewish world, can never again be the same.

The event therefore resists explanation—the historical kind that seeks causes, and the theological kind that seeks meaning and purpose. More precisely, the better the mind succeeds with the necessary task of explaining what can be explained, the more it is shattered by its ultimate failure. What holds true of the Holocaust holds true also of its connection with the state of Israel. Here, too, the explaining mind suffers ultimate failure. *Yet it is necessary, not only to perceive a bond between the two events but also so to act as to make it unbreakable.*

Historians see a causal connection between the Holocaust and the foundation of the state of Israel. The reasoning is as follows. Had it not been for the European Jewish catastrophe, all the centuries of religious longing for Zion, all the decades of secularist Zionist activity, together with all such external encouragement as given by the Balfour Declaration, would have produced no more than a Palestinian ghetto. This might have been a community with impressive internal achievements but, rather than a "national home" for homeless Jews, it would have been itself at the mercy of some alien government of dubious benevolence. Only the Holocaust produced a desperate determination in the survivors and those identified with them, outside and especially within the *Yishuv,* ended vacillation in the Zionist leadership as to the wisdom of seeking political self-determination, and produced a moment of respite from political cynicism in the international community, long enough to give legal sanction to a Jewish state. Even so "the UN resolution of 1947 came at the last possible moment."[1]

This reasoning is plausible; no more so, however, than its exact opposite. Why were the survivors not desperate to stay away from Palestine rather than reach it—the one place on earth which would tie them inescapably to a Jewish destiny? (After what that destiny had been to them, the desire to hide or flee from their Jewishness would have been "natural.") Why did the Zionist leadership rise from vacillation to resoluteness rather than simply disintegrate? (Confronted by absolute enemies, it was at the mercy of its friends.) As for the world's respite from political cynicism, this was neither of long duration nor unambiguous while it lasted. Ernest Bevin and his Colonial Office were rendered more—not less—intransigent to Zionist pressures by the catastrophic loss of lives and power which the Jewish people had just suffered. And the five Arab armies that "surged in upon the nascent Israeli nation to exterminate it and make themselves its immediate heirs" were "encouraged by the way Hitler had practiced genocide without encountering resistance."[2] Thus while, as previously argued, the state of Israel after the Holocaust may be viewed as a near necessity, yet we now see that it may be viewed, with equal justice, as a near impossibility. Historical explanation falls short in this manner because all human responses to the Holocaust are ultimately incalculable.

If historical explanations (seeking merely causes) remain precarious, theological explanations (seeking nothing less than meaning and purpose) collapse altogether, not because they are theological but because they are explanations. They fail whether they *find* a purpose, such as punishment for sin, or merely *assert* a purpose without finding it, such as a divine will, purposive yet inscrutable. This theological failure is by no means overcome if the Holocaust is considered as a means, inscrutable but necessary, to no less an end than the "dawn of redemption," of which in turn the state of Israel is viewed as the necessary "beginning." No meaning or purpose will ever be found in the event, and one does not glorify God by associating his will with it. Indeed, the very attempt is a sacrilege. (I have elsewhere argued that Jewish thought at its deepest level, especially vis-à-vis catastrophe, does not express itself in explanatory systems but rather in conflicting Midrashim, the goal of which is not how to explain God but how to live with him. Radicalizing the midrashic approach, I have also argued that to find a meaning in the Holocaust is impossible, but to seek a response is inescapable.)[3]

What then must be said of such as Rabbi Israel Shapiro of the city of Grodzisk who told his Jews at Treblinka that *these* were at last the *real* birth-pangs of the Messiah, that they all were blessed to have merited the honor of being the sacrifices, and that their ashes would serve to purify all Israel?[4]

First, this response must be revered *as a response;* however—in equal reverence for all the innocent millions, the children included, who had neither the ability, nor the opportunity, nor the desire, to be willing martyrs—it must be *rid totally of every appearance of being an explanation.* Did God *want* Auschwitz? Even the ancient rabbis sometimes seem to view the messianic birth-pangs not as a means used by a purposive (if inscrutable) divine will, but rather as, so to speak, a cosmic catastrophe which must occur before divine power and mercy can find their redemptive manifestation.

Second, Rabbi Shapiro's extreme of pious hope must be juxtaposed by opposites no less pious and no less to be revered. The pious men of a *shtibl* in the Lodz Ghetto spent a whole day fasting, praying, reciting psalms, and then, having opened the holy ark, convoked a solemn *din Torah,* and forbade God to punish his people any further. (Elsewhere God was put on trial—and found guilty.)[5] And in the Warsaw Ghetto a handful of Jews, ragged, alone, poorly armed, carried out the first uprising against the Holocaust Kingdom in all of Europe. The rabbis showed religious piety when, rather than excuse God or curse him, they cited his own promises against him. The fighters showed secular piety when, rather than surrender to the Satanic Kingdom, they took up arms against it. The common element in these two responses was not hope but rather despair. To the rabbis who found him guilty, the God who had broken his promises in the Holocaust could no longer be trusted to keep *any* promise, the messianic included. And precisely when hope had come to an end the fighters took to arms—in a rebellion that had no hope of succeeding.

With this conclusion, every explanatory connection between the Holocaust and the state of Israel has broken down, the causal historical kind in part, the teleological religious kind entirely, and even the hope connecting the one event with the other competes with despair. Yet, as we have said, it is necessary not only to preceive a bond between the two events but also so to connect them as to make the bond unbreakable. Such a bond is *possible* because to seek a *cause or a meaning* is one thing, to give a *response* is another. And it is necessary because the heart of every *authentic* response to the Holocaust—religious and secularist, Jewish and non-Jewish—is a commitment to the autonomy and security of the state of Israel.

IIB. RESPONSE

The Chronicler Yosef Gottfarstein reports:

> The Jews of Kelmé, Lithuania, were already standing beside the pits which they had been forced to dig for themselves—standing ready to be slain for the Sanctification of the Name. Their spiritual leader, Rabbi Daniel, asked the German officer in command of the operation to allow him to say some parting words to his flock, and the latter agreed, but ordered Rabbi Daniel to be brief. Speaking serenely, slowly, as though he were delivering one of his regular Sabbath sermons in the synagogue, Rabbi Daniel used his last minutes on earth to encourage his flock to perform Kiddush Hashem in the proper manner. Suddenly the German officer cut in and shouted at the rabbi to finish so that he could get on with the shooting. Still speaking calmly, the rabbi concluded as follows: "My dear Jews! The moment has come for us to perform the precept of Kiddush Hashem of which we have spoken, to perform it in fact! I beg one thing of you: don't get excited and confused; accept this judgment calmly and in a worthy manner!"
>
> Then he turned to the German officer and said: "I have finished. You may begin."

Gottfarstein continues:

> . . . At Kedainiai the Jews were already inside the pit, waiting to be murdered by the Germans, when suddenly a butcher leaped out of the pit, pounced on the German officer in command, and sank his teeth into the officer's throat, holding on till the latter died.
>
> When Rabbi Shapiro, the last Rabbi of Kovno, was asked which of these two acts he thought was more praiseworthy, he said: There is no doubt that Rabbi Daniel's final message to his flock concerning the importance of the precept of Kiddush Hashem was most fitting. But that Jew who sank his teeth into the German's throat also performed the precept in letter and in spirit, because the precept includes the aspect of action. "I am sure that if the opportunity had presented itself, Rabbi Daniel would also have been capable of doing what the butcher did," Rabbi Shapiro added.[6]

"I have finished. You may begin." We search all history for a more radical contrast between pure, holy goodness and a radical evil utterly and eternally beyond all redemption. The German officer saw what he saw. He heard what he heard. So did his men, How then could even one go on with the shooting? Yet they all did.

This unredeemable evil must have been in Rabbi Shapiro's mind when he did not hesitate to rank a simple, presumably ignorant, and perhaps not very pious butcher with a saintly rabbi learned in the ways of the Torah and earnestly obeying its commandments. For us who come after, the resistance as faith and dignity of Rabbi Daniel and his flock, the *kiddush ha-Shem* of the butcher, and the judgment concerning these two forms of testimony made by Rabbi Shapiro of Kovno, itself a form of testimony, are nothing less than a dual revelation: a holy dignity-in-degradation, a heroic war against Satanic death—each a resistance to the climax of a millennial, unholy combination of hatred of Jews with Jewish powerlessness which we are bidden to end forever.

To listen to this relevation is inevitably to be turned from the rabbi who had only his faith and the butcher who had only his teeth to the Warsaw Ghetto fighters in their ragged dignity and with their wretched arms. Of the second day of the uprising one of the leaders, Itzhak Cukierman (Zukerman) reports:

> ... By following guerrilla warfare theory, we saved lives, added to our supply of arms and, most important, proved to ourselves that the German was but flesh and blood, as any man.
>
> And prior to this we had not been aware of this amazing truth! If one lone German appeared in the Ghetto the Jews would flee *en masse*, as would Poles on the Aryan side. ...
>
> The Germans were not psychologically prepared for the change that had come over the Jewish community and the Jewish fighters. They were seized with panic.[7]

Amazingly, the Holocaust Kingdom was breached. At least in principle, the millennial unholy combination was broken.

This fact recreated in Zuckerman hope in the midst of despair: "We knew that Israel would continue to live, and that for the sake of all Jews everywhere and for Jewish existence and dignity—even for future generations—only one thing would do: Revolt!"[8]

Another leader of the uprising, Mordecai Anielewicz, was to perish in the flames of the Ghetto. Yet in his last letter he wrote: "My life's aspiration is fulfilled. The Jewish self-defense has arisen. Blissful and chosen is my fate to be among the first Jewish fighters in the Ghetto." "Blissful" and "chosen" are almost exactly the words used by Rabbi Israel Shapiro of the city of Grodzisk as he led his flock to the crematoria of Treblinka, sure that their ashes would hasten the coming of the Messiah.

But *was* Jewish destiny so much as touched by the handfuls of desperate men and women in the ghettos and camps? And is it *true in any sense whatever* that the millennial, unholy combination of hatred of Jews and Jewish powerlessness has been so much as breached? Rabbi Shapiro was unable to sustain his faith in God without also clinging to the "aspect of action" in *kiddush ha-Shem*, as performed by the butcher. The fighters were unable to persist in their fight without staking their faith on future Jewish generations. Was not, in both cases, the faith groundless and hollow, overwhelmed by despair?

Mordecai Anielewicz died in May 1943. Named after him, kibbutz Yad Mordekhai was founded in the same year. Five years after Mordecai's death, almost to the day, a small band of members of the kibbutz bearing his name held off a well-equipped Egyptian army for five long days—days in which the defense of Tel Aviv could be prepared, days crucial for the survival of the Jewish state. The Warsaw Ghetto fighters had not, after all, been mistaken.

Their hope, however, had not been a rational one, much less a calculated prediction. It had been a blessed self-fulfilling prophecy, for the heroism and self-sacrifice of the prophets had been the indispensable element without which the prophecy could not have been fulfilled. The battle for Yad Mordekhai began in the streets of Warsaw. To this day the justly larger-than-life statue of Mordecai Anielewicz dominates the kibbutz named after him, reminding the forgetful and teaching the thoughtless that what links Rabbi Daniel, the butcher, the two Rabbis Shapiro, and the Ghetto fighters with Yad Mordekhai is neither a causal necessity nor a divine miracle, if these are thought of as divorced from human believing and acting. It is a fervent believing, turned by despair from patient waiting into heroic acting. It is an acting which through despair has recovered faith.

Behind the statue stands the shattered water tower of the kibbutz, a mute reminder that even after its climax the combination of hatred of Jews and Jewish powerlessness has not come to an end. However, the shattered tower is dwarfed by the statue, and is at its back. The statue faces what Mordecai longed for and never despaired of—green fields, crops, trees, birds, flowers, Israel.

> Our Father in Heaven, the Rock of Israel and her Redeemer, bless Thou the state of Israel, the beginning of the dawn of our redemption. Shield her with the wings of Thy love, and spread over her the tabernacle of Thy peace. . . ."

NOTES

1. Walter Laqueur, *A History of Zionism* (London: Weidenfeld & Nicolson, 1972; New York: Schocken, 1976), p. 593.

2. M. Sperber, . . . *Than a Tear in the Sea* (New York: Bergen-Belsen Memorial Press, 1967), p. XIV.

3. Emil Fackenheim, *Quest for Past and Future* (Bloomington: Indiana University Press, 1968; Boston: Beacon, 1970), chap. 1; and *God's Presence in History* (New York: New York University Press, 1970; New York: Harper Torchbook, 1973), chaps. 1 and 3.

4. Cited in M. M. Kasher, ed., *Haggadat Pesah Azri-Yisraelit* (New York: American Biblical Encyclopedia Society, 1950), p. 137.

5. *Ani Ma'amin* (Jerusalem: Mosad Ha-Rav Kook, 1965), p. 206.

6. "Kiddush Hashem over the Ages and Its Uniqueness in the Holocaust Period" in *Jewish Resistance during the Holocaust* (Jerusalem: Yad Vashem, 1971), p. 473.

7. Meyer Barkai, tr. and ed., *The Fighting Ghettos* (New York: Tower, 1962), pp. 26 ff.

8. Ibid., p. 30.

A. ROY ECKARDT

◼ Christians and Jews

Along a Theological Frontier

LECTURE I: FAITH UNDER THE JUDGMENT OF HISTORY

I am deeply appreciative of being allowed a place in the Hugh Th. Miller Lecture series. I should like to dedicate my presentations to the memory of a dear friend. Heinz David Leuner of Breslau and London.

It is now thirty-five years since I started to think about the Christian-Jewish relation. That may be a foolhardy announcement, in view of the limitations in what I have to say. The truth is that I can be of no primary aid in the historical and biblical areas; I may be of some help from ideational and moral standpoints.

I

In addressing ourselves to theological-frontier questions for Christians and Jews of today, we shall concentrate, first, upon "Faith under the judgment of history" and then in the second lecture upon "History under the judgment of faith." As a subtitle for both presentations (or, as I think about it, perhaps a substitute title for our whole time together), I submit "The Story of Some Children."

A passage of Elie Wiesel's work, *A Beggar in Jerusalem*, helps bring our whole problem into relief: " . . . the crowd keeps getting larger. Military personnel and officials, celebrities and journalists, all are streaming by in one continuous procession, along with rabbis and students, gathered from all over the city, from

---

From "Christians and Jews: Along a Theological Frontier," *Encounter* 40 (2): 89–127 (Spring 1979).

every corner of the land. Men, women and adolescents of every age, every origin and speaking every language, and I see them ascending toward the [Western] Wall, toward all that remains of their collective longing. Just like long ago, at Sinai, when they were given the Torah. Just like a generation ago, in the kingdom of night, when [the Torah] was taken back."[1]

Herein is focused our entire problem: The Torah, vehicle and treasure of faith, yet here taken back, evidently because of another event in time and place, an event called the kingdom of night. (Could it be that the kingdom of night saw, as well, the taking back of the Cross and the Resurrection?)

Is it so, then, that history—defined as realized event—is the judge of faith? Or is it so, contrariwise, that faith remains the judge of human history? Or, for that matter, are we obliged to sustain a dialectic between the two? When historical event is enabled to supervise and determine faith, will not the transcending and saving resources and norms of faith eventually dissipate? But when faith is permitted to determine the status and import of historical event, are not the values of a God-created humanity and of human obligation assailed? Conceivably, a worthful dialectic between faith and history will implement a required tension, or at least an unavoidable one, between spiritual affirmation and worldly humaneness.

The overall theological justification for the subjecting of faith to the judgment of history is the persuasion that God himself acts through the happenings of time and place. Here is exactly what it means to denominate Christianity and Judaism as historical religions. The judging of faith by historical event is nothing new in the story of Christianity. Indeed, this was precisely the method put forward by the church in her original evaluations of Judaism. We are met by the consequent paradox that the judging of faith by history may itself involve the work of faith. According to the Christian faith, the ultimate disposition of the dramas of history must come from beyond the stage of history. Nevertheless—to fill out our paradox—the critical assessing of history at the hands of faith is itself a historical act. As Martin Buber used to say, all religion is history.

II

A certain theological schema has intruded itself powerfully within the Christian tradition, a schema according to which the triad of Cross-Resurrection-Parousia is made into a solely determinative series of faith-events. As Professor Heinz Kremers of Germany's University of Duisburg comments adversely, in the thinking of many Christians such a concatenation as this transcends the ordinary realm of history, with the consequence that it will forever marshall priority, soteriologically speaking, over all historical happenings.[2] It is in keeping with this outlook that Alan T. Davies of Toronto University identifies the Crucifixion and the Resurrection—lying as they reputedly do along "the margin of history"—as qualifying "the extent to which Christian faith can accept new revelatory moments. . . ."[3] A ready consequence of this schema is that Christianity itself becomes a wholly transcendent "reality," which moves in entirely "spiritual" ways above the flux and vagaries of history. Events of the in-between time are treated interstitially: history is remanded to a collection of interstices between the original truth-event of sacred history and a decisive, coming truth-event. These latter become the only truth-events that count. From this perspective, such a happening as the kingdom of night, the German Nazi Holocaust of the Jews, possesses no significance for faith.

However, it would be most unwarranted to construe the dialogue between Christianity and Jewishness as involving, respectively, a transcendentalist outlook and a non-transcendentalist one. Jewish thinking and life are themselves not entirely devoid of the interstitial viewpoint—as witness those Jews who have identified their Holocaust as no different in kind from other evils that have beset the people of God throughout history. It is told, indeed, that certain pious Jews sang and danced their way into the gas chambers and crematoria—as though the Holocaust of their people were of no real consequence, were, in effect, a non-event.[4] Again, some ultra-Orthodox Jews, including, strikingly enough, certain ones who reside within *Eretz Yisrael* itself, wholly reject the legitimacy of today's Jewish state—for the reason that only the coming Messiah can implement a Jewish polity.

On the other side of the arena, the noted philosopher Emil L. Fackenheim recently confessed: "Authentic Jewish theology cannot possess the immunity I once gave it, *for its price is an essential indifference to all history between Sinai and the Messianic days."*[5] Fackenheim has been brought up short, and shatteringly so, by the cruciality of the Holocaust of his people. And I remember well the day a non-religious Jewish friend at Kibbutz Yad Mordechai in the western Negev took my wife and me through their museum exhibit of the Holocaust of Polish Jewry. As we emerged into the sunshine, his arm swept across the surrounding countryside, and he said, "You have seen our crucifixion; now, please, behold our resurrection."

It is obvious as well that some spokesmen of the Christian faith are prepared to find decisive theological meaning in contemporary happenings—as examples, the United Methodist historian Franklin H. Littell, who characterizes the Holocaust of the Jews and the establishing of the Third Jewish Commonwealth as "alpine events" within twentieth-century Christendom,[6] and the Episcopalian Paul van Buren, who writes that Christian "theology can shut its eyes and pretend that the Holocaust never happened and that Israel doesn't exist. . . . But if there are prospects for serious theology, for a theology not hopelessly blind to matters that pertain to the heart of its task, then the time has come for a reconsideration of the whole theological and Christian enterprise of the most radical sort. . . ."[7]

If we are correct that today's Christian-Jewish dialectic cannot be identified in simple terms as an instance of transcendentalism versus historicalness, nevertheless the very fact that the Holocaust of the Jews and the inaugurating of the Third Jewish Commonwealth involve primarily the Jewish community means that through these very events the issue may be joined today between a transcendentalist faith that boasts imperviousness to worldly happenings, and a faith confessedly open to the wounding contingencies of time and space. Is it the case that the Jewish Holocaust and a reemerging Israel are special events for Christians, and if they are, in what explicit ways are we called to speak of, and to relate to, these events?

III

The possible Christian relevance of the Holocaust of the Jews is sometimes held to turn upon the charge that something in Christianity, in Christian teachings, and in the life and behavior of Christians helped to bring about and to implement the German Nazi *Endlösung der Judenfrage*, the "Final Solution of the Jewish question." In recent literature a most oftcited historical aphorism is that of Raul Hilberg in his influential work *The Destruction of the European Jews:* "The missionaries of Christianity had said in effect: You have no right to live among us as Jews. The secular rulers who followed had proclaimed: You have no right to live among us. The German Nazis at last decreed: You have no right to live."[8]

The British scholar and Anglican clergyman James Parkes, greatest historian of the Christian-Jewish relation, writes: The hatred and denigration of the Jewish people

> have a quite clear and precise historical origin. They arise from Christian preaching and teaching from the time of the bitter controversies of the first century in which the two religions separated from each other. From that time up to today there has been an unbroken line which culminates in the massacre in our own day of six million Jews. The fact that the action of Hitler and his henchmen was not really motivated by Christian sentiments, the fact that mingled with the ashes of murdered Jews are the ashes of German soldiers who refused to obey orders . . . , the fact that churches protested and that Christians risked their lives to save Jews—all these facts come into the picture, but unhappily they do not invalidate the basic statement that anti-semitism from the first century to the twentieth is a Christian creation and a Christian responsibility, whatever secondary causes may come into the picture.[9]

Why should Professor Littell characterize the Holocaust of the Jews and the reestablishing of political Israel as "alpine events" within contemporary Christendom? He declares:

> The cornerstone of Christian Antisemitism is the superseding or displacement myth, which already rings with the genocidal note. This is the myth that the mission of the Jewish people was finished with the coming of Jesus Christ, that "the old Israel" was written off with the appearance of "the new Israel." To teach that a people's mission in God's providence is finished, that they have been relegated to the limbo of history, has murderous implications which murderers will in time spell out. The murder of six million Jews by baptized Chris-

tians, from whom membership in good standing was not (and has not yet been) withdrawn, raises the most insistent question about the credibility of Christianity. The existence of a restored Israel, proof positive that the Jewish people is not annihilated, assimilated, or otherwise withering away, is substantial refutation of the traditional Christian myth about their end in the historic process. And this is precisely why Israel is a challenge, a crisis for much contemporary Christian theology.[10]

And why should Paul van Buren argue that the *Endlösung* necessitates a radical reconsideration of the entire Christian theological enterprise? He explains: "The roots of Hitler's final solution are to be found in the proclamation of the very *kerygma* of the early Christians. . . . [The command out of Auschwitz] is that we accept a judgment on something false lying close to the very heart of our tradition. . . ."[11]

Finally, the Canadian Catholic scholar Gregory Baum is cited: "What Auschwitz has revealed to the Christian community is the deadly power of its own symbolism." The "anti-Jewish thrust of the church's preaching" is not a historical, psychological, or sociological matter; "it touches the very formulation of the Christian gospel." Along with Parkes, Littell, and van Buren, Professor Baum concentrates upon the realities of Christian triumphalism and supersessionism in the presence of the Jews and Judaism, or upon what Father John Pawlikowski of Chicago calls "the theology of substitution," which (again citing Baum) "assigns the Jews to the darkness of history,"[12] rejected by God and man, in ways that could only end in the camps of murder. In the Nazi Final Solution "the theological negation of Judaism and the vilification of the Jewish people" within the Christian tradition were, at the last, translated into the genocide of the Jews.[13]

Of the multiplying of citations there is no end. And that practice may not settle very much. Historical analysis, however expert, does not end disputation—although in the present case the varied backgrounds of the many new historiographers (I have quoted only a few[14]) and the weighty consensus of their findings combine to demand careful and sober attention. One counterpoint may be inserted: That the anti-Jewish element in Christianity is not beyond exception is illustrated in the fact—if I may venture a personal note—that through all the years my wife and I were growing up actively in the Methodist Church, we never heard any such thing as Christian anti-Jewishness, and we did not really learn of it until Christian and other scholars apprised us of the phenomenon in our twenties.

The general question of the nature and *élan vital* of causation, not excepting historical causation, has been enigmatic for a long time—particularly since David Hume (though not "because" of him!). However, a salient fact travels as a silent and haunting partner with the new historiography: so large a number of the contemporary analysts are Christians. They are speaking of the historical fate of Jews. But in the very act of doing this, they summon attention to their own identity. For their identity as human beings is tied to someone who was himself a Jew, someone who, had he by some miracle been living in the "right" time and place, would have been dispatched to a Nazi gas chamber or crematorium. And, in all probability, his execution would have been brought off by men who were themselves Christians, and who were thus related to the very one whom they would have been destroying.

Thus does the new historiography of the church's place in the Holocaust of the Jews convey, *in and of itself, and quite independent of the specific historical theorization*, a metahistorical dimension, a dimension by means of which such categories as incredibility and revulsion and mystery inexorably gain entry, not to mention the categories of relevance, of moral decision, of culpability. "Jesus was a Jew"—in these four short words is established forever the bond between Christianity and the Holocaust of the Jews (as also the Third Jewish Commonwealth). These events become "alpine events" for Christians in a most elementary way: by the mere facts of the Jewishness of these events and, more importantly, by the very nature of Christian historical identity and destiny. How often are elementary and plain truths obscured by the artifices of history and the machinations of men!

The consequence indicated, the alpine character of the events under discussion, appears against the aura of an absolutely singular development within *Heilsgeschichte* (the story of salvation). For the effort was now carried forward to ensure that there would not be a single Jew upon Planet Earth.[15] The *ganze Einzigartigkeit*, the unique uniqueness, the only-ness of the Final Solution is disclosed in the fact that all Jewish babies were to be killed along with all children and grownups. This had never been the case, in 4,000 years. It is the historical *identity* of these victims that marks off this event from other horrible events, including other "holocausts." But the only-ness of the *Endlösung* is also, ultimately speaking, theological in nature. As William Jay Peck writes, after Auschwitz "the very being of God" is "tied up with the problem of murder."[16]

The Holocaust of the Jews splits the story of our world into two epochs: B.F.S., "Before the Final Solution," and F.S., "In the Year of the Final Solution." We are meeting in the year 38 F.S., since the traditional date 1941 is probably best identified as year one of the Holocaust of the Jews.[17]

IV

What are the possible judgments of the Holocaust of the Jews upon the life of faith? Earlier Professor Fackenheim was cited: Authentic Jewish theology can no longer be granted immunity to the history between Sinai and the messianic days; the *Endlösung* has intervened. And what about Christians? Can they permit themselves to retain an essential indifference to the history between Jesus of Nazareth and the End of days?

In order to face up to these questions, we shall single out five themes: the Jewish people and the person and claim of Jesus; Christian conversionism and the Jews; the Covenant and the trial of God; the Crucifixion of Jesus; and, lastly, the Resurrection.

In the first place, among socially fateful religious teachings has been the allegation that the Jewish people have failed to honor the divine opportunity to accept Jesus as the Messiah, and are deservedly chastised by God for the rejection.

What are we to say to this? Martin Buber has written: "Standing bound and shackled in the pillory of mankind, we [Jews] demonstrate with the bloody body of our people the unredeemedness of the world."[18] The Jew "feels this lack of redemption against his skin, he tastes it on his tongue, the burden of the unredeemed world lies on him."[19] The original, majority Jewish response to the possible messiahship of Jesus was, and stays so today, that his subjection to the Roman overlords, in contrast to his potential role of helping to destroy Rome, indicated the non-messianic character of Jesus. Jewish insistence that Jesus of Nazareth could not possibly be the promised Messiah of Israel, sustained as this conviction is by several thousands of years experience of the unredeemedness of the historical order, gained terminal authentication in the *Endlösung*. Climactic and, indeed, eschatological proof was furnished in and through the Holocaust of the Jews, administered as that event was by those who represented redemption of both a Christian and a non-Christian kind.

Jewish non-acceptance of Jesus as Messiah remains among the most sublime and heroic instances of Israel's faithfulness to her Covenant with God.[20]

V

A second theme is Christian conversionism directed at the Jewish people. This theme is a striking case of the convergence of faith and history, and a reminder that our present division between those two areas is analytical as much as it is substantive. On the one hand, it may be argued that any Christian attempt to missionize Jews comprises an implicit assault upon the Israel of God, the foundation of the church, and accordingly is self-refuting and self-destructive. If the Jewish people are not the elder brothers and sisters within God's family, it would appear that the gentiles as reputedly adopted younger brothers and sisters are still in their sins, and remain lost and without hope, "outside God's covenants and the promise that goes with them" (cf. Ephes. 2:1–13). The Covenant into which the gentiles are ostensibly led by the event of Jesus the Jew becomes a delusion.

From the standpoint of this reaction, the effort to convert Jews to Christianity is identifiable as a veiled attack, perhaps unknowingly, upon the Christian faith itself. Conversionism is a Christian impossibility—not for those pragmatic reasons so dear to the hearts of Americans, but for reasons of Christian theological principle.

On the other hand, the *Judenmission*, the organized effort to "save" Jews, is confronted by the judgment of history. The Final Solution helps to bring home the dreadful consequences of the entrenched program to convert Jews. Among some Christians of contemporary Germany, a shattering phrase has gained currency: *eine geistliche Endlösung*, "a spiritual Final Solution." Within the front rank of concerned Christian scholars in Germany today stands Rudolf Pfisterer of Schwäbisch-Hall. Dr. Pfisterer emphasizes that the *Judenmission*, the Christian mission to the Jews, is, in his words, "nothing more than the continuing work of the Final Solution." For, in the last resort, what is the moral difference between stuffing Jews into gas chambers and mass graves, and striking at the very heart of their religious integrity?[21] Here is a terrible reminder that Christian supersessionism and triumphalism, which helped ensure the Holocaust of the Jews, are also contemporaneous embodiments and fulfillments of the German Nazi program. Yet we should never have been led to think in these terms had it not been for the *Endlösung*. The judgments of history are strange, and sometimes they are saving judgments.

VI

A third theme is the Covenant and the trial of God.

We have referred to the taking back of the Torah in the kingdom of night. Could it be that it was God himself who withdrew the teaching and turned his face, because of the acts of his people? Did Israel betray the divine Covenant, and thus stand condemned? The Council of the Evangelical Church of Germany meeting in Darmstadt solemnly asserted that the suffering of the Jews under the Nazis was God's punishment. The Council called upon the Jewish people to desist from their rejection of Christ and from their ongoing crucifixion of him.[22] The date of the meeting? Three years after the ending of the Holocaust.

The *Beggar in Jerusalem* speaks again to us. There is much laughter in that tale. For the most part, it is terrible, maniacal laughter. According to Rabbi Nachman of Bratzlav, somewhere in the world there is a certain city that encompasses all other cities. In this city is a street that contains all the other streets of the city; on that street is a house dominating all the other houses; it contains a room that comprises all the other rooms of the house. "And in that room there lives a man in whom all other men recognize themselves. And that man is laughing. That's all he ever does, ever did. He roars with laughter when seen by others, but also when alone."[23]

Is there something special for this man to laugh at now, in 1978? (By "1978," we mean, of course, 1933 to 1945, or 8 B.F.S. to 5 F.S.) Yes, there is a special occasion for laughter. The man is particularly laughing in this moment because of the context of the withdrawing of the Torah: it was *in the kingdom of night* that the Torah was taken back. Accordingly, it would appear that someone who identifies the *Endlösung* as God's act of condemnation of his people is subject to confinement, where he will be obliged to listen, without surcease, to the laughter of that man in that room in that house upon that street within that city which is the world. For, just a few pages earlier in *A Beggar in Jerusalem*, a young madman, one of only three survivors who had escaped the deportation, has put the ineluctable question: "How does God justify himself in his own eyes, let alone in ours? If the real and the imaginary both culminate in the same scream, in the same laugh, what is creation's purpose, what is its stake?"[24] The character Gregor in Wiesel's *Gates of the Forest* finally grasped the meaning of the Jewish Holocaust: the event implicated not only Abraham and his son Isaac, "but their God as well."[25] If, indeed, the *Endlösung der Judenfrage* is an act of judgment, must not the judgment be addressed, in the very first instance, to God himself, as against the people of God? Could it be, then, that when the Torah was withdrawn, it was taken away, not from Israel, but instead from the King of the Universe?

In recent thinking, Jewish and Christian, no one has posed this kind of query more relentlessly than our colleague Richard L. Rubenstein. The question is here raised, not of the impossibility or objective negation of all divine-human covenants (as Rubenstein goes so far as to conclude), but instead of the obliterating of the Covenant of special demands upon Israel—this, in contradistinction to a Covenant of promise, of assurance.

From this standing-ground, a moral indictment is entered against the Lord of hosts—this God who, as Rabbi Eliezer Berkovits puts it, "is responsible for having created a world in which man is free to make history."[26] Once upon a time God mandated that his chosen ones be "a kingdom of priests and a holy nation" (Exod. 19:6). As a consummation of this demand, in the kingdom of night his elect could be transubstantiated into *Unmenschen*, the bacilli from below. The original sin of God—a sin in which Christians, Muslims, and others were to become most ready and available accomplices—was the sin of applying the absolute divine perfection to the lives of ordinary human creature. The accusation entered against God is no less than one of implicit Satanism. No plea of innocence appears open to him. No appeal seems available to him. He stands condemned, guilty as charged. All that is left for him is an act of penitence. In the shadow of the gas chambers and the crematoria, God is required, not alone to express genuine sorrow for his place in the unparalleled agony of his people, but to promise that he will not sin again, that he won't have anything to do with such suffering in the future. In Elie Wiesel's *Souls on Fire* Rabbi Levi-Yitzhak reminds God that he had better ask forgiveness for the hardships he has inflicted upon his children. This is why the phrase Yom Kippur also appears in the plural, Yom Kippurim; "the request for pardon is reciprocal."[27]

The consequence of the juridical-moral trial of God is the eclipse of the Covenant of demand. The myth of the Jews as "suffering servant" will surrender its loathsomeness only as that Covenant is granted a proper funeral.[28]

VII

Let us consider the theme of the Cross of Jesus. Could it be, the question was raised at the beginning, that with the advent of the kingdom of night, the Cross was also taken back?

A study by Jürgen Moltmann of the University of Tübingen, entitled *The Crucified God*, is of first importance, illustratively and substantively, to this our fourth theme. The theme has two aspects: on the one hand the historical-moral fate of the Cross as a Christian symbol, especially in its linkage to the Resurrection, as emphasized by Professor Moltmann; and, on the other hand, the historical-moral difficulty created by Moltmann's advocated link between the Cross and ultimate horribleness.

We are told by Moltmann that Christ's "death is the death of the one who redeems men from death, which is evil."[29] No, in the Nazi time the message of the Cross assisted in *bringing* death, the polar contrary of the "pains of love." The "crucified Christ" simply cannot be separated from what has happened to, and been done to, the Cross. Professor Moltmann tries to argue that the Cross "does not divide Christians from Jews."[30] In truth, countless Jews of our world will never be enabled to distinguish the Cross from the *Hakenkreuz* (the "hook-cross," the swastika), nor can they be expected to do so. It was after the Holocaust of the Jews that a Jewish woman, catching sight of a huge cross displayed in New York City at Christmastime, said to her walking companion, Father Edward H. Flannery: "That cross makes me shudder. It is like an evil presence."[31] It was in and through the *Endlösung* that the symbol of the Cross was taken captive by ultimate devilishness. When asked by two bishops in 1933 what he was going to do about the Jews, Adolf Hitler could readily answer that he would do to them exactly what the Christian church had been advocating and practicing for almost two thousand years.[32]

Professor Moltmann declares: "The poverty and sufferings of Christ are experienced and understood *only* by participation in his mission and in imitating the task he carried out. Thus the more the poor understand the cross . . . as the cross of *Christ*, the more they are liberated from their submission to fate and apathy in suffering."[33] No, in stark truth the millions of Jews[34] were *not* liberated, from death or from other suffering. They were not liberated at all, through "understanding" or any other factor. Moltmann goes on: "'Resurrection, life, and righteousness' come through the death of this one man in favor of those who have been delivered over to death through their unrighteousness." No, history replies. The Jews did not "qualify" as unrighteous—nor, for that matter, as righteous. They were just murdered. And they were murdered just because they were Jews—not good Jews or bad Jews or any other kind of Jews, but just Jews. What does it mean to tell the inmates of Buchenwald or Bergen-Belsen, as this Christian theologian does, that "through his suffering and death, the risen Christ brings righteousness and life to the unrighteous and the dying?"[35]

However, the truly decisive consideration is that in the presence of Auschwitz, the claims that Jürgen Moltmann makes for Christian symbols and "virtues" have come to have the very opposite meanings and consequences from those he indicates. For now, within his own German history and within ours, the categories of "weakness"—he supplies them all—"weakness," "impotence," "vulnerability," "openness to suffering and love," "divine protection"[36] have all been transubstantiated into demonic structures. As Rabbi Irving Greenberg observes, in *our* world suffering only helps to "strengthen rampant evil and to collaborate in the enthronement of the devil."[37] The endlessly woeful consequence is that the Cross is robbed of its redemptiveness. All that remains upon the hill of Golgotha is unmitigated evil. After Auschwitz, a question mark is nailed to the Cross as the reputedly determinative symbol of redemptive suffering. From the point of view of the Holocaust of the Jews, God is not met on the Cross—even in his "Godforsakenness." Once upon a time he may have been met there, but he is met there no longer. For as we seek to behold Golgotha now, our sight is blocked by huge mounds of torn bodies and their ashes.

The other aspect of the question of the Cross—Moltmann's effort to link the Cross with ultimate horribleness—is the more weighty of the two, because it is not eligible for the possible rejoinder that, after all, the Cross transcends and is immune to a certain historical-moral fate, and thereby is able to retain its redemptive power, come what may.[38] Professor Moltmann also puts the Cross of Golgotha in unique association with Jesus' (allegedly) total Godforsakenness. Jesus' abandonment and deliverance up to death are held to constitute the very torment of hell.[39]

It may be suggested that this particular abomination simply does not stand up as the absolute horror upon which the Christian faith can and should, dialectically, build its hope. It may be contended that in comparison with certain other sufferings, Jesus' death becomes relatively nonsignificant.

The tale is told of a scene in Auschwitz in the late Summer of 1944. The gas chamber near the crematorium was out of order; it had been wrecked in a Jewish commando operation in August.

> The other gas chambers were full of adults and therefore the children were not gassed, but just burned alive. There were several thousand of them. When one of the SS sort of had pity, he would take a child and beat the head against a stone before putting it on the pile of fire and wood, so that the child lost consciousness. However, the regular way they did it was by just throwing the children onto the pile. They would put a sheet of wood there, then sprinkle the whole thing with petrol, then wood again, and petrol and wood, and petrol—and then they placed the children there. Then the whole thing was lighted.[40]

How is it still possible, if it ever was possible, to make the passion of the Jewish man, Jesus of Nazareth, *the* foundation of Christian faith? Jesus was at least a grown man, a mature man, a man with a mission, and by all the evidence a courageous man, who set his face steadfastly to go up to Jerusalem (Luke 9:51). In contrast, there has occurred within this world and within the present epoch an evil that is more terrible than other evils. This is the evil of small children witnessing the murders of other small children, *whilst knowing that they also are to be murdered in the same way*, being aware absolutely that they face the identical fate. Jürgen Moltmann's claim concerning Jesus and his Godforsakenness reads like theology from before the Holocaust of the Jews. Though he writes today, Moltmann appears, at this juncture, to be living as though the events of the kingdom of night never transpired. The Godforsakenness of Jesus has proven to be non-absolute, if it ever was absolute, for there is now a Godforsakenness of Jewish children which is a final horror.

VIII

Our fifth and last theme, and the most crucial one, is that of the Resurrection. At the beginning we raised the question of whether not alone the Torah and the Cross, but also the Resurrection, were taken back in the kingdom of night.

James Parkes reminds us again and again that there is no way to build good theology upon bad history. Sometimes Parkes's counsel causes no special difficulties, since many theological testimonies have a solid base in historical fact: the Exodus from Egypt did occur, the Crucifixion of Jesus did take place. But what about the Resurrection of Jesus? Is that a historical event, an event of time and place, *of the same order* as the Crucifixion?

To seek to grapple with this question by making reference to the Holocaust of the Jews would appear to be absurd. But is it actually so that there are no connections?

In a piece in the *Journal of the History of Ideas* entitled "The Nazi Holocaust as a Persisting Trauma for the Non-Jewish Mind," Emil Fackenheim argues that in the post-Holocaust time, *the* central question for Christianity remains the link between Christian affirmation and Christian antisemitism.[41] No dogma is more central to traditional Christian affirmation than the Resurrection of Jesus Christ. It is as a means of facing up to such shattering allegations as this one from Fackenheim that some Christian theologians have been calling for a recovery of Jewishness within the church. But what is that recovery to mean? Christian spokesmen of today will sometimes be heard to stress that the scourge of Christian antisemitism demands a wholehearted rethinking of Christian teachings. Yet once these people have finished their presentations, they often have done little more than repeat, in attractive words perhaps, the very doctrines that have caused all the trouble. It seems to be a case of continuing Christian triumphalism—complete with guilt feelings.

The ultimate test case is the Resurrection—for three solid and related reasons. One of these was intimated just above. The faith of countless Christians has as its center the achieved Resurrection of Jesus. "If Christ has not been raised, . . . your faith is vain"—so writes the Apostle Paul to the Corinthians (I Cor. 15:14). Second, and accordingly, the one place where a reaffirmation of Jewishness could occur, were it to occur at all, would be in conjunction with the Resurrection. For, thirdly, in this context the recovery of Jewishness can only mean a certain interpretation of the applicability of historical judgment to the Resurrection, the radical assertion that the Resurrection has not happened.

In the presence of historical judgment the Resurrection is made problematic, quite apart from the Christian-Jewish encounter, and problematic in a unique way that does not apply to our earlier themes. The same Apostle Paul who insisted that without the Resurrection of Jesus Christ the Christian faith is vain, did not himself believe in the Resurrection—in the way that the writer of Luke 24 did. To Paul, the body that is sown is not the body that is raised. "Flesh and blood can never possess the kingdom of God, and the perishable cannot possess immortality" (I Cor. 15:35–57). But according to Luke 24—some are now arguing that Luke is the earliest Gospel[42] —"Jesus himself stood among them. . . . 'See my hands and my feet, that it is I myself; handle me, and see; for a spirit has not flesh and bones as you see that I have.' And while they still disbelieved for joy, and wondered, he said to them, 'Have you anything here to eat?' They gave him a piece of broiled fish, and he took it and ate before them" (Luke 21:36, 39–43). The controversy has never ceased. Christian Fundamentalism insists upon "the resurrection of the same body of Jesus which was three days buried."[43] Other Christians, unable to underwrite the resuscitation of a corpse, find consolation, or claim to in some form of Pauline transformationism, often aided by mythologistic, spiritualist, or experientalist contentions. This latter view is most difficult to sustain from the standpoint of strictly historical judgment, or logical historicist judgment, which holding as it does that an event is either realized or unrealized, either happens or does not happen, will suggest that either the Fundamentalists are correct or the Resurrection has not occurred.[44] There is not, alas, any third choice. This state of affairs brings us back to the Christian-Jewish confrontation.

In the frame of reference of our present subject, a particularly serious question arises: Is it really possible for the Christian church to preach the Resurrection in a non-triumphalist way? From the very wording of this question, the traditional message of Easter Day and the German Nazi *Endlösung* are seen to be fatefully linked.

The overall Christian plight respecting the Jewish people and Judaism is brought into clear focus in the combination of ideas presented by Wolfhart Pannenberg of the University of Munich. Pannenberg asserts that "through the cross of Jesus, the Jewish legal tradition as a whole has been set aside in its claim to contain the eternal will of God in its final formulation."[45] The "law" is consummated, fulfilled in Jesus. Typifying as he does the accustomed (and false) allegation within German and other biblical scholarship that Jesus himself stood in opposition to a hardened Jewish "law,"[46] Pannenberg calls upon the Resurrection to prove his charge: Jesus came into fundamental conflict "with the law itself, that is with the positive Israelite legal tradition which had become calcified [*sic!*] as 'the law' after the exile." However, through the resurrection of Jesus "the emancipation from this law was confirmed by the God of Israel himself."

Professor Pannenberg employs exactly the same reasoning in the matter of Jesus' alleged claim for his own person, and he uses this opportunity to resort to the old canard of Jewish complicity for Jesus' death: Jesus' "claim to authority, through which he put himself in God's place, was blasphemous for Jewish ears. Because of this, Jesus was then also slandered by the Jews before the Roman governor as a rebel. If Jesus really has been raised, this claim has been visibly and unambiguously confirmed by the God of Israel. . . ."[47]

In Wolfhart Pannenberg, we are supplied in a single package, with the major elements of the entire Christian historical-moral predicament vis-à-vis the Jewish people and Judaism: the Cross, the setting aside of "the law" through its "fulfillment" in Jesus, Jesus' own "opposition" to "the law," Jesus' "authority' as equal to that of God, and then the Resurrection[48] as the divine validation of these various points at which Christianity stands in judgment upon the Jewish people and their faith.[49] A value of Pannenberg's exposition is its pointing up the truth that the teaching of the achieved Resurrection of Jesus lies at the heart of Christian opposition and hostility to Judaism and the Jewish people. For only with that teaching does Christian triumphalism reach fulfillment. Only here are the various human and divine-human claims making up the church's dogmatic structure furnished with the capstone of an event which is said to be exclusively God's and that in this way vindicates every other claim. The representative of this ideology declares, in effect: 'It is not the Christian theologian to whom you Jews are to listen. The theologian is, after all, a fallible and sinful human being. Rather, let us have God decide the matter. But God's decision proves to be on the Christian side, not yours. *He* raised Jesus from the dead. Thus is the Christian shown to be right and you are shown to be wrong. In the Resurrection God himself *confirms* the Christian gospel, the Christian cause."

IX

The question is repeated, for it stands at the heart of history's judgment upon the Christian faith: Is it possible, or how is it possible, for the Christian church to proclaim the Resurrection of Jesus Christ in a non-triumphalist way? It is clear that although Professor Pannenberg is a Christian of Germany (or perhaps because he is a Christian of Germany?[50]), his theologizing is in no essential way affected by the Holocaust of the Jews. However, this is not the necessary fate of Christian thinkers and scholars in Germany or elsewhere. A passage from the young New Testament scholar Peter von der Osten-Sacken. Director of the *Institut Kirche und Judentum*, Berlin, will exemplify the opposite possibility and at the same time bring to summary-focus our initial lecture: "In view of the experience of history . . . the Gospel's claim to exclusive truth must be open to theological criticism inasmuch as it lends the Gospel . . . totalitarian features that are doomladen and destructive. This and nothing else is the issue when we seek to come to terms with the matter of Christian anti-Judaism. Once the link between the Gospels' totalitarian claim and Christian hostility to the Jews is realized, a new light falls on the relationship between political anti-Judaism as a totalitarian ideology and Christian anti-Judaism. Both are then seen to be closely and unsuspectedly akin."[51]

NOTES

1. Elie Wiesel, *A Beggar in Jerusalem*, translated from the French by Lily Edelman and the author, New York: Random House, 1970, pp. 199–200.

2. Heinz Kremers, communication to author, 19 November 1975.

3. Alan T. Davies, "Response to Irving Greenberg," in Eva Fleischner, ed., *Auschwitz: Beginning of a New Era? Reflections on the Holocaust.* New York: Ktav, 1977, pp. 61–62.

4. Cf. Moshe l'arger, *Sparks of Glory*, translated by Mordecai Schreiber, New York: Shengold Publishers, 1974, chap. 27 "The Dance in the Shadow of the Gas Chamber."

5. Emil L. Fackenheim, "The People Israel Lives," in Frank Ephraim Talmage, ed., *Disputation and Dialogue: Readings in the Jewish-Christian Encounter*, New York: Ktav, 1975, p. 304.

6. Franklin H. Littell, *The Crucifixion of the Jews*. New York: Harper & Row, 1975, p. 2.

7. Paul van Buren. "The Status and Prospects for Theology," *CCI Notebook* (Philadelphia), 24 (November 1975), 3. Van Buren's article is based on a paper read before the annual meeting of the American Academy of Religion in Chicago, November, 1975.

8. Raul Hilberg, *The Destruction of the European Jews*. Chicago: Quadrangle Books, rev. ed., 1967, pp. 3–4.

9. James Parkes, *The History of Jewish-Christian Relations*, unpublished address to the London Society of Jews and Christians, p. 3.

10. Littell, *The Crucifixion of the Jews*, p. 2. An example of a New Testament passage sometimes utilized to support the view that the Jews were dispersed from their land in keeping with God's punishment is Luke 21:20–24, where it is adjudged that "this people will be taken captive "among all nations; and Jerusalem will be trodden down by the Gentiles, until the times of the Gentiles are fulfilled."

11. Van Buren, "The Status and Prospects for Theology," p. 3.

12. Gregory G. Baum, *Christian Theology After Auschwitz* (Robert Waley Cohen Memorial Lecture), London: The Council of Christians and Jews, 1976, pp. 8, 9, 11.

13. Gregory Baum, Introduction to Rosemary Radford Ruether, *Faith and Fratricide: The Theological Roots of Anti-Semitism*, New York: Seabury Press, 1974, p. 8.

14. Others include Willehad P. Eckert, Edward H. Flannery, Eva Fleischner, Malcolm Hay, Friedrich Heer, Jules Isaac, Charlotte Klein, H. David Leuner, Guenther Lewy, Fadiey Lovsky, Reinhold Mayer, Rudolf Pfisterer, Léon Poliakov, Rosemary Ruether, Michael Ryan, Frederick M. Schweitzer, Marcel Simon, Martin Stöhr, and Karl Thieme.

15. Cf. Emil L. Fackenheim: "The Nazis were not antisemites because they were racists, but rather racists because they were antisemites" ("The Human Condition After Auschwitz: A Jewish Testimony a Generation After." *Congress Bi-Weekly* [New York], XXXIX, 7 [27 April 1972], 9).

    Any who doubt the singularity of the *Endlösung* may well reflect upon the current conspiracy to deny that it ever took place. Reference is made to the tacit murderers who are now engaged in killing the sufferers a second time, by taking away the victims' first death from them. Thus do these parties comprise a grisly witness to the distinctiveness of the Holocaust. The unique uniqueness of the event is validated through the pretense that it did not happen. Of what other monstrous event in human history has there ever been a plot by reputedly civilized people to say that the thing never transpired? (An example of the effort to deny that the Holocaust ever happened is a book by a professor of electrical engineering at Northwestern University, Arthur R. Butz, *The Hoax of the Twentieth Century*. Richmond, Surrey: Historical Review Press, n.d.).

16. William Jay Peck, "From Cain to the Death Camps: An Essay on Bonhoeffer and Judaism," *Union Seminary Quarterly Review* (New York), XXVIII. 2 (Winter 1973), 159–160.

The only-ness of the Holocaust is likewise seen in its subjecting of the ultimate truth to the ultimate lie. In May 1933 Hitler said that "the Jew cannot be a human in the image of God, the eternal one; the Jew is the image of the devil" (as quoted in "Federal President honours woman who saved Jews," *Deutschland-Berichte* [Bonn-Holzlar], XIV, 3 [March 1978], 13).

17. It was early in 1942 that the resolve was officially made to implement the *Endlösung der Judenfrage in Europa* ("the Final Solution of the Jewish Question in Europe"). The formulation was put forth on the 20th of January in that year, at a conference at Cross-Wannsee, although the actual decision was probably made sooner (so Gerald Reitlinger argues: of his *The Final Solution: The Attempt to Exterminate the Jews of Europe 1939–1945*, New York: A. S. Barnes. 1961, p. 102). Raul Hilberg speaks of the fateful step across the "dividing line" that inaugurated the "killing phase," and he refers to two all-decisive orders by Hitler in 1941 that were to doom all European Jewry (*The Destruction of the European Jews*, pp. 177ff.). The Wannsee agreement was simply the logical consummation of, or it merely gave expression to, a resolve whose roots are traceable to 1919, when Adolf Hitler declared that his ultimate objective was "the removal of the Jews altogether."

18. Martin Buber, *Ereignisse und Begegnungen*, Leipzig: Insel-Verlag, 1920, p. 20.

19. Martin Buber, *Israel and the World: Essays in a Time of Crisis*, New York: Schocken Books, 2nd ed., 1963, p. 35.

20. There is the allied question of the Jews and the fate of Jesus. The question of the "responsibility of the Jews" for Jesus' death rates no more than summary comment; the "charge" against them should have been placed long ago upon the refuse heap of historical falsehood. That the Jewish people of Jesus' time and their leaders had nothing to do with any maltreatment or crucifixion of him is discussed in a definitive but predictably ignored study by Justice Haim Cohn of the Supreme Court of Israel, a volume entitled *The Trial and Death of Jesus* (New York: Harper & Row, 1971). Cohn shows the inconceivability of any Jewish legal or religious condemnation of Jesus. The very notion that Jesus was brought to trial by the religious authorities on a charge of blasphemy, was convicted on his own confession, and was given a capital sentence is wholly out of the question, on no less than seven fundamental provisions of Jewish law: 1. No Sanhedrin was permitted to try criminal cases outside the temple precincts, in any private home. 2. No criminal case could be conducted at night. 3. No one could be tried on criminal charges on the eve of a festival. 4. No one could be convicted on his own testimony or on the basis of his own confession. 5. A person could be convicted of a capital offense only on the testimony of two lawfully qualified eyewitnesses. 6. The eyewitnesses were required to have warned the accused of the criminality of his intended act and the legal penalties for it. 7. The meaning of "blasphemy" is the pronouncing of the name of God; and it is irrelevant what alleged "blasphemies" are uttered as long as the divine name is not expressed (pp. 95–96, 97–98, 105, 112, 116; cf. A. Roy Eckardt, *Your People, My People: The Meeting of Jews and Christians*, New York: Quadrangle/The New York Times Book Co., 1974, p. 34 and, in general, chap. 3).

On the basis of the foregoing considerations, plus such others as the falsity of the tradition that the Romans were accustomed to release malefactors at Jewish festival times (cf. the account about Barabbas), the thoroughgoing speciousness of the New Testament on the subject of Jesus' trial and death is underscored. It is necessary, however, to insert a caveat here, in the name of realism. Regrettably, historical analysis is a highly limited weapon in disposing of human emotional commitments and in counteracting volitional prejudices. The New Testament documents are not objective history; they are polemical, evangelical tracts. But this datum cuts two ways. On the one hand, it reflects the fact that the records cannot be trusted as bearers of objective truth. But, on the other hand, and lamentably, it points up the consideration that the Christian world is wedded to these documents. Scholarly analysis is severely restricted in its ability to overcome the human bias that is derived from, and sustained by, these sources. In a word, the Christian reformer has his work cut out for him. Insofar as he may be tempted to limit himself to the disseminating of historical truth, his chances of creative influence are not terribly great. It is most essential, therefore, that he not hamstring himself by adhering to one method alone. In a single sentence Ignaz Maybaum points up this need for extra-historical strategies, and also authenticates the judgment made above that the alleged Jewish responsibility for Jesus' death rates only summary treatment. Maybaum writes: "the ancient tradition that 'the Jews killed Christ' . . . has its origin in the twilight between myth and history and is therefore not accessible to historical research" (*The Face of God After Auschwitz: The Encounter of Jews and Christians*, New York: Scribner, 1967, Schocken, 1973, pp. 157–158).

21. Alice and Roy Eckardt, "German Thinkers View the Holocaust," *The Christian Century*, XCIII, 9 (17 March 1976), 251.

22. "Ein Wort zur Judenfrage, Der Reichsbruderrat der Evangelischen Kirche in Deutschland," Darmstadt, 8 April 1948, in *Der Ungekündigte Bund. Neue Begegnung von Juden und christlicher Gemeinde*. Dietrich Goldschmidt und Hans-Joachim Kraus, Herausgeber, Stuttgart; Kreuz-Verlag, 1962, pp. 251–254.

Over the intervening years, the Evangelical Church of Germany has moved far from the position reported. In *Christen und Juden*, a recent official pronouncement from the Council of that Church, the authors reveal an acute awareness of the *Endlösung*; plainly, it is much on their conscience. They speak of the deep trauma that the event created for Christians, of the church's latter-day rediscovery of its Jewish roots, and of the abiding integrity of the faith of Judaism. They confess the appalling role of the Christian world in the historic persecution of the Jewish people, including the causative power of Christian antisemitism in the annihilation of the Jews of Europe. The contributors emphasize that a special obligation falls upon the Christians of Germany to oppose the new antisemitism that appears in the form of politically and socially motivated anti-Zionism. Christians have a particular duty to support the independence and security of the State of Israel—not alone as a political reality or human achievement, but also within the very frame of reference of the people of God (*Christen und Juden, Eine Studie des Rates der Evangelischen Kirche in Deutschland*, Gütersloh: Gütersloher Verlagshaus Gerd Möhn, 1975, pp. 23, 28–31).

23. Wiesel, *A Beggar in Jerusalem*, p. 30.

24. *A Beggar in Jerusalem*, p. 28.

25. Elie Wiesel, *The Gates of the Forest*, trans. Frances Frenaye, New York: Avon Books, 1967, p. 168.

26. Eliezer Berkovits, "The Hiding God of History," in Yisrael Gutman and Livia Rothkirchen, eds., *The Catastrophe of European Jewry: Antecedents-History-Reflections*. Jerusalem: Yad Vashem, 1976, p. 704.

27. Elie Wiesel, *Souls on Fire: Portraits and Legends of Hasidic Masters*, trans. Marion Wiesel, New York: Random House, 1972, p. 107.

28. A. Roy Eckardt, "Is the Holocaust Unique?" *Worldview* (New York), XVII, 9 (September 1974), 34–35.

29. Jürgen Moltmann, *The Crucified God: The Cross of Christ as the Foundation and Criticism of Christian Theology,* trans. R. A. Wilson and John Bowden. New York: Harper & Row, 1974, p. 51.

30. *The Crucified God,* p. 134.

31. As cited in Edward H. Flannery, *The Anguish of the Jews: Twenty-three Centuries of Anti-Semitism,* New York: Macmillan. 1965, p. xi.

32. Frederick M. Schweitzer, *A History of the Jews Since the First Century A.D.,* New York: The Macmillan Company, 1971, p. 222.

33. Moltmann, *The Crucified God,* p. 52; emphasis added to the word "only."

34. We must beware of falling into a numbers game. Taken in and of itself, there is nothing singular or impressive in the figure of "six million Jews." For example, out of five and a half million Russian prisoners of war in Germany, some four million were killed. Many more non-Jews than Jews died in the course of the Nazi period. The singularity of the *Endlösung* lies in the *identity* of the victims, not in their numbers.

35. Moltmann, *The Crucified God,* p. 185.

36. *The Crucified God,* p. 303.

37. Irving Greenberg, "Lessons to Be Learned from the Holocaust," unpublished paper at International Conference on the Church Struggle and the Holocaust, Haus Rissen, BRD, 8–11 June 1975.

38. In answer we may point out that such a rejoinder is not able to overcome ideology, because, no matter how valiantly we human beings twist or turn, *the* "truth" always proves in the end to be *our* "truth."

39. Moltmann, *The Crucified God,* pp. 148, 151.

40. This account is taken, with some minor changes, from a representation in the unpublished paper by Irving Greenberg. "Lessons to Be Learned from the Holocaust."

41. Emil L. Fackenheim, "The Nazi Holocaust as a Persisting Trauma for the Non-Jewish Mind," *Journal of the History of Ideas,* XXXVI, 2 (April–May 1975), 375.

42. Robert L. Lindsey contends for the chronological primacy of Luke (in e.g., "A New Approach to the Synoptic Gospels," *Christian News From Israel* (Jerusalem). XXII. 2 [1971]). 56–63. Lindsey is supported by David Flusser (in e.g., "The Crucified One and the Jews." *Immanuel* (Jerusalem), No. 7 [Spring 1977]. 23–37).

43. J. Paul Williams, *What Americans Believe and How They Worship,* rev. ed., New York: Harper & Row, 1962, p. 103.

44. If the one who was reputedly raised from the dead was not the psychosomatic Jesus of Nazareth, we are forced to ask: Who was he? But if he was the psychosomatic Jesus, we have to inquire: Where did he go? What became of him?

45. Where has such a claim ever been made in the Jewish community? The real Jewish point of view is diametrically opposite to Pannenberg's caricature of it. The constant need to rethink and reformulate the legal tradition, a need that lies at the center of ongoing interpretations by scholars and rabbis, is itself the proof that the tradition does *not* "contain the eternal will of God in its final formulation."

46. See Charlotte Klein, *Theologie und Anti-Judaismus, Eine Studie zur deutschen theologischen Literatur der Gegenwart,* München: Chr. Kaiser Verlag, 1975, espec. chaps. 2–3. A

thoroughly documented and formidable work, written in a semi-popular way, is Jules Isaac, *Jesus and Israel*, ed. Claire Huchet Bishop, New York: Holt, Rinehart and Winston, 1971, espec, parts I–III on the wholly positive relation of Jesus of Nazareth to Judaism, Torah, and the Jewish people. Among other relevant works, see Ben Zion Bokser. *Judaism and the Christian Predicament*, New York: Alfred A. Knopf, 1967, espec. pp. 181–209: David Flusser, *Jesus*, New York: Herder and Herder, 1969, espec. pp. 41–61: Krister Stendahl. "Judaism on Christianity: Christianity on Judaism," in Talmage, ed., *Disputation and Dialogue*, pp. 330–312: and Joseph B. Tyson, *A Study of Early Christianity*, New York: Macmillan, 1973, pp. 373–380.

47. Wolfhart Pannenberg, *Jesus—God and Man*, trans, Lewis L. Wilkins and Duane A. Priebe, Philadelphia: The Westminster Press, 1968, pp. 67, 257, 258.

48. There is great irony in the fact that Pannenberg's own understanding of the Resurrection is a version of Pauline transformationism (*Jesus—God and Man*, pp. 75, 77).

49. Pannenberg writes that the Jewish people "represent humanity in general in its rejection of Jesus as a blasphemer in the name of the law." "In fact, the reproach of blasphemy (Mark 14:64) through the claim of an authority belonging only to God was probably the real reason why the Jewish authorities took action against Jesus . . . The rejection of Jesus was inevitable for the Jew who was loyal to the law so long as he was not prepared to distinguish between the authority of the law and the authority of Israel's God" (*Jesus—God and Man*, pp. 246, 247, 252, 253, 263). In the Foreword to a commentary on the Apostles Creed, Pannenberg tells of a fundamental change in his views, as against a position he had expressed in 1964, according to which the Resurrection of Jesus meant the end, in principle, of the Jewish religion. He has come to believe that a basic distinction is required between a religion of law and the Jewish faith. The God of Jewish history can surmount "the law" (*Das Glaubensbekenntnis, ansgeiegt und veranticortet vor den Fragen der Gegenwart*, Hamburg: Siebenstern Taschenbuch Verlag, 1972, p. 6). However, in the same year Pannenberg wrote elsewhere that "Jesus Christ was not only the prophet of the coming Kingdom, but also became its Messiah and the pioneer and head of a new humanity" ("Zukunft und Einheit der Menschheit." *Evangelische Theologie* [München]. 32. Jahrgang, Heft 4 [Juli/August 1972], 389). On the other hand, several years later Pannenberg lamented the "eschatological exclusiveness of the Christian understanding of election" as a root cause of many wrong turnings in the history of Christianity. And he fully acknowledged that the *Endlösung* had antecedents in the Christian persecution of Jews (communication to author, 29 November 1975).

In a massive volume entitled *Christsein (Christian Existence,)* München: R. Piper Verlag, 1974, identified by its author as a "small *Summe*," a Swiss scholar, Hans Küng, includes a chapter on Christianity and Judaism in which he says many of the "right things" about Judaism and the Jews, e.g., that "all anti-Judaism is treason against Jeaus himself" and that after Auschwitz, Christendom cannot avoid a "clear admission of its guilt" for the centuries of antisemitism, a guilt that contributed to the coming of Nazism. Yet even in this chapter—a quite brief one—Küng suggests that in the discussion between Christians and Jews today, it would be well for Jews to give heed to the question of the person of Jesus, and he concludes the chapter by emphasizing that it is "as the Christ, the finally decisive, critical, authoritative one" that Jesus of Nazareth makes Christianity what it is (pp. 161, 162, 164, 166). However, the real difficulties with *Christsein* lie in Küng's analysis outside this particular chapter. To choose a few among a great many examples, we are told that Jesus set himself against the Mosaic "law" and its current interpreters; that the Jewish law "sought his death" and indeed "executed him": and that "in the still-living crucified one" a disgraceful death has become a death "of redemption and liberation" (pp. 281–284, 328, 387). Küng's repeated efforts to soften some of these conclusions both in his book—for instance, we are assured in *Christsein* that the Jews of today can hardly be held guilty for Jesus' death—and in a lengthy conversation with the writer and his wife (Tübingen, 5 December 1975) are not very convincing. He cannot avoid having presented these judgments as constituting the truth. Küng's problem may be associated with the fact that, as he granted to us, his rethinking of Judaism has been prompted not by the Holocaust itself but by the Second Vatican Council. Most fatefully of all, the reinterpretation of Jesus as *das massgebende Grandmodell* (the authoritative, basic model) for all human beings (*Christsein*, pp. 542–544) does not overcome the vice of Christian supersessionism in any way essentially different from the Christian claim of the divinity of Christ in the "from above" sense criticized by Küng. His reinterpretation may actually comprise a more dangerous kind of supersessionism than other traditionalist views, because it presents itself in a non-supersessionist spirit.

50. Cf. Klein, *Theologie und Anti-Judaismus.*

51. Peter von der Osten-Sacken, "Anti Judaism in Christian Theology." *Christian Attitudes on Jews and Judaism* (London, No. 55 (August 1977), 6.

PART 3

◙ Developments: The 1970s and 1980s

The fit between the following selections and those that have preceded it is not strictly chronological. Some of the thinkers represented in this section were certainly already thinking about the impact of the Holocaust when the central positions were being articulated. But, for a variety of reasons, it seemed better to collect examples of their work here, in a single section that might be broadly conceived as a representation of the subsequent work of the 1970s and 1980s that built on the foundation of the central systematic thinking of the late 1960s and early 1970s.

It would be difficult to identify a common thread that runs through all of these thinkers and their work. To be sure, they are collected here as representative of thinking oriented around the Holocaust and its impact. But even here there is no uniformity in the role that that event plays and how it structures or determines their thought. What I mean by this caveat is this: There is no one who began to think about the Holocaust and its impact without already having appropriated and sharpened certain intellectual skills and developed various positions, conceptions, and categories. The point that I am raising here concerns the degree to which these thinkers expose their established modes of inquiry, positions, and so on to the event itself and its unprecedented character. It also, in a sense, concerns the role that the Holocaust comes to play for them, how determinative it is, what influence it has, and how easily it is for them eventually to *incorporate* the event into the old scheme, suitably revised, or into a new one.

For some of the people we have included in this volume and discussed in earlier introductions—such as Eckardt, Greenberg, and Fackenheim, and one could also include Levi, Appelfeld, Celan, and Wiesel—once the Holocaust imposed itself and was confronted, it remained central, determinative, an undeniable center, as it were. With these thinkers, then, the centrality of the Holocaust is unique, imposing, and continuous.

But we have already noticed that this was not so, say, for Rubenstein or for Berkovits and even for Arendt. Indeed, Arendt is an especially interesting case. At times, the death camps and concentration camps so influence her thinking and unsettle her accepted categories that she is really at a loss to clarify and arrive at firm, precise conclusions. This occurs, I think, in the final pages of *The Origins of Totalitarianism* when she tries to bring to some conclusion her reflections on radical evil. Even later, when in reporting and reflecting on the Eichmann trial she introduces the notion of the "banality of evil," it is not without unclarity and confusion. For at least on one reading of that difficult phrase, it really is meant to capture the understanding of the Nazi criminals which Arendt had identified in the 1945 article on guilt and responsibility and developed in *The Origins of Totalitarianism*; hence, the banality of evil is what she had earlier called its radicality. Overall, however, Arendt is a political philosopher with a systematic interest in understanding the relations among our conceptions of human nature, political reality, and morality. Her views are steeped in Kant, Aristotle, and Heidegger and concern rationality, intention, action, and purpose. At the same time, she developed a view of Jewish history and Zionism that invoked this political philosophy and judged Jewish history to display the divorce between Judaism and the political and hence between Judaism and the ideal of rational human conduct, the morally good life. All of this comes together in a tremendously controversial way in her treatment of Eichmann and of the *Judenrate* during the Holocaust. The judgment of complicity or accommodation that she levels is a product of all of this theory and not just a matter of historical description. In all of this, the role of the Holocaust is confusing and complex.

With the thinkers represented in the current section, the issue of the centrality of Auschwitz arises again and again, and in different ways. In the 1970s and 1980s, for example, there is a widespread movement afoot towards what we might call historicism, of one variety or another. Its indications are everywhere; the vocabulary of truth, certainty, and knowledge is being replaced by the notions of understanding, interpretation, and paradigms. Realisms and objectivisms are being displaced by pragmatisms and various forms of idealism. And it is occurring everywhere, in anthropology, the history and philosophy of science, literary theory and criticism, philosophy, history, and on and on. The major figures provide names for a list of our culture's intellectual luminaries— Kuhn, Rorty, MacIntyre, Taylor, Skinner, Pocock, Fish, Derrida, Foucault, and then back to Nietzsche, Heidegger, Gadamer, and Habermas. Some of those who have recognized the importance of the Holocaust come to that recognition out of this pluralistic, pragmatic movement. One wonders whether the event has moved them in a primary and determinative way or whether they see it as a powerful case of historical influence (or both), and to what degree.

Others come to the Holocaust with different intellectual equipment and dispositions and needs, some moral, some theological, some philosophical, some social scientific, and so forth. At the same time that they may very well appreciate the undeniable character of Auschwitz, they may also see how their own positions or views are receptive to acknowledging the special role of the event. There may be, then, an intersection of historical honesty and receptivity and intellectual direction, a fortunate intersection perhaps. In such a case, the Holocaust may be treated as unprecedented but not unique, and the response to it can become part of a general view concerning history, modern culture, and more. One wonders which if any of the thinkers represented in this section can be described in this way.

One surprising feature of these readings is that they show how slim are the really superior Jewish contributions to the enterprise of rethinking Judaism after Auschwitz. Perhaps this is a function of the powerful and deep responses by the central thinkers. Rubenstein's views have generally been taken to exhibit one extreme, the use of theodicy to reject the transcendent God of history and the traditional notion of covenant. Many may agree with this view, which is really a caricature of Rubenstein, but there are no new statements along these lines that deserve special notice. Often the others—Fackenheim, Greenberg, and Berkovits—are grouped together as theists or such, and while many sympathize, no one has really developed or revised their views. There are many pretty superficial summaries but few penetrating analyses and only a few criticisms worth even casual notice.

This is not the appropriate place to reflect on why there has been so little serious Jewish development of post-Holocaust Jewish thought; the reasons doubtless have much to do with deep tendencies in American and Israeli Jewish life, with general views among Jewish scholars about the nature of Jewish scholarship and Jewish thought, and with changes in the rabbinate and with Jewish leadership generally. One need only look at the impressive dictionary *Contemporary Jewish Religious Thought*, edited by Arthur Cohen and Paul Mendes-Flohr, to realize how historical, diverse, and nonphilosophical modern Jewish thought has become; for most people, long-range historical surveys and textual analysis have taken the place of anything one might call serious Jewish theology or self-understanding.

Hence, there are few Jewish materials. The sole new work of significance is Arthur Cohen's *The Tremendum*. Wyschogrod's criticisms of Fackenheim and others represent the most widely accepted attack, one unquestionably appropriated, for example, by Jacob Neusner in a frequently cited but insubstantial article.[1] The writings of Marc Ellis and Michael Lerner should be consulted as representing certain politically inspired critiques; references are in the bibliography.

In contrast, for a short period of time, there was extensive and serious Christian reflection. I have selected from a much greater number of figures and writings that discuss the impact of the Holocaust, usually as part of a larger project to rethink Christianity in terms of its relation to Judaism and the Jewish people. There is no need to examine each of the Christian thinkers represented here. They invariably deal with the important themes that are raised by the Holocaust and by the prior involvement of the Church in two millennia of anti-Jewish attitudes and activity. These issues concern supersessionism, triumphalism, missionary activity, anti-Jewish interpretation and preaching, and more. The most influential statement of the textual entrenchment of anti-Jewish attitudes can be found in Rosemary Reuther's *Faith and Fratricide*, a book that generated heated debated about its scholarship and general agreement about its thesis, that anti-Judaism is the "left hand" of Christology and that negative views about the Jews are present in the New Testament and continually thereafter in normative and influential works, from the Church Fathers through Luther and beyond.

David Tracy's heterodox and subtle defense of Christian pluralism is featured in his books *Blessed Rage for Order* and *The Analogical Imagination*. The latter is a hermeneutically sophisticated analysis of the complexities of traditional

Christian interpretation. Responsive to Gadamer, Ricouer, and others, Tracy shows how each stage of Christian self-understanding involves complex recovery of the past, sometimes receptively and sometimes in opposition. Not surprisingly, then, Tracy comes to appreciate the impact of the Holocaust on this process of Christian self-interpretation, suggesting that various features of the tradition must be approached using a "hermeneutics of suspicion," to use Ricouer's apt phrase. These features include supersessionism, anti-Jewish attitudes in the New Testament and later, missionizing among Jews.

Many years ago Alan Montefiore, a moral and political philosopher at Balliol College, Oxford, published an article on moral philosophy after the Holocaust.[2] Outside of that article and the work of Fackenheim, there was little genuine philosophical discussion of the event until the 1980s. Then there occurred several important developments. First, Berel Lang edited a double issue of *The Philosophical Forum* wholly devoted to the Holocaust. Secondly, Emil Fackenheim was invited to present a major paper at the Eastern Division Meetings of the American Philosophical Association, and that paper, "The Holocaust and Philosophy," was published in *The Journal of Philosophy*. Thirdly, an anthology has recently been published that deals with philosophical reflections on the Holocaust. And finally, a special group of the American Philosophical Association has been formed to discuss issues that arise out of the Holocaust. Moreover, as philosophy has broadened in scope and changed in character, issues about agency, representation, and historiography have captured the interest of philosophers, as well as literary critics and others (see the next section), and the increasing influence of European and especially French philosophy has also led to more and more philosophical reflection on Nazism and the death camps.

One issue of importance has come to the fore, and the work on it has already given signs of importance. Philosophers, historians, and social scientists have turned to the relationship between the Holocaust and genocide. Recently, especially with the flourishing discussions of applied ethics—among the topics of which are included war, terrorism, and violence—there has been some attention paid to the category of genocidal acts. As might have been expected, the Nazi attempt to exterminate Jewry often is cited as a prime example. Hence, scholars and thinkers are naturally drawn to ask in what sense the event was genocidal, how it compares to other genocidal acts, before and after, and what, if anything, might be essential to the notion of genocide and to understanding the Holocaust and its role in our study of the phenomenon of genocide. An article by Steven Katz is one example of this type of discussion; it focuses on the intentions of the perpetrators and compares the Holocaust to other genocidal acts. His conclusion is the interesting one that while the Holocaust does exhibit unprecedented intentional features, these are not theologically significant. Berel Lang, in a sensitive article reprinted in his fine book *Act and Idea in the Nazi Genocide*, explores our concept of genocide, and Fackenheim's paper, already cited, elaborates a case he has been trying to make for nearly two decades, that the Holocaust is both unprecedented as a case of radical evil and powerfully determinative for that reason.

For Jewish and Christian thinkers especially, confronting the Holocaust has come to mean, at least since 1967, confronting the reality and significance of the State of Israel as well. In one sense, this fact has so politicized the reflection about the Holocaust and its impact that genuine dialogue among discussants has become increasingly rare. Those who take the Holocaust to be determinative of the historical situation of contemporary Jews and Christians have tended to take the survival of the State of Israel very seriously, indeed as the centerpiece of contemporary Zionist commitment. For them, the reestablishment and defense of Israel may be revelatory; at least it is an expression of vigorous self-reliance, of defense of a homeland, and of protection of human dignity. Hence, the threats to Israel's survival and any denial of Israel's right to exist become, in effect, an inheritance from the Nazi past. Others, who typically hail from the left and have long worried about Israel's political posture and moral character, drawing frequently on traditional liberal sentiments, prophetic morality, and perhaps a lingering allegiance to new left radical postures, find in this apparently unconditional commitment to Israel's survival a lapse in moral sensitivity. To them, the Palestinian Arabs, like other oppressed peoples whose human rights are being violated, form the nexus of a complex moral-political dilemma that Israel is failing to resolve. Hence, an intractable obstacle to genuine discussion and reflection among the varieties of contemporary religious thinkers, to the point where a serious attentiveness to the horror and atrocity of Auschwitz comes to be associated with right-wing reactionary politics and the belittling of Auschwitz with knee-jerk liberalism.

Still, it is unavoidable that Jewish and Christian life after Auschwitz is also Jewish and Christian life in the age of a new Jerusalem. The thinkers represented in this section, as well as Rubenstein, Fackenheim, Eckardt, Littell, Berkovits, and Greenberg, have written about the role the state of Israel. Berkovits, for example, sees in the state of Israel a virtual miracle, whereby the Jewish commitment to bring moral probity to history, seriously diminished by the victory of power and domination that was Auschwitz, is rejuvenated and revived. Others, like Fackenheim and Greenberg, see in Israeli self-defense an expression of secular self-reliance cooperating with a sense of religious purpose. Indeed, we can even return to Améry, who saw himself exclusively as a secular Jew, but who felt a powerful sense of solidarity with the Zionist cause precisely because it was, for him, the primary vehicle of the singled-out Jew to oppose the forces that threatened human dignity. Solidarity with Israel, that is, was exactly what opposing Nazi purposes and serving the cause of humanity meant for Améry.

NOTES

1. Jacob Neusner, "The Implications of the Holocaust," *Journal of Religion* 5 (3): 293–308 (July 1973).
2. Alan Montefiore, "The Moral Philosopher's View on the Holocaust," *European Judaism* 11 (1977): 13–22.

MICHAEL WYSCHOGROD

◼ Faith and the Holocaust

Speaking of the Holocaust, Emil Fackenheim writes in *God's Presence in History: Jewish Affirmations and Philosophical Reflections*[1]: "Silence would, perhaps, be best even now, were it not for the fact that among the people the flood-gates are broken, and that for this reason alone the time of theological silence is irretrievably past."

The flood-gates are, indeed, broken and silence no longer surrounds the Holocaust. Whether it was the people who broke the flood-gates or whether it was a small number of Jewish writers who, in recent years, have not permitted the people to forget what many have very much wanted to forget, remains an open question. From their side, the Holocaust thinkers (Fackenheim, Elie Wiesel and one or two others) have been driven above all by the terror that the people will forget, that the Holocaust will cease to be the central event of contemporary Jewish existence and become, instead, one memory among the many others that make up Jewish history. The people, for their part, have been ambivalent. On the one hand, they have certainly wanted to forget: Jewish life, after all, has not been transformed by the Holocaust, business continues as usual and time has shown once again that it heals all wounds—a fact for which men cannot help thanking God while recognizing the horror of the process when such wounds as the Holocaust are involved. On the other hand, the Jewish public has also wanted to remember: the reception accorded the writings of Elie Wiesel demonstrates the point. Whoever addresses Jewish audiences with any frequency can testify to the kind of charge generated when the Holocaust is mentioned. This is the one common experience of the Jewish people today, believing and unbelieving, learned and simple, young and old. Not to be addressed by the Holocaust is the one sure sign of exclusion from the Jewish people, it is the great divide that separates those in from those out. It is this ambivalence of forgetting and remembering that characterizes, it seems to me, the attitude of the people.

It was the philosopher Ludwig Wittgenstein who announced that concerning those matters of which we cannot speak we ought to remain silent. While, of course, he had nothing like the Holocaust in mind, it is difficult, as Fackenheim well understands, not to apply the rule of silence to it. The peril is blasphemy. In

"Faith and the Holocaust," *Judaism* 20 (Summer 1971): 286–294

fact, it seems to me that nothing but blasphemy can be the result if we view the Holocaust from the human point of view. If we find ourselves continuing to believe in the Biblical God after the Holocaust, we can neither forgive Him nor love Him. Or, following Richard Rubenstein, we blaspheme by denying the existence of the God of history and are driven into some form or other of atheism.

Fackenheim, for his part, has little sympathy for Rubenstein. He speaks (p. 71) of "the view of a 'radical' Jewish theologian who asserts that . . . the Midrashic framework is shattered by Auschwitz; the God of history is dead." Without mentioning Rubenstein's name in the body of the text (though he is identified in a footnote), Fackenheim calls him to task for having the temerity to speak: "What assures him [Rubenstein] of his capacities to deal with the trauma—or stills his fear that some other mechanism may cause him to utter words which should have never been spoken?" Fackenheim's lack of sympathy for Rubenstein's total rejection of the "for our sins are we punished" theology would make good sense if Fackenheim could see his way to embracing this standpoint, a standpoint which is, after all, not unhallowed by Jewish history. The fact of the matter, however, is that Fackenheim, too, finds it impossible to embrace the theology of "for our sins are we punished." As a response to Auschwitz, this doctrine, according to Fackenheim, "becomes a religious absurdity and even a sacrilege" (p. 73). Fackenheim buttresses this contention by reference to the work of N. N. Glatzer who had claimed, in his *Untersuchungen zur Geschichtslehre der Tannaiten* that the "for our sins are we punished" view was rejected by the ancient rabbis, "perhaps not in response to the destruction of the Temple by Titus, but in response to the paganization of Jerusalem by Hadrian" (Fackenheim, p. 73). This being so, what is so dreadfully wrong with Rubenstein's rejection of the Biblical God once he found himself rejecting the view that, in Hitler, Israel was once more feeling the scourge of God?

In the section of the book entitled "The Midrashic Framework and the Holocaust" (pp. 69–79), Fackenheim examines the various standpoints that attempt to deal with the Holocaust from within the circle of faith and finds them all lacking. He then examines "Jewish Secularism and the Holocaust" (pp. 79–84) and finds that Jewish secularism, in stubbornly persisting in its Jewish identity after the Holocaust, is also involved in a profound contradiction, because the logic of its position would dictate assimilation, a solution that would seem to be indicated by the cost of Jewish survival, especially in the twentieth century, but which the Jewish secularist nevertheless refuses to embrace. The two frameworks, the theological and the secular, from which the Holocaust can be approached are, therefore, rejected by Fackenheim, and this explains his dissatisfaction with Rubenstein to the extent that he reads Rubenstein as simply representative of the secular option. It should, however, be kept in mind that Fackenheim rejects with equal firmness the standpoint of simple faith, be this in the "for our sins are we punished" form or perhaps an even more simple faith which refers to the inscrutability of God's will. All these are inadequate. What then, is adequate?

Only obedience to the Voice of Auschwitz. This voice, as heard by Fackenheim, commands the survival of Jews and Judaism. Because Hitler was bent upon the destruction of both, it is the duty of those Jews who survived Hitler to make sure that they do not do his work, that they do not, by assimilation, bring about the disappearance of what Hitler attempted but ultimately failed to destroy. For the religious Jew, this means that he must go on being religious, however inadequate Auschwitz has shown his frame of reference to be. And for the secular Jew, the voice of Auschwitz commands not faith, which even the voice of Auschwitz cannot command, but preservation of Jews and Judaism. Speaking of the significance of the voice of Auschwitz for the secular Jew, Fackenheim writes: "No less inescapable is this Power for the secularist Jew who has all along been outside the Midrashic framework and this despite the fact that the Voice of Auschwitz does not enable him to return into this framework. He cannot return; but neither may he turn the Voice of Auschwitz against that of Sinai. For he may not cut off his secular present from the religious past: The Voice of Auschwitz commands Jewish unity" (pp. 88–89). The sin of Rubenstein is, therefore, that he permits Auschwitz further to divide the Jewish people at a time when survival is paramount if Hitler is not to be handed a posthumous victory, and survival demands unity. Because this is so, Rubenstein should presumably soft-pedal his doubts so as not to threaten the Jewish people at a time when everything must be secondary to the issue of survival.

What can be said about all this?

Since all criticism proceeds from a point of view, it would be best for me to state mine. I do not think that a voice can be extracted from the Holocaust which will speak to believer and non-believer alike. I do not think that the question of faith can be circumvented by means of Auschwitz. Finally, I do not think that Judaism can be given a new hold on life by means of Auschwitz. For me, the Holocaust was a totally destructive event which makes my remaining a Jew infinitely more difficult than it has ever been. I can only marvel at Fackenheim's effort to extract a positive result from the Holocaust, a kind of negative, natural theology with the survival of the people, rather than the existence of God, as the conclusion.

Let us first examine the contention that the voice of Auschwitz speaks to the secular Jew and commands him to adhere to his Jewishness so as not to hand Hitler a posthumous victory. At the risk of drawing simplistic analogies, it is necessary to examine the logic of the argument. Let us imagine that there arises a wicked tyrant who sets as his goal, for his own depraved and psychotic reasons, the extermination of all stamp collectors in the world. It is clear that it would be the duty of every decent person to do everything in his power to frustrate the scheme of that tyrant. Let us further imagine, however, that before the tyrant is made harmless, he succeeds, in fact, in murdering a large proportion of the world's stamp collectors. Does it now follow that subsequent to the tyrant's demise it becomes the duty of the remaining stamp collectors not to lose interest in their stamp collecting so as not to hand the tyrant a posthumous victory? Isn't there all the difference in the world between exterminating persons who wish to be stamp collectors just because they wish to be stamp collectors and the right of individuals or groups to lose interest in something they no longer wish to remain interested in? Would it be a posthumous victory for the tyrant were stamp collecting to disappear from the world as long as this disappearance is due, not to force, but to free choice? I cannot see why, if I am a secular, non-believing Jew, it is incumbent upon me to preserve Judaism because Hitler wished to destroy it. What was incumbent upon me was to destroy Hitler, but once this is accomplished, the free choice of every individual is restored and no further Hitler-derived burdens rest on the non-believing Jew.

It is, of course, true that there are secularist Jews who insist on remaining Jews even after the Holocaust. Fackenheim seems to be convinced that, if not for the voice of Auschwitz, these secularist Jews would have every reason to embrace assimilation in light of the price that Jewish existence extracts. The desire of some secularist Jews to remain Jews may be due, however, to the fact that they find positive value in remaining Jews independently of the Holocaust. Jewish secularism, with its national and ethnic identification, existed long before the Holocaust, when surely no voice from Auschwitz could be heard. In such circles, assimilation was resisted, partly because of a genuine and deep pride in the historic contribution of the Jewish people to civilization and, partly, I would think, because assimilation was never quite as possible as Fackenheim seems to think it was and is. And finally, there is the possibility that there is something slightly irrational about the desire to perpetuate Jewish existence when this desire is combined with secularist premises. To the believer, this can be taken to demonstrate that Jews remain in the service of God even in their state of disbelief and that forces deeper than those known to the individuals concerned shape Jewish existence. But all this is a far cry from turning this state of affairs into an ideology, which is precisely what Fackenheim attempts to do.

I have already termed Fackenheim's enterprise "negative natural theology," a phrase which deserves brief explanation. Traditionally, natural theology has been the enterprise whereby the existence of God is demonstrated on the basis of some rational evidence, without recourse to faith or revelation. Most commonly, the point of departure for such an attempt was some "positive" feature of the world as it appears to man: its order, its beauty, or its harmony. It was then argued that such characteristics could not be the result of pure chance and that it was, therefore, necessary to posit some all-powerful and rational being as the author or creator of a universe possessing the respective positive characteristics. Such an argument was presumably persuasive to the nonbeliever and could force him to concede the existence of an intelligent creator, all without having to leave the framework of reason with which we started.

Fackenheim's point of departure is, of course, the opposite of the "positive." Instead of being the order, beauty, harmony or justice of the universe, it is a totally unique crime, unparalleled in human history. But once we get over this initial difference, similarities appear. In the positive version, a positive characteristic of the universe is noted and it is argued that no natural explanation for it is adequate. In negative natural theology, an evil is pointed out for which also, it is alleged, no natural explanation is possible. Of course, the conclusion in negative natural theology cannot be identical with that of positive natural theology, inasmuch as the problem of theodicy cannot here easily be ignored. Nevertheless, the conclusion which Fackenheim draws, the sacred duty to preserve the Jewish people, is the functional equivalent of the existence of God in positive natural theology, inasmuch as it becomes a total foundation for the continued existence of Judaism, a foundation as fully serviceable to the secularist as to the believer. One is almost driven to the conclusion that in the absence of the Holocaust, given Fackenheim's profound understanding of the irreversibility of the secular stance, no justification for the further survival of Judaism could have been found. With the Holocaust, amazing as this may appear, Judaism has gotten a new lease on life.

Because the Holocaust becomes, for Fackenheim, the fulcrum of his negative natural theology, he apparently finds it necessary to claim that it was, and remains, a unique event in human history. Strictly speaking, this is not necessary, since any sufficiently terrible negative event can become the foundation of a negative natural theology so long as it can be argued that it is not amenable to natural explanation. Nevertheless, it is understandable that an overwhelmingly terrible event such as the Holocaust would be even more useful if it could be demonstrated that in addition to everything else it was totally unique. Now this is precisely what Fackenheim maintains. According to him, the uniqueness of the Holocaust consists of the fact that there was no "rational" purpose in the crime. "Whole peoples," writes Fackenheim "have been killed for 'rational' (however horrifying) ends such as power, territory, wealth, and in any case supposed or actual self-interest. No such end was served by the Nazi murder of the Jewish people" (p. 70). In a footnote, he adds: "I feel constrained to stress once again that I assert only that the Nazi genocide of the European Jews is unique, not that it is a greater or more tragic crime than all others. Thus, for example, the fate of the gypsies at the hand of the Nazis (itself an 'ideological' project) is at least in one sense more tragic—that no one seems to bother to commemorate them. Even this example of genocide, however, though itself a product of Nazi ideology, still differs from the Nazi genocide of European Jewry: no comparable hate propaganda was directed by the Nazis against the gypsies. Whence this groundless, infinite hate, indiscriminately directed against adults and children, saints and sinners, and so relentlessly expressed in action" (p. 100). What are we to make of this claim?

It would be rather beside the point, though not without logical force, to argue that, in one sense, all events are unique, since there can be no event which does not have at least one characteristic not shared by any other event—if only its exact place and time of occurrence. In another sense of the word "unique," no event is unique for there is no event which does not share at least one characteristic with at least one other event—if only the fact that both are events. This being so, it might not be altogether unreasonable to expect some discussion of the sense of the word "unique" in such a vehement claim by a philosopher of the uniqueness of an event. Even so, the issue far transcends such relatively technical considerations. The crux of the matter is a moral one.

Although, as we have seen, Fackenheim restricts himself to the claim that the Holocaust was a unique crime and not that it was a greater or more tragic crime than all the others, the claim of uniqueness reflects an existential fact: that for Fackenheim the focus of his life is the destruction of European Jewry and not the extermination of the gypsies or of the residents of Hiroshima in World War II, the Armenians in World War I or the illiterate peasants of Vietnam in the recent past. In some way, the fate of European Jewry is for Fackenheim in a class by itself, having an existential significance for him that these other horrors do not have. We will soon have to ask why this is so or, perhaps, more to the point, what justification Fackenheim can offer for this being so. It is not to be expected that the obvious reply, namely, that since Fackenheim is a Jew he is more reached by the fate of Jews than by that of others, will satisfy either Fackenheim or his critics. Fackenheim's insistence on the uniqueness of the Holocaust indicates that he feels constrained to justify his preoccupation on grounds other than simple ethnic or national partiality. And he feels constrained to justify his preoccupation because he senses an accusation in the air, an accusation emanating from those who present themselves as equally reached by the death of any child, be he in Warsaw or Biafra, in 1943 or 1970. To this sensibility such dwelling on a catastrophe of the past is an evasion of the crimes—as they see it—being committed today about which something can still be done but about which Fackenheim does not write books and articles. For such people, the ultimate object of reverence is man wherever he appears, rather than just "one's own," which is the light in which they see Fackenheim's enterprise.

It is at this point that Holocaust theology as practiced by Fackenheim finds itself on the defensive. At this point, it is essential to be scrupulously honest. It is necessary to admit that we are fixated on the Holocaust to an extent quite unacceptable in a universalistic framework. The moral force of those who cannot share this fixation must be recognized. It is, I believe, necessary to abandon the attempt to find "objective" criteria in accordance with which such a fixation on the Holocaust will be made plausible, simply because any and all such criteria bestow uniqueness on the Holocaust at the expense of diminishing the other occasions of human suffering. To argue that one is asserting only the uniqueness of the Holocaust and not that it is a greater or more tragic crime than all others, simply won't do because the uniqueness which is asserted ("groundless, infinite hate indiscriminately directed against adults and children, saints and sinners, and so relentlessly expressed in action") turns out to be morally decisive and not just an attribution of abstract uniqueness. It is necessary to recognize that, from any universally humanistic framework, the destruction of European Jewry is one notable chapter in the long record of man's inhumanity against man, a record which compels the Holocaust to resign itself to being, at most, a first among equals.

If we therefore remain fixated on the Holocaust it must be for another reason. It is true that the Holocaust is *our* catastrophe and one is entitled to mourn more intensely for the death of a relative than for that of another. But this consideration cannot have ultimate significance. On the psychological plane such partiality is understandable; on the final, moral plane, all men enjoy the same dignity as my relatives and it therefore follows that crimes against them cannot be qualitatively different from those against others.

To justify Emil Fackenheim's and my fixation with the Holocaust, I must resort to theology. To make clear my meaning, I must recount an episode that I witnessed quite recently.

A devout Catholic philosopher of my acquaintance returned from mass one Sunday morning in a state of agitation. Some progressive members of the parish had removed the crucifix from its usual position and substituted for it a contemporary crucifix on which, instead of the suffering Jesus, there was affixed a collage depicting suffering Vietnamese men, women and children. My friend was outraged. "How can they," he asked, "equate human suffering with the suffering of the Incarnate Son, a person of the Godhead?" I had no doubt of his deep and genuine compassion for the suffering of man, wherever and whenever it occurs. But it was only the suffering of the Son of God at Golgotha that, he argued, redeemed the sins of the world and healed the suffering of man. To substitute the suffering of man for this saving event was to confuse man with God, something that benefits neither.

Must we not say something at least somewhat similar if we are to remain really honest? The fate of Israel is of central concern because Israel is the elect people of God through whom God's redemptive work is done in the world. However tragic human suffering is on the human plane, what happens to Israel is directly tied to its role as that nation to which God attaches His name and through which He will redeem man. He who strikes Israel, therefore, engages himself in battle with God and it is for this reason that the history of Israel is the fulcrum of human history. The suffering of others must, therefore, be seen in the light of Israel's suffering. The travail of man is not abandoned, precisely because Israel suffers and, thereby, God's presence is drawn into human history and redemption enters the horizon of human existence.

Can we deny that all this must be a scandal in the eyes of nonbelief? Can we expect the non-believer to concede that somehow the fate of Israel is more central, more decisive, more important than the fate of any other people? We cannot and must not expect this; we must learn to live with the knowledge that there is an abyss between belief and nonbelief, that for non-belief Auschwitz is a member of a large and tragic class of human evil whose voice, if it commands anything, commands men to struggle against evil and injustice wherever perpetrated. When we observe the Holocaust fading from the consciousness of men, as it inevitably will, when we observe it fading to some extent even from the consciousness of our young, we must be neither surprised nor outraged. To remember is not, after all, the really natural inclination of man. Were this not so, the Torah would not find it necessary to command the remembering of the Amalekite assault on Israel. The Torah commands it precisely because it is natural for man to forget, for memories to fade, for emotions to be calmed and for wounds to heal. The Torah commands remembering because only a believing community can transcend time, can fixate on events of very limited "historic" significance (how "significant" was the Exodus to the ancient world whose records never mention it?) and find in them the significance of a redemption history apparent only to the eyes of faith. For believing Israel, the Holocaust is not just another mass murder but, perhaps, the final circumcision of the people of God. But how else, except by the power of God, can anyone believe that?

One final word about the theology of Emil Fackenheim. Israel's faith has always centered about the saving acts of God: the election, the Exodus, the Temple and the Messiah. However more prevalent destruction was in the history of Israel, the acts of destruction were enshrined in minor fast days while those of redemption became the joyous proclamations of the Passover and Tabernacles, of Hannukah and Purim. The God of Israel is a redeeming God; this is the only message we are authorized to proclaim, however much it may not seem so to the eyes of non-belief. Should the Holocaust cease to be peripheral to the faith of Israel, should it enter the Holy of Holies and become the dominant voice that Israel hears, it could not but be a demonic voice that it would be hearing. There is no salvation to be extracted from the Holocaust, no faltering Judaism can be revived by it, no new reason for the continuation of the Jewish people can be found in it. If there is hope after the Holocaust, it is because to those who believe, the voices of the Prophets speak more loudly than did Hitler, and because the divine promise sweeps over the crematoria and silences the voice of Auschwitz.

NOTE

1. Emil L. Fackenheim, *God's Presence in History* (New York: New York University Press, 1970).

AMOS FUNKENSTEIN

▣ Theological Interpretations of the Holocaust

A Balance

THE MEANING OF MEANING

That the extermination of the Jews in Europe ought to arrest the attention of theologians seems obvious. That it has actually done so, especially in the last decade, and continues to do so, is a fact. But what we *mean* when we ask about the theological "meaning" of the Holocaust is far from obvious. For some it means the meaning of the catastrophe in inherited theological terms: an attempt to salvage a theodicy from the rubble left by the eruption of evil as an apparently autonomous force. For others it means the meaning of the catastrophe *for* theology: either in a polemical vein, when they address the failure or even complicity of rival theologies; or critically, when they question the legitimacy of their own theological heritage in the shadow of the systematic destruction of human life and dignity. I shall call these trends, in turn, the direct, the polemical, and the critical-reflexive modes of theologizing about the Holocaust. And I shall argue that the first is offensive, the second hypocritical, and the third not radical enough even in its most radical manifestations.

THE HOLOCAUST AS PUNISHMENT AND SIGNAL

One of the few who dare to state that the Holocaust is perfectly comprehensible in traditional theological terms shall serve as our starting point. From the extreme case we may learn something about seemingly more reasonable attempts in the same direction.

Shortly after the foundation of the state of Israel, there appeared a book with the typical rabbinical title *And It Pleased Moses (Vayo'el Moshe).*[1] Its author,

From *Unanswered Questions*, edited by François Furet. Copyright © 1985 by Editions de Seuil. Reprinted by permission of Schocken Books, distributed by Pantheon Books, a division of Random House, Inc.

R. Yoel Taitlbaum, was the leader of an ultra-Orthodox, anti-Zionist, cohesive movement whose branch in Israel is known as the "Guardians of the City" (Neture Karta). It summarizes all traditions in support of passive messianism— I shall explain the term immediately—and concludes that the Holocaust was an inevitable consequence of, and punishment for, a formidable sin: the transgression of the divine warning not to seek redemption by one's own hands, through human initiative. His argument is as follows:

"Because of our sins we have been exiled from our land." The dispersion and oppression of the Jewish nation in the diaspora has a punitive-cathartic function, and only God can call an end to the punishment. Those who wish to "precipitate the end" and force God's hand through human action are, whether or not they know it, rebels. Three times the Song of Songs repeats an oathlike formula: "I put you under oath, the daughters of Jerusalem, in the name of the deer and the gazelles of the field, not to hasten nor to precipitate love until it desires." An old exegetical tradition justified the inclusion of such eminently secular love songs in the canon of sacred scriptures on the grounds that it ought to be read *only* allegorically, as a dialogue between God and the spirit of Israel (or, in other quarters, the *ecclesia*). The three oaths, we are taught in the tractate Ketubot of the Babylonian Talmud, have a particular allegoresis.[2] The threefold repetition of the formula refers to three oaths imposed on Israel and on the nations of the world after the destruction of the temple. Israel was held by oath not to rebel against the nations among which it is held as a "prisoner of war," and not to try and "hasten the end." In return, the nations of the world were held by the third oath not to oppress Israel *too* much.

From these premises Taitlbaum draws an outrageous conclusion. Because, in the course of the Zionist movement, an ever growing number of Jews broke the oath and took their fate into their own hands—they wished to turn, in Herzl's words, "from a political object into a political subject"—the nations of the world, in turn, likewise felt themselves free of the oath not to oppress Israel too much, and oppress they did. Why did they? Taitlbaum assumes, as a matter of course, that "Esau always hates Jacob," inherently and incessantly. The Holocaust is the inevitable consequence of the Jewish spontaneous drive toward sovereignty or even autonomy. It is not even the last catastrophe: The perpetration of the sin continued with the foundation of the state of Israel. A catastrophe is imminent, after which only a few, the "remnants of Israel," will survive to witness the true redemption. Indeed, Taitlbaum's whole argument is embedded in the apocalyptical premise that the true redemption, through divine miracle, is very close at hand. The times preceding it are, in the traditional imagery, times of extreme wars and tribulations, times replete with false hopes and false Messiahs.

In a curious way Taitlbaum shares the belief that the messianic days are at the threshold with his Orthodox adversaries, the "Bloc of the Faithful" (Gush Emunim).[3] They too assume that hatred against Jews is inherent in the nations of the world because the choice of God fell upon Israel, or, in the more secular version of U. Z. Greenberg, because Israel is "the race of Abraham, which had started on its way to become master."[4] They regard the Holocaust and the subsequent formation of the state of Israel and its wars as a divine signal for an active preparation in "the dawn of our redemption." Since our time is the time of the messianic war, and redemption has already started, it is incumbent upon Jews to conquer and hold to the promised borders of their holy land, to shape it into a *civitas dei*. For Taitlbaum the Holocaust came because Jews were too active; for the Gush Emunim, because Jews were too passive; for both it is a portent of the Messiah.

Two distinct traditions of Jewish messianism clash here in their exaggerated forms: the passive-utopian messianic tradition as opposed to active-realistic messianism. The former has been by far the predominant tradition, an antidote of the rabbinical establishment against dangerous messianic eruptions; the latter, although a minority tradition, has had a continuous career and some notable authorities on its side: Maimonides, Jacob Berab, Zvi Kalisher. Maimonides, to whom world history is a continuous history of the monotheization of the world guided by God's *"List der Vernunft"*—i.e., "Miracles of the category of the possible"—saw also in the messianic days a period within history without change in cosmic or human nature.[5] He believed that there were some ways to precipitate them through human initiative, as by the reconstruction of the old court system in the land of Israel. Jacob Berab, who tried to implement this plan through the attempt to renew the pristine ordination, was rebuked by the Jerusalemite head of the court, who insisted that the messianic days can come only as a package deal: no element of them can be taken out of its miraculous context to be implemented now.[6] Kalisher, in the nineteenth century, devoted his life to encouraging settlement in Israel or even the renewal of some sacrifices in the present for the very same reasons. Note that this "active messianism" is not a precursor of Zionism. On the contrary: Zionism started with an antimessianic claim, a desire for sovereignty irrespective of messianic expectations. Both Taitlbaum and the Gush Emunim represent pre-Zionistic mentalities. Both are, in different ways, fossils of the past, albeit poisonous fossils.

The ideology of passive messianism, to which Taitlbaum is an heir, should not be confused with the myth of the physical passivity of diaspora Jewry. Why did Jews not offer resistance in the face of their extermination? Raul Hilberg, in the introduction to his monumental book,[7] refers to the alleged two thousand years of mental conditioning in appeasement. Passivity, he believes, was an intrinsic mental feature of diaspora Jewry. This is a myth as widespread as it is dangerous; dangerous it is because it suggests an artificial gap between the passive diaspora mentality and the active, healthy mentality of the new species of Jew in Israel. Neither in antiquity nor in the Middle Ages did Jews abstain from physical resistance in the face of persecution, whenever feasible. They resisted during the Crusaders' pogroms, the Chmielnicki pogroms, and modern pogroms. Resistance during the Nazi occupation was no less than among most other occupied populations. At best, one could ask why German Jews were not more active in the resistance movement until 1939, or why there was more cooperation than necessary later. But if there was passivity, it was not a heritage of diaspora mentality but rather of modern vintage. To the modern European Jew, who identified himself with the state he lived in, resistance against his state seemed outside the universe of discourse; nor could he conceive of a state acting against the *raison d'état*. The preemancipation Jew, by contrast, always saw himself as an alien, as a "prisoner of war," and was always on the alert. The legal principle, "the law of the kingdom is valid law," which was quoted by some reformers of the nineteenth century to prove the priority of state law even in Jewish terms, originally meant the opposite. It pertained to property only and delineated a *Widerstandsrecht*: only if a ruler acts in accord with the law of the land is one obliged to obey him.[8] The ideology of passive messianism is the only true nucleus of the myth of passivity: it served to emphasize the lack of acute political aspiration. In a way, then, the political emancipation and acculturation of Jews in Europe opened the way for two extreme, new possibilities: total passivity and total self-assertion. In the language of Sartre, the postemancipation Jew may be said to live in a constant "situation" of "*être-vu*"[9]: he shunned it by identifying with the aggressor, or defined it by becoming Zionist.

At best, passive messianism was an ideology, not a legally binding position. It was prevalent once, but is obsolete today even among the Orthodox. Why then dignify Taitlbaum's insult to common sense and decency with a detailed discussion? Because in theology, as in the law, much can be learned from extreme-limit cases. An overt absurdity is better than a covert one. Jewish theologians who are less extreme than either Taitlbaum or the Gush Emunim, such as E. Fackenheim or E. Berkovits,[10] admit that they can see no theological rationale to the Holocaust. The Holocaust is incomprehensible, they say, and defies all theodicies. But they do find a theological meaning in the survival: the survival of each man or the survival of the nation and the rebirth of the state. In both they find a confirmation of the divine presence and a promise to preserve Israel.

Even these diluted versions of a theodicy are offensive. Having survived while others—close family and friends—have not is a terrible burden to many survivors. Haunted by excruciating memories, many of them refused to talk or reminisce in the years following interment; some of them do so only now, fearing that true memories will be lost within their generation. It may well be that the state of Israel too owes its establishment in part to the Holocaust; but this also is a terrible burden, not a sign of chosenness or divine grace. Similar perceptions may have moved George Steiner in his recent book, tasteless as it may otherwise be.[11] There is only one instance of theologizing in Primo Levi's account of his survival in Auschwitz. It reads:

> Now everyone is busy scraping the bottom of his bowl with his spoon so as not to waste the last drops of the soup; a confused, metallic clatter, signifying the end of the day. Silence slowly prevails and then, from my bunk on the top row, I see and hear old Kuhn praying aloud, with his beret on his head, swaying backwards and forwards violently. Kuhn is thanking God because he has not been chosen.
>
> Kuhn is out of his senses. Does he not see Beppo the Greek in the bunk next to him, Beppo who is twenty years old and is going to the gas chamber the day after tomorrow and knows it and lies there looking fixedly at the light without saying anything and without even thinking any more? Can Kuhn fail to realize

that the next time it will be his turn? Does Kuhn not understand that what has happened today is an abomination, which no propitiatory prayer, no pardon, no expiation by the guilty, which nothing at all in the power of man can ever clean again?

If I was God, I would spit at Kuhn's prayer.[12]

. . .

THE DIALECTICAL THEOLOGY OF MEANINGLESSNESS

To the most courageous among recent theologians, the very meaninglessness of the Holocaust constitutes its theological meaning. To lose faith in the face of the Holocaust is itself, they say, a manner of faith, a positive religious act. When, in the eleventh century, Anselm of Canterbury advanced his ontological proof of God's existence, he also gave a new meaning to the Psalm's verse: "The fool [wicked] hath said in his heart: there is no God." Since God's existence is necessarily implied by his very concept, whoever thinks of God yet denies his existence cannot but be foolish (wicked). The modern theologians I have in mind—Rahner, Baum, Rubenstein, and others—turned Anselm on his head. "A person deeply troubled by the Holocaust and made unable to affirm God's presence is caught in an essentially religious question and hence already under the influence of God's grace. If a person were shallow, or wholly pragmatic, or egotistical, or only concerned about protecting his own interests, he would not be troubled at all. He is troubled because he is religious."[13] Even atheists, Vatican II reminds us, may be touched by grace.

The admission that God—or ethical theism—died in Auschwitz because Auschwitz defies all meaning calls, we are told, for a radical change of the most fundamental premises.

> What has emerged in our theological reflection based on Karl Rahner is a rather different religious imagination. Here God is not conceived of as a lord ruling history from above, but as the vitality at the core of people's lives making them ask the important questions and moving them toward their *authentic* existence. God is conceived here as the *ground* of human existence, as the summons operative in their lives, and as the *horizon* toward which they move. God is not so much lord of the universe as heart of the world. What is emphasized in this theology is what theologians call Divine immanence, which in ordinary [!] language means God's being *in-and-through the world*. . . . God's presence to people changes them, severs them from destructive trends, and moves them towards a more creative future. . . . But the in-and-throughness of God does not leave the world as it is; it judges the world and *summons* it to new life.[14]

Yet even here, where theologians are most courageous, false tunes are unavoidable. The key phrases underlined by us point unmistakably to a definite philosophical source. Exchange "God" for "being" (*Sein*); the rest of the vocabulary is Heidegger's. Seemingly without ethical judgments, Heidegger distinguishes two modes of human existence, the inauthentic and the authentic. So does the quoted passage. *Dasein*, "Being-there" or existence, is the only form in which the elusive *Sein*, "being" (in contrast to *Seiendes*, "entities") is concerned with itself: "[*Das Dasein ist ein Seiendes*], *dem es in seinem Sein um dieses Sein selbst geht.*"[15] Yet in its first and average occurrence it is alienated from itself, lost in the world (*In-der-welt-sein*) in such a manner that it uses things in the world (*Zuhanden-sein*) and is absorbed in it. With every man are inseparably others with whom he shares the concern (*Sorge*) with the mundane. *Dasein* is inauthentic in that state, it is "man"—everyone—characterized by *Seinvergessenheit*, disconcern with its true self-being. It flees fear (*Angst*) rather than facing it, facing its basic feature as *Geworfen-sein*, being "thrown into" (as well as "projected into": *geworfen*) the world. Only the authentic self, in contrast to the inauthentic "everyone" (*man*), and moved by fear and trembling (*Angst*), is capable of asking the question-of-being (*Daseinfrage*), the question to which there is ipso facto no answer because its answer is for that particular being to be no more. Here too the meaninglessness of the question constitutes its very meaning. Here too it is the characteristic of the authentic self which is not "lost in trivial concerns" to ask such questions to which there is no answer. Rather than the "chatter" (*Gerede*) of "everyone" (*man*), the authentic self lets Being which is in itself speak for itself through his very futile question of being.

Few who read Heidegger's *Sein und Zeit* failed to be caught by its spell. The fascination with Heidegger's thought is similar in many ways to the fascination with Spinoza's *Ethics*; both have a uniquely comforting power. In both, the ultimate meaning of everything that is resides in itself only. Spinoza's *Deus sive natura* reifies the logic of the Megarians to the utmost: only that which is, is possible; that which is not is impossible, even meaningless. Like Spinoza's God, Heidegger's being is always expressed through beings (*Seiende*), and is never capable of expressing "itself" immediately and without them; it illuminates without being seen, just as (if one may borrow a metaphor from Wittgenstein) a picture never points at itself. In contrast to Spinoza's substance, however, Heidegger insists on the necessary temporal structure of being. The acquiescence with the total immanence of the meaning of the world—including, for Heidegger, the temporality of being—means that there is no more to the life of a subject than itself; it cannot be endowed with a transcendent meaning or value; when it comes to its individual end, its meaning will be no more nor less than *that* and *what* it was. Annihilation does not deprive that which is from having meaning; it rather constitutes an integral part of that meaning.

This having been said, we turn back to the call for authenticity which some of the more courageous theological reflections on the Holocaust borrowed from Heidegger.

It is precisely at this point, namely with the distinction between authentic and inauthentic existence, that the ethical critique—a critique from the vantage point of ethics—must commence. Heidegger promises us that no moral judgment is implied in that distinction.[16] In an almost Hegelian manner, he even sees in the alienation of *Sein* in *Dasein* from itself through the flight into unauthentic existence a necessary stage for its return (*Kehre*) unto itself. Yet consider the further attributes of inauthenticity. Only the authentic self can be said to possess conscience or even to be capable of "sinning." The anonymous "everyone" lives in a continuous degeneration and fall (*Verfall des Daseins*), a fall "into the world" (*in die Welt verfallen*). "Everyone" is, literally, interchangeable with everyone else.

Without entering a sustained discussion about the nature of moral speech, let me assume that we ought to start with some "concrete absolutes" in an ethical discourse if we wish to navigate between relativization and empty, formal abstractions. Let me also assume that human life and human dignity are such absolutes—be it in a cognitive or axiomatic-thetic, descriptive or normative sense. They command our relentless respect; they are the "infinite right" of each subject. We may conceive of situations, such as the necessity of self-defense, in which we would be justified in violating them: it would be an evil act, even when justifiable.

Human life and the incommensurable value of each individual were assaulted in infinite ways in Nazi Europe. An ethical perspective of this sort cannot avoid being extremely narrow-minded, rigorously one-sided. It can make no concessions to higher gods and higher values, and it cannot permit any distinction between individuals based on higher values. Life, the life of each individual, must be taken to be always meaningful in and of itself. The everyday reality of Heidegger's "everyone," the person who never attends to the question of being but is "lost unto the world," must be endowed from the one-sided vantage point of ethics with as much dignity and intrinsic value as the life of the searcher for fundamental existential truths. The man who cultivates his garden and does all the things in the way he is supposed to cannot be called inauthentic except by his author. From an ethical point of view, *every life is authentic*, a value in and of itself, not interchangeable with any other human life, a mode *sui generis*. Once discrimination is permitted even in theory, its consequences are difficult to foretell. If the person of "everyone" is interchangeable with everyone else, let alone if he is classified a nonperson—that is, without personality—then he is less valuable. And if less valuable, then perhaps also dispensable. Or again: is not crisis—say, war and destruction—beneficial in Heidegger's terms, because it "calls" man to his true self? Heidegger himself drew such conclusions after 1933.

But, you may object, the possible or even real abuses of a theory (even by its promoter) need not be held against it: in part, this has been my own argument. My critique, however, goes deeper than that. The very distinction between authentic and inauthentic existences, not only its possible career, is an intrinsic assault on the *dignitas hominis*, the integrity and worthiness of each concrete individual life, however lived. The latter attitude, with its difficulties and paradoxes, must constitute the absolute center of humanistic ethical theories, even at the cost of subscribing to a one-dimensional, flat philosophical anthropology.

At best, Heidegger's distinction diverts from this focus; at the worst, it undermines it.

I do believe, however, that much of the force of Heidegger's insistence on the immanence of being, of which we spoke earlier, can be saved without redundant discriminations. An ethical monadology is conceivable in which the life of each is a unique and significant point of view of human possibilities for better and worse; each situation, individual and collective, is such that it is significant and something can be learned from it about man; and, should all human history have, finally, come to pass and leave behind no record, its meaning will be that and what it was, as replete with good and evil, the beautiful and the ugly, as it then will have been.

Mutatis mutandis, the flaws in the thought of Heidegger are also the flaws in those dialectical theologies which speak in Heidegger's idiom. Why is the person who "asks important questions," say, concerning God's presence in the face of massive evil, "more authentic" than the person who does not? And why are the questions of the *homo religiosus*, however broadly we define him, more important than the purely human questions asked by others about their experience in the concentration camps? Consider, for example, the most moving and reflective account written about the experience of Auschwitz, Primo Levi's *Se questo è un uomo* (published in English as *Survival in Auschwitz*). It asks many questions, but none of them theological. It refuses to see the concentration camp as meaningless: "We are in fact convinced that no human experience is without meaning or unworthy of analysis, and that fundamental values, even if they are not positive, can be deduced from this particular world which we are describing." Indeed, the religious-theological questions, were he to ask them, would distract from the power of Levi's reflections, which are centered around man, not around God.

As against the distinction between the begraced and those who lack grace, between authentic and inauthentic existences, the reality of the concentration camps taught Levi other distinctions, distinctions which are purely homocentric, such as the distinction between "the drowned and the saved."

We do not believe in the most obvious and facile deduction: that man is fundamentally brutal, egotistic and stupid in his conduct once every civilized institution is taken away, and that the *Häftling* is consequently nothing but a man without inhibitions. We believe, rather, that the only conclusion to be drawn is that in the face of driving necessity and physical disabilities many social habits and instincts are reduced to silence.

But another fact seems to us worthy of attention: there comes to light the existence of two particularly well-differentiated categories among men—the saved and the drowned. Other pairs of opposites (the good and the bad, the wise and the foolish, the cowards and the courageous, the unlucky and the fortunate) are considerably less distinct, they seem less essential, and above all they allow for more numerous and complex intermediary gradations.

This division is much less evident in ordinary life; for there it rarely happens that a man loses himself. A man is normally not alone, and in his rise or fall is tied to the destinies of his neighbours; so that it is exceptional for anyone to acquire unlimited power, or to fall by a succession of defeats into utter ruin. Moreover, everyone is normally in possession of such spiritual, physical and even financial resources that the probabilities of a shipwreck, of total inadequacy in the face of life, are relatively small. And one must take into account a definite cushioning effect exercised both by the law, and by the moral sense which constitutes a self-imposed law; for a country is considered the more civilized the more the wisdom and efficiency of its laws hinder a weak man from becoming too weak or a powerful one too powerful.

But in the *Lager* things are different: here the struggle to survive is without respite, because everyone is desperately and ferociously alone. If some *Null Achtzehn* vacillates, he will find no one to extend a helping hand; on the contrary, someone will knock him aside, because it is in no one's interest that there be one more "mussulman" dragging himself to work every day; and if someone, by a miracle of savage patience and cunning, finds a new method of avoiding the hardest work, a new art which yields him an ounce of bread, he will try to keep his method secret, and he will be esteemed and respected for this, and will derive from it an exclusive, personal benefit; he will become stronger and so will be feared, and who is feared is, ipso facto, a candidate for survival. . . .

They crowd my memory with their faceless presence, and if I could enclose all the evil of our time in one image, I would choose this image which is familiar to me: an emaciated man, with head dropped and shoulders curved, on whose face and in whose eyes not a trace of thought is to be seen.

If the drowned have no story, and single and broad is the path to perdition, the paths to salvation are many, difficult and improbable.[17]

Among the "saved" then are both the noble (such as his friend Alberto) and the ignoble, the cunning and the less cunning. Levi employs the theological idiom ironically: as if to say that being saved is not of a theological or other transcendental character; it is a most basic human property. Out of the experience of the concentration camp, Levi crystallized the building blocks of a true philosophical anthropology, more genuine and accurate than either Heidegger's or any recent theologian's. The power of his reflections, I repeat, lies in that they are centered around the concrete man, not around a chimera of the authentic self nor around God.

Indeed, religious questions may even be detrimental to ethical human concerns. They are detrimental, I believe, in the following sense. The assumption is made by even the most self-critical theologians that there exists a particular virtue in the commitment to values higher than human life and human integrity, that the person who lives his life *veluti pecora*, without asking existential-religious questions, lacks "grace." But the table may be turned as follows. A commitment to higher values above the sanctity of the individual not only distracts from the study of man, but can and did lead to abuses and crimes of much greater extent than selfish self-interest ever perpetrated. Concededly, this is not a *necessary* consequence of commitments to absolutes, but it has often enough been so. Now it matters little whether the higher values were transcendent or immanent, God, fatherland, race or the ideal society of the future. In the name of all of them crusades were fought, genocides committed, persons degraded. No major religion I know of was immune. Perhaps then dialectical theologians are not radical enough. Perhaps theology itself is one source of that very danger which they contemplate. William of Ockham, whose ethical theory recognizes very clearly the need for a concrete absolute if one wishes to navigate between the Scylla of relativization and the Charybdis of empty, formal abstractions, claimed it is wrong to say that God wants that which is good. Rather, it is good because God wanted it. The God of the Bible wanted, as it were, a genocide against the Amalekites, including women, children, and cattle. A more refined God of later centuries wanted heretics to be "compelled to enter" or be abolished. An even more refined God may demand the self-sacrifice of the believer so as to sanctify the name of God. A secular age translated such demands into world-immanent terms, among them race. *Tantum religio potuit suadere malorum.*

Again, I do not argue that religious commitments do, of necessity, lead to abuse. But neither should it be argued that because of lack of religiosity (so to say, as an "outburst of paganism") concentration and extermination camps became possible. I rather argue that the focus on the religious-theological implications of the Holocaust is intrinsically the wrong focus. The question of what it teaches us about God or any other higher norms and values is insignificant beside the question of what it teaches us about man, his limits, his possibilities, his cruelty, his creativity, and his nobility. In human terms the Holocaust was not meaningless. To say that it was seems as offensive as to say that it had a theological meaning, that is, a divine purpose.

For similar reasons we ought to object to the characterization of the Holocaust as "incomprehensible." It is one of the most prevalent predicates in the theological literature about the Holocaust—and not only in the theological literature. On the contrary: historians, psychologists, sociologists, and philosophers ought to make every effort to comprehend the catastrophe, and they ought to be guided by the reasonable expectation that they can comprehend it. The crime committed by the Nazis was of immense proportions: the horror and the suffering transgress our capacity of imagination, but it is possible to understand them rationally. Even if the perpetrators of the crime were madmen who lost all touch with reality, a reconstruction of their mentality and patterns of action would be possible. But they were not madmen, at least not in the clinical sense of the word: if madness entails loss of the sense of reality, then no society can be called mad, because reality is a social construct through and through. The prehistory of the genocide, its necessary conditions, can be illuminated more and more. The mental mechanisms by which Nazi ideology justified mass murder can be followed step-by-step. Germany stood fast in its illusion of apocalyptic "total war." The Jews, they were certain, are not only an inferior race on the order of Slavs and blacks, they are even more dangerous, because they are a universal, destructive parasite which (unlike other races) cleverly adapts to become almost indistinguishable from the host society in order to destroy the healthy texture of that society from within. Their extermination was spoken of in terms of hygienic medicine: Jews were labeled a dangerous bacteria. *"Entlausung"* (delousing) was the terrible realization of an ideological metaphor in the concentration camps. By degrading the inmates of the camps, by robbing them of their personalities, the victims were supposed to turn into that which the Nazi ideology claimed they had always been: subhuman. It was a mechanism which functioned to concretize, to visualize, the rationale for extermination. Nor is it true that the extermination of the Jews was carried out at the cost of the war effort, as Hilberg and others once believed. We cannot excuse ourselves from the obligation to understand the Nazi mentality if we want to condemn it, let alone if we want to prevent similar crimes from being committed again.

Theologians seem to emphasize the "incomprehensibility" of the Holocaust and the "madness" of those who caused it because they cannot find any theological meaning in it. Perhaps also it is because they hardly dare to say that if one were to believe in transcendent forces, the Holocaust would prove the autonomy of evil, an evil manifested not only or primarily by the number of its victims but by its sheer inexhaustible inventiveness, by the almost infinite number of methods found for systematic killing and degradation. If, however, we turn from God to man, the Holocaust is neither incomprehensible nor meaningless. It was neither bestial nor indeed pagan. It was, instead, an eminently human event in that it demonstrated those extremes which *only* man and his society are capable of doing or suffering. It pointed at a possibility, perhaps unknown before, of human existence, a possibility as human as the best instances of creativity and compassion.

NOTES

1. Joel Taitlbaum, *Vajoel Moshe* (New York, 1952; 2nd ed., 1957).

2. Bab. Talmud, *Ketubot* 111a; *Cant. Rabba* 2,7. Literally, the formula is an oath, but a playful imitation of one: wherefore the invocation of God (*el Shaddai, el Tseva'ot*) is replaced by a phonetical simile (*aylot ha'sade tsviot*). Cf. R. Gordis, "The Song of Songs," in Mordecai M. Kaplan, *Jubilee Volume* (New York, 1953), pp. 281–397, esp. 308–9.

3. Menachem M. Kasher, *Hatekufa hagdola* (Jerusalem, 1969); it contains explicit polemics also against Taitlbaum.

4. U. Z. Greenberg, *Rehovot hanabar, Safer hailiot veha'koah* (Tel Aviv, 1957), p. 7; "father of the superior race," p. 31 and passim. *Geza* is the accepted modern Hebrew term for "race"; a racial ideology will be called *torat geza*. In 1957 it had other connotations than in 1920, when Zabotinsky promised: "With blood and with sweat / A race will be formed for us / proud, magnanimous, and cruel."

5. A. Funkenstein, "Maimonides: Political Theory and Realistic Messianism," *Miscelanea Medievalia* II (1977), pp. 81–103.

6. R. Levi ben Habib, *Responsa* (Venice, 1565), appendix (*Kuntres hasmicha*); on the ideological background cf. J. Katz, "Mahloket hasmicha ben Jacob-Berab veha Raloah," *Zion* 17 (1951), pp. 34 ff.; Funkenstein, op. cit. p. 102.

7. R. Hilberg, *The Destruction of the European Jews* (Chicago: Quadrangle Books, 1967). We elaborated some of the following remarks elsewhere (*The Passivity of Diaspora Jewry: Myth and Reality*, Aran Lecture 11, Tel Aviv, 1982).

8. Bab. Talmud, *Nedarim* 28a; *Gittin* 10b; *Baba Kama* 111; *Baba Batra* 54b–55a; Cf. Sh. Shiloh, *Dina demalchuta dina* (in Hebrew) (Jerusalem, 1974).

9. J. P. Sartre, *Réflexions sur la question juive* (Paris, 1947).

10. E. Fackenheim, *God's Presence in History* (New York, 1970); *The Jewish Return into History* (New York, 1978). E. Berkovits, *Faith After the Holocaust* (New York: Ktav, 1973).

11. George Steiner, *The Portage to St. Christobel of A. H.* (New York: Simon & Schuster, 1982).

12. Primo Levi, *Survival in Auschwitz* (orig. title, *Se questo è un uomo*), trans. S. Woolf, (New York: Macmillan, 1961), pp. 151–52.

13. G. G. Baum, *Christian Theology After Auschwitz* (Robert Waley Cohen Memorial Lecture) (London, 1976), esp. pp. 7–15.

14. Ibid., p. 19.

15. M. Heidegger, *Sein und Zeit* (Tübingen, 1957), p. 12.

16. Ibid., p. 175: "Der Titel (Das Verfallen, etc.), der keine negative Bewertung ausdrückt . . ."

17. Primo Levi, op. cit., pp. 100–103.

ARTHUR A. COHEN

◼ Thinking the Tremendum

Some Theological Implications of the Death Camps

There is something in the nature of thought which is alien to the enormity of the death camps. There is something no less incommensurable in the reality of the death camps which repudiates the attentions of thought. Thinking and the death camps are opposed. The procedures of thought and the ways of knowing are confounded. It is to think the unthinkable, which is not alone contradictory but hopeless, for thought entails as much a moral hope (that it may be triumphant, mastering its object, dissolving the difficulties, containing and elucidating the conundrum) as it is the investment of skill and dispassion in a methodic procedure. The death camps are a reality which, by their very nature, obliterate thought and the humane program of thinking. We are dealing, at the very outset, therefore, with something unmanageable and obdurate—a reality which exists, which is historically documented, which has specific beginnings and ends, located in time, the juncture of confluent influences which run from the beginnings of historical memory to a moment of consummating orgy, never to be forgotten, but difficult to remember, a continuous scourge to memory and the future of memory and yet something which, whenever addressed, collapses into tears, passion, rage. The death camps are unthinkable, but not unfelt. They constitute a traumatic event, and like all decisive trauma, they are suppressed but omnipresent; unrecognized but tyrannic; silted over by forgetfulness, but never obliterated; rising like a shade in dreams, allusions, the imagination to plague consciousness without end.

Nearly thirty years have passed since the closing of the death camps. The first decade after the revelation of the murder of the Jews (and their no less misfortunate but unsung confederates, the Gypsies) was passed in defining the language of formal-description and formal judgment. It was the time of the statistical accounting, the development of an accurate historical language, the numbering of the victims, the definition of the grammar of genocide, and the no less wall-eyed, benumbed dealing of judgment to the accused, the trials, the executions, culminating in the Eichmann trial of 1961. The second period saw the rescue of a literature, the beginnings of the controversies of interpretation, the publication of fictional accounts of the camps and autobiographic documents, by the quick and the dead, from Chaim Kaplan, Emmanuel Ringelbaum, André Schwarz-Bart, J. P. Steiner, Elie Wiesel, Katzetnik, Pyotr Rawicz, to mention but several among countless others. The task of this literature was neither to astonish nor to amaze, neither to exalt nor to abase, but to provide a vivifying witness to the mortal objectivity of the statistics.

It is during the present and third decade, now drawing to a close, that a new moment in the assimilation of the historical reality has begun. Another generation, those who knew not, has grown up—a generation that knows the birth and struggle of the State of Israel, but knows nothing directly of the Hitler years and the immediate shock of their ferocity. To this generation the question of meaning has become critical. It is the generation that sees upon its flesh the scar without the wound, the memory without the direct experience. It is this generation that has the obligation, self-imposed and self-accepted (however ineluctably), to discern a meaning and an instruction from the historical, not only lest the events recur, but more importantly that, if they do, they never recur in the same way. To achieve this prophylactic sense, this preventive vision, is the task not alone of energizing memory, hearing the witnesses, attending to their words and warnings, but is a task of thinking. It is not enough to deal with the reality of the death camps viscerally, with passion and anguish, with guilt for surviving and abashment before the enormity, with rage and anger, sublimated, as Jewish anger has always been. These are not enough, nor are they even sufficient. It is simply not adequate to *feel* this *tremendum*. One must live with the *tremendum*, and living with it requires that it be perceived accurately (to the extent that accuracy is possible about events as charged as these), clearly (to the extent that looking into the charnel house can ever be unclouded and precise), and distinctly (to the extent that it can be confronted as a constellated phenomenon which both does and does not indict all of Western civilized history, all of Christianity, all of silent humanity, and most of all, the history and faith of Israel). There was a time when it was understandable that one's reaction to the asking of the meaning of the *tremendum* was the fervid wish that it had none, that it implicated nothing beyond itself, that it described an historical horror, but that it did not tear apart the fabric of the larger universe where men create, make art, think, love, ransoming the human from the mud and muck of the concrete and particular. That time is past.

We are in the third decade. The distance between our selves and the events of the *tremendum* has grown. The survivors persist, most in private communication with their memories, most silent; others vigorously, often desperately, trying to bridge the chasm which opened beneath them then, thirty years ago, talking to us well and badly, convincingly and shrilly, patiently and irritably, superior to us and supercilious, guarding as they do a body of uncommunicate images and imaginings or else vaguely and mystically, floating beyond us, palpable ghosts and specters of a world we never knew. To the side of the survivors have come, however, in recent years, other aides and interpreters, the thinkers. It is as someone who is trying to think about the *tremendum* that I address you this evening. My observations fall into two general and primary categories: thinking about the historical and thinking about the meaning of the historical.

The predicament one faces at the very outset is that the procedures of traditional thought afford us very little assistance. Historiography is a patient accumulation of relevant information with a view to describing and interpreting events. The Dutch historian Pieter Geyl made it abundantly clear in his ongoing argument with Leopold von Ranke that history may be value-free, but that historiography is never so. History is not simply telling what happened. The historian always tells what happened from the historian's point of view. Geyl, writing of Napoleon while detained in a privileged concentration camp throughout the war, showed how European historians of Napoleon and of the Napoleonic era—Taine, Quinet, Sorel, and others—constructed a Napoleon who was true to some facts, but not to all, accurate to part of the reality, but not to the whole, and in the process a liberal Napoleon, a reactionary Napoleon, a bourgeois Napoleon, a middle-class or an elitist Napoleon rose and fell. The facts were all there, but historians select. When a work of history refuses to select, when it has no point of view, it cannot construe history. Instead, it retires into chronicle and accumulation, telling all and obfuscating everything. Historiography must always select and combine, reconstruct and pattern, establish causalities and coincidences. One judges the acuteness and probability of truth by the ability of the historian to contain more of the reality, to reconcile its living contrariety and dissolve its palpable confusion, rather than by whether the story it tells is what one has all along believed or wants to believe. Great historiography renovates familiar readings of history and however parti pris, whatever its loyalties to one or another ideological movement or doctrinaire position, the great history declares its patent.

Traditional historiography does not help our dealing with the *tremendum* of the genocide of European Jewry precisely because the reality exceeds the causalities. Nothing before, not the French revolution, not the unification of Germany, not the emancipation of the Jews, not the rise of capitalism, not the teaching of contempt according to Gospels and church fathers, none of these, causalities though they may be, achieve more than a gloss of the enormity—explicating this or that figure in the Nazi movement or interpreting this or that current of mob psychology or popular ideology, but leaving intact and unexplained the singularity of a machinery conceived and constructed to destroy a whole people.

If historiography is not a satisfactory tool, are there not other disciplines of inquiry, the investigation of the psychological and linguistic conceits of the perpetrators and their victims, which will assist us? Is it not relevant to understand the modes of deviance which released the psyche and language of a civilized society from the bonds of morality to the development of which its own traditions of *kultur* had so profoundly contributed? What allowed, such a course of inquiry might investigate, the degeneration of German speech over the length of a half-century from the rich, imbricated, responsible pursuit of truth into the garbled, vulgarized German authorized and distributed by the Nazi press, Nazi literature, and official bureaucratic speech?

Such an inquiry would be illuminating, but ultimately ineffectual, since the debasement of language and the traducing of the psyche, dependent as it is upon the organ of speech, is a process observable in varying degrees in every Western language. Germany is only a case of more so and earliest, but there is little doubt that the same has been true in the Soviet Union, and one notes that even the *New York Times* often prints news which is not "fit" to be printed. The debasement of language, the stripping of its subtlety and moral intention, is a procedure which began in the West long before Hitler and continues after he is gone. It will help us to explain a kind of cauterization of conscience by the use of metaphor and euphemism to understand that in official Nazi language the extermination of Jews was precisely that—the disinfectant of lice, the burning of garbage, the incineration of trash, and hence language never had to say exactly what acts its words commanded: kill, burn, murder that old Jew, that middle-aged Jew, that child Jew. Language created its own rhetoric of dissimulation, and a conscience which was no longer required to hear accurately, a result not unique to Nazi Germany, but, indisputably, an efficient aspect of its discipline.

The point is that whatever we may learn from history, linguistics, psychopathology, political science, or social anthropology about the conditions which preceded and promoted the death camps or the behavior of oppressors and victims which obtained within the death camps is unavailing. All analysis holds us within the normative kingdom of reason and however the palpable irrationality of the events, the employment of rational analysis is inappropriate. I do not feel the calm of reason to be obscene, as some critics of the rational inquiry into the *tremendum* have described it. It is not obscene for human beings to try to retain their sanity before an event which boggles sanity. It is a decent and plausible undertaking. It is simply inappropriate and unavailing. Probative reason, dispassionate reason have no place in the consideration of the death camps, precisely because reason possesses a moral vector. To reason, that is, to evaluate, is to employ discernment and discrimination, and reasoned discrimination entails the presence of a moral ambiguity and its resolution. There is no possibility of regarding the *tremendum* as standing within the parsings of moral judgment. It is not simply that the death camps were absolutely evil. Such judgments do not help. It is not enough to pronounce them absolutely evil. Absolute evil is a paradigm. There is little to which we can point in the history of men and nations which is absolutely evil, although the criterion of that abstraction has helped moralists to pronounce upon the relative evils of history.

The relativity of evil in the temporizings of moralists rarely entails the exposition of the relative good. Relative evils do not complete themselves by the description of relative goods. Relative evil is measured in the mind against absolute evil. Of course, such a logic of moral expedience has an ultimate reckoning. If it is too commonplace for men to release themselves from the paradigm of the absolute, it is even easier to excuse transgression—the erosion of moral sensibility (that human ether in which the conscience breathes) is clogged and stifled; men rationalize and justify so long and so well that the time passes quietly, unobserved, when they should have stopped and shouted, "no, not this, not this." But, of course, it is hard in a shouting and busy world, continuously assaulted by interests and needs, for any single man to be heard crying against the flood. In such a time, the recognition that there are absolute evils abstractly described, and formulated in commandments whose very authority guarantees transgression, has not prevented us from accumulating a mountain of small evils which, like the bricks of the Tower of Babel, might one day reach up and pierce the heavens. The point of this is to suggest that moral convention, a pragmatic regimen of norms and *regulae* of behavior, have authority only so long as the absolute evil of which they are *exempla* remains abstract and unrealized. When the absolute evil comes to be, the sphere of the moral and immoral ceases to be efficacious. Can one doubt this in the politics of the twentieth century? Until the end of the eighteenth century the political theory of Europe centered about philosophies of law, right, duty, and freedom. It was understood that the relation of citizen and state was somehow a moral relation, that the citizen was a person educated to freedoms and informed by responsibilities. In our time, such language has virtually disappeared from public debate and inquiry. The language of politics is not that of moral interaction and representation, but the calibration and weighting of power, influence, need, and control in such fashion as to guarantee for one's own constituency a larger and measurably greater security both for and against uncontested aggression. Questions of right and law, of justice and equity have virtually disappeared as criteria for social and political action. The consequence of all this—the process of the demoralization of the political—is the irrelevance of the absolute and the utter, as the adjectival thunder to the nominally relative. What men once called murder, barbarism, cruelty, or sadism is simply useless rhetoric. Not one of us can summon these words with the authority with which John Milton or Voltaire might have uttered them and few can hear the English rendering of the Hebrew prophets with little more than a recognition of their immense eloquence. Words no longer command us precisely because they no longer reflect concepts and convictions which directly agitate conscience.

If this analysis is correct, it will be readily understood why I have come to regard the death camps as a new event, one severed from connection with the traditional presuppositions of history, psychology, politics, and morality. Anything which we might have known before the *tremendum* is rendered conditional by its utterness and extremity. At this juncture, let me remark why I have chosen the word *tremendum* to identify the death camps and why, most particularly, I have not and cannot refer to Auschwitz as the name by which to summarize and transmit the reality. Auschwitz is only one among many sites of death. It was not even the largest death camp, although it may well have claimed the largest number of victims. Auschwitz is a particularity, a name, a specific. Auschwitz is the German name of a Polish name. It is a name which belongs to *them*. It is not a name which commemorates. It is both specific and other. And, if my perception is correct, what occurred then, from the time of the conception of the "Final Solution" until the time that surreal idealism was interrupted, is the transmutation of chosen persons into chosen people, of the scandal of Jewish particularity and doggedness into the scandal of Jewish universality. What might have been, until the time of the "Final Solution," a controversy about the particularism and insularity of Judaism in contradistinction of the dogma of nationalist anti-Semites who wanted a Jewry divested of Judaism and Jewish identity, a theological reform which wanted Jews rehabilitated by Western humanism and *kultur*, or a Zionism which wanted Jews tied both to self-determination and Socialist class-consciousness in the struggle against Jewish temerity and timorousness, became in the death camps the brute factuality of the universal. Not the individual Jew, not the martyred Jew, not the survived Jew—not a Jew by any name or fortune—not such a Jew of particularity was chosen. Jew, simple Jew, nominative universal describing and containing all mankind that bears that racial lineament until the third generation of ancestry, became chosen and was universalized. The death camps ended forever one argument of history—whether the Jews are a chosen people. They are chosen, unmistakably, extremely, utterly.

The uniqueness of the death camps, that which makes them a novelty in extremis, severed from all normative connections to historical precedent and causality, imparts to them a phenomenological simplicity. The death camps are a reality quite literally sui generis, and insofar as their reality is concerned, it is not necessary for us to perform phenomenological surgery, to bracket them, to excise their connections from the welter of historical conditions, to clarify the standpoint of perception in order not to confuse their manifestation with that of any other seemingly comparable phenomenon, like the social institution of the prison or the army. Simply defined (and the simpler the better for our purposes), the death camps were constructed to fulfill one purpose: to kill the greatest number of Jews at the least possible cost in money and material. To the side of Jews were added Gypsies, another "degenerative and infectious race," and the work was undertaken and, by war's end, almost completed. It was a task pursued with lethal self-sacrifice since, quite clearly, as many historians have noted, the war effort of the German army was severely impaired by the preference given to the transport of Jews. The simplicity of the phenomenon is no less its enormity. To kill Jews, any and all, defines the reality and clarifies its uniqueness. In the long history of "the teaching of contempt," in Jules Isaac's telling epitomization of the Christian doctrine of the rejection and humiliation of the Jewish people, the church never undertook to kill the Jews. Certainly the church had the opportunity; it did not have the intent. As Professor Yosef Hayim Yerushalmi pointed out recently, the anti-Jewish massacres of medieval times were "principally the work of the mob and the rabble" and, as he elaborates elsewhere in the same remarks, were often interrupted and contained by the appeals of cardinals and popes, rather than being the outcome of their direct instigation. This is not to say that Jews and Judaism were beloved to the church. It is merely to indicate what should not be forgotten, that the practice of the church was as ambiguous toward the Jews as was its theology. It acknowledged that Judaism was a *religio licita*, a legally permissible religion, even though a deluded one; that it worshipped the true God, although inadequately; that it was a primary faith, although one humiliated and superseded. The most telling observation of Professor Yerushalmi in this context is his ironic suggestion that had the church not rejected the Marcionite heresy, that which specifies the distinct and unrelated dualism of the God of Creation (that of Hebrew scriptures) and the God of Redemption (the Jesus of the Gospels), the Jews might well have been destroyed. Precisely because the church did not disdain its origins, did not repudiate the God of Israel, the Jews survived. Indeed, the novelty of the death camps is further underscored. The medieval tradition of anti-Semitism was *contra-Judaeos*, against the faith and the belief of the Jews, and, only by inference, against the people and the ethnicity that sustained that faith. The older traditions of anti-Semitism, those that stretch back into Roman times, the rage of Apion and Manetho, the confusions of Tacitus and others, signify an uncritical perception of the Jews as a political unit, a religious commonwealth that refused Rome, not allegiance, but moral capitulation. The ancient Jews annoyed Rome less because they were different than because they regarded that in which they were different to be superior to Rome. Perhaps there, well before Christianity, the seedbed of racial contempt is to be found, the ultimate historical ground of Sartre's contention in *The Anti-Semite and the Jew* that the anti-Semite chooses to make himself nondescript, to attach himself to the solidarity of the miserable mob, to make himself mediocre precisely because he cannot make himself individual. The anti-Semite takes upon himself the vulnerability of the state, the difficulties of an abstract, national pride and whatever there is, out there, that offends against the few values that give him identity, those he calls the menace of the Jew. Of course, Sartre's analysis is undergirded by historical assumptions with which we would take issue, but what seems to me most profound in his inquiry is the perception of racism as an instrument of insulating and aggrandizing the empty man, or, as is more appropriate to the anti-Semitism of figures of undeniable weight and influence—figures such as Marx, Bakunin, and Kautsky, to name but three revolutionary intellectuals whose anti-Semitism reached grotesque proportions—their anti-Semitism was a means of interpreting their ressentiment, their unreasonable contempt for the slowness, the intractability, the stubborn obduracy of the old order which refused to cave in on schedule.

State-instituted racism and racial anti-Semitism is a modern phenomenon, whose origins may lie in the classical tradition which knew no efficient distinction between the political manipulation of religion and the religious validation of the state. In the Middle Ages, the doctrine of the two powers, the king and the bishop, in continuous tension and embattlement, the king warring to win the loyalty and the blessings and benefices of the church, and the church using the weapons of popular agitation and excommunication to manipulate the powers of the king, maintained a healthy imbalance in which the Jews, *servi camerae*, bond servants to both crown and cross, were more often maintained as financial and political intermediaries to their disputes than cast into the fires of either. All this delicate tension dissolved with the victory of the secular state, the state which could conceive, administer, and propagate throughout its realm quickly and efficiently, employing the press, the clergy, the law, the army, and the civil service as instruments of disseminating policy. If that policy were racist, the Czars could with ease send the Black Hundred into the streets; it could distribute the Protocols of the Elders of Zion; the army could condemn Dreyfus and hold the government ransom for his condemnation; and National Socialism could institute the program of ultimate anti-Semitism, the death camps.

What must be understood is that the irrational phenomenon of racism can still be made intelligible—psychologically, socially, historically. Any Jew reading Graetz's *History of the Jews* before 1939 would, I think (seduced as he might be by Graetz's eloquence and narrative gifts), regard his summation of the many hundreds of pogroms, massacres, and riots which fill his pages as being antiphonic and unremarkable: 9 Jews were slain, 11 Jews died; 157 Jews were thrown into the moat and perished; 411 Jews were burned; 31 Jews died at the stake; 1 Jew died from his wounds. Indeed, the familiar litany of Jewish history until the death camps was predictable—whatever the violence, Jews died. The history of the Jews could be read as the history of Jewish dead from Ibn Verga's *Shevet Jehudah* until the beginning of the era of the death camps. The fact that the numbers were compassable, variant, incidental, rising and falling, great or few, without apparent pattern or consistency enabled us to regard Jewish history as a continuous narrative of Jewish lives being paid for Jewish life. Throughout it all, it could be said that Jews died *al kiddush ha-Shem*, in sanctification of the Name of God, as martyrs to faith, although undoubtedly many there were who were ignorant Jews, Jews without faith, even assimilated and unconscious Jews, killed no less as Jews, ennobled no less as martyrs.

The death camps changed all that as well. We are given a fixed number. We deal with a single inconceivable enormity, one figure of six million, that has neither grown nor varied, remaining a stationary imponderable. It is no less clear that the Jews who died cannot be called martyrs. This is not to say that they are not martyrs; it is only to say that the theological implication of such a martyrdom is as catastrophic for one's conception of God as it is trivializing of one's notion of martyrdom. If the reality is inconceivable, if we cannot encompass the decision of one people to congregate and destroy another, attended by the complicity and inattention of all the rest of mankind, equally inconceivable is any language of compensation or heroic transfiguration. The human beings who died are not made more sacred nor more innocent by being called martyrs; indeed, in martyrizing them we dismiss them, having given them their histrionic due. The only people who have the right to call the dead in the camps martyrs are those who believe in the sanctity of martyrs and are willing themselves to be martyrs. I know such people and I believe them when they speak of the martyrs of the camps, but I also know that very often they separate out from the company of those martyrs the no less murdered Jews who were nonbelieving Jews, Jews without *mitzvot*, even assimilated Jews, Socialist Jews, Jews with changed names and non-Jewish identities. It will not do to call them martyrs just yet.

I have come to the point in my remarks when the hopelessness of this inquiry seems insurmountable. I have done everything I can to make the death camps not only unique, incomparable, sui generis, but, more to the point, beyond the deliberations of reason, beyond the discernments of moral judgment, beyond meaning itself. It is precisely for this reason that I have used one unexplained term throughout this lecture, employing it conspicuously, but never defining it. I have spoken of the death camps. That is clear. A factual phenomenological description, a phrase almost neutral in its factuality. But I have also used the term *tremendum*.

Quite recently I had occasion to reread, as I do frequently, Rudolf Otto's magisterial essay, *The Idea of the Holy* (Das Heilige). That essay, a late product of German idealism, an early achievement of phenomenological analysis, is turned to the investigation of our knowledge of the holy. The holy is not simply a cognomen for God; it is not God's other name, a name among many names, standing alongside Merciful or Judge. The holy is the dimension of God's presence. The presentness of God is his holiness. Rudolf Otto, using the Hebrew Bible, with a sovereign control and a warming love of its nuance and texture, elicits from that text revelations of the presence of God which are astonishing. Indeed, astonishment, surprise, and amazement are the very terms by which

Otto underscores the shattering perception of God's nearness. God is near, Otto indicates. God is present, Otto evinces, but God is not for those reasons any the less terrifying and unfathomable. It is for this reason that Otto describes God in a single phrase as the *mysterium tremendum*—the utter mystery, the enormous mystery, indeed, the terror-mystery, for *tremendum* has as well not only the aspect of vastness, but the resonation of terror. The phenomenology of the holy begins with the perception of the terror-mystery of God and radiates from there, qualified, moderated, and textured by the traditional modes of mercy, love, and justice, until the utter God becomes the Father God of *Tatenu*, until the shattering presence becomes the still, small voice, until the terror-mystery becomes a God with whom men can coinhabit the universe.

The terror-mystery of God, the *mysterium tremendum* of divinity has always, in the phenomenology of religion, been offset and contested by under-divinities, potencies, and dominions in the universe which loath such ultimacy. The perception of the demonic coexisted with the perception of the holy. Indeed, part of the terror-mystery of God is that his manifestation in whirlwinds and at seas, in fires and in floods was often perceived at the outset as the work of his opponent, his demiurge, his particular devil. No wonder that God, in his *magisterium*, often appears under the aspect of his terror. The ferocity of God appears to resemble the demonic. It is no less the case if one listens, as the text unfolds its narrative, that what begins in ferocity ends in a bird with an olive branch and a rainbow. The terror-mystery of the holy becomes the love-mystery of the holy and the terror dissolves into grace.

This is one reading of the aspect of the holy as *mysterium tremendum*. But, let us put the case that we of the modern age no longer can deal with the holy, cannot perceive it, do not, justifiably one would think, authenticate its presence, but most contrary and fractious, regard ourselves as alone and autonomous in the universe, unbounded by laws except as conventions of power, unhedged by moralities except as consent and convenience dictate, is it not the case that in such a civilization all that was once permitted to the infinite power of God and denied to the finite and constrained power of men is now denied to the forgotten God and given over to the potency of infinite man? Caution: I am not proposing in this yet another gloss to the familiar discussion of Faustian man compacted to the Devil, with all its attendant critique of technology, machine-culture dehumanization. The argument here is different. It is the proposal of a counter to the *mysterium tremendum*. It is the human *tremendum*, the enormity of an infinitized man, who no longer seems to fear death or, perhaps more to the point, fears it so totally, denies death so mightily, that the only patent of his apparent indifference is to build a mountain of corpses to the divinity of the dead, to placate death by the magic of endless murder.

I call the death camps the *tremendum*, for it is the monument of a meaningless inversion of life, to an orgiastic celebration of death, to a psychosexual and pathological degeneracy unparalleled and unfathomable to any man bonded to life. And of the nations and cultures of the West, is there any so totally committed to life, to the choice of life and its enlargement as a system of conduct and behavior as that of the Jews? The Jew may well be the ideal victim because of his mere persistence, his sheer endurance, his refusal to die throughout four millenia until the *tremendum* was a celebration of the tenacity of life. Every Jew who has left Judaism for Christianity has invariably—and the literature is astonishing in its confirmation of this perception, from Paul to Tarsus to Boris Pasternak—argued that the old Jew is dead, that Judaism has no more life to speak, no more novelty to contribute, nothing vital and energetic any longer to transmit to the species. The Jew is, in such literature, construed as though dead, whereas no less clearly it is necessary to mortify Judaism in order to rationalize and excuse its abandonment. The living Jew must become the dead Jew in order that the non-Jew be saved. The covenant with life must be severed in order that the divinization of men and their proof against death be confirmed.

Martin Buber has written in a passage often cited that there is no caesura in the history of the Jews, no midpoint, no intermediation, no gap to be filled by the Holy Spirit, no descending dove of grace, no yawning time waiting for the divine incursion. Most specifically, in this teaching, Buber was addressing the absence of penultimate messianic moments. "In our view," Buber wrote, "redemption occurs forever, and none has yet occurred. Standing, bound and shackled, in the pillory of mankind, we demonstrate with the bloody body of our people the unredeemedness of the world. For us there is no cause of Jesus; only the cause of God exists for us." Buber tried to deal with the *tremendum* on several occasions, always obliquely, always *b'derech agav.* He spoke of our times as the eclipse of God, times when between men and God a veil had been dropped, a veil of confusion, obstinacy, or demonism through which the Word of God could not penetrate. He believed until the end of his life that God continued to speak, but that no man heard. Moreover, he continued to believe that God's speech was his action, and that not hearing that speech was, in effect, to destroy the efficacy of God. God spoke and created the world. God spoke and the people covenanted themselves to his service. Six million died and God's speech was not heard. Not enough. Moving rhetoric, but unfortunately not theology, not thinking. It has to be tougher than that. It has to be more than the eclipse of God. It has to be more than the death of God. It has to be more even than Nietzsche's madman proclaiming that "we have slain him." Not enough. And we know that now.

Buber's assertion that there is no caesura in Jewish history is accurate insofar as it concerns the eschatological vision of the perfecting and redemption of history, but wrong insofar as it misses the underside of history, the corrupting caesura, the abyss rather than the heavens of the historical. For the holy, there may be no caesura, but for the unholy, its name is caesura. The discontinuity of the abyss is precisely what insures that it is both caesura and *tremendum.* The abyss of history is, in this view, also a gap in normal time, no less a gap, no less a decisive gap than would be the messianic redemption. In the time of the human *tremendum,* conventional time and intelligible causality are interrupted. In that time, if not redemption, then the demonic tears the skein of events apart and man (and perhaps God no less) is compelled to look into the abyss. The Jews, for reasons no longer curious, have looked into the abyss several times in their long history. Tradition counts the destruction of the Temple and the obliteration of the Jewish settlement in ancient Palestine as one abyss. There was a caesura. The abyss opened and the Jews closed the abyss by affirming their guilt, denying the abyss, and assuming the culpability of the demonic. Not the "beyond reason," but the "within providence" became the satisfactory explanation. The expulsion of the Jews from Spain is accounted another. There was a caesura. The abyss opened and the Jews closed the abyss once again, not only by reaffirming their guilt, but more by transforming the event into an end-time of ordinary history and the beginning-time of mystic gnosis in which a new heaven was limned and the unseen order became transparent to mystical understanding. The death camps of the modern world are a third. There was another caesura of the demonic. This time the abyss opened and one-third of the Jewish people fell in.

It is not possible to respond as did the survivors of the first abyss. We do not hold ourselves guilty. We cannot say, as an incomparably stupid rabbi is quoted as having said of the Maalot massacre, that it occurred because the school in which the twenty-four children were slain contained twenty-four unkosher *mezzuzot*. That extremity of magical, talismanic thinking is hopeless, and all the degrees of talismanism up to the doctrine of "for our sins are we slain" is insupportable. But that was an old doctrine of providence, simplistic, but not without counterbalance of innumerable Midrashim which saw quite clearly into the nature of the mystery. The real point is that for our ancestors, whatever the deficiencies of their popular doctrine, they lived in the presence of the *Mysterium Tremendum*, the Holy God, and knew quite intimately the shudder and trembling of his immediacy. Nor do we respond as did the survivors of the second abyss. The kabbalistic transfiguration of the Spanish exile and the decimation of Sephardic Jewry represented an overwhelming and ingenious reinvestment of the historical process with a new significance, one which was adept at reading the sign language of events and determining an arcane and previously impenetrable language of hope. The third abyss is read, however, neither with guilt nor with hope.

To read the event with neither guilt nor hope is a pitiless conclusion. It lets the event lie meaningless, unrescued, unransomed. The death camps are meaningless, but they are also instructive. This is obvious, but I do not wish to complete my discussion with a recourse to homiletics or consolations. I could (and I believe it would be fruitful on another occasion) undertake to apply the analysis of Franz Rosenzweig to the ahistorical character of life within Torah in contrast with the holocaustal normality of life after the death camps, but I am frankly not ready for the personal implication of such an inquiry.

For the moment I must allow the brutal summation to emerge as it must. The death camps cannot be transcended. There is no way of obliterating their historicity by overleaping them. Quite the contrary. If there is no transcendence beyond the abyss, the abyss must be inspected further. The descent deeper into the abyss must take place; in a word, the abyss must be *subscended*, penetrated to its perceivable depths. The task of the excavation of the demonic is no metaphor. How can we regard the atomic bomb, or Vietnam, or the revelations of Solzhenitzyn's *Gulag*, if not as modalities of the abyss, excavations and elaborations of the human penchant to self-infinity, to the ultimate hubris which brings not only Jews, but all men to the borderlands from which there is no return for any.

It begins with the Jews and it can end with the habitable world. There is no way of making the genocidal totality of the death camps meaningful to the non-Jew as such, precisely because every Jew that has endured to this hour is a survivor in fact or an accidental survivor at least, whereas for the non-Jew the genocide of the Jews is an objective phenomenon which, on the face of it, by its definition appears to exclude him. The non-Jew would be slain only by having become a Jew (as occurred to many); otherwise he is able to contemplate but not share in either the fate of the victim or the perpetual unease of the survivors. This is a critical distinction which makes all effort of the Christian or the non-Jewish secular opponent of racism fail to understand what exactly the death camps mean to the Jews. For the non-Jew the death camps are still, so he imagines, a paradigm of human brutality, at least an epiphenomenon. For the Jew, however, it is historically real. The Bible commands that every Jew consider himself as though he went forth in exodus from Egypt. The grammatical authority of the Haggadah makes clear that this is no metaphor, whatever our wish to make biblical language metaphoric. The authority is clear: I was really, even if not literally, present in Egypt and really, if not literally, present at Sinai. God contemplated my virtual presence, then, thirty-odd centuries ago. The fact that history could not prevision and entail my presence is irrelevant. No less the case that the death camps account my presence really, even if not literally, hence my obligation to hear the witnesses as though I were a witness, to be with the witness as though I were a witness. It is mandatory that this real presence of all Israel in the death camps, experiencing the *tremendum*, enter the liturgy as surely as it entered the narration of the Exodus. Within us there is always hope and despair, and within faith that twin constellation must be honored, the hope extended by God to man and the despair returned by man to God—the dialectic most grimly enacted in our time.

Beyond all these considerations, we return again and again to break our head upon the *tremendum* of the abyss, a phenomenon without analogue, discontinuous from all that has been, a new beginning for the human race that knew not of what it was capable, willing to destroy and to be destroyed. We must create a new language in which to speak of this in order to destroy the old language which, in its decrepitude and decline, made facile and easy the demonic descent. When the preparations are completed, then the new beginning of the race which started in that quintessential perfection of the abyss must be thought (lest it be considered unthinkable) and redescribed (lest it be considered indescribable) and reconnected to the whole of the past, lest the abyss never be closed, and projected into the future, lest the future imagine it has no share in that past. In that way, first by separating the *tremendum* from all things and descending into the abyss, then by rejoining the *tremendum* to the whole experience of mankind as end point of the abyss and new beginning of the race, it is possible to link again the death camps, the *tremendum* of the abyss, to the *Mysterium Tremendum* of God who is sometimes in love with man and sometimes loathes him.

FRANKLIN SHERMAN

▣ Speaking of God after Auschwitz

The fact that we are able to take up a topic such as "speaking of God after Auschwitz" indicates that a certain stage of maturity has been reached in Lutheran-Jewish conversations. It was not very long ago, after all, that doubt was widely expressed as to whether the deep issues of faith could be dealt with at all within such an interreligious setting. Were not these matters too personal, too particular, too burdened with the baggage of our respective histories to be the appropriate subject of a dialogue that envisioned a fresh start in our relations with one another?

It is to the credit of the planners of the Lutheran-Jewish conversations that from the start, they were bold enough to plunge into biblical and theological topics on which the deepest convictions of both sides could come to expression. Many of these topics, however, were ones on which there was so definite a body of conviction on both sides, worked out through centuries and even millennia of discussion, that the spokesmen for the two faith communities could to a large extent serve simply as reporters of the received doctrine on the matter. Perhaps this has been more true for Lutheranism, which has been much more ready to encapsulate its faith in doctrinal or dogmatic form than has Judaism. But with a topic such as the present one we confront a question to which there are no ready-made answers.

Even for Judaism, which has lived now with the memory of the Holocaust for a generation, it can hardly be said that there is a consensus as to its meaning— if the term "meaning" can be applied to so irrational and so tragic an event.

Among Lutherans, at least American Lutherans, it is doubtful if the question has even been faced in a serious way. Thus its appearance on our agenda here should not be taken as an indication that the time is ripe for a final word to be spoken, but on the contrary, that the time is at hand for a real engagement with the problem to begin. The present paper, therefore, has the character of an essay—being an effort to open up the question, rather than a definitive statement.

Our topic would be easier to deal with if it read, "Speaking of Man after Auschwitz." For I think it is rather clear what must be said about man after the experience of the Holocaust. Let me put it in terms of the thought of one of the lesser figures of the Lutheran Reformation, one Matthias Flacius Illyricus.

Both Lutheran and Calvinistic theology of the sixteenth century, as is well known, held to a very realistic, not to say pessimistic, doctrine of man. But Flacius pushed this anthropological realism too far. Sin, he said, has become man's very nature and substance, and the image of God in man has become the image of Satan. For this he was condemned by the Lutheran fathers, as may be seen in the First Article of the Formula of Concord of 1577; and this rejection was highly significant in preserving for Lutheranism a higher estimate of man's cultural and historical possibilities than it has sometimes been credited with. (One thinks here particularly of Reinhold Niebuhr's critique of what he calls the "cultural defeatism" of Lutheranism.)

But from the perspective of this age "after Auschwitz" we may have to say that Flacius simply was a man in advance of his time. When he said that the image of God in man had become the image of Satan, he was wrong in applying this to the whole human race. But he had what now must be considered a correct provision of the depths to which man would fall in the persons of the mass murderers of our own age.

Listen to these words of Elie Weisel, in which he describes this phenomenon:

> It is possible to be born into the upper or middle-class, receive a first-rate education, respect parents and neighbors, visit museums and attend literary gatherings, play a role in public life, and begin one day to massacre men, women, and children, without hesitation and without guilt. It is possible to fire your gun at living targets and nonetheless delight in the cadence of a poem, the composition of a painting. One's spiritual legacy provides no screen, ethical concepts offer no protection. One may torture the son before his father's eyes and still consider oneself a man of culture and religion. And dream of a peaceful sunset over the sea.[1]

That is Satan garbed as an angel of light. And as the reports of the Vietnam atrocities have shown, it is not only in Germany that such things happen, nor is it only by Germans that they are done. If we wish to speak honestly of man as we have come to know him in our time, we dare not forget what we have learned of these demonic depths of human nature.

But what of *God*? That is the question with which we are confronted here today. Very bluntly put, the question is this: How can we believe any longer in a God of love and a God of power, a God who is "king of the universe," when six million Jews—almost the whole of European Jewry—could be slaughtered without the slightest sign of intervention, either from abroad or from above. (I am sure that the suffering inmates of the concentration camps would not have minded whether God worked mediately or immediately to save them—whether by lightening bolts from heaven or by the intervention of the U.S. government or of the papacy. *Neither* occurred.)

Here is the problem of theodicy on a cosmic scale. "Theodicy"—Leibnitz is thought to have coined the term, and the word itself contains the essence of our problem: how to reconcile our notion of God, *theos*, with our notion of justice, *dikē*. Or: how to justify the ways of God to man.

Put that way, the question sounds blasphemous; who is man that God should justify himself to him? Yet this is a question that is integral to biblical religion itself, from Job to St. Paul. Indeed, the problem of Auschwitz may be said to be *the problem of Job magnified six millionfold.*

It is significant that the profoundest treatment of the problem of evil in the Hebrew Bible is one that is couched in terms of a dramatic narrative about one single individual and his family. It is true also today that the terror and mystery of Auschwitz are brought home to us more by the story of one boy and one family, as told to us autobiographically by Elie Weisel, than by all the statistics or more generalized conclusions of those who have tried to analyze the problem as a whole. Perhaps this is because the human mind simply finds it impossible to work with both the *intensity* and *extensity* of the problem. Once one has entered to any extent into the suffering of one single individual caught in the nameless terror of the pogroms and the persecutions, the deportations and the death camps, it is difficult to multiply this, say, by sixtyfold and still retain one's grasp upon the problem. To multiply it by six hundredfold, by six thousandfold, by sixty thousandfold, by six hundred thousandfold, by six millionfold, is impossible. And so one's mind, reeling, returns to the picture of the single individual. We see him then, not only in himself, but as prototypical of the whole number of sufferers.

The figure of Job is pertinent to our inquiry above all for the chief characteristic with which the narrative endows him: his innocence. "There was a man in the land of Uz, whose name was Job; and that man was blameless and upright, one who feared God, and turned away from evil" (Job 1:1). It is this which gave the lie to the retributory doctrine represented by Job's friends—the idea that suffering is to be explained as the punishment for sin. Job protests his innocence, and in this he is vindicated, at the conclusion of the drama, by God himself. He does not claim to be wholly sinless; he is, after all, human. But he is in no way chargeable with transgressions of such a magnitude as to account for the suffering that is his. In this he is comparable to the victims of the Holocaust. For it is above all their innocence that is so moving, and so puzzling for a theodicy.

The doctrine of retribution dies hard, however. Note that it can work in two ways: (a) as a warning: "If you sin, you will suffer." This no doubt has some truth and can serve a useful hortatory purpose. But (b) it can also be used as an *ex post facto* explanation: "Because you are suffering, you must have sinned." Logically, this doesn't make sense. If all A is B, this in no way implies that all B is A. Psychologically, however, the retributory theory makes a great deal of "sense" in that it serves the sadistic impulse to increase the sufferings of others by adding to the suffering a further load of guilt for having brought it on oneself. Alternatively, it can serve masochistically to increase one's own suffering in this way.

How is God spoken of according to this theory? As a *God of judgment*, or even more, as a *God of vengeance*. The line between judgment and vengeance is this: in both, the suffering is related to antecedent sin; but "judgment" implies some reasonable proportion between the sin and the punishment, while "vengeance" implies a disproportion.

Is it possible to think of the Holocaust as God's judgment upon the Jews, or as his vengeance upon them? One's heart and mind and soul instinctively reject such a thought. Even to mention it is bitter to the tongue. Yet Christians must recognize that for centuries the church promoted just such a theory to explain the fall of Jerusalem and the destruction of the Jewish state. The besieging Romans, it was taught, were God's instrument of judgment upon the Jews for not accepting the Messiah.

It is true that some Jewish thinkers themselves accepted the theory that Israel's suffering and its dispersal by the Romans was to be interpreted as punishment for its sins. That does not make the theory any more correct. Its inadequacies must be clearly exposed. Toward this end, the statement of the Second Vatican Council which lifts from the Jews and Judaism as such the charge of responsibility for the crucifixion makes a great contribution, as do the similar Lutheran statements. But much remains to be done through education among the broad masses of church membership to break the last threads of this guilt-and-punishment theory. This must be done as preventive therapy, lest at any time in the future there is a temptation to apply it once again.

If the doctrine of retribution was the chief theory represented by Job's interlocutors, there was also another theory, a subordinate motif, which we may call the *theory of moral education*. In a word, suffering is good for you! "Behold, happy is the man whom God reproves; therefore despise not the chastening of the Almighty. . . . He delivers the afflicted by their affliction, and opens their ear by adversity" (Job 5:17; 36:15). Again, this theory has some truth to it, but only a limited truth. It is a true statement of what a man of faith can make out of his suffering—but only up to a certain point. When his very humanity begins to be destroyed, as was the case in the concentration camps, then it is fruitless to talk of the ennoblement of his character.

In both these instances (the theory of retribution and the theory of moral education) we have a case of the extension of what Robert K. Merton, in another context, called "theories of the middle range" into all-inclusive explanatory principles; and that extension simply is not justified. If it were, it would leave us with the picture of a monstrous God who tortures his creatures in order to perfect them, a cosmic version of the American commander in Vietnam who declared that he had to "destroy the village in order to save it."

It is most interesting to discover that parallels to these two theories represented by Job's interlocutors echo down through the history of Christian thought. The most substantial recent volume dealing with this problem is John Hick's *Evil and the God of Love.*[2] Consulting Hick's analysis, we find that he distinguishes between two major theories of evil (which is to say, two major types of theodicy) in Christian thought. The first he denominates the Augustinian theory, and the second the Irenaean, after the second century church father Irenaeus.

The Augustinian view is oriented to the categories of sin and punishment. The existence of suffering and evil in the world is attributable to the fall, i.e., to the fault of men. The Irenaean view, in contrast, looks not to the past but to the future for its explanation. It "finds the justification for evil in an infinite (because eternal) good which God is bringing out of the temporal process."[3] Life is a vale of soul-making, and all will eventually be to the good. Hick offers the following contrast between the two points of view:

> Instead of the [Augustinian] doctrine that man was created finitely perfect and then incomprehensibly destroyed his own perfection and plunged into sin and misery, Irenaeus suggests that man was created as an imperfect, immature creature who was to undergo moral development and growth and finally be brought to the perfection intended for him by his Maker. ... Instead of the Augustinian view of life's trials as a divine punishment for Adam's sin, Irenaeus sees our world of mingled good and evil, as a divinely appointed environment for man's development. ....[4]

Irenaeus's own words convey this "optimistic view" quite graphically:

> How, if we had no knowledge of the contrary, could we have had instruction in that which is good? ... For just as the tongue receives experience of sweet and bitter by means of tasting, and the eye discriminates between black and white by means of vision ... so also does the mind, receiving through the experience of both the knowledge of what is good, become more tenacious of its preservation, by acting in obedience to God.[5]

A very interesting theory, but in no way sufficient as an explanation of the Holocaust.

Those who are acquainted with the thought of Teilhard de Chardin will recognize that he stands within this Irenaean tradition. All of life tends toward the Omega Point, and is justified in its partial value by that total fulfilment toward which all things move. An inspiring cosmic vision—but one that is only able to deal with the tragedies along the way by, in effect, minimizing them. Teilhard has been widely criticized for being unable to interpret in terms of his cosmic evolutionary theory the tragic events of the twentieth century, which seem to have thrown into reverse what might have appeared to the nineteenth century as human progress.

If the first theory speaks of God as *the God of judgment,* the second speaks of God as *the God of creative purpose.* But neither is adequate to explain, much less to justify, Auschwitz. Neither, in fact, was found adequate by Job to explain his own suffering. The only answer Job receives is the theophany: an experience of the overwhelming majesty and awfulness of God. In this sense, the answer to Job's question is that there is no answer: I am God and you are man; and the fact that you are man is reflected precisely in the fact that you cannot comprehend my ways. Job bows to the dust, in humility and faith.

What does this mean for our speaking about God? It means that we speak of God as *the God of mystery;* that we acknowledge the inscrutability of God.

If we return to John Hick's analysis for a moment, we find that although he adopts, on the whole, the Irenaean viewpoint that the sufferings of this present time are justified by their eventual result, it is precisely the Holocaust which he acknowledges cannot be fit within this context of explanation. He has to allow it to remain as a surd, as something unexplainable.

It is to be noted as a grievous failing of Hick's whole study that in a four hundred page volume on "Evil and the God of Love," published in 1966, he does not refer to the Holocaust until page 397! His discussion up to this point is altogether too much in the domain of the personal, the psychological, and the metaphysical rather than the historical and the political realms. If he had taken this greatest example of the upsurge of evil in modern times into account earlier in his analysis, it might have affected the whole result; it might have destroyed the relative optimism of his Irenaean viewpoint.

Nevertheless, when he does refer to the Holocaust, he does not balk at describing it for what it is. Hick has been describing the way in which we are helped to bear our own suffering when we understand it within the context of God's ultimate loving purpose. "What, however," he asks, "of the sins and sufferings of others?" And he continues:

> When we ask such a question today we almost inevitably think of the Nazi programme for the extermination of the Jewish people, with all the brutality and bestial cruelty that it involved and evoked. What does that ultimate purpose of divine purpose and activity mean for Auschwitz and Belsen and the other camps in which, between 1942 and 1945, between four and six million Jewish men, women, and children were deliberately and scientifically murdered? Was this in any sense willed by God?
>
> The answer is obviously no. These events were utterly evil, wicked, devilish and, so far as the human mind can reach, unforgivable; they are wrongs that can never be righted, horrors which will disfigure the universe to the end of time, and in relation to which no condemnation can be strong enough, no revulsion adequate.... Most certainly God did not want those who committed these fear-

ful crimes against humanity to act as they did. His purpose for the world was retarded by them and the power of evil within it increased.[6]

Thus Hick can offer no explanation for the Holocaust. The most he can offer is a word of hope and consolation regarding the individuals who were caught up in it. His words to this effect are worth a further extended quotation.

> Our Christian awareness of the universal divine purpose and activity does, however, affect our reaction even to these events. First, as regards the millions of men, women, and children who perished in the extermination programme, it gives the assurance that God's purpose for each individual has not been defeated by the efforts of wicked men. In the realms beyond our world they are alive and will have their place in the final fulfillment of God's creation. The transforming importance of the Christian hope of eternal life—not only for oneself but for all men—has already been stressed above, and is vitally relevant here.
>   Secondly within the situation itself, the example of Christ's self-giving love for others should have led Christians to be willing to risk their own lives to help the escape of the threatened victims; and here the record is partly good but also, unhappily, in too large part bad. And third, a Christian faith should neutralize the impulse to meet hatred and cruelty with an answering hatred and cruelty. . . . Such a renouncing of the satisfaction of vengeance may be made possible to our sinful hearts by the knowledge that the inevitable reaction of a moral universe upon cruelty will be met, within this life or beyond it, without our aid. "Vengeance is mine, I will repay, says the Lord."[7]

Thus Hick has recourse to a doctrine of eschatological reward and retribution, and he ends, as we began, with a reference to the God of vengeance; now, however, not of vengeance upon the Jews, but upon their oppressors.

Without entering into a discussion of that motif as such, let us observe once more that in this major effort at a theodicy by a contemporary Christian theologian, he cannot comprehend the Holocaust within his framework of explanation. We are thus left to speak of God, so far as his relation to this event is concerned, in terms of mystery. Like Job, we bow in awe before his inscrutability.

There is a category in Lutheran theology which is intended as an acknowledgment of this mystery, this inscrutability. This is the notion of the *Deus absconditus*—the hidden God. Luther derived the phrase from the Latin of Isa. 45:15: *Vere, tu es Deus absconditus.* "Truly, thou art a God that hidest thyself."

For Luther, the will of God is not evident in the ordinary course of world events. His will is known only where he chooses to make it known; only in revelatory moments, not in life as a whole. We live by those moments, but in so doing, we walk by faith, not by sight. And faith is usually contrary to experience.

We spoke of the *Deus absconditus* as a category in Lutheran thought. It is more than a category: it is the background or undertone of all that is said in this theology. It was Miguel de Unamuno, I believe, who coined the phrase "the tragic sense of life"; but we may say that Luther, above all other theologians, possessed this tragic sense. All his assertions of faith, of courage, and of victory were rooted in what one Luther interpreter has called "the grand nevertheless." *Trotzdem*—in spite of all—I will believe!

Let us recapitulate the discussion thus far. The problem of Auschwitz, like the problem of evil as such, is the problem of how such things can happen if God is both good and powerful. If he is not good, then he looks upon these matters with indifference or even, if this is conceivable, with delight. But such a God would in no way be the God we worship. Luther suggests that the very word *Gott* ("God") is rooted in the concept of *Gut* ("good"). *Gut und Gott*: the two cannot be torn apart, or all that we know as Christian or Jewish faith would turn into its opposite. If the goodness of God is not to be given up, if he is truly all-loving and at the same time all-powerful, then Auschwitz cannot be explained. It remains in the domain of mystery. It is not surprising, therefore, that attention has been paid to the other pole of the equation, and it has been asked, Is God in fact all-powerful, or in what sense is he all-powerful?

We enter here upon a realm of theological questions which we can in no way treat adequately within the framework of the present paper. We can only briefly pass in review some of the major forms which reflection about this question has taken—the question being that of the nature and limits of God's power or of the exercise thereof.

The first is the conception of a finite God. This is a notion which, needless to say, has never found residence in any body of official Christian teaching. The idea no doubt has a long history. In American theology, its chief spokesman, in fact its sole spokesman of any prominence, was Professor Edgar Sheffield Brightman of Boston University. Brightman posited an element which he called "the Given," with which God himself has to deal, either using it as an instrument or, if that is impossible, acknowledging it as an obstacle.

> The Given consists of the eternal uncreated laws of reason and also of equally eternal and uncreated processes of nonrational consciousness, . . . disorderly impulses and desires, such experiences as pain and suffering, the forms of space and time, and whatever in God is the source of surd evil.[8]

The last sentence is significant. By "surd evil" Brightman means evil that is *not* explainable as the means to a greater good. He speaks of this as having its source "in God"; yet it constitutes for God a limit upon his own nature, a limit upon his will to love.

Brightman's view, as we have already indicated, has found little if any acceptance. I mention it precisely because it is so little known, and yet so precisely directed to our problem.

The second view of which we must take note speaks not of a finite God, but of a self-limited God. Unlike Brightman's conception, this one has a long and venerable history in Christian thought, and indeed in Jewish thought as well. I am speaking of God's self-limitation simply in this sense: in that he has created a world with two interrelated characteristics—freedom and lawfulness. Man is free: free to choose good or evil. But nature is bound, bound to act in accordance with cause and effect. Thus man is free to conceive and to construct the gas chambers at Auschwitz. And when the handle is turned, gas will flow through the nozzle. God is powerless, unless he wishes to contravene either human freedom or physical natural law. And this he does not wish to do.

Involved here is the whole question of grace and free will, of providence and predestination, indeed a whole metaphysic and a whole theology. My purpose here is simply to suggest that the problem of "speaking of God after Auschwitz" can hardly be dealt with apart from this range of considerations. It is a question that goes to the heart of our conception of God and man, and of their relations one to the other.

Speaking quite personally, I should have to say this: that in an intellectual sense, this solution (that of a self-limiting God) may be satisfying; but in a religious sense, and in a moral sense, it is not. For when the horrors grow so extreme as was the case in Auschwitz, then one's conscience cries out for God, if necessary, to put an end to history itself to stop the slaughter.

Yet, on further reflection, we may not really wish that. When we consider the relative meaningfulness of our own lives despite the pall of sadness from such horrors as the Holocaust, and when we consider the resurrection of Israel itself after the catastrophe—that is, the return of the Jews to their ancient homeland and their rebirth as a nation—we realize that we would *not* have wanted history to stop at some point in the early 1940s. And so we sympathize, if one may say so, with the dilemma in which God found himself, and in which he continually finds himself, confronted with a world which he has chosen to endow with mixed characteristics of freedom and lawfulness.

We have spoken of the finite God and the self-limited God. The third conception is that of the embattled God. I am speaking here of views that posit a demonic force that struggles against the divine. Paul Tillich may be credited with reintroducing the concept of the demonic into contemporary theology. It represents a demythologized version of the traditional notion of the devil, or Satan. There is no personal devil, but the demonic is terribly real. It consists in what Tillich has called "structures of destruction"—forces, trends, powers, irrational movements and instances of mass hysteria, all leading to the awful possibility of the pursuit of evil simply for evil's sake.

The rediscovery of this factor was not in the first instance an intellectual event; it was a historical event, based on the outcropping in the twentieth century of the dark underground of human history. Paul Tillich had the prescience to articulate this concept already in the 1920s, on the basis both of his experience in the First World War, and also on the basis of his long-term analysis of trends in modern life and thought that were to coalesce in the phenomenon of Nazism, and that had already begun to gain momentum in that very decade. His estimate of Nazism and his struggle against it were very clear, so much so that when the Nazis assumed power in 1933, the name of Paul Tillich was on the very first list of university professors to be dismissed from their posts.

The rediscovery of the demonic has had a tremendous impact on our image of man, since it is through man that the demonic works. But it also has an impact on our concept of God. It causes us to think of God as an embattled God, still struggling against the powers of evil in the world. Among Lutheran theologians, Gustaf Aulén has been prominent among those giving voice to this conception. He was professor of theology at the University of Lund and later a bishop of the Church of Sweden.

Aulén, in his book *Christus Victor*[9] and in his systematic theology, has set forth a dualistic-dramatic theory of the atonement. It is dualistic in that it posits a radical opposition between God and the powers of evil. It is dramatic in that it sees this opposition as working itself out on the stage of history in terms of the concrete clash between destructive and constructive powers. It is a theory of the atonement in that it posits a decisive significance for the event of Christ, seeing in his crucifixion and resurrection the decisive battle in this warfare between the divine and the demonic.

Aulén and others in the period after the Second World War used to employ the following illustration. Our present situation in history, they said, after the resurrection and before the parousia—that is, between the "first" and "second" comings—is like the situation of occupied Europe when the successful Allied invasion of Normandy was announced. The people of occupied Europe knew at that point that their liberation was at hand. Indeed, the victory had already begun, and even though setbacks might yet occur, the final triumph of the Allied cause was certain. So it is, said these Christian theologians, in the interim between the advent of the Messiah and the total victory of his kingdom. We live between D-Day and V-Day.

This theory, it may be pointed out, can be read in either of two ways. It is like the proverbial half-full glass of water, which may equally well be viewed as half-empty. On the one hand, there is a note of confidence in what God has done. On the other hand, there is a very sober realism about the battles that may yet lie ahead. To speak in this way of God is to speak of an embattled God. But that is perhaps to accentuate the negative. Let us speak more positively and biblically, with a slight turn of the phrase, by speaking rather of a "God of battles."

We have reviewed three "solutions" to our problem which left the divine sovereignty unimpaired, but thereby failed to answer the question of how the reality of God and the fact of Auschwitz can be held together. These were the sin-and-punishment theory, the character-education theory, and the theory that declines to answer the question, leaving the matter in the realm of mystery. Then we surveyed three positions which in some way do qualify God's sovereignty, at least with respect to the present age. These were the theories of the finite God, the self-limited God, and the embattled God.

With all this, however, we still have not spoken of God in the way that corresponds most closely to the nature of the problem, and that corresponds too to the deepest insights of the Christian—and also, I believe, of the Jewish—faith. This is to speak of the suffering God.

The late Abraham Joshua Heschel taught us to speak of the "divine pathos." He reminded us of how different is the Greek concept of God dwelling alone in *apatheia* ("without feeling"), or "thinking on thinking," from the Hebraic conception of a living and active God who is vitally concerned with the affairs of men. Heschel urged us not to be afraid to speak of God—not anthropomor-phically to be sure—but "anthropopathically." God too knows wrath and love and jealousy and joy, according to the Bible. If the danger of this line of thinking is God's humanization, even worse, said Heschel, would be his anaes-thetization.

Above all it is Jeremiah, according to Heschel's study of the prophets, who taught us of God's involvement in the sufferings of men. It is intriguing to note that precisely the same point is made by the Japanese theologian Kazoh Kitamori in his book *Theology of the Pain of God*. This work, published in English transla-tion in 1965,[10] is believed to be the first work of Christian theology ever trans-lated from Japanese into English, rather than the other way around. Kitamori writes:

> It is said that Isaiah saw God's holiness, Hosea saw God's love, and Amos saw God's righteousness. We wish to add that Jeremiah saw God's pain. . . . [11]

This is a pain, says Kitamori, which is at the same time God's love.

This is for me, religiously, the solution to the problem. God participates in the sufferings of men, and man is called to participate in the sufferings of God. Per-haps it is the only adequate solution intellectually as well. It was the German philosopher Friedrich Schelling who said in his book *Of Human Freedom*, that "all of history is virtually an enigma without a concept of an agonizing God." That, I think, is a memorable statement.[12]

For Christianity, the symbol of the agonizing God is the cross of Christ. I think that it is tragic that this symbol should have become a symbol of division between Jews and Christians, for the reality to which it points is a Jewish reality as well. I mean the reality of suffering and martyrdom.

The cross is not the instrument upon which the Jews put Jesus or anyone else to death; it was the Roman overlords who did so. Rather, the cross was the instru-ment upon which Jews were put to death. And this long antedates the time of Jesus. According to Josephus, Cyrus introduced into his edict for the return of the Jews from Babylon the threat of crucifixion for any who interfered with the exe-cution of his edict. Darius the Persian threatened this death to those who refused obedience to his decrees. Antiochus Epiphanes crucified faithful Jews who would not abandon their religion at his bidding. And after the siege of Jerusalem by the Romans, Titus crucified so many Jews that, says Josephus, "there was not enough room for the crosses, nor enough crosses for the condemned."[13]

The cross thus refers in the first instance to a *Jewish* reality: to the reality of suffering, all too well known to this people, from the time when they cried out in their affliction under Pharaoh, down to the time of their yet more unspeak-able sufferings under the modern Pharaoh. The further interpretations which Christians give to the cross of Christ are well known, but what I wish to do is to point us back behind the interpretations to the reality of this man who suffered as a Jew, and on the basis of whose sufferings the Christian should be the first to identify with the sufferings of any Jews.

The fact that this has not been the case, and that the cross has been the symbol not of identification but of inquisition, is a matter for the deepest shame on the part of Christianity. One thing is clear as to how we may speak of God after Auschwitz. We may not speak, and we cannot speak, in terms of any kind of triumphalism. We can speak only in repentance. A God who suffers is the opposite of a God of triumphalism. We can speak of God after Auschwitz only as the one who calls us to a new unity as beloved brothers—not only between Jews and Christians, but especially between them.

At an interfaith service held at the Lutheran School of Theology at Chicago on May 29, 1973, to commemorate the thirtieth anniversary of the Warsaw uprising, a prayer was offered which expresses very well this spirit of repentance and renewal. It was said antiphonally between the leader and the congregation:

> With those who grade any people as "superior" or "inferior" . . .
> *We share the guilt, O Lord.*
> With those who would "solve" any problem by destroying a group . . .
> *We share the guilt, O Lord.*
> With those who pretend not to know what a leader who traffics in fear and
>   hatred will do . . .
> *We share the guilt, O Lord.*
> With those who exult when their group does what they individually
>   would be ashamed to do . . .
> *We share the guilt, O Lord.*
> With those who wait until defeat to condemn what they accept in victory
>   . . .
> *We share the guilt, O Lord.*
> We share the guilt, and ask your help, O Lord . . .
> *To stand today against what we condemned a generation ago.*
> We share the guilt, and ask your help, O Lord . . .
> *To stand in our own country against what we condemn in another.*
> We share the guilt, and ask your help, O Lord . . .
> *To know that what all evil persons have done, we too could do.*
> We share the guilt, and ask your help, O Lord . . .
> *To know that what all good and brave persons have done, we too could do.*
> We share the guilt . . .
> *And the glory, O Lord.*
> In the holocaust . . .
> *May the I-who-am-opposed-to-you be consumed.*
> From the ashes of the holocaust . . .
> *May the I-who-am-with-you arise.*[14]

We have surveyed various aspects of the question of "Speaking of God after the Holocaust." Perhaps much of this speculation has been futile. In conclusion, we may refer to Karl Marx's famous remark in the last of his "Theses on Feuerbach." "The philosophers," he said, "have only *interpreted* the world, in various ways; the point, however, is to *change* it."

It may be questioned whether it is proper at all to employ God as an explanatory hypothesis, as some of the thinkers whom we have surveyed have done. God is not in the first instance an explanatory hypothesis; he is an impelling force. The very best way to speak of God after Auschwitz, therefore, is to speak of him in such a way that men are moved to see to it that such a thing never happens again. Unfortunately, in a world in which human freedom and human perversity are both very real, we cannot say that it *could* not happen. Therefore we say that it *must* not happen.

We have treated the problem of the Holocaust, as our topic demanded, in terms of the problem of God. But we need to return from this ultimate level of the question to the proximate level, on which the phenomenon of the Holocaust will be treated in terms of its more immediate historical causes. That is a task, however, not for one or two brief sessions of a conference, but for an ongoing inquiry that, despite all the work that has already been done, will require yet more years and decades until the significance of this event is really understood. Let us as Jews and Christians dedicate ourselves to joint participation in that ongoing task.

NOTES

1. Elie Weisel, *One Generation After*, tr. Lily Edelman and the author (New York: Avon Books, 1972), p. 10. Copyright © 1970 by Random House, Inc. Reprinted by permission.

2. John Hick, *Evil and the God of Love* (New York: Harper and Row, 1966).

3. Hick, *Evil and the God of Love*, p. 263.

4. Ibid., pp. 220 ff.

5. Irenaeus *Against Heresies* 4.1. Quoted by Hick, *Evil and the God of Love* p. 220.

6. Hick, *Evil and the God of Love*, p. 397.

7. Ibid., pp. 397 f.

8. Edgar Sheffield Brightman, *A Philosophy of Religion* (New York: Prentice-Hall, 1940), p. 337.

9. Gustaf Aulén, *Christus Victor* (New York: Macmillan, 1956).

10. Kazoh Kitamori, *Theology of the Pain of God* (Richmond: John Knox Press, 1965).

11. Ibid., p. 161.

12. This wording is taken from the English version of Kitamori's book, and is presumably a translation of the Japanese translation of Schelling. The reference is to *Of Human Freedom*, p. 403 of the German original; in the English translation by James Gutmann (Chicago: Open Court, 1936), it reads: "All history remains incomprehensible without the concept of a humanly suffering God."

13. Josephus, *The Jewish War* 5.11.2.451. Quoted by Maurice Goguel, *The Life of Jesus*, tr. Olive Wyon (London: Allen & Unwin, 1933), p. 534.

14. The author of this litany is Robert Blakely.

ROBERT E. WILLIS

◼ Auschwitz and the Nurturing of Conscience

It has been argued recently that it is not possible to ground Jewish theology legitimately in the Holocaust.[1] Whatever the significance of that event might be for Jewish life and thought, it is asserted, it cannot, in itself, provide the basis for a revitalized faith. Jacob Neusner, for example, is particularly blunt in rejecting that possibility:

> One who did not believe in God before he knew about the Holocaust is not going to be persuaded to believe in Him on its account. One who believed in the classical perception of God presented by Judaic theologians is not going to be forced to change his perception on its account.... Jews find in the Holocaust no new definition of Jewish identity because we need none. Nothing has changed. The tradition endures.[2]

Thus, Neusner categorically sets aside the efforts of Emil Fackenheim and Richard Rubenstein, among others, to see in the Holocaust an utterly unique event requiring a new departure for Jewish theology. Rubenstein's suggestive metaphor of the Holocaust as a time bomb ticking within the Jewish community[3] is neutralized when placed within the salvific contours of the tradition, and Fackenheim's urging of a new and commanding word from Auschwitz—that Jews continue to exist as Jews, lest Hitler be handed a posthumous victory[4]—is silenced by the sustaining power of the original 613.[*]

---

*Editor's note: The number "613" refers to the traditional *mitzrot* or commandments found in the Torah.

Reprinted by permission of Robert E. Willis.

Whether or not Neusner is ultimately proved correct in his view of the insignificance of Auschwitz for the Jewish story and its accompanying metaphors, and of the enduring sufficiency of tradition, no such appeal will suffice when the focus shifts to the implications of that event for the Christian story. What then becomes clear is that the tradition that has informed and shaped the sensibility of the Christian community through time has itself contributed to the development of anti-Judaic and anti-Semitic attitudes and actions. Rosemary Ruether has attempted to describe the form of that contribution in her suggestion that "anti-Judaism in Christian theology stands as the left hand of Christology."[5] Moreover, she continues,

> the stance of church leadership toward the results of theological anti-Judaism has been one which might be described as "the right hand not knowing what the left hand is doing," and that continues to be the attitude of the Christian church toward the history of anti-semitism in Christian history up to our own time, despite the Holocaust.[6]

Ruether's analysis of the ambiguity present within the Christian tradition raises what is surely the most difficult and agonizing question of all: the degree to which the church is to be held accountable for the Holocaust. Did Christian theology—the developing (and developed) explication of the Christian story, which began with the New Testament writings—prepare the way, wittingly or unwittingly, for that horror? For A. Roy Eckardt, at least, the answer is unequivocal:

> The Holocaust remains merely the final act of a uniquely unique drama. It is simply the hour that succeeds the drawing up of all the doctrinal formulations. It is the attaining of the "right time" (*kairos*) following upon all those *practice sessions* of crusade, inquisition, and the like. The Holocaust is *no more than* this consummation. Yet in that very simplicity, in that very absence of originality, there is contained all the insane complexity. Only in these latter years could we fully and finally ready ourselves for the eschatological deed (*Endlösung*). Only the final destruction was left to be carried out. . . . The Nazis were nothings. They could only provide concrete, practical implementation of the dominant theological and moral conclusions of the Church, with the aid of technological devices not previously available to Christendom.[7]

And, with regard to the impact wrought by the Holocaust on the subsequent thinking of the church, Eckardt finds no basis for optimism. "Very largely," he asserts, "the churches continue to live in the midst of the *Endlösung*."

It is impossible to conceive a more massive or absolute indictment of the Christian conscience and the story framework within which it is set. Indeed, if it is really the case that the Holocaust—the acting out of the "final solution"—can be seen as no more than the necessary expression of what was present implicitly in that story from the beginning, then it is hard to see what hope remains for any sort of fundamental reorientation or reshaping of it. The only possible conclusion would have to be that the Christian tradition, despite its ostensibly positive intent, and the contributions it may have made to human well-being, is in its very essence evil, the final embodiment of the Antichrist. Moreover, both the claims advanced on behalf of the capacity of the Christian conscience to respond in a morally fitting way, and the presumed ability of the Christian community to give it appropriate shape and direction, would have to be rejected.

Understandably, one shrinks from embracing so stark a conclusion. Not even Richard Rubenstein, in his analysis of the fateful relationship that has existed between Judaism and Christianity, found it necessary (or possible) to see in the death camps a *necessary*, and therefore unavoidable, consequence of the Christian outlook.[8]

Even so, we must not move too quickly to neutralize Eckardt's judgment, for it represents a profound *cri de coeur*, a resounding *mea culpa* spoken on behalf of the Christian community as a whole. At the very least, it serves as a dramatic reminder of the burden of guilt and responsibility which must be shouldered for the contribution which the church's theology did, in fact, make to the *Endlösung* of the Nazis. The fact that that event cannot fairly be seen as a direct entailment of the Christian story does not lessen the evil consequences it helped to produce.

It seems clear, at any rate, that the response of the Christian community to the moral crisis represented by the Nazis and their policies was at best ambiguous, and at worst the most explicit embodiment to date of the limited power of the Christian story to shape conscience and behavior in a morally appropriate fashion. Indeed, what emerges from that piece of history is a precise indication of the ambiguity and the complexity of the relationship between moral agency (in both its corporate and individual forms) and the story, or stories, by which it is shaped and directed.[9] To put it differently, we can say that it exposes dramatically the gap between the ideal and the actuality of the church, a gap which gains specific embodiment in the tension between what, from a moral point of view, is required and what in fact is done.

What is required now is the effort of attempting to expand the content and the dynamics of the Christian conscience through an absorption of the lessons conveyed to it by Auschwitz. To put it differently, the church must allow its conscience and those of its members to be nurtured by the Holocaust to a new embodiment of the relationship between story and moral agency. The urgent need for such an exploration has been expressed forthrightly by Friedrich Heer: "For the Church to assume her share of permanent co-responsibility for the whole Jewish community presupposes an illumination of the Christian conscience which is only just beginning. To put it into practice, a complete revision of Christian theology is needed."[10]

It has been proposed—by Stanley Hauerwas and Michael Novak, among others—that a theory of the moral life which seeks to do justice to the intentionality of moral agency must take seriously the particular story that has come to be embodied in the life of the self. It is only in relation to the complex story that is lived by the self, and the ways in which that informs and shapes the overall direction of its life, that moral assessment and action can occur.

To stress the relationship between story, intentionality, and action is not to reject the place of principles and rules in the moral life. It is, rather, to focus attention on what may be called the aesthetic component of morality—that larger and richer background which comprises its ethos, and which enables the specific actions of the self to be displayed as part of an ongoing character pattern rather than merely a discrete series of actions. As Hauerwas puts it:

> Our moral lives are not simply made up of the addition of our separate responses to particular situations. Rather we exhibit an orientation that gives our life a theme through which the variety of what we do and do not do can be scored. To be agents at all requires a directionality that involves the development of character and virtue. Our character is the result of our sustained attention to the world that gives a coherence to our intentionality.[11]

The story that we come to embody and make our own is not, however, self-generated. The formation of character and the shaping of intentionality occur within a social context, or, more accurately, within the several communities—family, nation, church—with which we have to do. The moral biography of the self is thus to be understood in relation to the stories, symbols, and metaphors generated by those communities, and appropriated as one's own.

It goes without saying that the process of appropriation will be complex rather than simple, for although there may well be points at which the various stories presented will mesh, there will also certainly be others where conflict and tension will arise—the claims of the family against those of the nation, those of nation and family against those of the religious community, and so forth.

It is in relation to this welter of potentially conflicting claims, loyalties, and obligations that the self must attempt to forge a coherent and durable pattern of moral response. That necessity points to the cruciality of a story which both transcends our undertakings and grounds us in them, providing an outlook whereby we are enabled to resist the tendency to identify completely (and immorally) with partial stories, and the roles and demands they present to us.

For the Christian moral self, such a transcending story is unfolded within the Christian community, which provides a setting within which moral awareness can be nurtured to a potential, albeit always provisional, embodiment of maturity.[12] It is within such a setting that the moral self *in its wholeness* can be specified in terms of the category of conscience. "Conscience" then serves as a shorthand designation for the complex of factors that impinge on the moral identity of the self, and points to the possibility of actions that exemplify continuity between character (virtue) and obligation. As James Nelson has remarked: "If we think of conscience with its several interrelated and social dimensions, then it is obvious that we are pointing not only to one particular element or faculty but to the entire moral self in all its richness and complexity."[13]

The understanding of conscience suggested above has certain obvious affinities with the views of such thinkers as Lehmann, Tillich, H. R. Niebuhr, and Bonhoeffer. In each, though not in precisely the same way, there is a concern to view the moral identity of the self—the totality of which I have designated by the term "conscience"—in relation to the social reality of the Christian community, and the meaning-complex of symbol, metaphor, and story by means of which it carries on the process of reflection, self-criticism, and action. The theonomous or trans-moral image of the self as moral agent that emerges here points to the transcendent ground of the moral life in the sovereignty of God (or God-in-Christ), and to that final level of accountability which must be exhibited faithfully throughout its duration.

One way of expressing the force of that accountability is to say that the understanding of the moral agency of the self that is projected within the Christian story entails the concept of deputyship. James Gustafson has indicated in a precise way the connection that holds therein between conviction and accountability.

> Our convictions are that God, made known through his deeds in Israel's perceptions of them, and in the face of Jesus Christ as the apostles have depicted it to us, is the sovereign Lord of all things. To be deputized by him is to be particularly responsible to him for the things over which he is Lord. No person, no event can be arbitrarily left out of our concern. And certainly the particular events and persons in our particular spheres of life give location to our deputyship. To fulfill this is to think carefully about God's will and way, to be perceptive with reference to our world, to be sensitized and directed by our faith and conviction, and to shape our intentions and actions with clarity. It is also to acknowledge that we are *only* deputies, and subject to the limitations and perversions of agency. God remains sovereign, and we live in hope as well as in solemn moral obligation.[14]

The nurturing context provided by the Christian community and its story is thus possessed, in principle, of the power to affect the dispositions and characters of its members. Within that setting, the universal and the personal dimensions of moral responsibility and accountability can be maintained and brought to the level of conscious reflection and enactment. Therein we find a perspective inclusive enough to relativize, without submerging, our lesser, though unavoidable, loyalties, so that our tendency to settle into some form of either moral polytheism or moral henotheism is transformed.

It is obvious, however, that we are dealing here with an ideal view. The requirements of deputyship are beset, as Gustafson notes, by our "limitations and perversions," and by our persistent tendency to fall into self-deception with respect to the implications of Christian moral identity and the way in which it ought to penetrate the various roles we inhabit, and define the limits of their claims upon us.

Nor is the possibility of self-deception an eradicable element in our lives. Despite the nurturing efficacy of the religious community, it remains a potent force in the very being of the moral agent. As David Burrell and Stanley Hauer-was have noted, "To be is to be rooted in self-deception." Given that fact, it becomes clear that "the moral task involves a constant vigilance: to note those areas where the tendency has taken root. This task is made more difficult by the illusions of the past which we have unsuspectingly inherited."[15]

Coming to an awareness of those aspects of our lives which contain the seeds of self-deception involves more than mere self-examination. It must encompass, as well, an insight into the ways in which the basic story by which persons are nurtured within the Christian community has itself contributed to the development of a deficient conscience, so that the venture of deputyship becomes fundamentally distorted.

That point applies with especial force to Auschwitz, for, as Burrell and Hauerwas have noted,

> the complicity of Christians with Auschwitz did not begin with their failure to object to the first slightly anti-semitic laws and actions. It rather began when Christians assumed that they could be the heirs and carriers of the symbols of the faith without sacrifice and suffering. It began when the very language of revelation became an expression of status rather than an instrument for bring-ing our lives gradually under the sway of "the love that moves the sun and the stars." Persons had come to call themselves Christians and yet live as though they could avoid suffering and death. So Christians allowed their language to idle without turning the engines of the soul, and in response, their lives were seized by powers that they no longer had the ability to know, much less to combat.[16]

The perversion of language into a story exposed to the risk of being inter-preted as an indication and guarantee of status—the triumphalist posture con-tained, implicitly if not explicitly, within much Christian theology—brings again into view the other side of that image. A story which evokes the motif of triumph requires the counter-motif of defeat and rejection. In short, it requires what became an increasingly prevalent component of Christian theology after A.D. 70: the assertion of the covenant unfaithfulness of Judaism and the Jewish people, and their subsequent rejection and replacement by Christianity.

What seemed a development with the power to counteract that pattern, the rejection by the church of Marcion's position in the second century, in fact proved to be an ironic certification of it. Marcion was judged heretical by the emerging orthodox consensus, the Jewish scriptures were affirmed as part of the Christian canon, but Judaism, viewed subsequently, was granted no continuing validity or worth. The only avenue of escape from the crime of deicide and a perverted story lay in conversion. The refusal to turn down that road provided additional proof, if any were needed, of Jewish hardness of heart, and made possible the emergence of a conscience within the church which could entertain, with only an occasional loss of equanimity, the spectacle of Jewish persecution and suffering.

Nor have the anticipation of the eventual conversion of the Jewish community, and the withering away of Judaism which it presupposes, yet been laid to rest, as Franklin Littell has noted: "Both during the conflict and in church gatherings after the war, even the best and most courageous churchmen continued to define the Jew's place in history for him, refusing to recognize Judaism as a religion in its own right, stressing a provisional tolerance based on expectation of the Jew's coming conversion to Christ."[17]

And the most recent effort on the part of the Vatican, announced in January of this year, to develop a more cordial atmosphere for Jewish and Christian relations, remains captive, despite its positive aspects, to that model. Marc Tannenbaum's comment is apt: "The assertion of a conversionary intention within the framework of guidelines for the improvement of Catholic-Jewish relations cannot but cast doubts about the motivations of the entire program."[18]

If, after Auschwitz, it is still possible for Christians to cling to the pretension that their story undergrids a responsibility for the conversion of Jews, then it is questionable whether we can learn anything from the events of history. For unless the consciences of those who profess to live out the Christian story can be reawakened by a consideration of these events—and the Holocaust in particular—then it would appear that there is a fated quality to the outlook the Christian story engenders which prohibits significant revision. If that is the case, however, we are doomed to achieve not only an ambiguous, but a perverted and evil embodiment of the deputyship entailed by that story. The range of responsible, conscientious caring is foreshortened to exclude fellow humans who happen to be Jews, and the silence of Pius XII becomes, as Arthur Cochrane suggests, the symbol of collective disobedience and failure.[19]

We are faced, at this point, with the alternative posed earlier by Paul Lehmann: either to dispose of the conscience altogether, or to transform it. Lehmann's solution was to present a vision of the theonomous conscience, grounded in the life of the *koinonia*, and responsive to the humanizing action of God in the world. In that setting, faith (i.e., response to the story) provides the basis for human actions in conformity with the directionality of the divine movement toward humanization, in an atmosphere set free from the demands of prescriptive legalism and from strict dependence on the guidance afforded by moral principles and rules. However, Lehmann's prospectus for a refashioned conscience does not avoid the danger of "forgetting the difference between the ideal church and the real church," as Alan Davies has pointed out.[20]

The possibility of overcoming that difference is, at best, limited. If self-deception is part of the given nature of human existence, then it follows that *any* story elaborated by a community and embodied in the lives of its members will suffer from partial insight and wisdom, and will run the risk of producing evil effects as well as good. Given that fact, it is perhaps understandable that historians like J. H. Plumb have tended to view the category of story in strongly pessimistic terms, arguing that it serves *only* the process of self-aggrandizement, thereby leading inevitably to over-simplification and distortion. The only reasonable course of action, then, is to reject story entirely, and to replace it with history, which (as Plumb sees it) can provide a true and impartial recounting of the facts.[21]

In view of the relationship that exists between story and conscience in the religious community, however, such a move would be both inadmissible and disastrous to the enterprise of moral agency. Whatever its distorting capacities—and they are both real and persistent—it is hard to see what sense could be attached to the concept of Christian moral action (or any other, for that matter) apart from the storied context within which it is set. It is doubtless true that "a person who habitually thinks in terms of parable and fable, most of all a fable of the highly organized sort which we call a religion, has a difficulty about altering an individual moral judgment, which is not experienced by the follower of principles."[22] That difficulty applies *a fortiori* to the sorts of moral assessments Christians have been led to make about Judaism and the Jewish people under the tutelage of their dominant story. What is required, then, is that the pattern laid down within it become "open to moral claims from without," so that it is empowered to "admit its own inadequacy."[23]

The approach taken by H. Richard Niebuhr provides a useful way of coming to grips with the problem. In *The Meaning of Revelation*, he underscores the importance of the inner history of the Christian community (its own story), and indicates also the significance, potentially, of outer, external views of it for limiting the tendency toward self-deception and for heightening moral awareness:

> Every external history of ourselves, communicated to us, becomes an event in inner history. . . . The church has had to respond to them. Though it knew that such stories were not *the* truth about it, it willingly or unwillingly, sooner or later, recognized *a* truth about it in each one. In so far as it apprehended these events in its history, these descriptions and criticisms of itself, with the aid of faith in the God of Jesus Christ it discerned God's judgment in them and made them occasions for active repentance. Such external histories have helped to keep the church from exalting itself as though its inner life rather than the God of that inner life were the center of its attention and the ground of its faith. They have reminded the church of the earthen nature of the vessel in which the treasure of faith existed. In this practical way external history has not been incompatible with inner life but directly contributory to it.[24]

There is a difference, of course, between what Niebuhr means by outer history and the event of Auschwitz. It is a difference, however, which serves to heighten the tragedy of that occurrence. For although the Holocaust was not, in any intentional sense, an "external history of ourselves, communicated to us," it ought to become such, for what is presented there is the dreadful irony of a community, long accused of the crime of deicide, embodying totally the image of crucifixion claimed by the church as the most potent symbol of God's love and the meaning of discipleship.

That judgment must be followed immediately by the recognition that the image of the crucifixion can be applied to Auschwitz only imperfectly, as something *imposed*, not chosen. The possibility of the Christian story and conscience receiving instruction from that event depends on seeing it properly. Only if it is seen for what it was and is—a radical calling into question of the credibility of Christianity—can its significance begin to be unpacked. When it is so seen, however, when Christians allow the horror of Auschwitz to penetrate their consciousnesses steadily and without flinching, then they are enabled to receive a new training in Christianity.

That training must begin with the shock of recognition, the willingness to accept guilt and admit complicity. Does this imply a concept of collective guilt? I believe that it does, but at the level of shared memory and participation in the ongoing life of a community rather than at the level of interpersonal assessment and judgment of the actions of others. It is obviously true that none of us here were directly involved in the policies that led to the death camps. Nevertheless, the effects of the Christian story through time in creating a potent seedbed for contemporary anti-Semitism, and the actions of those who professed allegiance to it during that crisis, can become, through intentional appropriation, part of my (and our) history as well. Theodore R. Weber has expressed the point well: "The self's memory . . . provides a track on which the guilt of other persons in other ages can run into the present, and the identification of the self with selected or given historical antecedents provides the coupling mechanism by which their guilt becomes my guilt."[25]

The acceptance of one's complicity in Auschwitz provides no basis for assessing the intentions and actions of others. It is an action that each of us must perform for herself or himself, but it is done in the name of, and on behalf of, our participation in the community as a whole. Nevertheless, it is not a merely religious action devoid of moral import. Rather, it is, following Karl Barth's analysis, the *primary* moral deed—repentance, *metanoia*—which must precede and inform all subsequent thinking and doing.

Once that act has been performed, there are further implications that follow from the training in awareness afforded by Auschwitz. To begin with, we are forced to a radical reopening of the question of the relationship between God and evil. It is ironic, in that respect, that the emergence of Christian theologies of the death of God took their departure, not from that event, but rather from various assumptions about the state of contemporary consciousness in a secularized world. That fact, surely, provides a stunning indication of the degree to which Auschwitz has failed to penetrate the minds of Christian thinkers.

Franklin Sherman and A. Roy Eckardt have grappled recently with the problem of belief in God after Auschwitz, with strikingly different proposals.

Sherman's approach is to stress the participation of God in human sufferings and the moral imperative that follows, viz., that women and men are called upon to become active participants in that suffering. Nor is he unaware of the moral ambiguity involved in appealing to that symbol, centering, as it does, in the cross: "It is tragic that this symbol should have become a symbol of division between Jews and Christians, for the reality to which it points is a Jewish reality as well, the reality of suffering and martyrdom." Nevertheless, an emphasis on voluntary suffering, divine and human, can, Sherman believes, cut through the pretentiousness of a triumphalist outlook, and recall us to a remembrance of our shared humanity under God: "A God who suffers is the opposite of a God of triumphalism. We can speak of God after Auschwitz only as the one who calls us to a new unity as beloved brothers—not only between Jews and Christians, but especially between Jews and Christians."[26]

It is clear that Sherman's proposal assumes the continuing validity of traditional covenant theology, now corrected and chastened by an acknowledgment of the ambiguities latent within it and the need for continual repentance for the evils they have produced.

Eckardt, by contrast, maps out a position which stresses God's voluntary *abrogation* of the covenant as the only (morally) proper act of repentance for his complicity in the evil of involuntary suffering to which it has led. That must mean, however, that "the myth of the Jew as 'suffering servant' can surrender its horrible power only as the erstwhile Covenant is given a decent and moral burial."[27] Following Emil Fackenheim, Eckardt argues for a new understanding of Jewish existence in which the primary motif is that of survival rather than suffering, and in which the categories of traditional theology give way to the process of moralization and secularization.

There are problems in both Sherman's and Eckardt's approaches. The former must confront the challenge of making credible, after the Holocaust, *any* appeal on the part of Christians to the efficacy of the cross, and the image of sacrificial, voluntary suffering it presents. At the very least, it is an image which must, for the time being, be embodied in the *life* of the Christian community, rather than merely proclaimed.

The latter must wrestle with the implications for Christians of a Jewish identity set free from the storied framework of the covenant, in view of the continuing reality of secular anti-Semitism. In short, it is possible, in this case, to do the wrong thing for the right reasons. If the first Holocaust occurred, in a sense, under Christian auspices, the possibility of a second under secular sponsorship must be taken seriously. Thus, the judgment that the symbol of covenant can be accorded neither credibility nor place in Christian language about Judaism and Jewish existence must be weighed with care, lest it provide the basis for an indifferent, rather than an informed, conscience.

Perhaps the safest, and most obvious, point to be made at this time is that the Holocaust looms, unavoidably and consumingly, as a mystery for the Christian thinker, and that the first response must be a respectful silence. When the effort is undertaken of bringing that event into conjunction with the God professed to be the center of value within the Christian story, then the process of exorcising those elements within it which contribute to and sustain, however subtly, either a presumed superiority or anti-Semitism, presents itself as the first task for a renewed conscience.

Auschwitz can also be seen as the final exposure of the dangers that attend the privatization of religion, a development that must be judged an important contributing factor to the inability of the church to respond properly to the threat posed by Hitler and his policies. To put it differently, the Holocaust presents a stark reminder of the consequences of making the Christian story one's own without at the same time appropriating a consciousness of its grounding in community and its universally inclusive potency.

There is at present a good deal of interest in various approaches to the spiritual life which stress individual effort, concentration, or meditation; and the task of "getting one's head together" has achieved the status of moral obligation for the young, and, perhaps, for the not-so-young as well. If Peter Berger is correct, we are witnessing the flowering of impulses set in motion at the time of the Reformation.[28]

In short, the privatization of religion emerges, albeit ironically, out of the Protestant emphasis on the sole sovereignty of God's grace and the corresponding need to search diligently in scripture in order to discover the access routes that enable one to experience a sense of contact and relationship with it. The contemporary secular view of the religious life as essentially an affair between the isolated individual and whatever sources of transcendence he or she can discover may well be a perversion of the Protestant outlook, but it is, at any rate, a perversion from which the church is not free.

This side of Auschwitz, there is a pressing need to recover a sense of the importance of the institutionalization of the Christian story, that is, an awareness of the ways in which it shapes persons into a community of nurture, and provides a sense of identity which cuts across their various offices and roles, thereby informing moral agency at every point in their lives.

The consciences of Christians can receive further instruction from Auschwitz when it is seen as the parable par excellence of human vulnerability. As Rubenstein has pointed out, the Holocaust represented the bringing together of the concept of superfluous persons with heightened technological efficiency and power.[29]

Thus, it was not only the question of Jewish survival that was posed at Auschwitz. The death camps point to the question mark hanging over the collective future of us all, for they expose our penchant for falling back on various kinds of "final solutions" to the problems that confront us, with their attendant evils. The process remains the same, whether it takes the form of the continued insanity of believing that the best road to peace is through a continually increasing defense budget and stockpiles of nuclear arms, through bombing the Vietnamese back to the Stone Age, through adopting policies of "benign neglect" toward black people and "termination" toward Native Americans, or through a calculated indifference to the sanctity of the environment and the legitimate needs of others in order to satisfy the consumption level of the United States and other presumably "developed" countries.

Moreover, it is sobering to consider that just now, when death education and the process of dying have found a receptive audience in the schools and churches of our society, we are witnessing a growing tendency to expand the limits of permissible death. Regardless of one's position on the issue of the morality of abortion, it should at least be conceded that it raises profound and complex issues about the meaning and status of developing life, and that those are not even seriously broached, much less engaged, by talk about "fetal tissue," the risk factor in various surgical procedures, and the like.

Equally profound and complex issues are now surfacing as the result of new discoveries and techniques in the biological and medical professions: the appropriateness and limits of experimentation on human beings; the proper range to be allowed to genetic planning and control; the guidelines, surgical and moral, that must be observed in relation to organ transplantation; and the moral appropriateness of employing procedures of direct euthanasia.[30]

To view these developments from the perspective of human vulnerability bodied forth at Auschwitz is not to reduce their complexity or to provide ready-made solutions. What can happen is that the conscience informed by that image will remain more sensitive to the potentially serious threats they pose to our capacity to endure as morally sensitive persons. The lure of technological efficiency that made Auschwitz a reality has not, certainly, departed from our midst.

Nor need one be an alarmist to make that point. That one may be accused of falling into that posture by the simple act of asserting that there are perhaps some actions that ought to be (even if they are not for all) both unthinkable and undo-able, is surely a mark of the times, and of a growing tendency to embrace the notion that some lives are indeed superfluous (provided only that they are not our own), and thus expendable.

Finally, in the light of the restoration of Israel, Auschwitz can instruct the consciences of Christians of a fact which has, often enough, been denied: the ongoing durability and existence of Judaism and the Jewish people. It is tempting to view the relationship between the Holocaust and a restored Israel in terms of the model of crucifixion and resurrection. It is, I am convinced, a model, which should be approached with extreme caution. At the very least, it is not something which Christians are in any sense permitted to say to Jews, for it manages simultaneously both to deepen and to make innocuous the horrors of Auschwitz, by making them a condition for eventual rebirth and liberation. It is additionally offensive, moreover, in that it attempts to make sense of, and perhaps to justify, events which simply cannot be fitted into any tidy conceptual scheme. Elie Wiesel's comment is apt:

> Israel, an answer to the holocaust? It is too convenient, too scandalous a solution. First, because it would impose a burden, an unwarranted guilt-feeling, on our children. To pretend that without Auschwitz there would be no Israel is to endow the latter with a share of responsibility for the former. And second, Israel cannot be an answer to the holocaust, because the holocaust, by its very magnitude, by its essence too, negates all answers. For me, therefore, these are two distinct events, both inexplicable, unexplained, mysterious, both staggering to the mind and a challenge to the imagination. We shall never understand how Auschwitz was possible. Nor how Israel, scarcely a few years later, was able to draw from itself the strength and vision to rebuild its home in a world adrift and in ruins.[31]

The challenge posed for the Christian conscience by the restoration of Israel is, quite simply, whether we have the capacity to learn, in however limited a fashion, from the past, or whether we are, as Eckardt asserts, still living in the *Endlösung*, the time of the "final solution." For the simple fact of the matter is that the difficulties occasioned for Christian consciousness by a Judaism and a people who refused to cease existing in conformity with the story informing that consciousness are, if anything, intensified by their continuation—despite the time and effort expended during the Holocaust—as a definite and (potentially) enduring political and geographical reality.

I am not suggesting that Israel as a nation is exempt, or to be exempted, from the sorts of factual, empirical analyses and judgments ordinarily applied to nation states. A recognition of the symbolic import for the Christian conscience of Israel's reappearance among the nations need not, and should not, entail automatic acceptance of every policy decision made by its government. Nor on the other side, should it mean that Israel is to be judged by standards of conduct which are not expected of others. The right of a nation and its people to exist cannot justifiably be tied to the condition that their behavior should exhibit moral superiority to others at every point.

The crucial question, then, is whether Christians can endorse, wholeheartedly and without reservation, the right of the Jewish people to exist *in that particular, definite form.* For the image of the Jew presented by Israel represents the incarnation of a potential and a dream (within the Jewish story) which has simply had no place in the traditional Christian outlook: Jewish identity and existence *despite* Christianity; the land restored and made fruitful *despite* the destruction of the temple; the possibility of hope *beyond* despair; the burden of precariousness *removed*, to a degree, by the freedom to be; and the having of a place within which being can receive form and extension through time.

If that dream and its fulfillment can become a part of the consciousness of the Christian community, then it will be possible to understand from within, as it were, why there is continued anxiety in Israel today over the possibility of a second Holocaust, and why it is possible for someone like Golda Meir to express the unimaginable dread aroused by that vision in terms of a "Masada complex." It is doubtless true, as Robert Alter has argued, that Masada, with its image of mass suicide, comes into sharp conflict with the value placed on life within the Jewish tradition.[32] It is also important, however, to see in that image a symbol of the final rejection of passivity. In short, if there is to be a second destruction of the Jewish people, it will at least occur, this time, by their own hands, not by those of others.

In the end, the degree to which the Christian story and conscience are informed by the reality of Israel will provide a measure of what has been learned from the Holocaust. The moral imperative that ought to result from the latter has been put succinctly by Franklin Sherman: "In a world in which human freedom and human perversity are both very real, we cannot say that it *could* not happen. We say that it *must* not happen."[33]

This article represents at best a beginning in what must become an ongoing process of appropriation and reflection. For the God who summons us to community and obedience in the Christian story is envisioned as the universal center of value whose valuing knows neither partiality nor limit. To make that story one's own while continuing to exclude from consciousness the implications it carries for us as moral agents who bear a special burden and responsibility for Judaism and the Jewish people, and thereby for all persons, signifies only that we have, to our shame, missed the point.

NOTES

1. See, e.g., Michael Wyschogrod, "Faith and the Holocaust," *Judaism*, XX, 286–94; and Jacob Neusner, "The Implications of the Holocaust," *Journal of Religion*, LIII (1973), 293–308.

2. Neusner, "The Implications of the Holocaust," p. 308.

3. Richard Rubenstein, *After Auschwitz* (Indianapolis: Bobbs-Merrill, 1966), p. 223.

4. Emil L. Fackenheim, *Quest for Past and Future* (Boston: Beacon Press, 1968), p. 20.

5. Rosemary R. Ruether, "Anti-Semitism in Christian Theology," *Theology Today*, XXX (1974), 365.

6. Ibid., p. 380.

7. A. Roy Eckardt, "Is the Holocaust Unique?" *Worldview*, XVII (1974), 33–34.

8. Ibid., p. 34.

9. Rubenstein, *After Auschwitz*, pp. 20–21.

10. See Stanley Hauerwas, "The Self as Story: Religion and Morality from the Agent's Perspective," *Journal of Religious Ethics*, I (1973), 71–85.

11. Friedrich Heer, "The Catholic Church and the Jews Today," *Midstream*, XVIII (1971), 27.

12. See Paul Lehmann, *Ethics in a Christian Context* (New York: Harper & Row, 1963).

13. James B. Nelson, *Moral Nexus* (Philadelphia: Westminster Press, 1971), p. 38.

14. James M. Gustafson, *The Church as Moral Decision-Maker* (Philadelphia: Pilgrim Press, 1970), p. 108.

15. David Burrell and Stanley Hauerwas, "Self-Deception and Autobiography: Theological Reflections on Speer's *Inside the Third Reich*," *Journal of Religious Ethics*, II (1974), 111.

16. Ibid., p. 100.

17. Franklin H. Littell, "Christendom, Holocaust, and Israel," *Journal of Ecumenical Studies*, X (1973), 487.

18. *St. Paul Pioneer Press*, January 3, 1975.

19. Arthur Cochrane, "Pius XII: A Symbol," in Eric Bentley, ed., *The Storm Over the Deputy* (New York: Grove Press, 1964), pp. 157–62.

20. Alan T. Davies, *Anti-Semitism and the Christian Mind* (New York: Herder and Herder, 1969).

21. J. H. Plumb, *The Death of the Past* (Boston: Houghton Mifflin, 1971).

22. R. W. Hepburn, "Vision and Choice in Morality," in Ian T. Ramsey, ed., *Christian Ethics and Contemporary Philosophy* (New York: Macmillan, 1966), p. 193.

23. Ibid., p. 190.

24. H. Richard Niebuhr, *The Meaning of Revelation* (New York: Macmillan, 1941), pp. 62–63.

25. Theodore R. Weber, "Guilt: Yours, Ours, and Theirs," *Worldview*, XVIII (1975), 21.

26. Franklin S. Sherman, "Speaking of God After Auschwitz," *Worldview*, XVII (1974), 29–30.

27. Eckardt, "Is the Holocaust Unique?" in ibid., p. 34.

28. See Peter L. Berger, *The Sacred Canopy* (Garden City: Doubleday, 1969), part II, "Historical Elements."

29. See Richard Rubenstein, "Religion and the Origins of the Death Camps," in *After Auschwitz*, pp. 1–44.

30. See James B. Nelson, *Human Medicine* (Minneapolis: Augsburg, 1973).

31. Elie Wiesel, *One Generation After* (New York: Bard Books, 1965), pp. 166–67.

32. Robert Alter, "The Masada Complex," *Commentary*, LVI (1973), 19–24.

33. Sherman, "Speaking of God After Auschwitz," p. 30.

DAVID TRACY

◼ Religious Values after the Holocaust

A Catholic View

CATHOLIC THEOLOGY

The expression *Catholic theology* means, of course, the self-interpretation of the Catholic Christian religious tradition. And yet this seemingly obvious description of the task of Catholic theology needs further explanation. Only then can we hope to clarify the explicitly theological task of Catholic Christianity in relation to that event of sheer negativity we hesitatingly call the Holocaust—an event which, with Arthur Cohen, we might more fittingly name theologically the *tremendum* of our age.[1]

To assume that Catholic theologians practice Catholic theology by engaging in the self-interpretation of the Catholic tradition is, in fact, to imply several factors needing explication. The principal task of the theologian is one of interpretation of both the tradition and the contemporary situation. Theology is a task, therefore, for finite, historical interpreters living in a particular cultural situation and attempting to render fitting interpretations of their religious tradition for and in that situation.[2]

Second, theologians as interpreters in this case are also, by definition, those who in some recognizable manner participate in that religious tradition. Thereby do theologians commit themselves to appropriate the tradition's own authoritative norms (its classics) as guides to interpretation.

Third, in the case of Catholic theology, this appropriation is likely to stress the need for taking account of the classics of the whole tradition from the original apostolic witnesses in the New Testament to the present experience of the entire church community, as well as (in the language of the Second Vatican Council) the "signs of the times" in one's own age. It is also the case historically that Catholic theologians have tended to emphasize the trustworthiness of the whole tradition (usually under the rubric of "the development of doctrine"). Catholics have generally, therefore, emphasized interpretation as a hermeneutics of retrieval of the resources of the tradition for the present. In recent years, however, another mode of interpretation has come to play a more and more central role in Catholic theology. This second kind of interpretation can be called a hermeneutics of suspicion upon the possible errors, illusions, and distortions that may also be present in so long, so rich, so complex, and so ambiguous a tradition as that of Catholic Christianity.[3]

In terms of our historical experience, it hardly seems necessary to recall that every tradition, including every religious tradition, is properly described as ambiguous in its reality. For any particular participant in a religious tradition, therefore, two realities will operate. First, a fundamental trust in the disclosive and transformative religious realities of the tradition. That trust and loyalty are named faith. Faith's self-interpretation is called theology. Second, a recognition that alongside fundamental trust in and loyalty to the tradition lies a suspicion upon the possible presence of errors, illusions, distortions in the tradition itself.

Yet my appeal to the need for a Catholic hermeneutics of suspicion, based on a recognition of ambiguities in the tradition alongside (not replacing) a hermeneutics of retrieval based on a fundamental trust in the tradition, is not simply an appeal to our contemporary experience. Rather the familiar appeal in Catholic theology to the *theological* need to "discern the signs of the time" is only the first indication of this demand for suspicion. The traditional Catholic themes of *ecclesia semper reformanda* ("the church always in need of reform") and the theme, well formulated by Catholic theologians from Augustine to Rahner, of the theological reality of a "sinful church" (not only a "church of sinners"), alongside the theological understanding of church as eschatological sacrament of Christ and world, already indicate the need for a Catholic hermeneutics of suspicion. Sin, after all, is a far more radical charge than error, illusion, distortion in our earlier formulation.

Moreover, as the Catholic-Protestant polemics of the past fade into unmourned memory, it becomes clear that the reformatory principle has become a major moment in Catholic theology itself. As Paul Tillich stated years ago on the Protestant side, Reformation theology needs to appropriate "Catholic substance" along with its "Protestant principle." As one should also add, Catholic theology needs to appropriate far more than it often does that Protestant principle as part of its own Catholic Christian substance. As both Catholic and Protestant theologians, moreover, have entered into serious dialogue with Jewish theologians, both Catholics and Protestants have learned anew how Jewish a religion Christianity finally is. Above all, they have learned that the Jewish prophetic, the self-critical, self-reformatory, both suspicious and retrieving eschatological reality of our own Christian and Jewish authoritative biblical faith must be more fully retrieved.

To retrieve those prophetic and eschatological Jewish strains in Christianity is to demand that a major part of contemporary Christian theological interpretation should be a hermeneutics of suspicion upon the actual realities of the religious tradition, a tradition recognized *theologically* as fundamentally trustworthy yet also recognized theologically as ambiguous and demanding constant prophetic self-reform. The route from the anti-Judaic statements of the New Testament through the revolting anti-Jewish polemics of John Chrysostom and others in the patristic period through the explicit (and yet more deadly, the implicit) "teaching of contempt" tradition in the Christian tradition to the virulent, revolting anti-Semitism that can pervade and clearly has pervaded many a Christian unconscious are merely the most obvious examples of the radical ambiguities within the Christian religious tradition.

As the prophetic strain is religiously appropriated and theologically employed in contemporary Catholic theology, moreover, the disclosures—both painful and necessary—of further ambiguities in the very tradition which Catholics fundamentally trust and to which they remain loyal increase. The attempts to reform church structures in the prophetically oriented theologies of Küng and Schillebeeckx, for example, are grounded in a profound faith and trust in the tradition's own norm, Jesus Christ, as these theologians attempt to free the "dangerous" prophetic memory of Jesus upon the actualities of present church life. The attempts to disclose the repressed ideologies of sexism, classism, oppression, and alienation in traditional and modern Christian life and thought by the Third World liberation theologians, the black theologians, and the feminist theologians are *theologically* grounded in this biblical prophetic strain in Christianity itself. The liberation theologians seek to release the half-forgotten, often repressed memory of the suffering of the oppressed—those who are special, privileged to God, from the great prophets to Jesus. They release this prophetic hermeneutics of suspicion in order to charge the church to be faithful to its own possibility and command. Those Catholic theologians who have exposed the ideological distortions of anti-Judaism and anti-Semitism in the tradition—such theologians as Flannery, Ruether, Baum, and Pawlikowski—live in and by that prophetic demand, that inner-Catholic demand for the religious reality of constant self-criticism and self-reform. They live in and by the theological reality of both retrieval and suspicion. It is crucial to see that all these Catholic theologians are as deeply engaged in a hermeneutics of retrieval of the tradition as their curiously untroubled colleagues. Yet what these theologians see is precisely that really to retrieve the prophetic, eschatological strain which empowers Christianity as a religion is also to retrieve the theological necessity for a hermeneutics of suspicion upon the radical ambiguities of the tradition—the whole tradition from its beginnings to the present. No less than more "traditional" Catholic theologies of retrieval are these theologies of both retrieval and suspicion (indeed, often retrievals of the prophetic strain itself through its release of religious suspicions upon the ideological distortions in the tradition) grounded in Catholic faith. That faith bears all the marks of authentic faith: a fundamental trust and loyalty to the tradition mediating the dangerous memory of Jesus, the prophetic memory of the suffering of the oppressed, and the hope released by the proleptic eschatological event of the ministry-death-resurrection of Jesus Christ.

My original description of the task of Catholic theology, therefore, as "the self-interpretation of the Catholic religious tradition" must yield to the fuller description suggested by these theological remarks. Involved in the self-interpretation of the tradition, the systematic theologian as a participating member of the tradition will be grounded in a fundamental trust and loyalty to the tradition itself and will be engaged, therefore, in a fundamental hermeneutics of retrieval of the tradition's own founding, classic, authoritative resources. As thus grounded, the theologian must also retrieve the prophetic strain empowering the whole tradition. Thereby must the theologian engage in a hermeneutics of suspicion as well—suspicion upon, in, and for the sake of the tradition itself. Like any interpreter of any cultural or religious tradition, the theological interpreter remains a radically finite, historical being. Like any finite, historical persons, theologians as well remain rooted in their own ambiguities: attempting to provide critical reflections and appropriate interpretations for and in the tradition; recognizing that each of us bears a personal and cultural history that both frees and binds us; recognizing that not only finitude and historicity but error, illusion, distortion, and even sin are as much a part of the theologian's actuality as of anyone else's; recognizing, therefore, that no theologian can claim to speak for the whole church but that each must attempt to develop interpretative proposals for the church. Those proposals can be grounded in a fundamental trust and loyalty yet formulated hermeneutically as both retrieval and suspicion. To attempt more is to deny the radical historicity of every theological interpreter. To attempt less is to deny the risk that every theological interpretation must be.

For these reasons, like some other Catholic theologians, I have formulated the task of the theologian in the following terms: the attempt to develop mutually critical correlations between interpretations of the tradition and our contemporary experience. Such, for myself, is the principal interpretative task of every theology. Such, on the tradition's own terms (its demand to discern the signs of the times, to engage in prophetic discernment) is the demand and the risk imposed upon every theology.

I have spoken so far of the Catholic theologian's relationship to the tradition. I have argued that the tradition itself demands that our contemporary experience operate in the appropriation and interpretation of the tradition. It is time, however, to shift the focus to that contemporary experience, more exactly to that overwhelming "sign" of our times we call the Holocaust, to see what differences that event might make for the reinterpretation of the Catholic tradition.

THE HOLOCAUST AND CATHOLIC THEOLOGY

I understand the historical event called the Holocaust as an event of sheer, unmitigated negativity: an event disclosing an evil that is incommensurable, incomprehensible—indeed, as Fackenheim, Cohen, Greenberg, and others have persuasively argued, a unique event.[4] Arthur Cohen's expression for that event—the *tremendum*—seems to me to capture the religious and theological dimensions of the event itself. The event is tremendous in the original meaning of that word—earthshaking and frightening. The event is tremendous in the religious meaning of the word—awesome, incomprehensible, frightening, and world shattering. The Holocaust, in Catholic theological terms, discloses the classic countersign of our age. That negative countersign changes the optimistic, secure, consoling signs of the times in our age into signs of radical ambiguity. How can we simply praise what the theological tradition calls the world when the world produced this? How can we simply stand by and continue optimistic theologies of the world when we recall that our Western humanist world either collapsed in the face of that vile destruction of all traditional Greek, Latin, and German humanist cultural values and traditions or else stood by and did little or nothing to stop the horror? How can we stand by and continue to develop theologies of the church and the tradition as if the Holocaust did not happen? How can we do so, as Christians, when we recall that the Christian churches, both Protestant and Catholic, stood by, watched, and did little or nothing to stop the *tremendum*. That individual Christians and individual humanists heard that call and acted, suffered, and died can give the rest of us some heart that the ideals of those traditions did live even then. But that the official churches or whole groups of church congregations did little or nothing in the face of that reality is a fact which commands profound religious repentance and demands genuine theological response.

I submit that the Holocaust is the classic negative event of our age, an event that bears the religious dimension of the *tremendum*; an event that does not displace the founding religious events of either Judaism or Christianity; yet an event that demands the release, for Christians, of a profound Christian hermeneutics of suspicion upon many traditional interpretations of the Christian tradition. Through the work of the theologians mentioned above, that hermeneutical task, that painful and necessary theological task, has already begun. Through the person of Pope John XXIII after his encounter with Jules Isaac, through the recent statements of the French and Dutch bishops, that task

has already begun in the official church. But it would be dishonest to state anything more than that the task has begun. If one can infer from the silence of most
theologians the fact that they still stand back and refuse to face this *tremendum*,
we must conclude that for many theologians and many Christians, the painful,
necessary disclosures of unrelieved evil of the Holocaust have not been allowed
to touch their interpretations of either the world or the Christian tradition.

The fact remains, however, that the hermeneutics of suspicion released by
the Holocaust can and should become for Christians a demand for a Christian
theological hermeneutics of suspicion upon both tradition and world. In the
light of that suspicion, we may yet find the possibilities for new hermeneutics of
retrieval of half-forgotten or even repressed aspects of the Christian tradition.

Allow me to give some examples of both the suspicions raised by the Holocaust and the possibilities of retrieval of sometimes forgotten aspects of the tradition which the reality of the Holocaust does disclose. I will concentrate my
major attention on the fundamental doctrines of salvation, Christ, and God.
Before those more controversial aspects of my proposal, however, allow me to
note some prior issues that demand further and continuous reflection.

The first factor is the most obvious and perhaps the most deadly: Christianity has explicitly allowed in the writings of some of its most cherished fathers of
the faith (Saint John Crysostom being only the most famous example) a long
teaching of contempt for the Jews and for the Jewish religion. Christianity has
implicitly allowed more popular expressions of this contempt to perdure even
in its catechisms and its popular piety. The liturgical reforms of the Good Friday
service initiated by Pope John XXIII and the catechetical reforms initiated since
Vatican II are merely the first expressions of the suspicions that must be cast on
this revolting tradition of both implicit and explicit teachings of contempt.
Every vestige of that tradition should not only be removed but repented for.
Repentance and reformatory action alone are worthy of a tradition that honors
the prophetic spirit now released upon the tradition's own sins—sins, to recall
the traditional Catholic vocabulary, of both omission and commission. The story
told by Edward Flannery in *The Anguish of the Jews*, as well as the histories of the
church during the Nazi period, calls not only for reform (as almost all admit) but
for profound and meaningful repentance—as some official church leaders
(notably the Dutch and French bishops) now insist.

Moreover the painful, repressed memories of Christian anti-Semitism have
also been aided by the anti-Judaic statements of the New Testament, especially
but not solely in the Gospel of John. If those scriptural statements cannot be
excised, then minimally they should always be commented upon whenever
used in liturgical settings and noted critically in every Christian commentary on
the Scriptures. The history of the effects of those New Testament anti-Judaic out-
bursts should signal the need for Christians, singly and communally, to reflect
upon ways to banish forever this bad side of the good news of the New Testament. Those anti-Judaic statements of the New Testament bear *no* authoritative
status for Christianity. Even the most "fulfillment"-oriented Christology has no
real theological need for them. The heart of the New Testament message—the

love who is God—should release the demythologizing power of its own prophetic meaning to rid the New Testament and Christianity once and for all of all these statements.

To release a Christian hermeneutics of suspicion, I suggested earlier, can also release a Christian hermeneutics of retrieval. These first examples of suspicion, in fact, also suggest the necessity of retrieval. In a real sense, this has begun to occur powerfully among Christian theologians—that is, among all those (I include here the liberation theologians) who have begun to recognize the profoundly Jewish character of Christianity itself. The Christian God is none other than the God of Israel, the God of Abraham, Isaac, and Jacob. Our Christ is none other than Jesus the Jew of Nazareth. Our sacred texts are none other than the Hebrew Scriptures, which also serve as our Old Testament, and the apostolic writings—the apostolic writings of the early Jewish Christians, which we call the New Testament.

Yet to retrieve the Jewishness of Christianity is also to retrieve the possibility of recalling, on Christian grounds, that for the Christian the Jews are and will remain God's chosen people. The Christian as Christian can and, I believe, must affirm that chosenness of the Jews as a theological reality. The contemporary Christian can do so, I also believe, without the ambiguities, if not incoherence, in Paul's real but confusing affirmation of that chosenness. The earlier attempts to revive the notion of two covenants of Hans Urs von Balthasar and Jacques Maritain on the Catholic side of the dialogue and the extraordinary theological position of Franz Rosenzweig on the Jewish side indicate that this aspect of the Pauline notion can perhaps be retrieved without Paul's own ambiguities. At any rate, these noble theological developments of Rosenzweig, von Balthasar, Maritain, and others already indicate that every Catholic (even such relatively conservative Catholics as Maritain and von Balthasar) can and should affirm, on inner Catholic grounds, that the Jews were, are, and will remain God's chosen, covenanted people. Entailed by this theological commitment are others. Catholics should learn the history of the Hebrew Scriptures not only through the Christian eyes of the New Testament and Christian Old Testament scholars but through the eyes of Jewish scholars as well; Catholics should learn—which means practically that Catholic institutions, especially colleges and seminaries, should teach—the history of postbiblical Judaism. When we learn, for example, more about the rabbinical teaching, we will be unlikely to repeat the poisonous clichés in the law that still inflict Christian biblical scholarship and theology (especially, as E. P. Sanders has persuasively shown,[5] Pauline scholarship).

A second theological issue relates to the first. In terms of my rubric of the hermeneutics of suspicion released by the Holocaust upon the tradition, the issue can be formulated as the nature of Christian salvation in the world. Insofar as one kind of Catholic spirituality is spiritualizing (or unworldly) and privatizing (or nonpublic) and insofar as that spirituality aided individual Christians to avoid their historical responsibilities in the situation of the Holocaust, contemporary Catholic theological reflection on salvation and spirituality needs to become yet more suspicious of all nonworldly, nonpolitical forms of spirituality. It should be added, of course, that at least since the document *Gaudium et Spes* at Vatican II (and the prior work of theologians like Teilhard de Chardin), any unworldly and surely private spirituality has already been under Catholic theological suspicion.

And yet it is clearly not the case, in the perspective of the Holocaust, that the proposed solutions of Teilhard or other incarnationalist and Christian humanist theologians or even the optimistic appraisal of the world in *Gaudium et Spes* (or, it might be added, the too optimistic appraisal of secularity in my own *Blessed Rage for Order* and in similar "secular" theologies) can any longer suffice. For the suspicions released by the Holocaust are radical suspicions not only upon unworldly and privatizing spiritualities. They also cast suspicion upon the this-worldly and antiprivatizing spiritualities which accord too optimistic a portrait of the world.

In that sense, theological reflection upon the Holocaust reinforces and indeed, as we shall see below, radicalizes the kind of Catholic liberation and political theological appraisal of the systematic distortions present not only in the church tradition but in the secular, worldly tradition as well. This point is worth dwelling upon. For in the present neoconservative resurgence in both Catholicism and the wider culture, the exposé of the radical ambiguity of the world and the secular can often become an occasion (and sometimes an excuse) to return to a purely spiritual, unworldly, and finally private spirituality. The latter cases range from a retrieval of the *fuga mundi* tradition of an earlier asceti-cism through the temptations (not necessity) or charismatic renewals to the more moderate, but no less deadly, retreats from the world of neoconservative theologians.

Just as George Steiner's profound critique of Western humanism in the light of the Holocaust or the Frankfurt school's analysis of the dialectic of the Enlightenment suggest for secular culture, theological analyses of the profound distortions revealed in the world and secular culture should not become the occasion to retreat from a spirituality for and in the world. The example of Catholic liberation and political theologies is instructive here. For these theo-logical critiques from the Left do disclose through their analyses of the classism, racism, sexism, anti-Semitism, oppression, and alienation present in both church traditions and secular traditions that any theological account of the rad-ical ambiguity of the world cannot occur without a radical affirmation of the world. In theological terms, we are freed *from* the world *for* the world. The vio-lence of this language (freed from) is exact and does cast profound suspicion on any optimistic appraisal of the world. But we are freed from the world for the world. To ignore that "freedom for" is to risk developing spiritualities and the-ologies of salvation which will betray the retrieval of the worldly, historical, political character of the central biblical and traditional understandings of sal-vation in the world. In short, the Holocaust piercingly casts a radical hermeneu-tics of suspicion upon any optimistic theological appraisals of the world. That event also casts a suspicion upon any pessimistic spiritualities of retreat from our historical and political responsibility.

The Catholic "return to history and the world" initiated by Vatican II has received its proper corrective from those political and liberation theologians. For these theologians have developed profound theological hermeneutics of suspicion upon the world and an equally profound hermeneutics of retrieval of the this-worldly reality of Christian salvation. They have retrieved half-forgotten (and, it should be noted, almost always Jewish rather than Greek) resources of the tradition. The recent theology of the Catholic political theologian Johann Baptist Metz is instructive here.[6] Metz has attempted to retrieve the apocalyptic tradition insofar as apocalyptic both negates all complacency in contemporary history and at the same time demands action in and for the world in that same history. Metz has appealed as well to the profoundly Jewish theological sensibilities of Walter Benjamin's retrieval of eschatological narratives. Narrative—a traditional form of Jewish but rarely Christian theology—is retrievable precisely in Benjamin's sense: keeping alive the prophetic memory of the suffering of the oppressed. Moreover, the appeal of Latin American liberation theologians that the New Testament can be read properly only in the light of the this-worldly and historical character of the Jewish notion of redemption is yet another sign that in our post-Holocaust age the suspicions released on any optimistic appraisal of the world can become further retrievals (if often unconscious ones) of the Jewish, this-worldly, ethical, and historical side of Christian salvation itself.

I suggested above that the event of the Holocaust has released a hermeneutics of suspicion that reinforces the suspicions of the liberation and political theologians on the world. At the same time, the Holocaust radicalizes those suspicions and those possibilities of retrieval. This point is important to note theologically for, with the notable exceptions of Baum and Ruether, Catholic liberation and political theologians have not yet noted the radicalization of the more usual liberation suspicions upon the world that the event of the Holocaust demands. In short, the Latin American theologians as well as the Euro-American political theologians have generally not allowed the profound suspicions released by the Holocaust upon traditional christological formulations to inform their perspective. Rather, in spite of their radical critique of traditional and modern liberal theologies of salvation, these theologians formulate their Christologies with a seemingly untroubled use of such biblical and traditional categories as the New Covenant, fulfillment, and the law-gospel contrast. And yet the question must be raised—as Baum, Pawlikowski, and Ruether have properly raised it for Catholic theology—whether so untroubled a retrieval of traditional christological language can be any more countenanced than an untroubled use of traditional salvation language.

For myself, the suspicion which the Holocaust discloses for traditional christological language is this: does the fundamental Christian belief in the ministry, death, and resurrection of Jesus Christ demand a Christology that either states or implies that Judaism has been displaced by Christianity? As we saw above, Franz Rosenzweig gave one famous suggestion on how both Christianity and Judaism can be recognized as two covenants from the viewpoint of

Judaism. Hans Urs von Balthasar and Jacques Maritain made analogous suggestions from the Catholic side. In a post-Holocaust situation, however, it does become questionable whether the history of the effects of Christian theological fulfillment language or law-gospel language or even the New Covenant language can really be retrieved without seeming to imply that God's covenant with the chosen people, the Jews, is abrogated and that Judaism becomes, in the new covenantal Christian perspective, a spent religion.

Clearly the intent of New Covenant language need not imply the latter and does not for von Balthasar, Maritain, and others. Still, the historical effects of that language, including the effects of Christian caricatures of Judaism as a legalistic religion, the effects of Christian ignorance of postbiblical Judaism in its full richness and complexity, the effects of the easy if often implicit move from fulfillment or New Covenant language to displacement or substitution language should render Christian theologians suspicious even of these noble theologies of retrieval based on a real Jewish-Christian dialogue.

The post-Rosenzweig Jewish "return into history" must be matched, on the Catholic side with a Catholic return into history. In sum, it is not possible on scriptural grounds to so spiritualize the notion of Messiah that that office loses all relationship to the central Jewish concept of "Messianic times." Any purely realized eschatology (including those informing purely incarnationalist theologies) can maintain itself only at the price of ignoring two central realities: first, the clear presence of the eschatological "not yet" in the New Testament itself, and second, the stark negativity of the radical not yet in our age disclosed in all its horror by the Holocaust.

For Christians to recognize the reality of the negative is to retrieve, theologically, the eschatological reality of the not yet. For Christians to retrieve the reality of the not yet as a historical reality is to recall that the concept Messiah cannot (by being spiritualized) be divorced from the reality of Messianic times. The presence of several Christologies in the New Testament itself (including Christologies where the not yet plays a crucial role, as in Mark's suffering-Messiah Christology) demands the following recognition: however influential in later Christian history, theological pure fulfillment models and ahistorical Messiah models are not the only New Testament models that can be employed to express the fundamental Christian belief in the ministry, death, and resurrection of Jesus Christ.

To employ the language of a proleptic Christology seems to me an appropriate route to take. For to affirm the belief in Jesus Christ is, for the Christian, to affirm the faith that in the ministry, death, and resurrection of Jesus the decisive token, manifestation, prolepsis of the future reign of God (and, thereby, of Messianic times) is both already here in a proleptic form (indeed, for myself, has been manifested as always already here) and, just as really, not yet here.

This Christological belief—fundamental to Christianity—is a belief that, of course, no Jewish believer can accept. And yet what the Jew can, I believe, recognize in this is that however really this Christian belief divides these two faith communities (as it does), this Christian belief in no way implies the displacement of Judaism by Christianity. Christology thus reformulated as proleptic reaffirms on inner-Christian grounds the status of the Jews as God's chosen, covenanted people. Christology can and should resist the Christian temptation to so spiritualize the notion of Messiah as to wrench it from real history and thereby from the notion of Messianic times. The always/already/not yet structure of belief pervading Israel's covenant with God and Israel's expectancy of Messianic times remains the fundamental always/already/not yet structure of Christian belief as well. Where the two religious communities divide remains as clear as ever. For the Christian, it is in Jesus as the Christ that the prolepsis of those future times is decisively glimpsed. For the Christian, to believe in Jesus as Messiah and Christ is to state the Christian belief in the worthwhileness of the risk of a life of discipleship of this Jesus—a life modeled on the ministry of and words of Jesus. That risk is grounded in the Christian belief in the necessity for action in history and for the world. That action is grounded, for the Christian, in the cross and its disclosure of the reality of suffering for those who will risk that life and in the resurrection and its disclosure of hope for the future—both the future of real history and the future of an afterlife. The individual Christians who took the risk of that model—that *imitatio Christi*—in the struggle for the Jews against the blasphemous and obscene evil of Nazism are those Christians whose lives should remind us that the very life of Christianity endures not by resting in the theologically false security of an ahistorical triumphalist Christology. Christianity lives religiously only by its faith, risk, hope in the always, already, not yet event of the ministry, death, and resurrection of Jesus Christ.

Revisionary suggestions for Christology in a post-Holocaust age similar to that suggested above have already occurred among Catholic theologians. But as far as I am aware, the ultimate theological issue, the understanding of God, has yet to receive much reflection from Catholic theologians. And yet, as Schleiermacher correctly insisted, the doctrine of God can never be "another" doctrine for theology but must pervade all doctrines. Here Jewish theology, in its reflections on the reality of God since the *tremendum* of the Holocaust, has led the way for all serious theological reflection.

I will not presume to comment upon the inner-Jewish theological debate on this central theological issue. I will presume to state, however, that no Christian theologian can afford to ignore that discussion as if it were simply an inner-Jewish theological issue.

Rather, as I have urged throughout these reflections, the event of the Holocaust is at least as much a theological challenge for Christian self-understanding as it is for Jewish. The hermeneutics of suspicion released by the Holocaust upon Christian self-understanding touches, I have suggested, theological interpretations of such central Christian doctrines as the nature of salvation and the doctrine of Christ. Yet for Christian theologians to stop there would, I believe, be to forget that theology is finally and at every moment *theo*-logy. The concentration of Jewish theological reflection on the doctrine of God in the light of the Holocaust must become, for both Jew and Christian, the heart of the theological matter. There is no other God for the Christian than the God of Israel—the God of Abraham, Isaac, Jacob, and Jesus Christ. The Scriptures we share—the

Hebrew Scriptures—are an authoritative source for the reflection upon the reality of God for us both. No Christian theologian can still feel free to ignore the extraordinary complexity of those Scriptures' reflection on God—the anger at God in Lamentations 3, the God of love and justice in Deuteronomy and the great prophets, the contrast, if not conflict, in the portraits of God in Amos, Hosea, and Job. Any Christian theologian who, in this post-Holocaust age, can repeat the specious claim that the New Testament understanding of God as a God of love is either radically different from the God of love of Deuteronomy or Hosea, or contradicts the God of justice and wrath of Amos, or eliminates the profound problematic of Job or Lamentations 3 is at best a Marcionite, at worst one who will not face the sheer negativity of the Holocaust and its painful demand upon every Christian believer in the God of Abraham, Isaac, Jacob, and Jesus Christ.

The first step, therefore, for Christian theologians to take in reflecting upon the reality of God in the light of the Holocaust is to retrieve, once again, our Jewish roots. We need to retrieve those roots in such manner that we take with full theological seriousness the complex portrait of God in the Hebrew Scriptures. We can also hope that in the light of the reflections of post-Holocaust Jewish theologians, Christian theologians begin to take more seriously as well the postbiblical resources of Judaism in its diverse and complex reflections on the reality of God: from the subtleties of rabbinical Judaism through the mystical negativity in God of cabalistic Judaism through the retrieval of mad midrash in Elie Wiesel and Emil Fackenheim.

Moreover, the very negativity of the event of the Holocaust forces a suspicion upon many traditional Christian theological understandings of God which do not seriously take account of that kind of overwhelming evil. Surely we should suggest that yet another half-forgotten tradition in Christian theology needs retrieval after the release of those suspicions: I refer especially to the so-called negative or apophatic theological traditions. I refer as well to the recognition and theological appropriation of different kinds and degrees of negativity in the theological understanding of God: in the radical incomprehensibility tradition of Aquinas and Rahner, the hidden-revealed God of Luther and Calvin, God as ground and abyss in Schelling and Tillich, God as absent and present in John of the Cross and Teresa of Avila.

Christian theology, I believe, is just at the beginning of this properly theological reflection on the reality of God. That such reflection is forced upon us is the result of any serious theological reflection upon the Holocaust. Such reflection may also find resources in our common Scriptures with our Jewish colleagues; resources in the reflections of postbiblical Jewish thought as they are now being retrieved by the daring, necessary, painful enterprise of post-Holocaust Jewish theology; resources as well in the negative theologies of Christian theological tradition and in the negativity embedded, if widely overlooked, in such classic Christian theological understandings of God as Pseudo-Dionysius, Aquinas, Luther, Calvin, Hegel, Schelling, Tillich, and Rahner. If we are merely at the beginning of this theological reflection on God, then it becomes imperative to recognize the reality of suspicion and the possibilities of retrieval. I can make no further claim for my own reflections on this ultimate theological question at the present save to state, briefly and tentatively, how that suspicion has affected my own theological understanding of the reality of God.

No more than a heuristic sketch of a direction for thinking of the reality of God after the Holocaust seems possible here. Yet that much, at least, should be attempted. Otherwise we may be tempted to forget that all theological thought is finally the always inadequate and always necessary attempt to understand the God who revealed God's very self to us.

For myself, the question of God in the light of the Holocaust is not principally a question of theodicy. I can understand and respect the posing of questions of theodicy in the classical theological tradition in two primary cases: when the question of natural evil is raised, the question can be posed sharply; when the question of human evil is raised (as in the paradigmatic case of the Holocaust), the classic reflections seem to me to reveal their inadequacy. More exactly, those classic reflections are appropriate as reflections not on genuine, concrete evil but on the condition for the possibility of evil, namely, the divine gift of human freedom which allows the frightening misuses of that freedom in human evil. Indeed, classical philosophical and theological reflections on the nature of evil are usually also transcendental or metaphysical in character—as in the honorable tradition of understanding evil metaphysically (as nonbeing) in Aquinas.

These classic reflections continue to provide real resources for reflection upon metaphysical or transcendental conditions of possibility on the question of God and evil. Yet the Holocaust as a sheer evil perpetrated by human beings on human beings also discloses the real limitations of all such metaphysical or transcendental reflection on conditions of possibility. Rather the overwhelming horror in the historical concreteness of the Holocaust makes us recognize that even if we begin with classic theological reflections on the conditions of possibility of freedom, human evil (as nonbeing), and on God's transcendence and immanence or the divine permissive will, we could not end there. With the tradition, we can recognize after the Holocaust that there is no philosophical solution to the question of evil. Even the classic analyses of the nonbeing of evil indicate, not a solution, but the radicalization of the insight (the inverse insight) that there is no philosophical solution. With the tradition, we can also recognize that any properly theological understanding of God's reality must allow for three factors: philosophical coherence, appropriateness to the scriptural portrait of God, and existential resonance with human beings' concrete experiences of both God and radical evil.

Yet as soon as we mention this last requirement we also recognize the profound question which the Holocaust poses to the religious believer as ultimately a religious, not a philosophical, question. For the religious experience of God as, for example, an immanent-transcendent God of love clashes with the equally religious sense of the mystery of the profound evil disclosed in the *tremendum* of the Holocaust. The appeals to Job, to Lamentations 3, to "mad midrash" and to the suffering servant of Second Isaiah or the crucified God of the Christian symbolism are profoundly religious-theological responses to the issue. Each of these responses challenges either explicitly or implicitly the possibility of a philosophical response. And here, surely, they are correct. For the real conflict we sense in the Holocaust as Jews and Christians is not a philosophical conflict between human freedom and divine transcendence, or between evil as a nonbeing and God's permissive will, but a profoundly religious conflict. That conflict is a sense of being torn apart religiously: by the radically disorienting experience of unmitigated evil in the Holocaust on the one hand and a sustaining experience of God as revealed as a God of pure, unbounded love on the other.

Religiously and theologically considered, therefore, the Holocaust is not primarily a problem of theodicy in the classic mold but a problem of anthropodicy. Yet to say this is not to suggest that there is no rethinking necessary for the doctrine of God in the *tremendum* darkness of the Holocaust. I have argued elsewhere and at length that even before considering the Holocaust, Christian theology should accept a process understanding of God as more coherent, more faithful to the scriptural portrait of God as really affected and affecting human beings (that is, really a God of love) and as more resonant to our contemporary experience of change as a responsible candidate for perfection language and, therefore, for God language.[7] But even this now familiar process theological proposal must itself be rethought and radicalized in a post-Holocaust age.

Even those theologians like myself who continue to believe that process categories are, in fact, more philosophically coherent than classically theistic categories; that they are more appropriate categories for understanding the scriptural affirmation of God as a God of love; and that they are more existentially resonant to our postclassical understanding of change and process as anthropological constants and marks of perfectibility, not imperfection, cannot after the Holocaust rest in an affirmation of a process understanding of God, much less a process theodicy. What those theologians who accept these process categories (for example, God as "all-powerful" and "all-knowing" means the greatest power and knowledge coherently conceivable not verbalizable) can do, I suggest, is to radicalize the process understanding of God *as love*. Thus would the negativity present in the suffering always/already present in genuine love be deliberately rethought in relationship to God's own reality.

I mentioned earlier that for Christian theology, the Holocaust releases a suspicion upon theology. Here it releases a suspicion upon any easy (and easily sentimentalized) notions of God as a God of love and, through that suspicion, releases as well a recognition of the need for theologians to reconsider the possibility of retrieving often-overlooked resources in three areas: first, in the Hebrew Scriptures (Job, Lamentations 3, Amos, Isaiah); second, in the usually overlooked resources of negative theologies in the later Christian tradition itself (Pseudo-Dionysius, Eckhart, Boehme, Schelling); third, in the often-noted but too seldom employed negative elements in the classical theologies of Augustine, Aquinas, Luther, Calvin, Barth, Rahner. It is these resources, I believe, that most need reflection and, if possible, retrieval in the post-Holocaust reflections of all Christian theologians, whether traditional or process. I cannot pretend to have undertaken that necessary reflection on possibilities of retrieval with anything like adequacy. Yet I can and do suggest that even my own process theological understanding of God must radicalize its own self-understanding of the reality of the negative in God.

For myself that means that we must rethink anew the reality of suffering in the reality of God's own self as the self who is love. I believe, with Dietrich Bonhoeffer, that "only a suffering God can help us now." I believe, with the often-repressed strains of the Scriptures of both traditions, Jewish and Christian, that our God is none other than pure, unbounded love—the God who radically affects and is affected by (that is, suffers) the evil we, not God, persist in inflicting upon God's creation. I believe, therefore, that the unspeakable suffering of the six million is also the voice of the suffering of God. It is for us to hear that cry—the cry at once of our fellow human beings and the cry of God's chosen people become the cry of God. Like all the commands of God, this command to hear that lament and that suffering is a command which can enable and empower all who hear it to real action in real history. For all those who hear that voice—the voice of our suffering, betrayed God (betrayed by us) and the voice of God's suffering, betrayed people (betrayed by us)—that voice can become the bond that unites us all in calling out together, with them and with our God, "Never again!"

NOTES

1. See Arthur Cohen, *The Tremendum: A Theological Interpretation of the Holocaust* (New York, 1981).

2. I have defended this interpretation of the nature of systematic theology in *The Analogical Imagination: Christian Theology and the Culture of Pluralism* (New York, 1981).

3. The categories "hermeneutics of retrieval" and "hermeneutics of suspicion" are Paul Ricoeur's; inter alia, see his *Freud and Philosophy* (New Haven, 1970). For my own use of these categories in relation to the event of the Holocaust, see the hermeneutical companion piece to this present article, "History, Historicity and Holocaust," from the Indiana University conference on the Holocaust (forthcoming from Indiana University Press).

4. See Cohen, *The Tremendum*; Emil Fackenheim, *God's Presence in History* (New York, 1970); idem, *The Jewish Return into History* (New York, 1978); Irving Greenberg, his several essays on the covenantal theme in post-Holocaust Jewish thought.

5. See E. P. Sanders, *Paul and Palestinian Judaism: A Comparison of Patterns of Religion* (Philadelphia, 1977).

6. Johann Baptist Metz, *Faith in History and Society: Toward a Practical Fundamental Theology* (New York, 1980).

7. See my *Blessed Rage for Order* (New York, 1975).

◼ Christians and Jews after Auschwitz

Being a Meditation Also on the End of Bourgeois Religion

A MORAL AWARENESS OF TRADITION

I am no expert in the field of Jewish-Christian ecumenism. And yet my readiness to voice an opinion on the question of Jewish-Christian relations after Auschwitz is motivated not least by the fact that I no longer really know—faced with the catastrophe of Auschwitz—what being an expert can possibly mean. So already that name has been uttered which cannot and should not be avoided when the relationship between Jews and Christians in this country—or in fact anywhere else—is being formulated and decided. It is a name which may not be avoided here, nor forgotten for an instant, precisely because it threatens already to become only a fact of history, as if it could be classified alongside other names in some preconceived and overarching history and thereby successfully delivered over to forgetfulness, or—amounting in the end to the same thing—to selective memorial celebrations: the name "Auschwitz," intended above all here as a symbol of the horror of that millionfold murder done to the Jewish people.

Auschwitz concerns us all. Indeed what makes Auschwitz unfathomable is not only the executioners and their assistants, not only the apotheosis of evil revealed in these, and not only the silence of God. Unfathomable, and sometimes even more disturbing, is the silence of men: the silence of all those who looked on or looked away and thereby handed over this people in its peril of death to an unutterable loneliness. I say this not with contempt but with grief. Nor am I saying it in order to revive again the dubious notion of a collective guilt. I am making a plea here for what I would like to call a moral awareness of tradition. A moral awareness means that we can only mourn history and win from it standards for our own action when we neither deny the defeats present within it nor gloss over its catastrophes. Having an awareness of history and attempting to live out of this awareness means, above all, not evading history's

From *The Emergent Church*, by Johann Baptist Metz, © 1981 by The Crossroad Publishing Company. Used with permission of The Crossroad Publishing Company.

disasters. It also means that there is at least *one* authority that we should never reject or despise—the authority of those who suffer. If this applied anywhere, it applies, in our Christian and German history, to Auschwitz. The fate of the Jews must be remembered as a moral reality precisely because it threatens already to become a mere matter of history.

AUSCHWITZ AS END POINT AND TURNING POINT?

The question whether there will be a reformation and a radical conversion in the relations between Christians and Jews will ultimately be decided, at least in Germany, by the attitude we Christians adopt toward Auschwitz and the value it really has for ourselves. Will we actually allow it to be the end point, the disruption which it really was, the catastrophe of our history, out of which we can find a way only through a radical change of direction achieved via new standards of action? Or will we see it only as a monstrous accident within this history but not affecting history's course?

Let me clarify the personal meaning I attach to Auschwitz as end point and turning point for us Christians by recalling a dialogue I shared in. At the end of 1967 there was a round-table discussion in Münster between the Czech philosopher Machovec, Karl Rahner, and myself. Toward the end of the discussion, Machovec recalled Adorno's saying: "After Auschwitz, there are no more poems"—a saying which is held everywhere today to be exaggerated and long since disproved—unjustly, to my mind, at least when applied to the Jews themselves. For were not Paul Celan, Thadeus Borowsky, and Nelly Sachs, among others—all born to make poetry as few others have been—destroyed by the sheer unutterability of that which took place at Auschwitz and the need for it somehow still to be uttered in language? In any case, Machovec cited Adorno's saying and asked me if there could be for us Christians, after Auschwitz, any more prayers. I finally gave the answer which I would still give today: We can pray *after* Auschwitz, because people prayed *in* Auschwitz.

If this is taken as a comprehensive answer, it may seem as exaggerated a saying as Adorno's. Yet I do not consider it an exaggeration. We Christians can never again go back behind Auschwitz: to go beyond Auschwitz, if we see clearly, is impossible for us of ourselves. It is possible only together with the victims of Auschwitz. This, in my eyes, is the root of Jewish-Christian ecumenism. The turning point in relations between Jews and Christians corresponds to the radical character of the end point which befell us in Auschwitz. Only when we confront this end point will we recognize what this "new" relationship between Jews and Christians is, or at least could become.

To confront Auschwitz is in no way to comprehend it. Anyone wishing to comprehend in this area will have comprehended nothing. As it gazes toward us incomprehensibly out of our most recent history, it eludes our every attempt at some kind of amicable reconciliation which would allow us to dismiss it from our consciousness. The only thing "objective" about Auschwitz are the victims, the mourners, and those who do penance. Faced with Auschwitz, there can be no abstention, no inability to relate. To attempt such a thing would be yet another case of secret complicity with the unfathomed horror. Yet how are we Christians to come to terms with Auschwitz? We will in any case forgo the temptation to interpret the suffering of the Jewish people from our standpoint, in terms of saving history. Under no circumstances is it *our* task to mystify this suffering! *We* encounter in this suffering first of all only the riddle of our own lack of feeling, the mystery of our own apathy, not, however, the traces of God.

Faced with Auschwitz, I consider as blasphemy every Christian theodicy (i.e., every attempt at a so-called "justification of God") and all language about "meaning" when these are initiated outside this catastrophe or on some level above it. Meaning, even divine meaning, can be invoked by us only to the extent that such meaning was not also abandoned in Auschwitz itself. But this means that we Christians for our very own sakes are from now on assigned to the victims of Auschwitz—assigned, in fact, in an alliance belonging to the heart of *saving history*, provided the word "history" in this Christian expression is to have a definite meaning and not just serve as a screen for a triumphalist metaphysic of salvation which never learns from catastrophes nor finds in them a cause for conversion, since in its view such catastrophes of meaning do not in fact exist at all.

This saving history alliance would have to mean, finally, the radical end of every persecution of Jews by Christians. If any persecution were to take place in the future, it could only be a persecution of both together, of Jews *and* Christians—*as it was in the beginning.* It is well known that the early persecutions of Christians were also persecutions of Jews. Because both groups refused to recognize the Roman Emperor as God, thus calling in question the foundations of Rome's political religion, they were together branded as atheists and haters of the human race and were persecuted unto death.

THE JEWISH-CHRISTIAN DIALOGUE IN REMEMBRANCE OF AUSCHWITZ

When these connections are seen, the question becomes obsolete as to whether Christians in their relations to Jews are now finally moving on from missionizing to dialogue. Dialogue itself seems, in fact, a weak and inappropriate description of this connection. For, after all, what does dialogue between Jews and Christians mean in remembrance of Auschwitz? It seems to me important to ask this question even though—or rather because—Christian-Jewish dialogue is booming at the present time and numerous organizations and institutions exist to support it.

1. Jewish-Christian dialogue in remembrance of Auschwitz means for us Christians first: It is not we who have the opening word, nor do we begin the dialogue. *Victims* are not offered a dialogue. We can only come into a dialogue when the victims themselves begin to speak. And then it is our primary duty as

Christians to listen—*for once to begin really listening*—to what Jews are saying of themselves and about themselves. Am I mistaken in the impression I have that we Christians are already beginning in this dialogue to talk far too much about ourselves and our ideas regarding the Jewish people and their religion? That we are once again hastening to make comparisons, comparisons separated from concrete situations and memories and persons, dogmatic comparisons which may indeed be better disposed and more conciliatory than before but which remain equally naïve because we are once more not listening closely? The end result is that the dialogue which never really achieved success is once more threatened with failure. And is not the reason for this that we are once again unable to see what is there, and prefer to speak about "Judaism" rather than to "the Jews"?

Have we really listened attentively during the last decades? Do we really know more today about the Jews and their religion? Have we become more attentive to the prophecy of their history of suffering? Or is the exploitation not beginning again, this time in a more sublime fashion because placed under the banner of friendliness toward the Jews? Is it not, for example, a kind of exploitation when we pick out fragments of texts from the Jewish tradition to serve as illustrations for our Christian preaching, or when we love to cite Hassidic stories without casting a single thought to the situation of suffering out of which they emerged and which is obviously an integral part of their truth?

2. No prepared patterns exist for this dialogue between Jews and Christians, patterns which could somehow be taken over from the familiar repertoire of inner-Christian ecumenism. Everything has to be measured by Auschwitz. This includes our Christian way of bringing into play *the question of truth*. Ecumenism, we often hear, can never succeed if it evades the question of truth: it must therefore continually derive from this its authentic direction. No one would deny this. But confronting the truth means first of all not avoiding the truth about Auschwitz, and ruthlessly unmasking the myths of self-exculpation and the mechanisms of trivialization which have been long since disseminated among Christians. This would be an ecumenical service to the one undivided truth! In general, Christians would be well advised, especially in dialogue with Jews, to show particular sensitivity in using the notion of truth. Too often, in fact, has truth—or rather what Christians all too triumphantly and uncompassionately portrayed as truth—been used as a weapon, an instrument of torture and persecution against Jews. Not to forget this for a moment belongs also to the respect for truth in the dialogue between Christians and Jews!

Something else has to be kept in mind, too: When we engage in this Christian-Jewish dialogue, we Christians should be more cautious about the titles we give ourselves and the sweeping comparisons we make. Faced with Auschwitz, who would dare to call our Christianity the "true" religion of the suffering, of the persecuted, of the dispersed? The caution and discretion I am recommending here, the theological principle of economy do not imply any kind of defeatism regarding the question of truth. They are rather expressions of mistrust in relation to any ecumenism separated from concrete situations and devoid of memory, that so-called purely doctrinal ecumenism. After Auschwitz, every theological "profundity" which is unrelated to people and their concrete situations must cease to exist. Such a theology would be the very essence of superficiality. With Auschwitz, the epoch of theological systems which are separate from people and their concrete situations has come to its irrevocable end. It is for this very reason that I am hesitant about all systematic comparisons of respective doctrines, however well-intentioned and gentle in tone; hesitant also toward all attempts to establish "theological common ground." Everything about this is too precipitate for my liking. Besides, did this common ground not always exist? Why, then, was it unable to protect the Jews from the aggressive scorn of Christians? The problems must surely lie at a deeper level. We have to ask ourselves the question: Can our theology ever be the same again after Auschwitz?

3. There is yet another reason why the Jewish-Christian dialogue after Auschwitz eludes every stereotyped pattern of ecumenism. The Jewish partner in this sought-after new relationship would not only be the religious Jew, in the confessional sense of the term, but, in a universal sense, every Jew threatened by Auschwitz. Jean Améry expressed it thus, shortly before his death: "In the inferno [of Auschwitz] the differences now became more than ever tangible and burned themselves into our skin like the tattooed numbers with which they branded us. All 'Arian' prisoners found themselves in the abyss *elevated* literally light-years *above* us, the Jews. . . . The Jew was the sacrificial animal. He had the chalice to drink—to its most bitter dregs. I drank of it. And this became my existence as Jew."

CHRISTIANITY AND THEOLOGY AFTER AUSCHWITZ

The sought-after ecumenism between Christians and Jews does not, of course, depend only on the readiness of Christians to begin at last to listen and to let Jews express themselves as Jews, which means as the Jewish people with their own history. This ecumenism contains also a fundamental theological problem regarding Christianity's own readiness, and the extent of this readiness, to recognize the messianic tradition of Judaism in its unsurpassed autonomy; as it were, in its enduring messianic dignity, without Christianity betraying or playing down the christological mystery it proclaims. Once again, this question is not to be handled abstractly but in remembrance of Auschwitz. Does not Auschwitz compel Christianity and Christian theology toward a radical inquiry into their own condition, a self-interrogation without which no new ecumenical evaluation of the Jewish religion and of Jewish history will be possible for Christians? I would like briefly to develop certain elements of this self-interrogation which seem important to me; these contain, moreover, just as many indications of constantly recurring and therefore quasi-endemic dangers within Christianity and its theology.

1. In the course of history, has not Christianity interpreted itself, in abstract contrast to Judaism, far too much as a purely "affirmative" religion, so to speak, as a theological "religion of conquerors" with an excess of answers and a corresponding lack of agonized questions? Was not the question of Job so repressed or played down within Christology that the image of the Son who suffers in relation to God and God's powerlessness in the world became all too adorned with the features of a conqueror? Does not the danger then arise of a Christological reduction of the world's history of suffering? I want to illustrate what this means by a brief quotation from the German synodal document, "Our Hope": "In the history of our church and of Christianity, have we not taken . . . Christ's suffering, in its hope-inducing power, and then separated it too much from the one history of suffering of humanity? In connecting the Christian idea of suffering exclusively with his cross and with ourselves as his disciples, have we not created gaps in our world, spaces filled with the unprotected sufferings of others? Has not our attitude as Christians to this suffering often been one of unbelievable insensitivity and indifference"—as though we believed this suffering fell in some kind of purely profane sector, as though we could understand ourselves as the great conquerors in relation to it, as though this suffering had no atoning power, and as though our lives were not part of the burden placed upon it? How else, after all, is that history of suffering to be understood which Christians have prepared for the Jewish people over the centuries, or at least not protected them against? Did not our attitude in all that time manifest those typical marks of apathy and insensitivity which betray the conqueror?

2. Has not Christianity, precisely in comparison with the Jewish religion, concealed time and again its own *messianic weakness?* Does there not break through within Christianity, again and again, a dangerous triumphalism connected with saving history, something the Jews above all have had to suffer from in a special way? But is this the unavoidable consequence of Christian faith in the salvation definitively achieved in Christ? Or is it not true that Christians themselves still have something to await and to fear—not just for themselves, but rather for the world and for history as a whole? Must not Christians too lift up their heads in expectancy of the messianic Day of the Lord? This early Christian doctrine about expecting the messianic Day of the Lord—what level of intelligibility does it really have for Christian theologians? What meaning does it have—not only as a theme within Christian theology (one mostly dealt with in a perplexed or embarrassed way), but rather as a principle of theological knowledge? If this meaning were operative, or if Christians had rediscovered it in the light of Auschwitz, it would at once make clear that messianic trust is not identical with the euphoria about meaning often prevalent among Christians, something which makes them so unreceptive toward apocalyptic threats and perils within our history and allows them to react to the sufferings of others with the apathy of conquerors. And this meaning of the messianic Day of the Lord would make Christian theology perhaps more conscious of the extent to which the apocalyptic-messianic wisdom of Judaism is obstructed and repressed within Christianity. If the danger of Jewish messianism resides for me

in the way it continually suspends all reconciliation from entering our history, the inverse danger in a Christian understanding of messianism seems to me to be the way it encloses the reconciliation given to us by Christ too much within the present, being only too prepared to hand out to its own form of Christianity a testimony of moral and political innocence.

Wherever Christianity victoriously conceals its own messianic weakness, its sensorium for dangers and downfalls diminishes to an ever greater degree. Theology loses its own awareness for historical disruptions and catastrophes. Has not our Christian faith in the salvation achieved for us by Christ been covertly reified to a kind of optimism about meaning, an optimism which is no longer really capable of perceiving radical disruptions and catastrophes within meaning? Does there not exist something like a typically Christian incapacity for dismay in the face of disasters? And does this not apply with particular intensity to the average Christian (and theological) attitude toward Auschwitz?

3. Is there not manifest within the history of our Christianity a drastic deficit in regard to political resistance and a corresponding excess of political conformity? This brings us, in fact, to what I see as the central point in the self-interrogation of Christians and of theology in remembrance of Auschwitz. In the earliest history of Christianity, as was already mentioned, Jews and Christians were persecuted together. The persecution of Christians ended, as we know, fairly soon, that of the Jews continued and increased immeasurably through the centuries. There are certainly numerous reasons for this dissimilar historical development in regard to Christians and Jews, and not all of them are to be used in criticism of Christianity.

Yet in making this observation, a question regarding our Christianity and its theology forces its way into my consciousness, a question that has long disturbed me and must surely affect every theology after Auschwitz: Has Christianity not allowed too strict an interiorization and individualization of that messianic salvation preached by Jesus? And was it not precisely this extreme interiorization and individualization of the messianic idea of salvation which placed Christianity—from its Pauline beginnings onward—at a continual advantage over against Judaism in coming to an arrangement with the political situation of the time and in functioning more or less without contradiction as an intermediary and reconciling force in regard to prevailing political powers? Has Christianity, perhaps for this reason only, been "in a better position"? Has the two-thousand-year-old history of Christianity contained less suffering, persecution, and dispersion than the history of the Jews for the very reason that with Christianity one could more easily "build a state"?

In a sense, Bismark was on the right track when he said that with the Sermon on the Mount "no one can build a state." But has it then been an advantage, I mean a messianic advantage, that Christians have obviously always been more successful than Jews in knowing how to accommodate their understanding of salvation to the exigencies of political power by using this extreme individualization and interiorization? Should we not have expected to find in the history of Christianity many more conflicts with political power similar to the history of suffering and persecution of the Jewish people? Does not Christianity, in fact, manifest historically a shattering deficit in political resistance, and an extreme historical surplus of political accommodation and obedience? And finally, is it not the case that we Christians can recognize that concrete destiny which Jesus foretold for his disciples more clearly in the history of suffering undergone by the Jewish people than in the actual history of Christianity? As a Christian theologian, I do not wish to suppress this question, which disturbs me above all in the presence of Auschwitz.

This is the question that compelled me to project and work on a "political theology" with its program of deprivatization (directed more toward the synoptics than to Pauline traditions), to work against just these dangers of an extreme interiorization of Christian salvation and its attendant danger of Christianity's uncritical reconciliation with prevailing political powers. This theology argues that it is precisely the consistently nonpolitical interpretation of Christianity, and the nondialectical interiorizing and individualizing of its doctrines, that have continually led to Christianity taking on an uncritical, as it were, postfactum political form. But the Christianity of discipleship must never be politicized postfactum—through the copying or imitation of political patterns of action and power constellations already present elsewhere. Christianity is in its very being, as messianic praxis of discipleship, political. It is mystical and political at the same time, and it leads us into a responsibility, not only for what we do or fail to do but also for what we allow to happen to others in our presence, before our eyes.

4. Does not Christianity conceal too much the *practical core* of its message? Time and again we hear it said that Judaism is primarily oriented toward praxis and less concerned with doctrinal unity, whereas Christianity is said to be primarily a doctrine of faith, and this difference is held to create considerable difficulty for Jewish-Christian ecumenism. Yet Christianity itself is not in the first instance a doctrine to be preserved in maximum "purity," but a praxis to be lived more radically! This messianic praxis of discipleship, conversion, love, and suffering does not become a part of Christian faith postfactum, but is an authentic expression of this faith. Ultimately, it is of the very essence of the Christian faith to be believed in such a way that it is never just believed, but rather—in the messianic praxis of discipleship—enacted. There does, of course, exist a Christianity whose faith is only believed, a super-structure Christianity serving our own interests—such a Christianity is bourgeois religion. This kind of Christianity does not live discipleship but only believes in discipleship and, under the cover of merely believed-in discipleship, goes its own way. It does not practice compassion, but only believes in compassion and, under the screen of this merely believed-in compassion, cultivates that apathy which allowed us Christians to continue our untroubled believing and praying with our backs to Auschwitz—allowed us, in a phrase from Bonhoeffer, to go on singing Gregorian chant during the persecution of the Jews without at the same time feeling the need to cry out in their behalf.

It is here, in this degeneration of messianic religion to a purely bourgeois religion, that I see one of the central roots within contemporary Christianity for our failure in the Jewish question. Ultimately, it is the reason why we Christians, as a whole, have remained incapable of real mourning and true penance, the reason also why our churches have not resisted our society's massive repression of guilt in these postwar years.

Presumably, there are still other Christian and theological questions posed to us in remembrance of Auschwitz, questions which would open a way to an ecumenism between Christians and Jews. We would certainly have to uncover the individual roots of anti-Semitism within Christianity itself, in its doctrine and praxis. A continual and significant part of this is that relationship of "substitution within salvation history," through which Christians saw themselves displacing the Jews and which led to the Jews never being really accepted either as partners or as enemies—even enemies have a countenance! Rather, they were reified into an obsolete presupposition of saving history. However, this specific inner Christian research cannot be undertaken here; it would go far beyond the limits of this paper. I must also rule out here any investigation of the roots of anti-Semitism in those German philosophies of the nineteenth century which in their turn have lastingly marked the world of theological ideas and categories in our own century.

What Christian theologians can *do* for the murdered of Auschwitz and thereby for a true Christian-Jewish ecumenism is, in every case, this: Never again to do theology in such a way that its construction remains unaffected, or could remain unaffected, by Auschwitz. In this sense, I make available to my students an apparently very simple but, in fact, extremely demanding criterion for evaluating the theological scene: Ask yourselves if the theology you are learning is such that it could remain unchanged before and after Auschwitz. If this is the case, be on your guard!

REVISIONS

The question of reaching an ecumenism between Christians and Jews, in accepting which the Jews would not be compelled to deny their own identity, will be decided ultimately by the following factor: Will this ecumenical development succeed within the church and within society? Theological work for reconciliation remains nothing more than a surface phenomenon when it fails to take root in church and society, which means touching the soul of the people. Whether this ecumenism successfully takes root, and the manner of its success, depends once again on the way our churches, as official institutions and at the grass-roots level, relate to Auschwitz.

What is, in fact, happening in our churches? Do not the "Weeks of Christian-Jewish Fellowship" threaten gradually to become a farce? Are they not a witness to isolation far more than to fellowship? Which of us are really concerning ourselves about the newly emerging fears of persecution among the Jews in our country? The Catholic Church in West Germany in its synodal decree, "Our Hope," declared its readiness for a new relationship with the Jewish people and recognized its own special task and mission. Both the history behind the preparation of this section of the synod's text and its finally accepted form could show how tendencies to hush up and exonerate had a powerful impact. Nevertheless, if we would only take this document really seriously even in this final version! "In that time of national socialism, despite the exemplary witness of individual persons and groups, we still remained as a whole a church community which lived its life with our backs turned to the fate of this persecuted Jewish people; we let our gaze be fixed too much on the threat to our own institutions and remained silent in the face of the crimes perpetrated on the Jews and on Judaism."

Yet, in the meantime, has not a massive forgetfulness long since taken over? The dead of Auschwitz should have brought upon us a total transformation; nothing should have been allowed to remain as it was, neither among our people nor in our churches. Above all, not in the churches. They, at least, should necessarily have perceived the spiritual catastrophe signified by Auschwitz, one which left neither our people nor our churches undamaged. Yet, what has happened to us as Christians and as citizens in this land? Not just the fact that everything happened as if Auschwitz had been, after all, only an operational accident, however deplorable a one. Indications are already appearing that we are once more beginning to seek the causes for the Auschwitz horror not only among the murderers and persecutors, but also among the victims and persecuted themselves. How long, then, are we to wear these penitential garments? This is a question asked above all by those who have probably never had them on. Has anyone had the idea of asking the victims themselves how long we have to drag out our penance and whether something like a general "limitation of liability" does not apply here? The desire to limit liability in this area is to my mind less the expression of a will to forgiveness from Christian motives (and indeed *we* have here hardly anything to forgive!) than it is the attempt of our society and of our Christianity(!) to decree for itself—at last—acquittal and, poised over the abyss of horror, to get the whole thing—at last—"over with."

Faced with this situation, one thing is clear: The basis for a new relationship between Christians and Jews in remembrance of Auschwitz must not remain restricted to the creation of a diffuse sense of reconciliation nor to a Christian friendliness toward Jews which is as cheap as it is ineffective (and is itself, in fact, not seldom the sign of an unfinished hostility to Jews). What must be aimed at is a concrete and fundamental revision of our consciousness.

To take one example: This new dialogical relationship we are seeking, if it is truly to succeed, must not become a dialogue of theological experts and church specialists. This ecumenism must take root in the people as a whole, in the pedagogy of everyday life, in Sunday preaching, in church communities, families, schools, and other grassroots institutions. Everyone knows that new traditions are not established in advanced seminars nor in occasional solemn celebrations. They will only emerge if they touch the souls of men through a tenacious process of formation, when they become the very environment of the soul. But what is actually happening here in our churches and schools? Not least in our churches and schools in the rural areas which are held to be so "Christian"? Certainly anti-Semitism in rural areas has varied causes; yet not the least of these are related to religious education. In my own rural area, in a typically Catholic milieu, "the Jews" remained even after the war a faceless reality, a vague stereotype; representations for "the Jews" were taken mostly from Oberammergau.

Some historians hold the view that the German people in the Nazi era were not, in fact, essentially more anti-Semitic than several other European peoples. Personally, I doubt this, but if it were true, it would raise an even more monstrous possibility, something already put forward years ago by one of these historians: Might the Germans have drawn the ultimate consequences of anti-Semitism, namely the extermination of the Jews, only because they were *commanded to;* that is, out of sheer dependence on authority? Whatever the individual connection may have been, there is manifest here what has often enough been established as a "typically German danger." And this is the reason why the question being dealt with here demands the highest priority being given by both society and the churches to an energetic educational campaign supporting critical obedience and critical solidarity, and against the evasion of conflict and the practice of successful conformism, opportunism, and fellow-travelling.

In this context I want to quote, without pursuing her argument further, the thoughts of a young Jewish woman, who worked as a teacher in West Germany, regarding the Week of Fellowship: "There are two expressions I learned in the school without having the least idea of their significance. One of them is 'in its juridical form,' and the other is 'legal uncertainty.' Every event in the school, and I assume in all other institutions, has to be confirmed in its juridical form, even when this leads to senseless behavior. . . . Wherever I look, I see only exemplary democrats who, according to the letter and without any reason or emotion, observe laws and ordinances, instructions, directions, guiding lines and decrees. The few who protest against this and display some individualism and civil courage are systematically intimidated and cowed. . . . That is the reason why I do not fraternize with the Germans, why I reject the Week of Fellowship, and why my soul boils over at the empty babble about our dear Jewish brethren; the same people who today speak eloquently of tolerance would once again function as machines which had been presented with a new and different program!"

At the beginning, I mentioned that Auschwitz can only be remembered by us as a moral reality, never purely historically. This moral remembrance of the persecution of the Jews touches finally also on the relationship of people in this country to the *State* of Israel. Indeed, *we* have no choice in this matter (and I stand by this against my left wing friends). *We* must at all events be the last people to now accuse the Jews of an exaggerated need for security after they were brought in the most recent history of our country to the edge of total annihilation; and *we* must be the first to trust the protestations of the Jews that they are defending their state, not from reasons of Zionist imperialism but as a "house against death," as a last place of refuge of a people persecuted through the centuries.

ECUMENISM IN A MESSIANIC PERSPECTIVE

The ecumenism between Jews and Christians in remembrance of Auschwitz, which I have been discussing here, does not lead at all to the outskirts of inner Christian ecumenism, but rather to its center. It is my profound conviction that ultimately ecumenism among Christians will only make progress at all, and certainly will only come to a good conclusion, when it recovers the biblical-messianic dimensions of ecumenism in general. This means it must learn to know and recognize the forgotten and suppressed partner of its own beginnings, the Jewish people and their messianic religion. It is in this sense that I understand Karl Barth's warning in his 1966 "Ecumenical Testament": "We do not wish to forget that there is ultimately only one really central ecumenical question: This is our relationship to Judaism." As Christians, we will only come together among ourselves when we achieve together a new relationship to the Jewish people and to its religion; not avoiding Auschwitz, but as that particular form of Christianity which, after Auschwitz, is alone permitted to us and indeed demanded of us. For, I repeat: We Christians can never again go back behind Auschwitz. To go beyond Auschwitz is, if we see clearly, impossible for us of ourselves; it is possible only together with the victims of Auschwitz.

And so we could arrive one day, although I suggest this cautiously, at a kind of *coalition of messianic trust* between Jews and Christians in opposition to the apotheosis of banality and hatred present in our world. Indeed, the remembrance of Auschwitz should sharpen all our senses for present-day processes of extermination in countries in which on the surface "law and order" reigns, as it did once in Nazi Germany.

FURTHER READING

Arendt, Hannah. *Eichmann in Jerusalem: A Report of the Banality of Evil.* Rev. ed. Penguin, 1977.

Fleischner, Eva, ed. *Auschwitz—Beginning of a New Era? Reflections on the Holocaust.* Ktav, 1977.

Glucksmann, Andre. *The Master Thinkers.* Harper & Row, 1980.

Haffner, Sebastian. *The Meaning of Hitler.* Macmillan, 1979.

Horkheimer, Max, and Theodor W. Adorno. "Elements of Anti-Semitism: Limits of Enlightenment." In *Dialectic of Enlightenment.* Continuum, 1975, pp. 168–208.

Küng, Hans, and Walter Kasper. *Christians and Jews* (=*Concilium* 98). Seabury 1976.

Kogon, Eugene. *The Theory and Practice of Hell.* Repr. Octagon, 1972.

Metz, Johannes B., and Jürgen Moltman. *Meditations on the Passion.* Paulist, 1979.

Mitscherlich, Alexander, and Margaret Mitscherlich. *The Inability to Mourn: Principles of Collective Behavior.* Grove, 1975.

Pratt, G., et al. *Peace, Justice and Reconciliation in the Arab-Israeli Conflict: A Christian Perspective.* Friend, 1979.

Rubenstein, Richard J. *After Auschwitz: Essays in Contemporary Judaism.* Bobbs-Merrill, n.d.

Reuther, Rosemary. *Faith and Fratricide: The Theological Roots of Anti-Semitism.* Seabury, 1974.

Sartre, Jean-Paul. *Anti-Semite and Jew.* Schocken, 1965.

Stendahl, Krister. *Paul Among Jews and Gentiles.* Fortress, 1976.

EMIL L. FACKENHEIM

■ The Holocaust and Philosophy

Philosophers have all but ignored the Holocaust. Why?

1. Attuned to universals, they have little use for particulars, and less for the unique. The Holocaust thus becomes at most one case of genocide among others. *However,* philosophers *have* attended to the *momentously* unique. Hegel and Marx have treated the French Revolution, not revolutions-in-general.

2. Philosophers seldom consider things Jewish. As regards Judaism, the term "Judeo-Christian" rarely signifies more than token recognition. As regards Jews, they are one "ethnic" or "religious group" among others, just as antisemitism is reduced to a "prejudice." Rare is a work such as Jean Paul Sartre's *Antisemite and Jew,*[1] and even this treats "antisemite" more adequately than "Jew." *However,* the Third Reich, not merely its Holocaust component, was "the only German regime—the only regime ever anywhere—which had no other clear principle than murderous hatred of Jews, for 'Aryan' had no clear meaning other than 'non-Jewish.'"[2] (The Japanese were honorary "Aryans," and the "Semitic" Mufti of Jerusalem was a welcome guest in Nazi Berlin.)

Emil L. Fackenheim, "The Holocaust and Philosophy," *Journal of Philosophy* 82 (10): 505–514 (October 1985). Reprinted by permission of the *Journal of Philosophy* and Georges Borchardt, Inc., Literary Agency.

3. The French Revolution, though momentous, is a positive event. The Holocaust is devastatingly negative. Qua humans, philosophers are tempted to flee from this into some such platitude as "man's-inhumanity-to-man-especially-in-wartime." (Arnold Toynbee[3]: "What the Nazis did is not peculiar.") Qua philosophers, having always had problems with evil, they have a new problem now. *However,* philosophers must confront *aporiae,* not evade or ignore them.

This paper will treat the Holocaust as unique; as anti-Jewish not accidentally but essentially; and as a *novum* in the history of evil.

I. THE UNIQUENESS OF THE HOLOCAUST

The World War II Jewish genocide resembles most closely the World War I Armenian genocide. Both were (i) attempts to murder a whole people; (ii) carried out under cover of war; (iii) with maximum secrecy; (iv) after the deportation of the victims, with deliberate cruelty, to remote places; (v) all this provoking few countermeasures or even verbal protests on the part of the civilized world. Doubtless the Nazis both learned from and were encouraged by the Armenian precedent.

These are striking similarities. As striking, however, are the differences. The Armenian deportations from Istanbul were stopped after some time, whether because of political problems or the logistical difficulties posed by so large a city. "Combed" for Jews were Berlin, Vienna, Amsterdam, Warsaw. In this, greater Teutonic efficiency was secondary; primary was a *Weltanschauung.* Indian reservations exist in America. Jewish reservations in a victorious Nazi empire are inconceivable: already planned instead were museums for an "extinct race." For, unlike the Turks, the Nazis sought a *"final* solution" of a "problem"—final only if, minimally, Europe and, maximally, the world would be *judenrein.* In German this word has no counterpart such as *polenrein, russenrein, slavenrein.* In other languages it does not exist at all; for whereas Jordan and Saudi Arabia are in fact without Jews, missing is the *Weltanschauung.* The Holocaust, then, is but one case of the class "genocide." As a case of the class: "intended, planned, and largely successful *extermination,*" it is without precedent and, thus far at least, without sequel. It is unique.

Equally unique are the means necessary to this end. These included (i) a scholastically precise definition of the victims; (ii) juridical procedures procuring their rightlessness; (iii) a technical apparatus culminating in murder trains and gas chambers; and (iv), most importantly, a veritable army of murderers and also direct and indirect accomplices: clerks, newspapermen, lawyers, bank managers, doctors, soldiers, railwaymen, entrepreneurs, and an endless list of others.

The relation between direct and indirect accomplices is as important as the distinction. The German historian Karl Dietrich Bracher[4] understands Nazi Germany as a dual system. Its inner part was the "S.S. state"; its outer, the traditional establishment—civil service, army, schools, universities, churches. This latter system was allowed separate existence to the end, but was also increasingly penetrated, manipulated, perverted. *And since it resisted the process only sporadically and never radically, it enabled the S.S. state to do what it could never have done simply on its own.* Had the railwaymen engaged in strikes or sabotage or simply vanished there would have been no Auschwitz. Had the German army acted likewise there would have been neither Auschwitz nor World War II. U.S. President Ronald Reagan should not have gone to Bitburg even if no S.S. men had been buried there.

Such was the army required for the "how" of the Holocaust. Its "why" required an army of historians, philosophers, theologians. The historians rewrote history. The philosophers demonstrated that mankind is "Aryan" or "non-Aryan" before it is human. The theologians were divided into Christians who made Jesus into an "Aryan" and neo-pagans who rejected Christianity itself as "non-Aryan"; their differences were slight compared to their shared commitments.

These were direct accomplices. But here too there was need for indirect accomplices as well. Without the prestige of philosophers like Martin Heidegger and theologians like Emanuel Hirsch, could the *National-Sozialistische Weltanschauung* have gained its power and respectability? Could it have won out at all? The Scottish-Catholic historian Malcolm Hay asks why what happened in Germany did not happen in France forty years earlier, during the Dreyfus affair. He replies that in France there were fifty righteous men.[5]

What *was* the "why" of the Holocaust? Astoundingly, significantly, even the archpractitioners rarely faced it. *Archpractitioner* indisputably fits Treblinka Kommandant Franz Stangl. (Treblinka had the fewest survivors.) In a postwar interview Stangl was asked: "What did you think at the time was the reason for the extermination of the Jews?" Stangl replied—as if Jews had not long been robbed naked!—"they wanted their money."[6] Did Stangl *really* not know? Yet, though Treblinka itself was secret, its raison d'être had always been public. In the Nazi *Weltanschauung* Jews were vermin, and one does not execute vermin, murder it, spare its young or its old: one *exterminates* vermin—coldly, systematically, without feeling or a second thought. Is *vermin* (or *virus* or *parasite?*) a "mere metaphor"? In a 1942 "table-talk," right after the Wannsee conference that finalized the "Final Solution," Hitler said:

> The discovery of the Jewish virus is one of the greatest revolutions . . . in the world. The struggle we are waging is of the same kind as that of Pasteur and Koch in the last century. How many diseases can be traced back to the Jewish virus! We shall regain our health only when we exterminate the Jews.[7]

For racism, "inferior races" are still human; even for Nazi racism there are merely too many Slavs. For Nazi antisemitism Jews are not human; they must not exist at all.

Stangl failed with his interviewer's first question. He failed with her second as well. "If they were going to kill them anyway," he was asked, "what was the point of all the humiliation, why all the cruelty?" He replied: "To condition those who actually had to carry out the policies. To make it possible for them to do what they did." The interviewer had doubted Stangl's first answer, but accepted his second as both honest and true. Honest it may have been; true it was not. The "cruelty" included horrendous medical nonexperiments on women, children, babies. The "humiliation" included making pious Jews spit on Torah scrolls and, when they ran out of spittle, supplying them with more by spitting into their mouths. Was all this easier on the operators then pulling triggers and pushing buttons? *Treblinka—the Holocaust—had two ultimate purposes: extermination* and also *maximum prior humiliation and torture.* This too—can Stangl have been unaware of it?—had been part of the public *Weltanschauung* all along. In 1936 Julius Streicher declared that "who fights the Jew fights the devil," and that "who masters the devil conquers heaven" (MW 188). And this basest, most pornographic Nazi only echoed what the most authoritative (and equally pornographic) Nazi had written many years earlier:

> With satanic joy in his face, the black-haired Jewish youth lurks in wait for the unsuspecting girl whom he defiles with his blood ... By defending myself against the Jew, I am fighting for the work of the Lord.[8]

To "punish" the "Jewish devil" through humiliation and torture, then, was part of "Aryan" salvation. Perhaps it was all of it.

"Jewish devil" and Jewish "vermin" (or "bacillus," "parasite," "virus") existed side by side in the Nazi theory. For example, this single Hitler-passage of 1923:

> The Jews are undoubtedly a race, but they are not human. They cannot be human in the sense of being in the image of God, the Eternal. The Jews are the image of the devil. Jewry means the racial tuberculosis of the nations (cited by Fest, op. cit.).

Side by side in the theory, "devil" and "vermin" were synthesized in the Auschwitz praxis, and this was a *novum* without precedent in the realm of either the real or the possible. Even in the worst state, punishment is meted out for a *doing*—a fact explaining Hegel's statement, defensible once but no more, that any state is better than none. And, even in the hell of poetic and theological imagination, the innocent cannot be touched. The Auschwitz praxis was based on a new principle: *for one portion of mankind, existence itself is a crime, punishable by humiliation, torture, and death.* And the new world produced by this praxis included two kinds of inhabitants, those who were given the "punishment" and those who administered it.

Few have yet grasped the newness of that new world. Survivors have grasped it all along. Hence they refer to *all* the "punished" victims as *k'doshim* ("holy ones"); for even criminals among them were innocent of the "crime" for which they were "punished." Hence, too, they refer to the new world created by the victimizers as a "universe" other than ours, or a "planet" other than the one we inhabit. What historians and philosophers must face is that Auschwitz was a kingdom not of this world.

II. THE HOLOCAUST AND THE HISTORIAN

But the Holocaust took place *in* our world. The historian must explain it, and the philosopher must reflect on the historian's work.

Raul Hilberg[9] has studied closely the "how" of the Holocaust. In answer to the "why" he has said: "They did it because they wanted to do it."[10] This stresses admirably the respective roles of Nazi *Weltanschauung* and Nazi decision-making. But how accept *such a Weltanschauung*? How make decisions *such as these*? As if in answer to these further questions, Bracher (op. cit.) writes:

> The extermination [of the Jews] grew out of the biologistic insanity of Nazi ideology, and for that reason is completely unlike the terrors of revolutions and wars of the past (430).

Again further questions arise. What or who was insane, the ideology or those creating, believing, implementing it? If the latter, who? Just the one? Or the one and the direct accomplices? Or the indirect accomplices as well? And, climactically, is "insanity" *itself* an explanation, or merely a way of saying that attempts to explain have come to an end?

Historians will resist this conclusion. Has not the "Jewish devil" a long tradition, harking back to the New Testament? (See especially John 8:44.) As for the "Jewish vermin" (or "virus" or "parasite"), Hitler got it from antisemitic trash harking back decades. Doubtless without these factors the Holocaust would have been *impossible*, a fact in itself sufficient to mark off the event from other genocides. *But do these (and other) factors suffice to make the Holocaust possible? To explain an event is to show how it was possible; but the mind accepts the possibility of the Holocaust, in the last analysis, only because it was* actual. Explanation, in short—so it seems—moves in circles.

In his unremitting search for explanations the historian must respond to this challenge by focusing ever more sharply on what is unique in the Holocaust. The philosopher must ponder Hans Jonas's paradoxical Holocaust-dictum: "Much more is real than is possible" (MW 233). Minimally, what became real at Auschwitz was *always* possible, but is now *known* to be so. Maximally, Auschwitz *has made possible* what previously was *impossible*; for *it is a precedent*. In either case, philosophers must face a *novum* within a question as old as Socrates: what does it mean to be human?

III. THE MUSELMANN

Allan Bullock stresses that Hitler's originality lay not in ideas but in "the terrifying literal way in which he ... translate[d] fantasy into reality, and his unequalled grasp of the means by which to do this."[11] One original product of this "translation" was the so-called *Muselmann*. If in the Gulag the dissident suffers torture-through-psychiatry, on the theory that in the workers' paradise such as he must be mad, then the Auschwitz praxis reduces the "non-Aryan" to a walking corpse covered with his own filth, on the theory that he must reveal himself as the disgusting creature that he has been, if disguisedly, since birth. To be sure, the *Muselmänner* included countless "Aryans" also. But, just as "the Nazis were racists because they were antisemites" is truer than the reverse, so it is truer that non-Jewish *Muselmänner* were Jews-by-association than that Jewish *Muselmänner* were a sub-species of "enemies of the Reich."

The process was focused on Jews in particular. Its implications, however, concern the whole human condition, and, therefore, philosophers. Among these few would deny that to die one's own death is part of one's freedom; in Martin Heidegger's *Being and Time* this freedom is foundational. Yet, of the Auschwitz *Muselmann*, Primo Levi[12] writes:

> Their life is short, but their number is endless; they, the Muselmänner, the drowned, form the backbone of the camp, an anonymous mass, continually renewed and always identical, of non-men who march and labor in silence, the divine spark dead within them, already too empty really to suffer. *One hesitates to call them living; one hesitates to call their death death.*

To die one's own death has always been a freedom subject to loss by accident. On Planet Auschwitz, however, the loss of it was made essential, and its survival accidental. Hence Theodor Adorno[13] writes:

> With the administrative murder of millions death has become something that never before was to be feared in this way. Death no longer enters into the experienced life of the individual, as somehow harmonizing with its course. It was no longer the individual that died in the camps, but the specimen. *This must affect also the dying of those who escaped the procedure* (355; my translation; italics added).

Philosophers are faced with a new *aporia*. It arises from the necessity to listen to the silence of the *Muselmann*.

IV. "BANAL" EVIL AND PLANET AUSCHWITZ

From one new way of being human—that of the victims—we turn to the other, that of the victimizers. Since Socrates, philosophers have known of evil as ignorance; but the Auschwitz operators included Ph.D.s. Since Kant philosophers have known of evil as weakness, as yielding to inclination; but Eichmann in Jerusalem invoked, not entirely incorrectly, the categorical imperative.[14] From psychiatry philosophy learns of evil as sickness; but the "SD intellectuals" who so efficiently engineered the "Final Solution" abominated Streicher-type sadists, "wanted to be regarded as decent," and had as "their sole object . . . to solve the so-called Jewish problem in a cold, rational manner."[15] Philosophy has even had a glimpse of what the theologians call "radical" or "demonical" evil—the diabolical grandeur that says to evil "be thou my good!" However, just as people the world over experienced human shock when they watched newsreels of the big Nazis at the Nuremberg trials, so Hannah Arendt—a belated owl of Minerva—experienced philosophical shock when, more than a dozen years later, she observed Eichmann at his Jerusalem trial. *Of grandeur, there was in them all not a trace.* The characteristic Nazi criminal was rather a dime-a-dozen individual, who, having once been an ordinary, nay, respected citizen, committed at Auschwitz crimes of a kind and on a scale hitherto unimaginable, only to become, when it was over, an ordinary citizen again, without signs of suffering sleepless nights. Eichmann was only one such person. Others are still being discovered in nice suburbs, and their neighbors testify how they took care of their gardens and were kind to their dogs. Himmler himself, had he escaped detection and the need for suicide, might well have returned to his chicken farm. The philosopher in Arendt looked for some depth in such as these, and found none.[16] It was "banal" people who committed what may justly be called the greatest crime in history; and it was the system that made them do what they did.

The concept "banal evil," however, is only half a philosophical thought. Who created and maintained the system, if not such as Himmler and Eichmann, Stangl, and the unknown soldier who was an S.S. murderer? In reply, many would doubtless point to one not yet mentioned by us among the banal ones. And, it is true, Adolf Hitler *did* have an "unequaled grasp of the means" by which to "translate fantasy into reality." To go further, the whole Nazi Reich, and hence Planet Auschwitz, would doubtless have disintegrated had some saintly hero succeeded in assassinating just this one individual. Even so, it is impossible to trace the monstrous evil perpetrated by all the banal ones to some monstrous greatness in the Fuehrer of them all. For if it is a "superstition . . . that a man who greatly affected the destiny of nations must himself be great,[17] then Hitler is the clearest illustration of this truth. His ideas, though blown up into a pretentious *Weltanschauung,* are trite; so, for all the posturing intended to disguise the fact, is the man. Other than a low cunning, his one distinguishing mark is a devouring passion, and even that is mostly fed by a need, as petty as it is limitless, to show them—whom?—that the nobody is somebody. Were even the beliefs of this "true believer" truly held? Did he ever dare to examine them? Certainly—all his biographers are struck by the fact—he never *re*-examined them. As likely, they too were part of a Wagner-style posturing, right up to his theatrical death.

Such historical considerations aside, we must face a philosophical problem. If we accept and philosophically radicalize Eichmann's plea to have been a mere "cog in the wheel," we end up attributing to the few—even to just one?—a power to mesmerize, manipulate, dominate, terrorize that is *beyond* all humanity and, to the many, a mesmerizability, manipulability, and craven cowardice that is *beneath* all humanity. Yet, whereas Auschwitz *was* a kingdom not of this world, its creators and operators were neither super- nor subhuman but rather—a terrifying thought!—human like ourselves. Hence, in however varying degrees, the mesmerized and manipulated *allowed themselves* to be so treated, and the dominated and terrorized *gave in* to craven cowardice. Not only Eichmann but *everyone* was more than a cog in the wheel. The operators of the Auschwitz system were *all* its unbanal creators even as they were its banal creatures.

A moment of truth relevant to this occurred during the 1964 Auschwitz trial held in Frankfurt, Germany. A survivor had testified that, thanks to a certain S.S. officer Flacke, one Auschwitz subcamp had been an "island of peace." The judge sat up, electrified: "Do you wish to say that everyone could decide for himself to be either good or evil at Auschwitz?," he asked. "That is exactly what I wish to say," the witness replied (MW 242).

Then why were such as S.S. officer Flacke exceptions so rare as barely to touch and not at all to shake the smooth functioning of the machinery of humiliation, torture, and murder? And how could those who were the rule, banal ones all, place into our world a "kingdom" evil without precedent, far removed from banality and fated to haunt mankind forever? We cannot answer the first question. Gripped by the *aporia* of the second, the philosopher is unlikely to do better than fall back on a familiar dictum: Auschwitz—like the Reich as a whole, especially as revealed in the endless, empty *Sieg Heils* of the Nuremberg *Parteitage*[18]—was a whole that was more than the sum of its parts.

Philosophers have applied this dictum without hesitation to animal organisms. To human realities—a society, a state, a civilization, a "world"—they have applied it with hesitation, and only if the whole enhanced the humanity of all beyond what would be possible for the parts, separately or jointly, alone. It is in contrast to this that the *novum* of the Holocaust-whole is revealed in all its stark horror. It did not enhance the humanity of its inhabitants. On the contrary, it was singlemindedly geared to the destruction of the humanity (as well as the lives) of the victims; and in pursuing this goal, the victimizers destroyed their own humanity, even as they yielded to its being destroyed. Pursuing his own age-old goal, the Socratic quest, "What is Man?," the philosopher, now as then, is filled with wonder. But the ancient wonder is now mingled with a new horror.

NOTES

1. New York: Schocken Books, 1948.

2. Leo Strauss, Preface to the English edition of Spinoza's *Critique of Religion*, reprinted in Judah Goldin, ed., *The Jewish Expression* (New York: Bantam Books, 1970), p. 347.

3. In a debate with Yaacov Herzog. See Herzog, *A People that Dwells Alone* (London: Weidenfield & Nicholson, 1975), p. 31.

4. *The German Dictatorship* (New York: Praeger, 1969), esp. ch. viii.

5. *The Foot of Pride* (Boston: Beacon Press, 1950), p. 211.

6. Gitta Sereny, *Into that Darkness* (London: Andre Deutsch, 1974), p. 101.

7. Cited by Joachim C. Fest, *Hitler* (New York: Vintage, 1975), p. 212.

8. Hitler, *Mein Kampf*, Ralph Manheim, tr. (Boston: Houghton Mifflin, 1943), pp. 325, 365.

9. See his magisterial *The Destruction of the European Jews* (Chicago: Quadrangle, 1961).

10. In private conversation with this writer.

11. Cited by Herbert Luethy, "Der Fuehrer," N. Podhoretz, ed., in *The Commentary Reader* (New York: Atheneum, 1966), p. 64.

12. *Survival in Auschwitz*, S. Woolf, tr. (New York: Orion, 1959), p. 82, italics added.

13. *Negative Dialektik* (Frankfurt: Suhrkamp, 1975).

14. Referred to in Hannah Arendt, *Eichmann in Jerusalem* (New York: Penguin, 1977), pp. 135 ff.; analyzed in MW 270 ff.

15. H. Hoehne, *The Order of the Death's Head* (London: Pan, 1972), pp. 301 ff. Analyzed in *To Mend the World*, pp. 211 ff. and also in my *The Jewish Return into History* (New York: Schocken Books, 1978), pp. 69 ff.

16. See especially *Eichmann in Jerusalem*, passim, and R. Feldman, ed., *The Jew as Pariah* (New York: Grove Press, 1978), p. 251.

17. Luethy, op. cit., p. 65. Luethy's brilliant essay is worth more than many a whole Hitler biography.

18. I have tried to grasp and to capture the idolatrous compact between *Volk* and *Fuehrer*, manifested most clearly in the endless yet empty *Sieg Heils* of the Nuremberg *Parteitage*, in "Idolatry as a Modern Possibility," *Encounters between Judaism and Modern Philosophy* (New York: Schocken Books, 1980), pp. 171–198, esp. pp. 192–195.

HANS JONAS

▣ The Concept of God after Auschwitz

A Jewish Voice[1]

When, with the honor of this award, I also accepted the burden of delivering the oration that goes with it, and when I read in the biography of Rabbi Leopold Lucas, in whose memory the prize is named, that he died in Theresienstadt, but that his wife Dorothea, mother of the donor, was then shipped to Auschwitz, there to suffer the fate that my mother suffered there, too, there was no resisting the force with which the theme of this lecture urged itself on my choice. I chose it with fear and trembling. But I believed I owed it to those shadows that something like an answer to their long-gone cry to a silent God be not denied to them.

What I have to offer is a piece of frankly speculative theology. Whether this behooves a philosopher is a question I leave open. Immanuel Kant has banished everything of the kind from the territory of theoretical reason and hence from the business of philosophy; and the logical positivism of our century, the entire dominant analytical creed, even denies to the linguistic expressions such reasonings employ for their purported subject matters this very object-significance itself, that is, any conceptual meaning at all, declaring already—prior to questions of truth and verification—the mere speech about them to be nonsensical. At this, to be sure, old Kant himself would have been utterly astounded. For he, to the contrary, held these alleged nonobjects to be the highest objects of all, about which reason can never cease to be concerned, although it cannot hope ever to obtain a knowledge of them and in their pursuit is necessarily doomed to failure by the impassable limits of human cognition. But this cognitive veto, given the yet justified concern, leaves another way open besides that of complete abstention: bowing to the decree that "knowledge" eludes us here, nay, even waiving this very goal from the outset, one may yet meditate on things of this nature in terms of sense and meaning. For the contention—this fashionable contention—that not even sense and meaning pertain to them is easily disposed of as a circular, tautological inference from first having defined "sense" as that which in the end is verifiable by sense data or from generally equating "meaningful" with "knowable." To this axiomatic fiat by definition only he is bound who has first consented to it. He who has not is free, therefore, to work at the *concept* of God, even knowing that there is no *proof* of God, as a task of understanding, not of knowledge; and such working is philosophical when it keeps to the rigor of concept and its connection with the universe of concepts.

But of course, this epistemological laissez-passer is much too general and impersonal for the matter at hand. As Kant granted to the practical reason what he denied to the theoretical, so may *we* allow the force of a unique and shattering experience a voice in the question of what "is the matter" with God. And there, right away, arises the question: What did Auschwitz add to that which one could always have known about humans and from times immemorial have done? And what has it added in particular to what is familiar to us Jews from a millennial history of suffering and forms so essential a part of our collective memory? The *question of Job* has always been the main question of theodicy—of general theodicy because of the existence of evil as such in the world, and of particular theodicy in its sharpening by the riddle of election, of the purported covenant between Israel and its God. As to this sharpening, under which our present question also falls, one could at first invoke—as the prophets did—the covenant itself for an explanation of what befell the human party to it: the "people of the covenant" had been unfaithful to it. In the long ages of faithfulness thereafter, guilt and retribution no longer furnished the explanation, but the idea of "witness" did instead—this creation of the Maccabean age, which bequeathed to posterity the concept of the martyr. It is of its very meaning that precisely the innocent and the just suffer the worst. In deference to the idea of witness, whole communities in the Middle Ages met their death by sword and fire with the *Sh'ma Jisrael*, the avowal of God's Oneness on their lips. The Hebrew name for this is *Kiddush-hashem*, "sanctification of the Name," and the slaughtered were called "saints." Through their sacrifice shone the light of promise, of the final redemption by the Messiah to come.

Nothing of this is still of use in dealing with the event for which "Auschwitz" has become the symbol. Not fidelity or infidelity, belief or unbelief, not guilt or punishment, not trial, witness and messianic hope, nay, not even strength or weakness, heroism or cowardice, defiance or submission had a place there. Of all this, Auschwitz, which also devoured the infants and babes, knew nothing; to none of it (with rarest exceptions) did the factory-like working of its machine give room. Not for the *sake* of faith did the victims die (as did, after all, "Jehovah's Witnesses"), nor *because* of their faith or any self-affirmed bend of their being as persons were they murdered. Dehumanization by utter degradation and deprivation preceded their dying, no glimmer of dignity was left to the freights bound for the final solution, hardly a trace of it was found in the surviving skeleton specters of the liberated camps. And yet, paradox of paradoxes: it *was* the ancient people of the "covenant," no longer believed in by those involved, killers and victims alike, but nevertheless just this and no other people, under which the fiction of race had been chosen for this wholesale annihilation—the most monstrous inversion of election into curse, which defied all possible endowment with meaning. There does, then, in spite of all, exist a connection—of a wholly perverse kind—with the God-seekers and prophets of yore, whose descendants were thus collected out of the dispersion and gathered into the unity of joint death. And God let it happen. What God could let it happen?

Here we must note that on this question the Jew is in greater theoretical difficulty than the Christian. To the Christian (of the stern variety) the world is anyway largely of the devil and always an object of suspicion—the human world in particular because of original sin. But to the Jew, who sees in "this" world the locus of divine creation, justice, and redemption, God is eminently the Lord of *history*, and in this respect "Auschwitz" calls, even for the believer, the whole traditional concept of God into question. It has, indeed, as I have just tried to show, added to the Jewish historical experience something unprecedented and of a nature no longer assimilable by the old theological categories. Accordingly, one who will not thereupon just give up the concept of God altogether—and even the philosopher has a right to such an unwillingness—must rethink it so that it still remains thinkable; and that means seeking a new answer to the old question of (and about) Job. The Lord of history, we suspect, will have to go by the board in this quest. To repeat then: What God could let it happen?

For a possible, if groping, answer, I fall back on a speculative attempt with which I once ventured to meet the different question of immortality but in which also the specter of Auschwitz already played its part. On that occasion, I resorted to a *myth* of my own invention—that vehicle of imaginative but credible conjecture that Plato allowed for the sphere beyond the knowable. Allow me to repeat it here.

In the beginning, for unknowable reasons, the ground of being, or the Divine, chose to give itself over to the chance and risk and endless variety of becoming. And wholly so: entering into the adventure of space and time, the deity held back nothing of itself: no uncommitted or unimpaired part remained to direct, correct, and ultimately guarantee the devious working-out of its destiny in creation. On this unconditional immanence the modern temper insists. It is its courage or despair, in any case its bitter honesty, to take our being-in-the-world seriously: to view the world as left to itself, its laws as brooking no interference, and the rigor of our belonging to it as not softened by extramundane providence. The same our myth postulates for God's being in the world. Not, however, in the sense of pantheistic immanence: if world and God are simply the same, the world at each moment and in each state represents his fullness, and God can neither lose nor gain. Rather, in order that the world might be, and be for itself, God renounced his being, divesting himself of his deity—to receive it back from the odyssey of time weighted with the chance harvest of unforeseeable temporal experience: transfigured or possibly even disfigured by it. In such self-forfeiture of divine integrity for the sake of unprejudiced becoming, no other foreknowledge can be admitted than that of *possibilities*, which cosmic being offers in its own terms: to these, God committed his cause in effacing himself for the world.

And for aeons his cause is safe in the slow hands of cosmic chance and probability—while all the time we may surmise a patient memory of the gyrations of matter to accumulate into an ever more expectant accompaniment of eternity to the labors of time—a hesitant emergence of transcendence from the opaqueness of immanence.

And then the first stirring of life—a new language of the world: and with it a tremendous quickening of concern in the eternal realm and a sudden leap in its growth toward recovery of its plenitude. It is the world-accident for which becoming deity had waited and with which its prodigal stake begins to show signs of being redeemed. From the infinite swell of feeling, sensing, striving, and acting, which ever more varied and intense rises above the mute eddyings of matter, eternity gains strength, filling with content after content of self-affirmation, and the awakening God can first pronounce creation to be good.

But note that with life together came death, and that mortality is the price which the new possibility of being called "life" had to pay for itself. If permanence were the point, life should not have started out in the first place, for in no possible form can it match the durability of inorganic bodies. It is essentially precarious and corruptible being, an adventure in mortality, obtaining from long-lasting matter on its terms—the short terms of metabolizing organism—the borrowed, finite careers of individual selves. Yet it is precisely through the briefly snatched self-feeling, doing, and suffering of *finite* individuals, with the pitch of awareness heightened by the very press of finitude, that the divine landscape bursts into color and the deity comes to experience itself.

Note also that with life's innocence before the advent of knowledge God's cause cannot go wrong. Whatever variety evolution brings forth adds to the possibilities of feeling and acting, and thus enriches the self-experiencing of the ground of being. Every new dimension of world-response opened up in its course means another modality for God's trying out his hidden essence and discovering himself through the surprises of the world-adventure. And all its harvest of anxious toil, whether bright or dark, swells the transcendent treasure of temporally lived eternity. If this is true for the broadening spectrum of diversity as such, it is even truer for the heightening pitch and passion of life that go with the twin rise of perception and motility in animals. The ever more sharpened keenness of appetite and fear, pleasure and pain, triumph and anguish, love and even cruelty—their very edge is the deity's gain. Their countless, yet never blunted incidence—hence the necessity of death and new birth—supplies the tempered essence from which the Godhead reconstitutes itself. All this, evolution provides in the mere lavishness of its play and the sternness of its spur. Its creatures, by merely fulfilling themselves in pursuit of their lives, vindicate the divine venture. Even their suffering deepens the fullness of the symphony. Thus, this side of good and evil, God cannot lose in the great evolutionary game.

Nor yet can he fully win in the shelter of its innocence, and a new expectancy grows in him in answer to the direction which the unconscious drift of immanence gradually takes.

And then he trembles as the thrust of evolution, carried by its own momentum, passes the threshold where innocence ceases and an entirely new criterion of success and failure takes hold of the divine stake. The advent of man means the advent of knowledge and freedom, and with this supremely double-edged gift the innocence of the mere subject of self-fulfilling life has given way to the charge of responsibility under the disjunction of good and evil. To the promise and risk of this agency the divine cause, revealed at last, henceforth finds itself committed; and its issue trembles in the balance. The image of God, haltingly begun by the universe, for so long worked upon—and left undecided—in the wide and then narrowing spirals of prehuman life, passes man's precarious trust, to be completed, saved, or spoiled by what he will do to himself and the world. And in this awesome impact of his deeds on God's destiny, on the very complexion of eternal being, lies the immortality of man.

With the appearance of man, transcendence awakened to itself and henceforth accompanies his doings with the bated breath of suspense, hoping and beckoning, rejoicing and grieving, approving and frowning—and, I daresay, making itself felt to him even while not intervening in the dynamics of his worldly scene: for can it not be that by the reflection of its own state as it wavers with the record of man, the transcendent casts light and shadow over the human landscape?[2]

Such is the tentative myth I once proposed for consideration in a different context. It has theological implications that only later unfolded to me. Of these I shall develop here some of the more obvious ones—hoping that this translation from image into concept will somehow connect what so far must seem a strange and rather willful private fantasy with the more responsible tradition of Jewish religious thought. In this manner I try to redeem the poetic liberties of my earlier, roving attempt.

First, and most obviously, I have been speaking of a *suffering God*—which immediately seems to clash with the biblical conception of divine majesty. There is, of course, a Christian connotation of the term "suffering God" with which my myth must not be confounded; it does not speak, as does the former, of a special act by which the deity at one time, and for the special purpose of saving man, sends part of itself into a particular situation of suffering (the incarnation and crucifixion). If anything in what I said makes sense, then the sense is that the relation of God to the world *from the moment of creation*, and certainly from the creation of man on, involved suffering on the part of the God. It involves, to be sure, suffering on the part of the creature too, but this truism has always been recognized in every theology. Not so the idea of God's suffering with creation, and of this I said that, prima facie, it clashes with the biblical conception of divine majesty. But does it really clash as extremely as it seems at first glance? Do not we also in the Bible encounter God as slighted and rejected by man and grieving over him? Do not we encounter him as ruing that he created man, and suffering from the disappointment he experiences with him—and with his chosen people in particular? We remember the prophet Hosea, and God's love lamenting over Israel, his unfaithful wife.

Then, second, the myth suggests the picture of a *becoming God*. It is a God emerging in time instead of possessing a completed being that remains identical with itself throughout eternity. Such an idea of divine becoming is surely at variance with the Greek, Platonic-Aristotelian tradition of philosophical theology that, since its incorporation into the Jewish and Christian theological tradition, has somehow usurped for itself an authority to which it is not at all entitled by authentic Jewish (and also Christian) standards. Transtemporality, impassibility, and immutability have been taken to be necessary attributes of God. And the ontological distinction that classical thought made between "being" and "becoming," with the latter characteristic of the lower, sensible world, excluded every shadow of becoming from the pure, absolute being of the Godhead. But this Hellenic concept has never accorded well with the spirit and language of the Bible, and the concept of divine becoming can actually be better reconciled with it.

For what does the becoming God mean? Even if we do not go so far as our myth suggests, that much at least we must concede of "becoming" in God as lies in the mere fact that he is affected by what happens in the world, and "affected" means altered, made different. Even apart from the fact that creation as such—the act itself and the lasting result thereof—was after all a decisive change in God's own state, insofar as he is now no longer alone, his continual *relation* to the creation, once this exists and moves in the flux of becoming, means that he experiences something with the world, that his own being is affected by what goes on in it. This holds already for the mere relation of accompanying knowledge, let alone that of caring interest. Thus, if God is in any relation to the world—which is the cardinal assumption of religion—then by that token alone the Eternal has "temporalized" himself and progressively becomes different through the actualizations of the world process.

One incidental consequence of the idea of the becoming God is that it destroys the idea of an eternal recurrence of the same. This was Nietzsche's alternative to Christian metaphysics, which in this case is the same as Jewish metaphysics. It is indeed the extreme symbol of the turn to unconditional temporality and of the complete negation of any transcendence that could keep a memory of what happens in time, to assume that, by the mere exhaustion of the possible combinations and recombinations of material elements, it must come to pass that an "initial" configuration recurs and the whole cycle starts over again, and if once, then innumerable times—Nietzsche's "ring of rings, the ring of eternal recurrence." However, if we assume that eternity is not unaffected by what happens in time, there can never be a recurrence of the same because God will not be the same after he has gone through the experience of a world process. Any new world coming after the end of one will carry, as it were, in its own heritage the memory of what has gone before; or, in other words, there will not be an indifferent and dead eternity but an eternity that grows with the accumulating harvest of time.

Bound up with the concepts of a suffering and a becoming God is that of a *caring God*—a God not remote and detached and self-contained but involved with what he cares for. Whatever the "primordial" condition of the Godhead, he ceased to be self-contained once he let himself in for the existence of a world by creating such a world or letting it come to be. God's caring about his creatures is, of course, among the most familiar tenets of Jewish faith. But my myth stresses the less familiar aspect that this caring God is not a sorcerer who in the act of caring also provides the fulfillment of his concern: he has left something for other agents to do and thereby has made his care dependent on them. He is therefore also an endangered God, a God who runs a risk. Clearly that must be so, or else the world would be in a condition of permanent perfection. The fact that it is not bespeaks one of two things: that either the one God does not exist (though more than one may), or that the one has given to an agency other than himself, though created by him, a power and a right to act on its own and therewith a scope for at least codetermining that which is a concern of his. This is why I said that the caring God is not a sorcerer. Somehow he has, by an act of either inscrutable wisdom or love or whatever else the divine motive may have been, forgone the guaranteeing of his self-satisfaction by his own power, after he has first, by the act of creation itself, forgone being "all in all."

And therewith we come to what is perhaps the most critical point in our speculative, theological venture: this is not an omnipotent God. We argue indeed that, for the sake of our image of God and our whole relation to the divine, for the sake of any viable theology, we cannot uphold the time-honored (medieval) doctrine of absolute, unlimited divine power. Let me argue this first, on a purely logical plane, by pointing out the paradox in the idea of absolute power. The logical situation indeed is by no means that divine omnipotence is the rationally plausible and somehow self-recommending doctrine, while that of its limitation is wayward and in need of defense. Quite the opposite. From the very concept of power, it follows that omnipotence is a self-contradictory, self-destructive, indeed, senseless concept. The situation is similar to that of freedom in the human realm; far from beginning where necessity ends, freedom consists of and lives in pitting itself against necessity. Separated from it, freedom loses its object and becomes as void as force without resistance. Absolute freedom would be empty freedom that cancels itself out. So, too, does empty power, and absolute, exclusive power would be just that. Absolute, total power means power not limited by anything, not even by the mere existence of something other than the possessor of that power; for the very existence of such another would already constitute a limitation, and the one would have to annihilate it so as to save its absoluteness. Absolute power then, in its solitude, has no object on which to act. But as objectless power it is a powerless power, canceling itself out: "all" equals "zero" here. In order for it to act, there must be something else, and as soon as there is, the one is not all powerful anymore, even though in any comparison its power may be superior by any degree you please to imagine. The existence of another object limits the power of the most powerful agent at the same time that it allows it to be an agent. In brief, power as such is a *relational* concept and requires relation.

Again, power meeting no *resistance* in its relatum is equal to no power at all: power is exercised only in relation to something that itself has power. Power, unless otiose, consists in the capacity to overcome something; and something's existence as such is enough to provide this condition. For existence means resistance and thus opposing force. Just as, in physics, force without resistance—that is, counterforce—remains empty, so in metaphysics does power without counterpower, unequal as the latter may be. That, therefore, on which power acts much have a power of its own, even if that power derives from the first and was initially granted to it, as one with its existence, by a self-renunciation of limitless power—that is, in the act of creation.

In short, it cannot be that all power is on the side of one agent only. Power must be divided so that there be any power at all.

But besides this logical and ontological objection, there is a more theological, genuinely religious objection to the idea of absolute and unlimited divine omnipotence. We can have divine omnipotence together with divine goodness only at the price of complete divine inscrutability. Seeing the existence of evil in the world, we must sacrifice intelligibility in God to the combination of the other two attributes. Only a completely unintelligible God can be said to be absolutely good and absolutely powerful, yet tolerate the world as it is. Put more generally, the three attributes at stake—absolute goodness, absolute power, and intelligibility—stand in such a logical relation to one another that the conjunction of any two of them excludes the third. The question then is: Which are truly integral to our concept of God, and which, being of lesser force, must give way to their superior claim? Now, surely, goodness is inalienable from the concept of God, and not open to qualification. Intelligibility, conditional on both God's nature and man's capacity, is on the latter count indeed subject to qualification but on no account to complete elimination. The *Deus absconditus*, the hidden God (not to speak of an absurd God) is a profoundly un-Jewish conception. Our teaching, the Torah, rests on the premise and insists that we can understand God, not completely, to be sure, but something of him—of his will, intentions, and even nature—because he has told us. There has been revelation, we have his commandments and his law, and he has directly communicated with some—his prophets—as his mouth for all men in the language of men and their times: refracted thus in this limiting medium but not veiled in dark mystery. A completely hidden God is not an acceptable concept by Jewish norms.

But he would have to be precisely that if together with being good he were conceived as all powerful. After Auschwitz, we can assert with greater force than ever before that an omnipotent deity would have to be either not good or (in his world rule, in which alone we can "observe" him) totally unintelligible. But if God is to be intelligible in some manner and to some extent (and to this we must hold), then his goodness must be compatible with the existence of evil, and this it is only if he is not all powerful. Only then can we uphold that he is intelligible and good, and there is yet evil in the world. And since we have found the concept of omnipotence to be dubious anyway, it is this that has to give way.

So far, our argument about omnipotence has done no more than lay it down

as a principle for any acceptable theology continuous with the Jewish heritage
that God's power be seen as limited by something whose being in its own right
and whose power to act on its own authority he himself acknowledges.[3] Admittedly, we have the choice to interpret this as a voluntary concession on God's
part, which he is free to revoke at will—that is, as the restraint of a power that he
still and always possesses in full but, for the sake of creation's own autonomous
right, chooses not fully to employ. To devout believers, this is probably the most
palatable choice. But it will not suffice. For in view of the enormity of what,
among the bearers of his image in creation, some of them time and again, and
wholly unilaterally, inflict on innocent others, one would expect the good God
at times to break his own, however stringent, rule of restraint and intervene
with a saving miracle.[4] But no saving miracle occurred. Through the years that
"Auschwitz" raged God remained silent. The miracles that did occur came forth
from man alone: the deeds of those solitary, mostly unknown "just of the
nations" who did not shrink from utter sacrifice in order to help, to save, to mitigate—even, when nothing else was left, unto sharing Israel's lot. Of them I shall
speak again. But God was silent. And there I say, or my myth says: Not because
he chose not to, but because he *could* not intervene did he fail to intervene. For
reasons decisively prompted by contemporary experience, I entertain the idea
of God who for a time—the time of the ongoing world process—has divested
himself of any power to interfere with the physical course of things; and who
responds to the impact on his being by worldly events, not "with a mighty hand
and outstretched arm," as we Jews on every Passover recite in remembering the
exodus from Egypt, but with the mutely insistent appeal of his unfulfilled goal.

In this, assuredly, my speculation strays far from oldest Judaic teaching.
Several of Maimonides's Thirteen Articles of Faith, which we solemnly chant in
our services, fall away with the "mighty hand": the assertions about God ruling
the universe, his rewarding the good and punishing the wicked, even about the
coming of the promised Messiah. Not, however, those about his call to the
souls,[5] his inspiration of the prophets and the Torah, thus also not the idea of
election: for only to the physical realm does the impotence of God refer. Most of
all, the *Oneness* of God stands unabated and with it the "Hear, O Israel!" No
Manichaean dualism is enlisted to explain evil; from the hearts of men alone
does it arise and gain power in the world. The mere permitting, indeed, of
human freedom involved a renouncing of sole divine power henceforth. And
our discussion of power as such has already led us to deny divine omnipotence,
anyway.

The elimination of divine omnipotence leaves the theoretical choice between the alternatives of either some preexistent—theological or ontological—
dualism, or of God's *self*-limitation through the creation from nothing. The dualistic alternative in turn might take the Manichaean form of an active force of evil
forever opposing the divine purpose in the universal scheme of things: a two-
god theology; or the Platonic form of a passive medium imposing, no less universally, imperfection on the embodiment of the ideal in the world: a form-
matter dualism. The first is plainly unacceptable to Judaism. The second

answers at best the problem of imperfection and natural necessity but not that of positive evil, which implies a freedom empowered by its own authority independent of that of God; and it is the fact and success of deliberate evil rather than the inflictions of the blind, natural causality—the use of the latter in the hands of responsible agents (Auschwitz rather than the earthquake of Lisbon)— with which Jewish theology has to contend at this hour. Only with creation from nothing do we have the oneness of the divine principle combined with that self-limitation that then permits (gives "room" to) the existence and autonomy of a world. Creation was that act of absolute sovereignty with which it consented, for the sake of the self-determined finitude, to be absolute no more—an act, therefore, of divine self-restriction.

And here let us remember that Jewish tradition itself is really not quite so monolithic in the matter of divine sovereignty as official doctrine makes it appear. The mighty undercurrent of the Kabbalah, which Gershom Scholem in our days has brought to light anew, knows about a divine fate bound up with the coming-to-be of a world. There we meet highly original, very unorthodox speculations in whose company mine would not appear so wayward after all. Thus, for example, my myth at bottom only pushes further the idea of the *tzimtzum*, that cosmogonic centerconcept of the Lurianic Kabbalah.[6] *Tzimtzum* means contraction, withdrawal, self-limitation. To make room for the world, the *En-Sof* (Infinite; literally, No-End) of the beginning had to contract himself so that, vacated by him, empty space could expand outside of him: the "Nothing" in which and from which God could then create the world. Without this retreat into himself, there could be no "other" outside God, and only his continued holding-himself-in preserves the finite things from losing their separate being again into the divine "all in all."

My myth goes farther still. The contraction is total as far as power is concerned; as a whole has the Infinite ceded his power to the finite and thereby wholly delivered his cause into its hands. Does that still leave anything for a relation to God?

Let me answer this question with a last quotation from the earlier writing. By forgoing its own inviolateness, the eternal ground allowed the world to be. To this self-denial all creation owes its existence and with it has received all there is to receive from beyond. Having given himself whole to the becoming world, God has no more to give: it is man's now to give to him. And he may give by seeing to it in the ways of his life that it does not happen or happen too often, and not on his account, that it "repented the Lord"[7] to have made the world. This may well be the secret of the "thirty-six righteous ones" whom, according to Jewish lore, the world shall never lack[8] and of whose number in our time were possibly some of those "just of the nations" I have mentioned before: their guessed-at secret being that, with the superior valency of good over evil, which (we hope) obtains in the noncausal logic of things there, their hidden holiness can outweigh countless guilt, redress the balance of a generation, and secure the peace of the invisible realm.[9]

All this, let it be said at the end, is but stammering. Even the words of the great seers and adorers—the prophets and the psalmists—which stand beyond comparison, were stammers before the eternal mystery. Every mortal answer to Job's question, too, cannot be more than that. Mine is the opposite to the one given by the Book of Job: this, for an answer, invoked the plenitude of God's power; mine, his chosen voidance of it. And yet, strange to say, both are in praise. For the divine renunciation was made so that we, the mortals, could be. This, too, so it seems to me, is an answer to Job: that in him God himself suffers. Which is true, if any, we can know of none of the answers ever tried. Of my poor word thereto I can only hope that it be not wholly excluded from what Goethe, in "Testament of Old-Persian Faith," thus put into Zarathustra's mouth:

All that ever stammers praising the Most High
Is in circles there assembled far and nigh.[10]

NOTES

1. This is my translation of a lecture I delivered in German on the occasion of receiving the Dr. Leopold Lucas Prize for 1984 at Tübingen University. It was published in Fritz Stern and Hans Jonas, *Reflexionen finsterer Zeit* (Tübingen: J. B. C. Mohr, 1984). The lecture expanded and recast an earlier paper with the same title ("The Concept of God after Auschwitz," in *Out of the Whirlwind*, ed. A. H. Friedlander [New York: Union of American Hebrew Congregations, 1968], 465–76), which in turn incorporated portions of my 1961 Ingersoll Lecture, "Immortality and the Modern Temper."

2. Hans Jonas, "Immortality and the Modern Temper," the 1961 Ingersoll Lecture at Harvard University, first printed in *Harvard Theological Review* 55 (1962), 1–20; now in Hans Jonas, *The Phenomenon of Life* (Chicago: University of Chicago Press, 1982), 262–81.

3. The same principle has been argued, with slightly different reasoning, by Rabbi Jack Bemporad, "Toward a New Jewish Theology," *American Judaism* (Winter 1964–65), 9ff.

4. An occasional miracle, i.e., extramundane intervention in the closed causality of the physical realm, is not incompatible with the general validity of laws of nature (rare exceptions do not void empirical rules) and might even, by all appearances, perfectly conform to them. On this question, see Hans Jonas, *Philosophical Essays* (Chicago: University of Chicago Press, 1980), 66–67, and, more extensively, my Rudolf Bultmann Memorial address of 1976 at Marburg University, "Is Faith Still Possible?: Memories of Rudolf Bultmann and Reflections on the Philosophical Aspects of His Work," *Harvard Theological Review* 75, no. 1 (January 1982), 1–25, esp. 9–15; see also 17–18 of this address for a statement of the religious objection against thinking of God as "Lord of History."

5. For more about this inalienable postulate of revealed religion—the possibility of revelation itself, i.e., of God's speaking to human *minds* even if debarred from intervening in physical *things*—see Jonas, "Is Faith Still Possible?" pp. 15–20.

6. Originated by Isaac Luria (born 1534–died 1572).

7. Genesis 6:6–7.

8. Sanhedrin 97b; Sukkah 45b.

9. The idea that it is we who help God rather than God helping us I have since found movingly expressed by one of the Auschwitz victims themselves, a young Dutch Jewess, who validated it by acting unto death. It is found in *An Interrupted Life: The Diaries of Etty Hillesum, 1941–43* (New York: Pantheon Books, 1984). When the deportations in Holland began in 1942, she came forward and volunteered for the Westerbork concentration camp, there to help in the hospital and to share in the fate of her people. In September 1943 she was shipped, in one of the usual mass transports, to Auschwitz and "died" there on 30 November 1943. Her diaries have survived but were only recently published. I quote from Neal Ascherson ("In Hell," *New York Review of Books* 31, no. 13 [19 July 1984], 8–12, esp. 9): "She does not exactly find God, but rather constructs one for herself. The theme of the diaries becomes increasingly religious, and many of the entries are prayers. Her God is someone to whom she makes promises, but of whom she expects and asks nothing. 'I shall try to help you, God, to stop my strength ebbing away, though I cannot vouch for it in advance. But one thing is becoming increasingly clear to me: that You cannot help us, that we must help You help ourselves. . . . Alas, there does not seem to be much You Yourself can do about our circumstances, about our lives. Neither do I hold You responsible. You cannot help us, but we must help You and defend Your dwelling-place in us to the last.'" Reading this was to me a shattering confirmation, by a true witness, of my so much later and sheltered musings—and a consoling correction of my sweeping statement that we had no martyrs there.

10. "Und was nur am Lob des Höchsten stammelt, / Ist in Kreis' um Kreise dort versammelt" (Goethe, "Vermächtnis altpersischen Glaubens").

PART 4

◼ The Holocaust and Western Culture: The 1980s and 1990s

There are some diseases—malaria, for example—that, once contracted, can never be eradicated from the victim's body. The virus or bacteria that causes them lies dormant in the body, erupting at any given moment, when some condition occurs that provokes them into action.

In North America, during the last two decades of the twentieth century, the memory of the Holocaust has been like these viruses or bacteria; it has been a "persisting trauma" that is ever-present in our culture, our consciousness, our sense of who we are, erupting into public display and debate when some event occurs to stimulate our sensitivity, our guilt, our pain. These moments of engagement have temporarily transported the Holocaust from the book review sections of our journals and magazines to their featured articles and editorials, from the "Holocaust" shelves of our bookstores to their prominent display tables, from occasional news items in the papers and on television to the front pages and the featured editorial programs. As we look back, then, on the intellectual responses to the Holocaust that have dotted our cultural landscape over the past twenty years, we note that they have occurred in conjunction with such events.

Some of these events, provocative and contentious, have been public ones, political or cultural, widely influential. Here I am thinking of Ronald Reagan's response to Bitburg, the construction and opening of the United States Holocaust Museum in Washington, the television miniseries *Holocaust* of the later 1970s, and Steven Spielberg's movie *Schindler's List*. These and similar high-profile events have flashed like comets across the sky of public interest, generating widespread discussion in newspapers, magazines, on television, and in innumerable public forums. Eventually too, scholars have turned to them in symposia, books, and anthologies, and this is especially so now, in the time of "postmodernism," when cultural studies, issues of identity, and the examination of popular, nonliterary culture have become so prominent. Whenever such an event occurs, scholars are quick to ask what it means, what it tells us about the ways personal and public memory work, and what it shows about our capacity to deal with the memory of Auschwitz and the death camps, to incorporate it, to work through it, to live with it.

Others of such events are somewhat more arcane, more academic. Here I am thinking, for example, of Holocaust revisionism and denial, which does have its popular side, especially in communities where there are large populations of survivors who find such denial particularly repulsive, but also has its scholarly side, in journals, forums, and books where the methods, claims, and credentials of deniers are examined and challenged. Another such episode is the German *Historikerstreit*. It has often been noted that this seemingly academic debate about the historical treatment of Nazism and the extermination procedures became in Germany a matter of general public interest and concern precisely because of its political significance and its role in the neo-conservative effort to minimize and even negate the memory of Nazism in favor of a sense of renewed German pride. In short, in Germany, in the 1980s, the debate became part of the public controversy over the role of the Nazi past in contemporary German identity, and was contested over the relationship between politics and historiography.

A further venue, so to speak, for the eruption of scholarly discussion of the Holocaust has involved figures like Martin Heidegger. During the 1980s and 1990s in the English-speaking world, Heidegger has become increasingly prominent. His influence on the French—from Levinas to Derrida—together with his importance for philosophers like Richard Rorty and Charles Taylor, has made him an essential icon of contemporary "postmodern" reflection. At the same time, ever since the publication in America of Victor Farrias's controversial book on Heidegger and the Nazis, the issue of Heidegger's Nazism has become a matter of tremendous interest. Partly this interest has arisen because of the question whether Heidegger's Nazi commitments are so deeply intertwined with his philosophical views that the latter are somehow compromised or even refuted by that connection. Partly it has arisen because of the more general question about the nature of the relationships between philosophy and theory, on the one hand, and politics and history, on the other. One outcome, regardless of the motive, has been extensive discussion about the death camps, Nazi totalitarianism, and modernity. Several anthologies have been published, and a host of books, often focused on the question of what the meaning of Heidegger's political views were and what their relationship is to his philosophical views, especially those of his later period, after the publication of *Being and Time*. The role of the subject, of Spirit, and the totalization of Heidegger's turn to Being—these have been major subjects of discussion.

Western intellectual culture, then, has had to wait for the theological discussion to abate and for the Holocaust to find its way into popular culture and everyday life. Moreover, as it has itself become more consumed by the issues of difference, otherness, and particularity as well as history and politics, secular intellectuals have felt drawn to the Holocaust as an historical event that is inescapably particular and yet momentous for Western culture. The recent controversy over Daniel Goldhagen's *Hitler's Willing Executioners* is both surprising and unsurprising within this context. As a work of historical scholarship, it is hardly in the class of the work of Saul Friedlander, Christopher Browning, Omer Bartov, or a host of others. Yet its publication was an event with volatile, explosive repercussions, both in the United States and in Germany. At one level, it was a publicity achievement, indicative of how easily and how extensively public attitudes are shaped, directed, and exploited by the media. At another, Goldhagen's book had the virtue of a simple but incendiary theme, the dominant role of antisemitism in Nazi criminal agency. No matter how pretentious, how academic, how repetitious the presentation of this theme, it is simply stated, easily understood, and easily publicized. It is also controversial in its simplicity and tied to group, national, and religious identification, a theme of powerful current interest.

In this section I have not tried to provide sample responses to all these events—Bitburg, Holocaust denial, *Schindler's List*, the Holocaust Museum, and so forth—or to offer readings that refer to them in significant ways. The bibliography lists many of the books and anthologies that have emerged from these debates. Rather, I have tried to include exemplary discussions of many of the most important and interesting themes that have arisen out of this literature.

The deepest and most central issue has to do with language, art, and, in general, representation. Past events retain their power for us through contemporary memory. We speak of them, portray them, memorialize them, ritualize them, and more. But the Holocaust is an event of unmitigated darkness and horror. How can we honestly, responsibly capture it in our systems of representation without distortion? Is symbolic representation even possible without such distortion? If not, how can we minimize the distortion in order to prevent the event's total loss? Most of the articles in this section deal with these problems, some or all, in one way or another. I have chosen them because they have done so in especially interesting ways or because the author is someone with whom we should all become acquainted or because the essay raises central questions in a clear and powerful way. In short, in my estimation, this section collects some excellent work produced during the past decade or so.

The large issue of representation and memory fragments into a variety of more local concerns. One is about historiography. The *Historikerstreit* ("historians' controversy") was in part about historiography of the Nazi period and what is should be like. Should it focus on the extermination process, the death camps, and antisemitism? Or can it—indeed, should it—deal with other aspects of life in Germany during the period in such a way that the overarching political policies of the government are set aside? What role does historiography play in the way a society and culture "remembers" past events? Does the historian have a moral or civic responsibility to this project of memory that ought to influence the way he or she engages in historical practice? Should moral concerns influence the historian's choice of subject matter, of issues to discuss, of evidence to use? These are serious and challenging issues, and some of the issues in this section focus on them. But they can be addressed from another angle. To some, all historiography is constructed. It is shaped by the interests and capacities of the historian and by the rhetoric of historiography at any given moment. If so, historical treatment of the Holocaust shares something with fictional, imaginative accounts. And the same responsibilities and concerns that guide fictional treatments should also apply to historical ones. These issues were discussed by several prominent historians at a conference convened by Saul Friedlander at UCLA; the proceedings were published in an important anthology, *Probing the Limits of Representation*, which includes many important essays on historiography but also on literature, film, art, and more.

This leads to a second area of concern, that of language. Five essays in this section, in one way or another, ask how the Holocaust can be represented in language, if at all, and what literary forms are most appropriate for responding to that event in writing. This has been a theme that Berel Lang has written about extensively; one should consult his fine book *Act and Idea in the Nazi Genocide* as well as the anthology which he edited, *Writing and the Holocaust*. Michael André Bernstein's book *Foregone Conclusions* examines the narrative dealing with the Shoah and delivers a powerful critique of the ways in which the Holocaust determines the treatments of its past. It is not surprising that writers like Primo Levi, Aaron Appelfeld, Dan Pagis, and Paul Celan have been the subjects of searching appraisal, and one of Bernstein's targets is Appelfeld's use of the Holocaust as the unmentioned, undiscussed vehicle for casting a shadow over the events he narrates.

Modernity has meant various things to us. We associate it with the modern world—its social and political developments, its secularization, industrialization, bureaucratization, rationalization, and more. We also associate it with the Enlightenment themes of freedom and rationality, the emergence of political forms and societies built on respect for all human beings, for their freedom and self-determination, their equality, and the respect due all people as human beings with common and fundamental rights. Furthermore, we associate modernity with modernism and the critique, complex and diverse, of modern society. Historians, political theorists, and sociologists have wondered where the roots of Nazi totalitarianism lie; it has been a theme for the Frankfurt School, for Arendt, and for recent thinkers too, including Zygmunt Bauman in his important book *Modernity and the Holocaust*. What do the death camps tell us about our Enlightenment conception of human nature, about modern society and culture, and about the modern social sciences? As a sociologist, Bauman is especially interested in what the Holocaust implies for sociology, as it emerged at the turn of the twentieth century in figures like Weber, Simmel, Durkheim, and others, and as it is practiced now.

In a sense, this too is a fragment of the larger issue about representation. For our modes of thinking are modes of representation, vehicles whereby we capture the past for the present. Canonical disciplines are frameworks for grasping, understanding, domesticating the world, and past events are part of that world, remaindered for us in texts, documents, cultural objects, remnants of all kinds. In one sense, the uniqueness of every event, every item, should make us worry about how much we sacrifice when we seek to think about it, to conceptualize it; we gain and we lose. But surely there is no choice. As beings with memory, the capacity for thought and language, and a sense for past and future, we are bound to generalize, to compare, to abstract from the particular in order to deal with it at all. Still, occasionally events come along whose particularity is so vivid, so powerful, so moving, and so dramatic that we wonder where the limits should be drawn. We are warned by such events that what we do is up to us and that the choices we make may have deeply moral implications. We are warned to think about this and not take it for granted. The Holocaust is one of these events, and its eruption into scholarly and intellectual consciousness has regularly taken the shape of such a warning. The readings in this section, which brings us up to the present, are intended as evidence of this warning and how it is being understood.

SAUL FRIEDLANDER

▣ The Shoah in Present Historical Consciousness

As we approach the end of the century, our vision of the Nazi epoch and the "Final Solution" may become significantly influenced by ongoing political and ideological transformations, as well as by an ever-more massive change in the production of the imaginary in Western societies. Seemingly well-anchored ideological and political structures are crumbling, and the evolution of the heartland of Europe, possibly of the entire Euro-Asian continent, is shrouded in an uncertainty in which historical interpretations of what appeared as a definitively closed past may again receive some sort of hearing. At least part of Western society has apparently reached a "posthistorical" plateau, the ideological foundation of which has been heralded as the "end of history," that is, as the end of the ideological confrontations which have dominated most of the world since the French Revolution and the early nineteenth century.

The gist of my argument is as follows: Since the end of the war, notwithstanding our considerable increase in historical knowledge, the catastrophe of European Jewry has not been incorporated into any compelling framework of meaning in public consciousness, either within the Jewish world or on the Western cultural scene in general. Indeed, if we exclude basic historical reconstruction, which is growing apace, there seem to be major obstacles confronting the very representation of the events as such. Under these circumstances, the present upheavals in Eastern and Central Europe and the openly expressed antisemitism accompanying them, as well as major simplifications in the representation of the Shoah within the increasingly ahistorical Western world, may lead to significant attempts at revising or degrading the memory of that past.

From Saul Friedlander, *Memory, History, and the Extermination of the Jews of Europe* (Bloomington: Indiana University Press, 1993).

THE ABSENCE OF CONVINCING FRAMEWORKS OF MEANING WITHIN THE JEWISH WORLD

The major increase in references to the Shoah from the late 1960s on, in the Jewish world and elsewhere, is a matter of massive evidence. Yet notwithstanding some systematic attempts, this increase in representation has not led to any compelling framework of meaning as far as public consciousness is concerned. Let us briefly consider this issue in the Jewish world, starting with the Israeli scene.

From the late 1940s on, systematic attempts were made to insert the Shoah within a major traditional framework of interpretation, carrying new significance as a result of the creation of the Jewish state: that of "Catastrophe and Redemption." This global framework was itself linked to an isomorphic, historically specific representation, that of "Catastrophe and Heroism." After some two decades, both structures started to dissolve.

The secular version of commemoration followed the overall traditional pattern of catastrophe and redemption. When, in 1951, the Knesset chose the twenty-seventh of Nisan as *Yom ha-Shoah* (Holocaust Remembrance Day), the Knesset committee dealing with this issue declared that the date was chosen to commemorate the heroism of ghetto fighters (it was the closest possible commemoration date to that of the Warsaw Ghetto uprising) as well as the massacres of Jews by the Crusaders, "forefathers of the Nazis."[1] The official date aimed, therefore, at memorializing values consonant with those of the new state by linking Catastrophe and Heroism. On a wider scale, it reinserted the Shoah in the historical sequence of Jewish catastrophes leading to the redemptive birth of a Jewish state. It was because of the death of the six million, according to Rabbi Nurock, the head of the committee, that "we have been privileged to have our state."[2] The date chosen inaugurates a series of three closely related commemorations. *Yom ha-Shoah* is soon followed by the Memorial Day for the Fallen in Israel's Jewish Wars. At sunset on that day, Independence Day celebrations begin, and the traditional mythic pattern of catastrophe and redemption is forcefully reaffirmed.

The "Catastrophe and Heroism" interpretation—with its explicit public comments on the passivity of the large mass of Jews led to extermination "like sheep to slaughter"; the heroism of a few ghetto fighters and partisans, mostly belonging to the Zionist youth movements; and the collaborationist policies of the appointed Jewish leadership, the Jewish Councils—was questioned from the very beginning by religious circles,[3] by some secular survivors,[4] as well as by distinguished outsiders such as the poet Natan Alterman.[5] Nonetheless, it was accepted by the vast majority of the Israeli population. This representation started crumbling with the Eichmann trial and subsequently lost its hold on public discourse. It is more difficult to identify the process which led to the increasing, albeit partial, dissolution of the catastrophe and redemption interpretive structure.

Several factors could be taken into account. First, the change of attitude of Israelis toward the Diaspora (i.e., the disintegration of the "negation of diaspora" ideology inherent in pre-state Zionism as well as in Ben-Gurion's oft-repeated position during the 1940s and 1950s), resulting in a growing sensitivity concerning the catastrophe of European Jewry as such, without the necessary reference to any redemptive aftermath.

Second, the rise, from the mid-1970s on, of a new authenticity in testimonies and literature about the Shoah, daring to challenge socially imposed codes of interpretation. "The individual sensibilities," writes one of the foremost inter-preters of this literature, "which had been rendered historically insignificant when juxtaposed with the socially ritualized codes, are now harnessed to an equally public enterprise of denationalizing memory and challenging exclusive claims to the inheritance. . . ."[6]

Third, the use of new metaphors based on ideological tenets concerning the conflict between Israelis and Palestinians. The Arabs were compared with the Nazis on the right side of the political spectrum; on the other hand, a "subver-sive" use of symbols appeared on the militant left, equating Jewish behavior with that of the Nazis. In both cases, the politicization of symbols eliminated the metahistorical dimension of the early official narrative. One could argue that such references created distorted but nonetheless effective frameworks of mean-ing. I would claim that they mainly offered an arsenal of transient metaphors.

In other words, the more time passed since the extermination of the Jews of Europe, the less compelling the initial interpretive frameworks became for Israeli historical consciousness. In my opinion, no relevant frameworks of meaning appeared in their stead, notwithstanding an upsurge in references to the Shoah both on the ideological level and in recent Israeli literature.

I can barely refer here to Jewish consciousness of the Holocaust in the Dias-pora, mainly in the United States. Again, whatever the amount of references and the semblance of public relevance, no compelling framework of meaning seems to have appeared in the public domain. Obviously, this does not preclude some specific significance of the Shoah for many Jews as individuals.[7]

One should recall, first of all, how far were the events of Europe from Amer-ican Jewish consciousness up to the very end of the war. Some have argued that since 1945, a mainly unexpressed but nonetheless very keen awareness of what had happened in Europe was taking shape within United States Jewry, particu-larly with the return of soldiers from Europe and with the arrival of Jewish sur-vivors to American shores. Whatever case may be made for subdued awareness, it did not find any echo on the public scene.

The survivors often got the impression that very few within the wider American Jewish public were interested in what they had to tell. The turning point appeared in the 1960s, with the Eichmann trial first and, particularly, on the eve of the Six-Day War. During the same period, moreover, the bolstering of Jewish identity, possibly as a result of the overall growth of ethnic identity in the United States, expressed itself both in American Jewry's rediscovery of its East European heritage and the closely related centrality of the Holocaust. What started to take shape in the 1960s found its full expression in the late 1970s and early 1980s. The survivors, by now mostly well integrated in American society, became increasingly intent on establishing various modes of carrying on the memory of the Shoah. Museums, monuments, and donations for Holocaust teaching were on their way. A second generation established its own frameworks of action to carry on their parents' cult of remembrance. Thus the Holocaust became part and parcel of American Jewish consciousness in the 1980s. Possibly as much as Zionism or religious affiliation, the catastrophic past of European Jewry seemed to be giving American Jewry a major element of self-identification, a mark of distinctiveness and status.

Much has been written about this instrumentalization of the Shoah by American Jewry.[8] This subject still awaits systematic inquiry. Yet in spite of sometimes simplistic commemorative endeavors, in spite of the functional use of the Shoah for Jewish identity-building, no meaningful interpretation emerges except for the general statement that "what happened once can happen again." This statement, rooted in what seems to be an ongoing fear of antisemitism among a vast majority of American Jews,[9] appears nonetheless as a rather weak instinctive reaction, because if it were deeply believed, it would create a major psychological barrier between American Jews and the society into which they long to integrate totally. Thus, the representation of the events is lacking clear terms of reference once we leave the level of historical reconstruction, which, let me say again, progresses apace. It may well be that, in Yosef Yerushalmi's terms, the Jews, as in the wake of the expulsion from Spain, are awaiting a new metahistorical myth to give meaning to the Shoah, in the same way the Kabbalah's cosmic myth gave meaning to the previous catastrophe.[10] For the time being, however, nothing of the kind seems to be emerging in the public domain.

MAJOR OBSTACLES IN REPRESENTING THE SHOAH ON THE WESTERN CULTURAL SCENE

In very schematic terms, the representation of the Shoah within Western culture over the last four decades could be said to display the following major characteristics: vague ubiquity, presence-absence on the ideological-cultural scene, and trivialization in mass awareness as a result of the growing impact of the culture industry.

Major catastrophes such as the Shoah become centrally significant for the collective self-perception of the groups directly involved in one way or another, while the reworking of these catastrophes through time mobilizes central symbolic systems at the disposal of these groups.

In the contemporary process of elaboration of historical consciousness, historiography may well be playing a secondary role to film and television, popular literature, state commemorations, monuments, and museums. In each case, the mobilization of symbols depends on ideological contexts and generational interactions as well as on various other social forces. However, the basic issue remains the same: the relation between the previously represented and the new, between established meanings and fundamental challenge.

In his study of the way the British experience on the Western Front from 1914 to 1918 has been remembered, conventionalized, and mythologized in literature, Paul Fussell shows how the writer, faced with events incredible and therefore incommunicable "in their own terms," has to use "precedent motifs and images" in order to communicate "unprecedented meaning." He states: "By an imaginative leap the unknown is assimilated to the known, and something genuinely new is realized."[11]

This process, usually valid and effective even in the case of massive and previously unimagined catastrophes such as the First World War, does not seem to have fully worked in the case of the Shoah: the unknown is not being assimilated by the known; the unprecedented, although constantly drawing upon precedent motifs and images, is not transformed into new understanding; the imaginative leap has only partly succeeded; the mind is not at rest. Unresolved questions persist as to the very status of the events, their commensurability or incommensurability, their exceptionality or nonexceptionality, their openness to generalization or their essentially non-relevant nature in terms of lessons and forecasts or simply of understanding something not yet understood about the nature of man and society.

One can attribute this uncommon burden of memory to the fact that for a whole age group, still active on the public scene, this past remains part of personal memory. With the passage of two or three decades at most, the memory of the Shoah will be essentially ritualized for some and historicized for the great majority, like any other past event saved from oblivion. The destruction of the Jews of Europe will become an empty formula and, in any case, "mere history."

However, the ongoing questions raised by younger age groups about this past still leave the question of the impact of time unresolved. It may well be that something in the nature of the events themselves gives it some of its apparent irreducibility and therefore of its persistence, something possibly identified by the German philosopher Jürgen Habermas, when he wrote:

> There [in Auschwitz] something happened that up to now nobody considered as even possible. There one touched on something which represents the deep layer of solidarity among all that wears a human face; notwithstanding all the usual acts of beastliness of human history, the integrity of this common layer had been taken for granted. . . . Auschwitz has changed the basis for the continuity of the conditions of life within history—and this not only in Germany.[12]

Although an almost imponderable element of incomprehension, as expressed by Habermas, may well be at the very core of this constant resonance of the "Final Solution," let me suggest some more immediately identifiable reasons for it.

A first element of incomprehension is very close to the issue as addressed by Habermas. It could be reformulated as the breaking of a taboo, possibly the most fundamental of all taboos: the Nazi perpetration of systematic, prolonged extermination of categories of human beings considered as non-human. Such behavior causes instinctive repulsion at the level of the species as well as at that of the individual. The very disappearance of these psychological (or sociobiological) barriers concerning the "scientific" mass killing of other human beings represents, it seems to me, the first and foremost issue for which our usual categories of interpretation are insufficient.

It is true that at the end of the war and more widely than ever over the past few years, it has been argued that such mass extermination is far from exceptional in human history, particularly in contemporary history. This very issue became the "hard core" of the German "historians' controversy." The by now classic answer to this argument was given by the Stuttgart historian Eberhard Jäckel:

> The National Socialist murder of the Jews was unequalled because never before has a State, with the authority of its responsible leaders, decided and announced the total killing of a certain group of people, including the old, the women, the children, the infants, and turned this decision into fact with the use of all the possible instruments of power available to the State.[13]

It is the perception of the exceptionality of this trespassing which seems to form the continuous subtext of some of the most persistent questions about Nazism and the Shoah, whether this is clearly perceived or not.

Since this fundamental issue has no clear answer, or more precisely, as the answers follow one another without ever carrying conviction, the stream of representations which constantly formulates the question (as well as the answer) swings between the incompatible categories of the mythical on the one hand and the banal on the other.

Let me suggest another set of issues, not as intractable as the previous one but nonetheless germane to the problem of the constant recurrence of that past: the relation between the achievements of civilization and the breaking of all the norms, values, and rules of that same civilization within the framework of Nazi extermination policies. In other words, were the "Final Solution" and other Nazi annihilations the ultimate stage in "the destruction of reason," or were they the ultimate stage of technological and bureaucratic "rationality"? Are they some kind of perverted use of the very discourse of scientific progress and ever-growing rationalization against the progress of rationality and modernity? If we accept this last hypothesis, we are faced with a series of unsettling contradictions. For whoever believes in the "unfinished project of modernity," Auschwitz may well be a major and essentially elusive obstacle on that envisioned path, as Horkheimer and Adorno had already perceived in their 1944 *Dialectic of Enlightenment*.

Neither is the mind left at rest when pondering the relationship between the traditional Christian attitude toward the Jews and the "Final Solution." Does Christianity bear a historic responsibility for the Shoah, or should Nazism be considered as a fundamental revolt against the "Judaeo-Christian" interpretation of the sense of human life and history? Any answer to these questions cannot but leave unresolved questions and continuous doubts.

One further point may be of the essence. When the "Final Solution" was implemented, metaphorically speaking, an apocalyptic dimension entered history, took place within history. In some remote areas of eastern Europe, the total annihilation of millions of human beings was being systematically implemented. But for those who were not the victims, life went on, during the events and after them: the apocalypse had passed by unnoticed. We are confronted with an "end" that happened, that was entirely consummated for millions of human beings, but which surrounding society hardly perceived, possibly did not want to perceive at all. Life continued—and continues—its normal flow.

The total dissonance between the apocalypse that was and the normality that is makes adequate representation elusive, because the human imagination stumbles when faced with the fundamental contradiction of apocalypse within normality. Most survivors, vaguely perceiving the total dissonance, fell into problematic rituals of commemoration. Others, sooner or later, were overwhelmed by the unredeemed past: Tadeusz Borowski, Paul Celan, Piotr Rawicz, Jean Améry, and more recently Primo Levi.

The arguments about problems of representation of the Shoah have been of the most various kinds. The points which will be discussed here are related to an initial and manifest fact: over the last four and a half decades, in the major debates which took place on the Western ideological and cultural scene, the representation of the Shoah does not seem to have played any significant role, whatever the excellence of some of the cultural productions stemming from it may be. Thus we have to admit a major discrepancy between the presence of that memory and the absence of its general cultural impact.

One could explain this discrepancy in rather simple historical terms. The immediate postwar period, dominated by the high tide of existentialism, was one of generalized cultural silence about the Shoah among Jews and non-Jews alike. In his recent book on the "Vichy Syndrome," the French historian Henri Rousso reminds us that in France, for instance, this particular aspect of the immediate past—the persecution of the Jews by Vichy, the deportations and the exterminations—was massively repressed in the years following the Liberation. Alain Resnais' film *Night and Fog*, first shown in the 1950s, did not mention the Jews specifically, and this sort of universalization of the extermination became the hallmark of the 1960s and the early 1970s when the cultural scene was conquered by the new wave from the Left.

In Germany, where Left-wing students confronted the misdeeds of their parents' generation, the equation of Nazism with fascism and capitalism—that is, the prolongation of the past into the life of the Federal Republic of Germany—became a common cliché which very soon covered the specificity of the extermination of the Jews. Peter Weiss' play *The Investigation* is possibly the best example of this confrontation/nonconfrontation with Auschwitz. The cultural reaction of the 1970s, with its nonpolitical and aestheticizing discourse, was certainly not an adequate framework for the integration of that facet of an unacceptable past. The growing awareness of the Shoah during those years came instead from the culture industry, about which there will be more to say later. This sociohistorical summary does not offer any explanation for the marginality of the Shoah.

Since the end of the Second World War, Nazi crimes have become the fundamental referent of State criminality. The full revelation of Nazi atrocities exerted such a massive impression on the contemporary imagination that, immediate political efficiency notwithstanding, the reference to any other mass terror, including Stalinism, thenceforth took Nazism as its ultimate point of reference and comparison. As Hannah Arendt expressed it in "Questions on Moral Philosophy": "The Nazi regime from a moral and not a social point of view was much more extreme than the Stalin regime at its worst." With the passage of time, the extermination of the Jews of Europe became the very core of this representation of criminality: a subject one could not be neutral about, a theme which could not be represented in any haphazard way.

This "moral imperative" which does not seem to fade away expresses itself concretely in two significant ways. To this very day, any compromise with Nazism, particularly so far as Nazi antisemitism and the "Final Solution" are concerned, immediately raises widespread moral condemnation and heated moral debates whenever some new facts are brought to light. The recent and ongoing controversy surrounding Paul de Man's wartime journalism is a case in point, whatever its real significance may be, as are the new revelations about the extent of Martin Heidegger's involvement with the Nazis beyond what was already known. The forceful reactions provoked by the "apologetic" tendencies in German historiography are another illustration of this condition.

These common reactions may well be the belated remorse of a society which went to any length of compromise during the events themselves. As Jean Baudrillard recently mentioned, we may be facing "a collective attempt to hallucinate the historical truth of evil . . . a desperate attempt to snatch a posthumous truth from history, a posthumous exculpation." This "moral imperative" leads to the common reticence toward dealing with the Shoah or with Nazism in general, outside of certain accepted norms of aesthetic expression or intellectual discourse.

This situation, in my view, creates a major obstacle to the representation of the Shoah within the main components of present-day cultural sensibility: the ironic mode and postmodern aesthetics.

Let me say a few words about the issue of the ironic mode. Paul Fussell has convincingly shown that at the level of elite culture at least, the most significant mode of representation to have emerged from the "Great War" was the ironic one. Although his examples are all taken from the British literary scene, the same argument would be valid for other European countries and literatures. The ironic mode is in part consonant with modern sensibility. In more ways than one, the contemporary conception of the absurd was an outgrowth of the "Great War." Fussell may have underrated the persistence of the monumental-didactic mode (in the Nietzschean sense of the term), even at the level of elite culture, whenever an ideological position informs the discourse. As far as the First World War is concerned, take for instance Ernst Jünger's *Storms of Steel*, or Jean Renoir's *The Grand Illusion*. We also find the resurgence of the monumental-didactic mode in the representations of the Spanish Civil War and, essentially, in those of the Second World War and of the various aspects of the fight against fascism and Nazism. But does this automatically include the representation of the Shoah? At first glance, the ironic voice should have been the adequate one. Let us consider this point somewhat more closely.

"The abridgement of hope," so poignantly described by Fussell, may well be the fundamental characteristic of the ironic mode. Almost by definition, it could have been at the very core of the representation of the Shoah. This, however, was not and is not the case: the "abridgement of hope" is not recognized as plausible or typical. The death of the airgunner in *Catch-22* is recognizable, but the long lines of Riga Jews marching to the extermination pits are not within an experiential field which encompasses the absurdity of expectations, the death of men in their prime or the shattered lives of soldiers surviving absurd wars.

One could object that some of the preeminent literary renditions of the annihilation of the Jews seem to be within the ironic tradition: Tadeusz Borowski's *This Way for the Gas*, Primo Levi's *If This Is a Man*, Aharon Appelfeld's *Badenheim 1939*, and what has been called Dan Pagis' "Poetics of Incoherence." However, the argument could be made, decisively I think, against the authenticity of the ironic voice even in these apparently exemplary cases. First, all of these writers seem to express, be it in an undertone, the most urgent need of all, the bearing of testimony. "What will the world know of us, if the Germans win?" the Pole Tadeusz Borowski wrote during the war. Secondly, even if they reject the search for historical coherence and the soteriological message, they seem to use "incoherence" in a profoundly didactic way, that is, in order to convey some message that cannot be defined but is nonetheless at the very core of their endeavors.

The overall representation of the Nazi era, and of the annihilation of the Jews in particular, tends therefore to flow back into the monumental-didactic mode, whatever the many forms of this mode may be. This means, in itself, a fundamental dissonance in relation to contemporary sensibility, as the ironic mode is an essential dimension of this sensibility and as the disconnection between moral judgment, aesthetic norms, and intellectual analysis represents a strong component of present-day Western culture.

I shall not dwell at any length on the difficulty of using post-modern aesthetics for an interpretation of the Shoah, since I have dealt with much of this issue through another lens—in my *Reflections of Nazism*.[14] In that essay, I pointed to the difficulties created by such approaches in relation to Nazism in general. Anything of the kind applied to the Shoah would but accentuate the dilemmas. The "moral imperative" seems to impose limits on aestheticization. These limits cannot be defined a priori, but their transgression is perceived by the reader or the viewer, and this very limitation seems particularly at odds with what may sometimes appear as the playful experiments of post-modernity.

Finally, there exists an inherent difficulty in the historical contextualization of these events. The "Final Solution," like any other historical phenomenon, has to be interpreted in its historical unfolding and within the relevant historical framework. A priori, therefore, we should be dealing with this epoch and these events as with any other epoch and events, considering them from all possible angles, suggesting all possible hypotheses and linkages. But as we know, this is not the case and, implicitly for most, this cannot be the case. No one of sound mind would wish to interpret the events from Hitler's viewpoint. Actually, even the "interpreters" belonging to the neo-Nazi lunatic fringe do not try to justify the "Final Solution"; they deny its very existence. Even in regard to much less extreme positions, there is a sense of self-restraint about the available interpretive repertoire.

This situation does not stem and could not stem from any ideological "orthodoxy" imposed by any group. What could have been argued during the years immediately following the war—the existence of an overall consensus imposed by victors and victims alike—certainly cannot be argued today. Thus the historian feels that, in this case, there are some undefined but clearly felt limits to interpretation. This very perception of limits—about the nature of which one can have any number of arguments, but the sense of which is compelling—may indicate that we are possibly facing an exceptional situation which calls for a fusion of moral and cognitive categories in the course of the historical analysis as such.

Let me clarify the questions raised by such limitations on interpretive strategies by one simple illustration: Could one write the history of the science produced by experiments made on human beings in Nazi camps as genuine history of science, or can one use the results of such experiments as elements in ongoing, normal scientific discourse?[15]

In more general terms, the limitation of the approaches to the interpretation of the "Final Solution" puts the historian in an essentially insoluble situation. Such difficulties are compounded by the variety of general theories which take this apparently exceptional situation into account and aim nonetheless at inserting it into a convincing explanatory framework. It is beyond the scope of this text to consider these various attempts and show their insufficiency. At the level of political ideological interpretations, as far as the historical contextualization of the "Final Solution" is concerned, the simplest argument is the following: the point is not that concepts such as "totalitarianism" or "fascism" seem inadequate for the contextualization of the "Final Solution," but, obversely, that these concepts fit much better the particular phenomena they deal with once the "Final Solution" is not included.

The only global historical interpretation which seems to "fit" is the most traditional one: the incremental effect of an ever-more radical antisemitic factor. But even those historians who still remain close to this view have to admit that because of the very nature of Nazi antisemitism and the "Final Solution," "the question of continuity becomes problematic."[16]

The gist of these difficulties has recently been expressed in a remarkably clear way by one of West Germany's leading historians, Reinhart Koselleck:

> I consider that the history [of the "Final Solution"] is confronted by demands that are moral, as well as political and religious, and which altogether do not suffice to convey what happened. The moral judgment is unavoidable, but it does not gain in strength through repetition. The political and social interpretation is also necessary, but it is too limited to explain what happened. The escape into a religious interpretation requires forms of observance which do not belong either to the historical, the moral, or the political domain. In my thoughts on this issue up to the present day, I did not manage to get beyond this aporetic situation. In any case, these considerations point to a uniqueness which, in order to be determined, creates both the necessity of making comparisons as well as the need to leave these comparisons behind.[17]

Ultimately we are confronted with the problem of language as such. I do not wish to refer again to Theodor Adorno's oft-quoted statement on poetry after Auschwitz. Suffice it here to recall the approach forcefully expressed by George Steiner in his *Language and Silence* and taken up again in his recent "The Long Life of Metaphor: An Approach to the Shoah":

> It may be that the Shoah has eradicated the saving grace, the life-giving mystery of meaningful metaphor in Western speech and, correlatively, in that highest organization of speech which we call poetry and philosophic thought. There would be a just logic and a logic of justice in such eradication.[18]

Steiner chose Paul Celan's poems to illustrate the ultimate boundary that the Jewish poet unavoidably reaches in his confrontation with this past. These limits cannot be trespassed. Let me rephrase the difficulty we are facing in the following terms: Why do we feel that Picasso's "Guernica" forcefully expresses the horror of the death and destruction brought about by the German attack on this peaceful Spanish town, whereas we do not know of any visual expression, nor can we clearly think of any, that would adequately express the utter horror of the extermination of the Jews of Europe? In Jean-François Lyotard's words concerning Auschwitz, how does one measure an earthquake which has destroyed all instruments of measurement?

NEW DILEMMAS

The dilemmas just outlined take a new dimension as a result of the political-ideological landscape alluded to at the outset and as a result, on the other hand, of the growing impact of the culture industry.

In contemporary Western societies, at least since the end of the 1960s, two contradictory aspects seem to characterize historical consciousness. On the one hand, "the past is . . . pervasive in its abundance of deliberate, tangible evocations."[19] History books for the general public abound; the media have developed a predilection for historical subjects; historical museums and memorials proliferate; all over the West, commemorations of major historical events follow each other in ever-growing pomp. On the other hand, it is common and no less true to consider our epoch, the last twenty years in any case, as essentially "post-historical." Is not the very notion of *post-histoire* a recent rediscovery meant to define our times in correlation with the concept "post-modernity"?[20] And does not *post-histoire* imply, almost by definition, a growing irrelevance of historical consciousness as a result of historical immobility?

The common denominator of these contradictory aspects is the overriding presence of the past within the commercially dominated sector of the culture industry, as previously mentioned. In this framework the past appears as both pervasive and apparently irrelevant.

The dichotomy just noticed takes an entirely new dimension in the light of the ongoing political-ideological changes taking place in Central and Eastern Europe. One could well argue that after a period of intensified historical aware-ness, Central and East European societies, in the wake of fundamental eco-nomic, social, and political transformations, will adopt the increasingly ahistor-ical stance of the West. The question facing us is the following: Are we moving toward a global society within which historical consciousness will progressively become the mere product of haphazard initiatives of the culture industry, or will we be confronted by new challenges about and from the past? An ongoing dichotomy in historical consciousness remains possible as well. In all these cases, the impact on the representation of the Shoah may be considerable.

Let us first consider the intensified references to the past, both in Central and Eastern Europe, in national, ethnic, and even religious terms. We are con-fronted with the possibility of a new German national self-assertiveness in cul-tural/ideological terms, and various expressions of a new Russian, Slavophile, "Pamyat"-like surge of historical interpretations cannot be avoided.

Whatever the long-term intensity of such tendencies may be, one perceives that even if more official openings are offered in Eastern Europe for referring to the fate of the Jews under the Nazi regime, old/new resentments are surfacing, blending the animosity against the Jews with the hatred of Bolshevism and thus possibly leading to a vision of the "Final Solution" as the result of a not entirely unjustified battle against Judeo-Bolshevik forces. In a recent report from the Soviet Union, Bill Keller of the *New York Times* reported:

> It is not just the weird paramilitary order, Pamyat, that is obsessed by the Jews. In conversations with educated, cultured Russians who would never be caught dead wearing a black T-shirt, in the pages of official magazines and newspapers favored by the nationalists, and in debates at the Russian Writers' Union, "the Jewish question" looms large. And with the coming of glasnost, discussion of it has become much less inhibited.
>
> "I think today the Jews here should feel responsible for the sin of having car-ried out the Revolution, and for the shape that it took," Valentin Rasputin, who had been chosen a member of the Congress of People's Deputies, told me in November. "They should feel responsible for the terror. For the terror that existed during the Revolution and especially after the Revolution. They played a large role, and their guilt is great. Both for the killing of God, and for that."[21]

All this may disappear with the tides of liberalization and westernization, but at this time, many signs seem to point the other way. My argument, however, goes one step further. The rise of the antibolshevik tide with its obvious antisemitic contents may remain limited to the East European sphere. But recent historical debates which took place in the Federal Republic of Germany concerning the "Final Solution," the reappearance of Right-wing movements in the German Democratic Republic as well as in the Federal Republic, and the widespread desire to normalize the representation of the Nazi epoch may turn a more self-assertive, reunited Germany into a favorable receptacle for strong groups favoring such revisionism. Such groups could possibly become a conveyor belt of the old/new themes to the West. These forecasts, one hopes, will be proven wrong; nonetheless, they should be kept in mind.

On the Western, particularly American, "post-historical" scene, the problems appear in a different light. The growing irrelevance of past ideological confrontations means of necessity the growing irrelevance of the period that was most intensely dominated by these confrontations: the epoch of Nazism. This does not mean that some of the most salient aspects of this period will disappear, as they have left an imprint on the imagination independent of their historical significance. As previously mentioned, we are witnessing the increase of mass media representations of the Shoah independent of any clear framework of meaning, whether because of the difficulties inherent in the construction of such a framework or because of the growing sense of nonexistential significance of that past. Such malleability and relative indifference to meaning may, however, create a ready ground for the penetration of the hostile themes rising in the East.

In the second of his "Theses on the Philosophy of History," Walter Benjamin writes:

> The past carries with it a temporal index by which it is referred to redemption. There is a secret agreement between past generations and the present one. . . . Like every generation that preceded us, we have been endowed with a *weak* messianic power, a power to which the past has a claim. That claim cannot be settled cheaply. . . . [22]

If Benjamin's view of historical redemption implies the construction of meaning, we may be confronted with an insoluble paradox when facing the extermination of the Jews of Europe: on the one hand, the most diverse modes of evocation of the events abound; on the other hand, both in the representations of this past as well as in its interpretation, we are facing dilemmas which paralyze our "weak redeeming powers." One may wonder, though, whether such a situation is not appropriate. In the last part of Claude Lanzmann's film *Shoah*, the structure of the narration seems to become ever looser, as if disintegrating. When, in the end, a leader of the Warsaw ghetto uprising speaks, nothing is left of the rhetoric of heroism, of symbolic redemption; there is only bitterness at heart. The inability to say, the apparent pathology of obsessive recall, the seemingly simplistic refusal of historiographical closure may ultimately be the only self-evident sequels of an unmasterable past.

NOTES

1. For these various quotes, see Saul Friedlander, "Die Shoah als Element in der Konstruktion Israelischer Erinnerung," *Beiträge zur Jüdischen Gegenwart* 2 (Babylon, 1987).

2. Ibid.

3. Ibid.

4. Ibid.

5. Nathan Alterman, *Al Shtei Hadrachim: Dapim min Hapinkas*, edited by Dan Laor (Tel Aviv, 1989).

6. Sidra Dekoven Ezrahi, "Revisioning the Past: The Changing Legacy of the Holocaust in Hebrew Literature," *Salmagundi* 68–69 (Fall 1985–Winter 1986), p. 270.

7. For testimonies concerning such an impact on Jewish-American intellectuals, see David Rosenberg, ed., *Testimony: Contemporary Writers Make the Holocaust Personal* (New York, 1989).

8. See, for instance, Jacob Neusner, "A 'Holocaust' Primer," *National Review*, 3 August 1979; Leon A. Jick, "The Holocaust: Its Use and Abuses within the American Public," *Yad Vashem Studies* 14 (Jerusalem, 1981); particularly, Robert Alter, "Deformation of the Holocaust," *Commentary* 71 (February 1981).

9. See the study by Seymour Martin Lipset reported in the *New York Times*, 8 March 1990.

10. Yosef Hayim Yerushalmi, *Zakhor: Jewish History and Jewish Memory* (Seattle: University of Washington Press, 1982), p. 98.

11. Paul Fussell, *The Great War and Modern Memory* (New York: Oxford University Press, 1975).

12. Jürgen Habermas, *Eine Art Schadensabwicklung* (Frankfurt a/Main, 1987), p. 163.

13. Eberhard Jäckel, "Die elende Praxis der Untersteller," *Historikerstreit* (Munich, 1987), p. 118.

14. Saul Friedländer, *Reflections of Nazism: An Essay on Kitsch and Death*, translated by T. Weyr (New York: Harper and Row, 1984; rpt. Bloomington: Indiana University Press, 1993).

15. Some aspects of this issue were discussed at a conference held by the Center for Biomedical Ethics at the University of Minnesota in May 1989.

16. Otto Dov Kulka, "Critique of Judaism in European Thought: On the Historical Meaning of Modern Antisemitism," *Jerusalem Quarterly* 52 (Fall 1989): 5.

17. Letter to the author, 29 June 1989.

18. George Steiner, "The Long Life of Metaphor: An Approach to 'the Shoah,'" *Encounter* 68/2 (February 1987): 61.

19. Richard Lowenthal, *The Past Is a Foreign Country* (Cambridge, England, 1985), p. xv.

20. See in particular Lutz Niethammer, *Posthistoire, Ist die Geschichte zu Ende?* (Reinebek bei Hamburg, 1989).

21. Bill Keller, "Yearning for an Iron Hand," *New York Times Magazine*, 28 January 1990, p. 48.

22. Walter Benjamin, "Geschichtsphilosophische Thesen," in *Illuminationen, Ausgewaehlte Schriften* (Frankfurt, 1961), pp. 268–269; English translation, *Illuminations* (New York, 1969), p. 254.

OMER BARTOV

▣ Intellectuals on Auschwitz

Memory, History, and Truth

When I came/From Circe at last . . . / No tenderness . . . nor pity . . . / nor . . . wedded love . . . / Could have conquered in me the restless itch to rove/And rummage through the world exploring it,/All human worth and wickedness to prove./ So on the deep and open sea I set/Forth . . . / I and my fellows were grown old and tardy . . . / . . . that none should prove so hardy/To venture the uncharted distances . . . /'Brothers,' said I . . . / Think of your breed; for brutish ignorance/Your mettle was not made; you were made men,/ To follow after knowledge and excellence.' . . . / Then we rejoiced; but soon we had to weep,/ For out of the unknown land there blew foul weather,/ And a whirlwind struck the forepart of the ship; . . . / And over our heads the hollow seas closed up."[1]

The urge to write this chapter can be traced back to several causes. A number of scholarly/polemical discussions on the difficulties with memory and forgetting, representation and commemoration of the Holocaust prompted me to attempt to articulate my thoughts on the subject and clarify to myself what it was that so disturbed me in those seemingly reasonable and detached ruminations.[2] Teaching a course on the Holocaust brought me once more face to face with the familiar, yet still jarring realization that neither teachers nor students, nor for that matter anyone who had either experienced it or studied it from some geographical or chronological distance could quite grasp the essence of the Holocaust or make it understandable to others.[3] Always remaining from without, on the margins of experience and comprehension, one was never actually speaking of the thing itself, one never dared (or found oneself unable) to put one's finger on the heart of the matter. Was this due to the elusive nature of the matter, or to the fears aroused in us by the prospect of direct confrontation? This predilection for the indirect or oblique approach could also be observed in some scholarly gatherings and subsequent publications, whether they consisted of the more down-to-earth variety of scholars or of those more inclined toward contemporary literary criticism.[4]

Finally, there were some texts by survivors, and especially those by Jean Améry and Primo Levi.[5] It was the immense gap between their thoughts on the experience and phenomenon of Auschwitz and those of the intellectual and academic community that suggested a deeper and more complex relationship, indeed, a multifaceted obstacle or disturbance, whose presence was being felt but not fully acknowledged, and whose origins and implications might reveal to us some failure in communication and understanding, an emotional block springing from an abyss of anxiety, that must be investigated, however little hope we may have of reaching its roots and exposing it fully to light.

In the larger background I have detected in myself a growing unease with the postwar and, more recently, the so-called postmodern representations of the Holocaust (and by implication also of fascism, war, and numerous other forms of violence), as well as with the choice of focus, tone, and methodology evident in the literary-intellectual discourse on Auschwitz and in the new (or not so new) historiographical trends emerging especially, but by no means exclusively, from Germany. Conversations with survivors (many of whom have only lately become capable of speaking about their experiences), on the one hand, and recent manifestations of right-wing, xenophobic sentiments in Germany, on the other, along with the intensification of political abuses of the Holocaust in commemoration and demagogy, have greatly contributed to the urge to investigate the links between these seemingly unrelated phenomena that nevertheless all had one theme in common—namely, mass, industrial murder in the heart of Western civilization. Indeed, the experience of simultaneously teaching a course on German history demonstrated how difficult it was to bridge the gap between *that* and Auschwitz. Yet I have been plagued by the constant, nagging inability to point out what was the reason for my unease, what was actually wrong with the recent treatment of the Holocaust, and what were the alternatives. If there was one common denominator here, I felt, it was the widespread fascination, indeed the obsession, with perversity and obscenity, inhumanity and criminality, aggression and horror. Yet this was no fanatic fascination, no savage obsession; rather, it revealed a strange, but not wholly unfamiliar mixture of cool aesthetic pleasure and mild nausea at being confronted (or choosing to be confronted) with a highly stylized form of these phenomena, recreated on the page or in the studio in a manner assured to make them appear attractive, stimulating, *interesting*.[6] This was disturbing: an obsession with fascism and all its attributes whose psychological and intellectual motivations bore an uncanny resemblance to those that had accompanied the phenomenon itself.

The following cannot claim to be anything more than some reflections by one who until recently has avoided writing directly on the Holocaust. Belonging to a generation born after the event, I do not claim to profit from this biological coincidence as Helmut Kohl and many of his younger compatriots have done. Indeed, I am conscious of being anything but unscathed by the Shoah, whether personally, intellectually, politically, or morally. Moreover, I clearly realize that I cannot hope to understand the heart of darkness any better than the next person, and that every attempt to illuminate it must confront the horrifying tendency of the event to pollute and swallow any ray of light. Nevertheless, for us there is only the trying. By posing some questions and tying together some issues, I hope to point toward new paths of inquiry both regarding the Holocaust itself and its impact on our present intellectual, moral, and political predicament. Indeed, I believe that a critique of the intellectual discourse on and the historiography of the Holocaust can extend far beyond the limits of the death camps and encompass the general problems we face today in writing on the history of humanity and in seeking to distil its meaning for our own culture and society. For however small our individual contribution may be, this is, or should be, the task of the intellectual.

I. THE SURFEIT OF MEMORY AND THE USES OF FORGETTING

There seems to be a new trend, which at a second glance proves to be a rather old one, to remove the Holocaust from our view (or at least shift it aside a little) with the argument that it obscures our perception and prevents us from a more vivid understanding of the real issues and cardinal problems of the epoch in which we are living.[7] This view distinguishes itself from what is claimed to have been the dominant argument, or, rather, persuasion previously—namely, that the Holocaust is an ineffable, incomprehensible, and therefore somewhat ahistorical event. According to an extreme version of this view, the Holocaust is precisely that, a vast sacrificial act somehow meant to purge the world of evil by exercising it to the greatest conceivable degree; the Jewish people sacrificing itself for the ultimate good of humanity, just as Jesus had done two thousand years before; a sort of insanely (or Godly) logical circle finally closed, necessarily containing some kind of message to humanity and civilization, even if we wretched humans may not yet be capable of deciphering its meaning.[8] Conversely, the critics of this eschatological view contend with some degree of complacency that although they can sympathize with its proponents, they themselves apply more rational, scientific, and detached instruments to explain and put into perspective this historical event just like any other.[9] The Holocaust, then, is being pulled apart by two contending camps, either as a core event of the twentieth century, if not indeed of Western civilization or even humanity as a whole, with the tragic Jewish fate as its centerpiece, a culmination of (anti-

Jewish) persecution throughout the ages and of the unfolding of divine will[10]; or as a block that distorts and obscures our view of the past and our hopes, plans, and dreams of the future, that relegates all other barbarities and achievements to a secondary place, that overemphasizes the Jewish experience, human depravity, and ineffable (divine or Satanic) forces, that is backward, theological, emotional, nationalist, narrow-minded, and finally antihumanistic, and which therefore must absolutely be removed.[11]

Removed where? To forgetfulness. Not to be repressed, but instead to be consciously, rationally put into its proper context and perspective, with the appropriate scholarly tools ensuring us of good judgment, minimizing the weight of emotion and sensation, giving everyone their just historical due.[12]

Yet, strangely, there is a measure of impatience precisely among the proponents of the balanced and detached scholarly approach. This impatience is reflected both in the speed with which they would like to bring about that transformation of approaches they so persuasively propagate, and in their tendency to oversimplify the views they contend to be confronting. For their opponents are neither made of one mold, nor, for that very reason, can they be removed by the allegedly opposing arguments of scholarship, balance, and objectivity. Indeed, by presenting the other side as a monolithic body of opinion (or emotion), the proponents of the contextualized view are themselves paradoxically forced together and—mostly very much against their will and better judgment—are found sharing their scholarly abodes with very strange bedfellows indeed.[13]

Another characteristic of the discussion is that both survivors and scholarly critics seem to feel the urgency of their approaching demise. This of course brings to mind other aspects of the relationship between time, age, and death in confronting the Holocaust: arguments concerning the chronological distance between crimes committed and judgment handed down as regards the perpetrators; the effect of time on retelling their experiences, or, conversely, on their inability to go on living and consequent acts of suicide, as regards the survivors; the political legitimation time seemingly brings to German politicians, identity, and aspirations; and the effects of historical distance on scholarship. But, at this point, historians seem to be torn between the scholarly benefits of time, on the one hand, and its far less merciful effects on the individual. And it is here that we find that some of the most eloquent promoters of forgetting belong to the generation of both the perpetrators and the (more often than not potential) victims, that is, to those who presumably still retain vivid personal memories of the period.[14] Hence we, who cannot remember, are urged to recognize the merits of forgetting by those who cannot forget—all this with a sense of urgency springing from the realization that soon they will no longer be there to remember and may themselves thereafter be forgotten.[15]

Now the argument of the surfeit of memory is problematic on a number of counts. For one thing, it seems to follow too closely on the heels of other sensationalist theses, such as the pronouncement of the end of history and the assertion regarding the arrival of the post-national age, both of which must now come to terms with the melancholy restaging of pre-1914 nationalist, ethnic, and religious hatreds and passions. The same can be said about the strange revival of the idea of forgetting, so common immediately after the affair, at a time when it at least had the merit of helping both Jews and Germans to go about the business of reconstructing their lives[16]; for now, very few people remember anyway. It is only among select communities that memory, both personal and historical, still plays a major role, and it is to them that one should address oneself, rather than to some general audience that does not remember what it is being asked to forget. If there is a surfeit of memory, if there is a need to forget, it is in three communities, namely, the relatively limited intellectual/academic, often Jewish and left-liberal community in the United States; the much wider scholarly, intellectual, media, and political circles in Germany; and the corresponding, and perhaps locally even more influential groups in Israel.

To claim that there is a surfeit of memory of the Holocaust in the United States is highly debatable. Most Americans have only the vaguest possible notion of what the Holocaust was about.[17] Indeed, Americans are arguably the least well-informed people in the West on the Holocaust, Nazism, or, for that matter, the history of this (or any other) century. The Holocaust has also played a relatively minor role in American politics and foreign policy, though in this case it was given ample rhetorical consideration. Neither the decision to rearm Germany nor the decision to support Israel militarily have anything more than the most tenuous connection with the former's Nazi past and the latter's status as the political representative of its victims. Hence I would argue that it is wholly gratuitous to call for a new campaign of forgetting as regards a community notorious for the weakness of its historical memory.

When speaking of the Jewish community in the United States, the picture is naturally very different. However, even here I would argue that one has to differentiate between various groups. The Jewish orthodox community is neither influenced by any of the debates on memory and forgetting, nor does it seek an explanation for the Holocaust. On the other extreme, it would seem that not a small portion of the Jewish-American population feels only very loosely tied to Jewish experience and history, and is generally just as ignorant of the European past as the gentiles. This leaves us with the intelligentsia, a group whose discourse is really directed to its own members, the international scholarly and intellectual community, and most specifically to Germans and Israelis. As such, I feel that this discourse must be examined together with similar discourses in Germany and Israel, as well as among scholars of the period and intellectuals involved in writing on it.

The debate on the Holocaust tends to make use of a large number of commonly accepted but often either inaccurate or false assumptions. In what follows, I will therefore try to point out some problems relevant to the question of memory and history, forgetting and repressing, political abuse and commemoration, in Germany and Israel. I will then turn to the question of the representation of the Holocaust and to the scholarly, literary, and philosophical discourse on this theme.

II. THE HISTORIKERSTREIT AND THE IMPORTANCE OF MEMORY

The German historians' controversy has been relegated to the status of a "mere" political debate without any scholarly merit.[18] I would like to argue that the wider implications and repercussions of the *Historikerstreit* can only now be properly understood. Leaving academic rivalries and party politics aside, the deep-seated motivations and sentiments of German scholars manifested in the debate can now be seen to have had a major impact both on the discourse on history, memory, and identity in Germany and on the historical reevaluation of Nazism and the Holocaust. In another sense, the *Historikerstreit* clearly demonstrated the inability to make precisely those distinctions between detached scholarly pursuits, ideological persuasion, and personal memories and experience that some (if not most) of its participants had demanded.

Unlike the United States, Germany is a nation in which memory and history have always played a major role, at least since the beginning of the previous century. For a national culture so deeply attached to history the events of 1933–45 are obviously a seemingly insurmountable obstacle in the way of reconstructing both personal and national identity, both the political organization of the country and the scholarly analysis of past and present. Hence the calls for a more contextualized view of Hitler's regime presented in the mid-1980s as heralding a new approach to the past were in fact anything but new; the comparisons of German barbarism with other nations' brutalities and atrocities were current even in the Third Reich itself, serving as a legitimizing element and generating even greater destructive and nihilistic passions.[19]

Memory, as we all recognize, is elusive and ambiguous. Politicians have always relied on the shortness of people's memories. When some German scholars claimed less than ten years ago that it was time to cease treating the Third Reich as consisting first and foremost of Auschwitz, and that one should turn to other, no less important aspects of this period, an impression was created that indeed up to that point most historians had concerned themselves with the "Final Solution" to the exclusion of everything else.[20] Yet the same arguments were heard twenty years previously, despite the fact that even then a large body of research on many other facets of the Nazi regime already existed, while the scholarship on the Holocaust, especially in Germany, was anything but predominant or particularly impressive.[21] The wish to shift the emphasis was therefore not based on a real need to cease an obsessive preoccupation with the "Final Solution," but rather on the personal discomfort, the scholarly difficulties, and the political/ideological implications of coming to terms with this phenomenon in the first place. There was here once more an impatience with the necessity of confronting what one wished to do away with, rationalized by the perceived need to stop doing what had in fact been done only to a very limited degree in the past.

Many German historians involved in the *Historikerstreit* had very vivid memories of the period they now wished to historicize. They had internalized the period and now, in their late middle-age, those events came back to haunt them. They wished to understand that past, for, after all, those still were, at least in the biological sense, the best years of their lives. And yet they did not wish the history that was so much part of their formative years to consist only of the darkest aspects of Nazi rule, those very aspects to whose study they themselves had contributed so much. Thus, they turned to the more positive sides of the period: to resistance, nonconformity, finally to everyday life.[22] This direction of research was initially motivated or legitimized by the worthy aim of doing away with the conservative presentation of the Nazi regime as a brutal dictatorship ruled by a criminal clique with no relevance for German society or history as a whole. However, it soon transpired that once we investigate the experience of the common man and woman, we discover that even during abnormal times most people continue to live normal lives. The conclusion to be drawn could have been, of course, that this was precisely what was abnormal in Nazi society—namely, that people continued their normal existence under a terroristic and murderous regime whose actions were wholly or partly known to most people. But this was not always the conclusion drawn by these scholars; rather, some saw in their findings proof of some form of resistance to the regime, that is, that by living normally, people had refused to adopt the ideological fanaticism urged on them by the regime, and even, at times, made demands on the regime (such as the workers),[23] refused to carry out some of its orders (such as Catholic school teachers),[24] or adopted some forms of youthful nonconformity such as listening and dancing to forbidden music.[25] That this sort of resistance did not seem at any point to threaten the regime—indeed, that in most cases the same people who "resisted" also collaborated—was of course recognized, and yet one was left with a much more positive impression of German society under Nazism. And, naturally, when speaking of the *Alltagsgeschichte* of the simple German citizen, one did not speak of the "concentrationary universe" erected by the regime elsewhere.[26] Thus, a separation of existences was created; there was German history and there was the history of the victims of Nazism, or, as it was perceived both by Germans and Jews, Jewish history. Similarly, there was German memory (finally repossessed, to his own satisfaction, by Edgar Reitz in his film *Heimat*),[27] and there was Jewish memory (brought to us through Claude Lanzmann's *Shoah*). Moreover, while German memory got its due, often via the most respectable academic circles and most gifted artists, Jewish memory was condemned by both German and non-German, often also Jewish, scholars as constituting a sentimental, mythical obstruction to the understanding of the past.[28]

The repercussions of the *Historikerstreit* can be seen, for instance, in certain recent works by some younger German scholars who had no personal exposure to Nazism. Interestingly, however, they seem to have picked up and further developed ideas first proposed by their older colleagues. Among the more controversial is the theory that presents the Nazi regime as a modernizing agent in German history.[29] This is not the same argument raised some two decades ago—that the destruction brought on Germany by Hitler's war had compelled material and social reconstruction on a new and much more modern basis.[30] Rather, this is a positive view of some elements of Nazism, its industries, its social policies and legislation, its technological obsessions, its mobilization of women, and so forth. This relates to the recent appeals for a different periodization of German history, according to which the dates 1933–45 are obviously mere indications of political and military events, whereas most Germans would have considered the period between 1929–49 as much more crucial to their existence.[31] For, while the victims of the regime were naturally concerned with the political periodization, the majority of Germans remember the past as divided into the bad years of 1929–35 (economic depression and unemployment), the good years of 1935–41 (economic expansion and conquest), the catastrophe of 1941–49 (military defeats and economic devastation), and finally the economic miracle of the 1950s.[32] This division has the added merit of stretching into the present, as the argument is raised that the time has arrived to turn Germany's economic might into political clout.

To be sure, the modernizing theory of Nazism consistently ignores the most obvious contribution of the Third Reich to modernization, namely, mass, industrial murder. For while the Nazi contribution to the formulation of postwar German social policies, for instance, is debatable, the example given by the Nazi regime as to the ability of a modern state to destroy human lives with the same techniques used by modern industry, employing the bureaucratic apparatus readily available to any modern state, is one that can hardly be ignored. Because although history may not repeat itself, it is rare that anything introduced to human history is not used again. Whether the Holocaust was unique or not in terms of its precedents is one question; whether it will remain so is quite another.

The modernization theory, which has other aspects to it referring to the decision on the "Final Solution" that cannot be discussed here,[33] very much concerns German memory of, as well as wishful thinking on, the past. Memory and history are here closely bound, and we can extricate one from the other only with extreme care, if we do not wish to distort the outcome of the operation. For this reason, too, arguments regarding the surfeit of memory in Germany must come to terms with recent political events in that country. For while there is, of course, a memory of Nazism in Germany, what that memory consists of is quite a different matter. If some view Nazism as a past to be forgotten, perhaps because they remember its reality all too well, others would like to resurrect it because, lacking a personal memory of its horrors, they have reconstructed it in their minds as something horribly fascinating, anarchic, nihilistic, as well as containing the magic formula of bringing full employment, freedom from foreign influence, and national pride. How could some German youngsters today have constructed such an image of Nazism for themselves? Is this the kind of past that won't go away, that will keep haunting Germany (and its victims)?

Hence the calls for separating memory and history are based on a far too simplistic presentation of the issues involved.[34] First, because as historians we should know that memory plays a role in everything we do, think, or write, just as it did for the subjects of our research. Second, because the critics of memory do not in fact want to do away with it, but rather recommend a different *kind* of memory, of different *subjects,* and remembering in different *ways.* Hence the debate is in fact not at all on more or less memory, but on the politics of memory. And once in the realm of politics, arguably anyone's politics is as good as anyone else's: some people want to remember Jews and concentration camps, others want to remember German soldiers and their defense of the West against Bolshevism; some study memory through personal accounts, others distribute questionnaires, others still conduct studies of oral history; some speak of collective memory, some of national memory, some of personal memory. Thus the manner in which we speak of memory betrays our political beliefs, just as our political beliefs are molded to a large extent by our memories.

III. ISRAEL, COMMEMORATION, AND THE NORMALIZATION OF JEWISH EXISTENCE

The contention that Israel is strongly preoccupied, to some degree even obsessed, with the Holocaust, is undeniably true. Indeed, one could hardly expect things to be otherwise, considering the percentage of people living in Israel who have either personally experienced the Shoah, or whose family members survived the camps or perished in Nazi-occupied Europe. The question to be asked is, rather, how have the memory and history of the Holocaust, and the memory and history of Israel intermingled, and what are the results of this (potentially explosive) mixture? Clearly, this issue entails a wide array of psychological, sociological, and cultural dimensions, and retains a strongly emotional quality. Hence the simplistic portrayal of Israel as a society whose whole political culture and cultural identity are based on a manipulative commemoration of the Holocaust is somewhat off the mark. The argument that Zionism had found its legitimation in Nazism, that Israel owes its existence to the "Final Solution," that Israeli literary production offers a monolithic view of the proud, fighting Israeli as opposed to the Diaspora Jews who went like sheep to the slaughter, itself springs originally from assertions made by Israeli critics of what seemed to them the established view in that country in the 1960s, and even they had ignored quite different trends among the preceding literary generation. By now, the critics themselves are strongly identified with the political establishment and are in their turn under sustained attack from a younger generation of writers, poets, and playwrights.[35]

In point of fact, the obsession with the Holocaust in Israel has taken very different forms, especially over the last twenty-odd years. In a wide array of literary and artistic representations, Israelis have traced the complex, often disturbing connections between the Jewish experience in Europe and the Israeli experience in the Middle East. While in the past the dominant image was of the heroic Israeli, fighting against overwhelming numbers, and dying with a gun in his hand and the words "it is good to die for our land" on his lips, more recently the Israeli soldier has been represented as an occupier of another people (and in some of the more extreme versions made to appear as the equivalent of the Nazi), while the Palestinians have been portrayed as a persecuted and suppressed minority (with the implication, often adopted by the Palestinians themselves, that they are the contemporary equivalents of European Jewry).[36]

Conversely, the growing interest in the prewar Jewish existence in Europe finds increasing expression in Israeli intellectual life, literary representations, film, and university courses.[37] This of course reflects doubts about Israeli identity, as well as indicating the perceived need to connect Israel's short past with the much deeper roots of Jewish existence in Europe.[38] The early, so-called "synthetic" image of the Israeli, that heroic, handsome (somewhat Aryan-looking) youth who "was born from the sea,"[39] has been greatly complicated by growing anxiety about the present, skepticism about the future, and a sentimental longing for a vision of an idealized past. This has also been the occasion for, as well as one of the causes of, the meeting between grandchildren and grandparents, the new willingness of the elderly to remember, and the new interest awakened in the young to listen to those memories. Hence the self-perception of young Israelis is ambivalent and in constant flux, as they view themselves both as rebels against a vanished past and as strongly, inseparably (and increasingly less unwillingly) rooted in it, both as descendents of a persecuted minority in Europe and presently as oppressors in their own land.[40] This is not a comfortable, complacent attitude; rather it breeds tension, anger, frustration. But it does not reflect a simple, one-sided view of one's existence and makes for an intimate connection between memory and history, image and reality.

Nor can one accept the simplistic view of Israel as the epitome of the memorializing society, a nation that claims for itself a monopoly over the memory of the Holocaust as manifested in the Yad Vashem memorial and exhibit. For while the commemoration of the Day of Holocaust and Heroism (the official name of the Day of the Holocaust in Israel) has always been contentious in Israel, the Jewish state could hardly afford not to officially commemorate the murder of European Jewry.[41] Moreover, here too one should note that the Israeli media, scholars, and intellectuals have recently subjected previously held beliefs to a harsh critique, stressing the blindness of the *Yishuv* (the Jewish community in Palestine before the foundation of the state of Israel) to events in Nazi-occupied Europe, and shedding light on the reception of the survivors in Palestine, who were perceived by the public as "typical," cowardly Diaspora Jews whose main task must be to become rapidly socialized by means of repressing their past and assuming a new, "healthy" Israeli identity.[42] Just as the cult of the heroic Israeli has been greatly modified, so too has that of the heroes of the Holocaust. Recently the notion of heroism has been extended to include not only armed resistance, but also the very fact of enduring the most inhuman conditions.[43]

To be sure, Israeli youths are constantly exposed to a discourse on the Holocaust that serves as part of their identity-formation. This may create an image of humanity, history, and survival one would have preferred to be able to deny, yet it is unavoidable. Hence the point is to observe modifications in this discourse, rather than simply see it as an excess of memory, memorialization, and consequently biased history. The fact that this is indeed happening gives one room for hope, particularly if we consider the fact that a society one of whose central historical experiences is an event such as the Holocaust cannot be entirely "normal."

Normality is the other side of the coin. Here we reach another, Israeli-centered discourse that is deeply rooted in turn-of-the-century Zionism and has miraculously survived the crucial events of this century without shedding some of its more pernicious aspects. Paradoxically, precisely because this view presents the Diaspora Jew and the Israeli in radical opposition to each other, it is actually based on a complete avoidance of the Holocaust and its meaning. As such, although by now it is anything but a generally accepted opinion, it is of some interest in tracing the interplay of history, memory, and image in Israel.[44]

Zionism, like many other nationalist movements in the previous century, had to present a highly negative picture of the conditions it wished to transform so as to win adherents to its own ideology. For Zionism, this was the "abnormality" of Jewish existence in the Diaspora. This position was quite clearly related to the antisemitic rhetoric of the period. The Jew was presented as economically and socially parasitic, intellectually and physically degenerate, historically doomed. Borrowing both from the sociobiological and the Marxist discourses of late nineteenth-century Europe, the Zionists too spoke of the need to change both the material condition of the Jews and their physical constitution, to renew them mentally and biologically, to make them into a healthy race in mind and spirit, body and economic occupation.

Thus, Zionism strove to "normalize" the existence of the Jews by the creation of a national state. The notion of normalcy insinuates that the social and cultural life of the Jews in the Diaspora was "abnormal." It even seems that the Zionist image of the Jew confirmed antisemitic perceptions. Indeed, early Zionism accepted the seeming inevitability of antisemitism as inherent to the condition of statelessness. The affinity between antisemitic movements and Zionist intentions to concentrate the Jews in their own land made possible an ad hoc cooperation in the 1930s between Zionists and the Nazi regime concerning immigration from Germany to Palestine.[45] Moreover, among some Israeli intellectuals the early Zionist view of the "degenerate" Jews of the Diaspora persists to this day.[46] This perpetuation of an imagery that supposedly legitimizes the new, "normal" Jew in his homeland is clearly the result of both ignorance of the consequences such images had only fifty years ago and of a remarkable insensitivity produced by an unrelenting adherence to a political agenda. That such images are not the product of right-wing, revisionist circles, but rather of the Left, gives reason to pause before sketching a simplistic view of the effects of memory and its political abuses.[47] Let me repeat that this is not the predominant view, but rather one of several that are competing with each other in a society and a cultural environment still trying to come to terms with the events of the Holocaust and their meaning for Israeli existence.

Thus, memory and history, politics and prejudice, still play an important role both within Israeli society and in attitudes toward Israel and Jews abroad. The point is therefore not to appeal for a diminished preoccupation with memory, because such appeals will not and cannot have any effect on communities such as those of Germany and Israel that are understandably still obsessed with the past, but rather to try and understand what the interrelationship between memory and history is both on the personal and political level, as well as in scholarship and representation. For it is only by grasping the complexity of this phenomenon that we can enhance our insight into the political and cultural scene and perhaps begin to formulate our own intellectual and political response.[48]

IV. REPRESENTATION AND ITS DISCONTENTS

Ever since the end of the Second World War intellectuals have debated whether the Holocaust is at all representable, what are the motivations behind various representations of Auschwitz and to what extent such representations constitute an abuse of the historical truth and memory of the event. It has been said that figures such as Jean Améry, Primo Levi, and Paul Celan constantly wrote on their experiences so as to be able to (literally) keep body and soul together, and that finally their resistance broke down, leading them to suicide.[49] Yet this assertion hardly does justice to these figures or, for that matter, to many other survivors. Indeed, it seems to me to make a false distinction between those who write so as to rid themselves of a burden that otherwise would make their existence impossible and those who feel charged with a moral mission and direct their writing at the public. I see no reason to privilege one over the other. Writers who tend to be more inward-looking may well reflect on their personal experiences and question the understanding of such experiences and their wider implication both by themselves and by others; they can thereby fulfil also a social and moral function without becoming necessarily politicized. As for Levi and Améry (and in a different way also Celan), they stated quite unambiguously that the reason for their writing and the cause of their increasing despair had to do just as much with the political reality of the post-Holocaust world, perceived by them as constantly repeating at least some aspects of their own experiences in Auschwitz, as well as with the manner in which the horrors they had undergone were represented by artists, intellectuals, and politicians.[50] This is the important point: it was what happened after the Holocaust, when it became clear to the survivors that Auschwitz had not been the horror to end all horrors, but only signalled the beginning of a seemingly endless cycle of similar horrors (to which humanity was adapting itself with remarkable speed), which caused them such bottomless despair. And it was the newly emerging trends in representing their experiences in the Holocaust, which they saw not merely as being unfair to them, but perhaps more important as reflecting some fascination with extremity and with artificially recreating the most horror-filled situations so as to be able to observe them from the safety of one's armchair, that made them realize the extent to which Auschwitz was anything but the end, indeed merely the beginning of a new age.[51]

Jean Améry's collection of essays *At the Mind's Limits* consists not only, as the subtitle would suggest, of "contemplations by a survivor on Auschwitz and its realities," but is rather a series of melancholy ruminations on the situation of the intellectual as uprooted exile, as concentration camp inmate, and as a postwar voice feeling increasingly detached from the contemporary intellectual and cultural scene. It is, to my mind, the latter that is most painful and troubling, because Améry *wants* to communicate his experience, *wants* to draw conclusions from it and transmit them at least to the intellectual community, yet finds himself progressively isolated, misunderstood, marginalized, and finally rejected as a remnant of a past everyone is already trying to remold into a much more convenient, appropriately streamlined cast, one that would reflect the preoccupations of the postwar generation.[52] Many years after Auschwitz, Améry knows that millions of people are still suffering and dying in the most horrible ways all over the globe, and it is that which he cannot accept, the fact that Auschwitz and all its horrors did not even have the effect of mitigating the lot of posterity.

Anyone who reads Primo Levi's *Survival in Auschwitz* (an unhappy English rendering of the original Italian, *Is This a Man?*) should have no difficulties in recognizing that it *is* possible to represent the Holocaust. Having read several scholarly texts on the "Final Solution," my own students both in the United States and Israel agreed almost unanimously that it was only through Levi's memoir that they came close to understanding the experience of the individual in Auschwitz. And yet Levi himself was increasingly critical of his own account. As he wrote in his last published essays, *The Drowned and the Saved*, he had described life in the *Lager* from the position of one of the privileged, for it was only the privileged who had any chance at all of surviving.[53] Hence the vast majority, the "real" inmates who lacked any privileges, remained unrepresented. Moreover, Levi's late ruminations on Auschwitz are far darker and more ominous than the memoir written shortly after his return to Italy. In his essay "The Intellectual in Auschwitz," Levi comes to grips with Améry's forbidding visions of past and present. Intellectually, he refuses to agree with Améry, for during most of his post-Auschwitz existence Levi maintained an optimistic view of humanity. One must, and one could, retain one's humanity. This was the secret to survival, even if Levi's experience itself had given ample reason to qualify his belief. One must, and one could, learn from Auschwitz, draw the right conclusions (only, though, by knowing what happened there—hence the task Levi had set himself as informant) and thereby bring more humanity to the world. And one must not despair. Levi strongly objected to Améry's suicide, not on the personal level, but on the intellectual/moral one, that is, he rejected Améry's causes for despair. Yet his own late essays betray the same sort of despair, both concerning the veracity and fairness of his own depictions of the experience, the transmission of his experience in Auschwitz to a younger, uncomprehending generation, the political realities of the present, and, not least, the manner in which his experience was being represented.

Levi is very much concerned with what he has called "the gray zone," the regions where victims were also collaborators and where perpetrators could also show some signs of humanity. He looks into the "gray zone" with the eye of the humanist, he tries to derive comfort from the human element to be found even in the most brutal conditions, yet we somehow feel that the effect is quite the opposite. For as Levi himself says, the worst crime committed by the Nazis was to make the Jewish *Sonderkommandos* do their work for them in the gas chambers. Does Levi find a flicker of humanity even in the heart of darkness, or does he reveal the potential of barbarism even in the most humane? Initially, immediately after his release, his belief in humanity seems to have been greater than forty years after the event. What does this tell us about our reception of the survivors, our understanding of their existence, and the nature of the world we have built for ourselves with the benefit of knowing its barbaric potentials?

Whereas Levi and Améry do show that some sort of representation of the Holocaust is possible, there is little doubt that they rebel against much of what they see around them in postwar Europe. Levi clearly distinguished between his "gray zone" and Liliana Cavani's *The Night Porter* (1974). For him, the SS man who had shown a momentary compassion for the girl who survived the gassing is, nevertheless, a mass murderer who should be executed. He rebels against the allegedly intellectually stimulating zone of crime and sexual perversion, attraction and repulsion, subjugation and submission, so often exploited by filmmakers, and achieving such intellectual (and not so intellectual) popularity precisely due to its "dangerous" subject. This, to him, is abuse of the experience.[54]

There exists now a huge industry concerned with the representation of the Holocaust and its periphery, fascism, Nazism, and war, testifying to the morbid attraction to and fascination with the worst epoch in contemporary history. Our modern, or as some would have it, postmodern sensibilities seem no longer to be satisfied with simple, unambiguous images, and the alleged beauty of fascism, for which it itself had laid claim with such insistence, attracts the makers of filmic images and their viewers alike precisely because of the knowledge that behind that beauty lay the depths of horror and depravity. Hence such films as Luchino Visconti's *The Damned* (1969), Pier Paolo Pasolini's *Salo—The 120 Days of Sodom* (1975), Bernardo Bertolucci's *1900* (1976), Lina Wertmuller's *Seven Beauties* (1976), Hans Jürgen Syberberg's *Hitler, a Film from Germany* (1977), Rainer Werner Fassbinder's *Lili Marleen* (1981), and many more.[55] These are works whose message is as ambiguous as the sentiments they evoke in their viewers. They exploit our own mean instincts and then seem to blame us for possessing them; they fill us with anger, disgust, and frustration, yet we do not take our eyes off the screen. They shame and morally disarm us by making us accomplices to evil, at least as bystanders once removed. And they also sell very well since they possess the further ambiguous characteristic of attracting both intellectuals and professional peepers, both those of fine aesthetic sensibilities and individuals who like viewing brutalities, perversions, pain, and rape. They do not tell us much about the human experience under fascism, but rather about our own potential of being drawn to it. They are very much part of a relatively recent tendency toward detached, amoral, nonjudgmental, complacent, and yet highly dangerous morbid curiosity about extremity.

Yet this is not to say that the Holocaust is unrepresentable. Granted, memory can be abused. The German filmmaker Edgar Reitz vowed to undo the theft of German history allegedly committed by the American television series *Holocaust* and to "give it back" to his countrymen.[56] Hence his film *Heimat* (1984) spends sixteen hours telling us (or the Germans) what the *German memory* of the past is; predictably it hardly even mentions the Holocaust. Conversely, the French-Jewish filmmaker Claude Lanzmann produced his own eight-hour reconstruction of the Jewish memory of the Holocaust, in which he intentionally avoided using any German newsreels or other film material of the period, which obviously formed no part of the Jewish memory and presented the Jews as the Germans saw and remember them—as subhuman, faceless living or dead corpses.[57] Lanzmann's *Shoah* (1985) sets out to prove both the existence of the Holocaust as an historical event and as one that still lives on in the memories of all who were involved in it.[58] This is not a documentary, just as Levi's *Survival in Auschwitz* is not an autobiography. For these works reveal the immense importance of memory and show that the artificial distinction made between a so-called sacrilizing memory and a scientifically oriented history is invalid.

This was, of course, clearly recognized by both perpetrators and victims. For the accounts written during the Holocaust by *Lager* inmates were the very essence of the struggle between Nazism, which strove to annihilate both the Jews and their memory, and the victims, who refused to allow their memory to perish along with their physical existence. Such personal accounts are still being written today by survivors who had not been able either to verbalize or write down their experience until late middle-age. These too are representations, often filled with ruminations about human existence in the camps, belief in God, friendship and barbarism, selfishness and betrayal, sacrifice and loyalty.[59] No historian of the period, no one who seriously wishes to fathom human psychology or to understand the experience of humanity in this century, can afford to ignore them.[60]

Yet it is precisely for this reason that prose fiction on the Holocaust seems rarely to have the same effect as memoir literature and appears at best contrived, at worst cheap and sensationalist. For somehow fiction and imagination seem unable to confront what the Germans called "the arse-hole of the world"— Auschwitz, a place even those who had been there, both victims and perpetrators, kept describing as unimaginable.[61] If anything, *this* is the issue, much more than memory, for the historian is also called on to use his or her imagination, and the impossibility to imagine creates a block not easily overcome without precisely that distancing mechanism referred to by German historians who have "pleaded" for a historicization of the Third Reich.[62] Perhaps we can remember the unimaginable, but we cannot imagine it. It is precisely for this reason that we depend on other people's accounts, indeed, that we will not even begin to understand what we strive to clarify without constantly referring to those borrowed, tortured, at times inhumanly distorted memories.

The argument on the unrepresentability of the Holocaust was voiced in conjunction with one of the greatest single poems of the century. When Adorno asserted that poetry after Auschwitz was barbarism, the poem he appears to have had in mind was Paul Celan's *Todesfuge*.[63] Perhaps only those who have heard Celan reading this poem aloud can perceive the extent to which its relentless rhythm and stark imagery seem to recapture the whole experience of the death camp, the crazy logic of the extermination, the horrifying irony of installing the "chosen people" as smoke in the sky, this insane world of music and bloodhounds, of beauty and ashes, of total, endless, unremitting despair.

And yet Celan himself seems to have found his poem too coherent, too "poetic," too musical; it was taught in German schools as a good example of a poetic fugue; it was set to music; it did not, for him, recapture the essence of the unimaginable industrial annihilation, without any traces, of millions.[64] It is therefore his later poem, *Engführung* that wholly dispenses with any imagery, rhythm, balance, but is as disjointed, disoriented, verbally crippled, emotionally inexpressible as the memories of the survivors. It is a cry of pain, despair, boundless sorrow, which must remain mute because it is confronted with the wasteland of ashes and an indifferent world. Listening to Celan read this poem in Jerusalem, just a year before his suicide, one cannot forget the broken voice repeating "Asche, Asche Asche," for here one confronts not a surfeit of memory, not even a limit of representation, but the despair of not being able to remember, of trying to hold onto remnants of words spoken long ago, objects touched, feelings aroused, and yet constantly returning to the ashes. A world destroyed, turned into ashes, can never suffer from too much memory. That its representation—the true, impassioned attempt to resurrect it in words and images—cannot wholly succeed is testimony to the fragility of that memory and to the condition of what is being remembered, for it is blown away with every gust of wind.

V. DENIAL, RELATIVISM, TRUTH: THE FRUITS OF MORBID CURIOSITY

The French revisionist Robert Faurisson is an extreme case. His denial of the existence of the gas chambers is so preposterous that one would tend to shrug it off as irrelevant. But the fact is that the discussion on the question of the existence of gas chambers has become one of major importance not only regarding the murder of the Jews, but concerning the very nature of truth and its historical reconstruction. One might similarly reject offhand the application of theories of relativism to Auschwitz. But that too would be an error, for in Auschwitz the truth, as constructed by Western civilization, was shattered. Hence it is by applying whichever theory of historical explanation we consider useful and accurate to Auschwitz that we can test its validity. If we accept that Auschwitz happened in history, then theoretical generalizations that do not apply to it cannot apply anywhere else. If we do not accept that Auschwitz happened in history, then there is no reason to believe that anything else did.

Faurisson has argued that he had "tried in vain to find a single former deportee capable of proving to me that he had really seen, with his own eyes, a gas chamber."[65] This statement, as the philosopher Jean-François Lyotard has written, is based on the crazy logic that "in order for a place to be identified as a gas chamber, the only eyewitness I will accept would be a victim of this gas chamber; now, according to my opponent, there is no victim that is not dead; otherwise, this gas chamber would not be what he or she claims it to be. There is, therefore, no gas chamber."[66]

We are thus faced with a question of truth. Was there or was there not a gas chamber? Faurisson asserts that it did not exist, and we have to prove that it did. And in order to do so as historians, we need witnesses. Yet the very nature of the gas chamber makes witnesses a logical impossibility.

This is an issue of extreme importance and urgency. It confronts the historical profession, it confronts the intellectual, indeed, it confronts any human being with the peril of losing all control over the truth, of not being able to distinguish between what is false and what is true, of plunging into a dangerous abyss of an openended relativity, wherein there is no objective reality, but a multitude of subjective views, all legitimate. The historian Pierre Vidal-Naquet recognized this danger in his debate with Faurisson when he argued that although "everything should necessarily go through to a discourse . . . there was something irreducible which, for better or for worse, I would still call reality. Without this reality, how could we make a difference between fiction and history?"[67]

But can we make that difference? Vidal-Naquet, after all, called his own book on the subject *Assassins of Memory*, not of history.[68] And in the above-cited passage, we actually sense some despair, coming as it does from a distinguished scholar of antiquity who knows as well as (if not better than) most of us that truth is a highly ambivalent notion and that it can be reconstructed by the historian only on the most tenuous level. Is memory an integral part of history? Is history based on, or does it constitute at least a search for, truth? Is it, or should it be, an attempt to reconstruct reality? And how do we cope with a historical phenomenon in which one group of people consciously attempted to erase the memory, and therefore the history, of another group? Simon Wiesenthal writes that SS men in the *Lager* used to mock them by saying that "even if some proof should remain and some of you survive, people will say that the events you describe are too monstrous to be believed."[69]

Now we do have much evidence, both German and Jewish, as well as witnesses. But we cannot have testimonies of the gas chambers, from within, while they were operating. And if Faurisson's assertion may appear to us preposterous, Levi's admission, cited above, that he was not a true witness, for the true witnesses all perished, should be taken more seriously. So where is the truth? Even if we accept Levi's account of the labor camp as truthful, it does not tell us much about the gas chambers. And even if we accept the testimonies of the only survivors of the Chelmno death camp, they too, though they were inmates of the death camp, had never been inside an operating gas chamber, otherwise they would not have survived.

Faurisson does not claim that there is no truth, but rather that we need witnesses to establish it. And while Carlo Ginzburg, for instance, has argued that historians must rely even on the evidence of a single witness, and not insist on two,[70] the case we are confronted with is one of no witnesses at all. But there is another argument that has a direct bearing on this issue. For even after significantly modifying his position, most likely because he has clearly understood its implications when applied to the Holocaust, Hayden White has asserted that "There is an inexpungeable relativity in every representation of historical phenomena."[71]

At first glance, it is difficult to disagree with this position. Obviously, our choice of language, just as much as our choice of subject, point of view, our historical context, our own memories and education, and a whole series of other factors influence the way in which we write on an historical event. The question is, however, whether that event exists independently of our own reconstruction of it, and whether any reconstruction of an event is equally legitimate. Now while White finds the denial of the Holocaust "as morally offensive as it is intellectually bewildering,"[72] if he wishes to be consistent with his theory, there is no reason to reach that conclusion, for one could emplot the history of the Third Reich with the Holocaust taken out, or at least greatly modified; indeed, there are quite a number of such instances, whether in German school books that speak of the "persecution" of Jews by the "Nazis" or in films such as *Heimat*, which simply leaves the story of the Holocaust to others. If one is to argue that some kinds of emplotment are admissible and others are not, then one must propose some criteria in order to make that judgment.[73] Those can be criteria belonging to the realm of truth or to the realm of morality (and they are not mutually exclusive). But if one argues that all historical representation is relative, then one would be hard put to apply such criteria. Nor is it clear why certain modes of emplotment would be unacceptable, especially if we do not make a distinction between facts and interpretation, truth and lies, reality and image.[74]

Returning to the gas chambers, the question arises as to how we would emplot that phenomenon. We could tell it from the point of view of the victim, which might be imaginary (because the victim actually died) and yet factually accurate (this is done, for instance, in Schwarz-Bart's *The Last of the Just*). We might emplot it from the point of view of the Jewish *Sonderkommando*, some of whose members had actually survived to tell the tale; but we might also tell it from the point of view of the SS men present. Their view of their actions would be very different from that of the victims or the work-team, but it would be their reality and their understanding of what they were doing, their truth. Would we then be allowed to judge their representation of their actions against some objective reality?[75]

In his infamous speech in Posen in 1943 Heinrich Himmler told an assembly of SS officers that by their extermination of the Jewish people they had written a glorious page of German history, which, however, would never be recorded.[76] This would therefore constitute a fact that would never be admitted to have existed, a reality to be erased, a memory to be forgotten. This assertion brings me back to the unease I expressed at the opening of this chapter. The difficulty stems first and foremost, perhaps, from the realization that our own intellectual efforts to come to terms with the amorphous nature of reality can play so easily into the hands of those who have no qualms about producing realities of the most horrific nature and then claiming that they had never taken place.

Relativism has two other peculiar links. First, the issue of relativization. This is not to say that the relativists seek to relativize or that the proponents of historicization in Germany, who have been accused of trying to relativize Auschwitz, are in any way relativists. In fact, nothing could be farther from the truth, especially in the latter case. And yet, both schools, though without any visible direct ties, are part of the same intellectual discourse. If previously we found it immensely difficult to understand Auschwitz simply because of the nature and dimensions of the event itself, we are now faced with a new situation, whereby the event keeps slipping away from us either by being relativized as unoriginal, not central, not a focus of identification, indeed as a block to understanding both past and present; or by being given a relativistic treatment, whereby it can be remembered, imagined, and emplotted in so many different but equally acceptable ways that even if we would never deny it, at the same time we cannot say that one representation of it is more valid than another because the event is not recuperable as such.

Second, we are faced with a growing and highly disturbing fascination with extremity. This is linked both with relativism, due to the tendency of such theories to try and test their validity against extreme situations, and with the kind of fascination with violence that had triggered such extremities in the first place. The connection is also one of mood, or temperament. This is not an impassioned, engaged fascination, but rather a detached curiosity, devoid of any powerful emotion, a kind of peeping into the void from a safe theoretical distance, without risking even one's reputation, let alone physical injury. Finally, there seems to be a connection between this intellectual curiosity about extremity and the rise of violence and extremism in the West. For the fantastic realism of cinematic images, simultaneously purged of all real pain to the viewer, vivid and yet detached, arranged in such aesthetic forms so as to attract even the more feeble hearted, cannot fail to produce some reaction. And, as a quick glance at publishers' lists of books will reveal, intellectuals and academics are just as fascinated with death, suffering, perversion, and depravity.

We are thus faced, as I understand it, with several false dichotomies. One is the argument that an event cannot be proved to have taken place if no one who had experienced it directly, with his or her own eyes, can testify to it. This is the dichotomy between event and non-event. Another dichotomy is between naive realism and interpretation.[77] It is based on the contention that there are only two choices between a blind and uncritical belief in facts and a wholly skeptical view that refuses to accept them as anything more than previous interpretations. The last is between truth and relativity. The assumption is ultimately that the event took place and yet at the same time it did not. It did, in the sense that it can be emplotted in innumerable ways. It did not, in the sense that no one emplotment is better or, rather, more truthful, than another. If the event has no objective reality, then it is free to transform itself into whatever we may like.

It is here that I find myself beset by extreme unease. As historians, I believe we all know, or should know, that we can never achieve true objectivity, nor could we hope to discover true objective reality in the past. Obviously the past was, and is, made of numerous truths and realities, and it is highly difficult to distinguish between them, just as it is difficult for us to distinguish between our own motivations in studying a certain period in a certain manner. Obviously, there are numerous ways of telling the story of a murder, and those depend on the witnesses as much as on the person reconstructing the event. But a murder has taken place; we did not construct it in our imagination. In that sense, it is not relative. Moreover, it is important to adjudicate who was responsible (which is the real point of Akira Kurosawa's 1950 film *Rashomon*, of course).[78] The historian cannot escape the responsibility of acting as judge in this context.[79] And if we are told about it by way of a joke or informed that it did not happen, although we know that it did, or if we are told that the question of responsibility is so multifaceted as to defy definition, when we suspect that this position is evasive or duplicitous, then we have a right, indeed a duty, to be morally outraged both as historians and as human beings. Perhaps, too, we should examine whether we have ourselves made it possible for such assertions to be made. Perhaps what we believed to be interesting, intellectually stimulating, even playful, when applied to an extreme case proves to be morally dubious. And then, perhaps, we should admit that we had made an error, and that if our theory does not work here, it can no longer be called a theory, and might have to be discarded, or at least radically modified.

Proponents of relativism and indeterminacy often claim to be fighting a war of liberation against the tyranny of a totalizing discourse (in complicity with the authoritarian elements of society). Thus it has been argued that if we do not accept relativism, we are bound to end up as determinists. I believe that is wrong. Indeed, as Isaiah Berlin wrote more than twenty years ago, "Both [determinism and relativism] have, at times, succeeded in reasoning men or frightening men out of their most human moral or political convictions in the name of a deeper and more devastating insight into the nature of things."[80]

Hence, since relativism lacks a commitment to truth and morality and does not allow choice, it contains an element of cynicism; and while humanity is based on choice, relativism makes every argument allegedly possible. What is at stake is therefore not only what intellectuals say about the Holocaust, but how they view history and by extension how they perceive humanity. In this sense, the question of whether the gas chambers existed or not is vital, for if this can be doubted, or if it is a relative issue open to multiple emplotments, then everything is. Hence the question is not one of the limits of representation, but the limits of truth. If historians, as intellectuals, concede their moral neutrality, then they will finally concede their intellectual, political, and moral irrelevance. Thereby they will also abuse their function as educators, reconstructors of the past, and serious critics of the present. I do not see why historians or, more generally, intellectuals should doubt their role as critics of society, as representatives of a moral view, as persons seeking the truth and exposing lies. They must do so carefully, with integrity, with critical self-reflection, recognizing their weak-nesses and limitations, remaining open to criticism, to new ideas and new evidence. But once they surrender their claim for truth, they will end up serving those who will never be afraid of claiming the truth for themselves.

Let me conclude by way of some general remarks. I do not pretend to offer some new approach to the study of the Holocaust or to either the historical, literary-critical, or literary discourse on it. I do believe, however, that the issue is serious enough to merit consideration by any historical approach or literary theory that claims universal applicability. It is serious both because of the nature of the thing itself and because of its implications for the world in which we live.

By and large, none of us can really come to terms with the fact that modern civilization had been capable of perpetrating such an enormity. The conclusions to be drawn are so frightening, the anxiety into which we would plunge is so par-alyzing, that we simply must, as indeed we have done, think of our culture, tra-dition, civilization, with Auschwitz taken out. At the same time, however, I feel that when attempting to generalize about modern human experience and nature, one cannot afford to begin by a general theory and then see whether it conforms with the evidence from the Holocaust. For the obvious result of this would be either a significant modification of the theory or the assumption that Auschwitz does not belong to, or teach us anything about, humanity. On the other hand, I do not believe that we should generalize the Holocaust in a manner that would block all other avenues of human understanding and experience. Western civi-lization, even the twentieth century itself, consists of more than the Holocaust. If Auschwitz is central, indeed, if it signifies a "break of civilization,"[81] it never-theless must not be allowed to obscure our vision completely.

There has been a great deal of criticism of institutionalized memory, repre-sented either by certain individuals or institutions. Some aspects of this phe-nomenon are clearly lamentable, especially in cases where professional remem-berers make a material and moral profit from peddling their memories. In other cases this is problematic, but both inevitable and not wholly negative. A museum of the Holocaust may not be the most appealing idea to many of us. And yet, depending on the organization and didactic message of such institu-tions (and they all have one), I do not think we can a priori disapprove of them, for the simple reason that apart from a minuscule minority among even the more educated sectors of Western society, most people know hardly anything about the event and are not likely to take the trouble to learn about it in the future. If even a small minority does become exposed to some kind of well-arranged museum exhibit, that may not be so bad after all. For although I per-sonally believe that knowledge about the past does not at all necessarily prevent its recurrence, I also would claim that thinking about the future without a keen awareness of the past is even more perilous. This is, after all, one of the reasons why many of us have studied history.

But I do object to the assumed moral superiority of survivors (very few of them make such claims, of course, but it is that minority that is heard most loudly). I believe that the experience and memories of survivors give them insight not only into the event itself, but also into some aspects of human behavior and psychology, into the potential of each of us and into the potential of human society to create hell on this earth. However, though it is difficult to say, I do not think that the experience of Auschwitz gives one moral superiority, both for the reasons raised by Levi (that is, that the survivors often belonged to the "privileged," and those were not necessarily morally superior to those who perished), and because in many other areas of human experience and creativity Auschwitz had absolutely nothing to teach us. Hence, while we must take into account what survivors tell us about human behavior, we must also remember that this is a partial view, formed under the most extreme conditions. It is a warning, but it is not a whole picture of human action and potential.

It is partly for this reason that the artificial separation between those who study modern European history and those who study Jewish history or, even more precisely, the history of the Holocaust, is lamentable. Because just as the Holocaust was part of the European experience, so too Jewish history was part of European history. The way we study history now tends to separate the two, so that the Jews are kept out of the general stream of history, and the general stream of history is seen as having had nothing to do with the Jews. So too with the Holocaust. Just as Auschwitz was part of a general European scene, so too Jewish history does not simply lead to Auschwitz and therefore consist mainly of it.

Teaching a university course on the Holocaust has made me realize how important it is to expose young people, of whatever nationality, to this central event of our century. But the fact that one could teach Holocaust history in one class, and German history in another, with very few overlaps, made me understand once more that we are perpetuating an unfortunate and in some ways dangerous process.[82] Auschwitz must not be made into the focus of Jewish existence, for it is a black hole that sucks everything beautiful and hopeful into its void. By the same token, however, no member of Western civilization may study his or her history without knowing that one of its potentials was, indeed, Auschwitz.

NOTES

1. Dante Alighieri, *The Divine Comedy: Cantica I: Hell (L'Inferno)* (Harmondsworth, 1972 [1949]), pp. 235–37 (Canto xxvi). This chapter is a revised version of an article by the same name published in *H & M*, 5/1 (1993): 87–29; I would like to thank the editors of this journal and its publisher, Indiana University Press, for allowing me to reprint it here. For instructive comments on various earlier drafts thanks are due also to David Abraham, Guli Arad, Yehudit and Hanoch Bartov, James Buzard, Saul Friedlander, Paul Holdengräber, Peter Novick, Steve Pincus, Immanuel Sivan, Elona Zucker, and most especially Wai-yee Li.

2. See esp. Mayer, *Memory and History*; Maier, *A Surfeit of Memory?* See also L. Valensi, "Commentary on the Text of Arno Mayer," unpublished paper (1993); and the July 1993 issue of the journal *Esprit*, subtitled "Le poids de la mémoire: Comment transmettre le souvenir? Le pardon dans l'histoire."

3. For pertinent and insightful remarks on the problems and frustrations of teaching the most current and painful issues of the day to undergraduates, see L. Trilling, "On the Teaching of Modern Literature," in his *Beyond Culture: Essays on Literature and Learning*, 6th ed. (New York, 1965), pp. 3–30. More specifically on teaching the Holocaust, see M. R. Marrus, "'Good History' and Teaching the Holocaust," *Perspectives* 31/5 (1993): 1–12; A. S. Lindemann, "Anti-Semitism: A Case for Teaching about the manifestations of Prejudice," *Perspectives* 31/9 (1993): 15–20; J. Petropoulos, "Teaching the Holocaust in an Interdisciplinary Manner: Confronting the 'Holocaust as Hoax' Phenomenon," unpublished paper (1993). See also the March–April 1993 issue of *Esprit*, subtitled: "Métamorphoses du racisme et de l'antisémitisme: L'antisémitisme racial est-il appuru au XXe siècle? Comment peut-on être antiraciste?"

4. Good examples are the conference "The Origins of the 'Final Solution,'" held at the Institute of Contemporary History and Wiener Library in London in January 1992, whose proceedings have now been published in Cesarani, *The Final Solution*; and the conference on "Nazism and the 'Final Solution': Probing the Limits of Representation," held at the University of California, Los Angeles, in April 1990, whose papers were published in Friedlander, *Probing the Limits*.

5. J. Améry, *At the Mind's Limits: Contemplations by a Survivor on Auschwitz and its Realities*, 2d ed. (New York, 1986); P. Levi, *Survival in Auschwitz: The Nazi Assault on Humanity* (New York, 1959), and esp. his *The Drowned and the Saved*.

6. See, e.g., Friedlander, *Reflections of Nazism*. On Friedlander's sense of unease with recent modes of representation of and discourse on Nazism, see also his recent collection of articles, *Memory, History*, esp. Chapters 4, 6, and 7.

7. See, e.g., Mayer, *Memory and History*, and Maier, *A Surfeit of Memory?* But also, e.g., Primo Levi's comments throughout *The Drowned and the Saved* (1986); Martin Broszat's arguments in his *Plea*; Edgar Reitz's remarks in his *Liebe zum Kino: Utopien und Gedanken zum Autorenfilm, 1962–1983* (Cologne, 1984), p. 102, discussed also in E. L. Santner, "History Beyond the Pleasure Principle: Some Thoughts on the Representation of Trauma," in Friedlander, *Probing the Limits*, pp. 149–50, and in Kaes, *From Hitler to Heimat*, pp. 184–85; Jean Améry's comments in his 1977 preface to *At the Mind's Limits*; and Hannah Arendt's observations in her *Aftermath of Nazi Rule*. See further the arguments raised by Ernst Nolte, Andreas Hillgruber, and Michael Stürmer, in *Forever in the Shadow*. Yet Charles S. Maier, author of *The Unmasterable Past*, and Arno Mayer, author of *Why Did the Heavens Not Darken?* are both perfectly aware of what is at stake when discussing a memory which so many would like to see "go away." It is for this reason that I find their present positions somewhat bewildering. In this context, see also D. J. Goldhagen, "False Witness," *TNR* (April 17, 1989): 39–44.

8. Echoes of this view can be found, for instance, in Steiner, *Bluebeard's Castle*. See also G. Steiner, "The Long Life of Metaphor: An Approach to 'the Shoah,'" *Encounter* 68/2 (1987): 55–61. On Jewish history as a tale of constant persecution and martyrdom, see, e.g., Almog, *Antisemitism*; and Ettinger, *Modern Anti-Semitism*; Wistrich, *Antisemitism*. The classic critique of this view is H. Arendt, *Totalitarianism*, part I: "Antisemitism." A literary rendering of it can be found, e.g., in A. Schwarz-Bart, *The Last of the Just*, 5th ed. (New York, 1969).

9. Kershaw, *Nazi Dictatorship*, p. 80, differentiates between the difficulties faced by Jewish historians due to the fact that some of them tend toward "'mystification' and religious-cultural eschatology," and the "perspective of non-Jewish historians,"

which he finds "inevitably different." More strongly worded are the comments by Martin Broszat, in his correspondence with Saul Friedlander, now in Baldwin, *Reworking*, pp. 102–34.

10. Apart from note 8 above, see also Yerushalmi, *Zakhor*.

11. The contradictions between the various types of criticism of the eschatological view derive from the greatly differing political/ideological camps to which the critics belong; American (and in some cases Israeli) liberals on the one hand, German conservatives or "national liberals" on the other; as well as some radical left-wing circles in Germany and self-proclaimed "postmodern" historians in America.

12. Apart from the Broszat/Friedlander exchange in Baldwin, *Reworking*, and other contributions to that volume, see also Diner, *Nationalsozialismus*.

13. The most obvious case is the disturbing similarity between Arno Mayer's argument in *Why Did the Heavens Not Darken?* and Ernst Nolte's assertions in his *Past That Will Not Pass* and *Historical Legend*. See also Mayer, *Memory and History*, Maier, *A Surfeit of Memory?* and the arguments raised by all revisionist historians of the *Historikerstreit*, such as Joachim Fest and Klaus Hildebrand, in *Forever in the Shadow*. Broszat, who attacked the revisionists in 1986, had actually supplied quite a few arguments for their arsenal in his *Plea*, originally published in 1985.

14. Primo Levi was probably the most acute and honest observer of this problem. See his comments in *The Drowned and the Saved*, pp. 34–35.

15. Arno Mayer and Saul Friedlander, Martin Broszat and Andreas Hillgruber, to name but a few, had all experienced Nazism in one way or another; some as refugees, others as soldiers. Friedlander's *When Memory Comes*, 2d ed. (New York, 1991), demonstrates the acuteness of memory and the impact it has had on one's life; so does Hillgruber's *Zweierlei Untergang*, though in a very different manner. On the latter, see [Omer Bartov, *Murder in Our Midst: The Holocaust, Industrial Killing, and Representation* (New York, 1996)], Chapter 4. The importance of personal memory for historians writing on periods they themselves had experienced is discussed in the Friedlander/Broszat correspondence in Baldwin, *Reworking*, pp. 123, 129.

16. Repression of the immediate past both in Germany and in Palestine (later Israel) can be documented from a wide array of sources. See, e.g., Engelmann, *Hitler's Germany*, pp. 331–32; and Arendt, *Aftermath of Nazi Rule*. For some elements of Israeli repression, see Sivan, *The 1948 Generation*, and his *To Remember Is to Forget*. On soldiers of the Jewish Brigade confronting Holocaust survivors in Europe, see the novel by Hanoch Bartov, *The Brigade* (New York, 1968), and on confronting them in Israel, his *Shesh Kenafayim le-Ehad* (Each Had Six Wings) (Merhavya, 1954). On the perpetual silence of survivors in Israel, especially vis-à-vis their children, see David Grossman, *See Under: Love* (New York, 1989). For a comprehensive study of the Israelis and the Holocaust, see Segev, *The Seventh Million*.

17. Even the students who participate in my course on the Holocaust, a far more motivated group than the average, mostly admit to knowing very little about the event. This is not to say that there are no groups and organizations in the United States obsessed with the memory of the Holocaust and devoted to its institutionalization. But from a national point of view they seem marginal and of little influence on public opinion, let alone knowledge. In this context, see now the provocative unpublished paper by Peter Novick, "Pseudo-Memory and Dubious 'Lessons': The Holocaust in American Culture," (1995).

18. Richard Evans wrote as early as 1989 that the *Historikerstreit* "has very little to offer anyone with a serious, scholarly interest in the German past. It brings no new facts to light; it embodies no new research; it makes no new contribution to historical understanding; it poses no new questions that might stimulate future work." *In Hitler's Shadow*, p. 118. Similar remarks can be found in the introduction to Childers/Caplan, *Reevaluating*.

19. For numerous citations from soldiers' letters and propaganda material, see Bartov, *Hitler's Army*, pp. 106–78. See also Kershaw, *The "Hitler Myth,"* p. 209; Kaes, *From Hitler to Heimat*, pp. 3–35, on German cinema's confrontation with Nazism since 1945; and Friedlander, *Reflections of Nazism*. For interesting observations on the paths of German memory, see L. Niethammer, "'Normalisierung' im Westen. Erinnerungs-spuren in die 50er Jahre," in Diner, *Nationalsozialismus*, pp. 153–84, and U. Herbert, "'Die guten und die schlechten Zeiten': Überlegungen zur diachronen Analyse lebens-geschichtlicher Interviews," in L. Niethammer (ed.), *"Die Jahre weiss man nicht, wo man die heute hinsetzen soll": Faschismus Erfahrungen im Ruhrgebiet* (Berlin, 1983), pp. 67–96.

20. Broszat, *Plea*.

21. On such arguments, see, e.g., Améry, *At the Mind's Limits*, Preface to the 1977 edition. Also see D. Diner, "Between Aporia and Apology: On the Limits of Historicizing National Socialism" and "Negative Symbiosis: Germans and Jews After Auschwitz"; A. S. Markovits, "Coping with the Past: The West German Labor Movement and the Left," all in Baldwin, *Reworking*, pp. 135–45, 251–61, 262–75, respectively. K. D. Bracher's classic *The German Dictatorship: The Origins, Structure, and Effects of National Socialism* (New York, 1970), was originally published in 1969, as was the German original of Broszat, *The Hitler State*; J. C. Fest, *The Face of the Third Reich*, 3d ed. (Harmondsworth, 1979), was originally published in 1963. The publication of A. Speer, *Inside The Third Reich*, 2d ed. (London, 1979) in Germany in 1969 and its widespread popularity, is a case in point, as is Fest's 1977 film *Hitler: Eine Karriere*. None of these works devoted much space to the genocide of the Jews. Conversely, the most important work at the time on the Holocaust was Hilberg's *The Destruction of the European Jews*, published originally in 1961, and one of the most popular was Dawidowicz's *The War Against the Jews*, published in 1975; both were written in the United States, as was G. Reitlinger, *The Final Solution*, rev. ed. (South Brunswick, 1968), originally published in 1953. The shock of German audiences at viewing the film *Holocaust* (1979) testifies to their ignorance. See Kaes, *From Hitler to Heimat*, p. 184. Generally, German scholars contributed a great deal to the historiography of the Third Reich, and initially not much to that of the Holocaust; when they did turn to it, they often treated the subject in a highly controversial manner and in declared opposition to allegedly traditional, non-German, frequently Jewish historians. See, e.g., Adam, *Judenpolitik*; Broszat, *Genesis*; Mommsen, *Realization*.

22. In his correspondence with Friedlander, Broszat writes about his generation (the so-called Hitler Youth generation) that they were "old enough to be affected emotionally and intellectually to a high degree by the suggestivity . . . which the Nazi regime was capable of." After the collapse, they realized that they "had been cheated out of important years of our youth." They were, he argues, "Affected, yet hardly burdened" by their experience. How little burdened they felt is reflected in his assertion in another letter, that the "German historian . . . qua scientist and scholar . . . cannot readily accept that Auschwitz also be made, after the fact, into the cardinal point, the

hinge on which the entire factual complex of historical events of the Nazi period turns. He cannot simply accept without further ado . . . that Auschwitz even be made into the decisive measuring rod for the historical perception of this period." Baldwin, *Reworking*, pp. 123 and 116, respectively.

23. See T. Mason, "The Workers' Opposition in Nazi Germany," *HWJ* 11 (1981): 120–37; S. Salter, "Class Harmony or Class Conflict?" in *Government Party and People in Nazi Germany*, ed. J. Noakes (Exeter, 1980). See also my "The Missing Years: German Workers, German Soldiers," in *Nazism and German Society, 1933–1945*, ed. D. Crew (London, 1994).

24. The issue of conformity and collaboration is treated in detail in Kershaw, *Popular Opinion*. See also R. Gellately, *The Gestapo and German Society* (Oxford, 1990).

25. See D. J. K. Peukert, *Die Edelweisspiraten: Protestbewegungen jugendlicher Arbeiter im Dritten Reich: Eine Dokumentation* (Cologne, 1980), and *Inside Nazi Germany: Conformity, Opposition, and Racism in Everyday Life* (New Haven, 1987 [1982]), esp. Chapter 8.

26. See Nolan, *Historikerstreit and Social History*. See also Peukert, *Alltag und Barbarei*. On the writing of separate histories see Diner, *Aporia and Apology*.

27. Kaes, *From Heimat to Hitler*, pp. 163–92.

28. This is most strongly put by Broszat in the exchange with Friedlander, and now in Mayer, *Memory and History*, and more subtly also in Maier, *A Surfeit of Memory?*; and Kershaw, *Nazi Dictatorship*, esp. p. 80. See further in Dawidowicz, *Holocaust and the Historians*, esp. pp. 43–67; and Bauer, *Holocaust in Historical Perspective*, esp. pp. 30–49.

29. Aly/Heim, *Vordenker der Vernichtung*; and idem., "Deutsche Herrschaft 'im Osten': Bevölkerungspolitik und Völkermord," in *Erobern und Vernichten*, ed. P. Jahn and R. Rürup (Berlin, 1991), pp. 84–105; Zitelmann, *Hitler*; and Prinz/Zitelmann, *Nationalsozialismus*.

30. See mainly Dahrendorf, *Society and Democracy*; and Schoenbaum, *Hitler's Social Revolution*. Modernization is no longer viewed positively *as such* by the younger German generation; but as regards Nazism, it is represented as a non-ideological, progressive development.

31. See M. Broszat, K.-D. Henke and H. Woller, *Von Stalingrad zur Währungsreform. Zur Sozialgeschichte des Umbruchs in Deutschland* (Munich, 1988); Graml and Henke, *Nach Hitler*.

32. See Herbert, *Die guten und die schlechten Zeiten*; Niethammer, *"Normalisierung" im Westen*. For the "good years" from the point of view of women see A. K. Einfeldt, "Auskommen—Durchkommen—Weiterkommen. Weibliche Arbeitserfahrungen in der Bergarbeiterkolonie," in Niethammer, *Die Jahre*, pp. 267–96; and J. Stephenson, "'Emancipation' and its Problems: War and Society in Württemberg 1939–45," *EHQ* 17 (1987): 345–65; idem, *The Nazi Organization of Women* (Totowa, 1981). See also T. Mason, "Women in Germany, 1925–40: Family, Welfare and Work," Parts 1–2, *HWJ* 1 (1976): 74–113 and 2 (1976): 5–32; Koonz, *Mothers in the Fatherland*; R. Bridenthal, A. Grossmann, and M. Kaplan (eds.), *When Biology Became Destiny: Women in Weimar and Nazi Germany* (New York, 1984), part 2.

33. See [Bartov, *Murder in Our Midst*], Chapter 5, section I.

34. In this discussion the article by Pierre Nora is often invoked: "Between Memory and History: *Les Lieux de Mémoire*," *Representations* 26 (1989): 7–25. But Nora argues that

traditional memory (as exemplified according to him by the Jews) has been destroyed by modernity, and that this explains the current preoccupation *both* with memory and with history, both in scholarship and in other intellectual and artistic representations. This is not something that can be stopped by scholarly argument; it is a reflection of a certain cultural phase of Western society. In this context, see also J. Le Goff, *Histoire et mémoire*, 2d ed. (Paris, 1988).

35. See, for instance, the novels by Grossman, *See Under: Love*, Dorit Peleg, *Unah* (Tel Aviv, 1988); Omer Bartov, *Petihat Tsir* (Border Patrol) (Tel Aviv, 1988). For the monolithic portrayal, see Mayer, *Memory and History*. For comments on and analysis of the Israeli literary corpus, see S. D. Ezrahi, "Revisioning the Past: The Changing Legacy of the Holocaust in Hebrew Literature," *Salmagundi* (Fall/Winter 1985/86), and *By Words Alone*; and Y. S. Feldman, "Whose Story Is It, Anyway? Ideology and Psychology in the Representation of the Shoah in Israeli Literature," in Friedlander, *Probing the Limits*, pp. 223–39. See also Sivan, *The 1948 Generation*, and citations therein. The debate in Israeli in the 1960s had to do of course with the impact of the Eichmann trial, the first open confrontation of the Israeli public with the Holocaust. See Segev, *The Seventh Million*, pp. 323–66. See also, most recently, Hanoch Bartov, *I am not the Mythological Sabra* (Tel Aviv, 1995).

36. See, e.g., Yehoshua Sobol's play "Ghetto." Another instance of turning anti-semitism on its head is the Israeli film *Avanti Popolo*, where an Egyptian prisoner of war, an actor in civilian life (who is in turned played by an actor speaking Palestinian rather than Egyptian Arabic), recites Shylock's speech to a group of jeering Israeli reservists. See also the film *Behind Bars*, in which Palestinian prisoners in a high-security jail are portrayed as ideologically committed and educated freedom fighters, while the Israeli inmates are criminals. Another example of the mythical Arab and the awakening awareness of Israeli corruption is David Grossman's novel *Chiyuch Hagdi* (The Smile of the Lamb) (Tel Aviv, 1983). See in this context also E. Shprinzak, *Every Man Whatever Is Right In His Own Eyes: Illegalism In Israeli Society* (Tel Aviv, 1986 [Hebrew]).

37. Note the Diaspora museum in Tel-Aviv University (Beit Hatfutsot); the popularity of such authors as Shai Agnon and Beshevis Singer; the novels by Aharon Appelfeld; and works by younger writers trying to imagine a past they had never had (n. 35 above); the popularity of resurrected Yiddish songs, e.g., by the singer Hava Alberstein; recent re-issues and the enthusiastic reception of long-forgotten Jewish "Diaspora" literature, such as David Vogel's *Married Life* (London, 1988), originally published in Hebrew in 1929/30 as *Haye Nisuim*, reissued in Israel in 1986. There also seems to be a growing interest in studying the Yiddish language among Israeli students.

38. While in the past one spoke of an "Israeli culture" or folklore (much of which had been fabricated from foreign influences, such as the *Horrah* dance, which is a combination of Cossack and Beduin *Debka* dance), now the two major ethnic groups, the Ashkenazis and Sepharadis, each pull toward their respective cultures of origin, or at least the memory of what they had been decades ago, accompanied by the more common attraction to American popular culture. The growing popularity of Israeli renderings of Arabic music, on the one hand, and the influence of the new, massive Russian immigration, on the other, have further complicated the cultural scene.

39. As is the hero of Moshe Shamir's novel *Be-mo Yadav: Pirkei Elik* (With His Own Hands: Lessons of Elik) (Merhavya, 1951): "Elik was born from the sea." The hand-

some Sabra, often assuming a Siegfried-like look, is another of those ironies of national fate and literary imagination, whereby the ideal Israeli unburdened himself from the relics of the Diaspora, and yet used as his model the heroic Gentile (and former persecutor), combined with an idealized vision of Biblical figures.

40. The tendency to view the Diaspora with contempt has been replaced by a sense of curiosity, not least due to the fact that while the older generation had attempted to detach itself from its own (or its parents') European past, the younger generation have no direct knowledge of that past, and therefore derive it either from their own imagination or from tales by their grandparents. Thus the generational conflict between children and parents of the previous generation over the ties with the Diaspora has become a much more sentimental (or imaginary) discourse between grandchildren and grandparents, who often are similarly critical of the fabricated Israeli identity created by the middle generation, and express greater sympathy for the supposedly more "authentic" identity of the grandparents. There is here a strange resemblance with similar generational coalitions in Germany, where the grandchildren find it easier to sympathize with the grandparents (active in the Third Reich) than their parents, who had often rejected their own parents and all that they had stood for.

41. On Yom Hashoah Vehagvurah see, inter al., Young, *Texture of Memory*, pp. 263–81.

42. Porat, *The Blue and the Yellow Stars*; Segev, *The Seventh Million*; Shapira, *Land and Power*. One should follow the debates in the media around the publication of such studies, especially Segev's, to understand the immense interest and pain still aroused by this issue. See also Sivan, *The 1948 Generation*.

43. See, e.g., Yahil, *The Holocaust*, p. 379. For a recent investigation of Israeli icons of heroism, see Y. Zerubavel, *Recovered Roots: Collective Memory and the Making of Israeli National Tradition* (Chicago, 1995).

44. Here I refer especially to Yehoshua, *The Wall and the Mountain*, in which he compares the Wailing Wall and Mount Herzl, i.e. the wall of Jewish memory and faith as opposed to the mountain devoted to commemorating Israel's fallen soldiers and named after the visionary of Zionism. The author expresses his preference for the Mountain as embodying both nationalism and statehood and physical resistance to the enemy and rejects the Wall, which symbolizes for him blind belief in God and the helplessness of non-fighting Diaspora Jews. See my review of his book, "The Banality of Normality," and his reply, "In Favor of Answers," both in *Iton 77* 113 (1989): 6–10 (Hebrew).

45. Schleunes, *The Twisted Road*, pp. 192–213, which analyzes the *Haavara* agreement that created the financial incentives for the transfer of some 45,000 German Jews to Palestine by November 1938. The impact of Austrian antisemitism on Theodor Herzl has now been thoroughly documented in J. Kornberg, *Theodor Herzl: From Assimilation to Zionism* (Bloomington, 1993).

46. See note 44, above. Another version of the new Israeli identity was popularized especially in the 1950s by the so called Canaanites (*Kna'anim*), whose ideal combined the (imaginary) noble Arab warrior with the (mythical) Biblical Hebraic hero, postulating thereby total rejection of the intervening two thousand years of Jewish existence in the Diaspora; this in turn had roots in the earlier, pre-state *Hashomer* movement, whose members tried to adopt the perceived warlike virtues of the Beduin (they encountered in Palestine) and the Cossacks (they had left behind in Russia).

47. In this context see also the interesting discussion of the Warsaw memorial in J. E. Young, "Biography of a Memorial Icon: Nathan Rapoport's Warsaw Ghetto Monument," *Representations* 26 (1989): 69–106.

48. Further on memory, myth, and commemoration in Israel, see Sivan, *The 1948 Generation*; also see G. Shaked, *No Other Place: On Literature and Society* (Tel Aviv, 1988 [Hebrew]), a critique of an Israeli literary output that is far less certain about the absence of alternatives. And, most recently, Nurith Gertz, *Captive of a Dream: National Myths In Israeli Culture* (Tel Aviv, 1995 [Hebrew]).

49. This opinion was recently expressed in Maier, *A Surfeit of Memory?* But it is a rather common one.

50. Levi writes in *The Drowned and the Saved* that his book "sets itself a more ambitious goal, to try to answer the most urgent question, the question which torments all those who happen to read our accounts: How much of the concentration camp is dead and will not return . . . ?" (pp. 20–21). In speaking of feelings of guilt and shame, and of the suicides among survivors, he also notes that "there is another, vaster shame, the shame of the world," both as regards the Nazi period and other, more recent slaughters, such as in Cambodia. Significantly, but as we now know following the massacres in Bosnia (and even more recently in Chechniya), erroneously, he believes that mass slaughter is unlikely in the Western world because "the Lagers of World War II are still part of the memory of many, on both the popular and governmental levels, and a sort of immunization defense is at work which amply coincides with the shame of which I have spoken" (pp. 85–87). For Levi's criticism of representations of the Holocaust, see his remarks on Liliana Cavani's "Beautiful and false film," referring to her 1974 *The Night Porter* (p. 48). Améry writes in his 1977 preface to *At the Mind's Limits* that the preceding thirteen years "were not good years. One need only follow the reports from Amnesty International to see that in horror this period matches the worst epoches of a history that is as real as it is inimical to reason. Sometimes it seems as though Hitler has gained a posthumous triumph" (p. xvii). On Celan's unease with the public status achieved by his poem *Todesfuge* in Germany, his despair in the face of accusations by Germans that his poetic rendering of the Holocaust was too elegant and took too much pleasure in art, and his inability to express and communicate the horror, perceived by him as a reflection of the world he no longer could share, see J. Felstiner, "Translating Paul Celan's 'Todesfuge': Rhythm and Repetition as Metaphor," and S. D. Ezrahi, "'The Grave in the Air': Unbound Metaphors in Post-Holocaust Poetry," both in Friedlander, *Probing the Limits*, pp. 240–58, and 259–76 respectively.

51. This of course makes one think of the presumed innocence of the bystanders in the Holocaust, who could also be described as participants, once removed, since passively observing atrocities amounts to complicity. The element of curiosity involved in such passive watching, reflected in much of the documentation of the period, also ties in with our current curiosity in watching either staged horrors or horrific documentaries. See Klee, "The Good Old Days"; and interviews made by Claude Lanzmann in Shoah with Polish peasants living near death camps. See also his book, *Shoah: An Oral History of the Holocaust* (New York, 1985), pp. 24–40.

52. Levi rejects "the term *incommunicability,* so fashionable in the 1970s, first of all because it is a linguistic horror," and finds it "frivolous and irritating," an expression of "mental laziness." He argues that "silence, the absence of signals, is itself a signal, but an ambiguous one, and ambiguity generates anxiety and suspicion." *The Drowned and the Saved*, pp. 88–89.

53. Levi writes: "The worst survived, that is, the fittest; the best all died." Moreover, he stresses: "we, the survivors, are not the true witnesses. . . . We survivors are not only an exiguous but also an anomalous minority: we are those who by their prevarications or abilities or good luck did not touch bottom. Those who did so, those who saw the gorgon, have not returned to tell about it, or have returned mute, but they are the 'Muslims,' the submerged, the complete witnesses, the ones whose deposition would have a general significance." *The Drowned and the Saved*, pp. 83–84. See also [Bartov, *Murder in Our Midst*], Chapter 5, section IV.

54. Levi quotes Cavani as expressing her belief "that in every environment, in every relationship, there is a victim-executioner dynamism more or less clearly expressed and generally lived on an unconscious level." He replies: "I do not know, and it does not much interest me to know, whether in my depths there lurks a murderer, but I do know that I was a guiltless victim and I was not a murderer. I know that murderers existed, not only in Germany, and still exist, retired or on active duty, and that to confuse them with their victims is a moral disease or an aesthetic affectation or a sinister sign of complicity; above all, it is precious service rendered (intentionally or not) to the negators of truth." *The Drowned and the Saved*, pp. 48–49.

55. It is interesting to compare, for instance, Bernardo Bertolucci's *The Conformist* (1970) and István Szabó's *Mephisto* (1981). Whereas the first film creates sympathy with the wretched victim of fascism (who is nevertheless a collaborator and an accomplice to a murder), the second distances itself from the protagonist to a point of creating disgust in the viewer. Moreover, Bertolucci recreates scenes of such aesthetic beauty that even the most horrible events, such as the murder in the forest, retain a dream-like quality in our memory and do not cause anger or revulsion.

56. See Reitz, *Liebe zum Kino*.

57. In Harriet Eder's and Thomas Kufus' 1990 film *Mein Krieg*, for example, we are shown privately filmed scenes from the war with a running commentary by those who had filmed them made to the filmmakers forty or fifty years after the event. See my review in the *AHR* 97/4 (1992): 1155–57.

58. This relates to the revisionist arguments in France that I will refer to in the next section.

59. The constant theme, for instance, in R. Kraemer, *A Girl Whose Name I Fail to Recall: Notes of a Young Girl During the Holocaust* (Tel Aviv, 1992 [Hebrew]). In this context, see also the extraordinary account by H. M. Kovály, *Under a Cruel Star: A Life in Prague, 1941–1968*, 2d ed. (New York, 1989).

60. American undergraduate students participating in my course on the Holocaust tend to find that Levi's *Survival in Auschwitz* gives them "a feel" for what Auschwitz was like, but distinguish between his account and scholarly texts, which they find more objective, and hence more reliable, even if slightly "boring" or "dry." On the American predilection for objectivity in history, see P. Novick, *That Noble Dream: The "Objectivity Question" and the American Historical Profession*, 2d ed. (New York, 1989).

61. One of the two survivors of Chelmno, returning to the site forty years later, says in Lanzmann's film *Shoah*: "It is hard to recognize, but it was here. . . . Yes, this is the place. . . . No one can describe it. . . . And no one can understand it. Even I, here, now . . . I can't believe I am here. No, I just can't believe it." Cited in Friedlander's Introduction to *Probing the Limits*, p. 17. See also B. Lang, "The Representation of Limits," in ibid., pp. 300–317.

62. Broszat, "Plea."

63. See Felstiner, *Translating Paul Celan*, and Ezrahi, *The Grave in the Air*.

64. This is discussed in Felstiner and Ezrahi, ibid.

65. Cited in J. F. Lyotard, *The Differend: Phrases in Dispute* (Minneapolis, 1988), p. 3.

66. Ibid., pp. 3–4.

67. Cited in Friedlander, introduction to *Probing the Limits*, p. 8.

68. See [Bartov, *Murder in Our Midst*], Chapter 5, for a discussion of this book.

69. Cited in Levi, *The Drowned and the Saved*, pp. 11–12.

70. C. Ginzburg, "Just One Witness," in Friedlander, *Probing the Limits*, pp. 82–96.

71. H. White, "Historical Emplotment and the Problem of Truth," ibid., p. 37. See Martin Jay's regret at White's retreat from his more radical relativist position, which he characterizes as "a failure of nerve," in Jay, "Of Plots, Witnesses, and Judgements," ibid., p. 98.

72. White, *The Content of the Form*, p. 76.

73. White writes that "Hillgruber's suggestion for emplotting the story of the defense of the eastern front did not violate any of the conventions governing the writing of professionally respectable narrative history. He simply suggested narrowing the focus to a particular domain of the historical continuum, casting the agents and agencies occupying that scene as characters in a dramatic conflict, and emplotting this drama in terms of the familiar conventions of the genre of tragedy." *Historical Emplotment*, p. 42. That is, this is *also* possible, though we may not *like* it. There is nothing wrong in this emplotment per se. One can emplot the Wehrmacht troops as heroes or as villains, and there is no obvious reason to accept one and object to the other. For a discussion of Hillgruber's book, see [Bartov, *Murder in Our Midst*], Chapter 4.

74. White obviously does not accept the "traditional historical discourse" for which "there is presumed to be a crucial difference between an 'interpretation' of 'the facts' and a 'story' told about them," nor does he see the need for such "notions of a 'real' (as against 'imaginary') story and a 'true' (as against a 'false') story." Ibid., p. 39. Hence, presumably, truth and falsehood are relative: what was true for Höss, commandant of Auschwitz, namely, that the Jews were *Untermenschen*, was not true for Primo Levi. Depending on the circumstances, both could have been right or wrong, and we, as historians, cannot be judges of such moral positions because we too will emplot them according to our own biases. For Nazi emplotment, see M. Broszat (ed.), *Kommandant in Auschwitz: Autobiographische Aufzeichnungen des Rudolf Höss*, 10th ed. (Munich, 1985), by which time the book had sold more than 100,000 copies.

75. White claims that some plot types—e.g., pastoral or comic—are inadmissible. But of course his theory does not provide for criteria of inadmissibility. It seems to me that the "middle voice" he recommends has intrinsic elements of paradox, ambiguity, and irony. But with a kind of sleight of hand he attributes the "middle voice" to Levi, thus linking such elements to a self-critical, reflective moral seriousness. In this sense he wants to retain a margin of uncertainty, but subsumes it as an integral component of self-questioning and self-examination. Put simply, he wants to have it both ways: he tries to remain relativist while claiming moral high ground. It should be added that Nazism has probably been emplotted in all conceivable ways. (One especially controversial representation was provided in Hans Jürgen Syberberg's seven-hour film *Hitler, a Film from Germany* (1977). See also G. Steiner, *The Portage to San Cristòbal of A. H.* (London, 1981)).

76. See discussion of this in P. Haidu, "The Dialectics of Unspeakability: Language, Silence, and the Narratives of Desubjectification," in Friedlander, *Probing the Limits*, pp. 285–86.

77. White and Jay set up a bogey enemy in the form of the naive realism, positivism, and claim for absolute objectivity of the historian, when in fact any historian knows that his or her craft is only the art of the possible. On this, see the brilliant essay by Marc Bloch, *The Historian's Craft* (New York, 1953).

78. As well as of the original story. See R. Akutagawa, *Rashomon, and Other Stories* (Tokyo, 1952).

79. This seems to me the whole thrust of C. R. Browning, "German Memory, Judicial Interrogation, and Historical Reconstruction: Writing Perpetrator History from Postwar Testimony," in Friedlander, *Probing the Limits*, pp. 22–36, and especially of his *Ordinary Men*, where he reconstructs the crime and places the guilt where it belongs, but not without doing his best to explain the motivation and circumstances of the murders. See also [Bartov, *Murder in Our Midst*], Chapter 5.

80. I. Berlin, *Four Essays on Liberty*, 2d ed. (Oxford, 1979), p. 106.

81. See Diner, *Zivilisationsbruch*; also Yerushalmi, *Zakhor*.

82. In this context, see the illuminating remarks in Lang, *Act and Idea*, pp. 234–40.

KENNETH SEESKIN

▣ What Philosophy Can and Cannot Say about Evil

With few exceptions, academic philosophers have had little to say about the Holocaust. There was a time when I considered this outrageous. How could a discipline that examines human values and aspirations ignore one of the most significant, if not *the* most significant, events of the century? We are rightly disdainful of the scientists and professors in Germany who continued their studies amid some of the most fiendish evil ever imagined. How can we criticize them if the present philosophical community sees nothing in the Holocaust worth discussing? Unless we entertain the dubious proposition that philosophy has nothing to do with the historical circumstances in which it is written, we must ask how the events in Germany force a reexamination of philosophical categories.

I say *there was a time* when I considered philosophy's silence outrageous because at present the whole issue seems more complicated than it once did. It is not that I have given up the conviction that philosophy reflects the historical context in which it is written. Nor have I come to doubt that the Holocaust is critical for understanding the history of the twentieth century. But it is one thing to say that an event like the Holocaust demands philosophic reflection and another to identify the philosophic issues it raises.

There is an obvious respect in which genocide and mass murder are beyond the scope of philosophic analysis. As the late Arthur Cohen put it: "There is something in the nature of thought—its patient deliberateness and care for logical order—that is alien to the enormity of the death camps."[1] If, as Cohen and others have argued, reason is overwhelmed by evil on this scale, it is unclear what philosophy can contribute to the discussion. It can clarify terms like *genocide, murder,* or *intention.* For example, unlike mass murder, genocide is directed to a specific group. It seeks the destruction of every member of the group without regard for individual differences. It may be said, therefore, that the "crime" that genocide attempts to punish is not what a person has done but what a person is. How large the group must be for the killing to count as genocide, and whether the group must constitute a biological division, are open to question. I believe, however, that when people ask philosophers to think about the Holocaust, what they want is not sharper-edged concepts. Rather than wishing us to claim that we have a firmer grasp of the categories at our disposal, they want to claim that these categories have somehow broken down. Thus Cohen speaks of a caesura, Emil Fackenheim of a rupture. In both cases, there is an underlying conviction that the philosophic paradigms of the Enlightenment are no longer valid. We cannot talk about reason, history, evil, or the liberal state in the way our forebears did. According to Fackenheim, the Holocaust poses radical "countertestimony" to traditional philosophy.[2] He concludes that "where the Holocaust is, *no* thought can be, and where there is thought it is in flight from the event."[3]

Behind this talk of conceptual breakdown is the assumption that the Holocaust constitutes a unique form of evil and is without precedent in human history. For many writers, uniqueness is the central issue. Affirm it and you force people to take the Holocaust seriously. Deny it and you relegate the Holocaust to the back burners of the modern intellectual's agenda. Unfortunately there are no available criteria for deciding what makes a complex event unique. As Alan Rosenberg has argued, the whole question of uniqueness is a peculiar one.[4] Decisive events like the Peloponnesian War, the Renaissance, or the Protestant Reformation are unique in the sense that they involved specific people acting in unrepeatable circumstances. No one doubts that they changed the course of history.

But any historian will admit that there were precedents and contributing factors. Although they may be unrepeatable in a strict sense, events like these are not anomalous. So if a person were to press us on the question of their uniqueness, the obvious response would be that the question has to be reformulated. To a religious believer, Sinai and Calvary were unique because they involved special cases of divine intervention. In secular events, like the Peloponnesian War, however, the participants are subject to general laws or at least some type of observable regularity. We would therefore have to ask: unique in respect to what?

It is also worth noting that some events that could be called unique do not require categorial revision, for example, the first moon launch. Some events that do require categorial revision are part of recurrent patterns. The massacre of the civilian population of Melos in 416 B.C. exposed the ruthlessness of Athenian imperialism in a shocking way. In one respect, the massacre was unique—it was a turning point in the war and the ultimate expression of Athenian hubris. But to an astute observer, the Melian massacre was the outcome of policies in effect since the time of Pericles. According to Thucydides, the importance of the Melian massacre is not that it was a one-time-only event outside the course of history but exactly the opposite: It is indicative of patterns that will repeat themselves as long as human behavior remains the same.

What all of this goes to show is that uniqueness and importance are not the same—at least not if uniqueness means that nothing comparable to the event has ever happened before. On the other hand, if uniqueness means that an event is strange or alien, that it pushes our sensibilities to the limits, then a unique event can be an important one. In this sense, we can say, with Berel Lang, that genocide is *always* unique—even if there have been or could be multiple instances.[5] It is unique because we cannot respond to it in the way we respond to murder, lying, promise breaking, or other normal varieties of evil. I do not think people have paid sufficient attention to this distinction; as a result, much of what is said about the uniqueness of the Holocaust is beside the point. Genocide poses philosophic questions. The frequency with which it occurs does not. The questions posed by genocide amount to this, Is there a rational way of responding to the *irrational*? Can we devise a strategy for preventing future occurrences or must we simply recoil in horror? Notice, however, that these questions are practical in nature. They do not call for another attempt at theodicy, for a general account of why people are attracted to the demonic, or for a rupture of the philosophic paradigms we inherit from the Enlightenment. Some authors assume that unless one calls for sweeping revision of our moral vocabulary, one is not taking the six million deaths seriously. I believe this is a terrible mistake.

THE LIMITS OF MORAL DISCOURSE

I repeat: The Holocaust is unique in the sense that thought is overwhelmed by evil on this scale. But for precisely that reason, the practice of comparing the Holocaust to other instances of mass murder is suspect. Mass murder is always overwhelming. We can compare the historical context in which one instance of it occurs to the contexts in which other instances occur. But can we say that one instance is unique in respect to evil—that it is somehow worse than the others?

I submit that the answer is no. Moral reason is not infinitely extendible. It reaches a threshold at which comparisons of this sort either make no sense or are reprehensible in their own right. In the *Nicomachean Ethics* (7.5), Aristotle refers to incomprehensible evil as *bestiality* and claims it falls beyond the limit of vice or any other human shortcoming. To continue with his insight, we can distinguish murder from manslaughter, and murder without remorse from murder simpliciter; but when murder is indiscriminate, when it takes on the dimensions of a sacrament, a work of art, or a national purpose, our capacity to understand, to see nuances, breaks down. Unless we adopt the crudest sort of utilitarianism and look to body count or units of pain, the Western moral tradition offers no principle according to which "better" or "worse" have any meaning here. The loss of even one innocent life is outrageous. It does not follow, however, that lives are additive. Hitler's actions would be no more bearable if he had killed "only" five million Jews rather than six. By the same token, I do not think anything would be changed if he had killed his victims with swords or permitted some to live if they espoused Nazism. There would still be a Holocaust to talk about and a debate over its implications.

Let me be more specific, even graphic. What follows are three accounts of mass murder. The historical contexts in which they occur are quite different. The issue is whether one raises moral questions not raised by the others. The first is Thucydides' account of the massacre at Mycalessus. In reading it, keep in mind that the invaders were never in physical danger and that taking the town served no military objective.[6]

> The night he [Diitrephes] passed unobserved near the temple of Hermes, not quite two miles from Mycalessus, and at daybreak assaulted and took the town, which is not a large one; the inhabitants being off their guard and not expecting that any one would ever come up so far from the sea to molest them, the wall too being weak, and in some places having tumbled down, while in others it had not been built to any height, and the gates also being left open through their feeling of security. The Thracians bursting into Mycalessus scaled the houses and temples, and butchered the inhabitants, sparing neither youth or age, but killing all they fell in with, one after the other, children and women, and even beasts of burden, and whatever other living creatures they saw; the Thracian race, like the bloodiest of the barbarians, being ever most so when it has nothing to fear. Everywhere confusion reigned and death in all its shapes; and in particular they attacked a boys' school, the largest that there was in the place, into which the children had just gone, and massacred them all.) In short, the disaster falling upon the whole town was unsurpassed in magnitude, and unapproached by any in suddenness and in horror.

The second is taken from *The Brothers Karamazov* by Dostoevsky.[7]

"By the way, a Bulgarian I met lately in Moscow," Ivan went on, seeming not to hear his brother's words, "told me about the crimes committed by Turks and Circassians in all parts of Bulgaria through fear of a general rising of the Slavs. They burn villages, murder, outrage women and children, they nail their prisoners by the ears to the fences, leave them so till morning, and in the morning they hang them all—all sorts of things you can't imagine. People talk sometimes of bestial cruelty, but that's a great injustice and insult to the beasts; a beast can never be so cruel as a man, so artistically cruel. The tiger only tears and gnaws, that's all he can do. He would never think of nailing people by the ears; even if he were able to do it. These Turks took pleasure in torturing children too, cutting the unborn child from the mother's womb, and tossing babies up in the air and catching them on the points of their bayonets before their mother's eyes. Doing it before the mother's eyes was what gave zest to the amusement. Here is another scene that I thought very interesting. Imagine a trembling mother with her baby in her arms, a circle of invading Turks around her. They've planned a diversion; they pet the baby, laugh to make it laugh. They succeed, the baby laughs. At that moment a Turk points a pistol four inches from the baby's face. The baby laughs with glee, holds out its little hands to the pistol, and he pulls the trigger in the baby's face and blows out its brains. Artistic, wasn't it? By the way, Turks are particularly fond of sweet things, they say."

The third is an eyewitness account of a Polish guard at Auschwitz and is part of the official record of the Nuremberg trials.[8]

WITNESS: ... women carrying children were [always] sent with them to the crematorium. [Children were of no labor value so they were killed. The mothers were sent along, too, because separation might lead to panic, hysteria—which might slow up the destruction process, and this could not be afforded. It was simpler to condemn the mothers too and keep things quiet and smooth.] The children were then torn from their parents outside the crematorium and sent to the gas chambers separately. [At that point, crowding more people into the gas chambers became the most urgent consideration. Separating meant that more children could be packed in separately, or they could be thrown in over the heads of adults once the chamber was packed.] When the extermination of the Jews in the gas chambers was at its height, orders were issued that children were to be thrown straight into the crematorium furnaces, or into a pit near the crematorium without being gassed first.

SMIRNOV: (Russian prosecutor): How am I to understand this? Did they throw them into the fire alive, or did they kill them first?

WITNESS: They threw them in alive. Their screams could be heard at the camp. It is difficult to say how many children were destroyed this way.

SMIRNOV: Why did they do this?

WITNESS: It's very difficult to say. We don't know whether they wanted to economize on gas, or if it was because there was not enough room in the gas chambers.

Clearly there are historical differences between these events. My point is that there are no grounds for making moral comparisons. In a recent article, the historian Charles S. Maier tells us that numbers *are* important.[9] This remark occurs in a context in which Hitler is compared to Stalin and the Khmer Rouge. The question is whether extermination based on class is fundamentally different from extermination based on race. When confronted by the fact that Stalin killed several times more than Hitler, and by his own criterion should be a "worse" case of evil, Maier quotes Raymond Aron as follows: "Hostility based on the class struggle has taken on no less extreme or monstrous forms than that based on the incompatibility of race. . . . But if we wish to 'save the concepts,' there is a difference between a philosophy whose logic is monstrous, and one which can be given a monstrous interpretation." I do not know what "concept" is being saved or what relevant difference there is between a monstrous philosophy and a monstrous interpretation of an otherwise acceptable philosophy. There is no question that extermination based on class has often taken on racial overtones so that, in the last analysis, it is difficult to say whether we have the theory or its interpretation. Racial murder is confined to a specific group and is therefore easier to administer than an effort to kill the entire bourgeoisie. Yet why should that make a difference? Indeed, why did this discussion ever get started? When one considers the moral implications of such comparisons and recognizes the awful details of what is involved in exterminating any group of people, the mind simply boggles.

In this respect, I am in agreement with Elie Wiesel: Tragedies do not cancel each other out as they succeed one another.[10] The evil of the Holocaust does not make the massacre of Bulgarians any less detestable or any more understandable. Nor does the evil of the Bulgarian massacre make the Holocaust any less important from a philosophic standpoint. To the degree that Jewish tradition is relevant, radical evil in the person of Amalek has been with us since the Exodus and has reared its ugly head in century after century. If what people expect from philosophers is a way of distinguishing one encounter from another, then disappointment is inevitable. This does not mean that, to use Maier's term, I am "relativizing" the Holocaust. On the contrary, extermination based on race, class, or just plain fun is still extermination. It is supremely evil. If relativizing the moral depravity of the Nazis is objectionable—and it is—so is relativizing the depravity of Stalin, the Khmer Rouge, and anyone else who undertakes the systematic murder of innocent human life.

EVIL AND EVILDOERS

It will be objected that we can compare instances of mass murder by considering the intentions of the perpetrators. Intentionality is a moral category, and if there are important differences in what the murderers are trying to do, there are grounds for making philosophic distinctions. On this issue, there is important work by Steven Katz arguing that the intentionality of the Nazis has no precedent in human history, that the Holocaust was, indeed, a *novum*.[11] To establish the unique intentionality of Nazi genocide, he compares the policies and official propaganda of the Nazis to those of other groups. This strategy is informative up to a point. As one would imagine, the Nazis' justification for killing Jews was based on a particular ideology. For all I know, it was unprecedented. But propaganda is not always a reliable way of establishing intentionality. Sometimes propaganda is nothing but hyperbole, sometimes it obscures well-established facts. In the case of Hitler, there is an extended debate on when a consistent policy of extermination was formulated, whether it was the result of a single set of factors, and whether there was an unbroken continuity from Hitler's anti-Semitism to the construction of the gas chambers.[12] I refer to this debate not to pronounce on the historical evidence but to point out that however difficult it may be to ascribe intentionality to a single agent, these problems are nothing compared to those of ascribing it to an entire nation.

We do talk about the will of the German people or their national purpose. There is, however, a great risk in talking about *the* intentionality of the Holocaust—as if it were a single act or isolatable phenomenon. Did the bureaucrats who ordered the gas have the same intention as the people who turned it on? Did either have the same intention as the officers who designed ingenious methods of torture, or the citizens who looked the other way? As long as intentionality is the deciding factor, there is no reason why the circle should not include people in occupied countries who did not participate in the extermination of Jews but wished they could—or those in previous ages who tried to exterminate the Jews but lacked the physical means. All would agree that Jews should be disposed of. But can we really speak of a single intention?

For my part, the horror of the Nazi death machine does not become visible until we move from intention to action. We can talk all about abstractions like, "All Jews should be exterminated"—but there is a gap between proposing such a policy and the day-to-day activity of taking human life. We are told that even virulent anti-Semites became ill upon seeing the piles of charred bodies. It is the people who actually turned on the gas, killed the babies, and operated the crematoria who push our moral sensibilities to the limit. But when we move from intention to action, the claim of unprecedented evil weakens. A case in point is the fate of Gypsies. We can accept the arguments that show that Nazi policy regarding Gypsies did not call for total extermination. Some Gypsies were permitted to live. Yet surely the action of killing the hundreds of thousands slated for death is as loathsome and as incomprehensible as that of killing Jews. The same can be said for homosexuals, Marxists, intellectuals, "decadent" artists, and all other enemies of the Reich. Whether their deaths fall within the technical meaning of *genocide* is irrelevant. Moral reason shudders the second killing of this sort begins.

To his credit, Katz tries to avoid ethical or theological conclusions. He admits that numbers alone do not tell the full story. In his survey of mass murder, he refrains from judgments of better or worse. Unlike Maier and Aron, he does not get tangled in distinctions between an ideology and its interpretation. His thesis is simply that the uniqueness of the Holocaust consists in its "genocidal intent against the Jewish people." The question is whether he can employ a concept like *genocidal intent* without falling victim to moral comparisons he does not want to make. If the Nazi extermination of Jews is the first and only case of genocidal intent in history, how can we not conclude that it unleashed a new and previously unimagined form of evil? One cannot refer to a term like *genocidal intent* without expecting the audience to draw moral inferences for itself—particularly when writing on the Holocaust. So while Katz is anxious to stay clear of these inferences, his language gives him away. This is more than a verbal dispute. Even if Katz were to replace a charged word like *intentionality* with a neutral one like *policy*, the same problems would arise. Nazi policy regarding the Jews may have no precedent in history, but it is the evil of carrying out that policy that matters. And if we look at the action of killing Jews, it is neither better nor worse than that of killing other peoples. In fact, it is neither better nor worse than the actions described by Thucydides and Dostoevsky. All of these actions are unique in the sense of being radically alien.

UNIQUENESS AND IMPORTANCE

Many people will balk at this conclusion and regard it as a form of heresy. They are adamant that the Holocaust not be seen as "just another massacre." But the powerful emotions that accompany this issue suggest that for many people uniqueness is a cover for importance. The extermination of six million Jews can never be forgotten and demands some kind of adequate response. It will not do to look at the smokestacks or mass graves and return to business as usual. The Holocaust must be given the same attention we give events like the French Revolution or the First World War.

Nowhere is this more evident than in the work of Lucy Dawidowicz. In the foreword to *The Holocaust and the Historians*, she explains how she came to write the book:

> While I was working on *The War against the Jews 1933–1945* and *A Holocaust Reader*, I was dismayed to find how inadequately the murder of the European Jews had been recorded in history books. I became haunted by the fear that the history of 6 million murdered Jews would vanish from the earth as they themselves and their civilization had vanished.[13]

And a legitimate fear it was. The resulting study is a shocking account of how contemporary historians have ignored, distorted, or undercut an event of such magnitude. Some books on the history of Europe do not mention it at all, some mention it only in passing, some discuss Nazi genocide without mentioning that it was directed against the Jews, some suggest, in not very subtle ways, that the Jews were responsible for their own fate. The reasons are various but they boil down to two factors: (1) in the Eastern bloc, state-sponsored anti-Semitism is so prevalent that the facts of Jewish suffering under Hitler must be covered up or presented in such a way that the Jews are transformed from victims to victimizers; (2) in the West, there seems to be an unwritten rule according to which anti-Semitism is a Jewish problem best left to Jewish authors. The result is that research on the Holocaust is sketchy and heavily biased. Although Dawidowicz's book was published in 1981, four years before Reagan visited Bitburg cemetery, the rise of revisionist history in Germany underscores her point.

Yet her way of arguing for more research and greater rigor is to insist on the lack of historical precedent, and her way of arguing for that is to fall back on the notion of intention.[14] Here she opens herself to the same problems that beset Katz. Her case would be strengthened if she put uniqueness aside. To return to Thucydides, an event may be important because it reveals tendencies in human behavior that were always present but never displayed in such a stark way. To the degree that the Holocaust reveals such tendencies and forces us to look at history from the standpoint of the victim, it would constitute a turning point. Serious reflection on it would affect our understanding not only of the events of 1933–45 but of prior and subsequent events as well. We could no longer look at centuries of officially sponsored anti-Semitism in Europe without seeing them as a contributing factor nor discuss absolute forms of government without looking into the fate of "undesirables." Put otherwise, the importance of the Holocaust would derive from the fact that it is *not* an anomaly. That is why no competent historian can ignore it.

If, on the other hand, historians have ignored the concentration camps, there is reason to suspect they have ignored other atrocities as well—or used them for blatantly political purposes. How extensive is our evidence on the Gulag or the Khmer Rouge? I suspect that like our evidence on the Holocaust, it is sketchy. The feeling that the Holocaust not become "just another massacre" is legitimate in the sense that we cannot shrug our shoulders at the loss of six million people. To the degree that it is a turning point, we can no longer regard it or other events like it as aberrations—no matter how unpleasant it is to discuss them nor how damaging to one's cherished ideology. History must reflect the dark side of human behavior as well as its high spots. Notice, however, that all of this can be said, and the importance of the Holocaust affirmed, without claiming that nothing like it happened before.

CONSEQUENCES AND IMPLICATIONS

If historical studies on the Holocaust are rare, then, in the words of Dawidowicz, "its theological implications have proliferated." The event is so wrenching and leaves such an indelible impression on one's memory that any number of people have tried to appropriate it. The Holocaust refutes moral relativism by showing that at least one judgment is absolute. The Holocaust refutes moral absolutism by showing what can happen when people do not question orders. The Holocaust shows that the traditional understanding of God is bankrupt. The Holocaust shows that the traditional understanding of God is needed now more than ever before. The Holocaust shows that the theory of the liberal state is unacceptable because it has nothing to guarantee that such a catastrophe will not be repeated. The Holocaust shows that the absolute state is an abomination. The Holocaust shows that many of the dominant notions of rationality are false. The Holocaust shows that irrationality is too dangerous to contemplate. The Holocaust reveals the inherent evil in modernism, capitalism, fascism, nationalism, industrial technology, or refutes the theories of Hegel, Nietzsche, and Heidegger. The Holocaust proves once and for all the truth of Zionism, atheism, socialism, or liberal democracy.

Enough. People predisposed to anti-Semitism still find ways to hate and oppress Jews. Mass murder is still an option for world governments. Those who are suspicious of science, modernity, and technological progress would be so even if the Holocaust had never occurred. Those who are committed to the ideals of the Enlightenment and the theory of the liberal state will see in the Holocaust another reason for affirming them. It is only by putting our faith in these ideals that we have any chance of avoiding another catastrophe. Those who think the Holocaust proves the futility of capitalist production have said this about a thousand and one other things. To see how easily the Holocaust can be appropriated by people of all descriptions, one has only to consider the title of Andreas Hillgruber's book *Two Sorts of Destruction: Shattering of the German Reich and the End of European Jewry*. This work, which transforms victimizers into victims, is a good example of the revisionist history now popular with conservative movements in Germany.[15] It is, in fact, nothing but the mirror image of the Marxist interpretation which cites Jewish compliance with the Nazis to transform victims into victimizers. According to Saul Friedlander: "Three decades have increased our knowledge of the events as such, but not our understanding of them. There is no clearer perspective today, no deeper comprehension than immediately after the war."[16]

Even the people arguing for conceptual upheaval have reached a stalemate, as evidenced by Fackenheim's *To Mend the World*. Having mantained for hundreds of pages that the Holocaust constitutes a rupture in the fabric of rationality and a break with traditional philosophy, he finds near the end of the book that he must invoke the very concepts he earlier rejected in order to make sense of the heroism of concentration camp victims, the idea that resistance to evil is an ontological category, and the faith that the world can, in fact, be mended. By his own admission, he is faced with the dilemma that he can neither accept the traditional categories nor get along without them.[17] If we accept them, there is no rupture; if we get along without them, there is no repair. According to Fackenheim, there is little choice but to dwell between the extremes of this dilemma and endure the tension to which it gives rise.

My own suspicion is that the Holocaust leaves much of traditional philosophy intact. Even if Cohen is right, and the enormity of the death camps is alien to the deliberateness of philosophic reflection, the traditional philosopher still has a reply: Our inability to appropriate evil of this magnitude does not mean there is something wrong with our normal categories. We can still talk about freedom, virtue, and rationality even though there are people whose actions put them outside the boundaries of these determinations. If the traditional philosophers are right, we *have* to talk about freedom, virtue, and rationality or we will have no grounds for saying why events like the Holocaust terrify us. Try reading the historical passages cited above without thinking about the dignity of human life.

It is no accident, therefore, that Fackenheim cannot get along without the conceptual machinery he earlier repudiated. The old categories are still adequate for the situations they were meant to describe. They tell us what sort of actions can be praised or blamed and for what reasons. They offer principles on the basis of which one can make rational decisions. The fact that they cannot describe the universe of the mass murderer or enable us to understand why he does what he does does not mean that the categories themselves are at fault. If there were categories to explain this universe, if we could understand what makes people throw babies into a fire, then the Holocaust would no longer be alien. Thought would have a purchase on it. From a moral perspective, this is an impossibility. We *ought* to be overwhelmed by evil on this scale. If so, the old categories do exactly what we want them to: permit us to be rational when rationality is indicated and prevent us from thinking we understand what is too horrible to contemplate. There is, I submit, no "countertestimony" to them.

On the other hand, the *existence* of something that the old categories cannot explain may be philosophically significant. If we cannot comprehend evil on this scale, if mass murder is so alien that our mind boggles, then there are things that reason cannot penetrate, things that will remain forever absurd. These things are not supersensible realities or secrets of nature; they are human actions. The human mind can create a world that is orderly and efficient but irredeemably evil. Is this not a sufficient ground for revision?

In one respect, the answer is yes. According to the Neo-Platonic tradition, evil has no reality of its own: it is a lack or privation of goodness. On this view, it is impossible to have order where goodness is lacking. A completely evil society would soon destroy itself. If this tradition is wrong about the metaphysical status of evil, it is importantly right about the epistemological. Irredeemable evil may exist, but it is not comprehensible. We cannot compare one instance to another. We do not know why people are attracted to it, let alone a whole nation of people. To the degree that there is nothing about it of which we can approve, there is nothing about it that we can understand.

Kant defines the ultimate evil as a case where a rational agent chooses to undermine the grounds of rationality.[18] But this evil, which he terms *radical*, is at bottom a mystery. Unlike the Neo-Platonists, Kant does not deny its existence; in fact, he emphasizes how prevalent it is. But he insists that no explanation of it will ever be forthcoming. If so, we cannot use evil as the foundation of a world view. Unlike the Exodus from Egypt, the Renaissance, or the French Revolution, the Holocaust is not a formative event. It does not disclose a new set of values or give rise to a new set of aspirations. The only thing it "reveals" is its own radical negativity, which is to say that it does not reveal anything. It does not follow that historians are justified in ignoring it. The point is that we cannot expect new philosophic paradigms to emerge as a result. Once we admit the incomprehensibility of this kind of evil, there is little we can do except turn to the question of how to oppose it—a point that Fackenheim concedes as one of the horns of his dilemma.

The question then becomes, How can reason oppose something it cannot understand? Can we forgive mass murder? Should we extend legal protections to those who advocate it? Can we ally ourselves with someone who is considering it? Should we risk everything to prevent it? In true philosophic fashion, I have raised questions but not answered them. My point is that *these* are the questions we should be asking, not the ones that require comparisons between one atrocity and another. If we are going to take the Holocaust seriously, at least let us do so in a way that informs the choices we have to make in the future. We can then hope that the relative silence that has characterized the philosophic community up till now will give way to open discussion.

NOTES

1. Arthur A. Cohen, *The Tremendum* (New York: Crossroad, 1981), p. 1. The claim of incomprehensibility is common in the literature. It is challenged by Dan Magurshak in "The 'Incomprehensibility' of the Holocaust: Tightening up Some Loose Usage," *Judaism* 29 (1980): 233–42. Space limitations prevent me from taking up the claim of incomprehensibility in greater detail. I address this issue in an as yet unpublished paper entitled, "Coming to Terms with Failure: A Philosophic Dilemma."

2. Emil L. Fackenheim, *To Mend the World: Foundations of Future Jewish Thought* (New York: Schocken, 1982), p. 13.

3. Ibid., p. 200.

4. Alan Rosenberg, "Was the Holocaust Unique? A Peculiar Question?" in Isidor Wallimann and Michael Dobkowski, eds., *Genocide and the Modern World: Ideology and Case Studies of Mass Death* (Westport, Conn.: Greenwood Press, 1987), pp. 145–61.

5. Berel Lang, "The Concept of Genocide," *Philosophical Forum* 16 (1984–85): 1–18.

6. Thucydides, *The Peloponnesian War*, trans. Crawley (New York: Random House, 1951), 6.21.29.

7. Feodor Dostoevsky, *The Brothers Karamazov*, trans. Constance Garnett (New York: Random House, 1950), p. 283.

8. Taken from Irving Greenberg, "Cloud of Smoke, Pillar of Fire: Judaism, Christianity, and Modernity after the Holocaust," in *Auschwitz: Beginning of a New Era? Reflections on the Holocaust*, ed. Eva Fleischner (New York: KTAV, 1977), pp. 9–10.

9. Charles S. Maier, "Immoral Equivalence," *New Republic*, December 1, 1986, pp. 36–41.

10. Elie Wiesel, "Job: Our Contemporary," in *Messengers of God* (New York: Random House, 1976), p. 221.

11. Steven T. Katz, "The 'Unique' Intentionality of the Holocaust," in *Post Holocaust Dialogues* (New York: New York University Press, 1983), pp. 287–317.

12. For a discussion of this issue, see Michael R. Marrus, "The History of the Holocaust: A Survey of Recent Literature," *Journal of Modern History* 59 (1987): 114–60.

13. Lucy S. Dawidowicz, *The Holocaust and the Historians* (Cambridge, Mass.: Harvard University Press, 1981), p. 1.

14. Ibid., p. 14.

15. For further comment, see Jürgen Habermas, "Defusing the Past: A Politico-Cultural Tract," in *Bitburg in Moral and Political Perspective*, ed. Geoffrey Hartmann (Bloomington: Indiana University Press, 1986), pp. 43–49.

16. Saul Friedlander, "Some Aspects of the Historical Significance of the Holocaust," *Jerusalem Quarterly* 1 (1976): 137.

17. Fackenheim, *To Mend the World*, pp. 309–10.

18. Immanuel Kant, *Religion within the Limits of Reason Alone*, trans. with introduction and notes by T. H. Greene and H. H. Hudson (1934; rpt. New York: Harper & Row, 1960), pp. 20, 25, 27–29. Note Kant's conclusion (p. 38): "But the rational origin of this perversion of our will whereby it makes lower incentives supreme among its maxims, that is, of the propensity to evil, remains inscrutable to us."

KENNETH SEESKIN

▣ Coming to Terms with Failure

A Philosophical Dilemma

... We are no closer to answering the question of *why* evil occurs than we were in the time of Plato. Let me qualify this by saying that we are no closer to explaining how lucid, stable, and well-integrated personalities can choose to subvert the moral law. The reason is not that the various attempts to understand evil have been halfhearted. It is rather that this sort of evil cannot be incorporated into rational structures. To return to the character of Iago, one of the distinguishing features of the demonic is that it resists our efforts to understand it. The final words he speaks to Othello are an ultimate act of defiance. We can explain evil as ignorance, but the cost of doing so is that we assume the evildoer is pursuing the same ends we are. To the person who scoffs at those ends, we have nothing to say. Or we can explain evil as a self-originating act. But then we concede Iago's point: the decision to subvert the moral law is essentially surd. Between the conditions that permitted extermination and extermination itself, there is, as Claude Lanzmann remarked, a hiatus or abyss. It is that abyss which prevents us from saying we understand what happened in the Holocaust.

The understanding I speak of is philosophical. To say that the enactment of the Final Solution is incomprehensible is not to deny that historians can keep accurate records or that jurists can find cause for assessing blame. We have much to learn about the events that led from traditional hatred of Jews to the construction of gas chambers. What I am denying is that we will have a general theory to answer the questions we most want to ask. How could people with outward signs of rationality drive the trains or drop the crystals into the gas chambers? How could millions of other people look on as they did so? We want to probe the psyche of the perpetrators and claim we understand the logic of genocide. I submit, however, that all of the film clips, interviews, personal accounts, and philosophical reflections have not made that logic any more comprehensible. The universe they describe is rule-governed and internally consistent.[1] But it is a universe without redeeming value, a universe whose existence does not make it any more accessible.

It will be objected that the comparison between Iago and the Nazis is instructive only to a point. If there is no explanation of why an agent chooses to subvert morality and revel in human degradation, then the Holocaust is not the only event for which the philosopher must plead ignorance. Put otherwise, if there is no explanation for Iago's activity, there is no explanation for the activities of any psychopathic criminal. But then there is nothing distinctive about the Holocaust—at least not from a philosophical perspective. Of course, we cannot explain how people with outward signs of rationality could plan and execute the Final Solution. Still, if Kant is right, we cannot explain many of the brutal crimes reported in the daily newspaper, either. From Kant's perspective, the problem is not changed by increase in size. In one case, we have a brutal murder committed by a seemingly rational person; in the other, a nation has chosen to put a *group* of murderers in power and assist them with their work. Kant would argue, however, that philosophy is as incapable of explaining one as it is of explaining the other. So the people who maintain that the Holocaust is at bottom unintelligible do not establish that it is unique. There may be a thousand other events in history for which the claim of unintelligibility can be made. Although they may not be as comprehensive as the Final Solution, they, too, defy understanding. It is like the discovery of surd numbers. There was a great upheaval when the first one was found; but eventually mathematicians came to see that there were many others.

Needless to say, there is long and heated debate on the uniqueness of the Holocaust. It should be understood that I am not here taking sides in that debate. The immediate conditions that led to the death of the 6 million may have no historical precedent. Nazi ideology may be without equal in depravity. There may be no other case in which demonic forces took hold of an entire nation. My argument is simply this: if it is unique, it is not its unintelligibility that makes it so. Iago's actions are unintelligible, as well. And even though there is a world of difference between the plot to humiliate Othello and the attempt to destroy European Jewry, Iago is not any easier to understand when we point out those differences.

It may be said, therefore, that the person writing on the Holocaust confronts the unintelligible on a grand scale. Here it is realized not in the person of a disgruntled lieutenant, but in the national will. But the problem of writing about the Holocaust remains. If we can never understand it, we are back to the same dilemma: either (1) silence or (2) another attempt to complete an impossible task.

We may regret that the majority of philosophers have chosen silence, but their decision is not irrational. The history of philosophy is laden with examples of people extending human reason beyond its limits. The notion that there *are* limits that can be formulated in a precise way is one of the insights we inherit from the Enlightenment. To some philosophers, intellectual limits are like forbidden fruit. Once a person recognizes them, there is an immediate urge to ask about the territory that lies beyond. But, strong as that urge might be, a critical philosopher has to resist it. Having questioned Socrates' account of evil, we can agree with him on this much: there is an obligation to admit what we do not know. In fact, the recognition that there is something we do not know is itself a philosophical achievement.

On the other hand, if there is an obligation to admit what we do not know, there is an equally strong obligation not to remain silent in the face of mass murder. Some issues loom so large in the minds of modern intellectuals that a discipline such as philosophy cannot ignore them without running the risk of marginalization. That is, it cannot ignore them and still claim to provide a global perspective on culture. If the Holocaust has become an important issue for historians, theologians, filmmakers, novelists, and literary critics, then silence on the part of philosophers would indicate that the discipline has relinquished its position as cultural overseer. In many instances, this is exactly what has happened. According to Richard Rorty, people still believe it would be a good idea to have a view of how different parts of culture "hang together."[2] But, he continues, few people in this century have turned to philosophy to provide one. The Holocaust is no exception.

It seems that the philosopher's dilemma resolves itself into a choice between intellectual dishonesty, on the one hand, and marginalization, on the other. I suggest that the only exit from this dilemma is to adopt the Kantian strategy of shifting the focus from theory to practice. The goal of the philosopher writing about the Holocaust is not to probe the psyche of a concentration camp guard and say what makes it tick. It is to offer a program by which we can oppose the concentration camp guard and everything he stands for. This move is already apparent in the work of Emil Fackenheim. At a crucial place in *To Mend the World*, he writes: "The truth is that to grasp the Holocaust whole-of-horror is not to comprehend or transcend it, but rather *to say no to it, or resist it.*"[3]

The greatness of Fackenheim is, as his critic Jacob Neusner once remarked, that he discusses the Holocaust in such a way that theodicy is not the issue.[4] Unanswerable questions about God are ignored in favor of more pointed questions about humans. But here, too, Fackenheim knows when reason has met its limits. The real question is not why it happened, but what we do after we have seen what happened. This is not to say that Fackenheim is entirely successful. There are well-known problems associated with the 614th Commandment, Fackenheim's position on the State of Israel, and the claim that resistance to evil is an ontological category. The problem is that Fackenheim's shift from theory to practice is not as clean as we might like, so that often he avoids one dilemma only to find himself faced with another.[5] But that is a subject for another occasion. The basic insight—that we must try not to comprehend, but to resist—is sound.

On the question of writing, this insight implies a second one: writing itself can be an act of resistance. The Holocaust is not like the issues one finds in an introductory textbook on philosophy. It does not call for sharper-edged concepts or more elegantly formulated axioms. The person who discusses the meaning and implications of evil on this scale has one overriding concern: to bring the world to its senses. The hope is that having shown people the destructive potential of the human mind, the philosopher can set a course for a world in which such potential will never again be realized. If so, the philosophical implications of the Holocaust are normative. The task is to defend the values that the Nazis denied their victims—to explain what respect for human life requires of us. It should be said that this project, too, involves the possibility of failure. Pol Pot and the Gulag are evidence enough that it is unfinished.

The point is, however, that in this case, failure is not inevitable. Unlike the task of pushing the rock up the hill, that of bringing the world to its senses has a chance of success. To the degree that it does, the predicament of the philosopher writing about the Holocaust is not tragic, but prophetic—the correct analogue is not Sisyphus but Jeremiah. The difference is that if Jeremiah used a vision of the future to make his point, the philosopher writing about the Holocaust uses a vision of the past. Still, their functions are the same. Both have looked into a bottomless pit and returned with a call to action. The responsibility of the philosopher is to be specific about what such action requires. Unless we recognize this, the writing we produce will be an exercise in futility. If I am right, the author confronting an incomprehensible subject can do more than point out its incomprehensibility. Having looked into the bottomless pit, it is the job of such an author to lead us out of it.

NOTES

1. On the Nazi "logic of destruction," see Emil Fackenheim, *To Mend the World* (New York: Schocken Book 1982), pp. 130–131, 206–215.

2. Richard Rorty, *Consequences of Pragmatism* (Minneapolis: University of Minnesota Press, 1982), pp. 168–169.

3. Fackenheim, *To Mend the World*, p. 239.

4. Jacob Neusner, "The Implications of the Holocaust," in Neusner, ed., *Understanding Jewish Theology* (New York: KTAV, 1973), p. 187.

5. See the dilemma into which Fackenheim's argument (*To Mend the World*) forces him at p. 309ff.

MICHAEL ANDRÉ BERNSTEIN

◼ Narrating the Shoah

... In spite of the appeal of ... a principled silence, I became increasingly convinced that categorically refusing to represent the Shoah in fiction is a far more menacing position. On one level, I found myself resistant to the idea that anyone, whether a survivor of the camps or not, should undertake to speak for the whole category of Hitler's victims and generalize a set of principles, whether ethical, religious, or aesthetic, on their behalf. Such a scruple troubled me not only with regard to Adorno's formulation, but still more forcefully with Emil Fackenheim's attempt to derive a new, 614th commandment for contemporary Jewry that takes account of its situation after the genocide. In the original wording of his 614th commandment, Fackenheim, perhaps the most distinguished philosopher of the Shoah, proclaims, *"The authentic Jew of today is forbidden to hand Hitler yet another, posthumous victory."*[1] To the scarcely disguised coerciveness of Fackenheim's taking upon himself the decision of who are "authentic" Jews, and then enjoining upon them the requirement to live their Jewishness to the full precisely in order to deny Hitler a "posthumous victory," a frivolous answer might be that having contested most of the earlier 613 commandments, it is hardly surprising that Jews would not be particularly eager to embrace a new one. But beyond the dubiousness of promulgating new commandments, there is something that cries out to be resisted in Fackenheim's invocation of the murdered babies and *Muselmänner*[2] of Auschwitz in his writing. No one can speak for those murdered, and no one can determine what would count as a further betrayal of their suffering. The freedom to choose—one's own philosophy,

---

faith, communal affiliation, and historical sense, as well as one's mode of remembering and representing that memory—is precisely what Nazism made impossible for Jews, and although the affirmation of that freedom can do nothing for the victims of the Shoah, it is the only coherent rejection of the Nazi principle of nondifferentiation among Jews.

But to focus specifically on the issue of the moral legitimacy of aesthetic representation of the Shoah, I suspect that almost everyone who has wrestled with this question and decided against any prohibition of fictionalizations has come up with similar arguments. Nonetheless, it is important to make explicit the basis of one's conclusions. For me, the following considerations finally prevailed over my initial agreement with Adorno's interdiction.

Since the generation of survivors will soon die out, to prohibit anyone who was not actually caught in the Shoah from representing it risks consigning the events to a kind of oblivion interrupted only occasionally by the recitation of voices from an increasingly distant past. Any tribal story, if it is to survive as a living part of communal memory, needs regularly to be retold and reinterpreted. To keep silent would be still worse than a necessarily denaturing, because too "composed," speech, since it was precisely with the permanent silence of universal disbelief that the SS used to taunt the Jews in the camps—if any prisoners were to survive, the Nazis boasted, no one would believe their account. "Many survivors," Primo Levi writes, "remember that the SS militiamen enjoyed cynically admonishing the prisoners: 'However this war may end, we have won the war against you; none of you will be left to bear witness, but even if someone were to survive, the world will not believe him. There will perhaps be suspicions, discussions, research by historians, but there will be no certainties, because we will destroy the evidence together with you. And even if some proof should remain and some of you survive, people will say that the events you describe are too monstrous to be believed: they will say that they are the exaggerations of Allied propaganda and will believe us, who will deny everything, and not you. We will be the ones to dictate the history of the Lagers.'"[3] Even among themselves, the SS usually maintained a complex rhetoric of indirection, bureaucratese, paranomasia, euphemism, and displacement when referring to the Shoah. Thus, for example, the murder squads organized by Heydrich were called *Einsatzgruppen* (task forces) while the delicate phrase *Sonderbehandlung* (special treatment) was the standard term for physical annihilation. Even in Himmler's notorious speech of October 3, 1943, delivered to his senior officers at Posen, he first carefully refers to the *Judenevakuierung* (the "evacuation" or "deportation" of the Jews) before calling it *die Ausrottung* (extermination). Himmler announces that the genocide constitutes "ein niemals geschriebenes und niemals zu schreibenes Ruhmesblatt unserer Geschichte" (a never-written and never-to-be-written page of glory in our [SS] history) and declares that although he will, this one time, discuss it openly ("Unter uns soll es einmal ganz offen ausgesprochen sein"), nonetheless it can never be talked about in the outside world ("und trotzdem werden wir in der Öffentlichkeit nie darüber reden").[4] It is by public words, not by silence, that Himmler's boast is rejected, and in this sense, the retelling by other voices, voices of those who were never in German hands, crystallizes the continuing legacy of the Shoah, and confirms its wider importance as part of our collective memory.

Secondly, even the most scrupulous first-person "factual" testimony does a certain injustice to the other victims, if only by making its narrator the primary observing consciousness of both the tale and the events, thereby slighting the anguish of everyone else to a certain degree. Since survival itself was largely accidental, and since far more prisoners died in the camps than returned, the testimony of anyone who survived is necessarily both partial and, in the harshest sense, unrepresentative. (Primo Levi's *The Drowned and the Saved* [1986], for example, is haunted by the awareness that his own earlier account of Auschwitz, *If This Is a Man* [1947], is that of "an anomalous minority," necessarily excluding the perspective of the vast majority of inmates who perished without leaving any record of their ordeal.)[5] Moreover, since one of the Nazi mechanisms of controlling the prisoners depended on isolating each of them as much and for as long as possible to keep them ignorant of the full scale of their predicament, the testimony of any single survivor, no matter how vivid and thoughtful, will be fragmentary and in need of supplementation from other sources and narratives. Indeed, Levi points out that most of the survivor narratives he has come across have already been influenced, often unconsciously, by "information gathered from later readings or the stories of others."[6] Even the seemingly strictest first-person narratives often bear *from the outset* the markings of other stories, other interpretations encountered after the Liberation, and bear those markings as part of the minimum necessity of being able to tell a story at all. As the Israeli author and concentration camp survivor Yehiel De-Nur (Ka-Tzetnik) makes clear, "even those who had been there did not know Auschwitz. Not even someone who was there two long years, as I was."[7] But in its turn, each "supplementary" narrative, whether fictional or "documentary," will itself also contain stylization, figurative language, aesthetic ordering, and a distinct point of view, and thus provide, amid the shock of the information it conveys, a certain formal "seemliness." If the text succeeds in moving its reader at all, then these writerly choices must have yielded a kind of readerly "pleasure," strange though the term may be in this context. Irrespective of the genre, a reader necessarily remains someone who responds with emotions and ideas to words encountered in a printed text, no matter how imaginatively unsettling the subject matter of the narrative.

Indeed, I think it is fair to argue that one of the most pervasive myths of our era, a myth perhaps even partially arising out of our collective response to the horrors of the concentration camps, is the absolute authority given to first-person testimony. Such narratives, whether by camp survivors or by those who have endured rape, child abuse, or any devastating trauma, are habitually regarded as though they were completely unmediated, as though language, gesture, and imagery could become transparent if the experience being expressed is sufficiently horrific. Testimony wrung out of a person under extreme duress is thus seen as the most true, the most unmediated, the most trustworthy. In contemporary aesthetics, for example, the force of much "performance art" relies precisely—and I think precariously—on just such a faith in the authenticity of first-person testimony. Indeed, it is not stretching a point to argue that recent American art in general has been marked by a strong, even if unconscious, Platonic suspicion of aesthetic mediation, imitation, and stylization. Often this mistrust takes the form of a new kind of Puritanism directed against style-as-artifice and against the imagination as being able to give shape to experiences not autobiographically grounded. But the severity of the suspicion at the claims of the imagination is balanced by an utterly naive faith in first-person narratives, as though they were "really true" and untouched by figuration and by the shaping of both conscious and unconscious designs on the speaker's part. Adorno's injunction against representing Shoah experiences in fiction *because of the attendant stylization* assumes that testimonial accounts have no such stylization, which is, of course, only a specific example of what has become an increasingly prevalent criterion of judgment. So deep-rooted has the anxiety of figuration become that even a recent memoir, *A Time to Speak*, by Helen Lewis, a Theresienstadt and Auschwitz survivor, is accompanied by a foreword assuring the reader that the book contains no novelistic "tricks." More surprisingly still, the foreword, which bristles with scorn at literary self-consciousness, is written by Jennifer Johnston, herself one of Ireland's more distinguished contemporary novelists: "All the baggage of the novelist is here—joy and despair, good and evil, death and survival—but there is no fiction, none of the novelist's attention-seeking tricks, nothing is manipulated as a novelist would manipulate, the pattern is inherent not imposed. Helen Lewis . . . never invents; there is only Truth, witnessed Truth."[8]

Yet surely there is no reason to assume that first-person testimony about the horrific is more unmediated and complete than any other kind of speech. For example, concentration camp victims have many reasons, both conscious and unconscious, to amend and shape their narratives (guilt about having survived at all, shame for any acts they committed that may have been essential to their survival but which deeply violated the ethics of their ordinary lives, and even a degree of traumatization so severe as to make them incapable of recalling crucial aspects of their own experience). If, for instance, as the Israeli Supreme Court ruled on July 29, 1993, there is reasonable ground to doubt that John Demjanjuk really was "Ivan the Terrible" of Treblinka, then the misidentification by his surviving victims may be due not only to the long interval between "Ivan's" acts and Demjanjuk's arrest, but equally, to the very nature of the victims' suffering, which made them perhaps *less* able to identify their tormentor correctly, rather than, as the official myth has it, more certain of accurately remembering him. Perhaps the very need to find, and see punished, whoever made them suffer so terribly, persuaded the witnesses to identify positively a likely, but not necessarily the correct, candidate.[9] It is important to admit, moreover, that even the survivor-witness's testimony moves us not just by its factual and evidentiary material, but by fitting that material into a specific ideological/narrative framework. Readers respond very differently to autobiographical accounts of the Shoah, depending to a significant degree on the way the particular survivor's philosophical, religious, and socio-political perspectives color the documentary testimony. Primo Levi's liberal and scientifically trained Italian bourgeois worldview is unmistakably different from that of an Austrian literary intellectual like Hans Meyer (who wrote under the name Jean Améry after the war), let alone from that of an Eastern European Hasid, a Russian Bundist, or a committed Polish Zionist. All of the Shoah's victims may have shared the same fate, but as James Young rightly notes, "each victim 'saw'—i.e., understood *and* witnessed—his predicament differently, depending on his own historical past, religious paradigms, and ideological explanations." What we reconstruct through our reading is never the event as an absolute, but what Young goes on to call "the [contemporary writer's] understanding of them—that is, the epistemological climate in which they existed [for him] at the time."[10]

But so, too, every reader's response is shaped by the "epistemological climate" in which the testimony is read. As Jonathan Boyarin shrewdly observes, "in popular-culture representations of the Holocaust, the particular horror of the Nazi genocide is emphasized by an image of Jews as normal Europeans, 'just like us.' In fact we can only empathize with, *feel ourselves into*, those we can imagine as ourselves."[11] But the affective force of identification through perceived similarity is as powerful in high art as it is in popular culture. Secular Jewish intellectuals often react negatively, for example, to certain ultra-orthodox accounts of the Shoah (especially the theological explanation that it was the pre-war violation of the ritual laws and commandments by the assimilated Jews of Europe that was being expiated in the camps). Similarly, more religiously observant Jews often find Primo Levi's secular humanism shockingly blind to the anti-Semitic tendencies in the authors upon whom he drew for moral sustenance in Auschwitz. One of my colleagues, for example, told me that when he gave a talk on Levi's *Se questo è un uomo* to a local Jewish community, he was bitterly attacked by several members of the audience for praising the scene where the author rediscovers his fundamental humanity by recalling Dante's description of Ulysses in *Inferno* 26. Dante, in their eyes, was one of the central authors of the culture whose anti-Semitism had "culminated" in the camps, and they regarded Levi's invocation of Dante in such a setting as an index of an alienation from his people so complete that even Auschwitz could not teach him the futility of assimilationism. It is also instructive, if not particularly encouraging, to see that Levi is now under equally severe attack from quite a different source, not because of his lack of Jewish faith, but because he is so out of step with current American academic pieties. So, for example, Dominick LaCapra, a prominent history professor and theoretician, writes with breath-taking condescension, "It may also be useful to quote Levi on silence, for his words are instructive despite their dubious indebtedness to a largely unexamined tradition of high culture, overly analytic rationality, teleological assumptions and restrictive humanism."[12]

This disparity in responses should alert us to a fundamental paradox: all of the writers on the Shoah speak of its *incomprehensibility* and basic *incommunicability*; in fact, though, accounts of the Shoah, even more strictly than narratives of less extreme events, rely on the witness and his listener sharing the same code of values and explanatory models of individual and social behavior in order to render convincing the assertion that something "incommunicable" has been experienced. There is, in other words, no single order of memorable testimony, no transparent paradigm of representation, that can address the different narrative needs of all those gripped by the subject. Prohibitions of any kind inevitably—and futilely—try to erect the individual "legislator's" personal and ideological perspective as the only acceptable model.

Notwithstanding the extent to which theoretical reflection qualifies and ultimately rejects the insistence on purely factual narratives, the exploitation of the Nazi genocide in countless mediocre books and films is clearly a thoroughly depressing phenomenon. Revealingly though, the authors of many of the most clumsy fictionalizations are often at great pains in their prefaces or in separate interviews to insist that they have used the fullest available historical records and tried to be totally faithful to the facts as they have learned them through scrupulous research. In Thomas Keneally's *Schindler's List*, for example, we are told that the author has used "the texture and devices of the novel to tell a true story" and that he has wished "to avoid all fiction, since fiction would debase the record."[13] Berel Lang, who has discussed this issue with particular lucidity, notes that while the belief that "literature has moral presuppositions and consequences is not startling . . . moral accountability has rarely been pressed against the writer for the very *act* of writing. . . . [Writers on the Shoah demonstrate a felt] obligation (morally, but also intellectually) to establish their *right* to address that event as a subject."[14] Critical to establishing this right, as Lang remarks in a subsequent study, is "not so much [the writers'] success in achieving historical authenticity, as their acknowledgment of that as a goal—their deference to the conventions of historical discourse as a literary means."[15] Implicit in all such arguments is the sense that while *no* actual testimony could "debase the record," *all* "fictionalizations" inevitably do so.

Yet there is an unexplored absence of correlation between the argument against literary stylization, which says that the element of aesthetic pleasure contradicts the meaningless horror of the Shoah, and the argument against fictionalization, which says that the figuration of events not directly experienced by the artist debases all those who actually have undergone them. Both of these positions are equally vulnerable, it seems to me, to one or more of the counterarguments outlined above, but the lack of any logical connection between the two principal injunctions against all representations not authenticated by direct experience is itself striking. Moreover, there is a phenomenon as depressing in its own way as the entertainment industry's commercialization of the Shoah, but which, because of the misplaced aura of wisdom with which we endow any survivors of such unprecedented suffering, has rarely been publicly discussed. I am thinking here of what George Steiner has described as the "disturbingly commercialized pathos of horror [that] has arisen around certain survivors and their all-too-eloquent and sometimes even theatrical witness."[16] But if the biographical veracity of testimony does not guarantee its ethical significance, and if the element of stylization is inherent in any representation, fictional or not, then there is actually no single, global issue or injunction to be debated. There is only a series of specific works including poems, films, sculptures, drawings, novels, historical studies, and autobiographical memoirs, each of whose seemliness needs to be considered on its own terms without recourse to any overarching formulae. Instead of a single problem, there are the constantly changing questions raised by each new work that addresses the Shoah, and instead of a set of criteria determined in advance, only a kind of extreme localism of attention can come to terms with the variety of ways the Shoah is figured in our historical and moral imaginations. . . .

Precisely [the] lack of penetration into the lived moral world and choices of Appelfeld's characters is why the effect of their inevitable, if only partially narrated, destruction at the end of *Badenheim 1939* differs so fundamentally from the equally foreseeable and calamitous fates of fictional figures like Hektor, King Lear, or Balzac's Lucien de Rubempré. There is a crucial and often unacknowledged distinction between the "inevitability" of an anticipated climax in classical epic and tragedy, or in densely "realistic" novels like those of the *Comédie humaine*, and the retrospective, backshadowing historicomoral judgments of a book like *Badenheim 1939*. In works like *The Iliad*, *King Lear*, or *Splendeurs et misères des courtisanes*, the grim ending is not used retroactively to constitute the primary source of judgment on the characters. What the characters in these works do is seen as good or bad, evil or virtuous, at the moment their actions are committed. Lear is manifestly wrong and morally at fault right from his first speech—even if Goneril and Regan had kept their pledges and even if Cordelia were to have lived happily ever after in France, Lear's tyrannical self-indulgence would be palpably reprehensible. But if there had been no Shoah, the assimilationists vacationing in Badenheim might be considered, from certain perspectives, as weak or lacking in ethnic self-dignity, but from many other points of view, which probably included those of the majority of European Jewry, their self-definition as "Austrian citizens of Jewish origin" (21) would be entirely reasonable. To focus on one's private family ties, love affairs, careers, or artistic longings, is completely unobjectionable by normal, quotidian standards; only in the light of the genocide awaiting all of the characters can these kinds of priorities be found inadequate. In other words, the Shoah looming at the novel's end is used throughout the text, instant by instant and scene by scene, to judge everyone's behavior, and it forces us to interpret that behavior as escapist, futile, and ultimately self-destructive. This is not the case in a text, whether epic, tragedy, or novel, whose ending, once it has occurred, may seem retrospectively to have been predetermined but in which the episode-by-episode, moment-by-moment behavior of the characters is significant in its own right. So, for example, Hektor may be doomed in the judgment of the gods to die at the hands of Achilles, just as Achilles in turn must die before Troy falls, but their decisions and deeds throughout the poem have such resonance precisely because they are shown to be of momentous significance to themselves, to their companions, and even to the gods, irrespective of the end that awaits both warriors.

It should be abundantly clear from this discussion that nothing in my argument contests, let alone seeks to dismiss, the power of a literary tradition in which the audience's knowledge of the ultimate destiny of the characters is a crucial component in a work's aesthetic, emotional, and intellectual effect. But deterministic historical foreshadowing, unlike, say, classical tragic or heroic destiny, allows the already known end to minimize, not intensify, the actual choices of the characters, and it is as unlikely to succeed as are other attempts, in a secular age, to substitute historicist patterns of inevitability for the certainties of a theological world view. In part, no doubt, backshadowing often functions as our secular, historicist equivalent to the way a god can see the inevitability and interrelatedness of everything that happens. But in fact, stories about divine concern with the fate of time-bound mortals, whether set in the pagan world or in the Judeo-Christian one, with its insistence on the centrality of human "free will," make clear the importance of alternative choices in order to sustain any ethical judgment or even narrative interest. (Think, for example, of the story of Job, whose "test" depends entirely on the freedom that he does not exercise to curse God for the injustice of his sufferings.)

Of course my examples here are from works that we do not necessarily read for their historical specificity or analysis, but as I argued in my earlier discussion of Danto and Habermas, the ethical implications of backshadowing are registered as powerfully in historical as in fictional writing. As we have seen, in a sense it is clear that without a knowledge of what followed them, it is impossible to grasp the significance and implications of decisive past events (e.g., the first anti-Semitic laws passed by the Nazis). But it is not the course of a particular historical unfolding that is at issue here; rather, it is a respect for people living at a time *before* that unfolding was complete who could not, and should not, be expected to have any knowledge of the future. Sideshadowing is not concerned to deny to either the historian or the novelist a retrospective awareness of important events; but it *is* concerned (1) not to regard the future from which the writers speak as the inevitable outcome of the past, and (2) not to let retrospection impose a hierarchy of significant/insignificant, fertile/futile, etc., judgments on the actions and thoughts of the characters in their narratives when the terms of that hierarchy are entirely determined by the story's ending.

But against my plea for the legitimacy of sideshadowing even in so unpromising a setting as Austria at the time of the *Anschluss*, it is understandably tempting to argue that "to speak of the dialectic between freedom and necessity is to speak necessarily of a very one-sided dialectic."[17] Yet even at that moment in history there were other choices in Austria than denial of the impending catastrophe, as numerous contemporary memoirs detailing the flood of Jews seeking foreign visas makes clear. Even if most of the applicants were turned away, the trapped Jews were unlikely to have chosen to continue visiting vacation spas in utter indifference to the network of exclusionary and degrading legislation to which they were daily being made subject. Even if some Austrian Jews did refuse to acknowledge their perilous situation, the question of sideshadowing only indirectly concerns their likelihood of survival, which often was entirely out of their own hands; instead, sideshadowing seeks only to draw attention to the diversity of the stances they took toward their predicament and the particular ways they sought to maintain their existence and identity within their catastrophic new circumstances. It is crucial to recognize that the likelihood of success of any action is not the criterion by which a multiplicity of possibilities can be determined. Even if none of the available options has a very strong chance of succeeding, there are still differences among them (and since the issue here is one of saving individual human lives, surely even a small percentage is of enormous significance), and peoples' characters can be judged partially by which option they in fact attempt. This is a position Appelfeld himself logically, if not in the actual texture of his narrative, acknowledges, since otherwise he would not be able to ironize the assimilationist Jews of Badenheim. Clearly, if there actually had been no important individual choices left, then the Jews staying in places like Badenheim acted in the only way they could and are inappropriate targets for satire; but if there had been numerous different ways of reacting, as the historical record amply testifies, then Appelfeld's collapsing of the variety of Austro-German Jewish responses to Nazism into a single, monological model is too reductive to constitute a worthy or convincing satire.

I am claiming here that to acknowledge the validity of sideshadowing is not merely to reject historical inevitability as a theoretical model. Far more important, it means learning to value the contingencies and multiple paths leading from each concrete moment of lived experience, and recognizing the importance of those moments not for their place in an already determined larger pattern but as significant in their own right. This is what I have called a prosaics of the quotidian, and it is fundamentally linked to the historical logic of sideshadowing. At a crucial point in *Badenheim 1939*, the narrator sardonically observes that "the people were still preoccupied with their own affairs—the guests with their pleasures and the townspeople with their troubles" (20).[18] This "preoccupation with their own affairs," as much as the denial of their Jewishness, is the unpardonable sin of everyone in Badenheim, and in Appelfeld's narrative it leads to consequences like the characters' general refusal even to discuss the fact that overnight "a barrier was placed at the entrance to the town. No one came in or went out" (38). Concern with the immediate and local, the familial and private, is judged inherently unworthy, an act of betrayal of others and of blindness to one's own deeper interests. Measured against the Shoah, as is everything in *Badenheim 1939*, Appelfeld's charge carries an intuitive plausibility, but it only makes sense if we agree to that standard of measurement; his scale loses its meaning if we consider, for example, that concern with one's ethnic identity, with the welfare of others in one's community, and with the nature of the political dispensation under which one lives, are themselves also local and personal matters, as much a part of prosaics as our "daily pleasures and troubles." In his contempt for prosaics, or, more accurately, in his linking of prosaics with pure selfishness, Appelfeld again rejoins the very ethos of the Israeli ideology that he thought he had rejected: "Personal experience was simply not worthy of recall.

. . . Suffering by itself did not merit attention—unless it served a collective purpose." It is precisely distinctions like this that prosaics can not accept: a genuinely democratic, rather than a tyrannical, collective purpose can arise only out of the shared aims and hopes of the individuals who make up the larger group; such a purpose is the meeting point, not the liquidation, of the innumerable separate preoccupations and motives of everyone who agrees to work for the realization of the collective purpose.

Beneath the melancholy of its coolly appalled tone, the deeper irony of a work like *Badenheim 1939* is that while it finds a new idiom in which to narrate the margins of catastrophe, it also finds itself entrapped in the very explanations it deems unacceptable as soon as they are spelled out more clearly. Appelfeld himself has spoken with passion and sorrow about "this anti-Semitism directed at oneself. . . . Even after the Holocaust, Jews did not seem blameless in their own eyes. On the contrary, harsh comments were made by prominent Jews against the victims for not protecting themselves and fighting back."[19] (Appelfeld is presumably referring to Hannah Arendt, among others.) Although it is their assimilationism and lack of Jewish pride, not their inability to fight back, that is satirized, Appelfeld's characters collaborate so fully in their destruction that among those "prominent Jews" who make "harsh comments" about the victims of the Shoah, it is difficult not to include the author of *Badenheim 1939* himself. Even the most assimilated and self-denying Jews were still sufficiently Jewish to be murdered, and so the contempt of a novel like *Badenheim 1939* is just as "anti-Semitic" in its attribution of complicity as are the harshest judgments of the unnamed "prominent Jews."

What may seem like merely formal decisions about how much knowledge of the future to include in a narrative set in an earlier epoch, or about how much to let the narrative glance sideways and project forward to events that never happened, is already thematically charged and thereby morally significant. If it is absurd to see the "great world-historical event" of 1875 as Lenin's fifth birthday, and if we can smile at the idea of a secular angel arriving in Langres in 1713 to tell Mme. Diderot that she would soon give birth to a great encyclopedist, then we also have to learn to absolve from any blame those Jews who attended the summer festivals of Salzburg or Badenheim and went about dressed in *Trachten* rather than in the paramilitary gear of the *Haganah* or the *tephillin* of the orthodox. There is ample reason to find preposterous that it is now time to forgive the murderers. Recognizing the contingencies and uncertainties in human events can prevent us from blaming the victims for their disastrous choices, but it in no way mitigates the decisions and choices of their murderers. The consequences of evil actions may be unpredictable and continue long into the future, but they are committed by particular people at specific moments and can be recognized as evil as soon as they are performed. The murderers became such at the instant they participated in murder, and sideshadowing in no way minimizes—in fact, it only emphasizes—their moral culpability.[20] But enough time has passed for us to realize that it was always partially the shame of not having been there to help them survive that made blaming the victims of the Shoah so much a part of how the history of European Jewry has been figured since 1945. Sideshadowing eliminates neither historical responsibility nor moral judgment, but it insists we assign them prosaically: to individuals and individual actions where such judgments properly belong. It is these specific actions and choices made by individual people that constitute the history we inherit and with which our own actions and choices must ultimately come to terms.

NOTES

1. Fackenheim then spells out the implications of his commandment as follows: "We are first commanded to survive as Jews, lest the Jewish people perish. We are commanded, second, to remember in our very guts and bones the martyrs of the Holocaust, lest their memory perish. We are forbidden, thirdly, to deny or despair of God, however much we may have to contend with him or believe in him, lest Judaism perish. We are forbidden, finally, to despair of the world as the place which is to become the kingdom of God, lest we help make it a meaningless place in which God is dead or irrelevant and everything is permitted. To abandon any of these imperatives, in response to Hitler's victory at Auschwitz, would be to hand him yet other, posthumous victories." This injunction was originally delivered during the symposium "Jewish Values in the Post-Holocaust Future," held in New York City on March 26, 1967. It was subsequently published under the title "The 614th Commandment" in *Judaism*, vol. 16, no. 3 (Summer 1967): 269–73, and has been reprinted in Fackenheim's collection of essays, *The Jewish Return into History: Reflections in the Age of Auschwitz and a New Jerusalem* (New York: Schocken, 1978), 19–24.

2. *Muselmänner* (literally, "Muslims") is the term coined in the concentration camps for those "near-skeletons who, their feelings, thoughts, and even speech already murdered by hunger and torture, still walked for a while till they dropped to the ground." See Emil Fackenheim, *To Mend the World* (New York: Schocken, 1982), xix.

3. Primo Levi, *The Drowned and the Saved*, trans. Raymond Rosenthal (New York: Summit Books, 1988), 11. Levi attributes the story to "the last pages" of Simon Wiesenthal's *The Murderers Are Among Us*, but this must be a faulty recollection since Wiesenthal's account is significantly different. Wisenthal remembers being asked by SS Rottenführer (Corporal) Merz, "Suppose an eagle took you to America. . . . What would you tell them there?" After being repeatedly assured that he would not be punished for telling the truth, Wiesenthal told Merz, "I believe I would tell the people the truth." But to this, Merz calmly replied, "You would tell the truth to the people in America. That's right. And you know what would happen, Wiesenthal? . . . They wouldn't believe you. They'd say you were crazy. Might even put you in a madhouse. How can *anyone* believe this terrible business—unless he has lived through it?" Simon Wiesenthal, *The Murderers Are Among Us*, ed. Joseph Wechsberg (New York: McGraw-Hill, 1967), 334–35.

4. Himmler's speech is printed as "Document 1919-PS" in volume 19 of the *Trial of the Major War Criminals Before the International Military Tribunal: Nuremberg, 14 November 1945–1 October 1946* (New York: AMS Press, 1948), 110–173. The passages cited are on page 145 of the transcript. A partial translation of Himmler's talk can be found in Lucy T. Dawidowicz, ed., *A Holocaust Reader* (New York: Behrman House, 1976),

130–40. For a fine analysis of the speech, see Peter Haidu, "The Dialectics of Unspeakability: Language, Silence, and the Narratives of Desubjectification," in Saul Friedlander, ed., *Probing the Limits of Representation: Nazism and the "Final Solution"* (Cambridge: Harvard University Press, 1992), 277–99.

5. Levi, *Drowned and the Saved*, 83–84: "We survivors are not only an exiguous but also an anomalous minority: we are those who by their prevarications or abilities or good luck did not touch bottom. Those who did so, those who saw the Gorgon, have not returned to tell about it or have returned mute, but they are the 'Muslims,' the submerged, the complete witnesses, the ones whose depositions would have a general significance."

6. Levi, *The Drowned and the Saved*, 19.

7. Tom Segev, *The Seventh Million: The Israelis and the Holocaust* (New York: Hill and Wang, 1993), 8.

8. Helen Lewis, *A Time to Speak* (Belfast: Blackstaff, 1992), Foreword by Jennifer Johnston, ix.

9. Already before the Israeli Supreme Court ruling, District Judge Thomas A. Wiseman Jr., reviewing the case for the U.S. Sixth Court of Appeals, concluded in June 1993 that new evidence, largely from the secret police files of the former U.S.S.R., exculpated Demjanjuk from the "specific crimes" of Ivan the Terrible.

10. James E. Young, *Writing and Rewriting the Holocaust: Narrative Consequences of Interpretation* (Bloomington: Indiana University Press, 1988), 26, 31.

11. Jonathan Boyarin, *Storm from Paradise: The Politics of Jewish Memory* (Minneapolis: University of Minnesota Press, 1992), 86.

12. Dominick LaCapra, "The Personal, the Political, and the Textual: Paul de Man as Object of Transference," *History and Memory*, vol. 4, no. 1 (Spring/Summer 1992): 15.

13. Thomas Keneally, *Schindler's List* (New York: Simon and Schuster, 1982), 10. These examples were suggested to me by Berel Lang, *Act and Idea in the Nazi Genocide* (Chicago: University of Chicago Press, 1990), 133ff.

14. Berel Lang, ed., *Writing and the Holocaust* (New York: Holmes and Meier, 1988), 4–6.

15. Lang, *Act and Idea in the Nazi Genocide*, 135.

16. George Steiner, "The Long Life of Metaphor: An Approach to the Shoah," in Lang, ed., *Writing and the Holocaust*, 160.

17. I owe this phrase to a subtle, if ultimately hostile reading of this chapter by an anonymous reviewer for the journal *Common Knowledge*.

18. This motif is so central to Appelfeld's vision of Austro-German Jewry that it figures in almost every one of his novels on the theme. As an example, consider the similarity between the passage from *Badenheim 1939* quoted in the text and the following formulation from *The Age of Wonders* (trans. Dalya Bilu [Boston: David R. Godine, 1981], 163–64): "Since nobody knew that these were the last days in this house, on this street, and behind the grid of this lattice . . . since nobody knew, everyone buried himself in his own affairs as if there were no end to this life . . . even when everything teetered on the edge of the abyss."

19. Roth, "Talk with Aharon Appelfeld," 30.

20. One of the strengths of recent studies like Christopher Browning's *Ordinary Men: Reserve Police Battalion 101 and the Final Solution in Poland* (New York: Harper Collins,

1992) and *The Path to Genocide: Essays on Launching the Final Solution* (New York: Cambridge University Press, 1992) is how clearly they show the crucial role of individual decisions and choices in carrying out the genocide.

BEREL LANG

◼ The Representation of Evil

Ethical Content as Literary Form

WRITING AGAINST SILENCE

The discussion of the differences—conceptual, literary, moral—between imaginative and historical writing about the Nazi genocide has not addressed the more sweeping objection against *all* writing about the subject that motivates the "boundary question" referred to earlier. In most of its appearance this objection is conceptual rather than moral, asserting that the phenomenon of the Nazi genocide is beyond the grasp of human understanding, defying comprehension; the conclusion follows that *all* representation of those events, by the historian no less than the novelist, will fail. The indictment, then, does not question the intentions that underlie writing, nor is it based on limitations in the specific medium of literary representation. It is the opacity of the subject itself that is asserted, its inaccessibility either to reason or to the imagination. Even literary representations that acknowledge this constraint as part of their representation would not escape it; those that purport to overcome it would, in addition to exhibiting the limitation, be guilty of falsification. Imaginative writings with these failings, however, would not differ from texts in other kinds of writing, including that of history; on this account, the failure of representation is due not to the relation between a particular form of discourse and its subject but to the nature of the subject, which would be common to all such forms.

From Berel Lang, *Act and Idea in the Nazi Genocide* (Chicago: University of Chicago Press). Reprinted by permission of The University of Chicago Press.

It will be recognized that the description of an event as incomprehensible or inexplicable is often itself a figure of speech; the aporia, an extreme instance of hyperbole, asserts just this—that words cannot convey or encompass a given subject.[1] Since the grasp of language normally extends wherever experience does, to claim of an event by this means that it defies language and understanding is meant to attest to its extraordinary nature, and this purpose has been evident in many references to the incomprehensibility of the Nazi genocide. But these claims themselves often appear as part of accounts that go on to speak in detail about aspects of the Nazi genocide. This is evidence, apparently, of the figurative purpose of such statements; at least *something* in their subject, we infer, is comprehensible and available for representation.

This does not mean, of course, that all assertions of the ineffability of the events of the Nazi genocide are figurative. Its context makes clear, for example, that George Steiner's statement that "the world of Auschwitz lies outside speech as it lies outside reason"[2] was intended literally (although Steiner subsequently modified this claim). But even such literal references have room for significant differences in meaning. So, for instance, when Raul Hilberg, the author of what remains the single most important study of the Nazi genocide, speaks of the "historical incomprehensibility" of that event, he takes this to mean that there were no sufficient reasons, in terms of *rational self-interest*, for the decisions and actions of the Nazis resulting in the Final Solution.[3] Since reasons of this sort are in his view required for historical understanding, the Nazi genocide against the Jews is in this sense inexplicable—although that does not mean that *other* forms of explanation (for example, psychological or economic) are not relevant.

A different but also literal meaning of the claim of incomprehensibility appears in religious or theological analysis; here the Nazi genocide is viewed in the context of the problem of the existence of evil in a world ordered by a just and omnipotent God—with the question formulated once again as "How was it possible?" In this context, the claim of incomprehensibility is interpreted to mean that the events of the genocide are humanly unintelligible, although this conclusion would not be true—could not be true—within the larger framework of a divine will or understanding. (When the thesis of theodicy is extended to its logical conclusion, the phenomenon of the genocide becomes not only intelligible, but warranted—an inference that then raises its own problems for these authors.) On the more restricted issue of representation, however, the consequences of the literal claim of incomprehensibility are evident, pointing to the human inadequacy of the writer (and reader), not to an intrinsic opacity in the subject or any related inadequacy in the means of representation.[4] The events of the genocide are *humanly* incomprehensible (and thus ineffable), although this would not be true—could not be true—from the perspective of divine understanding.

The thesis that has been proposed concerning the limitations of imaginative writing about the Nazi genocide is not, however, tied in fact or principle to any more general claim of incomprehensibility or ineffability. The limitations described are associated with the forms of imaginative representation, and even then not equally among them. It may be, as certain theorists have proposed recently, that a characteristic distance and loss separates all literary representation from whatever that representation is "of," that language is always under-determined. It is obvious, quite apart from this theory of language, that discourse is not *identical* with its subject. But general claims of incomprehensibility have no special bearing on any particular subject of discourse, and it is the distance between discourse and subject, addressed to the connection between ethical content and literary form in the subject of the Nazi genocide, that has been the focus of the discussion here. Admittedly, if, as in the Platonic view, evil as such is unintelligible and consequently incapable of representation, then all attempts to write about the Nazi genocide would be bound to fail. But there would then be nothing exceptional about that particular subject. . . . Insofar as the view that evil as such is inexplicable is rejected, furthermore, the inadequacy of certain forms or instances of the representation of evil will be due to their specific features—in the subject or in the means or in the relation between them.

At least two questions crucial to the thesis proposed have so far been unmentioned. The first of these concerns the fact of imaginative writing about the Nazi genocide; that is, the widespread attention given to this writing by diverse audiences. Why, if the thesis asserted is warranted, should this active response to imaginative writings with the Nazi genocide as their subject not have been muted? (It is indisputable, moreover, that these writings have had wider currency than "historical" texts.) The second question addresses the logical basis of the thesis, specifically the distinction it assumes between "imaginative" and "historical" writing. It can reasonably be asked if historical discourse itself is not also imaginative. Does it not make use of the same figurative turns attributed to imaginative literature? Certainly there is strong evidence of the role of narrative structures and figurative discourse in historical writing—and this evidence only supplements the more basic fact that alternative historical versions invariably appear of the "same" event. Do not the objections that have been directed here at novels or the drama or poetry about the Nazi genocide hold with equal force against historical writing?

The first of these questions echoes a larger one that asks what it is in imaginative literature in general that draws readers to it. This is not the place to consider that question, however, except insofar as it bears immediately on the writing about the Nazi genocide. Admittedly, certain justifications have been given of a "Holocaust literature" which follow from a more general view of the significance of literature as such. But it is worth noting that these justifications, as they apply specifically to imaginative writings about the Nazi genocide, conclude precisely at the point where the objections that have been raised against such writings begin. So, for example, Lawrence Langer finds in the "art of atrocity" the value of creating "an imaginative reality possessing an autonomous dignity and form" that discloses perceptions about the "literal" world "which the mind ordinarily ignores or would like to avoid."[5] And Leslie Epstein finds in this writing an ability "to create a bond, a sense of connectedness between the reader and every aspect of the world that has been salvaged through imagination"; he remarks a "peculiar sense of responsibility" that the novelist, rather than the historian or theologian can instill.[6]

Neither of these statements implies that the novelist writing about the Nazi genocide uncovers new facts or information about its causes and means. Langer refers to the role of "perceptions"—what the writer calls attention to in his own response that others do not see (at least until the writer shows the way); and Epstein emphasizes the possibility of a shared consciousness or identity, which historical discourse would supposedly impede. Both these views reflect more general theories of the capacity of literature to affect its readers, and as was suggested earlier in this chapter, those theories themselves are open to question. But a more immediate difficulty faces the proposals by Langer and Epstein, inasmuch as the literary features which they stress might be judged liabilities where the subject of the Nazi genocide is concerned—not, as they would have it, positive achievements. It might be acknowledged, for example, that imaginative literature in general provides access to aspects of experience that readers might otherwise avoid or find blocked off. So, for example, the representation of human motivation is sustained in imaginative writing to an extent not usually found in other writing, and the explanation for this appears in the requirements of literature itself. Because of the requirement of continuity in the lives of their characters, authors of imaginative literature follow the sequences of psychological cause and effect more closely than the historian does (or could) and do so whether historical evidence exists or not.

That this aspect of literary representation tends to draw readers, however, does not ensure that the grounds of the attraction are themselves always warranted—and indeed, a conclusion opposite to the one reached by Langer and Epstein might be inferred as it bears on the specific subject of the Nazi genocide. It is precisely the individual consciousness that is denied in the act or idea of genocide—and the imposition of a representation of agency on that subject, involving also the persona of the author, conduces to a distortion that is both conceptual and moral. It is not only that in much quasi-historical fiction about the Nazi genocide, conversations or other evidence of individual motivation and character are "made up" in order to create a narrative where, given the absence of historical evidence, there would be only a chronicle (so, for example, in Steiner's *Treblinka* and Keneally's *Schindler's List*)—but that the literary role of subjectivity as such is arguably misplaced here, as the basis of what the representation is "of." This is, it seems, the more general implication of Adorno's comment specifically directed against the literary representation of fascism: "The impossibility of portraying fascism springs from the fact that in it . . . subjective freedom no longer exists. Total unfreedom can be recognized, but not represented."[7] What is crucial here is not that among fictional recreations of the genocide *particular* descriptions or statements can be shown to be unverifiable or false—although this is often the case and is disruptive when it occurs.[8] The more basic issues are literary and moral, not simply historical: that imaginative literature presupposes individuality and subjectivity in the representation of its characters and their actions, and that to represent certain literary subjects in those terms is a falsification. This does not mean that such representations are impossible; but it does mean that the moral strain within the literary subject, and between it and the historical subject, will disclose itself in the process of representation.

To be sure, the possibility always exists of literary and moral genius that may transcend these or any other supposedly intrinsic limitations. The history of literature provides notable examples of such accomplishment, and although even the most important writings on the Nazi genocide arguably fall short of this standard, they may nonetheless seem to overcome the limitations asserted here in the form of a general rule. To grant this possibility for figures like Celan, Borowski, or Appelfeld, however, need not undermine the main point of the thesis proposed. For there is no contradiction between conceding the possibility of literary significance and yet maintaining that no writer is immune to the moral and literary risks incurred when the subject of his writing is the Nazi genocide. The question remains to what extent writers are able to avoid these dangers, with the presumption that at best they will not escape entirely and that even insofar as they do the writings have to be read as a response to those dangers.

The second question mentioned at the beginning of this section concerns the privileged position that has been asserted here for historical writing relative to imaginative or figurative writing. This claim is based on the evidence that the potentiality of figurative discourse is limited where certain subjects or themes are concerned. But this assertion does not show that historical writing escapes the same objections. Without such evidence, which would have to demonstrate that historical writing is nonfigurative in at least some essential aspect of its composition, recent analyses of historical discourse which find in it a fundamental role for narrative—and thus literary—structure would hold.[9] The combination of moral and literary failure that, according to the thesis presented here, affects imaginative writing about the Nazi genocide would thus, for the same reasons, also apply to historical discourse.

There is a difference, however, between acknowledging that historical representation makes use of narrative and figurative means and asserting the stronger thesis that historical discourse, like the genres of imaginative literature, is essentially dependent on those means. It is in rejecting the latter characterization of historical discourse that the contrast between imaginative and historical discourse emerges here—and it is the *fact* of the events of the Nazi genocide that serves (here, but also for the more general principle) as a basis for the contrast. It may be true that there are no "bare"—that is, without the means of representation—historical facts; and it may also be that there is no writing (historical or imaginative) that does not in principle engender what has been referred to here as figurative space. But neither of these possibilities denies the possibility of representation that stands in a direct relation to its object—in effect, if not in principle, immediate and unaltered. It is *this* possibility that stands at the crux of the distinction between historical and figurative discourse.

The evidence for this last claim might draw on a number of sources, but for the discussion here, only one is necessary: the *fact* of the Nazi genocide itself.

Here, if anywhere, the difference between assertion and denial—on a different axis, between history and figuration—is clear, not only epistemically, but morally. To reject at this juncture the sharp distinction between historical and figurative discourse is, among its implications, to propose that reference to the Nazi genocide against the Jews is one of a number of possible figurative descriptions of a "fact" that does not exist outside such descriptions—or, more radically, to assert the possibility that the genocide did not occur, that it was not, is not a fact. Such implications hardly require elaboration; it seems clear that the existence of facts as such, the very possibility of knowledge, is at stake here. The enormity of denying the occurrence of the Nazi genocide is proportionate to the enormity of the occurrence itself; recognition of this proportion thus becomes itself part of the distinction between historical and figurative discourse proposed in this account.

This last claim does not mean that the occurrence of the Nazi genocide *cannot* be denied, and a number of writers, often grouped under the title of "revisionists," have done just this.[10] In one sense, this denial is insignificant: it has not gained many or very credible supporters, least of all among historians. But in the context of the discussion here, the denial is important for reasons that extend beyond the premises of methodological skepticism that can be used to question *any* historical claim—the contentions, for example, that "facts" have social or ideological origins, or that alternative descriptions are almost always possible for a single group of data. So far as concerns these issues, a denial of the occurrence of the Nazi genocide is no different than the rejection of any other generally accepted historical claim. But that denial *is* different, with the difference related to the moral significance of the fact of the genocide (and then also of its denial). What alters the balance here is not that the empirical evidence is so much fuller or more compelling for the occurrence of the Nazi genocide than for any other historical event, but that the consequences of the affirmation or denial of the claim of its occurrence add *their* weight to the evidence itself. On these grounds, it is no exaggeration to hold that to deny the occurrence of the genocide is in effect to deny the existence of facts—and, to that extent, of history.

It was evidently this consideration that stood behind the statement published by a group of thirty-four French historians in response to the revisionist claim—the latter epitomized for them by the denial that the gas chambers in the death camps did, or even could have been responsible for, the killings associated with them. After providing a brief outline of the historical unfolding of the "Final Solution," the historians direct their conclusion against the revisionists:

> Everyone is free to interpret a phenomenon like the Hitlerian genocide according to his philosophy. . . . Everyone is free to apply to it one or another means of explication; everyone is free, up to the limit, to imagine or to dream that these monstrous facts did not take place. They unfortunately did take place, and no one can deny their existence without outrage to the truth. The question should not be raised of how, *technically*, such mass murder could have been plausible. It was technically possible because it indeed took place. This is the obligatory

starting point of any historical inquiry on the subject. . . . It is impossible to have a debate on the existence of the gas chambers.[11]

The statement points to the basis for joining the moral and epistemic features in the revisionist denial. If ever there was a "literal" fact—beyond the possibility of alternative formulations, among which reversal or denial must always be one—it is here, in the act and idea of the Nazi genocide; and if the moral implication of the role of facts needed proof, it is also to be found here, again in the phenomenon of the Nazi genocide. Denial here traduces not only one truth, but the possibility of truth as such—an "impossible" debate. It is ultimately *this* necessity, then, that grounds the distinction between historical and figurative discourse—and then also the claim derived from that distinction of the failings in imaginative representations of the Nazi genocide. However it may be conceived beyond that point, the fact of the Nazi genocide is a crux that separates historical discourse from the process of imaginative representation and its figurative space, perhaps not uniquely, but as surely as any fact might be required or able to.

The privileged position of historical discourse in this distinction does not extend to other forms of critical or theoretical discourse; for example, to writing in the social sciences or philosophy. Some accounts of these other forms hold that they too are nonfigurative, unmediated in their representations of facts. But even aside from the question of whether this claim can be demonstrated (it may itself be figurative), those forms of discourse disclose at least one characteristic that was judged also in the imaginative writings about the genocide to distort its subject. This feature is the process of universalization, which is more commonly associated with theoretical inquiry than with literary expression. The dominant explanatory ideal in the social sciences proposes a general understanding of the aspects of behavior studied—an understanding that can be translated from one context to another or at the very least be placed in a general schema of culture and human conduct. The concern with even the most specific evidence, then, is a concern with its generalizable features, which, systematically, are prior to the evidence itself.

This subordination of the particular to the universal which characterizes theoretical discourse is usually effected as though the subject "theorized" made no difference to the process—as though *any* subject could be addressed in this way. But this contention seems false in general, and specific examples in writings about the Nazi genocide demonstrate its failure at least where *that* subject is concerned. So, for example, in The Informed Heart, Bruno Bettelheim examines the patterns of responses among concentration-camp captives in terms of Freudian psychology.[12] Against that background, Bettelheim asserts, a close likeness appears between the identities that concentration-camp captives took on and the reversion to infantile behavior in a standard form of neurosis. Those who escaped this reversion, Bettelheim contends, were enabled to do so first by achieving an understanding of the pressures exerted on them, and then by opposing it on the basis of that understanding—by the "informed heart." The criticism to which this analysis seemed open is not that its instantiation of behavior in the concentration camps under a general theory could not lead to conclusions that might then be confirmed but that even if it did, the cogency of those conclusions would in effect be accidental. The imposition of a theory requires the translation into its own terms of the evidence—that evidence for which it has no categories of its own as well as that for which it has. In this sense, theory dictates rather than discovers what is then formulated in its own conclusions. When in criticizing Bettelheim Terrence Des Pres calls attention to the role in the camps of altruism and cooperation which Bettelheim does not mention, then, his objection is not that Bettelheim's account is insufficiently general but that the form or structure of the analysis itself is problematic, that theory, in this sense, suffers from an intrinsic "blindness."[13]

Again, writing on a different aspect of experience in the camps, Richard Rubenstein applies the motif of the "death of God" to the possibility of religious belief "after Auschwitz."[14] In thus linking the refutation of religious commitment to the occurrence of the Nazi genocide, Rubenstein subsumes the individuality of that event under a general abstraction. History is here dramatized and universalized; the Nazi genocide is made not individual but unique. Like all other such claims, the underlying rationale requires the denial of individuality in order (ostensively) to emphasize it. So far as the occurrence of evil is a test of the existence of God, the Nazi genocide does not differ from an indefinite number of other historical occurrences of evil, most of them much slighter instances than the genocide. Again, Rubenstein's denial of this is the consequence of a method rather than of a failure to consider specific items of evidence.

These individual examples underscore the vulnerability of representations of the Nazi genocide to the distortion of generalization. Such theories as they preclude the possibility of disconfirmation, deny the particularity even of the evidence of which they are purportedly representations. This feature of theoretical explanation does not pose difficulties when what is "theorized" is not singular to begin with; indeed, generalizability in this sense is a basic presupposition in the natural sciences. But where particularity is an essential feature of a subject, the very concept of "explanation in general" comes into question—and it is also at this point that practical judgment diverges from theoretical judgment. Practical judgment—an inference leading to moral prescription and act—differs from theoretical judgment precisely on the ideal of universalization. It is the particularity of a decision or event that is the focus of practical judgment; the historically contingent features in the subject of moral discourse—the fact that any judgment about it is tied to an historical context—mean that the attempt to universalize those features also empties them of content. That theoretical or universal assertions can be abstracted from features of the Nazi genocide is not inconsistent with the conclusion that such assertions remain morally inadequate to that subject; they are as remote as the physiological composition of a human being is from his personality or moral character.

These last comments complete a full turn back to the issue of writing itself as an occasion of moral judgment. Once writing is viewed as an act, to be judged for what it "does" to its subject and to its readers, then the enormity of the Nazi genocide in its historical or nonliterary character necessarily affects—enlarges—the risks incurred in its literary representation. The judgment of literary representation depends, moreover, not only on its treatment of its subject, but on the alternatives from among which that one "act" was chosen and which might, in the critic's view, have included another one that was preferable. The most radical alternative to any particular representation of the Nazi genocide is not a different or contradictory one—but the possibility of not having written at all; that is, the writer's decision for silence. And this then provides a minimal but decisive standard by which all writing about the Nazi genocide can and ought to be judged, a standard that poses itself in the form of a question: Would silence not have been preferable, more valuable, than what was written? No writer could dispute the point of this question: in it, the stakes of writing are made proportionate to the weight of its subject.

Admittedly, this standard in a more general form is applicable to *all* writing. But for most literary subjects, a prima-facie presumption favors what might be contributed by its representation; it is the moral consequence of an event such as the Nazi genocide that opens this prima-facie presumption to question. The test of silence as an alternative, it should be noted, does not measure writing simply by an absence or denial of value. Silence may also "speak"; because of what silence both does and does not say, it is turned to as a means for honoring or commemorating the dead. This ritual use makes silence a still more compelling standard of judgment for writings about the Nazi genocide; they are always to be judged as having displaced the value of silence.

When religious writers refer to the nature or will of God as incomprehensible or ineffable, this is mainly an assertion of conceptual inadequacy, attesting to the difficulty of representing God in human thought or language. The theological traditions have made unusual efforts to show how deep-seated these constraints are; for example, Maimonides turns to the language of "negative theology" (what God is *not*), and Thomas, to the language of analogy: we can speak only of what god is *like*. But the dissonance in the relation between the events of the Nazi genocide against the Jews and the writing about them is not conceptual, but moral. In terms only of historical complexity, the Nazi genocide does not differ quantitatively from other large-scale events involving many countries and masses of people. Its difference is in the phenomenon of genocide—a difference reflected in the dissonance which appears when the act of writing is judged in terms of what it does to its readers, and together with that, of what it does to its subject—that is, on both counts, morally. The risk of failure here is constant.

NOTES

1. See Arthur Quinn, *Figures of Speech* (Salt Lake City: Gibbs M. Smith, 1982), 36.
2. George Steiner, *Language and Silence* (New York: Atheneum, 1966), 123.

3. Raul Hilberg, "Concluding Discussion," in Lang, *Writing* (see chap. 2, n. 8), 274.

4. See, e.g., Eliezer Berkovits, *Faith after the Holocaust* (New York: Ktav, 1973); Emil L. Fackenheim, *The Jewish Return into History* (New York: Schocken, 1978); Elisabeth Schüssler Fiorenza and David Tracy (eds.), *The Holocaust as Interruption* (Edinburgh: T. & T. Clark, 1984).

5. Lawrence Langer, *The Holocaust and the Literary Imagination* (New Haven: University Press, 1975), 30.

6. Epstein, "Writing about the Holocaust," in Lang (ed.), *Writing and the Holocaust* (New York: Holmes & Meier, 1988), 264.

7. Theodor Adorno, *Minima Moralia*, trans. E. F. N. Jephcott (London: NLB, 1974), 144.

8. Although criticism at this level also runs the risk of overliteralism; so, for example, Alvin Rosenfeld's objection to George Steiner's *The Portage of A. H. to San Cristobal*: "Why end it all . . . with Hitler's speech? Why give Hitler the last word?" (*Imagining Hitler* [Bloomington, Ind.: Indiana University Press, 1985], 98).

9. See Hayden White, *The Contents of the Form* (Baltimore, Md.: Johns Hopkins Press, 1987); Mink, "History and Fiction as Modes of Comprehension," in *Historical Understanding* (Ithaca, N.Y.: Cornell University Press, 1987).

10. The most widely known among these works include Arthur R. Butz, *The Hoax of the Twentieth Century* (Torrance, Calif.: Noontide Press, 1977); Robert Faurisson, *Mémoir en defense: Contre ceux qui m'accusent de falsifier l'histoire* (Paris: La Vieille Taupe, 1980)—this volume includes a supportive introduction by Noam Chomsky; Paul Rassinier, *Le Drame des juifs européens* (Paris: Les Sept Couleurs, 1964); and Serge Thion, *Vérité historique on vérité politique?* (Paris: La Vieille Taupe, 1980). See also the analyses of the revisionists by Nadine Fresco, "The Denial of the Dead: On the Faurisson Affair," *Dissent*, 1981, 467–83; and Pierre Vidal-Naquet, *Les Juifs, la mémoire et le présent* (Paris: Maspero, 1981).

11. *Le Monde*, 21 February 1979, 23 (Berel Lang's translation).

12. Bruno Bettelheim, *The Informed Heart: Autonomy in a Mass Age* (Glencoe, Ill.: Free Press, 1960). The method criticized leads elsewhere to an even more startling response to the evidence of the Holocaust: "Because of the nature of the psychoanalytic process, with its focus on libidinal and aggressive drives, psychoanalysts are in a unique position to guide the way in our attempt to master our enormous destructive potential, that is, the exacerbated and unrelieved urge for violence." (Steven A. Luel and Paul Marcus [eds.], *Psychoanalytic Reflections on the Holocaust* [New York: Ktav, 1984, 5.)

13. Terrence Des Pres, *The Survivor: An Anatomy of Life in the Death Camps* (New York: Oxford University Press, 1976).

14. Richard Rubenstein, *After Auschwitz: Radical Theology and Contemporary Judaism* (Indianapolis, Ind.: Bobbs-Merrill, 1966).

ANDREAS HUYSSEN

▣ Monuments and Holocaust Memory in a Media Age

I

Despite the growth of Holocaust revisionism in recent years,[1] the problem for Holocaust memory in the 1980s and 1990s is not forgetting, but rather the ubiquitousness, even the excess of Holocaust imagery in our culture, from the fascination with fascism in film and fiction, which Saul Friedlander has so persuasively criticized, to the proliferation of an often facile Holocaust victimology in a variety of political discourses that have nothing to do with the Shoah.[2] In a perverse way, even the denial of the Holocaust and the public debate surrounding that denial keep the Holocaust in the public mind. Short of denial, however, the original trauma is often reenacted and exploited in literary and cinematic representations in ways that can also be deeply offensive. Certainly, the unchecked proliferation of the trope itself may be a sign of its traumatic ossification, its remaining locked in a melancholic fixation that reaches far beyond victims and perpetrators.

If such proliferation, whether in fiction and film or in contemporary politics, actually trivializes the historical event of the Nazi Final Solution, as many would argue, then the building of more and more Holocaust memorials and monuments may not offer a solution to the problems of remembrance either. The attempt to counteract seeming trivializations such as the television series *Holocaust* (1979) by serious museal and monumental representations may only, once again, freeze memory in ritualistic images and discourses. The exclusive insistence on the true representation of the Holocaust in its uniqueness, unspeakability, and incommensurability may no longer do in the face of its multiple representations and functions as a ubiquitous trope in Western culture. Popularizing representations and historical comparisons are ineradicably part of a Holocaust memory which has become multiply fractured and layered.

The criteria for representing the Holocaust cannot be propriety or awe as would be appropriate in the face of a cult object. Awed and silent respect may be called for vis-à-vis the suffering of the individual survivor, but it is misplaced as a discursive strategy for the historical event, even if that event may harbor something unspeakable and unrepresentable at its core. For if it is our concern and responsibility to prevent forgetting, we have to be open to the powerful effects that a melodramatic soap opera can exert on the minds of viewers today. The post-Holocaust generations that received their primary socialization through television may find their way toward testimony, documentary, and historical treatise precisely via a fictionalized and emotionalized Holocaust made for prime time television. If the Holocaust can be compared to an earthquake that has destroyed all the instruments for measuring it, as Lyotard has suggested, then surely there must be more than one way of representing it.

The increasing temporal and generational distance, therefore, is important in another respect: it has freed memory to focus on more than just the facts. In general, we have become increasingly conscious of how social and collective memory is constructed through a variety of discourses and layers of representations. Holocaust historiography, archives, witness testimony, documentary footage—all have collaborated to establish a hard core of facts, and these facts need to be transmitted to the post-Holocaust generations. Without facts, there is no real memory. But we are also free to recognize that the Holocaust has indeed become dispersed and fractured through the different ways of memorializing it. An obsessive focus on the unspeakable and unrepresentable, as it was compellingly articulated by Elie Wiesel or George Steiner at an earlier time and as it informs the ethical philosophy of Jean François Lyotard today, blocks that insight. Even in its historically most serious and legitimate form, Holocaust memory is structured very differently in the country of the victims from the way it is in the country of the perpetrators, and differently again in the countries of the anti-Nazi alliance.[3]

All along, the same facts have generated significantly different accounts and memories. In Germany, the Holocaust signifies the absence of a strong Jewish presence in society and a traumatic burden on national identity. Genuine attempts at mourning, which have existed for some time, are hopelessly entangled with narcissistic injury, ritual breast-beating, and repression. Thus until recently there has been little public knowledge of, or even interest in, what was actually lost through the destruction. In Israel, the Holocaust became central to the foundation of the state, both as an endpoint to a disavowed history of Jews as victims *and* as a starting point of a new national history, self-assertion and resistance. In the Israeli imagination, the Warsaw Ghetto uprising has been invested with the force of a mythic memory of resistance and heroism unfathomable in Germany. The American imagination of the Holocaust focuses on America as the liberator of the camps and a haven for refugees and immigrants, and American Holocaust memorials are structured accordingly. In the Soviet account, the genocide of the Jews lost its ethnic specificity and was simply collapsed into the Nazi oppression of international communism. This was done to an extent which now requires a reconstruction of the narratives of East European and Soviet memorial sites.

Much of this, of course, is by now well-known, but it may not be fully grasped in its implications for the debate about remembrance, forgetting, and representation. Such multiple fracturing of the memory of the Holocaust in different countries and the multi-layered sedimentation of images and discourses that range from documentary to soap opera, survivor testimony to narrative fiction, concentration camp art to memorial painting has to be seen in its politically and culturally enabling aspects, as a potential antidote to the freezing of memory into one traumatic image or the mind-numbing focus on numbers. The new Holocaust museum in Washington D.C. is so successful because it is able to negotiate a whole variety of discourses, media, and documentations, thus opening up a space of concrete knowledge and reflection in the memories of its visitors.

II

What, then, of the monument in the larger field of Holocaust representations and discourses? Clearly, the Holocaust monument does not stand in the tradition of the monument as heroic celebration and figure of triumph. Even in the case of the monument to the Warsaw Ghetto uprising we face a memorial to suffering, an indictment of crimes against humanity. Held against the tradition of the legitimizing, identity-nurturing monument, the Holocaust monument would have to be thought of as inherently a counter-monument. Yet the traditional critique of the monument as a burying of a memory and an ossifying of the past has often been voiced against the Holocaust monument as well. Holocaust monuments have been accused of topolatry, especially those constructed at the sites of extermination. They have been reproached for betraying memory, a reproach that holds memory to be primarily internal and subjective and thus incompatible with public display, museums, or monuments. As a variation on Adorno, who was rightfully wary of the effects of aestheticizing the unspeakable suffering of the victims, it has been claimed that to build a monument to the Holocaust was itself a barbaric proposition. No monument after Auschwitz. And in light of fascist excesses with monumentalization, some have even gone so far as to suggest that fascist tendencies are inherent in any monument whatsoever.

All these critiques of the medium itself focus on the monument as object, as permanent reality in stone, as aesthetic sculpture. They do not, however, recognize the public dimension of the monument, what James Young has described as the dialogical quality of memorial space. There is no doubt that we would be ill-served by the Holocaust monument as death mask or by an aestheticization of terror. On the other hand, in the absence of tombstones to the victims, the monument functions as a substitute site of mourning and remembrance. How, after all, are we to guarantee the survival of memory if our culture does not provide memorial spaces that help construct and nurture the collective memory of the Shoah? Only if we focus on the public function of the monument, embed it in public discourses of collective memory, can the danger of monumental ossification be avoided. Of course, public discourse is most intense at the time of planning, designing, and erecting a new monument. There is no guarantee that the level of dialogic intensity can be maintained in the long term, and the Holocaust monument may eventually fall victim to the memory freeze that threatens all monuments.

The great opportunity of the Holocaust monument today lies in its intertextuality and the fact that it is but one part of our memorial culture. As the traditional boundaries of the museum, the monument, and historiography have become more fluid, the monument itself has lost much of its permanence and fixity. The criteria for its success could therefore be the ways in which it allows for a crossing of boundaries toward other discourses of the Holocaust, the ways it pushes us toward reading other texts, other stories.

No single monument will ever be able to convey the Holocaust in its entirety. Such a monument might not even be desirable, just as the Great Book about the Shoah, in Geoffrey Hartman's words, might "produce a deceptive sense of totality, throwing into the shadows, even into oblivion, stories, details and unexpected points of view that keep the intellect active and the memory digging."[4] There is much to be said for keeping Holocaust monuments and memorials site-specific, for having them reflect local histories, recalling local memories, making the Final Solution palpable not just by focusing on the sites of extermination, but on the lives of those murdered in the camps.

At some level, however, the question of the Holocaust as a whole, a totality, will reassert itself together with the problem of its unspeakability. After we have remembered, gone through the facts, mourned for the victims, we will still be haunted by that core of absolute humiliation, degradation, and horror suffered by the victims. How can we understand when even the witnesses had to say: "I could not believe what I saw with my own eyes." No matter how fractured by media, by geography, and by subject position representations of the Holocaust are, ultimately it all comes down to this core: unimaginable, unspeakable, and unrepresentable horror. Post-Holocaust generations can only approach that core by mimetic approximation, a mnemonic strategy which recognizes the event in its otherness and beyond identification or therapeutic empathy, but which physically innervates some of the horror and the pain in a slow and persistent labor of remembrance. Such mimetic approximation can only be achieved if we sustain the tension between the numbing totality of the Holocaust and the stories of the individual victims, families, and communities. Exclusive focus on the first may lead to the numbing abstraction of statistics and the repression of what these statistics mean; exclusive focus on the second may provide facile cathartic empathy and forget the frightening conclusion that the Holocaust as a historical event resulted, as Adi Ophir put it, from an exceptional combination of normal processes.[5] The ultimate success of a Holocaust monument would be to trigger such a mimetic approximation, but it can achieve that goal only in conjunction with other related discourses operating in the head of the spectator and the public sphere.

A monument or memorial will only take us one step toward the kind of knowledge Jürgen Habermas has described as an irreversible rupture in human history:

> There [in Auschwitz] something happened, that up to now nobody considered as even possible. There one touched on something which represents the deep layer of solidarity among all that wears a human face; notwithstanding all the usual acts of beastliness of human history, the integrity of this common layer had been taken for granted. . . . Auschwitz has changed the basis for the continuity of the conditions of life within history.[6]

Such knowledge is all too easily forgotten or repressed. To maintain it is all the more urgent since postmodern, post-Auschwitz culture is fraught with a fundamental ambiguity. Obsessed with memory and the past, it is also caught in a destructive dynamics of forgetting. But perhaps the dichotomy of forgetting and remembering again misses the mark. Perhaps postmodern culture in the West is caught in a traumatic fixation on an event which goes to the heart of our identity and political culture. In that case, the Holocaust monument, memorial, and museum could be the tool Franz Kafka wanted literature to be when he said that the book must be the ax for the frozen sea within us.[7] We need the monument and the book to keep the sea from freezing. In frozen memory, the past is nothing but the past. The inner temporality and the politics of Holocaust memory, however, even where it speaks of the past, must be directed toward the future. The future will not judge us for forgetting, but for remembering all too well and still not acting in accordance with those memories.

NOTES

1. For a compelling account see Deborah Lipstadt, *Denying the Holocaust: The Growing Assault on Truth and Memory* (New York: The Free Press, 1993).

2. Saul Friedlander, *Reflections of Nazism: An Essay on Kitsch and Death* (New York: Harper and Row, 1984).

3. See James Young's groundbreaking study *The Texture of Memory: Holocaust Memorials and Meaning in Europe, Israel, and America* (New Haven and London: Yale University Press, 1993).

4. Geoffrey Hartman, "The Book of Destruction," in Saul Friedlander, ed., *Probing the Limits of Representation: Nazism and the "Final Solution"* (Cambridge: Harvard University Press, 1992), 319.

5. Adi Ophir, "On Sanctifying the Holocaust: Anti-Theological Treatise," *Tikkun* 2:1 (1987): 64

6. Jürgen Habermas, *Eine Art Schadensabwicklung* (Frankfurt am Main: Suhrkamp, 1987), 163.

7. Kafka, *Letter to Oskar Pollak,* 27 January 1904.

BIBLIOGRAPHY

Altizer, Thomas J. J., and William Hamilton. *Radical Theology and the Death of God.* Indianapolis: Bobbs-Merrill, 1966.

Améry, Jean. *At the Mind's Limits.* Bloomington: Indiana University Press, 1980.

Arendt, Hannah. "The Concentration Camps." *Partisan Review* 15 (7): 743–763 (July 1948).

———. *Eichmann in Jerusalem: A Report on the Banality of Evil.* New York: Viking, 1963.

———. *Men in Dark Times.* New York: Harcourt, Brace and World, 1968.

———. "Thinking and Moral Considerations: A Lecture." *Partisan Review* 38 (3): 417–446 (Autumn 1971).

———. *The Origins of Totalitarianism.* 1951. Reprint. New York: Harcourt Brace Jovanovich, 1973.

———. "Organized Guilt and Universal Responsibility." In *The Jew as Pariah,* edited by Ron H. Feldman. New York: Grove, 1978.

Aschheim, Steven E. *Culture and Catastrophe: German and Jewish Confrontations with National Socialism and Other Crises* (New York: New York University Press, 1996).

———. "Nazism, Culture and *The Origins of Totalitarianism:* Hannah Arendt and the Discourse of Evil." *New German Critique* 70 (Winter 1997): 117–139.

Avisar, Ilan. *Screening the Holocaust.* Bloomington: Indiana University Press, 1988.

Aycoberry, Pierre. *The Nazi Question: An Essay on the Interpretations of National Socialism (1922–1975).* New York: Pantheon, 1981.

Baldwin, Peter, ed. *Reworking the Past: Hitler, the Holocaust, and the Historians' Debate.* Boston: Beacon, 1990.

Bartov, Omer. *Murder in Our Midst: The Holocaust, Industrial Killing, and Representation.* New York: Oxford University Press, 1996.

Bauer, Yehuda, and Nathan Rotenstreich, eds. *The Holocaust as Historical Experience.* New York: Holmes & Meier, 1981.

Baum, Gregory. "Theology after Auschwitz: A Conference Report." *The Ecumenist* 12 (5): 65–80 (July–August 1974).

———. "Catholic Dogma after Auschwitz." In *Antisemitism and the Foundations of Christianity,* edited by Alan T. Davies, 137–150. New York: Paulist, 1979.

Bauman, Zygmunt. *Modernity and the Holocaust.* Ithaca, N.Y.: Cornell University Press, 1989.

Benhabib, Seyla. *The Reluctant Modernism of Hannah Arendt.* London: Sage, 1996.

Berkovits, Eliezer. "Approaching the Holocaust." *Judaism* 22 (1): 18–20 (Winter 1973).

———. *Faith after the Holocaust.* New York: KTAV, 1973.

———. "Crisis and Faith." *Tradition* 14 (4): 5–19 (Fall 1974).

———. *With God in Hell: Judaism in the Ghettos and Deathcamps.* New York: Sanhedrin, 1979.

——— . "Rewriting the History of the Holocaust." *Sh'ma* 10 (198): 139–142 (October 3, 1980).

Bernstein, Michael André. *Foregone Conclusions: Against Apocalyptic History*. Berkeley: University of California Press, 1994.

Bernstein, Richard J. *Hannah Arendt and the Jewish Question*. Cambridge: MIT Press, 1996.

Borowitz, Eugene B. "God-Is-Dead Theology." In *The Meaning of the Death of God*, edited by Bernard Murchland, 92–107. New York: Vintage, 1967.

——— . "Hope Jewish and Hope Secular." *Judaism* 17 (2): 131–147 (Spring 1968).

Braiterman, Zachary. *(God) after Auschwitz*. Princeton: Princeton University Press, 1998.

Browning, Christopher R. *Fateful Months: Essays on the Emergence of the Final Solution*. New York: Holmes & Meier, 1985.

——— . *Ordinary Men: Reserve Police Battalion 101 and the Final Solution in Poland*. New York: HarperCollins, 1992.

——— . "The Decision Concerning the Final Solution." In *The Path to Genocide: Essays on Launching the Final Solution*, 96–118. Cambridge: Cambridge University Press, 1992.

——— . *The Path to Genocide: Essays on Launching the Final Solution*. Cambridge: Cambridge University Press, 1992.

Capp, Walter H., ed. *The Future of Hope*. Philadelphia: Fortress, 1970.

Cargas, Harry James, ed. *Responses to Elie Wiesel*. New York: Persea, 1978.

Clendinnen, Inga. *Reading the Holocaust*. Cambridge: Cambridge University Press, 1999.

Cohen, Arthur A. Commentary on Rubenstein, "Homeland and Holocaust." In *The Religious Situation: 1968*, edited by Donald R. Cutler, 87–91. Boston: Beacon, 1968.

——— . *The Tremendum: A Theological Interpretation of the Holocaust*. New York: Crossroad Publishing Company, 1981.

——— . "On Theological Method: A Response on Behalf of *The Tremendum*." *Journal of Reform Judaism* 31 (2): 56–65 (Spring 1984).

——— , ed. *Arguments and Doctrines: A Reader of Jewish Thinking in the Aftermath of the Holocaust*. New York: Harper & Row and Jewish Publication Society, 1970.

Cohen, Arthur A., and Paul Mendes-Flohr, eds. *Contemporary Jewish Religious Thought*. New York: Charles Scribner's Sons, 1987.

Cutler, Donald R., ed. *The Religious Situation: 1968*. Boston: Beacon, 1968.

Davies, Alan T. *Anti-Semitism and the Christian Mind: The Crisis of Conscience after Auschwitz*. New York: Herder and Herder, 1969.

——— , ed. *Antisemitism and the Foundations of Christianity*. New York: Paulist, 1979.

Davis, Moshe, ed. *World Jewry and the State of Israel*. New York: Arno, 1977.

Dawidowicz, Lucy. "American Public Opinion." *American Jewish Yearbook* 69 (1968): 198–229.

Des Pres, Terrence. *The Survivor: An Anatomy of Life in the Death Camps*. New York: Oxford University Press, 1976.

Dorff, Elliot. "A Response to Richard Rubenstein." *Conservative Judaism* 28 (4): 33–36 (Summer 1974).

Earley, Glenn David. "The Radical Hermeneutical Shift in Post-Holocaust Christian Thought," *Journal of Ecumenical Studies* 18 (1): 16–32 (Winter 1981).

Eckardt, A. Roy. *Elder and Younger Brothers: The Encounter of Jews and Christians*. 1967. Reprint. New York: Schocken, 1973.

——— . "The Devil and Yom Kippur." *Midstream* 20 (7): 67–75 (August/September 1974).

——— . "Is the Holocaust Unique?" *Worldview* 17 (1974): 31–35.

——— . *Your People, My People: The Meeting of Jews and Christians*. New York: Quadrangle, 1974.

———. "Jurgen Moltmann, the Jewish People, and the Holocaust." *Journal of the American Academy of Religion* 94 (4): 675–691 (1976).

———. "Christians and Jews: Along a Theological Frontier." *Encounter* 40 (2): 89–127 (Spring 1979).

———. "*Ha'Shoah* as *Weltwende:* The Attack of the Holocaust upon Christian Ideology." Revised version of paper given at Conference at Indiana University, November 3–5, 1980.

———. *For Righteousness' Sake: Contemporary Moral Philosophies.* Bloomington: Indiana University Press, 1987.

———. *Collecting Myself: A Writer's Retrospective.* Atlanta: Scholars, 1993.

Eckardt, A. Roy and Alice Eckardt. "Again, Silence in the Churches." Parts 1, 2. *The Christian Century* (July 26, 1967; August 2, 1967): 970–973, 992–995.

———. "The Holocaust and the Enigma of Uniqueness: A Philosophical Effort at Practical Clarification." *Annals, American Academy of Political and Social Science* 450 (July 1980): 165–178.

———. *Long Night's Journey into Day: Life and Faith after the Holocaust.* Detroit: Wayne State University Press, 1982.

Eckardt, Alice. "The Holocaust: Christian and Jewish Responses." *Journal of the American Academy of Religion* 42 (3): 453–469 (1974).

Edelheit, Joseph A., ed. *The Life of Covenant: The Challenge of Contemporary Judaism.* Chicago: Spertus College of Judaica Press, 1986.

Eisen, Arnold M. *The Chosen People in America: A Study in Jewish Religious Ideology.* Bloomington: Indiana University Press, 1983.

———. *Galut: Modern Jewish Reflection on Homelessness and Homecoming.* Bloomington: Indiana University Press, 1986.

———. "Jewish Theology in North America: Notes on Two Decades." *American Jewish Year Book* 91 (1991): 3–33.

Elazar, Daniel J. *Community and Polity: The Organizational Dynamics of American Jewry.* Philadelphia: Jewish Publication Society, 1976.

Ellenson, David. "The Continued Renewal of North American Jewish Theology: Some Recent Works." *Journal of Reform Judaism* 39 (1): 1–16 (Winter 1991).

Ellis, Marc H. *Toward a Jewish Theology of Liberation.* Maryknoll, N.Y.: Orbis, 1987.

———. *Beyond Innocence and Redemption: Confronting the Holocaust and Israeli Power.* New York: Harper & Row, 1990.

Evans, Richard J. *In Hitler's Shadow: West German Historians and the Attempt to Escape from the Nazi Past.* New York: Pantheon, 1989.

Ezrahi, Sidra DeKoven. *By Words Alone: The Holocaust in Literature.* Chicago: University of Chicago Press, 1980.

Fackenheim, Emil L. *The Religious Dimension in Hegel's Thought.* Bloomington: Indiana University Press, 1967.

———. "Idolatry as a Modern Religious Possibility." In *The Religious Situation: 1968,* edited by Donald R. Cutler, 254–287. Boston: Beacon, 1968.

———. *Quest for Past and Future.* Bloomington: Indiana University Press, 1968.

———. "The Commandment to Hope: A Response to Contemporary Jewish Experience." In *The Future of Hope,* edited by Walter H. Capp, 68–91. Philadelphia: Fortress, 1970.

———. *God's Presence in History.* New York: New York University Press, 1970.

———. *Encounters between Judaism and Modern Philosophy.* New York: Basic, 1973.

———. *The Jewish Return into History.* New York: Schocken, 1978.

————. "Concerning Authentic and Unauthentic Responses to the Holocaust." *Holocaust and Genocide Studies* 1 (1): 101–120 (1986).

————. *What Is Judaism?* New York: Summit, 1987.

————. *The Jewish Bible after the Holocaust.* Bloomington: Indiana University Press, 1991.

————. *To Mend the World.* 3rd ed. Bloomington: Indiana University Press, 1994.

Farias, Victor. *Heidegger and Nazism.* Philadelphia: Temple University Press, 1989.

Finkelstein, Norman G., and Ruth Bettina Birn. *A Nation on Trial: The Goldhagen Thesis and Historical Truth.* New York: Henry Holt and Co., 1998.

Fiorenza, Elisabeth Schüssler, and David Tracy, eds. *The Holocaust as Interruption.* Edinburgh: T. & T. Clark, 1984.

Fleischner, Eva, ed. *Auschwitz: Beginning of a New Era?* New York: KTAV, 1977.

Fleming, Gerald. *Hitler and the Final Solution.* Berkeley: University of California Press, 1984.

Fox, Marvin. "Berkovits' Treatment of the Problem of Evil." *Tradition* 14 (3): 116–124 (Spring 1974).

Friedlander, Saul. *Reflections of Nazism: An Essay on Kitsch and Death.* New York: Harper & Row, 1984.

————. *Memory, History, and the Extermination of the Jews of Europe.* Bloomington: Indiana University Press, 1993.

————, ed. *Probing the Limits of Representation: Nazism and the "Final Solution."* Cambridge: Harvard University Press, 1992.

Funkenstein, Amos. "Theological Interpretations of the Holocaust." In *Unanswered Questions*, edited by François Furet, 275–303. New York: Schocken, 1989.

Furet, François, ed. *Unanswered Questions: Nazi Germany and the Genocide of the Jews.* New York: Schocken, 1989.

Glanz, David. "The Holocaust as a Question." *Worldview* (September 1974): 36–38.

Graubart, Judah L. "Perspectives of the Holocaust." *Midstream* 24 (9): 53–64 (November 1973).

Green, Arthur E. "A Response to Richard Rubenstein." *Conservative Judaism* 28 (4): 26–32 (Summer 1974).

Greenberg, Irving. Commentary on Rubenstein, "Homeland and Holocaust." In *The Religious Situation: 1968*, edited by Donald R. Cutler, 91–102. Boston: Beacon, 1968.

————. "Judaism and Christianity after the Holocaust." *Journal of Ecumenical Studies* 12 (4): 521–551 (Fall 1975).

————. "Religious Values after the Holocaust: A Jewish View." In *Jews and Christians after the Holocaust*, edited by Abraham Peck, 63–86. Philadelphia: Fortress, 1982.

————. "Voluntary Covenant." *Perspectives, National Jewish Resource Center* (October 1982): 1–36.

————. "Will There Be One Jewish People by the Year 2000?" *CLAL Perspectives* (1985): 1–8.

————. *The Jewish Way: Living the Holidays.* New York: Summit, 1988.

Greenspan, Louis, and Graeme Nicholson, eds. *Fackenheim: German Philosophy and Jewish Thought.* Toronto: University of Toronto Press, 1992.

Habermas, Jürgen. *The New Conservatism: Cultural Criticism and the Historians' Debate.* Cambridge: MIT Press, 1989.

Hartman, Geoffrey H. *The Longest Shadow: In the Aftermath of the Holocaust.* Bloomington: Indiana University Press, 1996.

———, ed. *Bitburg in Moral and Political Perspective*. Bloomington: Indiana University Press, 1986.

———, ed. *Holocaust Remembrance: The Shapes of Memory*. Oxford: Basil Blackwell, 1994.

Hayes, Peter, ed. *Lessons and Legacies: The Meaning of the Holocaust in a Changing World*. Evanston, Ill.: Northwestern University Press, 1991.

Heyer, Robert, ed. *Jewish-Christian Relations*. New York: Paulist, 1974.

Hiden, John, and John Farquharson. *Explaining Hitler's Germany: Historians and the Third Reich*. 2nd ed. London: Batsford, 1989.

Hill, Melvyn A, ed. *Hannah Arendt: The Recovery of the Public World*. New York: St. Martin's, 1979.

Himmelfarb, Milton. Commentary on Rubenstein, "Homeland and Holocaust," in *The Religious Situation: 1968*, edited by Donald R. Cutler, 64–79. Boston: Beacon, 1968.

Huyssen, Andreas. *After the Great Divide: Modernism, Mass Culture, Postmodernism*. Bloomington: Indiana University Press, 1986.

———. *Twilight Memories: Marking Time in a Culture of Amnesia*. London and New York: Rootledge, 1995.

Insdorf, Annette. *Indelible Shadows: Film and the Holocaust*. 2nd ed. Cambridge: Cambridge University Press, 1989.

Isaac, Jules. *Teaching of Contempt: Christian Roots of Anti-Semitism*. New York: Holt, Rinehart, and Winston, 1964.

Jay, Martin. "Force Fields, Songs of Experience: Reflections on the Debate over *Alltagsgeschichte*." *Salmagundi* 81 (Winter 1989): 29–41.

Jens, Inge, ed. *At the Heart of the White Rose: Letters and Diaries of Hans and Sophie Scholl*. New York: Harper & Row, 1987.

Jonas, Hans. "The Concept of God after Auschwitz: A Jewish Voice." *Journal of Religion* (January 1987): 1–13. Reprinted in Lawrence Vogel, ed. *Mortality and Morality: A Search for the Good after Auschwitz*. Evanston, Ill.: Northwestern University Press, 1996.

Kaes, Anton. *From Hitler to Heimat: The Return of History as Film*. Cambridge: Harvard University Press, 1989.

Kaplan, Lawrence. "Rabbi Isaac Hutner's 'Daat Torah Perspective' on the Holocaust: A Critical Analysis." *Tradition* 18(3): 235–248 (Fall 1980).

Kateb, George. *Hannah Arendt: Politics, Conscience, Evil*. Totowa, N.J.: Rowman & Allanheld, 1983.

Katz, Steven T. *Historicism, the Holocaust, and Zionism*. New York: New York University Press, 1992.

———, ed. *Interpreters of Judaism in the Late Twentieth Century*. Washington, D.C.: B'nai B'rith Books, 1993.

Kershaw, Ian. *The Nazi Dictatorship: Problems and Perspectives of Interpretation*. 2nd ed. London: Edward Arnold, 1989.

Knowlton, James, and Truett Cates, trans. *Forever in the Shadow of Hitler?* Atlantic Highlands, N.J.: Humanities, 1993.

LaCapra, Dominick. *Representing the Holocaust: History, Theory, Trauma*. Ithaca, N.Y.: Cornell University Press, 1994.

———. *History and Memory after Auschwitz*. Ithaca, N.Y.: Cornell University Press, 1998.

Lacoue-Labarthe, Philippe. *Heidegger, Art and Politics*. Oxford: Basil Blackwell, 1990.

Lang, Berel. *Act and Idea in the Nazi Genocide*. Chicago: University of Chicago Press, 1990.

———. *Heidegger's Silence*. Ithaca, N.Y.: Cornell University Press, 1996.

————, ed. "Philosophy and the Holocaust." *The Philosophical Forum* 16 (1–2) (Fall–Winter 1984–85).

————, ed. *Writing and the Holocaust.* New York: Holmes & Meier, 1988.

Langer, Lawrence L. *The Holocaust and the Literary Imagination.* New Haven: Yale University Press, 1975.

————. *Versions of Survival: The Holocaust and the Human Spirit.* Albany, N.Y.: SUNY Press, 1982.

————. *Holocaust Testimonies: The Ruins of Memory.* New Haven: Yale University Press, 1991.

Lanzmann, Claude. *Shoah: An Oral History of the Holocaust.* New York: Pantheon, 1985.

Lerner, Michael. *Jewish Renewal.* New York: G.P. Putnam's Sons, 1994.

Levi, Primo. *Survival in Auschwitz.* New York: Orion, 1958.

————. *The Reawakening.* New York: Collier, 1965.

————. *The Periodic Table.* New York: Schocken, 1984.

————. *Moments of Reprieve.* New York: Penguin, 1987.

————. *The Drowned and the Saved.* New York: Vintage, 1989.

Levkov, Ilya, ed. *Bitburg and Beyond: Encounters in American, German and Jewish History.* New York: Shapolsky, 1987.

Lipstadt, Deborah E. *Denying the Holocaust.* New York: Free Press, 1993.

Littell, Franklin H. "Christendom, Holocaust and Israel: The Importance for Christians of Recent Major Events in Jewish History." *Journal of Ecumenical Studies* 10 (3): 483–497 (Summer 1973).

————. *The Crucifixion of the Jews.* New York: Harper & Row, 1975.

Loshitzky, Yosefa, ed. *Spielberg's Holocaust.* Bloomington: Indiana University Press, 1997.

Maier, Charles S. *The Unmasterable Past: History, Holocaust, and German National Identity.* Cambridge: Harvard University Press, 1988; 1997.

Marrus, Michael R. *The Holocaust in History.* Hanover, N.H.: University Press of New England, 1987.

Mayer, Arno J. *Why Did the Heavens Not Darken?: The "Final Solution" in History.* New York: Pantheon, 1988.

McGarry, Michael B. *Christology after Auschwitz.* New York: Paulist, 1977.

Metz, Johann Baptist. "Christians and Jews after Auschwitz." In *The Emergent Church: The Future of Christianity in a Postbourgeois World,* 17–33. New York: Crossroad, 1981.

Meyer, Michael A. "Judaism after Auschwitz." *Commentary* 53 (6): 55–62 (June 1972).

Milchman, Alan, and Alan Rosenberg, eds. *Martin Heidegger and the Holocaust.* Atlantic Highlands, N.J.: Humanities, 1996.

Mintz, Alan. *Hurban: Responses to Catastrophe in Hebrew Literature.* New York: Columbia University Press, 1984.

Morgan, Michael L. *Dilemmas in Modern Jewish Thought.* Bloomington: Indiana University Press, 1992.

————. "Reflections on Contemporary Jewish Thought." *CCAR Journal* 40 (4): 33–49 (Fall 1993).

————. "The Central Problem of Fackenheim's *To Mend the World,*" *The Journal of Jewish Thought and Philosophy* 5 (1996): 297–312.

————, ed. *The Jewish Thought of Emil Fackenheim.* Detroit: Wayne State University Press, 1987.

————, ed. *Jewish Philosophers and Jewish Philosophy: Essays by Emil Fackenheim.* Bloomington: Indiana University Press, 1996.

Munz, Christoph. *Der Welt ein Gedächtnis geben: Geschichtstheologisches Denken im Judentum nach Auschwitz*. Guttersloher, Germany: Chr. Kaiser, 1995.

Murchland, Bernard, ed. *The Meaning of the Death of God*. New York: Vintage, 1967.

Neske, Gunther, and Emil Kettering, eds. *Martin Heidegger and National Socialism: Questions and Answers*. New York: Paragon House, 1990.

Neusner, Jacob. "The Implications of the Holocaust." *Journal of Religion* 53 (3): 293–308 (July 1973).

———. *Stranger at Home: "The Holocaust," Zionism, and American Judaism*. Chicago: University of Chicago Press, 1981.

Niewyk, David L., ed. *The Holocaust*. 2nd ed. Boston: Houghton Mifflin, 1997.

Novak, Bill. "The Response Symposium." *Response* 4 (4): 17–123 (Winter 1970–71).

Novick, Peter. *The Holocaust in American Life*. Boston: Houghton Mifflin, 1999.

Ott, Hugo. *Martin Heidegger: A Political Life*. New York: Basic, 1993.

Ozick, Cynthia, and Harold Schulweis. "The Holocaust Dybbuk Debate." *Moment* 1 (10): 77–80 (May/June 1976).

Pawlikowski, John T. *The Challenge of the Holocaust for Christian Theology*. New York: Antidefamation League of B'nai B'rith, 1978.

Peck, Abraham J., ed. *Jews and Christians after the Holocaust*. Philadelphia: Fortress, 1982.

Podhoretz, Norman. "Hannah Arendt on Eichmann: A Study in the Perversity of Brilliance." *Commentary* 36 (3): 201–208, (September 1963).

Polen, Nehemiah. *The Holy Fire: The Teaching of Rabbi Kalonymous Kalman Shapira*. New York: Jason Aronson, 1999.

Rabinbach, Anson. *In the Shadow of Catastrophe*. Berkeley: University of California Press, 1997.

Rabinbach, Anson, and Jack Zipes, eds. *Germans and Jews since the Holocaust*. New York: Holmes & Meier, 1986.

"The Religious Meaning of the Six Day War: A Symposium." *Tradition* 10 (1): 5–20 (Summer 1968); participants—Shear Yashuv Cohen, Norman Lamm, Pinchas Peli, Michael Wyschogrod, Walter S. Wurzburger.

Rockmore, Tom. *On Heidegger's Nazism and Philosophy*. Berkeley: University of California Press, 1992.

Rockmore, Tom, and Joseph Margolis, eds. *The Heidegger Case: On Philosophy and Politics*. Philadelphia: Temple University Press, 1992.

Rosenbaum, Alan S. *Is the Holocaust Unique?* Boulder, Colo.: Westview, 1996.

Rosenbaum, Irving J. *The Holocaust and Halakhah*. New York: KTAV, 1976.

Rosenbaum, Ron. *Explaining Hitler*. New York: Random House, 1998.

Rosenberg, Alan, and Gerald E. Myers, eds. *Echoes from the Holocaust: Philosophical Reflections on a Dark Time*. Philadelphia: Temple University Press, 1988.

Rosenfeld, Alvin H. *A Double Dying: Reflections on Holocaust Literature*. Bloomington: Indiana University Press, 1980.

———. *Imagining Hitler*. Bloomington: Indiana University Press, 1985.

———. *Thinking about the Holocaust: After Half a Century*. Bloomington: Indiana University Press, 1997.

Rosenfeld, Alvin, and Irving Greenberg, eds. *Confronting the Holocaust: The Impact of Elie Wiesel*. Bloomington: Indiana University Press, 1978.

Roskies, David G. *Against the Apocalypse: Responses to Catastrophe in Modern Jewish Culture*. Cambridge: Harvard University Press, 1984.

Rubenstein, Richard L. "A Rabbi Visits Germany." *The Reconstructionist* 27 (1): 6–13 (February 24, 1961).

———. *Morality and Eros.* New York: McGraw-Hill, 1970.

———. "Job and Auschwitz," *New Theology* 8 (1971): 270–290.

———. *Power Struggle.* New York: Scribner, 1974.

———. *The Cunning of History: The Holocaust and the American Future.* New York: Harper & Row, 1978.

———. "Homeland and Holocaust: Issues in the Jewish Religious Situation." In *The Religious Situation: 1969,* edited by Donald R. Cutler, 39–64. Boston: Beacon, 1979.

———. *The Age of Triage.* Boston: Beacon, 1983.

———. "Naming the Unnameable; Thinking the Unthinkable (A Review Essay or Arthur Cohen's *The Tremendum*)." *Journal of Reform Judaism* (Spring 1984): 43–55.

———. *After Auschwitz: History, Theology and Contemporary Judaism.* 2nd ed. Baltimore: Johns Hopkins Press, 1992.

Rubenstein, Richard L. and John K. Roth. *Approaches to Auschwitz: The Holocaust and Its Legacy.* Atlanta: John Knox, 1987.

Ruether, Rosemary Redford. *Faith and Fratricide: The Theological Roots of Anti-Semitism.* New York: Seabury, 1974.

———. "The *Faith and Fratricide* Discussion: Old Problems and New Dimensions." In *Antisemitism and the Foundations of Christianity,* edited by Alan T. Davies, 230–256. New York: Paulist, 1979.

Rylaarsdam, J. Coert. "Jewish-Christian Relationship: The Two Covenants and the Dilemmas of Christology." *Journal of Ecumenical Studies* 9 (1972): 249–270.

Santner, Eric L. *Stranded Objects: Mourning, Memory, and Film in Postwar Germany.* Ithaca, N.Y.: Cornell University Press, 1990.

Schachter, Zalman M. Commentary on Rubenstein, "Homeland and Holocaust," in *The Religious Situation: 1968,* edited by Donald R. Cutler, 79–86. Boston: Beacon, 1968.

Schlant, Ernestine. *The Language of Silence: West German Literature and the Holocaust.* New York: Routledge, 1999.

Schulweis, Harold. "The New Jewish Right." *Moment* 1 (1): 55–61 (May/June 1975).

———. "The Holocaust Dybbuk." *Moment* 1 (7): 34–41 (February 1976).

Schwarzschild, Steven S., ed. "Jewish Values in the Post-Holocaust Future: A Symposium." *Judaism* 16 (3): 266–299 (Summer 1967).

Seeskin, Kenneth. *Jewish Philosophy in a Secular Age.* Albany, N.Y.: SUNY Press, 1990.

———. "Jewish Philosophy in the 1980's." *Modern Judaism* 11 (1991): 157–172.

Shandley, Robert R., ed. *Unwilling Germans?: The Goldhagen Debate.* Minneapolis: University of Minnesota Press, 1998.

Sherman, Franklin. "Speaking of God after Auschwitz." *Worldview* 17 (9): 26–30 (September 1974).

Siegel, Seymour. "Theological Reflections on the Destruction of European Jewry." *Conservative Judaism* 18 (4): 2–10 (Summer 1964).

———. "The Current Theological Situation." *Conservative Judaism* 23 (4): 11–24 (Summer 1969).

Silberman, Lou H. "Concerning Jewish Theology in North America: Some Notes on a Decade." *American Jewish Year Book* 70 (1969): 37–58.

Simon, Ulrich. *A Theology of Auschwitz: The Christian Faith and the Problem of Evil.* Atlanta: John Knox, 1967.

Singer, David. "The Case for an 'Irrelevant' Orthodoxy: An Open Letter to Yitzchak Greenberg." *Tradition* 11 (2): 74–81 (Summer 1970).

"Special Issue on the *Historikerstreit*." *New German Critique* 44 (Spring/Summer 1988).

"The State of Jewish Belief: A Symposium." *Commentary* 42 (2): 71–160 (August 1966).

Steiner, George. *In Bluebeard's Castle: Some Notes towards the Redefinition of Culture*. New Haven: Yale University Press, 1971.

———. *Language and Silence: Essays on Language, Literature and the Inhuman*. New York: Atheneum, 1974.

Swidler, Leonard, ed. "From Holocaust to Dialogue: A Jewish-Christian Dialogue between Americans and Germans." *Journal of Ecumenical Studies* 18 (1): 1–142 (Winter 1981).

Tiefel, Hans O. "Holocaust Interpretations and Religious Assumptions." *Judaism* 25 (2): 135–149 (1976).

Todorov, Tzvetan. *Facing the Extreme: Moral Life in the Concentration Camps*. New York: Metropolitan, 1996.

Tracy, David. *The Analogical Imagination: Christian Theology and the Culture of Pluralism*. London: SCM, 1981.

———. "Religious Values after the Holocaust: A Catholic View." In *Jews and Christians after the Holocaust*, edited by Abraham Peck, 87–107. Philadelphia: Fortress, 1982.

———. *Plurality and Ambiguity: Hermeneutics, Religion, Hope*. New York: Harper & Row, 1987.

Van Buren, Paul. "Christian Theology Today: Status and Prospects." *The National Institute for Campus Ministries Journal* 1 (2): 7–24 (Spring 1976).

———. *Discerning the Way: A Theology of the Jewish-Christian Reality*. New York: Seabury, 1980.

———. "Judaism in Christian Theology." *Journal of Ecumenical Studies* 18 (1): 114–127 (Winter 1981).

Vidal-Naquet, Pierre. *Assassins of Memory: Essays on the Denial of the Holocaust*. New York: Columbia University Press, 1992.

Whitfield, Stephen J. *Into the Dark: Hannah Arendt and Totalitarianism*. Philadelphia: Temple University Press, 1980.

Wiesel, Elie. *Night*. New York: Hill & Wang, 1960.

———. *The Town Beyond the Wall*. New York: Avon, 1964.

———. *The Gates of the Forest*. New York: Avon, 1966.

———. *The Jews of Silence*. New York: Holt, Rinehart and Winston, 1966.

———. *Legends of Our Time*. New York: Avon, 1968.

Williamson, Clark. "Process Hermeneutics and Christianity's Post-Holocaust Reinterpretation of Itself." *Process Studies* 12 (2): 77–93 (1982).

———, ed. "Issue on Post-Holocaust Theology." *Encounter* 42 (2): 103–167 (Spring 1981).

Willis, Robert. "Christian Theology after Auschwitz." *Journal of Ecumenical Studies* 12 (4): 493–519 (Fall 1975).

———. "Auschwitz and the Nurturing of Conscience." In *When God and Man Failed*, edited by Henry James Cargas, 147–167. New York: Macmillan, 1981.

Wolf, Arnold Jacob. "The Revisionism of Irving Greenberg." *Sh'ma* 13 (254): 104–106 (May 13, 1983).

Wolin, Richard. *The Politics of Being: The Political Thought of Martin Heidegger*. New York: Columbia University Press, 1990.

———, ed. *The Heidegger Controversy*. Cambridge: MIT Press, 1993.

Wyschogrod, Edith. *Spirit in Ashes: Hegel, Heidegger, and Man-Made Mass Death*. New Haven: Yale University Press, 1985.

Wyschogrod, Michael. "Some Theological Reflections on the Holocaust." *Response* 9 (1): 65–68 (Spring 1975).

———. "Auschwitz: Beginning of a New Era?: Reflections on the Holocaust." *Tradition* 17 (1): 63–78 (Fall 1977).

———. *The Body of Faith*. Minneapolis: Seabury, 1983.

Young, James E. *Writing and Rewriting the Holocaust: Narrative and the Consequences of Interpretation*. Bloomington: Indiana University Press, 1988.

———. *The Texture of Memory: Holocaust Memorials and Meaning*. New Haven: Yale University Press, 1993.

Young-Bruehl, Elisabeth. *Hannah Arendt: For Love of the World*. New Haven: Yale University Press, 1982.

Zimmels, H. J. *The Echo of the Nazi Holocaust in Rabbinic Literature*. New York: KTAV, 1977.

INDEX